D1478744

The Mythomanias:
The Nature of Deception
and Self-Deception

The Mythomanias:
The Nature of Deception
and Self-Deception

Edited by

Michael S. Myslobodsky
Tel-Aviv University

LEA **LAWRENCE ERLBAUM ASSOCIATES, PUBLISHERS**
1997 Mahwah, New Jersey

Lawrence Erlbaum Associates, Inc., Publishers
10 Industrial Avenue
Mahwah, New Jersey 07430

Cover design by Semadar Megged

Library of Congress Cataloging-in-Publication Data

The mythomanias : the nature of deception and self-deception / edited by Michael S. Myslobodsky.
      p.   cm.
    Includes bibliographical references and index.
    ISBN 0-8058-1919-3 (alk. paper)
    1. Deception. 2. Self-deception. 3. Mythoma-
nia. I. Myslobodsky, Michael.
    [DNLM: 1. Denial (Psychology) 2. Lying. Delu-
sions—psychology. 4. Self Concept. 5. Perceptual
Disorders—psychology. WM 193.5.D3 M999 1996]
    RC569.5.D44M98 1996
    616.89—dc20
    DNLM/DLC
    for Library of Congress   96-13605
                                    CIP

Printed in the United States of America
10 9 8 7 6 5 4 3 2 1

Contents

Foreword
Irving Maltzman   **vii**

Acknowledgments   **ix**
Contributors   **xi**

1   Living Behind a Facade: Notes on the Agenda   **1**
     Michael S. Myslobodsky

2   Self-Deception: A View From the Rationalist   **23**
     Perspective
     Joseph Agassi

3   Self-Knowledge and Self-Deception: **51**
     Further Consideration
     Anthony G. Greenwald

4   The Tricks and Traps of Perceptual Illusions   **73**
     Dan Zakay and Jonathan Bentwich

5   Wishful Thinking From a Pragmatic Hypothesis-   **105**
     Testing Perspective
     Yaacov Trope, Benjamin Gervey, and Nira Liberman

6   Identifying the Origin of Mental Experience   **133**
     Marcia K. Johnson

7   How Can We Be Sure? Using Truth Criteria to   **181**
     Validate Memories
     Michael Ross and Tara K. MacDonald

8   The Single-Mindedness and Isolation of Dreams   **203**
    Allan Rechtschaffen

9   Denial, Anxiety, and Information Processing   **225**
    Hasida Ben-Zur and Shlomo Breznitz

10 Imposture Syndromes: A Clinical View   **245**
    Lloyd A. Wells

11 Neuropsychology of Self-Deception: The Case   **277**
    of Prosopagnosia
    Israel Nachson

12 Mnemopoesis: Memories That Wish Themselves   **307**
    to Be Recalled?
    Leslie Hicks and Michael S. Myslobodsky

13 Phantom Limb Phenomena and Their Neural   **327**
    Mechanism
    Marshall Devor

14 Awareness Salvaged by Cunning: Rehabilitation   **363**
    by Deception in Audiovisual Neglect
    Michael S. Myslobodsky

    Author Index   **393**
    Subject Index   **400**

Foreword

Philosophers, social and clinical psychologists and psychiatrists, and, recently, neuroscientists, neurologists, and cognitive scientists have reflected on the broad and loosely bounded range of phenomena called *deception* and *self-deception*. Unexpectedly, I am immersed in the mood of the theme by virtue of civic duty and the human interactions it yields as I am sitting in a long L-shaped corridor in the courthouse of Culver City, California, the municipality where I live. I have been chosen at random from among the more than 14 million residents of Los Angeles County for jury duty, which must be completed within 1 month, 10 days in court, or service on a jury that reaches a verdict, whichever comes first. Three of the allotted weeks have passed, and I have been in the courthouse 6 different days.

The judge and deputy district attorney, as well as the public defender, repeatedly caution the panel to avoid biases toward or against police because of personal experiences and media events, toward or against members of minorities because the defendant is a member of such a subgroup, and so on. They are admonishing us to avoid self-deception, and ask us if we can do this. Everyone on the panel agrees that they can avoid bias. The deputy district attorney also points out that we have to use common sense and avoid being misled by possibly deceptive testimony from arresting officers or witnesses, or by possibly deceptive testimony of the defendant if he wishes to testify. Instructions are directed toward avoiding deception as well as self-deception. Is the defendant who says he did not commit the crime, where evidence seems to show that he did, lying, intentionally deceptive, or engaging in self-deception? Is it possible to deceive oneself, or is there always a glimmer of truth that is avoided? Must one have an intention to deceive oneself, and therefore know the truth? How else can it be avoided? Contemplate our minds. Do these questions not raise an old paradox? How can I consider self-deception and deception of others unless my own perceptions are subject to deception?

The problem of self-deception is nearby on any turn of the history of the human spirit. Its various aspects have been studied from the beginning of the experimental psychology of thinking: *Einstellung, mental set, Aufgabe, determining tendency, attitude*—an entire armamentarium of terms referring to a highly robust phenomenon is still with us. Among them are the lasting contribution of the Wurzburg school, "magical thinking" of Skinner, cognitive illusions, and "immanence illusion" of Minsky. Instructions to be on guard, "not to be blind," may reduce some kinds of mental set, as demonstrated years ago by Luchins in his classic series of experiments on Einstellung. In considering the other side of the coin, facilitation rather than inhibition, Lashley—in his seminal paper on serial order—suggested a solution to the problem of, for example, Horowitz playing a Beethoven sonata so rapidly that it would be impossible for his performance to be determined by recognizing more than each note, each stimulus, evoking its response. The solution must be in a form of preparedness—a mental set. Nowadays, it might be called *automatic*, as distinguished from *declarative learning*. What Lashley, a pioneer of behavioral neuroscience, did not know was that the Leningrad school of physiologists was already studying and theorizing about the physiological basis of mental set in terms of the phenomena and principles of the dominant focus; there was a massive amount of data and theorizing on the problem of set generated by Uznadze and his colleagues.

Epistemology aside, this book contains a fascinating array of problems. It displays the work of a diverse group of investigators marshaled by Myslobodsky to examine the various forms of "mythomania," deception, and self-deception ranging from the mundane to the bizarre (e.g., imposture, confabulations, minimization of symptomatology, denial, anosognosia). The outcome reflects the range of skills of its polymath editor—an experimental psychologist, neuroscientist, and physician, with efforts in art during his youth, who is equally at home in conducting wet and dry neuroscience, conducting research with rats as well as college sophomores, schizophrenics, and individuals suffering from epileptic seizures. Most assuredly, the book also reflects the versatility and skills of the authoritative authors of the individual chapters. Although the diverse phenomena discussed share a family resemblance, they are unlikely to have a common neurological machinery. To reach an explanation for these phenomena, a reliable pattern of lawful behavior must be delineated. It would then be possible to develop reasonable explanations based on the underlying neurobiological processes that give rise to the deficiencies designated as the mythomanias. The chapters herein provide an outline of such a development. The collection is consistent with the emerging gospel, indicating that neither the machinery of "nature" nor the forces of "nurture" taken alone are capable of explaining what makes cognition and behaviors aberrant. Enjoy the adventure-filled journey that awaits you.

Irving Maltzman
University of California, Los Angeles

Acknowledgments

There are many intellectual debts to my colleagues that this acknowledgment could hardly pay back.

This collection gives voice to my personal and professional appreciation of Seymour Kety, a great scholar, a man of deep humanity, a friend, and an inspiration. He helped in many kind ways.

My many friends at the National Institute of Mental Health, and particularly in the St. Elisabeth's Neuroscience Center of NIMH and Howard University deserve a special mention. With them I have spent my best time in Bethesda since 1985 and my sabbatical year of 1995. I wish to give my thanks to Llewellyn Bigelow, Richard Coppola, Terry Goldberg, Doug Jones, Fuller Torrey, Dan Weinberger, and Ivan Waldman (NIMH Neuroscience Center), and Loring Ingraham, Francois Lalonde and Alex Martin of Laboratory of Psychology and Psychopathology (NIMH) for their hospitality, company, support, and valuable discussions. The latter have covered just about everything, but eventually always settled on the issues of Neuropsychiatry, Psychopharmacology, and Brain Imaging. I have learned a great deal from them. Their cumulative effect in molding my interests and in toning my muscles on the tennis court during more than a decade of friendship is difficult to overestimate.

Leslie Hicks (Howard University) helped to channel my ambivalent interest in confabulations into a research paradigm uniting both of us. He and his students provided a vital backing for my research. Collectively, they contributed to an air of sophomoric optimism I experienced every time I came to Washington that eventually made the town my second intellectual home.

I was lucky to have the valuable counsel of Bill Hodos (University of Maryland) who pledged to give it gratis for the rest of his life or of mine (whichever ends first).

I record my gratitude to my students and associates who contributed to the conduct of experiments (they are listed in the published papers from this laboratory).

This volume was originally conceived as a product of a symposium to be sponsored by Adams Super Center for Brain Studies at Tel-Aviv University. Alas, this meeting proved impossible to organize in 1995, but the volume survived owing to the willingness of the contributors to expand and/or clarify their views. The majority of submissions were subjected to peer review. I wish to thank the referees who helped in making some painful decisions. Ms. Debbie Nir is gratefully acknowledged for expert secretarial assistance.

Still another institutional debt I owe is to the Bibliothéque Interuniversitaire de Médicine in Paris, and particularly to Allan Bissor, Pierre Sheela, and Sabine Labane who generously guided my meandering in the maze of French literature.

On the publisher's side, Judi Amsel and Kathy Dolan were patient with all my editorial whims and flaws. Teresa Horton read the manuscripts for the publisher with attention and skill. All of them did the job of carving a book out of a heap of paper and had to bear with the last minute changes, updatings, and additions.

Alexandra Parmet-Myslobodsky gave a hand in translating French sources and made my search for the Mythomanias in Paris a wonderful experience. Her unfailing poise, love, and care remain my major asset and most precious gift of all.

List of Contributors

Joseph Agassi, Department of Philosophy, York University, North York, Canada M3J 1P3.

Jonathan Bentwich, Tel-Aviv University, Department of Psychology, Tel-Aviv, 69978 Ramat-Aviv, Israel.

Hasida Ben-Zur, Center for Psychological Stress, University of Haifa, 31905 Haifa, Israel.

Shlomo Breznitz, Center for Psychological Stress, University of Haifa, 31905 Haifa, Israel.

Marshall Devor, Department of Cell and Animal Biology, Life Sciences Institute, Hebrew University of Jerusalem, Jerusalem 91904, Israel.

Benjamin Gervey, Department of Psychology, New York University, 6 Washington Pl., New York, NY 10003, USA.

Anthony G. Greenwald, Department of Psychology—Box 351525, University of Washington, Seattle, WA 98195-1525, USA.

Leslie Hicks, Department of Psychology, Howard University, Washington, DC 20059, USA

Marcia K. Johnson, Department of Psychology, Princeton University, Princeton, NJ 08544-1010, USA.

Nira Liberman, Department of Psychology, New York University, 6 Washington Pl., New York, NY 10003, USA.

Michael S. Myslobodsky, Tel-Aviv University, Psychobiology Research Unit, Tel-Aviv, 69978 Ramat-Aviv, Israel.

Israel Nachson, Department of Criminology, Bar-Ilan University, Ramat Gan, Israel.

Allan Rechtschaffen, University of Chicago Sleep Laboratory, 5741 South Drexel Avenue, Chicago, IL 60637, USA.

Michael Ross, Department of Psychology, University of Waterloo, Waterloo, Ontario, Canada N2L 3G1.

Yaacov Trope, Department of Psychology, New York University, 6 Washington Pl., New York, NY 10003, USA.

Lloyd A. Wells, Mayo Medical School, Department of Psychiatry, Rochester, MN 55905, USA.

Dan Zakay, Tel-Aviv University, Department of Psychology, Tel-Aviv, 69978 Ramat-Aviv, Israel.

1

Living Behind a Facade: Notes on the Agenda

Michael S. Myslobodsky

> *What is your substance, whereof are you made,*
> *That millions of strange shadows on you tend?*
> —W. Shakespeare, *Sonnet 53*

Deception is a perennial instrument of survival. For centuries, a cunning mind has been considered important in reaching individual and national goals, to the extent that is has been sanctified as a means of endurance in many cultures. By contrast, honesty went up in value with the development of social institutions and bonds, when deception was branded as an inferior, maladaptive, and inadequate individual coping strategy.

The word *honest* originates from the Latin *honestus*, which simply means "a man in an elite position," and thus approved by his fellow citizens because of his superior status. When Cassius, in a passionate tirade, incites Brutus against Caesar, he does not forget to mention: ". . . we petty men/Walk under his huge legs, and peep about/To find ourselves dishonourable graves./The fault, dear Brutus, lies not in our stars,/But in ourselves, that we are underlings" (W. Shakespeare, *Julius Caesar*, I; ii). The idea is that it should be unbearable for such a noble soul as Brutus to live as a small and timid "underling" (i.e., to live dishonestly), and Cassius gets his way. This connotation of honesty being reserved for the upper class guardians of public morality has long been dispelled. Truth became a dominant principle of behavior because it provided a better chance to adapt, grow, and evolve; it has acquired the rank of a drive that has made a difference in the world. Some adhere to what they perceive as truth even at the risk of personal doom. It has become socially unacceptable to persist in deceiving for personal gain, and it is either condemned or strongly resisted by society by education-

1

al, legal, or medical means. The departure from deception heralded a departure from nature to culture, or from nature to civilization.

Deception and truth are polar opposites on a continuum with various degrees of departure from blatant dishonesty to unbending truth. A small dose of duplicity may interfere little with family and social duties, particularly when triggered by difficult circumstances. It may either pass unnoticed or receive endorsement within a culturally stipulated range of conduct. By contrast, some flagrant falsities that violate cultural codes by their ineptitude, absurdity, or extravagance, so as to resemble carnival personalities, have long attracted the attention of the medical profession. Notice the proximity of French *un démenti* (lie, denial, contradiction, failure of effort) and *démence* (dementia, insanity)—a suggestive etymology.

This volume touches on several neuropsychiatric conditions in which deception or self-deception, in one form or another, play a visible role. They appear either as "positive-symptom" disorders (e.g., imposture, transvestitism, exhibitionism and obscene telephone calling, Münchausen's syndromes, delusional misidentification, confabulations) or "negative-symptom" conditions (e.g., denial, anosognosia, prosopagnosia, various anomalies of perception and memory). These disorders have diverse explanations, and their symptoms may be hidden behind a variety of diagnostic labels.

WHY THE MYTHOMANIAS

An interest in this theme dates back to Mandeville's (1730/1981) book, *A Treatise of the Hypochondriack and Hysterick Disease*. Dupré (1905) continued the theme and coined the term, originally to isolate an irresistible urge to lie, perhaps reminiscent of *pseudologia phantastica* ("*la tendance pathologique, plus ou moins voluntaire et consciente, au mensonge et à la création de fables imaginaires*"; p. 263). Later, the label of *mythomanias* metamorphosed to behavioral acts of pretense and impersonation (Dupré, 1925), and so included many who live in anguish behind a peculiar facade.

The boundaries of the syndromes of mythopsychopathology remain unchartered. The present volume is meant to convey the view that mythomania could be delineated in the spirit of "fuzzy logic" classification. This logic assumes that an object or event can have "fuzzy" boundaries, and thus can simultaneously belong to more than a single group and to a varying degree (Kosko, 1992). In reality, all psychiatric problems have fuzzy, rather than hard, boundaries. It is clear, however, that these symptoms may be abundant outside psychiatric hospitals, including bulimics who "binge and purge" in secret, emaciated anorexics who are convinced that their bodies are fat, and those who otherwise seem to be perfectly normal individuals even if with a penchant for self-dramatization (Wells, chap. 10, this volume). Their mode of coping, however, is so stigmatizing that it makes some of these individuals hopelessly lonely, unsure of their own significance, and unable to respond to cues of love or confide in parents, teachers, physicians, psychologists, or clergy. In a number of cases, the presence of mythopathology goes with (a) somewhat lacunar insight and a minimization of deficits, (b) defective feedback of actions, (c) misconception regarding immediate or remote goals, (d) proneness for magical ideation, (e) a lack of ability in setting priorities, (f) an inability to modulate drives, and (g) temptations ("irresistible urges") that run counter to what is good or what circumstances demand.

Consistent with Dupré, Merriam-Webster (1993) defines *mythomania* as "an excessive or abnormal propensity for lying and exaggerating." The word *excessive* implies a degree of tolerance to the message, its claim, or a claimant. *Trust* is the right word for the accepting attitude on the receiving end of any communication. Trust is a cumulative product of a collective effort with a biological and socioeconomic history of its own. It grants a promise that some allegations will receive a fair hearing, suspended disbelief, and even an initial acceptance. It is a form of faith that provides the binding glue for society and scientific community alike (Shapin, 1994). Trust is a buffer that permits the delay of disrespect or social punitive or medical actions unless the messenger defies the collective experience, by providing a completely garbled, inappropriate, excessive, and grotesque (i.e., untrustworthy) message. The scale of trust is a product of its society. Interestingly, Ambroise Paré, a giant of medieval medicine, did not challenge the accounts of others. He reproduced in his text an absurd story of the Countess Hagenan, who was said to give birth to 365 children (Haggard, 1946). Society has a score of individuals who are convinced of and even prompted into futile actions by their UFO experiences and the sense of once being abducted by extraterrestrial astronauts. Many share their beliefs.

Normalcy is portrayed as the disposition to emit dependable signals (e.g., verbal, postural, sexual) and reliably monitor the imperfections of memory, inadequate emotions, and flawed perceptions in oneself and/ or others. In contrast, mythomanias, in view of the foregoing, could be conceived of as behaviors (messages) that cannot be sustained by institutionalized trust of their witnesses. The catch here is that the threshold of trust may be set rather low. As Bruner (1986) observed, humans are so easily taken in that they must be described as *Home credens*. The allusion to institutionalized ("collective") wisdom poses additional problems. Societies are easily misguided by their gurus; occasional cases of mythomanias may remain undiscerned, whereas numerous others are facilitated. Agassi (chap. 2, this volume) shows self-deception in a historical perspective. His chapter is also a statement of awareness that the danger of self-deception lies in its becoming a part of organizational politics in scientific and medical practice alike. Societies impose or tend to recruit conformity, which is a misleading measure of accuracy. At times, it may even be a pernicious standard. Ross and MacDonald (chap. 7, this volume) indicate that an agreement between the parties provides convincing evidence only if the observations are independent. Some claims and motives may seem so compelling as to recruit substantial support, particularly if they are peddled by the professional "confidence tricksters" (see Agassi, chap. 2). The ability to subconsciously endorse falsities may lead to resounding pathology when someone endowed with authority "takes hold" of people's "memories" (see Ross & MacDonald, chap. 7; Wells, chap. 10). An illustrious example is the False Memory Syndrome of childhood—a troubling phenomenon akin to jatrogenic maladies promulgated by incompetent practitioners who maneuver their patients into the delusional plots of betrayal, incestuous love, and abuse. According to Wells, such cases could be viewed as a form of imposture by proxy on the part of zealous and poorly trained therapists. In their ineptitude, they kindle highly compelling scenarios by feeding into the inflamed imagination of their clients a piecemeal of low-probability events.

Beyond the episodes covered by psychiatric nosography, there are volumes of lay descriptions of daydreamers, saints and martyrs, plain hypocrites, puritan "commissars" with blasphemous erotic fantasies, pedophilic clergymen, vain terrorists, cyberpunks, promiscuous adventurists who cast themselves as victims, a spectrum of perverts, hardheaded ideologues, phony aristocrats, therapists who peddle seduction, and canny politicians who pursue their goals in contemptuous disregard of all evidence of the way the world operates. They all provide an exhibition of the "normal" range of mythopathology. They all show that the partition between normalcy and bona fide mythopathology is often paper thin, and what is codified as *mythomania* varies with the ways of society and its expectations, fears, and mores.

One of the reasons the mythomanias remain unexplored under their genuine name is that they look so normal. The other reason, perhaps, is that they are chameleons made of Shakespeare's "millions of strange shadows," and are described by dipping a pen into a dozen different inkpots. Thus, it is possible that the mythomanias are not less prevalent than other mental illnesses; they certainly could be both as devastating to an individual and as costly to society. Some of its forms may appear as remnants from a bygone age (e.g., astral and magical experience, demonic possessions, roles of a prophet, messiah, Satan, or God), whereas others are small bills for the changes of lifestyle in this century finally coming due (e.g., extraterrestrial encounters). There are efforts to rationalize Doppelgänger (heautoscopy) phenomena as a proof of the reality of an astral body state. More recently, the public was treated to a unique display of behavioral aberrations molded in "cyberspace." Cyberspace has become a "meal of the month," and now provides an alternative manner of communication where identities can be manufactured and concerns of appearance and posture drowned.

Despite its general interest, mythopathology has largely remained an obscure French affair (Bénézech, 1994; Douverger, Obler, Alric, & Wartel, 1991; Neyraut, 1960), not readily familiar to an English-language readership. The mythomanias seemed like a bit of curiosity that did not neatly fit into a specific deficit of central nervous system (CNS) processes. Nor were they intellectually compelling and academically rewarding in comparison with such conditions as schizophrenia or manic–depressive illness. With time, the name has become illegible as an old epitaph and ignored by the frontier neuropsychiatry preoccupied with its own molding. This oblivion has helped create a discipline at the price of overemphasizing the nosological confines. It is time to recognize that mythomania is among the last bastions of psychiatry that has little, if any, neurological authority and fuzzy boundaries. I believe that the "core" psychiatric disorders would be sooner transferred into the realm of neurology if such marginal issues were shifted into the center stage of neuropsychiatric research. Although with a little ingenuity one could group many forms of aberrant behaviors together, it is apparent that, apart from the homage to French psychiatry, the *mythomanias* provide a useful label for various remarkable signs of pathological duplicity and it is a term not difficult on the tongue to stay.

DECEIVING PROSPECTIVELY AND RETROSPECTIVELY

Any falsehood in behavior can be subdivided into two major categories: an "online" response and a long-term course of action. Dupré (1905) distinguished them by *duration* and *intensity*. Perhaps it is more accurate to designate the short-term episodes of duplicity as *reactive* or *retrospective*, whereas the long-term changes in behaviors are *prospective* maneuvers. This demarcation is based on the fact that these two manipulate different kinds of information, represent dissimilar strategies, and are established in response to unlike contingencies. Retrospective behaviors are aimed at deflecting punitive actions, avoiding embarrassment or an awkward social situation, obtaining something impossible to attain otherwise, protecting friends from trouble, demonstrating power over authority, and so on. An important point is that maneuvers of this kind are isolated, brief episodes that often elicit a compassionate smile from a witness and may not have any continuation in the future.

Prospective duplicity is directed at precluding future threats, fictitious, illusory, or real. It thus represents a lasting agenda set for gaining success of winning admiration or love of others. It becomes a fraudulent lifestyle when self-deception appears as the strategy of defense against depression and anxiety, rather than a fleeting tactical device. The mythomanias, by and large, fall into the category of *prospective duplicity*. Unlike the strategies used for benign retrospective deceit, which could be likened to a typical short-term withdrawal response, mythomanias could be conceived of as an approach strategy. It is frequently a disguised eruption to purchase social bonds, albeit on conditions of significant alterations of self-identity, behaviors, habits, or memory, and it may be associated with grotesque self-mutilation tendencies (Wells, chap. 10, this volume; Feldman, 1988).

Normal dimensions of self-deception in the realm of memory are exposed in the chapter by Ross and MacDonald (chap. 7, this volume). They have marshaled a wealth of evidence that people normally differentiate genuine from false memories at only slightly above chance levels. This is particularly evident in a case of episodic memory, which is one of the reasons that autobiography, or an unwritten autobiographical account (i.e., self-portraiture), as a genre is so problematic. As Bruner (1993) concluded: "There is no such thing as a 'uniquely' true, correct, or even faithful autobiography" (p. 39). To a neurologist, sane cases of "inadvertent misremembering" look like frank blunders of memory, known as *confabulations*. Perhaps they could legitimately be placed on one end of a continuum with the latter (see Johnson, chap. 6, this volume; Hicks & Myslobodsky, chap. 12, this volume). Ross and MacDonald (chap. 7) as well as Trope, Gervey, and Liberman (chap. 5, this volume) explain that people may tend to obscure the past instead of coming to terms with it.

Johnson (chap. 6, this volume) outlines a range of factors and conditions that make "episodic" memories bind to or dissociate from their origin (perceptual, contextual, affective, and semantic). She views cognitive processes underlying learning and memory within a complex framework—a multiple-entry, modular (MEM) memory system. This framework shows that memory could not be described without recourse to reflective activity. Its two reflective systems, R1 (refreshing, reactivating, shifting, noting) and R2 (rehearsing, retrieving, initiating, discovering), are driven by motivationally significant goals, designated as heuristic and strategic agendas. This framework is a gold mine of paradigms for examining when deficient source monitoring can make raw data of the senses produce biases and false beliefs and evolve into confabulations, delusions, and multiple personality in the context of age and individual differences.

Another kind of prospective self-deception may normally appear in the form of wishful thinking (Trope et al., chap. 5). Wishful thinking is the last hope of vanishing validity of people's decision-making process. On the scales of Trope's paradigm, philosophical dichotomy between romantics and rationalists (classical vs. recent, low-level vs. high-level); (see Agassi, chap. 2, this volume) does not exist; they appear to be the same group of folks. Both constantly err on the side of optimism. Trope et al. (chap. 5) point out that the distortion of reality is not a phenomenon limited to the mentally ill; everyone tends to maintain the illusion of their own rationality by seeing their freely chosen behaviors as desirable and then bolstering that opinion through selectively exposing themselves to information.

Wells (chap. 10) covers a number of prospective stratagems frequently observed by psychiatrists and clinical psychologists. The most articulate and all-inclusive representative is imposture. Impostors advance their goals almost as skillfully as mythological Proteus—a god who, as the legend has it, changed his form by will. I prefer to call the disorder the *Proteus syndrome* to avoid the derogatory label. In this group, Münchausen's patients are particularly striking in their persistent solicitation of the piercing brute force of invasive medicine. They are determined to obtain surgery as if it promises an erotic touch, a lascivious kiss, and loving bonds. It is still uncertain why these patients pretend to be what they are not. Do they redress their identity and expertly stage behaviors to minimize specific recognizable or imagined faults? How much do they monitor the degree of departure in their disguise from what they are? Alas, we do not know. To paraphrase Bruner (1986), the arguments of behavioral neurology convince one of their truth, clinical accounts of their lifelikeness. There are no neat and overpowering solutions in psychiatry and clinical psychology. However, the approach taken by social and cognitive psychologists (Johnson, Ross & MacDonald; Trope et al., Greenwald) helps demystify the mythomanias by pathologizing the norm—by showing that the syndrome does not develop de novo and that outlandish and extraordinary are frequently ordinary.

A SWEET SLAVERY OF SELF-DECEPTION

If self-deception originates in strategies of deception, whereas communication systems evolve to be reliable (Zahavi, 1993), then self-deception must be a unique trait. Somehow, however, most people are guilty of it. Everyone knows all too well that human beings are imperfect and fallible. They are frequently gullible; unrealistic in their expectations; imprecise in their recollections; inaccurate in assessing their chances for success, health, and individual contributions vis-à-vis roles played by others; and overly optimistic in their prospects for future gains in important, risky, or mundane, everyday events (see Agassi chap. 2; Trope et al., chap. 5). On top of what people experience during wakefulness, for a good portion of the nights, people's thinking and acting are jumbled, bizarre, and cannot be reflexively evaluated when the dreams take place (Rechtshaffen, chap. 8, this volume).

Self-deception begins with such staple of people's perceptual repertoire as illusions (Zakay & Bentwich, chap. 4, this volume). Being "tricked and/or trapped" by errors of perception while exploring "that great book" of the Universe, our sages were tempted to blame the Universe, which, in Galileo's words, "lies before our eyes." The falsities, of course, belong to all. As Asch (1952) mused: "We act and choose on the basis of what we see, feel, and believe. . . . When we are mistaken about things we act in terms of our erroneous notions, not in terms of things as they are" (pp. 64–65). The allusion to "our erroneous notions" is the comfortable way social psychology, in the past, implicated the ways of the brain, or top-down processes (i.e., experience, memory, motivation, inferences, beliefs perpetually enlisted in perception.)

Zakay and Bentwich (chap. 4) discuss the puzzling thing about illusions—that people continue to experience them without losing sight of the fact that they are illusions. Likewise, patients with parietal brain lesions are helped very little by "knowing" that they cannot have a supernumerary limb or experience pain in the missing extremity (Devor, chap. 13, this volume). Zakay and Bentwich suggest that some illusions are "adaptive" and aid in conforming to the reality, whereas others are not (or, perhaps remain in the rank of perceptual solutions in a search of a problem). Adaptive or not, illusions are a faithful caution that a joker is always hidden in the deck. It is likely that the inaccuracies of receptors have certain useful qualities; they may serve as a reservoir of contemplation and bold intuitive leaps of the scholar's thinking. One might wonder whether the deficits of self-knowledge, lack of insight, wishful thinking, and deviations from truth-telling are "anomalies" that sprout from the "prefabricated" deficit in sensory systems' design. That permits

8

the departure from sensation to perception, which virtually borders on imagination. In Johnson's (chap. 6) view, two reflective systems of her model (R1 and R2) permit manipulation of externally derived and self-generated information in memory to go well beyond perceptions to anticipate future events and imagine alternatives. Perhaps one general benefit of such strayed perception is that it permits one to stay delighted and have fun in situations of adversity.

The adaptive role of self-deception is exemplified here by denial, emotional numbness following trauma or medical illness. Denial is a continuation of the largely unconscious normal tendency to accept subjectively desired state of affairs ("optimistic biases") and wishful thinking (Trope et al.). Outright denial is typically a retrospective episode. It is believed to represent a motivated act (Gur & Sackheim 1979) and may thus be construed as a drive (pain)-reducing mechanism, sort of intracranial brain self-stimulation instantly recruited for self-repair. It is a symbolic adaptive mechanism, a guardian of hope, identity, and self-esteem in the face of distress (Ben-Zur & Breznitz, chap. 8, this volume).

Self-deception seems like an exclusion from the principle that brain avidly collects and updates information to create and shape within itself representations of the outside world. When brain works in the mode of the analytic, data-driven, bottom-up machine, it must be virtually immune to self-deception. But this is not a regular mode of its operation nor does it guarantee an enhanced viability. This was nicely shown by Feigenberg and Levy (1965) on the example of the size–weight illusion. The illusion is elicited when an individual is asked to compare weights (that are kept identical) of two objects of different volume. Feigenberg and Levy (1965) noticed that schizophrenic patients are insensitive to the illusion, which makes them more accurate than controls in the estimate of weights of handled objects. One reason this observation is so intriguing is that it is almost uncommon to find a task that schizophrenics execute better than normals. Yet this puzzle is predicated on the wrong assumption that an increment in perceptual accuracy is ever a sign of increased adaptation. The brain is programmed to use internalized beliefs. That makes its strength at the price of occasional self-deception. Thus, one cannot liberate the brain from self-deception. Without it, the brain has little left to do.

Self-deception either actively deflects relevant knowledge or turns on "top-down" processes that reach the circuits mincing fairly adequate information. When input information is blurred, the top-down processes are always ready to make sense of the message (Ross & MacDonald). Still another operation is to reject the unwanted or frankly harmful stimuli and dump for an infinite time the recall of this action (Ben-Zur & Breznitz). To limit the scope, Ben-Zur and Breznitz reserved the term *denial* for operations conducted on external input, or rather a recognizable "outside" event. Yet self-deception is hardly a homogeneous operation. More often, it is called to defuse damaging ("negative") inputs. That is why it is frequently seen in individuals with neurological and/or psychiatric disorders (Johnson). Some of these patients may minimize or completely disregard their condition, confabulate or manifest delusional misidentifications. For example, patients with troubling involuntary movements (e.g., Tardive dyskinesia) may be content with their state and report feeling fine when assessed with an indiscriminate (global) instrument such as Cantril's scale (Myslobodsky, 1993). Other kinds of self-deception may operate on representations, such as chronic painful memories and troubling distortions of body image. A good example is that of a child with cerebral palsy who omits one or two limbs when drawing pictures of humans from memory (Critchley, 1979). By contrast, some individuals develop crippling self-deception by suppressing "positive" inputs. Nachson (Chap. 12) draws attention to the case when patients deny their residual capability, but are explicitly aware of their deficit. Perhaps these are utterly different operations bearing the same name of self-deception.

Most of the time, the process of denial runs its routine job in the background. It mops behind the difficulty of consciousness to confront a problem, but deals with a particular assembly of cues, rather than specific issues. Greenwald (chap. 3, this volume) sees the strategy of knowledge avoidance as the operation of discarding "junk" mail. His example is that of a cancer patient who maintains the expectation of recovery against the overwhelming evidence of the incurable malignancy. This paradox prompts him to ask, "How could that defense be maintained so skillfully *without* using knowledge of the unwelcome fact to anticipate the forms in which it might try to intrude itself on consciousness?" If self-deception requires unconscious cognition, "how does that unconscious cognition relate to conscious cognition?" His theoretical account indicates that the paradox of self-deception was self-imposed by an attempt to explain the phenomenon from within the psychoanalytic view of coordinate conscious and unconscious cognition. The latter assumes a prior complete unconscious representation of threatening information and its control by a single agency. He draws attention to the fact that self-deception is part of knowledge avoidance, which derives from the initial and relatively weak step in a cascade of information processing within a complex neuronal network. It is thus a "pervasively ordinary phenomena" that appears in full color in a case of individual or global threats.

One might wonder, what is the evolutionary benefit in supporting a reproductive success of intrinsic inferiority in perception and self-perception? Why does such an inaccuracy fail to be mitigated by a more realistic assessment? What are the neurophysiological mechanisms of self-deception? When and why does the normal measure of self-deception reach pathological proportions? Who are the susceptible individuals? These questions have been addressed by a number of contemporary thinkers (Ceci, DeSimone Leichtman, & Putnick, 1992; Ekman, 1985; 1989; Festinger, 1964; Goffman, 1959; Gur & Sackeim, 1979; Lockard & Paulhus, 1988; Mele, 1994; Mitchell & Thompson, 1986; Taylor, 1989). Although much has been accomplished, the answers to these questions are unknown. It is certainly beyond this undertaking to give more than a sketch of an answer. There is surprisingly little to say about the nature of pathological duplicity. It is an obstinate problem, and it has been treated outside mainstream neurobiology.

BEHAVIORAL NEUROLOGY:
THE NECESSITY OF THE SECOND HAT

Some readers might find it worrisome and wonder why they have been asked to read about prosopagnosia, hemineglect, or phantom pain. The answer is that "Psychiatric systems, like religions, kinship systems, or political systems, are culturally constructed" (Gains, 1992, p. 3). Although somewhat disdainful, this statement is accurate in suggesting that psychiatry is an atheoretical discipline with low cross-cultural validity. It cannot provide exhaustive answers to many of the previous questions. When the "normal–abnormal" facades of behavior begin to thicken into a wall, the concepts, tools, vocabularies, and approaches taken by social and clinical psychology, or even psychiatry armed with the classical way of salvation by "inventing ever newer conjectures and their refutations" (Agassi, chap. 2), become insufficient to either understand or help a patient. Rather, a straightforward reductionistic assault in a search for brain mechanisms of the camouflage becomes an instrument of choice. Its goal is in "anatomizing the living" using a highly structured analysis; it is conducted by scrutinizing and/or experimentally reproducing neurological disorders which pathophysiology is isomorphic with different aspects of the mythomanias.

Johnson (chap. 6) consistently turns from the area of intelligent guesswork to that of verifiable anatomical claims. She discusses the contribution of several brain areas in monitoring memory for events. A number of the duties that earlier scholars confidently pronounced to be "hippocampal," "temporal," or "frontal" are carefully considered in her model.

Devor (chap. 13, this volume) shows how effective a fine-grained neurophysiology could be in resolving the mystery of neural processes behind the hallucinatory experience known as *phantom organs*. The clinical literature has long promulgated the belief that chronic phantom limb condition is a higher brain-level ("central") phenomenon. A classical example is that of a syndrome following an abrupt vascular lesion in the parietal lobe. Such a picture may be composed of sensory hemineglect and contralesional hemiplegia (the syndrome of loss commonly unappreciated by a patient), along with a phantom supernumerary limb that is personified as "the intruder," "that fellow," or something alien that imposes on a patient (i.e., the syndrome of acquisition, undesirable gain; Critchley, 1979). How this centrally created phantom—which looks more as partial heautoscopy (Grüsser & Landis, 1991)—forces its way on consciousness is difficult to understand. Likewise, the analysis of other falsities is almost hopeless unless a "mock-up" mythopathology is first explored (e.g., phantom organs, hemineglect, confabulations, or prosopagnosia). The beauty of Devor's model is that it permits a rigorous analysis. It helps demonstrate that abnormal firing, subserving phantom limb sensation, might arise, in principle, anywhere along the somatosensory projection pathway. Its ectopic sources in the periphery decide the sensory quality of the phantom percept. The activity of neurons in one or more CNS representations of the body, designated as the *neural matrix of conscious sensation*, determines its shape.

Three of the chapters herein take aspects of memory as their theme (Johnson, chap. 6; Ross & MacDonald, chap. 7; Hicks & Myslobodsky, chap. 12). They do not discuss the neurobiology of memory. However, they all allude to the fact that memory could hardly be conceived of as a system that is capable of flawless reading or "copying" of information from its storage. Normally these copies are surprisingly inaccurate. Yet a deviation from the template does not conflict with survival. Only occasionally, previous experience, as well as ongoing perceptual circumstances, are known to create grotesque "mutations" of a memory, so to speak, that could reach the stage of flagrant fantasies with no internal consistency. For some reasons, the latter products, called *confabulations*, are frequently harvested in frontal lobe patients (Johnson, chap. 6). Why should frontal lobe deficit be associated with confabulations? This volume provides only a few reductionist attempts to answer this question. All revolve around the shared belief that the frontal lobe is fundamental for voluntary control of attention, referencing of past experience, its organization, and evaluation. The crux of Johnson's argument is that an agenda (i.e., a cognitive script set by a combination of goals and component processes of the two reflective systems) is a pivotal agency for information source monitoring, introspection, self-control, and self-observation. The "agendas" are one's mind's eye that scrutinizes the self, and thus is instrumental in projecting and attempting to read through the minds of others, thereby contributing to awareness of awareness. Agendas are governed by the prefrontal circuits so that deficient frontal lobes make one incapable of pinpointing episodes when behavior and utterance become palpably implausible and psychologically unrealistic, imagery bizarre, logic muddled, and ethical system deranged. It is probably from this fertile soil of dwarfed insight, with an unintelligible, passionate yearning of a company and love, that the mythomanias (or at least some of their multifarious manifestations) come to bud, although it may be too simple a way of putting it. Yet even when making allowances for the contemporary scholarly leaning toward the primacy of prefrontal area in defining the anguished individual self-questioning in the steering between the rights and wrongs of life, Johnson does not seem to attribute confabulations solely to their inferior showing, nor does she tie her model irrevocably to the mast of frontal deficit. She conceives of frontal dysfunctions as jumbled transactions between different frontal areas and/or between frontal and extrafrontal regions.

By providing incongruous recollections, frontal lobe patients give themselves away: They concoct, rather than recall, their stories. They use memory storage to provide a response, but pick up its components in a fickle way. Hicks and Myslobodsky (chap. 12) wonder whether the fragments of information that appear in confabulations are random items (imagined or veridical) in the storage system that always appear with free recall, but normally remain suppressed as implausible. They acquire unusual allure because of patients' unusual bind to any fleeting recollection, in the same manner that irrelevant environmental objects "beg" to be handled by patients afflicted with environmental dependency syndrome (Lhermitte, 1986; Lhermitte, Pillon, & Serdaru, 1986). Consistent with the model of Lhermitte (1986), Hicks and Myslobodsky allow themselves to attribute the reduced sensitivity to dissimilar plausibility of recalled events and ongoing environmental cues following frontal lesion to the activity of the temporo-parietal cortex unopposed by the prefrontal inhibitory circuits. In a way, confabulations may be akin to denial: The process of retrieval is derailed such that alternative information is acquired instead of the needed one (Ben-Zur & Breznitz, chap. 9).

If we accept that there are certain benefits in denial, motivated "knowledge avoidance," or falsities in recollection, what is the benefit of confabulations? The answer is uncertain. Perhaps a satisfactory solution can be provided if, under the circumstances, a grave alternative might be in the loss of speech and consciousness. The experience of experimental and clinical neurology suggests that immense vitality and adaptability of the nervous system are achieved through an effort to function even if such a venture may initially seem pathetic and yield only confabulations. One might wonder whether confabulations spur cortical reorganization that helps recover function after CNS damage. This returns us to the point discussed earlier.

The overwhelming supremacy of cognition over perception might possibly suggest that the perfection of the senses was not an evolutionary target. As Milner and Goodale (1993) said: "Natural selection operates at the level of overt behavior: it cares little about how well an animal 'sees' the world, but a great deal about how well the animal forages for food, avoids predators, finds mates, and moves efficiently from one part of the environment to another" (p. 317). Thus, the brain may retain its gullibility if it assures advantage for survival. The perceptual world is brought into registry on the basis of knowledge and expectation of a dominant bias (a euphemism for deception) of one of the senses. Vision is one such coordinator. "Seeing is believing," goes on old bromide. As Ackerman (1991) maintained, the eye is always trying to make sense of life, "if it encounters a puzzling scene it *corrects the picture to what it knows. If it finds a familiar pattern, it sticks to it, regardless of how inappropriate it might be* in that landscape or against that background" (p. 230, italics added).

Hers is an adequate description (if with certain poetic license) of the way other senses succumb to vision. A remarkable, but seldom explored, example of visual dominance is the ventriloquist illusion. Struck by its robustness, Myslobodsky (chap. 14, this volume) showed how the illusion could overcome auditory neglect. Hemisensory neglect is a peculiar case of dissociation when a reasonably high level of sensory responsiveness may be combined with a profound oblivion of the stimuli. The patients were deceived as to the source of sounds by drawing attention to the dummy speaker on their "seeing side." As a result, they regained hearing of previously neglected sounds. In keeping with Festinger (1964), one could argue that perceptions shaped by existing knowledge are capable of overcoming a phenomenal disability. In the syndrome of unilateral audiovisual neglect, the ability to translate the tacit (inexpressible) information into explicit knowledge amounts to regaining consciousness. Here, too, the question of clinical utility of deception for the rehabilitation of patients with the syndrome of hemineglect cannot be resolved correctly without asking what the alternative would be.

METHOD OF MONSTERS

In keeping with Dupré (1905, 1925), it is recognized that some cases of mythopathology develop against the background of gross brain damage. Brain injury could also be conceived of as a model that permits the exploration of psychopathological syndromes, anchored in easily quantifiable brain abnormalities. The advantage of such models is that they relinquish the "realistic" etiology of maladies for plausibility of specific features. They tend to mutilate their target to emulate reality. Paradoxically, by sacrificing precision, or absurdly exaggerating certain elements, such models, like canvasses of Magritte, tend to arrive at understanding the generality. The whole idea of art is based on the validity of distortions of reality. Did not Henry Matisse utter the famous dictum, "Exactitude is not truth"? These deliberate distortions are at the heart of the "method of monsters" (see Lakatos, 1976), whose thesis is that the organization of normal systems is well served by scrutinizing their maladies, and that pathology is often capable of inflating the machinery operating in normalcy: "If we want to learn anything really deep, we have to study it not in its 'normal', regular, usual form, but in its critical state, in fever, in passion. If you want to know the normal healthy body, study it when it is abnormal, when it is ill. If you want to know functions, study their singularities" (Lakatos, 1976, p. 23). As Johnson (chap. 6, this volume) seconds, "much can be learned about a process from looking at 'normal' errors, or more serious errors that arise when the processes break down" (p. 71).

   Devor (chap. 13) provides the most convincing argument to support the claim that the analysis of the "seat of (somatosensory) consciousness" could be best advanced by scrutinizing the pathological alterations in the body schemata. Regrettably, not all kinds of hallucinatory experiences are ready for such exhaustive scrutiny as his "somatosensory ghost."

   Having analyzed the mechanism of denial in several planes—the plane of psychoanalytic theory, self-deception tactics, coping strategies developed in stress theory—Ben-Zur and Breznitz (chap. 9) demand, "How does the system know that it should not know?" This is a crucial question if one wishes to invite a neuroscientific debate. Although the answer is elusive, the authors hint at the possibility that contradictory strategies (i.e., different levels of knowing, different states of consciousness), or conscious and "verbally unreportable cognition" (Greenwald, 1992), represent a problem of brain laterality. The mere legitimacy of such a hunch is rooted in the split-brain operations in patients suffering from intractable epilepsy. An avalanche of neuropsychological evaluations spurred by the Sperry (1964, 1985) and Gazzaniga (1970) studies have shown that the two hemispheres have strategies and processing capacities of their own, and respond to different environmental cues. Future studies should explore whether denial is associated with the fact that the "dangerous aspects of the environment" give relative priority to the right hemisphere, presumably more competent in the matters of emotions, thereby reducing the ability of the verbal (i.e., conscious) processing of the "terrifying reality."

In a similar vein, questioning the assumption of unity within a personal knowledge system implicit in the term *self-deception*, Greenwald (chap. 3, this volume) indicates that the contrasting way in which the right and left hemispheres handle different input information is relevant for interpreting denial phenomena. In view of his allusion to the concept of orienting reflex (OR), it is tempting to juxtapose his sequential-stage view of information processing with the neo-Pavlovian doctrine of OR. There is no machinery in the brain other than OR to handle inputs for both spatial orientation and object identification whenever a novel, relevant, and/or sufficiently strong stimulus is encountered or severed internally by cognition (see Maltzman, 1977, for a review). The language of OR is a *lingua franca* of the brain that crosses several domains (e.g., perception, memory, motivation, motor control) before a less fixed-action pattern of organismal action is specified. At least two neuronal systems with different expertise are postulated for OR—the celebrated "where" and "what" steps. The latter have different meaning and frequently opposite motivational valence equivalent to the "withdrawal" and "approach" steps in behaviors. "Withdrawal OR" anticipates a detrimental conclusion regarding an event, whereas "approach OR" counts on an agreeable outcome of new circumstances. The OR network assumes a common metric of processing at different levels of the neuraxis. It requires the presence of numerous sources of information until the "neuronal model of stimulus" (Sokolov, 1963) is sufficiently updated to permit the transition to the "approach" stage of OR (see Soroker, Calamaro, & Myslobodsky, 1995, for a review). Based on the concepts of 'involuntary' and 'voluntary' orienting response of Maltzman (1977), it is possible to speculate that OR embodies aspects of signal processing that necessitate comparisons with mental representations, drives, and volition. The two kinds of OR may possibly have token borders with numerous interim steps between them so as to fit the network postulated by

Greenwald's model of self-deception. (Parenthetically, one might wonder whether Maltzman's internally generated OR is a psychophysiological version of Johnson's R1 and R2.) The possible role of the right hemisphere in the mediation of electrodermal-orienting responses was repeatedly on the agenda of research for its pertinence for the understanding of pre-conscious processing (see Mintz & Myslobodsky, 1983; Soroker et al., 1995, for a review).

Johnson (chap. 6, this volume) seeks to emphasize the divide between the neuronal mechanisms of reflective processes. Attributing reflective subroutines of her model (R1 vs. R2, or tactical-strategical or habitual-deliberate processes) to different degrees of control of the right- versus left-hemisphere networks, she is careful about proposing how this is achieved, and for good reasons. We have been slowly weaned from the idea that cognitive functions can be easily pinned on right versus left-hemisphere processes. In the end, the reader must wait for the time when functional brain-imaging techniques will preside over the debate. With the coming of age of brain imaging, these concepts are ready for a careful scrutiny.

Still another example of a puzzling deficit known as *prosopagnosia*— when familiar people are frequently identified by various nonfacial features, such as sounds of speech, manner of walk, odors, paraphernalia, and so on. It is one of other, more esoteric errors of facial perception (e.g., paraprosopia, pareidolias; see Grüsser & Landis, 1991, for a review). Nachson (chap. 11, this volume) proposes to conceptualize self-deception in prosopagnosia in terms of a dissociation between a (largely modular) face-recognition system and the (central) conscious-awareness system. He postulates a functional dissociation between cognitive functions, rather than a structural disconnection between distinct anatomical sites. Whether this is the mechanism of the syndrome remains to be elucidated. But if Nachson's cautious guesswork is near correct, it would not be difficult to nominate which of the presumed deficient brain sites should be selected for further analysis.

Virtually all people have a guaranteed place on a stage of insanity and imposture that is passionately played in their nocturnal dreaming. Such a rare kind of hallucinations as heautoscopy (hallucination of oneself) is an ordinary dream experience that appears in waking patients with temporal lobe epilepsy, drug intoxications, schizophrenia, parieto-temporal injuries, migraine, and other conditions. For Bliss (1986), the syndrome of multiple personalities is a process that has a quality of dream that "creates an inner world where 'magical' events may be encountered," thereby providing "an escape from intolerable realities." It is a small wonder that the notion of psychopathology as the intrusion of dreamlike states into wakefulness has been a target for investigation for some time. Somewhere along the road, however, it was quietly dropped without retraction. As Rechtschaffen (chap. 8, this volume) argues, this was done for worthy reasons. The parallel between the two might be legitimate only in a metaphorical sense due to the union between the change of consciousness and bizarre dream contents. Features of dreams, such as their nonreflectiveness, monothematicity, absence of intrusion of parallel thoughts or images, thematic coherence, and poor recall (i.e., their "single-mindedness," in Rechtschaffen's definition), do not look like psychotic hallucinations. Rather, the encapsulation of confabulational story and single-mindedness of dream experience seem so close that Rechtshaffen is tempted to suggest the similarity in mechanisms. The heuristic advantage of juxtaposing the two is in helping generate the neurological framework from which to consider one of the least understood features of sleep. This is done in his update. Yet if one searches for the nature of these staged nightly self-deceptions, and particularly the fact that they are kept below decks like the oarsmen of ancient galleons, visual hallucinations can hardly be discounted. One might profitably study the nature of single-mindedness in waking delusional patients.

Although this list could go on, it is not continued because this collation is fraught with ambiguities. Neurological models are not ready to cover the entire cast of the mythomanias, nor is it a goal of the present effort to map the psychiatric condition on a specific circumscribed neuronal deficit (e.g., brain regions, neurochemical system). This volume makes no pretense of being able to pinpoint lesions in specific brain sites that produce the whole complexity of the clinical syndromes discussed. Rather, it portends that only by neurologizing can we ever hope to give the mythomanias their place in the realm of neurosciences and provide answers regarding the brain machinery underlying deception and self-deception in general. A homely parable reiterated by Fuller Torrey (1989) may prove helpful in emphasizing the point:

One evening, a man was trying to read the newspaper. His little boy was making so much noise that he could not concentrate. Finally, in desperation, the father took a page of the newspaper showing a big map of the world and cut it into small pieces. "This is a puzzle," he said to his son. "Put the world together right." The little boy worked quietly in the next room, and in only a few minutes he returned with the map of the world put together exactly right. "How did you do it so quickly?" asked the father, in great surprise. "Oh," said the little boy, "there was a picture of a man on the other side of the page. I found that when I put the man together right, the world was just right, too." (p. 65)

I am hoping that the mythomanias can provide good service in the guesswork needed for reconstructing such a map. With its pieces glued together, a better picture of the brain's inner workings will be sketched.

ACKNOWLEDGMENTS

A. Martin, I. Maltzman, E. Valenstein, and F. Torrey performed me the service of reading the opening note to the book and offered intensely helpful suggestions and criticism. This is not to repudiate any error or opinions it contains. All are of my own making.

REFERENCES

Ackerman, D. (1991). *A natural history of the senses.* New York: Vintage.

Asch, S. E. (1952). *Social psychology.* Englwood Cliffs, NJ: Prentice-Hall.

Baker, R. A. (1992). *Hidden memories.* New York: Prometheus.

Bénézech, M. (1994). La mythomanie perverse de Pierre Molinier. En hommage à Ernest Dupré [Obstinate mythomania of Pierre Molinier. Dedication to Ernest Dupre]. *Annales médico-psychologiques, 152,* 239–242.

Bliss, E. L. (1986). *Multiple personality, allied disorders and hypnosis.* New York: Oxford University Press.

Bruner, J. (1986). *Actual minds, possible worlds.* Cambridge, MA: Harvard University Press.

Bruner, J. (1993). The autobiographical process. In R. Folkenflik (Ed.), *The culture of autobiography: Construction of self-representation* (pp. 38–36). Stanford, CA: Stanford University Press.

Critchley, M. (1979). Corporal awareness: Body-image, body scheme. In *The divine banquet of the brain and other essays* (pp. 92–105). New York: Raven.

Ceci, S. J., DeSimone Leichtman, M., & Putnick, M. (Eds.). (1992). *Cognitive and social factors in early deception.* Hillsdale, NJ: Lawrence Erlbaum Associates.

Dupré E. M. (1905). La mythomanie [The mythomania]. *Le Bulletin Médical, 23,* 263–268; *25,* 285–290; *27,* 311–315.

Dupré, E. M. (1925). *La mythomanie. Pathologie de l'imagination et de l'émotivité* [The mythomania. Pathology of imagination and emotion]. Paris: Payot.

Duverger, P., Obler, J. B., Alric, V., & Wartel, M. O. (1991). La question de la vérité. A propos d'un cas de pathomimie [Telling or withholding the truth in factitious disorder. Report of a case]. *Annales de Psychiatrie, 6,* 63–68.

Ekman, P. (1985). *Telling lies: Clues to deceit in the marketplace, politics, and marriage.* New York: Norton.

Ekman, P. (1989). *Why kids lie: How parents can encourage truthfulness.* New York: Scribner's.

Feigenberg, I., & Levy, V. L. (1965). An experimental investigation of probabilistic prognostication in pathological states. *Voprosi Psychologii, 1,* 42–54.

Feldman, M. D. (1988). The challenge of self-mutilation. A review. *Comprehensive Psychiatry, 29,* 252–269.

Festinger, L. (1964). *Conflict, decision, and dissonance.* Stanford, CA: Stanford University Press.

Gains, A. D. (1992). Ethnopsychiatry: The cultural construction of psychiatries. In A. D. Gains (Ed.), *Ethnopsychiatry: The cultural construction of professional and folk psychiatries* (pp. 3–49). New York: State University of New York Press.

Gazzaniga, M. (1970). *The bisected brain*. New York: Appleton-Century-Crofts.

Goffman, E. (1959). *The presentation and the self in everyday life*. New York: Anchor/ Doubleday.

Greenwald, A. (1992, June). Unconscious cognition reclaimed. *American Psychologist*, pp. 766–778.

Grüsser, O.-J., & Landis, T. (1991). *Visual agnosias and other disturbances of visual perception and cognition*. Boca Raton, FL: CRC Press.

Gur, R. C., & Sackheim, H. A. (1979). Self-deception: A concept in search of a phenomenon. *Journal of Personality and Social Psychology, 4*, 147–169.

Haggard, H. W. (1946). *Devils, drugs & doctors*. New York: Harper & Brothers.

Kosko, B. (1992). *Neuronal networks and fuzzy systems*. Englewood Cliffs, NJ: Prentice-Hall.

Lakatos, I. (1976). *Proofs and refutations: The logic of mathematic discovery*. Cambridge, England: Cambridge University Press.

Lhermitte, F. (1986). Human autonomy and the frontal lobes: II. Patient behavior in complex and social situations. The "environmental dependency syndrome." *Annals of Neurology, 19*, 335–343.

Lhermitte, F., Pillon, B., & Serdaru, M. (1986). Human autonomy and the frontal lobes: I. Imitation and utilization behavior: A neuropsychological study of 75 patients. *Annals of Neurology, 19*, 326–334.

Lockard, J., & Paulhus, D. (1988). *Self-deception: An adaptive mechanism?* Englewood Cliffs, NJ: Prentice-Hall.

Maltzman, I. (1971). The orienting reflex and thinking as determiners of conditioning and generalization to words. In H. H. Kendler & J. T. Spence (Eds.), *Essay in neurobehaviorism: A memorial volume to Kenneth W. Spence* (pp. 89–111). New York: Appleton-Century-Crofts.

Mandeville, B. (1981). *A treatise of the hypochondriack and hysterick disease* (2nd ed.). London: Hildesheim. (Original work published 1730)

Mele, A. (1994). Self-control and belief. *Philosophical Psychology, 7*, 419–435.

Merriam-Webster's Collegiate Dictionary. (1993). Springfield, MA: Merriam-Webster.

Milner, A. D., & Goodale, M. A. (1993). visual pathways to perception and action. *Progress in Brain Research 95*, 317–337.

Mintz, M., & Myslobodsky, M. (1983). Two types of hemisphere imbalance in hemi-Parkinsonism coded by brain electrical activity and electrodermal activity. In M. Myslobodsky (Ed.), *Hemisyndromes: Psychobiological, neurology, psychiatry* (pp. 213–238). New York: Academic Press.

Mitchell, R. W., & Thompson, N. S. (Eds.) (1986). *Deception: Perspectives on human and nonhuman deceit*. New York: State University of New York Press.

Myslobodsky, M. S. (1993). Central determinants of attention and mood disorders in tardive dyskinesia (tardive dysmentia). *Brain and Cognition, 23*, 88–101.

Neyraut, M. (1960). A propos de la mythomanie. *Evolution psychiatrique, 25*, 533–558.

Paré, A. (1996). *On monsters and marvels*. Chicago: The University of Chicago Press.

Shapin, S. (1994). *A social history of truth*. Chicago: University of Chicago Press.

Soroker, N., Calamaro, N., & Myslobodsky, M. (1995). Ventriloquist effect reinstates responsiveness to auditory stimuli in the "ignored" space in patients with hemispatial neglect. *Journal of Clinical and Experimental Neuropsychology, 17*, 243–255.

Sperry, R. W. (1964). The great cerebral comissure. *Scientific American, 210*, 42–52.

Sperry, R. W. (1985). Consciousness, personal identity, and the divided brain. In D. F. Benson & E. Zaidel (Eds.), *The dual brain: Hemispheric specialization in humans* (pp. 11–26). New York: Guilford.

Taylor, S. (1989). *Positive illusions. Creative self-deception and the healthy mind*. New York: Basic Books.

Torrey, E. F. (1989). *Nowhere to go. The tragic Odyssey of the homeless mentally ill.* New York: Harper & Row.

Zahavi, A. (1993). The fallacy of conventional signaling. *Philosophical Transactions of the Royal Society (London), B340,* 227–230.

2

Self-Deception: A View From the Rationalist Perspective

Joseph Agassi

SELF-DECEPTION IN GENERAL

In his "A Liberal Decalogue" Russell (1967, pp. 60–61) suggested not to envy people who live in a fool's paradise: It is a place only for fools. This saying invites detailed commentary. A fool's paradise is not a place, but a state of mind; it is a system of opinions, of assessments of situations, that calms one down, that reassures one into the opinion that all is well, even when all is far from well. Fools may be ignorant of the severity of their situations, perhaps because being well informed tends to get them into a panic. This happens regularly, and there is little that can be done about it, except that the wise would still prefer to be well informed so as to try to cope with the panic more constructively. They would not easily fall for the reassuring hypothesis, preferring to examine any reasonable alternative hypothesis about any risk that might invite action—so that if the hypothesis is corroborated, they can try to mobilize some appropriate action.

Alternatively, fools may tell themselves that there is no risk. This is self-deception, and the question is, why do people deceive themselves and take risks? To take a concrete example, people with weak hearts may avoid taking precautions and prefer to live like normal people and risk instant death from heart failure. This is possibly a rational choice. Yet some who suffer from weak hearts pretend, even to themselves, that they are normal. It is hard then to say whether they have chosen to live normally and take the risk. Perhaps they prefer to take precautions, and yet do not do so because they are unable to look the risk straight in the face.

More sophisticated ways of living in a fool's paradise are known. One may live there knowingly. One may feel that one does not share the reassuring received opinion, yet pretend that one does. This is what Russell warned against: Anyone who knowingly chooses to live in a fool's paradise is still a fool. Anyone who thinks that awareness of one's living in a fool's paradise immunizes one to its dangers is a fool. This is self-deception about one's ability to cope with deceit. Many philosophers have noted that people who habitually deceive finally fall for their own deceptions. This is the well-known phenomenon: confidence artists appeal to the willingness of their victims to deceive both themselves and others in one and the same act: The victims are encouraged to deceive themselves into thinking that they deceive only others while ignoring their own greed and the immorality of the way they choose to satisfy it. To this Russell added that the same holds true for all self-deception: Those who think they can live in a situation of self-deception without deceiving themselves finally fall for their own self-deception. The seemingly wise deceive themselves that they only pretend that they endorse the reassuring hypothesis: They do not know the cost of the pretense, which is the neglect of thinking out the viable alternatives.

The reason one endorses the reassuring hypothesis despite attempts to immunize oneself is complex. It is in part intellectual: One does not invest in the examination of alternative hypotheses. It is in part social: One cannot discuss alternative possibilities when one pretends to the world that one is committed to the reassuring hypothesis. It is in part psychological: One is ambivalent about matters, and one reassures oneself that one does not need the reassurance.

The case of self-deception, in brief, is complex. It involves error, impatience in thinking out detailed matters, unwillingness to examine each and every obvious option, and also deception proper. Yet clearly something is missing here: It is fear and obsession. As Freud was first to notice, self-deception usually rests on the stubborn reluctance to consider alternatives when these are suggested by others.

Not all cases of self-deception, however, are cases of life in fool's paradise. This phenomenon is usually associated with the self-deception that involves whole social groups. The social case is more complex than the personal case. The personal case of self-deception is puzzling because its victims refuse to consider corrections suggested by their environment. The case of the fool's paradise that is group self-deception, usually national, is different and more complex: A whole society declares a certain option not open to public discussion. Its given rationale is that it is dangerous to discuss different options—because it will help other people or discourage our people. Indeed, it is very similar to the case of the confidence artist: The group (national) leadership suggests that, although our case may be shaky, we may be able to succeed if it will be nevertheless accepted, and for this it should be presented with full confidence. All that is missing from the picture to complete it are two true observations. First, many political leaders are confidence tricksters, and they see themselves as such. Second, confidence tricksters make a profession of deceiving themselves that they deceive only others. In principle, then, the difference between the two cases—the private and the public—is only technical: Both are cases of reluctance—of not allowing oneself to examine views that deserve to be examined, where an excuse for this reluctance is left unexamined as well. The two cases differ as to the excuse offered for the reluctance. To make the difference purely technical, what is needed is to observe, as is explained in detail here, is that any effort to present a case authoritatively—be it personal, social, political, or intellectual—is in itself nothing short of self-deception.

In summary, when one deceives oneself, one does not know the cost of the self-deception, and it is usually this that makes the error significant. In other words, however irrational any case of self-deception looks, when one unpacks it, one finds it not very problematic. The inability to see this rests on a difficulty that enters the picture with the introduction of a theory of rationality. Two important theories of rationality are found in Western philosophy. The earlier of the two is the more important. It was known as the rationalist theory, and now it is known as *classical rationalism*. It identifies rational action with one based on rational belief and rational belief as that which rests on proof of sorts (Agassi, 1986a; Agassi & Jarvie, 1987, chap. 16). The other important theory is *romanticism:* It identifies rational action with one based on strong intuition: One acts rationally when one is true to one's inner self, when one listens to the right inner voice. This theory, be it true or false, is not given to rational discussion for the following reason. There is only one argument against it: By listening to one's inner voice, one can make tragic decisions. The followers of the romantic theory of rationality are not dissuaded by this argument for reasons that are good or bad. Whatever is the truth of the matter, the followers of the romantic theory are unshakeable. Hence, there is no point in pursuing this discussion unless and until someone comes up with a new suggestion (for details see Agassi, 1982).

The rest of this chapter is devoted to a discussion of the classical theory of rationality and of its implications for the case of self-deception. At the end, a new avenue for the theory of rationality is highlighted. The newer theory of rationality is more commonsensical, as it takes rationality to be a matter of trial and error. Thus, it permits the discussion to proceed along the lines suggested here.

RATIONALITY AND THE SOCIAL ORDER

The prevalence of self-deception is part of folk knowledge; it is the target of a rich folk literature, and of more sophisticated literature as well. It has not puzzled people, however, until the advent of modern times. The reason is not far to seek: The phenomenon began to puzzle people when it conflicted with received opinion and/or when it constituted a challenge that was surprisingly hard to meet. The surprising difficulty presented by a challenge testifies to the presence of a theory in the light of which it should be easily met. The theory that human beings are rational is the source of the trouble: Obviously, self-deception is not rational.

As long as the received opinion was that human beings are foolish, or unreasonable, it was expected that they should behave erratically, deceive themselves, and so on. Clearly, this traditionally received opinion was an unavoidable corollary to the traditionally received religious doctrines of the Western world prior to modern times: The wages of sin are slight and momentary and the cost of sin is eternal damnation; hence nothing is more rational than to behave properly. Yet people will sin ("the flesh is weak"). The prevalence of sin was taken by all the traditionally received religious doctrines of the Western world prior to modern times as conclusive evidence of human irrationality.

The situation was taken quite differently by most of the modern rationalistic philosophers, the classical rationalists: They considered the prevalence of sin to be evidence that sinners simply do not believe in eternal damnation. They reasoned thus: Rational people act in accord with their beliefs; people do not act in accord with the belief that their actions will lead to eternal damnation; hence, clearly, they do not believe in eternal damnation. Moreover, the classical rationalists taught that it is important to hold the right beliefs. To this end, beliefs should be adopted rationally, and then all will be as well as can be expected. Self-deception, however, does not fit the classical rationalist prescription: Classical rationalists always viewed it as the willful deviation from rational belief. Its prevalence, then, is, or seems to be, a refutation of their theory of rational belief. Hence its centrality for their theory of rationality—for the theory of rationality presented in the classical rationalist tradition (Agassi, 1977, 1991).

This last point deserves a slight elaboration. Practically all Western religious traditions and practically all folk wisdom constantly preach the restraint of natural human appetites on the ground of the (false) observation that selfish conduct obviously undermines social stability. The classical (Western) tradition of rationalist philosophy disagreed with this teaching and rejected this observation (as obviously the very opposite of the truth). It declared any desirable restraint better achieved by reason-

26

able, self-reliant individuals than by those frightened by hell fire and brimstone. Classical rationalists preferred, on the whole, not to prescribe restraint. They did not deny that some restraint is reasonable. Yet they considered particularly erroneous the demand to avoid greed and selfishness. The reasonable, self-reliant individual, they taught, will practice the necessary self-restraint anyway. The end of rational conduct is always selfish, as action comes to satisfy the natural appetites of actors. Hence, the best way to act, the best way to achieve one's end, is to behave intelligently—to act as a reasonable self-reliant individual (Agassi, 1986b).

In brief, the classical (Western) tradition of rationalist philosophy rejected as too strict the preaching of (Western) religious traditions and folk wisdom for the restraint of natural human appetites. It preached reasonable self-reliance, on the opposite view that reasonable, self-reliant individuals are better able to judge how strict their conduct should be. Rational action is best guided by thought; hence, the problem of rationality is less a question of the choice of a mode of conduct and more the question of the choice of the right belief to endorse. The problem then can be limited, at least initially, to rational belief.

The 17th- and 18th-century rationalist philosophers were liberals. They learned to argue against the traditional religious requirement for strictness, which was based on the observation that the unintended social consequences of selfish action are socially undesirable. The liberal philosophers suggested, on the contrary, that some social conditions ensure that the unintended social consequences of selfish action are socially desirable. Under such conditions, then, following natural appetites, selfish actions will (unintentionally) support social stability rather than undermine it. If so, instead of preaching to curb natural human appetites by the threat of hell fire and brimstone and eternal damnation, it is wiser to create conditions that will make selfish conduct socially beneficial: The readiness to act selfishly is more reliable than the readiness to curb selfish motives merely out of fear (Gellner, 1992, 1995, p. 8).

Initially, in the 17th and 18th centuries, the theory of rationality was prescriptive rather than descriptive. It became descriptive in the 19th and 20th centuries, with the advent of modern social science. It was recognized then that it is well worth investigating the facts of the matter, to observe what actions some extant ideas bespeak, and how. This created a need to distinguish explicitly between the two kinds of rationality: (a) the intellectual rational choice, the choice of beliefs or of opinions to endorse; (b) the practical rational choice, the choice of the right conduct. This distinction is briefly denoted as the choice between rational thought and rational action, or that between thought and action. The need to make this distinction explicit was first presented in modern sociology. It usually goes by the name of Max Weber, one of the acknowledged fathers of that field, who made his studies at the end of the 19th and the beginning of the 20th centuries. Now the classical rationalist assumption is that action is guided by thought, and rationally this is done as best as possible. Hence, the problem of rationality can be limited, at least initially, to the problem of rational thought: What opinions should one endorse? What is rational to believe in? What criterion of choice of a belief should one endorse? The best solutions to these questions, the classical rationalists taught, will ensure the best solutions to all problems.

RATIONALITY AND SELF-RELIANCE

Question: why did the classical rationalists find it so important to insist that, by the classical rationalist recipe, all is as well as can be expected?

Answer: Because throughout the history of classical rationalism, its adherents have opposed the religious doctrine that humans are evil and replaced it with the classical rationalist gospel of self-reliance as the road to salvation (Agassi, 1977).

Question: If all is as well as can be expected, why is the world still so frustrating, and why are people so disappointing as they are?

Answer: Because, says the classical rationalist, people are still not self-reliant.

Question: Why are people not self-reliant? What will make them so?

Answer: People are not self-reliant, says the classical rationalist, because they are captives of the [religious] doctrines they are taught, which makes them rely on their teachers. Only giving up these doctrines will enable people to become self-reliant. After the act of giving up received opinions, beliefs will be as rational as can be expected (for more details, see Agassi, 1991). The world may still not be perfect even when people will be as rational as possible, but it will be as perfect as possible. This is the classical theory of rationality: Rational conduct will bring about the best of all possible worlds, says the classical rationalist, particularly because it will advance scientific research, and thus increase self-knowledge and self-reliance.

It was in this way that self-deception was integrated into the broader system of the modern or classical rationalist movement, or of the Enlightenment movement, or the moderns. Self-deception, they taught, is irrational, and irrationality is due to the absence of self-reliance, and this absence is due to lies with which one is raised. Members of this movement were hardly ever explicit about religion. Few of those who were religiously skeptic dared hint at that fact. It only became permissible to refuse to assume the existence of God in the early 19th century, after the demise of that movement, and even then there was no attack on established religion until the mid-19th century. Nevertheless, this much is clear: The undercurrent of the gospel of Enlightenment was that of self-reliance; the educational system was blamed for teaching ideas that impede it. The education system was, of course, run and carefully monitored largely by the religious establishment. In the civilized world, this monopoly was broken by the French and American Revolutions, yet the monitoring of it by the religious establishment still goes on there to this day. However, few will blame the religious establishment for the wide spread of irrationality.

The situation merits careful analysis. The basic classical rationalist tenet is this: Self-reliance is the reliance on reason; therefore it is the same as rationality. It follows from this that self-reliance, or rationality, is the best guide to life. There is no substitute for thinking: Regardless of whether one is religious, it was suggested, one should not rely on any church or leader. Some modern rationalist philosophers preached and still preach religious self-reliance, or course ("God helps those who help themselves"). Yet is was this idea that undermined the authority of established churches and leaderships, regardless of whether and to what extent this authority was hostile to self-reliance.

The question then is, what is rationality? It was treated in a standard way within the classical rationalist tradition, and its current formulation is as follows. The question is first split into two: What is rational action? What is rational belief? The classical rationalist tradition took it for granted that people always act in accord with their beliefs; otherwise they are coerced by others, by the laws of the land, or by the laws of nature, and so they do not act freely, and so they do not really act. This is the distinction between action and behavior that entered the literature. (Behaviorism, accordingly, is the view that people never act in this sense of the word—that they are always coerced to move as they do by the combination of the general laws of nature and specific circumstances. The standard classical rationalist view rejects this doctrine, and takes for granted as a fact the repeated observation that people do act.) Assuming, then, that people act, it follows that they act rationally. It then follows that if their beliefs are rationally held, then their conduct is as good as can be reasonably expected. This seems reasonable, and even common sense. It is common sense, of course, only on the supposition that humans are naturally rational and self-reliant, that irrational conduct is due to childhood indoctrination in unreasonable beliefs, and that this indoctrination can be overcome for the asking. This means that people are rational unless they are deceived. Why, then, do people insist on being deceived? Why are people gullible? Classical rationalism offers no answer. This is the big gap in the classical rationalism of the Enlightenment movement. This doctrine is still very popular, and so the gap is still conspicuous.

Thus, the prevalence of self-deception is the major refutation to the doctrine of natural human rationality, which is at the root of the doctrine of the Enlightenment movement. Moreover, all deception is due to the fact that some of it is successful, and successful deception is possible only because many people allow themselves to be deceived. Why do they? Because they deceive themselves about other people's credibility. Admittedly, since rational opinion is at times erroneous, one may be deceived without self-deception. Yet, since reason is the best guide, if the rationalist philosophy is true, it will prevent constant systematic error. Systematic error is the result of insistence on it, of the mistrust of reason, and so it is due to self-deception. Even the trust in the teaching and indoctrination during childhood is a form of self-deception. It is possible and rationally obligatory to give it up and be set free. Yet people often cling to their education. They deceive themselves to trust it. The question that classical rationalism has to answer is, why then do people allow others to deceive them systematically? According to classical rationalism, what prevents bridging the gulf between the best, which is the life of reason, and the real, which is the practice of systematic error, is self-deception alone. This phenomenon deserves special attention: It is any systematic error that cannot be viewed as anything other than self-deception. All efforts to correct it are met with unintelligent excuses.

ERROR AND SIN

The ethics of the Enlightenment movement, of the modern philosophy of life, is simple: "Reason is and ought only to be, the slave of the passions," as David Hume aptly put it (Hume, 1980, Bk. 2, Pt. 3, Sec. 3). In this view, self-interest is the only right motive force for action, provided it employs reason to the full, which, of course, is eminently reasonable. Hence, all sin is violation of self-interest, and so, at bottom, all sin is error. This is the doctrine of enlightened self-interest. It is scarcely new. In antiquity it was know as the Socratic doctrine of eudaimony (*eu* is good and *daimon* is spirit; the name refers to the story, narrated in Plato's *The Apology of Socrates*—Socrates explains that he is the wisest by reporting that he has a good Fairy Godmother who prevents him from doing what he does not want to do, which is not good for him). This doctrine is particularly hard to defend, since experience is more in accord with the opposite doctrine, according to which humans are both wicked and self-destructive. Thus, the moral doctrine of classical rationalism appears to be empirically refuted.

The rejoinder to this criticism comes in two steps. The first move is to reduce all self-destruction to self-deception—on the supposition that as self-destruction hurts oneself, it is never desirable and so it is never reasonably desired. (It is unnatural.) The second move is to reduce wickedness to self-destruction. The way to effect this last reduction is to show that the wicked are sawing the branch on which they sit. This is shown by the claim that, as their need for friends requires, they should be benevolent not wicked. This is unsatisfactory, as it may work for friends, perhaps even for potential friends too, but not ever for enemies. It looks eminently reasonable to be vicious to them. Then different arguments are marshalled. An appeal is made to providence: It is in one's best interest to be on good terms with divine powers. This, too, is unsatisfactory, as it is an appeal to the wishes of the divine, not to those of a self-reliant actor. The holders of the monopoly on divine powers always oppose self-reliance. An appeal may then be made to one's need for peace of mind, and hence for peace with one's conscience (the conclusion of Hume, 1748/1980, explains martyrdom this way). This, too, is unsatisfactory: Conscience is based on religion, and the exercise of eudaimony was initially intended to do away with it, and for good reasons. Clearly, it is not conscience, but the sense of guilt, that disturbs the peace of mind. This sense of guilt is forcibly established by religious education to undermine self-reliance. All advocates of self-reliance recommend that the sense of guilt be eradicated (Agassi & Agassi, 1985; Kaufmann, 1973).

It is still possible to defend the doctrine of eudaimony, or enlightened self-interest: Self-destructive action is prevented by the sufficiently clear understanding of its consequences. The standard contemporary example is smoking, but any bad habit will do. The victims of a bad habit know that their conduct is not in their self-interest, but only in a vague manner: They often refuse to see it clearly until their physician convinces them that they are killing themselves. Then many of these people find themselves freed of their bad habit with no effort at all. Hence, the intensified energy and sense of guilt invested in efforts to stop a bad habit are forms of self-deception. What is needed is neither effort nor strong will, but clear understanding of the harm it causes, say the sages of the Enlightenment.

As it happens, all this is neither here nor there. Whatever the rule is for right behavior, it is clear that self-deception is not the right mode of conduct, yet it is prevalent. Even the assumption that all wickedness is due to self-deception does not help vindicate humanity very much, since self-deception is evidently wicked: The pure at heart will hardly fall for it. (Others are guilty of the sin of pride.) Hence, regardless of whether one should be as fully self-reliant as possible, and whether the canons of right conduct are those of enlightened self-interest, self-deception is both erroneous and sinful, yet it is regularly practiced. Why? In particular, is it the sin of it that brings about the error, or is it the other way around?

Before we proceed, we may wish to know, what does it matter? Imperfection is a familiar fact, as are both wickedness and stupidity. Why does the old party insist that all impropriety is sin, and why does the new party insist that all sin is error? Why not lump them together, or say that impropriety and misconduct are at times due to error and at other times due to sin (and often due to both)? After all, criminal law says exactly this: Criminal courts are often called to adjudicate and decide about the reason for some misdeed—is it due to sin or error? Moreover, such courts also distinguish between permissible and impermissible error. (This is the root difference between murder, premeditated or not, and involuntary manslaughter or accidental killing.) Why insist on reducing error to sin or the other way around?

The answer is this: Suppose that behind every sin lurks some error. The way to reduce sin is then not by preaching, but by enlightening. This is the explanation that historically stood behind the Enlightenment movement's optimistic view of humanity: Sinfulness is allegedly a part of human nature, whereas ignorance certainly is not. But this is questionable: Just as one may say that behind every sin is error, one may also say that behind every error is sin. Ignorance leads to excusable error only, whereas the error of people's ways are deviations from the straight and narrow. Established religion comes to prevent sin, and it teaches the true doctrine, but people who are wicked will not listen. Thus, according to all establishments that issue rules of proper conduct, self-reliance is the cardinal sin. (Hence, science can have no such establishment! This is conspicuously false, yet in the Age of Reason, in the time when classical rationalism flourished, it was much more reasonable than it is today to assume that science has no establishment whatsoever.) Here, again, we meet the source of the disagreement: It is this question—what is better to rely on, individual self-reliance or traditional wisdom?

This does not solve the problem at all. The fact remains that both morality and science are cultivated. Why try to eliminate one of these? The answer is that one depends on the other: Wisdom, says established religion, begins with the purity of heart ("the beginning of wisdom is the fear of God"); morality retort the enlightened, begins with the intelligent employment of reason. Does this dispute matter? Should it not be ignored and both morality and reason be employed?

All this will still not do. This discussion is stuck with the problematic phenomenon of self-deception; it is admittedly both stupid and wicked;

It is better eradicated, but no one knows how. Even the combined use of both explaining and preaching does not overcome it, and so there is a genuine need to learn more about it so as to cure it. The two common theories identify it as a sin as well as an error, yet they differ as to which one is the source of the other. Which is it then? In the hope of finding a better cure, a better understanding of self-deception may be sought. In this search, attempts may be made to criticize both theories.

BACON'S DOCTRINE OF PREJUDICE

The present discussion has got into a loop as sin and error are reducible to one another: Even if all error/sin is sin/error, it seems that the very disposition to err/sin lies in our moral/intellectual imperfection. All humans are disposed to both sin and error, and it is hard to decide which of the two dispositions lies deeper. Moreover, as this discussion concerns self-deception, it is important to note that possibly self-deception is inexplicable even were it known if error is the cause of sin or vice versa. The curious historical fact is that the presentation of the problem was first forcefully made by Sir Francis Bacon, around the year 1600. He solved it not by any attempt to choose between blaming sin for error and blaming error for sin but by blaming self-deception for both. He was not concerned with the question, which comes first, sin or error? He was not concerned with social and political philosophy. He had a tremendous vision: A great scientific revolution is in the offing, and it will bring about a great technological revolution. He was convinced that most social and political problems would be solved by the technological revolution. Until then, he recommended, a conservative attitude to politics should prevail.

As Bacon was convinced that technology would be revolutionized by the development of scientific knowledge proper, his sole concern in most of his writings was to help the advancement of learning (for a detailed discussion of all this, see Agassi, 1988b). Bacon took for granted the ancient doctrine of how enlightenment comes about: The pure mind is prepared to perceive the truth in an intuitive experience of sorts. This doctrine is generally known all over the world as mysticism (see Agassi, 1981b, chap. 23). There is much confusion here: The mystics proper do not claim that their knowledge is given to clear articulation, yet the Platonic and Aristotelian theories of learning do. Hence, these theories are not quite mystical; the neo-Platonic or cabalistic doctrines are mystical. The central question that this raises is, how is the mind purified? It engaged Bacon as it engaged many others before and after him. (Different mystics have offered different rituals for this purpose.) Everybody agrees, of course, that, to that end, the mind has to be of a righteous man—free of error. The question remains, how is the mind cleansed of its errors? Both Plato and Aristotle recommended critical debate as the means to that end. (Aristotle called this method *epagoge,* and this word was translated into *induction.*) It is the method of questioning that ends up with definitions, said Aristotle, as invented by the Pythagoreans and perfected by Socrates and Plato. Definitions are the foundations of science, Aristotle added, and they constitute the source of all true knowledge. Bacon agreed about all of this except for the ancient view of the efficacy of critical debate.

Critical debates, said Bacon, have gone on in universities for centuries, yet to no avail: Each party sticks to its guns. The reason is simple: One can always ignore criticism or dismiss it with a witticism ("this is an exception that proves the rule"), or, if one is obliged to take account of it, one can make a new subtle distinction, make a small exception, or otherwise belittle the worth of an argument.

This raises two central questions. First, is it always possible to belittle criticism? Second, why should one do that? The answer to the first question is in the affirmative. It is a powerful part of logic, known today as the Duhem–Quine thesis. Exceptions can always be classified in a different category. (To take a common example, the prejudiced who recommend the discrimination of any sort of people may admit that an instance of the sort in question is unjust; they will then place these counterinstances in a separate class and cling to their prejudice against the remaining members of the discriminated sort. For more details about the Duhem–Quine thesis, see Agassi, 1994.)

There are different attitudes to criticism. Duhem said science must accept criticism only in small doses so as to maintain its continuity. Why should science do that? Duhem did not explain, but the truth is that he was defending the same medieval method that Bacon was attacking because he greatly respected the same medieval thinkers Bacon despised. Bacon declared them enemies of progress; Duhem declared their contributions essential to the history of science. Bacon denied the existence of medieval science; Duhem was its first great historian. More important, Bacon agreed with the ancient revered philosophers that total scientific knowledge of the whole universe is possible; Duhem did not. Bacon declared the need for one and only one scientific revolution—the one that eradicates all prejudice and all error; Duhem advocated continuity and denied the possibility of scientific revolutions. Bacon envisaged a tremendous explosion of science; Duhem taught that science proceeds in small steps. Bacon ignored mathematics altogether and recommended for the mind free of prejudice to collect as many diverse observations of simple facts as possible, and to proceed slowly and carefully toward the goal of total scientific knowledge; Duhem saw this as naive and insisted on the need to develop the mathematical apparatus that is essential for scientific knowledge and fitting the facts within it.

How is one to judge between these views? Probably most people will reject both, at least because at least two scientific revolutions have occurred, contrary to both. Bacon was too radical in his demand to clean the slate with no theory left and Duhem was too conservative in his claim that science suffers no revolution as each stage of it depends on a previous stage (Agassi, 1957, 1963, 1981b; see also the biography of Duhem in Jaki, 1984).

Bacon was a Utopian visionary in the style of his time—the early 17th century. He based his vision on a new idea: He assumed that the rejection of all preconceived opinions and the accumulation of a vast collection of items of factual information will lead rapidly to the full growth of theoretical science. Further, he was deeply convinced that this growth will bring salvation, and that salvation is around the corner because everyone is naturally disposed to contribute to the growth of knowledge (Bacon, 1620/1994, Bk. I, Aphorisms 15–18). Why, then, is salvation not here already? Because there is a small obstacle to it: The sins of laziness and pride. People offer conjectures instead of working hard in the search for the truth, and then they refuse to admit criticisms as it puts them to shame. Thus, the demand for the purity of mind includes the demand for devotion and humility, caution, and resistance to the temptation to conjecture. Once one has made a conjecture, one sees the world as conforming to it, is then bound to endorse it as true, and is then trapped in it: It becomes a fixed feature of one's intellectual makeup. (This is corroborated by contemporary cognitive theory: One who endorses the theory that all is x, say cognitive psychologists, sees x everywhere; x can be atoms, life, sex, selfishness, or anything else.)

Prejudging matters instead of letting facts speak for themselves, Bacon explained, is the acceptance of a bribe. His explanation is subtle, and reminds one of what the Bible says of it (Exodus, 23:8): Bribery blinds the wise. That is, one says to oneself that one is wise enough not to be blinded by the bribe, but to no avail. The very bribe, argued Bacon, is what blinds one to the truth, as it is the flattery to oneself. It is only self-deception that stands between humanity and salvation through science. People flatter themselves that they are more clever and more knowledgeable than they are, thus getting blind to criticism. Moreover, the psychology of perception as first offered by Bacon, and as still taught today, suggests that nothing can be done about it. To become a good researcher, said Bacon, one must humbly admit ignorance, and relinquish all the preconceived notions that one happens to have; only then, he said, will one qualify to seek knowledge, and even then this holds as long as one does not pronounce opinions. Bacon's idea is generally rejected nowadays. It is generally agreed that people cannot live with empty heads. (Only some devotees of popular cheap versions of Oriental mysticism endorse the false view that some techniques empty the head of all ideas.)

The observation that theory blinds one to facts that offer criticism of it is a central part of contemporary psychology of perception and cognition. It often goes today by the name of the 20th-century psychologist Leon Festinger. This observation has led some thinkers, such as Giordano Bruno and Galileo Galilei of the 16th and 17th century, to the obvious conclusion that such observations spuriously validate the theories that invoke them. Bacon agreed but claimed that a theory can be properly validated—when it is rooted in unbiased observations: As long as theory precedes observation, he said, its validation by facts is assured for all those who propound it and for no other. Only if it emerges by itself out of many and diverse observations, he assured his reader, is the result truly assured and will convince all. Hence, proper observation begins with the cleaning of the observer's mind, and therefore observers must be humble and attend to small facts, not aspire to be the proud originators of great philosophical systems.

Why is the sin of pride so special in the scheme of things? Why are all sins to be viewed as errors, yet pride the sin at the root of error? Bacon answered that pride too is but error; of course it is a form of self-deception. It is the error that is the source of all errors, as it inhibits the natural disposition to learn the truth; it perverts the natural order of things by placing theory prior to observation, like building a house beginning from the roof.

Bacon stressed that the matter is subtle. There was no known reason to forbid the making of conjectures before he discovered that conjecture perverts the mind so that it is essential to relinquish all preconceived notions before one can contribute to the advancement of learning. Because the natural disposition to develop science is stronger than the disposition to make conjectures, Antiquity had knowledge and no reason to advance any conjecture. Then conjectures were advanced, especially those of Aristotle, and they were wicked. Once knowledge was perverted, it could not be restored without Bacon's new cure—his prescription of cleaning the slate and proceeding with caution. Naturally until then self-deception was the rule. Accordingly, Bacon called his philosophy "The Great Instauration," meaning the return to the golden age of Antiquity.

A SHORT HISTORY OF SELF-DECEPTION

Self-deception, to repeat, is ubiquitous, as is the folk literature about it. Also, folk literature presents self-deception as self-flattery. This is a point that Bacon's doctrine makes central. Bacon's proposal of a remedy had an old component and a new one. The old component is the following advice: Do not be gullible, trust no one but the facts and your own reason. The new component is: Discard all earlier opinions and start afresh. This is Baconian radicalism, and this is what characterizes modern, classical rationalist philosophy. Its most specific characteristic is its being Crusonian, as Popper and Gellner called it (Popper, 1945, vol. 2, pp. 219–220, 215; Gellner, 1995, p. 7; see also Agassi, 1981b, pp. 477–485, 488). As Descartes found out, after cleaning one's slate and before developing one's own philosophy, one is utterly alone. In the 19th century, Descartes' philosophy and his venture, the Baconian venture of starting afresh, were not as popular as in earlier centuries. One of its opponents was Kierkegaard (1985, preface), who nevertheless admired Descartes for having the courage needed for this venture. As this venture was deemed central to modern, classical rationalism, understandably, rejecting it led many, Kierkegaard included, to reject rationalism itself.

The reason that self-deception is the single obstacle, and such a formidable one at that, is simple. Almost any obstacles that may lie in the way of a self-reliant individual may be handled in the best manner available. The only unsurmountable obstacle to self-reliance is self-deception, since its victims are unaware of its very presence. Classical rationalists deemed the Baconian venture of cleaning the slate indispensable because it is easy to deceive oneself: As long as one holds to any opinion, to any opinion whatsoever, one is too well disposed toward it. Hence, those who rejected Bacon's radicalism were disposed to the view that self-deception is unavoidable. After Bacon had granted prominence and significance to the disposition for self-deception as the chief obstacle to the advancement of learning, and so to advancement in general, it became clear that the disposition to be rational depends on the single condition that self-deception be avoided. The irrationalists then centered, as they still do, on this question: Can this single condition ever be met? Irrationalism is the correct denial of the possibility of avoiding all self-deception and the erroneous conclusion that it is better to rely not on oneself but on tradition, the leadership or one's gut feelings or some other authority.

(Bacon's radicalism is not new: It is cabalistic in origin. Why did the performance of the cabalistic ritual fail to bring salvation? Because there is a catch here: To be valid, the ritual should be performed by a deserving individual who must be humble. But it is hard to be humble when one brings salvation to the world. Why do people end up in hell if they may repent even at the gates of hell? Because the wicked are haughty, and, at the gate of hell, they deceive themselves that they are there not deservedly, but out of good will—out of the will to save its inmates.)

The advocacy of self-reliance looks as if it were identical to the advocacy of rationality, and either looks as if it were identical to the advocacy of the avoidance of self-deception. The opposite of self-reliance is the reliance on others, who are not reliable, since there is nothing to rely on except one's own reason. Hence, the reliance on others is being deceived and all deception is self-deception at heart. According to Bacon, the transition from reliance on others to self-reliance takes effort, courage, and much good will. This is particularly so because, we remember, according to Bacon, self-reliance begins with the cleaning of one's slate—with starting afresh. This, as Kierkegaard stressed, is rather frightening. It also leaves too many questions unanswered, such as, what should one do in matters pertaining to one's means of livelihood and of one's religion? These questions were hardly ever dealt with. Descartes reported that he would not embark on the project of cleaning his slate before he had answered them to his own satisfaction. Today, almost all students of this matter agree that these questions were hardly ever dealt with, and they can never be satisfactorily answered.

This is a significant point. Children have faith in a Santa Claus of one sort or another, and in their having mothers. Somehow the faith in Santa Claus fades away, but having mothers is never questioned. (Feminists have a point, then, when they say there could never have been a female Descartes.) The demand that one should doubt even the existence of one's body, then, is only understandable in the sense that the extant scientific theories of bodies should be doubted. Indeed, the idealists who denied the existence of matter did not question the commonsense view of matter and of their own having emerged out of their mother's wombs. They questioned the theory of matter propounded by Descartes, by Newton, or by other physicists. It is no accident that the Baconian program and its execution by Descartes concerned the improvement of the natural sciences and technologies, hardly the improvement of the social sciences (or the *moral sciences,* to use the antiquated terminology), and even less so the social and political technologies. The application of the Baconian program to social and political studies came later, as an afterthought, and its application to political affairs was unexpected and bizarre.

The Baconian project—his plan to develop science—was a great success, as was his idea that technology will develop magnificently on scientific foundations. His view was echoed by his followers John Locke, David Hume, and, above all, Adam Smith (Halévy, 1955, p. 433). During the French Revolution it was echoed by Condorcet (1976; see also Schapiro, 1934). It was the faith that scientific-technological progress will inevitably improve social matters without much ado. This Baconian aspiration—to save humanity through the advancement of science and technology—failed totally, although not before it landed humanity in the modern world—industrial, postindustrial, and developing—for better or worse.

The first great fiasco of the Baconian program to save humanity through the advancement of science and technology was the French Revolution. The idea is not new that the revolution was the daughter of the ideas of the Enlightenment movement, especially its radicalism. This idea was advanced by the leading Reactionary thinkers, Edmund Burke and Georg Wilhelm Friedrich Hegel (see Agassi, 1977, pp. 218–220). They did not say it outright, but their followers did: People want to be deceived. They want that because they cannot practice self-reliance. This Reactionary idea helped the tyrants of the modern, developed world immensely, and caused untold harm.

The Reaction had much less of a vision and no program, yet being conservative it could always fall back on tradition. The central idea of the Reaction, then, was that people need tradition to tell them what to believe in. This takes the central idea of the Reaction out of the present discourse. The Reaction made a concession to the Enlightenment movement: Some individuals can be self-reliant. They prove it by going into the desert and staying there without food, drink, or company for 40 days and 40 nights. The Reaction deprived even the few self-reliant individuals of their reason: They are exceptional because they are extremely ambitious, and they follow their own bent no matter what. This is a recommendation for self-deception on a grand scale. It suggests that the exceptional must be lonely and stubborn, which is what characterizes many psychopathological cases. Indeed, Hegel said there is no way to distinguish between the exceptional who is a genius from the one who is crazy, or *alienated,* to use the term of Pinel: To be judged alienated (by accepted norms) is the price for one's decision to be self-reliant (until one manages to alter the norms and then be declared a hero). The Reactionary doctrine of dependence and self-reliance is a gross exaggeration. Let us return to a more commonsensical version of rationalism (Agassi, 1981b, chap. 15).

EXTREME RATIONALISM AS SELF-DECEPTION

No rule of logic is more potent than that which proscribes contradictions: They are deadly. Not only are they demonstrably false; declaring one true is the denial of all error, and so it is the admission of every possible statement. Nevertheless, a mathematical text can all too easily include one. In mathematics a misprint may introduce an error, and introducing an error into a mathematical system usually amounts to adding a contradiction to it (the equation $1 + 2 = 3$ becomes a contradiction when any one item in it is misprinted). Strictly, the rule banning all contradictions renders all texts that contain such misprints worthless. However, it is often easy to eliminate misprints by simply overlooking them, and this is done heedlessly unless and until they cause trouble. Even researchers whose ideas seem inconsistent are known to proceed working without worry about inconsistency, in the hope that this matter will be taken care of later. It is hard to judge how rational this attitude is; in the oversight of inconsistency, one risks the waste of time in the study of a worthless system. If the system under study happens to be consistent, or if the inconsistency in it is easy to remove, the result of the study may be useful. However, often a researcher investing much effort in some interesting question will obtain exciting results that rest on an inconsistency, so that the invested labor was sheer waste.

Here is an interesting corollary to the theory of self-deception. It is one thing to take a calculated risk, regardless of whether the end result is happy. It is quite another thing to pretend to have taken a calculated risk, be optimistic about matters, and forge ahead carelessly. Often the investment of effort is only of some pleasant hours of research that one may easily afford to lose. It is an observed fact that if stakes are high and the researcher is highly strung, self-deception steps in as the refusal to entertain the merest possibility of an error. It is hard to differentiate the reasonable cases of calculated risk from the cases of carelessness, as there is no theory that tells us when the risk is great and when not. Perhaps there can be no such theory regarding research.

So much for the requirement for consistency. It is more difficult to study other requirements, as these may be abandoned. This is the case with demonstrability—the supercriterion traditionally most generally adhered to and rightly most respected. It is invalid; adherence to it causes confusion and self-deception. Without the assumption that philosophers addicted to it are deluding themselves, it is hard to explain its popularity, despite its great allure. Historically, it is a central idea, and yet today it is recognized as most baffling. What is demonstrability? What theory of it is there? As its natural place is in mathematics, it can be examined there first.

The standard examples of demonstrations—of proofs—are mathematical, especially those of Euclid and of Archimedes. By modern standards, the quality of these demonstrations is very low. Russell (1917, pp. 66, 94–95) said that Euclid's proofs scarcely qualify. The first to have offered reasonable proofs, said Russell, was George Boole, at the mid-19th century (p. 74). In classical geometry, proofs consisted of deductions from the axioms of geometry. What follows from a theorem is a theorem, yet two nagging questions remained unanswered. First, what makes the axioms theorems? Axioms are self-evident: It is impossible to question their truth. Yet at least one axiom of Euclid was always questioned (for each straight line no more than one parallel line goes through a given point). In the 19th century, a system of geometry was constructed in which that axiom was relinquished. Early in the 20th century, Einstein developed a theory of gravity whose geometry is non-Euclidean. (It denies that space is the same everywhere, as it assumes that the properties of space differ where gravity differs.) So much for the self-evidence of axioms. The other question is, how is proof possible without axioms? It has to do with the theorems in the fields of arithmetic and of algebra. These were not based on axioms until early in the 20th century.

So much for proofs. As to proof theory, it was developed in the 1930s by combined efforts of a few great logicians. Their work was clouded by confusions, most of which were cleared decades later. Perhaps even now, proof theory is too problematic, so that perhaps we are still not entitled to claim possession of a clear proof theory, not even in logic and mathematics.

Yet the puzzling fact is that classical rationalist philosophy rested on the idea that rationality equals proof. An example of magnitude of the puzzlement may be useful, especially as it provides the flavor of the feeling that accompanies the situation. The classical and most popular work of Wittgenstein (1922, preface and famous last sentence) is accompanied by an air of tremendous tension: It declares that, on the one hand, what it says is so obvious that its articulation is neither possible nor called for, and on the other hand, it is so difficult that it is beyond words. Much controversy rages as to how to read his text, and much of it revolves around the question of proof and provability, and of what exactly the message about it is. Possibly, however, the literature in question is a mere expression of a tremendous sense of frustration at the inability of commentators to face their own inability to prove, which is to say that the literature in question is a mere exercise in the futility of self-deception.

As proof theory developed, it was proved that all effective proof procedures are limited, even in mathematics, let alone elsewhere, were proof elsewhere at all possible. The proof—Gödel's celebrated proof—was rejected by Wittgenstein. In the meantime, the matter has developed much further, and proof procedures and their limitations have become a field of intensive study within computer science. What is not provable in one system may be provable in another, as it can be added as an axiom; but the addition will create other unprovable theorems. Contrary to Wittgenstein, there is no comprehensive system in which the logical status of all that can be said is decided once and for all.

The idea that rationality equals proof is most basic. It is the source of much strength, but also of much self-deception—within philosophy as well as within science. Bacon said, and many others echoed, when in doubt one should refrain from endorsing any opinion, one should suspend judgment, and one should never express any opinion about what is doubtful, particularly not in public. Otherwise, self-deception is inevitable. This idea, hostile to self-deception as it is, looks immune to it. The fear that it is itself the malady it comes to cure is as frightening as the idea that physicians cause death. The fear that the medicine is worse than the ills it comes to cure produces a feeling of helplessness, and that feeling is a tremendous incentive for self-deception. Indeed, this is what happened when Semmelweis brought crucial empirical evidence to support the claim that physicians kill patients by not washing their hands. For decades, his view and his prescription were rejected by his peers. This is a clear case of a dangerous, irresponsible, grand-scale self-deception, practiced by a scientifically oriented group.

However erroneous classical rationalism is, it is still very popular among philosophers who like it for its advocacy of the use of reason and its support of science and of self-reliance. Yet it is itself a case of self-deception. These days, the rule of science is tacitly identified as the acceptance of the expert's authority. This is very disconcerting, as any acceptance of any authority is, as it conflicts with the demand for self-reliance. It is also silly. It is well known that the acceptance of the expert's authority may be fatal (see last paragraph for an example). The standard answer to this trite observation is that the reliance on experts is unavoidable in the modern world. Even if it were unavoidable, this does not make it less fatal. Moreover, the unavoidability of the reliance on experts has nothing particular to do with the modern world: It has always been the case, and it is much less so today, when the educated citizen knows more medicine than the best physician of a century ago. As the hypothesis that there is no choice but to rely on experts is refuted, it may be replaced with increasingly better hypotheses that will say how far and under which conditions the reliance on the expert's authority is worse than doing altogether without them. The reliance on experts' authority is clearly the worst superstition of the allegedly rationalist and the allegedly scientifically inclined, and this includes most research scientists (Feyerabend, 1970).

SELF-DECEPTION AS FIXATION

Bacon's doctrine of prejudice was limited to the prejudices of the researchers. Marx extended it to the views—the prejudices—extant in the general population, especially the extant philosophy of life. He labeled it *ideology.* Following Hegel, he denied the universalism of the Enlightenment movement, and replaced it with the view that the parochial views are locally valid. (Hegel called the views and attitudes agreeable to the state *the Universal.*) This theory is known as *relativism* or, more specifically, *epistemic and moral relativism* (see Agassi, 1992). Every period of history, Hegel said, has its own truths, as created by the heroes who are the leading lights of that period. These heroes together constitute the group of individuals who count—"the World Historical Figures." Marx accepted Hegel's epistemic and moral relativism only for the past—for class society. He declared the truth in a class society to be socially determined, but he taught that, in classless society, the truly universal would prevail. Hence, in a class society, all truths are relative and socially determined. Hence, all ideology is class prejudice. Being prejudices, ideologies are hard to shake off. This can only be done by individuals who can peer into the mechanisms of history, like Marx himself—they can divine the future society and the truths of that society.

According to Marx, the society of his day was ruled by employers, by the capitalists. He predicted that the ruling class of his day was destined to be replaced by employees, by the workers. He viewed other philosophers as captives of capitalist prejudices. He viewed himself as the mouthpiece of the future society. He viewed the prejudices of the capitalists inferior to those of the workers. He held the view that the views he was holding were superior to those held by other philosophers.

This is Hegelian: The top representative of humanity, be it the top nation (Hegel), top class (Marx), top civilization or culture (Spengler, Toynbee), or anything else that is tops, is tops in each and every respect. Hegel had a simple justification for this bizarre idea: The best is the militarily strongest, and the strongest takes all that is of value—the way Napoleon robbed the countries he conquered of their artwork. Hegel and Marx never explained why the arts and sciences always progress and they disregarded the historical facts of regress. The most conspicuous fact that Greek art and science are superior to medieval art and science was brushed aside with the aid of the claim for the superiority of the medieval political system or its agricultural technology over its predecessors. This is only evidence that being superior in one dimension is no guarantee for superiority in another. This option did not occur to Marx nor to Marxist scholars in the middle of the 20th century. (The famous scientist and historian of science J. D. Bernal (1939, chap. 2, sect. 1) declared flippantly that medieval science is superior to Greek science. (See also Bernal, 1952, 1954, p. 209; Agassi, 1963, chap. 7 and notes).

Traditionally, philosophy was reductionist: it recommended that events that belong to the different human sciences should be explained by theories from only one human science. Traditional reduction was to psychology: All human sciences, it was suggested, are at heart psychology: Sociology, politics, and economics are really parts of psychology. Bacon's doctrine of prejudice was perhaps behind this trend. When Hegel reduced the individual to society and declared political history the basic human science, he declared it essential for sanity to believe in national myths. Marx advocated the reduction of all human sciences to economics. He wanted to see all explanation of human affairs by reference to the economic conditions of the society in which they occur, chiefly in terms of the advancement of its technology. Freud, however, clung to the traditional recommendation to reduce all human phenomena to psychology. He attempted to explain the way some private prejudices have a strong hold on the minds of their victims. He was impressed by the fact that neuroses constitute intellectual blind spots, especially when the neurotics who sustain them are intelligent. He explained this by his theory of the emotional trauma (*trauma* means wound).

Freud's theory of the emotional trauma is simple. The cause of every neurosis, he suggested, is a trauma caused by some frightening, painful childhood event. Initially, the trauma leads to an attempt to cope with it by conjecturing a hypothesis. Being infantile, this hypothesis is not surprisingly of a low intellectual level. What is surprising is that the neurotic never gets over the initial hypothesis. This, Freud explained, is due to two facts. First, reliving the traumatic incident is painful. Second, one attempts to avoid that pain. For example, if one conjectures that the pain in question is caused by the rejection due to one's lack of achievement, one will increase one's efforts to achieve. The refutation of the hypothesis will only lead to redoubling the effort, rather than to recognizing that no effort will reverse the rejection (because one tries to achieve the wrong object, because the rejection is irreversible, because there was no rejection to begin with, or because of anything else). Therefore, the purpose of psychoanalytic treatment should be liberating neurotics from the prejudices that are at the base of their neurotic conduct, which incapacitates them. This, according to Freud, can be achieved only by helping them relive their initial traumatic experiences. Once this is achieved, patients experience strong relief and a sense of *catharsis,* and then, according to Freud, all is well.

This is Freud's celebrated catharsis theory. He later claimed to have refuted it to his own satisfaction. It is difficult to say what replaced catharsis as the aim of psychoanalytic treatment after that theory was abandoned. Possibly Freud was too hasty to reject the theory; possibly the fault was not in the ascription of therapeutic power to catharsis, but in the view that, after it, the patient is well and the treatment is over. I

(Agassi, 1981a) have suggested that the recovered mental patient needs treatment that is usually accorded to the physically convalescent. When a convalescent has weak muscles, it matters little why; the question is, how should they be strengthened? The same may be true of the mentally convalescent, whose decision power is small. If so, what precisely the prejudice was that the catharsis reveals is less important than the treatment accorded to willing mentally convalescents. This shows that Freud's theory is one of self-deception. It is a model for a number of such theories, yet not a sufficiently good one, as it does not take into account the atrophy of self-reliance due to prolonged neurosis. Freud has rightly observed that adolescents often get rid of their prejudices, but not those acquired under severe traumas—including morality, which is thus inculcated under the conditions of brainwashing, said Feyerabend (1968).

Self-deception can be treated in all generality. It is rational to inquire, to seek the truth, but perhaps not at any cost. At times, the search for the truth is too costly, and its outcome is of little significance. In these cases, it is reasonable to give up the quest. This is a troublesome catch. One remains ignorant, first, of the truth that one allows to remain hidden, and then also of the cost of giving it up—of relinquishing it. More than Bacon, Freud renders self-deception as the opposite of the search for the truth. He insisted more on the relentless search for the truth. Yet the limitation on the cost of the search for the truth remains. Selectiveness is unavoidable, and one about the search for the truth is inherently blind. What should be done about this? Freud was troubled by interminable analysis, which is an expression of both the excessive cost of analysis and its contribution to the increased atrophy of the patient's self-reliance.

This is where Freud got stuck. Bacon's doctrine relates to the search for the scientific truth. He said the search should not be selective, because any selection is guided by an idea, and that idea is a prejudice: It is judgment prior to the presentation of the relevant evidence. Even asking specific questions, Bacon said, is selective. The choice of a question is rooted in a prejudice. To avoid prejudice, research must be indiscriminate and all discovery accidental. Freud's view of his own research was orthodox Baconian; his claim that his theory evolved out of myriads of observations was clearly Baconian; his suggestion that analysts intervene minimally in the analytic process of self-discovery was based on his fear of prejudice. Yet his theory was related to everyday life, where the question about the search for the truth cannot be as all-encompassing as in research. Thus, he could not say how neuroses-free the average citizen should be (Freud, 1962, third paragraph from the end).

Freud appealed to simple common sense: One often deviates from the normal healthy views of things, and one is then normally corrected by circumstances or by peers. It is abnormal to resist this kind of correction. Abnormal resistance to common sense is at times intelligent, as in the case of a research scientist. Alternatively, it is sometimes unintelligent, at other times it is hardly a trouble, and still other times it incapacitates. This then requires treatment. Here then is the place for Freud's original contribution: The neurotic resistance is still rational, although it is obsessive (i.e., pathological). It is the insistence on avoiding the pain of reliving the trauma. This is a hurdle the incapacitated should be helped to clear. Reluctance to discuss one's opinions rationally is the outcome of the assessment that discussion will be painful. However, one is never able to assess properly the cost of the reluctance to acquire information for want of that very information. Therefore one should always be ready to reassess one's view that the pain is not worth the benefit. If common sense calls for this reassessment and is met with an obsessive refusal, perhaps the cause is psychopathological. Otherwise, the resistance is better diagnosed differently, especially when it expresses the fear of self-reliance (*decidophobia* is the apt term offered by Kaufmann, 1973).

CONCLUSION: THE NEW THEORY OF RATIONALITY

The discussion thus far is couched within common sense, or in a framework that differs radically from the classical theory of rationality. Since Freud fully endorsed that theory, his discussion was possibly inconsistent—in that it mixed common sense with the classical theory of rationality. Even if it is consistent, it is encumbered with irrelevant difficulties, and in its original wording it is much harder to comprehend than its (more general) variant reproduced here.

The discussion herein also deviates from the classical theory of rationality in its avoidance of the theory that the rational is the provable. Nor does it require an explicit wording of an alternative theory of rationality. The new theory of rationality that is required should share with common sense the idea that there is no human perfection. It should not assume any part or aspect of any product of the human mind to be perfect and above error. Briefly, it should include the idea that it is desirable to eliminate error as far as possible; it suggests that this is done by criticism. Criticism, then, should be viewed not as hostile, but as help. This idea is not new, and is clearly expressed in Plato's *Gorgias*. Yet in the writings of Plato (and Aristotle), the rationality of criticism is presented as a mere preliminary to the rationality of proof. Omitting this, we receive the new theory of rationality, or a variant of it: Critical discussion is not the appetizer, but the main course. Hence, it is not just concerning received opinions, as Plato and Aristotle suggested, but an endless process of inventing ever newer conjectures and their refutations—as much as is within the powers of the participants in the process (Agassi, 1995; Popper, 1945). (This raises the question, is logic perfect, and is mathematics? These matters are not discussed here, although they are of great philosophical interest.)

The assumption that criticism is rational is very rational, and its rejection by Bacon and his followers is a great pity, although Bacon was right to observe that critical discussion as practiced in the universities was an exercise in futility. The first modern variant of the fallibilist theory of rationality, which incorporates the assumption that rationality is critical debate, is due to Popper (1945, chap. 24). His theory is not free of objections, especially Bacon's. Criticism may be pointless at times. It can also be an unaffordable luxury. It is impossible to know if this applies to the case at hand. The theory under consideration may deserve criticism and it may not: Investing in criticism risks wasting valuable time.

Examples of irrational critical thinking abound, and at times they can be classified as pathological. Psychotherapists are familiar with many kinds of them. Patients are often ingenious at inventing new excuses that allow them to ignore or belittle criticism of their views and conduct. Patients are likewise ingenious at inventing criticisms of, and in finding lacunae in, the assumptions behind threatening proposals of therapists. People often use many tools—physical or mental—without bothering about their inner mechanisms. When patients are afraid of using a proposal made by their therapists, they suddenly show passionate interest in the mechanisms involved in the proposal and in critical debates about them. These passionate interests are delay tactics and expressions of fear. The observation of Konrad Lorenz is relevant here: Conduct under fear and pressure is less intelligent than the average in all animals. The claim made here is that even losing one's mind is a process due to rational conduct, but in fear and under great stress, and so with an ever-decreasing level of rationality (Fried & Agassi, 1976).

Thus, there are levels of rationality; the highest level available is hardly ever attained. It is approached only in some very leisurely, research-oriented discussions. Even then it is not always clear what avenue is best to take (contrary to classical rationalism), as there are many possibilities, some of them inherently blind. Thus, it is only seldom clear how the level of rationality can be raised. That the rationality of action may be a matter of degree is common sense, and if all rationality should be seen as a matter of degree, it is useful to view rational thought as a variant of rational action. Traditionally, rational thought, or rational opinion, was distinguished from rational action (including thinking). This is reinforced by the traditional distinction between states (of mind) and (mental) processes. This distinction is subtle and redundant: Jarvie and I

(Agassi & Jarvie, 1987) suggested viewing thought as a kind of action and the theory of rational thought as a part of the theory of rational action. This is meat to be a supplement to Popper's theory of rationality.

There are two points to mention before bringing this chapter to a close. First, unlike the classical theory of rationality, the fallibilist theory does not split rationality sharply to the scientific and the rest. It also recognizes common sense and its progress. (Think of the views of nutrition common a century ago, which recommended what is today viewed as empty calories and/or a cholesterol-rich diet; or of sexuality, which deemed masturbation self-destructive and the pleasure of sex undesired by decent women.) It also takes for granted that, in science as elsewhere, every significant criticism is an invention, so that it is important to see the difficulty of being critical (and so of being highly rational). This relates to the second point. The fear of criticism is rational, but not as rational as the effort to overcome it. Self-deception is thus a form of rational human conduct, but it is inferior to attempts to overcome fear and more so to fearless openness. This is not to say that every possible case of self-deception is equally harmful and to be equally harshly combatted. Often psychotherapists encounter cases that they judge—hopefully rightly—as not deserving treatment. The cases that do deserve treatment, even at a great cost, Freud noted, are those that grossly interfere with the ordinary course of life. Some cases are subtle and difficult to judge. A sense of proportion must prevail in discussing them. The pursuit of the truth is laudable, but it is not necessarily always the required treatment.

A sense of proportion is indispensable anyway, since there is no greater self-deception than the claim that one is utterly free of it, as is regrettably exemplified by the great thinkers Bacon, Marx, and Freud. This should be remembered as a warning against excessive self-confidence: Humans are all fallible and, as Plato already observed in great detail, it behooves us to be grateful for any attempt at criticism and correction.

APPENDIX

The editor has drawn my attention to a very recent essay by Mele (1996), that deserves notice because it comprises a very comprehensive survey of the most recent literature on self-deception, which is becoming increasingly fashionable these days. The literature is written from the viewpoint of the theory of rationality as the rational degree of belief and that as the degree to which the belief is justified by experience. This viewpoint was declared in this chapter as a version of self-deception, perhaps also an expression of some anxiety. The starting point of that literature is the so-called paradox of self-deception. Assume that successful deception occurs when one who thinks that some statement is true convinces someone else that it is not. Assume further that one successfully deceives oneself the same way. As a result, one does and does not think that the statement in question is true. As was explained here, it is easier to begin with self-deception and view most cases of deception as variants of it. As explained in this chapter, self-deception is always a form of ambiguity and/or confusion and ignorance, so that it is a spectrum, and there is no sharp division between those engaged in it and those who keep clear of it, although some people are very near one end of the spectrum and others on the other. Mele reported numerous experiments in self-deception, with no regard to the question, how well trained the subjects of the experiment are in the art of self-criticism. The absence of self-criticism, it was argued in this chapter, is not the same as self-deception, especially as all criticism is the result of some creative act. There is also the question of the cost of self-criticism that the experiments discussed by Mele disregard. The experimenters do not ask how important the self-deception under discussion is and how important the individuals in question considers it. Most engagement in astrology by modern educated people is a mild, harmless form of self-deception that cannot be taken as seriously as the case of self-deception that leads to disaster.

REFERENCES

Agassi, J. (1957). Duhem versus Galileo. *British Journal for the Philosophy of Science, 8*, 237–248.

Agassi, J. (1963). *Towards an historiography of science, Beiheft* 2. *History and theory.* Middletown, CT: Wesleyan University Press.

Agassi, J. (1969). Can religion go beyond reason? *Zygon, 4*, 128–168.

Agassi, J. (1975). *Science in flux. Boston Studies in the Philosophy of Science, 28.* Boston: Kluwer.

Agassi, J. (1977). *Towards a rational philosophical anthropology.* Boston: Kluwer.

Agassi, J. (1981a). Psychoanalysis As a human science: A comment. *British Journal of Medical Psychology, 54*, 295–296.

Agassi, J. (1981b). *Science and society: Essays in the sociology of science, Boston Studies in the Philosophy of Science, 65.* Boston: Kluwer.

Agassi, J. (1982). Irrationalism today. *Dialectica, 36*, 465–480.

Agassi, J. (1986a). On the fixation of beliefs. *Methodology and Science, 19*, 165–177.

Agassi, J. (1986b). Towards a canonic version of classical political theory. In M. Grene & D. Nails (Eds.), *Spinoza and the sciences, Boston Studies in the Philosophy of Science, 91*, 153–170.

Agassi, J. (1988a). *The gentle art of philosophical polemics: Selected reviews.* LaSalle, IL: Open Court.

Agassi, J. (1988b). The riddle of Bacon. *Studies in Early Modern Philosophy, 2*, 103–136.

Agassi, J. (1991). *The siblinghood of humanity: Introduction to philosophy.* Delmar, NY: Caravan Press.

Agassi, J. (1992). False prophecy versus true quest: A modest challenge to contemporary relativists. *Philosophy of the Social Sciences, 22,* 285–312.

Agassi, J. (1994). Minimal criteria for intellectual progress. *Iyyun, 43,* 61–83.

Agassi, J. (1995). The theory and practice of critical rationalism. In J. Misiek (Ed.), *Rationality: On the problem of rationality of science and its philosophy. Popper versus Polanyi, Boston Studies in the Philosophy of Science, 160,* 7–23.

Agassi, J., & Jarvie, I. C. (Eds.). (1987). *Rationality: The critical view.* Boston: Kluwer.

Agassi, J. B., & Agassi, J. (1985). The ethics and politics of autonomy: Walter Kaufmann's contribution. *Methodology and Science, 18,* 165–185.

Bacon, F. (1994). *Novum organum scientiarum.* LaSalle, IL: Open Court. (Original work published 1620)

Bernal, J. D. (1939). *The social function of science.* London: Routledge.

Bernal, J. D. (1952). *Marx and science.* London: Lawrence & Wisehart.

Bernal, J. D. (1954). *Science in history.* London: Watts.

Condorcet, M. J. A. N. C., Marquis de. (1966). *Selected writings.* Bloomington, IN: Bobbs Merrill.

Feyerabend, P. (1968). Science, freedom, and the good life. *Philosophical Forum, 1,* 127–135.

Feyerabend, P. (1970). Consolations for the expert. In I. Lakatos & A. Musgrave (Eds.), *Criticism and the growth of knowledge.* Cambridge, England: Cambridge University Press.

Freud, S. (1962). *Civilization and its discontent* (J. Strachey, Ed. & Trans.). New York: Norton.

Fried, Y., & Agassi, J. (1976). *Paranoia: A study in diagnosis, Boston Studies in the Philosophy of Science, 50.* Boston: Kluwer.

Gellner, E. (1992). *Reason and culture: The historical role of rationality and rationalism.* Oxford, England: Blackwell.

Gellner, E. (1995). Prometheus perplexed. In I. C. Jarvie & N. Laor (Eds.), *Critical rationalism, metaphysics and science: Essays for J. Agassi* (Vol. II), *Boston Studies in the Philosophy of Science, 162* (pp. 3–18). Boston: Kluwer.

Halévy, E. (1955). *The growth of philosophical radicalism* (M. Morris, Trans.). Boston: Beacon.

Hume, D. (1980). *Enquiries concerning human understanding and the principles of morals.* Westport, CT: Greenwood. (Original work published 1748)

Jaki, S. (1984). *Uneasy genius: The life and work of Pierre Duhem.* Boston: Kluwer.

Jarvie, I. C., & Laor, N. (Eds.) (1995). *Critical rationalism, the social sciences and the humanities, Essays for J. Agassi* (Vol. II), *Boston Studies in the Philosophy of Science, 162.* Boston: Kluwer.

Kaufmann, W. (1973). *Without guilt and justice.* New York: Weiden.

Kierkegaard, S. (1985). *Fear and trembling.* New York: Penguin.

Mele, A. R. (1996). *Real self-deception.* Preprint available on the World Wide Web.

Popper, K. R. (1945). *The open society and its enemies.* London: Routledge.

Russell, B. (1917). *Mysticism and logic and other essays* (2nd ed.). London: Allen & Unwin.

Russell, B. (1967). *The autobiography of Bertrand Russell: Vol. III. 1944–1967.* London: Allen & Unwin.

Schapiro, J. S. (1934). *Condorcet and the rise of liberalism.* New York: Harcourt.

Wittgenstein, L. (1922). *Tractatus logico-philosophicus.* London: Routledge.

3

Self-Knowledge and Self-Deception: Further Consideration

Anthony G. Greenwald

The term *self-deception* describes the puzzling situation in which a person appears both to know and not know one and the same thing. Consider as an example a cancer patient who maintains the expectation of recovery even while surrounded by the signs of an incurable malignancy. Presumably this patient knows unconsciously that the disease is incurable, but manages to prevent that knowledge from becoming conscious. Interestingly, one of the reasons for concluding that the patient unconsciously knows of the incurable malignancy is the very success of the defense. How could that defense be maintained so effectively without using knowledge of the unwelcome fact to anticipate the forms in which it might try to intrude into consciousness?

THE PARADOX OF SELF-DECEPTION

The sense in which this example is puzzling, or paradoxical, is shown in Fig. 3.1. Some encountered situation, or stimulus, is assumed to receive both unconscious and conscious analyses. The unconscious analysis, which is assumed to occur first, identifies a threatening, or anxiety-evoking, aspect of the stimulus. In Fig. 3.1, the anxiety-evoking stimulus is represented as some proposition, p—such as, "I have a terminal malignancy." Conscious analysis, however, fails to apprehend this proposition.

There are three puzzling aspects of this situation. First, how can the person manage unconsciously to reach the conclusion that proposition p is true while not also reaching that conclusion consciously? Second, what good does it do for the person not to know consciously that p is true? Should it not produce anxiety just to know unconsciously that p is

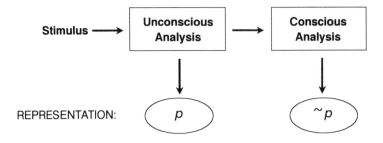

Three Questions

1. **How does the person both know and not know *p*?**
2. **What good does it do not to know *p* consciously?**
3. **Why is the faster, more accurate, system unconscious?**

FIG. 3.1.   The paradox (or puzzle) of self-deception. In this and other figures
in this chapter, theorized stages of cognitive analysis are represented by
rectangles, representation outputs are represented by ovals, and observable
events (stimuli and responses) are identified leading to or emerging from
these entities. In this figure, a proposition and its negation are represented
as *p* and ~*p*, respectively.

true? Third, and most puzzling of all, why does the unconscious system
give both a faster and a more thorough analysis than the conscious
system: Would it not be sensible to have one's most acute cognitive
abilities available to consciousness?

Interest in Self-Deception

Self-deception has attracted the interest of scholars of several different
disciplines, and for several different reasons. For clinical psychologists
and psychiatrists, self-deception is seen as a means of protection from
painful knowledge (Murphy, 1975; Sackeim & Gur, 1978; Schafer, 1976).
At the same time, it seems a strangely cumbersome method of defense.
That is, it appears to create more problems for the psyche than it can
possibly solve. How, therefore, can it protect? From this clinical perspective, understanding self-deception has implications for the conduct of
psychotherapy.

For cognitive psychologists and philosophers (e.g., Fingarette, 1969),
self-deception is seen as a paradoxical condition of knowledge. How
does a knowledge system accommodate an apparent internal contradiction? From this epistemological perspective, achieving an understanding of self-deception will shed light on the organization of human
knowledge.

For ethologists, self-deception is seen as a strategy that could provide an advantage in animal social interaction (e.g., Lockard, 1980; Trivers, 1985). By unconsciously deceiving itself, an animal might become a more effective deceiver of others. From this perspective, the investigation of self-deception might justify placing the psychological concept of the unconscious under the explanatory umbrella of sociobiology, making it a topic within the emerging subdiscipline of evolutionary psychology.

The intellectual perspectives of clinical psychology, psychiatry, cognitive psychology, epistemology, and sociobiology collectively yield a set of questions that might be answered by a successful analysis of self-deception. First, and most fundamentally, how is self-deception to be conceived of in terms of knowledge organization: If it requires unconscious cognition, how does that unconscious cognition relate to conscious cognition? Second, what is the function of self-deception: What psychic gain results from the combination of knowing something unconsciously while not knowing it consciously? Third, how common is self-deception: Is it an ordinary phenomenon of everyday life, or is it an exotic, even pathological phenomenon? And fourth, what empirical criteria can be used to identify self-deception: How can it be studied in the laboratory?

The theoretical analysis used in this chapter addresses these four questions and, in doing so, describes two theoretical alternatives to the paradox-laden psychoanalytic account of defenses against cognitive threat. One alternative borrows from cognitive psychology the well-established paradigm of an ordered series of *stages*, or *levels*, of information processing. The second theoretical account uses the newer paradigmatic approach of *parallel distributed processing*, or *neural network modeling*. Both of these theoretical approaches allow nonparadoxical interpretation of effective cognitive defenses.[1]

Previous Analyses

The most thorough intellectual analysis of self-deception was provided by philosopher Herbert Fingarette in the 1969 book *Self-Deception*. Fingarette sought to develop a paradox-free account of self-deception. Ultimately, Fingarette's attempt to avoid paradox must be judged unsuccessful. Nevertheless, Fingarette's review and analysis advanced the topic considerably, and provided a stimulating entry point for researchers. Notable among subsequent researchers were Gur and Sackeim (1979; see also Sackeim & Gur, 1978), who provided a careful statement of the

---

[1]The earlier version of this chapter (Greenwald, 1988b) described how the first of these two approaches (information-processing stages) could produce a nonparadoxical account of apparent self-deceptions. The second approach (network modeling) is newly included in the present chapter.

self-deception paradox and offered a laboratory procedure for its investigation.

Fingarette's (1969) Analysis. Fingarette started by criticizing previous attempts by philosophers to analyze self-deception, and concluded that previous attempts to resolve the paradox of self-deception either (a) had not addressed themselves to the proper phenomena of self-deception, or (b) rather than resolving the paradox, had merely portrayed it in a "variant form." Fingarette's own analysis went part of the way toward a solution, but unfortunately did not escape reintroducing the paradox. This reintroduction occurred in the form of an unnamed mechanism that analyzes the true (threatening) import of circumstances and, on the basis of the knowledge so obtained, purposefully prevents the emergence into consciousness of both the threatening information and the defense against it.

Fingarette's unnamed mechanism was capable of inference and intention in a way that required sophisticated symbolic representation. Yet Fingarette assumed that this mechanism operated outside of the ordinary machinery of inference and symbolic representation—that is, outside of conscious cognition. The paradoxical aspects of Fingarette's unnamed mechanism seem indistinguishable from the paradoxical aspects of Freud's censor (the agency of repression). For Freud, the censor operated from a base within the conscious ego, and although it appeared to have ego's reasoning powers, nevertheless was assumed to operate without ego's consciousness (Freud, 1923/1961). The three questions in Fig. 3.1, which define the paradox of self-deception, apply as much to Fingarette's analysis as to Freud's.

Gur and Sackeim's (1979) Analysis. In seeking to demonstrate the paradoxical character of self-deception, Gur and Sackeim (1979) adapted a voice-recognition task that had been developed about a half-century earlier by Wolff (1932; see also Huntley, 1940). In this task, after making recordings of samples of their own voice, subjects were asked to judge whether each of a series of played-back samples was or was not their own voice. The critical evidence comes from examining the relationship between occurrences of skin conductance response (SCRs) and overt verbal identification responses to the voice stimuli. The SCR is assumed to indicate unconscious own-voice recognition, whereas verbal identification indicates conscious recognition. Self-deception is judged to occur when the SCR occurs on an own-voice trial, yet the subject fails to identify the voice as self.

Why are such trials paradoxical? It is not simply that the SCR and verbal response appear to disagree. That disagreement could be explained nonparadoxically (and not very interestingly) by assuming, for example, that the skin conductance system is more prone to error (perhaps by influence from stray events), or that it is susceptible to sources of error that differ from those that disrupt verbal identification. The response disagreement becomes interestingly paradoxical, however, when one concludes that the SCR reflects an unconscious own-voice identification that plays a role in the purposeful blocking of conscious identification. It is therefore relevant that Gur and Sackeim demonstrated a correlation between individual differences in voice identification accuracy and scores on a Self-Deception Questionnaire measure, suggesting a motivated blocking of conscious voice recognition that is initiated by a knowing observer operating outside of conscious cognition.

Resolving the Paradox by Changing Assumptions

The Assumption of Personal Unity.   Paradoxes stimulate theoretical advance by making it apparent that there is a troublemaker lurking somewhere among one's theoretical assumptions. One candidate troublemaker, in the case of the self-deception paradox, is the assumption of personal unity that implicitly underlies much psychological theory (cf. Greenwald, 1982). This is the assumption that each person's knowledge is organized into a single, unified system. It is the assumption that implicitly justifies use of the word *individual* (i.e., an indivisible entity) to refer to the person. Alternatively, it might be assumed that there are dissociations within personal knowledge systems (Hilgard, 1977). For example, in the case of the voice-recognition task, one might assume that the right hemisphere (or some other modular brain subsystem; see Gazzaniga, 1985) controls the SCR independently of the left hemisphere's control of verbal-identification responses. With such an abandonment of the assumption of unity within the knowledge system, discrepancies between SCR and verbal identification of own-voice stimuli are no longer paradoxical—no more than it would be paradoxical for two different people to disagree in identifying the same voice.

Abandoning the assumption of personal unity seems a drastic step. At the same time that one gains the ability to explain findings of discrepancy between response systems, one gives up at least some of the ability to explain *relationships* between response systems—relationships of the sort that are heavily appealed to in psychological theory, for example, in the influential mediationist behaviorisms of Spence (1956), Mowrer (1960), or Osgood (1953), in the information processing theories of the cognitive revolution (e.g., Smith, 1968; Sternberg, 1969), and in cognitive interpretations of emotion such as those of Schachter and Singer (1962) or Lazarus (1984). In the last decade, however, the assumption of personal unity has received a substantial indirect attack, in the development of the concept of parallel distributed processing, or neural network modeling (e.g., Rumelhart & McClelland, 1986).

The Assumption of a Coordinate Unconscious.   There is another possible troublemaking assumption that many will find more easily sacrificed than the assumption of personal unity. This expendable troublemaker is the assumption of a *coordinate unconscious*—the assumption that unconscious and conscious cognition are coordinate, or equivalent in power, and therefore capable of the same types of mental operations. When the assumption of a coordinate unconscious is abandoned, it becomes possible to set unconscious cognition into a multilevel conception of mental representations—a conception that readily provides nonparadoxical explanations of phenomena to which the *self-deception* label has been attached.

An attractive alternative to the coordinate unconscious is a conception of unconscious cognition that is decidedly weaker in analytic power than conscious cognition—a *subordinate unconscious.* The subordinate unconscious assumption is described later after introducing a multilevel interpretation of human representational abilities. In the multilevel view, with its subordinate unconscious, unconscious cognition continues to play an important role in cognitive defense, but that role is served by mechanisms that are much weaker in analytic power than is the coordinate unconscious of psychoanalytically inspired theories of cognitive defense.

THE NONPARADOX OF KNOWLEDGE AVOIDANCE

This section explains in some detail how cognitive defenses, including ones that appear to involve paradoxical self-deception, can be explained theoretically without paradox when the assumption of a coordinate unconscious is replaced by the assumption of a subordinate unconscious.

Levels of Representation

The cognitive psychological concept of an ordered set of information-processing stages (e.g., Smith, 1968) provides the basis for a multilevel analysis of mental representations. Figure 3.2 shows a minimal levels-of-representation analysis, with just two stages or levels. The first stage produces a relatively crude representation of an experienced event. This initial representation can control some action directly while providing input for a second, higher, level of analysis. The second level, in turn, produces its own representation, which can control a different response to the event.

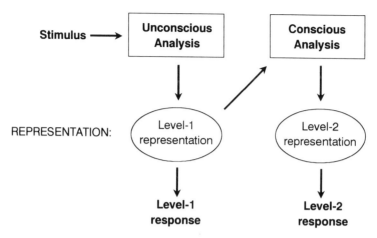

FIG. 3.2. Two-stage levels of representation scheme.

This familiar device of assuming that cognitive analyses occur in series or stages, illustrated minimally with two stages in Fig. 3.2, provides the basis for replacing the paradoxical concept of cognitive defense by self-deception with the nonparadoxical concept of cognitive defense by *knowledge avoidance*. To see how this levels-of-representation analysis avoids paradox, consider an analogy: a two-level model of behavioral (not cognitive) avoidance for the mundane problem of dealing with the contents of one's mailbox.

Junk-Mail Model of Knowledge Avoidance

The annoyance of dealing with unsolicited mass mailings—of material such as advertisements and requests for funds from various organizations—is partly captured by their common designation as "junk" mail. Fortunately, there are easily perceived cues that warn recipients of the likely uninterestingness of an envelope's contents. The postage may be lower than the rate for personal letters, the address likely printed by machine, the recipients's name given in unusual fashion (e.g., to "occupant"), and the envelope made from low-quality paper. Certainly many people have the habit of discarding, without opening, envelopes that provide such warnings. This is a useful avoidance response—one saves the time required to open and read the undesired contents of such mail.

The two stages of the junk-mail model (see Fig. 3.3) are (a) examining the exterior of the envelope, and (b) reading the contents. It is clear that the second stage's processing can be avoided by using results from the first stage's analysis. In other words, one need not know specifically what is inside the envelope to judge that it should be discarded.

In order to connect junk mail to self-deception, let us return to the

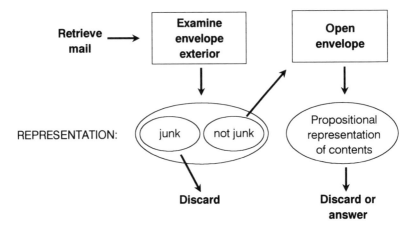

FIG. 3.3.   Junk-mail version of the two-stage model.

example of the terminally ill cancer patient. Perhaps the patient picks up cues indicating that *some* unwelcome knowledge may be available (like seeing the outside of the envelope), and then avoids learning precisely what the unwelcome knowledge is (like discarding the letter). There is no more paradox in the cancer patient's avoiding sure knowledge of terminal illness than there is in the junk-mail recipient's avoiding sure knowledge of the contents of an unopened envelope. This analysis, which proposes that an avoidance response can be based on partial analysis of a stimulus, is a close relative of ones offered previously by Allport (1955), Eriksen and Browne (1956), and Kempler and Wiener (1963), in their reviews of research on perceptual defense.

Nonparadoxical Account of the Voice-Recognition Experiment

Figure 3.4 analyzes Gur and Sackeim's (1979) voice-recognition procedure in terms of levels of representation. In the two-level model of Fig. 3.4, the SCR is controlled by the first level, which analyzes the acoustic features of a voice sample. The SCR may be elicited by voice-spectrum features that resemble one's own voice. This sensory-feature-based SCR is *not* equivalent to voice identification any more than examining the outside of an envelope is equivalent to reading its contents. Voice identification occurs only at the second stage of analysis, perhaps based on additional, more complex (paralinguistic) cues, such as accent, speech rate, and inflection. As was the case for the two levels of the junk-mail model, the two levels of the voice-recognition model involve different types of analysis. The second stage requires more complex analysis than

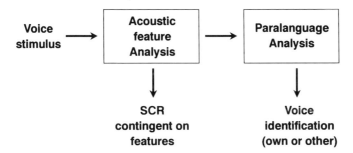

FIG. 3.4. Two-stage model of the voice-recognition experiment.

the first, and it produces a more abstract representation. Because the first-stage SCR and the second-stage self-identification can be based on different stimulus information, there is no paradox when a first-stage SCR is accompanied by nonidentification of own voice at the second stage.

Levels of Representation Elaborated

Figure 3.5 expands the two-level model of Fig. 3.2 into a four-level structure that is rich enough to account for a broad variety of human cognitive capabilities (based on Greenwald & Leavitt, 1984; elaborated further in Greenwald, 1988a). At the lowest level is sensory-feature analysis—a process that is assumed to operate automatically and without leaving memory traces—that is, unconsciously. In the model in Fig. 3.5, unconscious cognition is identified with this first (lowest) level, which does not produce representations more abstract than sensory features. The placement of a dividing line between unconscious and conscious cognition within the series of levels of analysis makes this model one of a subordinate, rather than a coordinate, unconscious. The second level identifies objects and accesses word meanings. The third level encodes verbal information into propositional representations (i.e., sentence meanings). The fourth and highest level uses stored conceptual knowledge to generate inferences from the third level's propositional representations.[2,3]

---

[2]In the more detailed development of this analysis (Greenwald, 1988a), the second level is split into two functions—object identification and categorization—that can be treated as separate levels.

[3]No attempt has been made in this chapter to relate the hypothesis of a series of cognitive stages of analysis, as in Fig. 3.4, to theorization concerning neural apparatus that could support such function. However, modern theorization concerning the orienting reflex (e.g., in the tradition of Sokolov, 1963) provides a conception of central nervous system organization that is quite compatible with the cognitive distinction between pre-attentional (unconscious) and attentional (conscious) levels.

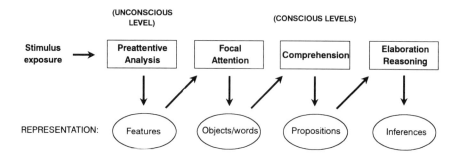

FIG. 3.5.   Four-level model of cognition.

"Self-Deception" as Avoidance of Inference

In the example of unawareness of terminal cancer, critical processing occurred at Figure 3.5's third level—the level at which events are analyzed in terms of propositions such as "The doctor said they removed all of the tumor." After that processing occurs, it is still necessary to use the fourth level—the level of reasoning from conceptual knowledge—to draw inferences such as "The doctor didn't tell me to expect complete recovery. That means my chances aren't so good." By not going beyond the third level—by not drawing inferences—one *avoids* an unwelcome conclusion. That is, cognition does not proceed to the level of identifying the threat specifically—the unwelcome news remains unknown. This avoidance of a painful conclusion differs fundamentally from the paradoxical self-deception of Fig. 3.1. In the self-deception analysis, the painful conclusion is simultaneously known (unconsciously) and not known (consciously). By contrast, in the avoidance analysis, the painful conclusion is not known at either a conscious or unconscious level.

In addition to providing an account of apparent self-deception associated with terminal illness, the cognitive-defense-by-avoidance-of-inference analysis applies to daily acts of avoidance that everyone must engage in routinely. Every time we hear news of personal risks—such as diseases associated with foods we eat (such as caffeine or eggs), or accidents associated with behavior in which we engage (flying or driving), or of possible local hazards (such as crime, earthquake, flood, or toxic waste spill), or even of global threats (such as terrorism, ozone depletion, or catastrophic nuclear reactor failure)—we can infer that our well being is threatened. However, most of us spend little time contemplating such threats. The analysis of this avoidance is quite similar to that of the terminally ill cancer patient. Our avoiding the unwelcome conclusion that we will fall victim to one of numerous threats may be credited to habits of interrupting trains of thought that lead to unpleasant conclusions (cf. Dollard & Miller, 1950). Of course, not all people avoid drawing frightening conclusions about their personal vulnerability. But, then, neither do all terminally ill patients avoid drawing the conclusion that they are dying.

Avoidance of Inference by Drawing Alternative Inference

Consider a possible example of cognitive defense that received much publicity in 1991, when Clarence Thomas was nominated to the position of Associate Justice of the United States Supreme Court. During Thomas's U.S. Senate confirmation hearing, law professor Anita Hill accused Thomas of sexual harrassment when Thomas had been her supervisor in a previous job. Thomas vigorously denied the accusation. The accusation and denial were such that it appeared that one of the two must be lying. A possibility that was not considered in the news and commentary accounts of the time is that both could have been telling what they perceived to be the truth! This would be possible if Hill and Thomas drew different inferences or conclusions from their participation in the same situation. What Hill concluded to be sexual harrassment might have been interpreted quite differently by Thomas, perhaps as an unsuccessful attempt to establish a friendly relationship with a colleague.

It has long been considered normal for different participants in a social interaction to draw different inferences (or make different attributions) about the interaction. Two well-researched sources of systematic variation in these attributions are associated with the differing perspectives of *actor* and *observer:* (a) Actors tend to interpret their actions as being responsive to events occurring in the situation, whereas observers are more likely to interpret the same behavior as indicating some characteristic personality trait of the actor (Jones & Nisbett, 1972); and (b) actors are likely to interpret and remember their own actions in a self-serving or self-enhancing way (Greenwald, 1980). The differences between Clarence Thomas's and Anita Hill's interpretations of their interaction could be a case of Thomas's drawing an inference that was self-servingly different from Hill's following interactions that they viewed and interpreted from different perspectives. As in the case of the terminal cancer patient, this can be a cognitive defense that is explainable in nonparadoxical fashion by the sequential-stage levels-of-representation model.

THE ORDINARINESS OF KNOWLEDGE AVOIDANCE

The illustrations of avoiding knowledge of terminal illness and avoiding anxiety about various risks and environmental hazards have been interpreted as cognitive defenses that occur between the third and fourth levels of the model in Fig. 3.5. Experienced events are analyzed to the level of propositions (such as "Amazon rain forests are being cut down"), but anxiety-producing inferences are avoided. Failure to draw such inferences may be the phenomenon that has most frequently been identified, in previous analyses, as involving (paradoxical) self-deception. In contrast with the present analysis, those previous analyses have assumed that the inference must be made at an unconscious level at the same time that it is avoided consciously. The model in Fig. 3.5, however, provides no mechanism for achieving inferences unconsciously, and does not require the occurrence of such inferences as a condition of successful avoidance.

The model in Fig. 3.5 allows knowledge avoidance to occur not only at the transition from its third to fourth level, but also in its lower level transitions. The following consideration of these possibilities suggests that cognitive defense by knowledge avoidance is a pervasively ordinary phenomenon.

Avoidance of Comprehension

Avoidance of third-level processing would occur if the words in a message were perceived individually (second-level processing), but the perceiver avoided comprehending their sentence-level meaning. Such avoidance of comprehension occurs commonly in dealing with the content of mass media. Television and radio programs are frequently interrupted by short commercial announcements in which one is uninterested; newspapers and magazines contain advertisements and uninteresting articles interspersed among their more interesting contents. In dealing with mass media, the perceiver may be consciously aware of the individual words of a message while nevertheless avoiding comprehension of their sentence-level meaning. Hearing or seeing a brand name may suffice to classify the surrounding message as uninteresting, which in turn leads to diverting attention elsewhere, thereby avoiding the effort of comprehending that message. Similarly, the title of a magazine article or the headline of a newspaper story may contain a name or topic word that is sufficient to forestall further analysis. Avoided comprehension after perceiving individual words may be what is happening when one reacts to another's "unattended" remark by asking for it to be repeated, but then readily retrieves the individual words in sequence and does the higher level work of comprehension before the remark before is actually re-stated.

Avoidance of Attention

Treisman and Gelade (1980) described the cognitive act of attention as involving the integration of sensory features into perceived objects. Avoiding attention can therefore occur when first-level analysis of sensory features is not followed by further perceptual analysis. The well-known "cocktail-party effect"—being able to focus on a single one of several simultaneously heard voices—is an example of avoiding attention. The listener successfully avoids attending to the words of extraneous conversations while nevertheless analyzing their sensory features, such as voice pitch and spatial location (Broadbent, 1958; Moray, 1970). A second example is an experience, familiar to most skilled automobile drivers, that occurs when, immediately after completing some portion of a familiar route, one is unable to recall stimuli that must have been processed recently, such as whether the last traffic light was red or green. In this case, it is not so much that perceiving the object is undesired as that it is unnecessary. For experienced drivers, driving is so well learned that it can be performed automatically, with habitual actions occurring in response to important stimulus features (i.e., after analysis only at the lowest level of Fig. 3.5), leaving those features unintegrated into perceptually attended objects.

Avoidance of Exposure

Perhaps the most common type of knowledge avoidance is one that cannot be located between stages of the levels-of-representation model because it involves complete nonexposure to stimuli that might lead to useless or otherwise unwelcome cognitive analyses. For example, consider the consequence of a heavy smoker not engaging in physical exercise. The smoker thus avoids encounters with stimuli (excessive fatigue, difficulty breathing, etc.) that could indicate adverse physical effects of smoking. In a similar fashion, by soliciting no student evaluations, a professor can avoid negative feedback that would injure self-esteem. And, to take an almost trivial example, many recreational tennis players effectively avoid discovering that they routinely commit the error of foot-faulting (i.e., stepping into the playing area before hitting a serve) because, consistent with good tennis form, they simply do not look at their feet while serving. Because there is no exposure to events that could lead to unwelcome knowledge, the avoiding-exposure strategy can be very effective. The avoider has no basis for suspecting that anything is being avoided. In terms of the four-level model, such behavioral avoidance of exposure to unwelcome stimuli preempts the first level of analysis. It is located off the left side of the model. The junk-mail model of Fig. 3.3 is itself an example of behavioral avoidance of exposure.

TWO NEW THEORETICAL DEVELOPMENTS

Neural Network Modeling

Since publication of the earlier version of this chapter, there has been active development of a new paradigmatic approach in psychology, alternatively labeled *parallel distributed processing, connectionism,* or *neural network modeling* (Rumelhart & McClelland, 1986). Figure 3.6 gives a schematic representation of this approach, indicating how it accommodates the distinction between conscious and unconscious cognition.

The extensive parallelism of the network model of Fig. 3.6 is its fundamental difference from the sequential-stage information-processing model of Fig. 3.5. The network model in Fig. 3.6 incorporates representations of two forms of conscious cognition.[4] One of these—conscious cognition as network operation that boosts activation to resonantly stable high levels in subnetworks—corresponds to an interpretation of *conscious cognition as a focus of attention* on some thought or percept. The network's second representation of conscious cognition is its possibility of having verbal outputs that, by virtue of their connections to inner nodes ("hidden units") of the network, are able to report (in some sense) on internal network status. These verbal outputs correspond to an interpretation of *conscious cognition as a capacity for introspective report* (or "self-consciousness"). Importantly, the structural principles of the neural network provide no assurance that these verbal reports will provide valid descriptions of network status.

In the information-processing form of theory (Fig. 3.5), cognitive defenses were explained nonparadoxically by supposing a hierarchical division between conscious and unconscious cognition, and assuming that unconscious cognition was associated with hierarchically lower and less complex levels of analysis. The neural network account avoids paradox by the more radical device of abandoning the assumption of personal unity. To illustrate: In a neural network account of the voice-recognition experiment (for which an information-processing account was portrayed in Fig. 3.4), the (nonverbal) SCR and the (verbal) voice-identi-

---

[4]The distinction between these two forms of unconscious cognition is developed more fully in Greenwald (1992).

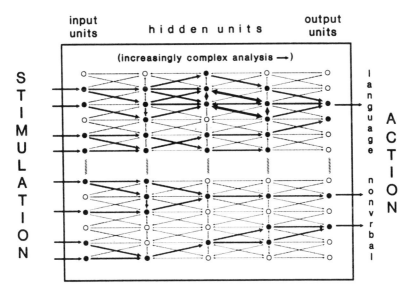

FIG. 3.6. Representation of conscious and unconscious cognition in the format of neural network (connectionist or parallel distributed processing) models. (This figure is duplicated with permission from Fig. 2 of Greenwald, 1992.)

fication response would be treated as outputs from analyses that occur in parallel. Because these two analyses might take independent paths through the network, they need be under no constraint to yield correlated outputs.

Implicit Cognition

In the early 1980s, cognitive psychologists began to investigate a large class of phenomena inspired by Edouard Claparède's (1911/1951) observation of a surprising manifestation of memory in a Korsakoff-syndrome patient. Characteristically for the illness, Claparède's patient lacked ordinary recollection, and was unable to recognize Claparède from one visit to the next. During one visit, Claparède deliberately pricked the patient's finger with a hatpin when they were shaking hands. On the next visit, the patient hesitated to shake hands with Claparède—whom, as usual, the patient did not recognize as a familiar acquaintance.

Jacoby and colleagues (Jacoby & Dallas, 1981; Jacoby & Witherspoon, 1982) have reported experimental tests that established the repeatability of observations (like Claparède's) of "remembering without awareness," not only with Korsakoff-syndrome patients, but also with normal undergraduate students. In Jacoby's research, unrecallable events have

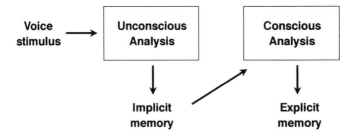

FIG. 3.7.   Two-stage analysis of implicit cognition.

been shown to potently influence judgments made in response to stimu-li that re-present some portion of the earlier event. A familiar example is that subjects will complete a word stem (e.g., *can___*) with a word that was presented earlier in the experiment (e.g., *candle*), even when they are unable to recall that *candle* was presented earlier.[5] Schacter (1987) reviewed the rapidly growing literature on such memory phenomena, and Greenwald and Banaji (1995) established that parallel forms of *implicit cognition* also occur pervasively in expressions of social attitudes, stereotypes, and self-esteem.

The defining characteristic of implicit cognition is that some judgment draws on information contained in past experience while the judge nevertheless remains ignorant of the influence of that past experience (see Greenwald & Banaji, 1995). This generic definition of *implicit cognition* encompasses the situation in which a skin conductance response to a playback of the subject's voice indicates that the subject is responding under the influence of past experience with the sound of own voice, even while not recognizing this influence. Not surprisingly, then, implicit cognition can be analyzed with a stage model of the same type used for the voice-recognition experiment (see Fig. 3.7).

EMPIRICAL ANALYSIS OF THE RELATIONSHIP BETWEEN CONSCIOUS AND UNCONSCIOUS COGNITION

Of the several procedures that have been used in attempted laboratory models of psychoanalytically conceived defense mechanisms, none has escaped criticism that the resulting evidence is inconclusive. For every sympathetic review of findings on topics such as perceptual defense (Dixon, 1981; Erdelyi, 1974) or repression (Erdelyi & Goldberg, 1979;

---

[5]The reader who completed this stem with *cancer* may have experienced the same kind of automatic influence routinely experienced by subjects in Jacoby's experiments.

Shevrin & Dickman, 1980), one can point to forceful opposing reviews (e.g., Eriksen, 1958; Holmes, 1974; Loftus & Loftus, 1980). In drawing conclusions from a review of the research literature, Erdelyi (1985) observed that a consistent shortcoming of laboratory models of cognitive defense was their failure to demonstrate that "the perceiver can intentionally and selectively reject perceptual inputs [of emotional stimuli]" (p. 256). Sackeim and Gur (1978) presented the following list of four criteria for an empirical demonstration of (paradoxical) self-deception:

1. The individual holds two contradictory beliefs (p and not-p).
2. These beliefs are held simultaneously.
3. The individual is not aware of holding one of the beliefs (p or not-p).
4. The act that determines which belief is and which belief is not subject to awareness is a motivated act. (p. 150)

The levels-of-representation analysis of knowledge avoidance (Fig. 3.3, 3.4, and 3.5) and the neural network model (Fig. 3.6) provide perspectives from which the difficulty of achieving research demonstrations that meet these four criteria is easily understood. In the levels-of-representation approach, because cognitive avoidance does not involve knowledge of what is being avoided, Sackeim and Gur's first, second, and fourth criteria are inappropriate. That is, the expectation of data patterns that match Sackeim and Gur's four criteria is contingent on the assumption of a coordinate unconscious—an assumption that seems quite unnecessary for the explanation of successful cognitive defense.

In the neural network approach, it is possible for conscious and unconscious cognition to be as independent of one another as if they were taking place in the left and right cerebral hemispheres of a split-brain patient. This possibility of independent, parallel cognitive paths bears on the reference to an individual (implying an indivisible entity) in Sackeim and Gur's first and third empirical criteria. In the neural network, there is no necessary assumption of personal unity, meaning that two mutually contradictory beliefs could be represented in the network without there being any system locus that has simultaneous access to them. This makes it possible for the neural network to account nonparadoxically for even exotic dissociations that could not be explained by information-processing models such as that in Fig. 3.5.[6]

---

[6]Greenwald (1992) described a variant information-processing approach that assumed the possibility of independent processing paths, each composed of sequential stages. (Information-processing models standardly assume only a single series of stages or levels.) When modified to permit multiple parallel paths, the information-processing approach may be paradigmatically indistinguishable from the neural network approach.

Recent empirical and theoretical developments have not only made cognitive psychologists much more comfortable with the idea of unconscious cognition than they were a decade ago, but have also shaped a view in which unconscious cognition is seen as operating alongside, and sometimes even independently of, conscious cognition. The theoretical development of neural network modeling has made the idea of parallel conscious and unconscious cognition decidedly nonparadoxical. In recent years, researchers have increasingly employed assumptions of independence (or dissociation) between conscious and unconscious cognition in their interpretations of experimental findings (e.g., Greenwald, Klinger, & Schuh, 1995; Jacoby, Lindsay, & Toth, 1992). These dissociations can be given nonparadoxical interpretation by either (or both) a levels-of-representation or a network approach.

In summary, Sackeim and Gur's (1978) list of criteria for an empirical demonstration of self-deception implies two assumptions that appear unneeded and excessive in light of cognitive psychological research of the past few decades. These two questionable assumptions are (a) *unconscious knowledge of threat*—that successful cognitive defense requires a prior, complete, unconscious representation of the knowledge that is being defended against; and (b) *single-agency coordination*—that successful cognitive defense represents the coordinated achievement of a single agency. In combination, these two assumptions comprise the view that was described earlier in this chapter as the "coordinate unconscious" conception. The knowledge-of-threat assumption is easily sacrificed in the context of a levels-of-representation view, in which low-level, partial analysis of a threatening stimulus allows avoidance or modification of a later, more complex analysis. The single-agency assumption survives in levels-of-representation models, but is unneeded in neural network models, which move away from a conception of personal unity and toward understanding the person as a distributed processor with multiple, concurrent cognitive processes.

CONCLUSION: A VIEW
OF UNCONSCIOUS COGNITION

This chapter has described a view of unconscious cognition that has evolved, in the last few decades, from a previously dominant view that rested on the psychoanalytic conception of coordinate conscious and unconscious cognition. The psychoanalytic view obliged the assumption that cognitive defense could involve paradoxical simultaneous knowledge and ignorance of threatening or anxiety-arousing situations. The assumed validity of this paradoxical psychoanalytic interpretation justified referring to some cognitive defenses as self-deceptions.

Contemporary cognitive psychology provides two theoretical interpretations of the relationship between conscious and unconscious cognition that provide nonparadoxical accounts of a wide variety of cognitive defenses, including those that have been labeled *self-deceptions*. The longer established of these interpretations is the concept of a hierarchical series of stages of information processing (or levels of representation). In this sequential-stage view, a low-level analysis can guide both the avoidance of threat and the avoidance of higher level processing that is needed to identify the exact nature of the threat. The more recently developed approach of neural network modeling, by accommodating independent paths of cognition initiated by the same stimulus, is theoretically powerful enough to provide nonparadoxical explanations of even exotic cognitive dissociations, such as multiple personality. One attraction of the sequential-stage information-processing view is its ability to provide a nonparadoxical account of cognitive defense, while accommodating the lay conception of unity of the normal personality. In the context of the neural network approach, personal unity may be treated merely as an illusion of the normal personality.

These new interpretations of unconscious cognition are important not only because they demystify phenomena previously considered to be paradoxical self-deceptions, but because they portray unconscious cognition as relatively weak in its cognitive analytic power. The conception of unconscious cognition as cognitively weak appears especially in the sequential information-processing interpretation, which associated unconscious cognition with early (and relatively crude) stages of processing. This conception of unconscious cognition as relatively weak in analytic power was implied by the junk-mail model, which was first described in the 1988 version of this chapter. The case for regarding unconscious cognition as weak in analytic power was developed in much more detail by Greenwald (1992).

ACKNOWLEDGMENTS

This chapter is a major revision and update of the author's contribution to the volume, *Self-Deception: An Adaptive Mechanism?*, edited by Joan S. Lockard and Delroy L. Paulhus (Englewood Cliffs, NJ: Prentice-Hall, 1988 [Greenwald, 1988a]). Preparation of the original chapter was aided by a grant from National Science Foundation (BNS-8217006). Preparation of this revision was aided by grants from National Science Foundation (SBR-9422242) and National Institute of Mental Health (MH-41328). The

author thanks Joan S. Lockard, Delroy L. Paulhus, and Prentice-Hall for
permission to use portions of the earlier chapter.

REFERENCES

Allport, F. H. (1955). *Theories of perception and the concept of structure*. New York: Wiley.
Broadbent, D. E. (1958). *Perception and communication*. London: Pergamon.
Claparède, E. (1951). Recognition and "me-ness." (E. Rapaport, Trans.). In D. Rapaport
  (Ed.), *Organization and pathology of thought* (pp. 58–75). New York: Columbia University
  Press. (Original work published 1911)
Dixon, N. F. (1981). *Preconscious processing*. London: Wiley.
Dollard, J., & Miller, N. E. (1950). *Personality and psychotherapy*. New York: McGraw-Hill.
Erdelyi, M. H. (1974). A new look at the new look: Perceptual defense and vigilance.
  Psychological Review, 81, 1–25.
Erdelyi, M. H. (1985). *Psychoanalysis: Freud's cognitive psychology*. New York: Freeman.
Erdelyi, M. H., & Goldberg, B. (1979). Let's not sweep repression under the rug: Toward
  a cognitive psychology of repression. In J. F. Kihlstrom & F. Evans (Eds.), *Functional
  disorders of memory* (pp. 355–402). Hillsdale, NJ: Lawrence Erlbaum Associates.
Eriksen, C. W. (1958). Unconscious processes. In M. R. Jones (Ed.), *Nebraska symposium on
  motivation: 1958* (pp. 169–227). Lincoln: University of Nebraska Press.
Eriksen, C. W., & Browne, C. T. (1956). An experimental and theoretical analysis of
  perceptual defense. *Journal of Abnormal and Social Psychology, 52*, 224–230.
Fingarette, H. (1969). *Self-deception*. London: Routledge & Kegan Paul.
Freud, S. (1961). The ego and the id. In J. Strachey (Ed. & Trans.), *The standard edition of the
  complete psychological works of Sigmund Freud* (Vol. 19, pp. 3–66). London: Hogarth.
  (Original work published in 1923)
Gazzaniga, M. S. (1985). *The social brain: Discovering the networks of the mind*. New York:
  Basic Books.
Greenwald, A. G. (1980). The totalitarian ego: Fabrication and revision of personal histo-
  ry. *American Psychologist, 35*, 603–618.
Greenwald, A. G. (1982). Is anyone in charge? Personalysis versus the principle of per-
  sonal unity. In J. Suls (Ed.), *Psychological perspectives on the self* (Vol. 1, pp. 151–181).
  Hillsdale, NJ: Lawrence Erlbaum Associates.
Greenwald, A. G. (1988a). *Levels of representation*. Unpublished manuscript, University of
  Washington, Department of Psychology, Seattle.
Greenwald, A. G. (1988b). Self-knowledge and self-deception. In J. S. Lockard & D. L.
  Paulhus (Eds.), *Self-deception: An adaptive mechanism?* (pp. 113–131). Englewood Cliffs,
  NJ: Prentice-Hall.
Greenwald, A. G. (1992). New Look 3: Unconscious cognition reclaimed. *American Psy-
  chologist, 47*, 766–779.
Greenwald, A. G., & Banaji, M. R. (1995). Implicit social cognition: Attitudes, self-
  esteem, and stereotypes. *Psychological Review, 102*, 4–27.
Greenwald, A. G., Klinger, M. R., & Schuh, E. S. (1995). Activation by marginally percep-
  tible ("subliminal") stimuli: Dissociation of unconscious from conscious cognition. *Jour-
  nal of Experimental Psychology: General, 124*, 22–42.
Greenwald, A. G., & Leavitt, C. (1984). Audience involvement in advertising: Four levels.
  Journal of Consumer Research, 11, 581–592.
Gur, R. C., & Sackeim, H. A. (1979). Self-deception: A concept in search of a phenome-
  non. *Journal of Personality and Social Psychology, 37*, 147–169.
Hilgard, E. R. (1977). *Divided consciousness: Multiple controls in human thought and action*.
  New York: Wiley.

Holmes, D. S. (1974). Investigations of repression: Differential recall of material experimentally or naturally associated with ego threat. *Psychological Bulletin, 81*, 632–653.

Huntley, C. W. (1940). Judgments of self based upon records of expressive behavior. *Journal of Abnormal and Social Psychology, 35*, 398–427.

Kempler, B., & Wiener, M. (1963). Personality and perception in the recognition threshold paradigm. *Psychological Review, 70*, 349–356.

Jacoby, L. L., & Dallas, M. (1981). On the relationship between autobiographical memory and perceptual learning. *Journal of Experimental Psychology: General, 110*, 306–340.

Jacoby, L. L., Lindsay, D. S., & Toth, J. P. (1992). Unconscious influences revealed: Attention, awareness, and control. *American Psychologist, 47*, 802–809.

Jacoby, L. L., & Witherspoon, D. (1982). Remembering without awareness. *Canadian Journal of Psychology, 36*, 300–324.

Jones, E. E., & Nisbett, R. E. (1972). The actor and the observer: Divergent perceptions of the causes of behavior. In E. E. Jones, D. E. Kanouse, H. H. Kelley, R. E. Nisbett, S. Valins, & B. Weiner (Eds.), *Attribution: Perceiving the causes of behavior* (pp. 79–94). Morristown, NJ: General Learning Press.

Lazarus, R. S. (1984). On the primacy of cognition. *American Psychologist, 39*, 124–129.

Lockard, J. S. (1980). Speculations on the adaptive significance of self-deception. In J. S. Lockard (Ed.), *The evolution of social behavior* (pp. 257–275). New York: Elsevier.

Loftus, E. F., & Loftus, G. R. (1980). On the permanence of stored information in the human brain. *American Psychologist, 35*, 409–420.

Moray, N. (1970). *Attention: Selective processes in vision and hearing.* New York: Academic Press.

Mowrer, O. H. (1960). *Learning theory and behavior.* New York: Wiley.

Murphy, G. (1975). *Outgrowing self-deception.* New York: Basic Books.

Osgood, C. E. (1953). *Method and theory in experimental psychology.* New York: Oxford University Press.

Rumelhart, D. E., & McClelland, J. L. (Eds.) (1986). *Parallel distributed processing* (2 vols.). Cambridge, MA: MIT Press.

Sackeim, H. A., & Gur, R. C. (1978). Self-deception, self-confrontation, and consciousness. In G. E. Schwartz & D. Shapiro (Eds.), *Consciousness and self-regulation: Advances in research* (Vol. 2, pp. 139–197). New York: Plenum.

Schachter, S., & Singer, J. E. (1962). Cognitive, social, and physiological determinants of emotional state. *Psychological Review, 65*, 379–399.

Schacter, D. (1987). Implicit memory: History and current status. *Journal of Experimental Psychology: Learning, Memory, and Cognition, 13*, 501–518.

Schafer, R. (1976). *A new language for psychoanalysis.* New Haven, CT: Yale University Press.

Shevrin, H., & Dickman, S. (1980). The psychological unconscious: A necessary assumption for all psychological theory? *American Psychologist, 35*, 421–434.

Smith, E. E. (1968). Choice reaction time: An analysis of the major theoretical positions. *Psychological Bulletin, 69*, 77–110.

Sokolov, E. N. (1963). *Perception and the conditioned reflex.* New York: Pergamon.

Spence, K. W. (1956). *Behavior theory and conditioning.* New Haven, CT: Yale University Press.

Sternberg, S. (1969). Memory scanning: Mental processes revealed by reaction-time experiments. *American Scientist, 57*, 421–457.

Treisman, A. M., & Gelade, G. (1980). A feature-integration theory of attention. *Cognitive Psychology, 12*, 97–136.

Trivers, R. (1985). *Social evolution.* Menlo Park, CA: Benjamin/Cummings.

Wolff, W. (1932). Selbstbeurteilung und fremdbeurteilung im wissentlichen und unwissentlichen versuch. *Psychologische Forschung, 16*, 251–329.

4

The Tricks and Traps of Perceptual Illusions

Dan Zakay
Jonathan Bentwich

> *Knowledge and error flow from the same mental sources, only success can tell the one from the other.*
>
> —Mach (1905/1976)

THE NATURE OF PERCEPTION

Most readers, looking at Fig. 4.1, would say they see a street with a house and pedestrians walking. When asked further which person is more distant, A or B, the common answer would be: "B." This answer would be given almost instantly, accompanied by a strong feeling of confidence. Nevertheless, the seemingly trivial perceptual experience, as reflected in the way Fig. 4.1 was perceived, raises some complex questions.

It is evident that people perceive such pictures as three-dimensional, but it is not clear whether this perception is a valid representation of the real stimulus. The perception of any visual stimulus is based on its retinal image—that is, "the two-dimensional distribution of light of various intensities and wavelength on the retina" (Coren, Ward, & Enns, 1993, p. 405). The retinal image can be considered a "pixel soup" from which some "primary sketch" (Marr, 1982) emerges. The translation of this pattern of brightness intensities, of which a perceiver is unaware, into a meaningful perception—like that of a street, houses at different distances, and people walking—is not self-evident. Let us focus on the level of correspondence between the retinal image of Fig. 4.1 and the perceptual experience evoked by it. It is possible to measure with a ruler

FIG. 4.1. A street. Computerized graphics of an original photo by Gad Rones.

the distances between the viewer and Persons A and B. Evidently, the distances are identical because both persons are on the same surface. Actually, any retinal image is two-dimensional because the retina is a two-dimensional surface. Thus, it can be claimed that there is no correspondence between the automatic three-dimensional interpretation given to a two-dimensional picture and the objective stimulus. Before reaching any conclusions, another common perceptual phenomenon is examined.

Many people have gazed at the moon on a semicloudy night. The immediate feeling is that the moon is moving while the clouds are standing still. Actually, the velocity of the moon's motion at any given moment, as reflected by the shift of its image on a perceiver's retina, is negligible. The stimuli that are really moving fast are the clouds, and so are their retinal image. With regard to the moon, people also see it much brighter at night, as compared with its perceived brightness during the day. Wrong again. From an objective point of view, the brightness of the moon, which is a dark gray rock, is the same by day and by night. What people perceive is the sun's light reflected by the moon with an equal intensity during the day or night (Rock, 1975).

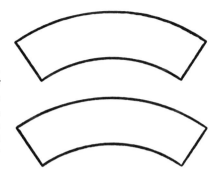

FIG. 4.2. The Jastrow illusion. From *The Psychology of Perception* by William N. Dember, copyright © 1960 by Holt, Rinehart and Winston, Inc., and renewed 1988 by William N. Dember, reproduced by permission of the publisher.

Let us now consider the Jastrow illusion (Rock, 1975) in Fig. 4.2. Its two forms presented are perfectly congruent, and yet the upper appears smaller than the lower. Révész (1924) demonstrated that this effect is not confined exclusively to human subjects. He trained chickens to peck only from the smaller of any pair of geometrical forms. After the chickens had acquired this habit, they were tested with the Jastrow figures. On their first experience, the chickens chose to peck the form that seems smaller to people. Thus, human perception, and probably that of animals as well, does not always correspond with the real objective stimuli. However, there is a difference in the way the three examples discussed so far are treated. The moon's apparent movement and the Jastrow phenomenon are usually designated as "illusions" and conceived of as errors with no perceptual benefit, whereas the three-dimensional interpretation of a two-dimensional picture is considered a "normal" and desirable perceptual experience. Individuals who are unable to experience the three-dimensional interpretation would be categorized as having abnormal perception, and frequently would find it difficult to adapt to the environment.

PERCEPTION AND ILLUSION

The *American College Dictionary* (1964) defined a *perceptual illusion* as "a perception of a thing which misrepresents it, or gives it qualities not present in reality" (p. 602). Another definition presented in *A Dictionary of Psychology* (Drever, 1974) is "a subjective perversion of the objective content or actual sense data" (p. 129). Rock (1975) defined an *illusion* as "a sensory impression or perception that is false or incorrect—what we experience does not correspond with the objective situation that can be determined by other means, e.g. measurement" (p. 390). A final example of how an *illusion* is defined is "Distortions or incongruencies between percept and reality" (Coren et al., 1993, p. 17). It is of interest that all definitions are quite similar to one declared in 1881 by the British scientist James Sully, one of the first to systematically explore the domain of illusions. According to Sully's definition, *illusion* is "any species of error which counterfeits the form of immediate, self-evident, or intuitive knowledge, whether as sense-perception or otherwise" (p. 6).

According to modern definitions as well as those of previous centuries, seeing a two-dimensional picture as three-dimensional is as much an illusion as seeing the upper form in the Jastrow figure as smaller than the lower form. One can even go further and claim that any perceptual experience is illusory in the first place, and is not an accurate representation of its corresponding physical stimuli. This can be demonstrated by the problem of resolution. Physics teaches that any object is composed of molecules, atoms, and elementary particles, yet whole objects are perceived. People's senses are limited; they are not sensitive to certain types of physical energy like magnetic fields or infrared light. Even that which is perceived is inaccurate, as the laws of psychophysics imply.

A basic phenomenon of the perceptual system is the Just-Noticeable-Difference (JND). People perceive a change in physical energy of any form not in an absolute way, but rather relative to the former intensity of physical energy experienced. Thus, a certain amount of physical energy, when added to an existing low amount of energy, might yield a sensation of change, but will not cause a feeling of perceived change when added to a higher current level of energy, as exemplified in a typical psychophysical function (Fig. 4.3). Such a psychophysical function,

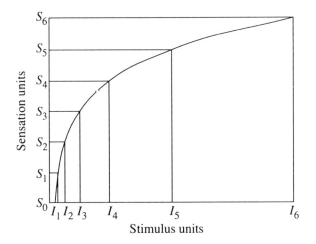

FIG. 4.3. A typical psychophysical function. From *Sensation and Perception* (p. 8) by H. R. Schiffman, 1982, New York: Wiley. Copyright © 1982 by Wiley. Reproduced by permission of John Wiley & Sons, Inc.

which is logarithmic in shape, reflects that sense organs transform physical energy into neural electrical activity by a logarithmic transformation. A basic property of psychophysical functions is that of the diminished return. This is the case not only regarding physical stimuli, but also an abstract stimulus like money, as exemplified in the shape of utility curves, which is similar to that of any perceptual psychophysical function. The JND phenomenon is thus a psychological misrepresentation of the physical world, and hence should be considered an illusion, but this is not the case.

The logarithmic property of people's perceptual system is an important tool of adaptation (no one would like to suffer pain as a linear function of the intensity of the physical energy causing it). Another example of the basic illusory nature of perception is the experience of a certain color or pitch. In the case of color, the corresponding physical stimuli are electromagnetic waves of a certain length; in the case of pitch, they are sound waves, but what is perceived is of an entirely different nature. Are colors an exact representation of electromagnetic waves? Perceptual dimensions are classified as *primary* (e.g., length), namely, characteristics, of objective stimuli independent of a perceptual system perceiving it; and *secondary* (e.g., color), which exist only when perceived. Consequently, the experience of secondary dimensions is illusional and yet a necessary condition for optimal survival. The former examples demonstrate that many of the "normal" perceptual experiences are illusory: They do not correspond directly to relevant physical stimuli. It seems, then, that existing definitions of *perceptual illusions* call for improvements.

THE PURPOSE AND TASK
OF PERCEPTUAL SYSTEMS

Protagoras, the Greek philosopher (450 BC), stated that "Man is nothing but a bundle of sensations." More recently, Coren et al. (1993) claimed that "the world is what your senses tell you. The limitations of your senses set the boundaries of your conscious existence" (p. 4). Therefore, people's knowledge of the external world is totally dependent on their senses. The knowledge that an organism obtains about his or her world is not incidental, but is related to what this organism needs to know to survive. The perceptual system is a purposive one, and its purpose is to enable an organism to survive and adjust to its relevant environment (Hochberg, 1970). Therefore, the purpose of a perceptual system is not to enable an exact representation of the external world, but rather to provide a useful one in terms of adaptation and survival. Returning once again to the example of viewing a two-dimensional picture, it should be noted that any two-dimensional image could represent an infinity of possible three-dimensional shapes; it is remarkable that, out of the infinity of possibilities, the perceptual system hits on just about the best one (Gregory, 1970). This selection is conducted by the brain, which acts like a decision-making system, choosing among all possible options the best one for survival or, as phrased by Gregory, "Perception involves betting on the most probable interpretation of sensory data, in terms of the world of objects" (p. 29). An illustration of this is the case of an increasing retinal image of an object, which can be caused by either an object increasing in size while keeping constant its distance from a perceiver, or by an object of unchanging size advancing toward a perceiver. The brain usually prefers the second interpretation because it is more useful to be prepared to meet an advancing object; this is also more frequent than that of an increasing-distant object. However, there are cases in which the brain does not have enough information to make a choice between two or more possible interpretations. In such cases, people experience the figures as reversible, shifting spontaneously from one configuration to the other.

Attneave (1971) proposed neural models of figural ambiguity, which assume that constant stimulation of a given figure results in adaptation or neural fatigue; after a period of time, this gives rise to the alternative percept. However, this interpretation is incompatible with findings showing that the processing of ambiguous figures can be influenced by cognitive factors, such as perceived intention, knowledge about the figure, and focus of attention (Tsal & Kalbert, 1985). Such findings support the notion of the brain's interpretive function. Paradoxical figures, like the one presented in Fig. 4.4, are possible only when physically perceived as two-dimensional. The paradoxical three-dimensional experience is possible as one of the infinite number of interpretations of a two-dimensional image (Gregory, 1970). Being presented fully as three-dimensional without hiding some crucial information, causes the paradoxical perception to disappear.

Some approaches to perception maintain that people perceive a direct reflection of physical properties of incoming stimuli (e.g., direct perception; Gibson, 1969). This approach, however, cannot account for complex illusory phenomenon like the kinetic depth effect. The *kinetic depth effect* is a phenomenon of perceiving a two-dimensional object as three-dimensional by seeing the rotation of its two-dimensional silhouette on a screen. Therefore, this is an illusion because there is no correspondence between the actual perceived depth and the two-dimensional property of the silhouette. The illusion is created by the way the brain analyzes the incoming pattern of perceptual cues, and it is very useful

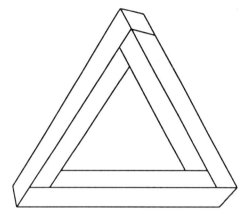

FIG. 4.4. A paradoxical figure. Computerized graphics
based on *Perception* (p. 71), by
A. Openhimer, Tel Aviv, Israel:
The Open University. Copyright 1989 by the Open University. Reproduced by permission.

for understanding the world. The direct perception approach is negated
by this phenomenon (Ullman, 1979). It is possible that perception is a
constructive process that entails the interaction of sensory stimulation
and the expectation, attention, and intention of the perceiver (Tsal &
Kalbert, 1985). These complex interactions evolve, in most cases, into
useful perceptual experiences that are sometimes based on mismatches
with corresponding physical stimuli, like in the three-dimensional perception of a flat picture or in the kinetic depth effect. In some cases,
however, the system produces "useless" discrepancies between the perceptual experience and the corresponding physical stimuli, due to the
existence of certain conditions and limitations. These are discussed in
the following sections, where it is claimed that veridical percepts, as well
as useful and profitless perceptual illusions, are all products of the same
basic perceptual processes.

TRANSACTIONALISM

In cases where an illusion might risk the optimal adjustment to the
environment, the perceptual system might try to correct it, sometimes
with success. An example is *aniseikonia*—an optical anomaly in which
the image in one eye is larger than the other, resulting in a significant
disparity between the images on each eye. Although optically there is a
difference in the size of the two ocular images, with confusing depth
cues, people who suffer from aniseikonia perceive the environment in a
relatively normal fashion. The mechanisms of perceptual constancies
(which are discussed later) are computational processes designed to prevent certain illusions from being experienced. Another example of how
the brain self-corrects an illusion is when one uses special prisms that

invert the perceived world upside down. Surprisingly, after a while, a person wearing these prisms gradually begins to see the world as usual. Actually, a similar process is occurring every second because a normal retinal image is an inverted image of the world, but the brain prevents this dangerous potential illusion from being experienced. The inverting prisms make a retinal image a more veridical representation of the world, but then the brain inserts its corrections, resulting in an illusion of an upside-down world. Fortunately, the brain is flexible enough to notice that this is not the familiar world, and to correct the perceptual outcome in the opposite direction. Ames (1946) and Kilpatrick (1961), who studied these phenomena, developed a transactional theory of perception. This theory suggests that, during an individual's active interactions and transactions with the environment, learning takes place. This learning is responsible for the fact that, despite the infinity of possible perceptions that might arise from a given retinal distribution, the actual perception is usually quite restricted; perceptual alternatives become limited in a way that corresponds closely to the familiar world.

ADAPTIVE AND MALADAPTIVE ILLUSIONS

The former analysis reveals that traditional definitions of *illusions,* focusing on the mismatch between perceptual experience and its corresponding physical stimuli, fail to distinguish between *adaptive* illusions, which—despite the existence of a mismatch—are useful for adapting to the environment, and *maladaptive* illusions. Examples of adaptive illusions are autokinetic depth effect, three-dimensional perception of a two-dimensional picture, the JND, and other psychophysical properties of perception, like the scaling of the intensity of perceptual experiences relative to a current adaptation level. Examples of maladaptive illusions are the apparent movement of the moon, the Jastrow illusion, and the phenomenon of paradoxical sensation of cold when skin spots sensitive to cold are stimulated with a temperature of 45°C (Schiffman, 1982). This chapter attempts to demonstrate that the same perceptual processes underlie adaptive and maladaptive illusions, and that the two types differ only in their ecological implications. A more adequate definition of *perceptual illusion,* then, should relate to these two types of illusions. Thus, *perceptual illusion* may be defined through a mismatch between a physical stimulus and its perceptual experience. When the mismatch aids an organism to adjust to its environment, the illusion is an adaptive one; when the mismatch causes a maladaptive consequence, the illusion is maladaptive.

FIG. 4.5.   Brightness contrast. Computerized graphics from *Sensation and Perception* (p. 265) by H. R. Schiffman, 1982, New York: Wiley. Copyright © 1982 by Wiley. Reproduced by permission of John Wiley & Sons, Inc.

CLASSIFICATION OF PERCEPTUAL ILLUSIONS

Contrasts and Aftereffects

Dember (1970) drew a distinction between two types of illusions: contrasts and aftereffects. An illusion of contrast occurs when "the value of a stimulus on an attribute is increased or decreased as a result of its being presented in the context of other stimuli with extreme values on that attribute" (p. 198). Both types of stimuli belong to the same sensory modality, feature the same physical properties, and are present simultaneously. Contrasts are typical in many sensory modalities. An example is brightness contrast (Fig. 4.5). All the inner squares in Fig. 4.5 are physically equal in brightness, but the inner square surrounded by the dark background appears brighter than the one surrounded by the light background. When a stimulus, *I*, is first visualized and after a while disappears, and a second stimulus, *t*, is then presented, an aftereffect occurs if some modification in the appearance of *t* takes place following inspection of *I*. There are figural, shape, and other types of after effects (Schiffman, 1982). For example, if one stares at a colored shape for about 30 seconds and one's gaze shifts to a neutral achromatic surface, the shape is still perceived, but in a reversed or complementary color.

   Aftereffects and contrasts are attributed to physiological processes of the sense organs, such as satiation. Some illusions might be caused by self-satiation. Any figure that undergoes inspection for more than a few seconds can produce satiation, which acts on the inspection figure (Dember, 1970). For example, Gibson (1969) found that a curved line viewed for several seconds tends to straighten. Similar aftereffects were found in other modalities (e.g., kinesthetic aftereffects; Wertheimer & Leventhal, 1958). If one hand is passed over a curved surface, a straight surface sensed immediately afterward would feel curved in the direction opposite to that of the exposure object. Dember's classification is interesting, but it is not sensitive to the variety of illusion-causing processes.

Some illusions may be very different from contrasts or aftereffects in terms of their causes.

Structural- and Strategy-Based Illusions

Beckett (1989) drew a distinction between two types of illusion-producing mechanisms: structural and strategy. Structural mechanisms are physiologically and/or anatomically based. Strategy, or cognitive, mechanisms represent higher computational information-processing programs that are responsible for the interpretation and meaning assigned to perceived stimuli. This classification, however, is too broad. In many cases, as is discussed later, both structural and strategy factors have a role in the illusion-producing process.

AN INFORMATION-PROCESSING-BASED CLASSIFICATION OF ILLUSIONS

Perceptual information processing advances through several distinct stages. The distal stimulus is actually a source of physical energy that lands on an appropriate sense organ, thereby forming a proximal stimulus. Physiological and biochemical processes in the sense organs transform the physical energy into electrical activity in the nerves. The neuronal signals are conducted to specialized areas in the cortex, and most probably these cortical regions are responsible for the emergence of a perceptual experience. From a cognitive point of view, the processing of incoming information starts by automatic, preattentive processes, in which stimuli are analyzed by their features (e.g., color). This is most probably done in parallel by feature-specific analyzers. The features are combined again to form basic perceptual objects (e.g., shapes, letters). But at this stage, attentional resources are already required. A crucial stage in the process is the organization of a perceptual field and its separation to figure and background. The final perceptual experience is emerging via complex pattern-recognition processes. The perceptual processes are influenced both by bottom-up processes (e.g., the direct properties of incoming information) and top-down processes (e.g., knowledge, expectations, etc.). This classification of illusions is begun by analyzing possible patterns of correspondence among the distal stimulus, the proximal stimulus, and the perceptual experience, as presented in Table 4.1.

Of the eight possible combinations types, only the six described in Table 4.1 represent real experiences:

TABLE 4.1
Types of Correspondence in Perception

Type of Perception	Distal Stimulus–Proximal Stimulus	Proximal Stimulus–Perceptual Experience	Perceptual Experience–Distal Stimulus
Veridical perception	+	+	+
"Corrected" veridical	—	—	+
Adaptive illusions	+;−	—	"+"
			(relevant distal stimulus)
Maladaptive illusions	+	—	—
Aftereffects	" − "*	+	—
Physical illusions	—	+	—

Note.   + denotes correspondence; — denotes noncorrespondence; +; − denotes possibility of either a "+" or a "−"; * denotes modified proximal stimulus.

Type 1: An example of veridical perception is the perception of pressure exerted on the skin, light intensity, sound intensity, and so on. In these cases, the three correspondence types are positive.

Type 2: When no correspondence exists between the distal and proximal stimuli, and between the proximal stimulus and the final perceptual experience, but yet the latter corresponds with the distal stimulus, it is called *corrected veridical perception.* The brain corrects the first two discrepancies. Examples are the perception of the world as a noninverted one, despite the retinal image being inverted, and all perceptual experiences corrected by perceptual constancies.

Type 3: This type describes the adaptive illusions. The final match between the actual distal stimulus (e.g., a two-dimensional picture, a two-dimensional shadow of a rotated three-dimensional object) and the perceptual experience is negative. However, it is positive regarding the stimulus for which the actual distal stimulus is a substitute, and which is the relevant one for adjustment, like the three-dimensional rotating object.

Types 4, 5, 6: Maladaptive illusions are represented by these types. In all three cases, the discrepancy existing in one or more of the stages of the perceptual processes is not corrected by the brain or any other perceptual process. In the case of aftereffects, the illusion is caused by a proximal stimulus that is modified due to the processes that took place in a former stage.

In the case of Type 6 (i.e., physical illusions), the illusion is caused by physical conditions external to the sensory and perceptual systems. Based on this analysis and the sequence of information-processing stages described earlier, a classification that reflects categories of illusion-producing factors is suggested.

Physically Based Illusions

These illusions cannot be attributed to perceptual processes, but rather to physical conditions that spoil the correspondence between the distal and proximal stimuli. Two examples of this category are mirage and distorted perceptions. These examples are based on viewing objects in water or through prisms because of physical properties characterizing the passage of light through a medium.

Illusions Caused by Low-Level Brain Processes

Looking at Fig. 4.6, a white square separated from the surrounding white of the paper with four black "pacmen"-like corners is most likely seen. Actually, this white square only exists in the observer's mind. This can be easily proved by covering the four black "pacmen." Surprisingly,

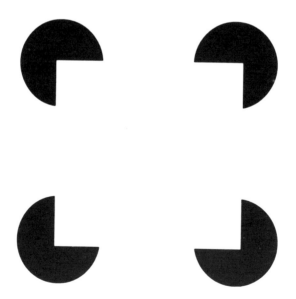

FIG. 4.6.   Illusory contours. From "The Perceived Strength of Illusory Contours" by T. Banton and M. D. Levi, 1992, *Perceptions and Psychophysics*, *52*, p. 678. Copyright © 1992 by Psychonomic Society. Reprinted by permission.

the white square disappears. This illusion is one example of illusory contour stimuli. The illusory contours are induced by the black forms, and are apparent edges that have no physically measurable properties, such as luminance or contrast (Banton & Levi, 1992). Siegel and Petry (1991) claimed that illusory contours are not related to processes causing brightness contrast. Rather, illusory contours are highly dependent on the angle and orientation of the black corners. Thus, if the black "pac-men" corners are rotated, the illusory contours become weaker or disappear. Explanations of illusory contours are far from clear. Van den Heydt, Peterhaus, and Baumgartner (1984) proposed a low-level hierarchical receptive field model. They stated that illusory contours are first defined by V_2 neurons that sum the inputs from line- or edge-sensitive V_1 neurons and end-stopped V_1 neurons oriented orthogonally to the illusory contour. This model obtained some empirical support by Banton and Levi (1992), who claimed that low-level processes account for 60% to 90% of the variance in measure of illusory contour strength.

Another illusion that is attributed, at least partly, to low-level brain processes is the Fraser illusion (Fig. 4.7; Stuart & Day, 1988). The segments constructing the letters are tilted, thus causing the letters to appear tilted, although actually the letters are not tilted. Stuart and Day suggested that the illusion results from lateral facilitation between orientation-selective cells. Another possible explanation is that the illusion is due to orientation being processed only at a local level. It should be emphasized, however, that attributing illusions to low-level brain processes is still speculative due to the methodological difficulties in this type of research.

FIG. 4.7.   The Fraser illusion. From "The Fraser Illusion" by G. W. Stuart and R. H. Day, 1988, *Perception and Psychophysics*, 44, p. 410. Copyright © 1988 by Psychonomic Society. Reprinted by permission.

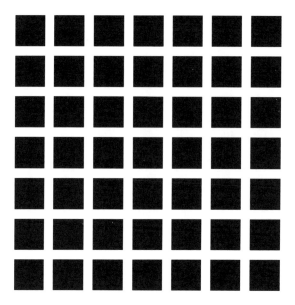

FIG. 4.8.   The Hering grid. Computerized graphics based on *Sensation and Perception* (p. 266) by H. R. Schiffman, 1982, New York: Wiley. Copyright © 1982 by Wiley. Reproduced by permission of John Wiley & Sons, Inc.

Illusions Caused by Physiological Processes at the Sensory Level and by Anatomical Structure

In Fig. 4.8 (the Hering grid; Schiffman, 1982), gray spots appear at each intersection except the one you are looking at. When looking at a pattern composed of a series of uniform bands graded from black to white, the Mach bands illusion is elicited. In this illusion, the lightness of each stripe does not appear uniform, although the intensity of each stripe is constant. One edge near the stripe's left-hand darker neighbor appears to be darker than the other edge, near the right-hand lighter neighbor. These three phenomena are presumably related to the process of lateral inhibition (Schiffman, 1982).

An example of an illusion attributed to anatomical properties of sensory receptors in the Purkinje shift, caused by the different properties of rods and cones. The resulting difference is in relative sensitivity to various wavelengths under photopic and scotopic illumination conditions. The outcome is that, as light intensity is changed, the apparent brightness of different wavelengths to which one is exposed is changed. An adaptive illusion based on anatomical structure is the "missing fundamental" in audition, which occurs as a result of the structure of the ear's basilar membrane. Two phenomena from tactile perception that are also caused by anatomical structure are the two-point threshold of touch and the Aristotle illusion. The latter is experienced when objects are touched with crossed fingertips (Benedetti, 1988). Two distinct touches are felt because stimulating the outside of the two fingers results in information being sent to two separate areas of the sensory cortex.

Perceptual Aftereffects

This type of illusion was already defined in a former section. Aftereffects can be found in many perceptual modalities. The McCallough color aftereffect (McCallough, 1965) can be induced when subjects view color patches overlaid with black bar grids or other geometric stimuli. After induction, presentation of the grid alone on a white ground evokes the complementary color aftereffect. The McCallough effect acquisition depends on the duration of exposure to inducing stimuli. A simpler way to experience color aftereffects is by staring at a brightly colored light for a while and then looking at a smooth, white surface. The image will be seen, but in the complementary color (e.g., a green afterimage to a red original one).

Illusions Caused by Interferences of Information Processing

Perceptual processing requires time and attentional resources to be carried out optimally. If these resources are not available, the perceptual process is disrupted, thereby leading to the experience of "maladaptive" illusions. The first phase of the perceptual information processing is the construction of perceptual objects. A description of this early stage is provided by feature integration theory (Treisman, 1986), which postulates that the construction of a perceptual object is done in two stages. The first one, which is preattentive, is analyzing separately and in parallel basic features that can be extracted from the proximal stimulus, such as color, shape, orientation of edges, and so on. All the features appearing in the same spatial location should now be combined to form one object. This is done in a second stage, in which focal attention is required to "glue" all the features together (some researchers [e.g., Tsal, 1989] do not agree that this "gluing" is done by focusing attention, but this discussion is beyond the scope of the present chapter).

If the focusing of attention in the second stage is disrupted, for example, because of time limitation, perceptual objects consisting of incorrect features might emerge. This illusion is termed *illusory conjunctions* (Treisman & Schmidt, 1982), and it can occur if an observer is presented with two separate, briefly flashed stimuli (e.g., a green O and a red X). The observer may end up reporting seeing a red O and a green X.

Another illusory phenomenon caused by interference with information processing is illustrated by the following experiment. A circular black disk and a ring circumscribing it are presented in sequence for a brief duration with a very short interstimulus interval (between 100–200 msec). The outcome of such an experiment is that the presence of the disk may not be perceived, or it may appear dimmer or less structured than if shown without the ring. This effect is called *masking* because the disk is masked by the ring (Lindsay & Norman, 1972). A possible explanation of masking is that the processing of each stimulus requires more than 100 msec to be completed. Because the masking stimulus is presented briefly after the target stimulus, the images of the two stimuli coincide and are processed simultaneously. The result is that they do not appear as two different stimuli, and thus the perception of the target stimulus is impaired (Eriksen & Collins, 1968). Thus, masking may be considered the result of temporal summation of physically successive components that appear concurrent. What was described here is *backward masking* because the masking stimulus followed the target stimulus. If the order is reversed, the process is termed *forward masking*. Masking effects are obtained in other modalities. For example, olfactory masking occurs when two different odorants with the concentration of one odor sufficiently surpass that of the other (Lindsay & Norman, 1972).

Organization of Perceptual Fields and Perceptual Illusions

One of the most important phases in the organization of a perceptual field is the discrimination of a figure from an amorphous background (Forgus & Melamed, 1976). The figure is that part of the perceptual field that appears as sharply delineated and distinct from the background, which is the remainder of the field. Selective attention plays a major role in this phase. Attention is focused on the figure that, as a result, is analyzed more fully than the background. At a cocktail party, a conversation with a friend becomes the figure; attention is focused on it while other voices are ignored. Nevertheless, a certain level of processing is always retained, which is enough for detecting one's name being called. At that moment, the organization of the auditory field is changed, and the voice calling one's name becomes the figure. The perceptual system remains perpetually active, trying to find meaningful patterns in any perceptual field because a homogeneous field does not transmit useful information.

The laws of Gestalt provide a good framework for understanding how perceptual organization occurs. This chapter is not the place for detailing these laws (a good coverage of them can be found in Coren et al., 1993), but a reminder is illustrated in Fig. 4.9. In Fig. 4.9a, either columns or rows of data can be perceived, whereas most people are likely to

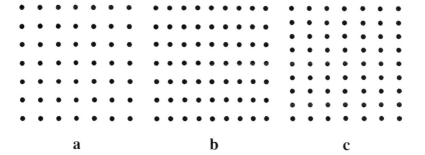

FIG. 4.9. Organization of perceptual fields by proximity. From *Perception* (p. 45) by A. Openhimer, 1989, Tel Aviv, Israel: The Open University. Copyright 1989 by The Open University. Reproduced by permission.

report seeing three rows of dots in Fig. 4.9b, due to spatial proximity, and two columns in Fig. 4.9c. This type of organization can be categorized as *adaptive illusion* because the organization exists only in a perceiver's mind, but it is useful.

There are other perceptual rules that govern the process of figure–ground separation. For example, a brighter part of a visual field is usually perceived as a figure, whereas its darker parts are perceived as background. This tendency could make one see something in an unfilled space between other figures, like the vase in the well-known reversible image in Fig. 4.10. The organization of perceptual fields is intimately connected with the place where attention is focused, as in the case of ambiguous figures. Tsal and Kalbert (1985) hypothesized that the formation of a given percept of an ambiguous figure results from focusing attention on a focal area that contains features significant for this percept, but not for the alternative one.

Gestalt laws of organization also apply to the auditory system. In hearing, too, proximity has been found to be the preferred organization when put in competition with both good continuation and spatial location. This is the essence of an auditory effect called the *scale illusion* (Radvansky, Hartman, & Rakerd, 1992). Using the rules of perceptual organization, it is possible to compose a musical piece played as solo by one instrument, which sounds as if it were playing two melodic lines at the same time. If the player alternates between a high series and a low series of notes, the listener perceives the alternating notes as two distinct themes.

Shortage of Information as a Cause of Illusions

Lack of Perceptual Variability. Information is the raw data processed by the perceptual system, and information is equivalent to stimu-

FIG. 4.10.   A reversible figure. From *Perception* (p. 48) by A. Openhimer, 1989, Tel Aviv, Israel: The Open University. Copyright 1989 by The Open University. Reproduced by permission.

lation variability and heterogeneity. A homogenous perceptual field is useless because it carries no information. Some illusions may be caused when stimulation is homogenous, even when, from an energetic point of view, the organism receives a normal level of stimulation. A homogenous visual field, or a stabilized image, causes perception to gradually fade away. A similar process has been found in tactile sensation (Zakay & Shilo, 1985).

Dearth of Information.   When the brain does not have sufficient information for a choice between two alternative interpretations of a shape, a viewer may experience a reversible figure, fluctuating between the two alternatives. A celebrated example is the Necker cube, with the two equally compelling possibilities of three-dimensional interpretation.

Context Effects

Generally, perceptive fields contain all information, either relevant or not (e.g., noise), at a specific moment in time. It is the role of attention to

a

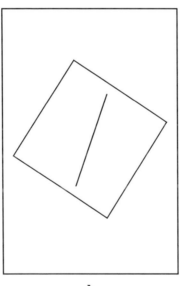

b

FIG. 4.11.   (a) Context effects. (b) The rod and frame experiment.

eliminate the noise. According to adaptation level theory (Helson, 1964), background stimuli influence the subjective intensity assigned to perceptual dimensions. Thus, contrasts are partly explained by context effects. Actually, context effects are one of the major causes of illusions. The "circle" in Fig. 4.11a is perceived either as a circle, the letter *o*, or the number *0*, depending on the context. In the classic rod-and-frame experiment (Fig. 4.11b), subjects are placed in a dark room with a luminous rod surrounded by a luminous frame (tilted at around 22°) and instructed to manually rotate the rod to true (gravity-based) vertical. Normally, the subjects place the rod at 8°–9° toward the tilt of the frame. This result has been described as an "automatic influence of the peripheral representation of the frame on the egocentric orientation-coordinate system," biasing the perception of true vertical toward the frame's own vertical and horizontal (Spivey-Knowlton & Bridgeman, 1993). Context effects play a role in some geometrical illusions, such as the well-known Müller–Lyer illusion, because the direction of the shifts induces some context on observers. Context effect may serve as another illustration of the basic argument—that normal, adaptive processes are cluttered by the same processes as maladaptive ones. In some cases, context effects are very helpful, such as in the case of speech perception (Coren et al., 1993).

Conflicting Perceptual Cues

If the views presented to the two eyes are significantly different, one might perceive only one or the other of the two images, but not both (a phenomenon termed *binocular rivalry*). In the domain of speech perception, conflicting audiovisual cues elicit the McGurk effect, as well as ventriloquist illusion (see Myslobodsky, chap. 14, this volume).

Improper Activation of Cognitive Processes

Perceptual experience is a joint product of both bottom–up and top–down processes. It is almost impossible to fully explain complex perceptions (e.g., depth perception or movement perception) by adopting a direct perception approach (Ullman, 1979). As outlined in Table 4.1, in some cases, specific cognitive processes evolve to correct potential erroneous perceptions. However, correcting processes are imperfect, and they cannot handle all stimulation patterns. Under some conditions, these processes are misled by the pattern of incoming stimuli, thereby eliciting maladaptive illusions. Two such cases are mentioned: improper activation of perceptual constancies and apparent motion. Both exemplify the unity of the processes underlying adaptive and maladaptive perceptual experiences.

Illusions Caused by Improper Activation of Perceptual Constancies. If perception were a direct reflection of proximal stimuli, people would live in a wobbly and continuously changing world. Someone advancing toward you would become increasingly taller. One's wardrobe would change its colors in different lighting conditions. The perceptual constancies depend on the integration of perceptual information of various sources with prior knowledge and experience. For example, size constancy prevents a distant adult from being perceived as a child due to depth cues indicating that the person is distant and due to prior knowledge about the size of adults. Shape constancy causes the shape of a familiar object to be perceived similarly from different viewing angles. Color constancy enables one to perceive the color of an object as similar under different lighting conditions. When a mechanism of perceptual constancy is activated when it should have been dormant, or when it is not turned on when it should have been, an illusion might emerge. A classical illusion of this sort is experienced in the Ames' room (Ames, 1951). The type of decision made by the brain in the latter case is dependent on the quality of information reaching it. Thus, tactual information about the actual trapezoid shape of the room will eliminate the illusion (Gregory, 1970).

Apparent Movement.   When one's eyes are fixed on a point of light in complete darkness, with time, one will perceive the light as moving. A possible explanation of that illusion, known as the *autokinetic movement,* is provided by Gregory (1970). It is proposed that a drift of the eyes away from the fixation point prompts the brain to maintain the fixation by sending motor commands. The "copies" of these commands, in the absence of signals from the image-retina system, cause the light to be perceived as moving. This explanation is supported by a recent finding by Assad and Maunsell (1995). These authors recorded activity from a monkey posterior cortex in the absence of either sensory or motor output. It has been proposed that activity of this sort could be related to either current or planned eye movements. This effect is an impressive illustration that illusions reflect the same perceptual processes that are responsible for normal perception of motion. It is only the condition and pattern of incoming stimuli that deceive the perceptual mechanism that causes the brain to make a wrong decision. The scenario is similar to the illusion of the moon passing over the clouds. In that case, the moon, perceived as smaller than the clouds and also a brighter target, is chosen to be the figure according to the Gestalt laws of organization, whereas the gray mass of clouds is treated as background. The apparent movement of the moon is an illustration of induced motion—an illusion of movement of a stationary object created by movement of the background or surrounding context (Michael & Sherrick, 1986).

Apparent movement can also be based on low-level physiological processes. If spatially separated static light flashed successively at appropriate interstimulus intervals, the two lights would be perceived as the directional movement of one spot of light. This apparent movement is termed the *Phi movement,* and it is what enables people to enjoy a movie (Broddick, 1974).

Motivation and Illusions

In 1947, Bruner and Goodman asked 10-year-old children to judge the size of various coins. One group of 10 children was taken from a low-income neighborhood; the second group of 10 children was taken from an affluent neighborhood. The results show that the poor children estimated the size of the coins to be larger, as compared with the wealthy children. The overestimation tended to go up with an increase in the monetary value of the coins. These results might suggest that perception is influenced by motivation because the value of money was probably much higher for the poor children than for the affluent ones. A possible methodological criticism here is that the sensitivity for size judgment is generally worse for the poor children than for the wealthy ones. Bruner and Goodman took care of this problem by having control groups judge the size of cardboard diskettes made the same size as the coins. There were no significant differences in size estimation in that case. Perhaps the poor children's familiarity with coins was lower than that of wealthy children, and perhaps the difference in size judgment could be attributed to differences in familiarity, rather than to motivational effects. Lambert, Salomon, and Watson (1949) controlled for the level of familiarity with coins, and concluded that size judgment was influenced by motivation. It should be noted, however, that not all researchers are convinced that these influences are purely motivational (e.g., Forgus & Melamed, 1976).

Top-Down Influences and Illusions

In some cases, illusions are caused by the interference of top-down processes associated with prior knowledge or expectations. The expectation theory of the size–weight illusion (Ross, 1969) states that prior experience with objects leads observers to expect that a larger object will be heavier than a smaller one. The learned correlation between large volumes and heavy weights results in an expectation or mental set that could affect the force an observer applies when lifting an object. A series of experiments by Davis and Roberts (1976) supported this cognitive theory.

High-Level Cognitive Processes

Temporal Illusions.   How does one know what time of day it is? Or how much time has elapsed since a certain event happened? Surprisingly, although time plays an important role in human life (Michon, 1985), no single sense organ or perceptual system mediates psychological time. Psychological time, in the range of seconds, minutes, and hours, seems to be another construction of the mind, and thus it is meaningless to speak about time perception. Subjective time is a product of cognitive processes of judgment and estimation. As such, subjective time is context-dependent, which can induce illusions. Present someone with two commands (e.g., "begin" and "stop") with a 10-second interval between them. Then ask the subject to estimate the duration of the interval. Present another subject with a similar task, but this time read a list of words during the 10-second interval. Most likely the second subject's duration estimation will be longer than the first's. In the first case, the subject was presented with "empty time," whereas in the second case, the time was filled with stimuli, thereby creating the "filled duration illusion." Filled time is estimated to be longer than empty time. Repeat the experiment with two more subjects, but this time tell them before the beginning of each interval that they will be asked to estimate the duration of the interval later on. In the latter case, the "filled duration illusion" was found to be reversed, such that the duration of the "empty" time interval was estimated as longer than that of the "filled" time interval (Zakay, Nitzan, & Glickshon, 1983).

In the first case, time was estimated retrospectively without awareness of the need to relate experience to time. In the second case, the subjects were prompted to make a prospective time estimation. Apparently, retrospective and prospective time estimations are modulated by different cognitive processes (Zakay, 1990). Retrospective time is a function of the amount of information representing meaningful changes, which can be retrieved from memory and attributed to the target interval. Prospective time is based on counting subjective time units in a cognitive counter—a process that requires attentional resources (Zakay & Block, 1995), but attentional resources are shared between all tasks that have to be performed at a given moment. Thus, when an "empty" time interval is presented, most attentional resources can be allocated for temporal information processing, whereas when a list of words is read, attentional resources are also allocated for analyzing and coding the words. As a result, less attentional resources can be allocated for temporal information processing, resulting in a shorter prospective estimation of "filled" time, as compared with "empty" time.

Perception of Causality.   Humans constantly strive to impose causality on their perceived world (Nisbett & Ross, 1980). Such causal interpretations are inferred from cues provided by movement and temporal order. Michotte (1963) extensively studied the necessary stimulus conditions for perceiving causality among moving stimuli. A major finding of

Michotte's work is that perception of causality in movement is produced by certain relations between interacting stimuli, in which no actual causal relation between elements need exist.

Individual Differences and Cultural Influences on the Perception of Illusions

The transactionalist view, described earlier, states that people who underwent different perceptual experiences during the critical years of perceptual development should have somewhat different perceptual experiences during adulthood. Thus, individual differences—reflecting both variability in the course of development and/or structural/cultural differences—should be expected in the perception of illusions.

Individual Differences.   Coren and Porac (1987) reported that, given any specific visuo-geometric illusion, observers range from high to low levels of measured illusion susceptibility. These differences are reliable, and can be attributed to differences in relevant abilities. Coren and Porac found that individual differences in the magnitude of visual illusion scores were significantly correlated with spatial ability measures. Other variables, such as age, gender, and education, were also found to be correlated with perceived magnitude of illusions, like in the case of the Poggendorff illusion.

Cognitive style is another variable that can cause differences in perceived magnitude of illusions. Witkin and Berry (1975) defined *cognitive style* as the overall personality and perceptual predispositions characteristic of a particular individual. Field-dependency is considered a dimension of cognitive style. People characterized as field-dependent are more susceptible to the influence of the frame-in-the-rod and frame tasks, as compared with field-independent people. However, perceptual illusions are not eliminated by personality characteristics; only the magnitude of the effect is affected. For instance, familiarity with the Müller–Lyer illusion does not prevent it from being experienced.

Cultural Effects.   The carpentered world hypothesis (Coren et al., 1993) states that individuals living in urban environments characterized by straight lines and angles tend to depend more on depth cues based on linear perspective than people living in rural environments characterized by curved lines. Indeed, investigations of cultural influences on perception reveal that people are dominated by the three-dimensional interpretation of two-dimensional pictures (Deregowski, 1980). Kilbride and Leibowitz (1975) tested Ugandan villagers belonging to the Baganda tribe. Their subjects were classified as two-dimensional, three-dimensional, or mixed perceivers based on their verbal responses to photographs portraying symbolic depth cues. They were presented with the Ponzo perspective illusion. Differences in the magnitude of the perceived illusion were found among the three groups. This was interpreted as reflecting the separation of cognitive factors determining responsiveness to symbolic depth cues in two-dimensional reproductions.

Do Maladaptive Illusions Cause Harm?

Maladaptive illusions are by and large harmless. However, this is only true when individuals act in their familiar environment under normal conditions. They appear deleterious when the environment becomes more demanding, such as at high velocity and/or weightlessness. An example of this is vertigo, which is felt as disorientation while flying at night or in clouds. Disorientation might result from stimulation of the vestibular and kinesthetic sense organs from acceleration and regular changes in directions. During changes in direction and velocity, the sensation of the vertical is felt more in relation to the aircraft than to the earth because of the manner in which the acceleration forces act on the vestibular organs. This effect may be so strong as to mislead a pilot into "perceiving" the plane as being oriented more vertically than it really is. When this happens without an external visual frame of reference, due to fog, clouds, or darkness, a pilot flying upside down might believe that he is actually flying facing up (McCormick, 1976). Other illusions of apparent movement might also endanger pilots who perceive a fixed light at night (e.g., a star) as a moving light. It has been reported that pilots have attempted to "join up" in formations with stars or street lights that appeared to be moving (Clark & Graybiel, 1955). Conditions of zero gravity, in the absence of any patterns of external stimulation, might result in the loss of body orientation. In extreme conditions, such as during exposure to free fall, even the sensation of falling might be lost (Lackner, 1992).

The Critical-Cue Versus the Multiple-Cue Approach

The critical-cue approach suggests that a single, "critical" cue can account for all perceptual illusions. In the case of the size–weight illusion, for example, a critical cue is the perceived size of an object. By contrast, the multiple-cue approach states that various sets of cues could be formulated to account for an illusion. For example, McCready (1986) demonstrated that factors like oculomotor efference might also be responsible for the moon illusion. By using multivariate techniques, it was revealed (McClellan & Bernstein, 1984) that different factors were responsible for judgmental errors in different classes of illusion. No critical stimulus is solely responsible for the illusion (Coren & Girgus, 1978), but rather a combination of several distinguishable aspects, each of which is separately capable of producing misperception (McClellan & Bernstein, 1984). This approach, derived from Brunswick's (1956) ecological approach, suggests that the reasons people misuse information about geometric figures are the same as the reasons they misuse information about more cognitive and less perceptual events, like in the case of clinical judgments (e.g., Hammond & Summers, 1972).

This point of view might be too extreme, but it seems true that a multiple-cue approach is more useful to understand a perceptual illusion than is a critical-cue approach. Even in the case of illusory contours, the basic low-level brain processes were found to account for 60% to 90% of the variability in the perceived strength of the illusion, but other factors like familiarity have an influence as well (Banton & Levi, 1992). Coren and Porac (1987) attempted to separate the relative contribution of structural and strategy mechanisms in the formation of the Müller–Lyer illusion. Their findings indicate that the involvement of structural factors significantly influences the observed illusion magnitude. This finding indicates that both types of mechanisms are involved in illusion formulation.

IS A GENERAL THEORY OF
PERCEPTUAL ILLUSIONS POSSIBLE?
THE CASE OF GEOMETRICAL ILLUSIONS

Visuo-geometrical illusions are errors in apparent length, area, direction, or curvature occurring in the perception of specific patterns of lines. Many integrative explanations for these illusions were offered during more than 100 years of investigation. Yet the nature of these illusions has yet to be elucidated (Rock, 1975). As a group, they seem to be a product of multiple cues (Hatopf, 1981). Thus, geometrical illusions can serve as a good demonstration of the multiple-cue approach. The following are explanations offered for geometrical illusions.

1. *The eye-movement theory.* Carr (1935) assumed that the impression of lengths is obtained by moving the eyes along a line from one end to the other. In the case of illusions, eye movements are interrupted by nonrelevant lines, such as the fins in the Müller–Lyer illusion. In this case, the eyes move more freely over the figure with the fins pointing inward than over the ones with the fins pointing outward. This theory was questioned by Evans and Marsden (1966), who demonstrated that

some of the geometrical illusions persisted under stabilized retinal image conditions.

2. *The empathy theory.* Lipps (1897) suggested that estimation of length is derived from emotional reactions aroused by a figure. For example, the Müller-Lyer illusion arises when the fins point outward and a feeling of expansion is evoked.

3. *The pregnance or good-figure theory.* This theory is based on the laws of Gestalt. It states that observers have a tendency to make a good continuation of patterns to achieve the best Gestalt allowed by the conditions. For example, if one of the Müller–Lyer figures is seen as consisting of two elements standing apart, the observer exaggerates the division. If the figure is seen as a single, compact object, the compactness is overstated.

4. *The confusion theory.* This theory attributes geometrical illusions to a confusion between the test and distracting elements. This confusion is created by the difficulty in discriminating and separating these elements. Empirical support for the confusion theory is provided by the "illusion-decrement" phenomenon, described later.

5. *Gregory's theory of central correction.* Gregory (1970) accounted for the illusions on the basis of the correction the perceiver makes in response to cues of distance and depth perception. His argument is that illusory figures are perceived as three-dimensional. Various depth cues would make parts of the figure appear farther away than others. Because the retinal sizes of all parts are the same, those that appear distant would be corrected to appear larger. This theory is not supported in some empirical studies, however. Ward, Porac, Coren, and Girgus (1977) claimed that depth processing may be evoked by some, but not all, classical illusion forms. To complicate the scenario, Coren, Porac, Aks, and Marikawa (1988) found that, under some conditions, lateral inhibition contributes to the magnitude of visuo-geometric illusions.

Another indication for the diversity of illusion-causing factors is provided by the illusion-decrement phenomenon mentioned earlier. The measured magnitude of an illusion seems to diminish with continued inspection. This is true for illusions like the Müller–Lyer, Poggendorf, Zoellner, the vertical–horizontal, and others. Several theories have been offered to explain illusion decrement, including cortical satiation and eye-movement theories. A differentiation mechanism was also suggested. Accordingly, observers learn to isolate various illusion-causing elements from the distorted figure simply through inspection. Empirical support for this explanation was provided by Coren and Girgus (1972). This also supports a "confusion" theory of visuo-geometrical illusions— namely, that illusions are the result of confusion between test and inducing elements. However, Coren and Girgus also argued that the differentiation mechanism alone is not sufficient to account for the diminishing of illusion magnitude with inspection.

In summary, the analysis of geometrical illusions, the factors that influence its perceived magnitude, and the phenomenon of illusion decrement suggest that illusions are caused by interactions among many factors, and that a general theory of illusions is hardly feasible. It was proposed here that illusions are not produced by any distinct mechanism other than the same perceptual machinery responsible for presumably undisturbed perception. Like perception, illusions obey the dictum that, "We act not so much according to what is directly sensed, but to what is believed" (Gregory, 1970, p. 11). Thus, hoping to present a general theory of illusions is as unrealistic as expecting that one general theory of perception would encompass the massive variety of perceptual processes.

REFERENCES

American College Dictionary. (1964). New York: Random House.

Ames, A. (1946). *Some demonstrations concerned with the origin and nature of our sensations: A lab manual.* Hanover, NH: Dartmouth Eye Institute.

Ames, A. J. (1951). Visual perception and the rotating trapezoidal window. *Psychological Monographs, 65,* (14, Whole No. 324).

Assad, J. A., & Maunsell, J. H. R. (1995). Neuronal correlates of inferred motion in primate posterior parietal cortex. *Nature, 373,* 518–521.

Attneave, F. (1971). Multistability of perception. *Scientific American, 225,* 62–71.

Banton, T., & Levi, M. D. (1992). The perceived strength of illusory contours. *Perceptions and Psychophysics, 52(6),* 676–684.

Beckett, P. A. (1989). Illusion decrement and transfer of illusion decrement in real- and subjective-contour Poggendorff figures. *Perception and Psychophysics, 45(6),* 550–556.

Benedetti, F. (1988). Exploration of a rod with crossed fingers. *Perception and Psychophysics, 44(3),* 281–284.

Broddick, O. A. (1974). Short range process in apparent motion. *Vision Research, 14,* 519–528.

Bruner, J. S., & Goodman, C. C. (1947). Value and need as organizing factors in perception. *Journal of Abnormal Psychology, 42,* 33–44.

Brunswick, E. (1956). *Perception and the representative design of psychological experiments.* Berkeley: University of California Press.

Carr, H. (1935). *An introduction to space perception.* New York: Longman.

Clark, B., & Graybiel, A. (1955). Disorientation: A cause of pilot error (Research Project No. NM001 110 100.39). USN School of Aviation Medicine.

Coren, S., & Girgus, J. S. (1972). Differentiation and decrement in the Müller–Lyer illusion. *Perception and Psychophysics, 12,* 446–470.

Coren, S., & Girgus, J. S. (1978). Visual illusions. In R. Held, H. W. Leibowitz, & H. L. Teuber (Eds.), *Handbook of sensory physiology* (Vol. 8, pp. 551–568). Berlin: Springer-Verlag.

Coren, S., & Porac, C. (1987). Individual differences in visual-geometric illusions: Predictions from measures of spatial cognitive abilities. *Perception and Psychophysics, 41,* 211–219.

Coren, S., Porac, C., Aks, D. J., & Marikawa, K. (1988). A method to assess the relative contribution of lateral inhibition to the magnitude of visual-geometric illusions. *Perception and Psychophysics, 43,* 551–558.

Coren, S., Ward, L. M., & Enns, J. T. (1993). *Sensation and perception* (4th ed.). New York: Harcourt Brace.

Davis, C. M., & Roberts, W. (1976). Lifting movements in the size–weight illusion. *Perception and Psychophysics, 20,* 33–36.

Dember, W. N. (1970). *The psychology of perception.* New York: Holt, Rinehart & Winston.

Deregowski, J. (1980). *Illusions, patterns and pictures: A cross-cultural perspective.* London: Academic Press.

Drever, J. (1974). *A dictionary of psychology* (rev. ed). London: Penguin.

Eriksen, C. W., & Collins, J. F. (1968). Sensory traces versus the psychological movement in the temporal organization of form. *Journal of Experimental Psychology, 77,* 376–382.

Evans, C. R., & Marsden, R. P. (1966). A study of the effect of perfect retinal stabilization on some well-known visual illusions, using after image as a method of complementing for eye movements. *British Journal of Physiological Optics, 23,* 242–248.

Forgus, R. H., & Melamed, L. E. (1976). *Perception: A cognitive-stage approach.* New York: McGraw-Hill.

Gibson, E. J. (1969). *Principles of perceptual learning and development.* New York: Appleton-Century-Crofts.

Gregory, R. L. (1970). *The intelligent eye.* New York: McGraw-Hill.

Hammond, K. R., & Summers, D. A. (1972). Cognitive control. *Psychological Review, 79,* 438–456.

Hatopf, W. H. N. (1981). Mistracking in alignment illusions. *Journal of Experimental Psychology: Human Perception and Performance, 7,* 1211–1246.

Helson, H. (1964). *Adaptation level theory: An experimental and systematic approach to behavior.* New York: Harper & Row.

Hochberg, J. (1970). The representation of things and people. In E. H. Gombrich, J. Hochberg, & M. Black (Eds.), *Art, perception and reality* (pp. 47–94). Baltimore: Johns Hopkins University Press.

Killbride, P. L., & Leibowitz, H. W. (1975). Factors affecting the magnitude of the Ponzo illusion among the Baganda. *Perception and Psychophysics, 17(6),* 543–548.

Kilpatrick, F. P. (1961). *Explorations in transactional psychology.* New York: New York University Press.

Lackner, J. R. (1992). Spatial orientation in weightless environments. *Perception, 21(6),* 803–812.

Lambert, W. W., Salomon, R. L., & Watson, P. D. (1949). Reinforcement and extinction as factors in size estimation. *Journal of Experimental Psychology, 39,* 637–641.

Lindsay, P. M., & Norman, D. A. (1972). *Human information processing—An introduction to psychology.* New York: Academic Press.

Lipps, T. (1897). *Raumaesthetik und geometrisch optische Täuschungen* [Spatial esthetics and geometrical optic illusions]. Leip: Barth.

Mach, E. (1976). *Knowledge and error.* Dordrecht: Reidel. (Original work published 1905)

Marr, D. (1982). *Vision.* San Francisco: Freeman.

McCallough, C. (1965). Color adaptation of edge detectors in the human visual system. *Science, 149,* 1115–1116.

McClellan, P. G., & Bernstein, I. H. (1984). What makes the Mueller a liar: A multiple-cue approach. *Perception and Psychophysics, 36(3),* 234–244.

McCormick, E. J. (1976). *Human factors in engineering and design.* New York: McGraw-Hill.

McCready, D. (1986). Moon illusions redescribed. *Perception and Psychophysics, 39(1),* 64–72.

Michael, S. F., & Sherrick, M. F. (1986). Perception of induced visual motion: Effects of relative position, shape and size of the surround. *Canadian Journal of Psychology, 40,* 122–125.

Michon, J. A. (1985). The compleat time experiencer. In J. A. Michon & J. L. Jackson (Eds.), *Time, mind, and behavior* (pp. 20–52). Berlin: Springer-Verlag.

Michotte, A. (1963). *The perception of causality.* New York: Basic Books.

Nisbett, R., & Ross, L. (1980). *Human inference: Strategies and shortcomings of social judgment.* Englewood Cliffs, NJ: Prentice-Hall.

Openhimer, A. (Ed.). (1989). *Perception.* Tel-Aviv: The Open University.

Radvansky, G. A., Hartman, W. M., & Rakerd, B. (1992). Structural alterations of an ambiguous musical figure: The scale illusion revisited. *Perception and Psychophysics, 52(3),* 256–262.

Révész, G. (1924). Experiments on animal space perception. *Proceedings of VIIth International Congress of Psychology, 29,* 56.

Rock, I. (1975). *An introduction to perception.* New Brunswick, NJ: Institute for Cognitive Studies, The State University of Rutgers Press.

Ross, H. E. (1969). When is weight not illusory? *Quarterly Journal of Experimental Psychology, 21,* 346–355.

Schiffman, H. R. (1982). *Sensation and perception* (2nd ed.). New York: Wiley.

Siegel, S., & Petry, S. (1991). Evidence for independent processing of subjective contour brightness and sharpness. *Perception, 20,* 233–241.

Spivey-Knowlton, M. J., & Bridgeman, B. (1993). Spatial context affects the Poggendorff illusion. *Perception and Psychophysics, 53(5),* 467–474.

Stuart, G. W., & Day, R. M. (1988). The Fraser illusion: Simple figures. *Perception and Psychophysics, 44(5),* 409–420.

Sully, J. (1881). *Illusions: A psychological study.* London: Routledge & Kegan Paul.

Treisman, A. M. (1986). Features and objects in visual processing. *Scientific American, 255,* 114–125.

Treisman, A. M., & Schmidt, H. (1982). Illusory conjunctions in the perception of objects. *Cognitive Psychology, 14,* 107–141.

Tsal, Y. (1989). Do illusory conjunctions support the feature integration theory? A critical review of theory and findings. *Journal of Experimental Psychology: Human Perception and Performance, 15,* 394–400.

Tsal, Y., & Kalbert, L. (1985). Disambiguating ambiguous figures by selective attention. *The Quarterly Journal of Experimental Psychology, 37A,* 25–37.

Ullman, S. (1979). The interpretation of structure from motion. *Proceedings of the Royal Society of London Series B, 203,* 405–426.

Van den Heydt, R., Peterhaus, E., & Baumgartner, G. (1984). Illusory contours and cortical neuron responses. *Science, 224,* 1260–1262.

Ward, L. M., Porac, P., Coren, S., & Girgus, J. S. (1977). The case for misapplied constancy scaling: Depth associations elicited by illusion configurations. *American Journal of Psychology, 90,* 609–620.

Wertheimer, M., & Leventhal, C. M. (1958). "Permanent" satiation phenomena with kinesthetic figural aftereffects. *Journal of Experimental Psychology, 55,* 255–257.

Witkin, H. A., & Berry, J. W. (1975). Psychological differentiation in cross-cultural perspective. *Journal of Cross-Cultural Psychology, 6,* 4–87.

Zakay, D. (1990). The evasive art of subjective time measurement: Some methodological dilemmas. In R. A. Block (Ed.), *Cognitive models of psychological time* (pp. 59–84). Hillsdale, NJ: Lawrence Erlbaum Associates.

Zakay, D., & Block, R. A. (1996). The role of attention in time estimation processes. In M. A. Pastor (Ed.), *Time, internal clocks, and movement*. Amsterdam: Elsevier.

Zakay, D., Nitzan, D., & Glickshon, J. (1983). The influence of task difficulty and external tempo on subjective time estimation. *Perception and Psychophysics, 34*, 451–456.

Zakay, D., & Shilo, E. (1985). The influence of temporal and spatial variation on tactile identification of letters. *Journal of General Psychology, 112(2)*, 147–152.

5

Wishful Thinking From a Pragmatic Hypothesis-Testing Perspective

Yaacov Trope
Benjamin Gervey
Nira Liberman

Wishful thinking, people's tendency to believe what they wish to be true, encompasses a broad, far-reaching range of phenomena. Social psychologists have approached wishful thinking from a variety of perspectives, ranging from lower level perceptual approaches (Bruner & Postman, 1947; Sackheim & Gur, 1977) to fairly elaborate issues of attributional bias (Brown, 1986; Ross & Fletcher, 1985; see also Taylor & Brown, 1988, for a review) and the evaluation of evidence (Kunda, 1990). This chapter first provides some examples of social-psychological research on wishful thinking, and then proposes a pragmatic hypothesis-testing framework that accounts for the origins of the phenomenon. Based on this proposed framework, the chapter then elaborates on the phenomenon, discussing some moderators of wishful thinking, the independence of accuracy and bias, the relationship between wishful thinking and mental health, and issues of subjectivity in wishful thinking.

Traditionally, distortion of reality has been seen as a hallmark of mental malfunctioning and pathology (Taylor & Brown, 1988). The belief that mentally healthy individuals engage in realistic self-appraisals has dominated psychology for most of its history (Fiske & Taylor, 1984; Jahoda, 1958; Jourard & Landesman, 1980; Kelley, 1955; Nisbett & Ross, 1980; see also Taylor & Brown, 1988, for a review). However, social psychologists have repeatedly found the distortion of reality to be more common than previously believed. In fact, it quickly became apparent that, instead of the exception, distorting reality is more often the rule (Greenwald, 1980; Lazarus, 1983; Nisbett & Ross, 1980; Taylor & Brown, 1988). Simply put, the majority of people seem to engage in wishful thinking, seeing themselves, their future, and those close to them through rose-colored glasses.

OUTCOMES OF WISHFUL THINKING

The outcomes of wishful thinking are among the most widely researched topics in social psychology today. Research on self-judgment, including current (Alicke, 1985; Brown, 1986; Festinger, 1957; Heider, 1958; Ross & Fletcher, 1985) and future (Weinstein, 1980) appraisals of the self, judgments of friends (Brown, 1986), and even judgments of ad hoc group members (Tajfel & Turner, 1986), show that people tend to be positively biased when they think of themselves and their environments. Although far from comprehensive, this section touches on several of the highlights from this area.

Unrealistic Optimism and Self Versus Other Comparisons

The literature on optimism and self–other comparisons suggests that people have a tendency to see themselves as possessing more positive qualities (e.g., traits and abilities) than other people, and to possess more positive than negative attributes (Alicke, 1985; Brown, 1986). For example, in comparison with the average person, most people believe they are smarter and friendlier, possess a better sense of humor, have a more promising future, and are better drivers (Brown, 1986; Campbell, 1986; Svenson, 1981; Weinstein, 1982). Concomitantly, people tend to judge others more harshly than they judge themselves (Lewinsohn, Mischel, Chaplin, & Barton, 1980). Obviously, these tendencies cannot reflect an undistorted reality: The majority of people cannot be above average. Yet they still tend to see themselves that way. Moreover, people tend to believe that their futures are even brighter than the present. When asked about what the future holds, one study found that participants listed four times more positives than negatives (Markus & Nurius, 1986).

Self-Serving Biases in Attribution

Not only do people tend to see themselves as possessing more positive qualities, but they see those qualities as causal in their successes, but not their failures. In essence, people attribute success to either their abilities or the amount of effort they put into the task, whereas people's failures get attributed to incidental, external factors (Bradley, 1978; Heider, 1958;

Ross & Fletcher, 1985; but see Dweck, Hong, & Chiu, 1993, for an individual-differences perspective). For example, winning a game of squash may get attributed to one's ability, whereas being beaten is attributed to the talents of the other player, not one's own lack of talent. In this way, succeeding at a task reinforces one's positive self-concept, providing further "proof" of one's better-than-average abilities. Conversely, failure becomes nondiagnostic, and can be deemed irrelevant to the desired conclusion. This is not to suggest that people are unaffected by failure, but that it is not deemed as indicative of their underlying qualities. Moreover, this tendency does not hold true when making attributions about others (Jones & Davis, 1965; Jones & Nisbett, 1972; see also Ross, 1977, for a review). When making attributions about others, people tend to see others' behaviors as being internally caused. Thus, when judging others, but not themselves, failures are just as indicative of underlying abilities.

Illusion of Control

People's assessments of the degree to which they affect success get extended to even random events. Given that some measure of skill or choice is involved in events as random as dice rolling and coin flipping, most people tend to believe that they have greater control over the outcome than they actually have (Langer, 1975; see also Crocker, 1982, for a review). For example, Langer (1975) found that people were more reluctant to part with a lottery ticket when they chose the numbers themselves, as compared with when the numbers were chosen randomly. In another study, participants playing a game of "high card" (in which two players randomly cut the deck, with the highest card winning) bet more when their opponent seemed nervous (Langer, 1975). In fact, people often employ strategies that imply some measure of personal control, like switching from one slot machine to another, blowing on dice, or talking to the roulette wheel to make it stop at the right number. Moreover, as suggested in the previous section, when the expected outcome actually occurs, people overattribute the degree to which they caused that outcome (Miller & Ross, 1975), but repeated failure to affect the outcome is treated as "bad luck."

Thus, it can be concluded that people's self-appraisals tend to reflect what they wish to be true, both for the present and the future. Moreover, people tend to assess the causes of their behavior preferentially, such that success is indicative of who and what they are, but failure is not as diagnostic. Further, people do not extend this preferential treatment to the average other. However, is it not also desirable to see those with whom they are close, or those with whom they identify, as better than average as well? In other words, is wishful thinking something that applies only to the self, or is it extended to encompass specific others?

In-Group Favoritism

The literature on the appraisal of those with whom people choose to associate, and even those with whom people are arbitrarily matched, indicates that wishful thinking is not limited to the self. Quite the contrary, people tend to see those they are close to as nearly as positively as they see themselves (Brown, 1986), and make similar assessments of the causes of their behaviors (Taylor & Kouvumaki, 1976). Moreover, even those with whom people are randomly placed in a group get preferentially judged. Research using the minimal intergroup paradigm, in which assignment is random, tends to show that "in-group" members are typically judged more favorably than members of the "out group" (Tajfel & Turner, 1986). In fact, it seems as if the mere classification of another person as an *us* instead of a *them* skews people's judgment (Perdue, Dovidio, Gurtman, & Tyler, 1990).

People primed with in-group designators like *us* and *we* tended to show an evaluatively positive mindset, such that positive person-descriptive adjectives were evaluated (Study 2) and responded to (Study 3) faster than negative person descriptors. Therefore, it seems that people do not simply see themselves as better than others, but those with whom they identify benefit from wishful thinking as well, and even associating in-group terms is enough to get people thinking more positively.

The Illusion of Rationality

One of the more basic, global assumptions people make about themselves is that they are essentially rational decision makers. This suggests that, given free choice, people will not do things they do not like to do, and that they will not contradict their own beliefs. However, even in the absence of external pressures, people often engage in behaviors that they do not find appealing, and they express attitudes that contradict what they believe about themselves. How does this inconsistency—between being rational actors who do not contradict themselves and choosing to engage in behaviors that belie this assumption—get resolved?

One possibility is suggested by the literature on cognitive dissonance (Comer & Laird, 1975; Festinger, 1957; Festinger & Carlsmith, 1959; Frey, 1986). This literature suggests that the inconsistency is resolved by changing one's preexisting attitude toward the discrepant behavior, so that people can maintain the illusion that they are rational. For example, Comer and Laird (1975) showed that freely choosing to participate in a study believed to be about personality and task performance aroused sufficient dissonance in their participants; it got them to change their attitude toward a behavior as extreme as eating worms. Over 40% of the respondents claimed that eating a worm was actually pleasant, whereas others rationalized their behavior by seeing the task as proof of bravery. Moreover, after deciding to engage in this behavior, it was difficult for the participants to reverse that decision. Given a choice between eating the worm and a simple perceptual task, 80% of Comer and Laird's participants asked to eat the worm.

These findings suggest that simply choosing to engage in a behavior makes people see that behavior as more appealing and, relatedly, the rejected alternative as less appealing (Brehm & Cohen, 1962, Festinger, 1957). Moreover, people tend to support and even strengthen that belief by selectively gathering information, seeking out evidence in support of their conclusions, and avoiding evidence that contradicts it (Frey, 1986). Thus, people are able to maintain the illusion of their own rationality by seeing their freely chosen behaviors as desirable and then bolstering that opinion through selectively exposing themselves to information.

Summary

Given this abbreviated overview of wishful thinking outcomes, it is quite evident that the distortion of reality is not a phenomenon limited to the mentally ill. Across a variety of contexts, even the mentally healthy tend to preferentially assess themselves and those close to them, and to positively bias their attributions of success and failure. However, it is not solely in decisions about the self and others that evidence for wishful thinking is found. There are several processes, or "stages of thought," that show evidence of wishful thinking as well.

WISHFUL THINKING PROCESSES

Perceptual Defense

Some of the earliest social-psychological research on perceptual defense suggests one process by which people may distort reality. *Perceptual defense* refers to people "not seeing" unpleasant things (Bruner & Postman, 1947). For example, it was found that people need longer exposure times to recognize "taboo" words, as compared with neutral words. Moreover, this tendency reverses for positive words: People need less time to recognize positive words than to recognize neutral words (see

Erdelyi, 1974, for a review). This work suggests that people tend to view their environments in the most positive light—in this case, by being predisposed toward processing desired stimuli and away from processing aversive stimuli.

Information-Retrieval Biases

Even when both positives and negatives are perceived, however, there is no guarantee that they will be equally available when people engage in self-evaluation. There is ample evidence to suggest that retrieval of autobiographical information from memory is biased toward the positive (Kunda, 1990; Taylor, 1991; see also Matlin & Strang, 1978, for a review). In one particularly compelling study by Sanitioso, Kunda, and Fong (1990), participants were led to believe that either introversion or extroversion were desirable characteristics. They were then asked to generate autobiographical memories indicative of their standing along this dimension. Those led to believe that introversion was desirable tended to generate introverted memories first as well as more introverted than extroverted memories, in contrast to those who were led to see extroversion as desirable. Thus, it seems that what people find desirable is both more accessible (Santioso et al., 1990) and better represented in memory (Isen, 1984; Matlin & Strang, 1978).

Biased Self-Testing

Another process in which wishful thinking is evident is biased self-testing. This process was particularly well illustrated in a study by Quattrone and Tversky (1984). In one of their studies, participants were told that a directional shift in their tolerance for cold after exercise was diagnostic of longevity. After a baseline measurement of tolerance for cold was taken, participants were then made to use a stationary bicycle for 1 minute, which was followed by the directional tolerance manipulation disguised as a psychophysics lecture. Participants who were told that an increase in tolerance was diagnostic of longevity held their arms immersed in cold water longer on the postexercise retest trial, whereas those told that a decrease in tolerance for cold was indicative of longevity showed a decrease in the amount of time they could tolerate the cold. Thus, the desirability of the conclusion motivated people to act in a manner consistent with that outcome, although the majority of the participants were unaware of the motivational influence. In other words, people's self-testing strategies were biased in favor of the most positive conclusion. By conforming to the demands of the longevity test, participants provided evidence for the desired conclusion.

Biased Search and Evaluation of Evidence

What happens when people are confronted with evidence that suggests an undesired conclusion, instead of choosing the behavior that suggests a desired conclusion? In other words, how do people maintain or arrive at the most favorable conclusion when confronted with disconfirming evidence? Research on the biased evaluation of evidence suggests that people tend to derogate the validity of unfavorable information to mitigate or even eliminate its impact (Ditto & Lopez, 1992; Frey, 1986; Kunda, 1990; Wyer & Frey, 1983). For example, Wyer and Frey (1983) showed that participants who were given failure feedback on an intelligence test evaluated the validity of that test lower than those who received success feedback. Although a compelling argument for wishful thinking, it could be argued that the prevalence of prior positive beliefs may have led to this effect. In other words, instead of being an instance of wishful thinking, the more elaborate and accessible knowledge people have about their own intelligence may have given them grounds to derogate the conclusion suggested by the failure feedback.

This issue was addressed by Kunda (1987), who found similar results in an experiment designed to control for the effect of prior beliefs—by making the aversive feedback (the dangers of caffeine) relevant for women but not for men in a factorial design on caffeine consumption. In her experiment, women high in caffeine consumption derogated the validity of an article citing the dangers of caffeine for women, whereas women low in caffeine consumption were convinced by the article. Moreover, men showed no such pattern, although they had equivalent prior knowledge about caffeine. Thus, wishful thinking was at work: Women, but not men, should be threatened by the anticaffeine message, and should therefore be motivated to derogate the article. These results were replicated in a conceptually similar study by Liberman and Chaiken (1992), in which high- and low-risk groups included both men and women, but for which prior beliefs were controlled.

Summary

Given the body of evidence on both outcomes of wishful thinking and the processes that contribute to them, it is hard to refute that the distortion of reality is a far more common phenomenon than traditionally supposed. From the motivation to avoid recognizing taboo words (Bruner & Postman, 1947) to the biased assessment of self and of aversive evidence (Brown, 1986; Kunda, 1987, 1990; Ross & Fletcher, 1985), one can clearly see wishful thinking at work. However, what remains unclear is how and why positivity bias—or wishful thinking—is so prevalent, and, as important, what limits and constrains this tendency.

The next section addresses these issues using a pragmatic hypothesis-testing model.

THE PRAGMATIC HYPOTHESIS-TESTING MODEL

This section interprets wishful thinking within a pragmatic hypothesis-testing framework (see Trope & Liberman, 1995). This framework views knowledge acquisition as a process of generating hypotheses and evaluating their validity by accessing, interpreting, and integrating information. Hypothesis testing is motivated by pragmatic concerns, in the sense that the costs of false acceptance and false rejection of a hypothesis determine whether hypothesis testing will be initiated, how much effort will be expended in the process, and when it will be terminated. Wishful thinking represents a tendency to accept positive hypotheses (i.e., hypotheses referring to subjectively desired state of affairs) rather than negative hypotheses (i.e., hypotheses referring to subjectively undesired state of affairs).

In this model, wishful thinking results from the same cognitive and motivational processes that bias testing of any hypothesis. One set of such processes involves confirmatory bias in hypothesis testing. Once a positive hypothesis is generated, it may implicitly bias accessing and interpreting information in favor of hypothesis confirmation. Because these processes are largely unconscious, they may persist even when perceivers are motivated to reach an accurate judgment and when they possess the processing resources required for systematic hypothesis testing.

A second set of processes suggested by the pragmatic hypothesis-testing model involves asymmetric error costs. Error costs are rarely symmetric. In some cases, false acceptance of a hypothesis is the more costly error, whereas in other cases, false rejection of a hypothesis is the more costly error. It is proposed here that perceivers often see failure to detect that a desired hypothesis is true (false rejection) as more costly than failure to detect that it is false (false acceptance). Given these asymmetric error costs, a pragmatic hypothesis tester will primarily seek to minimize failure to detect a subjectively desired state of affairs. Thus, asymmetric error costs contribute to wishful thinking by leading perceivers to require more information to accept a positive hypothesis than to reject it.

The following section discusses in more detail how confirmatory biases and asymmetric error costs bias perceivers toward accepting positive hypotheses.

CONFIRMATORY BIASES IN WISHFUL THINKING

Like Kunda (1990) and Pyszczynski and Greenberg (1987), it is assumed here that, when possible, people are likely to generate and choose desired, rather than undesired, possibilities as their focal hypotheses. For example, suppose a team member wants to determine why his or her team won a game. Some possibilities are desired (e.g., one's own performance is responsible for the victory) while other possibilities are less desired (e.g., the performance of other team members is responsible for the victory). The team member would be expected to answer this question by testing the hypothesis that it was his or her performance that was responsible for the victory; thinking of him or herself as responsible for a victory is more pleasant, more accessible, and subjectively more probable than the possibility that another team member was responsible for the victory. In general, people may initiate hypothesis testing with a desired possibility as their focal hypothesis. One reason is that desired possibilities are more cognitively accessible because they are associated with individuals' desired goals. Another reason is that desired possibilities are more pleasant to contemplate. Finally, desired possibilities often seem more probable on a priori grounds because individuals actively try to achieve them (see Miller & Ross, 1975).

As focal hypotheses, desired possibilities have an advantage in the hypothesis-testing process. Under optimal processing conditions, when perceivers have ample resources for systematic hypothesis testing, alternative hypotheses may be generated and evaluated. Hypothesis testing under these conditions can be characterized as *diagnostic,* in that it compares the focal hypothesis to alternative hypotheses (see Trope & Liberman, 1993, 1995). However, even in diagnostic testing, the focal hypothesis is considered earlier and receives more attention than alternative hypotheses. As described later, implicit processes—processes of which the individual is unaware—may act to produce evidential biases in favor of the focal positive hypothesis.

Mere Thinking About a Hypothesis

Recent research suggests that merely thinking about a hypothetical possibility and considering its plausibility enhances its subjective probability (see reviews by Gilbert, 1991; Koehler, 1991). For example, a number of studies have found that subjects who were asked to explain a hypothetical success in a future task expected to perform better on the task than subjects who were asked to explain a hypothetical failure on that task (Campbell & Fairey, 1985; Sherman, Skov, Hervitz, & Stock, 1981). Anderson (1983) asked subjects to imagine themselves engaging in a given behavior and to draw a sequence of cartoon sketches depicting the event. The estimated likelihood of actually engaging in the behavior increased after drawing. Finally, Gregory, Cialdini, and Carpenter (1982) asked one group of participants to imagine themselves subscribing to a cable television service; another group was given information about the service, but were not asked to engage in the imagination task. In the 6 months following the experiment, those subjects who engaged in the imagination task were more likely to subscribe to the service than other subjects. This research suggests that merely thinking "as if" a desired possibility is true may actually increase its subjective probability.

Behavioral Confirmation

Behavioral confirmation occurs when hypothesis-testing procedures elicit behavior that confirm one's hypotheses. Initial evidence suggestive of this possibility was obtained in Rosenthal and Jacobson's (1968) early research on the "Pygmalion effect." In the original study, teachers were induced to believe that randomly selected children were "late bloomers," and that they would show considerable improvement during the academic year. Initially, the achievement scores of these children did not differ from the rest of the class. However, at the end of the year, these kids scored higher than their peers on various achievement tests conducted by outside examiners. Apparently, the "late bloomers" received preferential treatment from the teachers, which, in turn, gave them an advantage over other children. Rosenthal's (1969, 1985) work on experimenter bias further demonstrated that experimenters' hypotheses influence their subjects' behavior. Experimenters presumably act in a manner that solicits from subjects the kind of behavior that confirms whatever hypothesis the experimenters are testing.

More directly relevant here is Snyder and Swann's (1978) research on self-confirming processes in lay hypothesis testing. Snyder and Swann asked subjects to test either the hypothesis that a target person is an introvert or the hypothesis that the target is an extrovert. Subjects could test their hypothesis by selecting from a list of questions that asked about introverted behaviors, extroverted behaviors, or behaviors that were irrelevant to introversion or extroversion. Snyder and Swann, as well as a number of researchers using variants of this paradigm, found that individuals preferred questions about behaviors that were consistent with the hypothesized trait, rather than with the alternative trait (see review by Trope & Liberman, 1995).

Subjects testing the hypothesis that the target was extroverted asked about extroverted behaviors, such as having many friends or going to parties, whereas subjects testing the hypothesis that the target was introverted asked about introverted behaviors, such as being quiet and enjoying solitary activities. These one-sided questions elicited hypothesis-confirming answers from the targets. Those tested for extroversion reported more extroverted behaviors, whereas those tested for introversion reported more introverted behaviors. Moreover, Snyder and Swann (1978) found that this resulted in hypothesis confirmation, so that subjects testing the extrovert hypothesis concluded that their target person was a relatively extroverted person, whereas subjects testing the introverted hypothesis concluded that their target was a relatively introverted person.

These findings suggest that the strategies people use to test their hypotheses are more likely to solicit hypothesis-confirming than hypothesis-disconfirming answers. Given that individuals tend to test positive rather than negative hypotheses, they will more often obtain evidence they like than evidence they dislike.

Biased Encoding and Retrieval

Even when hypothesis-testing procedures do not produce behavior confirmation, the hypotheses that individuals entertain may bias how the acquired evidence is encoded and subsequently retrieved from memory. One of the basic tenets of cognitive psychology is that encoding and retrieval processes are theory-driven. A hypothesis provides a mental model in terms of which evidence may be construed and retrieved. A large amount of research on social cognition has shown that, to the extent that evidence is ambiguous, its meaning will be assimilated to or disambiguated by the activated mental model (see Higgins, 1996b; Higgins & King, 1981). For example, Trope (1986) found that subjects who tested the hypothesis that a person was angry interpreted that person's facial expression as conveying anger, whereas subjects who tested the hypothesis that the person was happy interpreted the same facial expression as conveying happiness. Similarly, Snyder and Uranowitz (1978) demonstrated that subjects testing the suitability of another person for a job requiring an extroverted personality (e.g., salesperson) tended to recall that person's extroverted behaviors, whereas subjects testing the suitability of the same person for a job requiring an introverted personality tended to recall instances where that person acted in an introverted manner. Finally, Darley and Gross' (1983) subjects rated a child's performance as more successful when they tested the hypothesis that the child has high ability than when they were testing the hypothesis that the child has low ability.

It appears, then, that the same evidence may be construed and reconstructed in different and even opposite ways, depending on the perceiver's hypothesis. This makes hypothesis testing a subjective process, whose outcome depends on the mental models one brings to bear on the incoming evidence. The implications for wishful thinking are straightforward: Individuals testing positive hypotheses are likely to selectively encode and retrieve evidence that support what they want to believe. Such evidential biases may be independent of motivation to be accurate and the individual's processing resources. An individual may be highly motivated to reach accurate conclusions and may possess the prerequisite processing resources. However, because assimilative processes are largely implicit, they may be hard to detect and correct (see Trope & Liberman, 1993). Motivation for accuracy may lead individuals to generate alternative hypotheses and evaluate them relative to the desired hypothesis. However, because desired hypotheses are considered first, subsequent attention to alternative, less desired hypotheses is unlikely to undo the initial assimilative effect of the desired hypothesis (see Trope, Cohen, & Alfieri, 1991).

Thus, based on little supporting evidence, individuals may draw subjectively pleasing conclusions, but nevertheless maintain the impression that their conclusions are objectively justifiable by the available evidence. This obviously represents wishful thinking. But in the present framework, it is viewed as an integral part of normal, everyday hypothesis testing.

ASYMMETRIC ERROR COSTS
IN WISHFUL THINKING

The preceding section discussed cognitive mechanisms that produce evidential biases in favor of subjectively desired hypotheses. This section examines how individuals' pragmatic concerns—their attempt to minimize the cost of erroneous inferences—contribute to desirability effects. It is proposed that desirability effects occur when failure to detect that a desired hypothesis is true is costlier than failure to detect that it is false.

The pragmatic hypothesis-testing model assumes that hypothesis testing is motivated by the imagined outcomes of correct and incorrect inferences regarding a hypothesis (see Trope & Liberman, 1995). As shown in Table 5.1, an inference can be correct in two ways: correct acceptance and correct rejection. It can also be incorrect in two ways: false acceptance (errors of commission, false positives) and false rejection (errors of omission, false negatives). Each outcome has a positive or negative subjective value for the perceiver.

TABLE 5.1
Actual State of Affairs

Decision	Hypothesis True	Hypothesis False
Accept hypothesis	Correct acceptance	False acceptance (error of commission)
Reject hypothesis	False rejection (error of omission)	Correct rejection

The cost of a false rejection is the loss that results from rejecting rather than accepting a true hypothesis, whereas the cost of a false acceptance is the loss that results from accepting rather than rejecting a false hypothesis. For example, in testing the hypothesis, "Does my daughter have musical talent?", false rejection means failure to recognize that the child has musical talent. This error is costly when its consequences are worse than those of detecting that the child is musical. False acceptance would mean failure to detect that the child has no musical talent. This error is costly when its consequences are worse than those of recognizing that she is in fact not talented.

To reduce error costs, perceivers attempt to reach confident inferences. The minimal level of confidence (confidence threshold) a perceiver requires before terminating hypothesis testing depends on the relative costs of errors compared with the costs of information. A major assumption of this model is that perceivers set two different confidence thresholds: one for accepting the hypothesis and another for rejecting it. The acceptance threshold is the minimum level of confidence that the hypothesis is true, which a perceiver requires before accepting a hypothesis, rather than continuing to test it; the rejection threshold is the minimum confidence that the hypothesis is false, which a perceiver requires before rejecting the hypothesis, rather than continuing to test it. The acceptance threshold primarily depends on the cost of false acceptance relative to the cost of information. When wrongly accepting the hypothesis has high costs but the cost of information is low, the perceiver sets a high confidence threshold for accepting the hypothesis. Likewise, the rejection threshold primarily depends on the cost of false rejection relative to the cost of information. For example, when the consequences of failing to recognize a target's hostility are high, one will demand high confidence before rejecting that possibility. Correspondingly, when erroneously concluding that the target is hostile has particularly unpleasant consequences, one will demand high confidence before accepting that conclusion.

Whether a perceiver terminates or continues hypothesis testing also depends on his or her current confidence in the hypothesis prior to any new testing. This prior confidence reflects the perceiver's initial confidence in the hypothesis prior to any new information search. Perceivers will continue hypothesis testing as long as prior confidence is below both thresholds. Conversely, even perceivers with high confidence thresholds for accepting or rejecting their hypothesis will not engage in further testing if their prior confidence already exceeds either threshold.

The Combined Amount and Asymmetry of Error Costs

Two important aspects of inferential errors are their combined costs and their costs relative to each other. The total, or combined, error costs determine the overall extremity of the confidence thresholds and, thereby, the range of uncertainty at which a perceiver will continue to test his or her hypothesis, rather than simply making a decision to either accept or reject it. In some sense, the combined error costs represent one's overall concern with accuracy.

However, an important implication of the present analysis is that, whatever their combined level, the costs of false acceptance and false rejection may be unequal. Sometimes when the cost of a false acceptance is exactly the same as the cost of false rejection, avoiding false acceptance may be equally important as avoiding false rejection. But more commonly, the costs of the two errors are unequal so that the perceiver cares more about avoiding one type of error than the other (see Friedrich, 1993).

In the earlier example, the parent might be particularly concerned with providing the child with the opportunity to develop her potential musical talent. This parent's primary consideration, then, would be to minimize the likelihood of failing to detect the child's talent—namely, of a false rejection. Another parent might be more concerned about the potential of failures and frustration. For this parent, the premium would be on minimizing the likelihood of a false acceptance. One parent is focused on accurate detection of possible talent, whereas the other is focused on accurate detection of possible lack of talent. Thus, the two parents differ in the focus of their accuracy motivation, not in its overall amount.

Asymmetric costs of false acceptance and rejection will be reflected in asymmetric confidence thresholds for accepting versus rejecting a hypothesis. When false acceptance is more costly, acceptance thresholds will be higher than rejection thresholds. As a result, the hypothesis will have to be highly probable to be accepted, but only moderately improbable to be rejected. In contrast, when false rejection is more costly, rejection thresholds will be higher than acceptance thresholds, so that the hypothesis will need to be highly improbable to be rejected, but only moderately probable to be accepted.

The implications of these asymmetries for hypothesis testing are straightforward: The amount of information needed to accept a hypothesis may differ from the amount of information needed to reject it. When the acceptance threshold is higher, more information will be needed to accept the hypothesis than to reject it, and the opposite will hold when the rejection threshold is higher.

Thus, asymmetry in the costs of these two errors will lead to a bias in hypothesis testing. However, this bias is not identical with what is often thought of as biased motivation. That is, accuracy concerns need not lead to symmetric costs of errors and symmetric confidence thresholds. For example, in statistical decision making, the decision criteria for accepting a hypothesis are conventionally set much more strictly than the criteria for rejecting it. The scientist following these conventional criteria is therefore using biased decision criteria. The underlying motivation of the scientist is not usually considered biased, however. Objectivity is not compromised by these biased decision criteria. Indeed, the scientist who does not use conventionally asymmetric criteria, but instead decides to accept his or her hypothesis with the same leniency allowed to reject a hypothesis, would be widely regarded as demonstrating biased motivation. So, too, in lay hypothesis testing, symmetric decision criteria are not the hallmark of objective, unbiased motivation. Likewise, asymmetric—biased—decision criteria are not the hallmark of underlying biased motivation.

Desirability Effects

In the model discussed herein, the subjective desirability of a hypothesis—the extent to which one wants it to be true—can affect confidence thresholds for accepting and rejecting a hypothesis, based on the costs of false acceptance and false rejection, respectively. The two thresholds may either be symmetric (equally stringent) or asymmetric. Because the costs of the two possible errors may differ, one's acceptance thresholds may differ from one's rejection thresholds. For a variety of reasons, people may set their rejection thresholds more stringently than their acceptance thresholds, or they may set their acceptance thresholds more stringently, as in most scientific decision making. The desirability of the hypothesis is one of the factors that may lead to asymmetric confidence thresholds.

Why should desired hypotheses tend to have more lenient acceptance than rejection criteria (and the opposite for undesired hypotheses)?

First, falsely rejecting a desired hypothesis often means missing an opportunity to reach a desired goal. One may miss the opportunity to learn how to play the piano if one erroneously decides one lacks musical talent. One may miss the opportunity to get well if one erroneously decides that treatment is ineffective. One also may miss the opportunity to solve a problem if one wrongly decides it is unsolvable. When such goals are personally significant, missing the opportunity to reach them (the cost of false rejection) may seem worse than a futile attempt to reach them (the cost of false acceptance).

Second, as argued earlier, individuals are likely to think more about the state of affairs in which their desired hypothesis is true rather than false. This means that the possibility of failing to recognize a true desired hypothesis (false rejection) will be more salient than the possibility of failing to reject a false hypothesis (false acceptance). Therefore, with a desired hypothesis, the costs of erroneously rejecting it are likely to loom larger in one's mind than the costs of erroneously accepting it.

Third, the positive affect associated with accepting a desired hypothesis may attenuate the cost of a false acceptance, whereas the negative affect associated with rejecting a desired hypothesis may augment its costs. Thus, when someone aspires to achieve some goal, believing that the goal is achievable is more pleasing, at least in the short term, than believing it is not (see Friedrich, 1993).

In summary, when a conclusion is desired, the cost of false acceptance may seem lower than the cost of false rejection, leading to asymmetric confidence thresholds. One's overall motivation for accuracy may be quite high, but it may primarily stem from one's wish to avoid false rejection of the desired hypothesis. As a result, desired conclusions may be accepted more quickly and on the basis of less information and hypothesis testing than would be necessary to reject them. Moreover, one may selectively seek information that minimizes false rejections rather than false acceptances.

Earlier Termination Following Evidence Supporting Desired Hypotheses. A major implication of the assumption that desired hypotheses have costlier false rejection errors than false acceptance errors is that people should engage in more extensive and analytic processing before rejecting a desired hypothesis than before accepting it. Thus, evidence will often be evaluated more carefully and critically when it is inconsistent, rather than consistent, with a desired hypothesis. Evidence supporting the desired hypothesis is likely to bolster one's confidence to threshold, and may also lead to earlier termination of the hypothesis-testing sequence than evidence refuting it.

As discussed earlier, a number of recent studies evaluating self-relevant tests support this prediction. For example, Wyer and Frey (1983) and Pyszczynski, Greenberg, and Holt (1985) tested subjects and gave them either positive or negative feedback. Subjects then read reports concerning the tests' reliability. Those who had received positive test results judged reports supporting the tests as stronger, whereas those who had received negative test results judged reports refuting the tests as stronger. In these studies, then, subjects seemed more sensitive to unreliability when the test results were inconsistent, rather than consistent, with positive self-beliefs.

Comparable results have been found with evaluations of evidence concerning health issues relevant to some subjects. Kunda (1987) and Liberman and Chaiken (1992) had coffee drinkers and non-coffee drinkers read research reports concerning the risks of drinking coffee. Coffee drinkers judged results indicating that coffee was dangerous as weaker than did non-coffee drinkers, despite being matched on prior beliefs concerning coffee's health risks (Liberman & Chaiken, 1992). Exploring the mediating processes underlying these coffee drinkers' self-serving conclusions, Liberman and Chaiken found evidence that coffee-drinking subjects scrutinized the data more carefully and detected more flaws in the evidence.

Similarly, Ditto and Lopez (1992) told subjects about a purportedly dangerous medical condition that increases one's chances of pancreatic disease, "TAA deficiency." They then gave subjects yellow test papers to test their own saliva for TAA. Some subjects were told that the paper would turn green if they had the condition while others were told that it would turn green if they did not have the condition. Subjects were also told that the test's accuracy might be affected by irregularities in lifestyle, such as diet or sleep. When subjects tested their own saliva, none of the test papers changed color because they were actually just slips of yellow construction paper. When asked whether they had any life irregularities that might render the test inaccurate, subjects whose tests implied that they had (vs. did not have) TAA deficiency generated more life irregularities and rated the test as less accurate. Again, subjects seemed more sensitive to alternative interpretations when evaluating evidence that favored rejection of desired self-relevant hypotheses.

These findings are consistent with the idea that, in testing desired hypotheses, people are primarily concerned with minimizing false rejections. As a result, they need a smaller amount of information and less critical hypothesis-testing procedures to accept a desired hypothesis than to reject it.

Biased Information Search. Asymmetric confidence thresholds for desired hypotheses may produce an asymmetric information search.

Specifically, the stringent threshold for rejecting a desired hypothesis favors a search that is unlikely to leave the hypothesis undetected (i.e., unlikely to falsely reject the hypothesis). For example, consider the desired hypothesis that one's child is competent. The primary concern here is to minimize the likelihood of undetected competence. Given this goal, the hypothesis tester will observe the partner performing tasks in which it is relatively easy to succeed. In such tasks, failure is unlikely to occur unless the child is really incompetent. The likelihood of false rejection of the competence hypothesis is thus minimized. Stated otherwise, success, the likely outcome, is not very diagnostic, but it may be sufficient to exceed the lenient threshold for attributing competence to one's child. Failure is less likely, and can occur only if the child is incompetent. This makes failure sufficiently diagnostic to exceed the stringent threshold for rejecting the competence hypothesis. Similarly, the hypothesis tester will search his or her memory by first looking for instances of successful performances. Retrieving few successes may be sufficient to accept the competence hypothesis, whereas many more failures would have to be retrieved to reject this hypothesis. Such testing is unlikely to miss the possibility that a desired hypothesis is true, but may miss the possibility that a desired hypothesis is false (see Sanitiso et al., 1990).

Quattrone and Tversky's (1982) study, described earlier, illustrated these biased information-search processes in self-testing behavior. Recall that subjects in this study held their hands immersed in cold water longer when they were told that high cold tolerance (vs. low cold tolerance) was indicative of longevity. In our terms, Quattrone and Tversky's subjects were testing the desired hypothesis that their true cold tolerance was high. By making an effort to tolerate the cold water, subjects in effect minimized the likelihood of false rejection of this hypothesis. If the subject's true cold tolerance was high, his or her efforts ensured that it would be expressed in the test results. However, this could come at the expense of detection of low cold tolerance (i.e., with sufficient effort, even a subject with low cold tolerance could still obtain favorable test results). Thus, subjects' self-testing behavior was biased against detection of the undesired possibility. In our framework, this is because they were more concerned with missing the possibility that they have a desired physical attribute (high cold tolerance) than with missing the possibility that they have an undesired physical attribute (low cold tolerance).

In summary, research on motivationally biased information search and processing is consistent with the present error costs analysis. For a variety of reasons, failing to detect that a desired possibility is true is subjectively costlier than failing to detect that it is false. These asymmetric error costs lead to setting asymmetric confidence thresholds for accepting and rejecting a desired possibility, with acceptance thresholds becoming increasingly more lenient relative to rejection thresholds as the hypothesis becomes more desired. In this framework, biased search and processing of information are direct consequence of this asymmetry.

MODERATORS OF WISHFUL
THINKING PHENOMENA

People do not always accept desired beliefs. The question, then, is what determines whether positivity biases will or will not occur? Based on the hypothesis-testing framework, two types of moderators are considered: confirmation-bias moderators and error-cost moderators.

Confirmation-Bias Moderators

The earlier discussion of when confirmation biases are likely to support desired conclusions suggests that, at times, confirmation biases actually work against desirability biases. Some individuals may start hypothesis testing with undesired possibilities seeming more probable and salient than desired possibilities. This may be induced by chronic orientation toward avoiding negative outcomes, rather than approaching positive outcomes, a history of negative outcomes, or a contextually induced framing of decisions in terms of negative outcomes (see Higgins, 1987, 1996a; Tversky & Kahneman, 1981). For example, individuals who are chronically depressed may habitually expect and think of events in terms of negative possibilities (see Andersen, Spielman, & Bargh, 1992). For these individuals, evidential biases will favor confirmation of undesired conclusions. Indeed, a considerable amount of research has demonstrated what has been termed *depressive realism* (i.e., a lower incidence of positivity bias and wishful thinking phenomena among depressed than nondepressed individuals).

Ambiguity of evidence is obviously another important determinant of positivity bias. A desired hypothesis that an individual might entertain will distort the interpretation of incoming evidence only when the evidence is ambiguous—when it can be interpreted in multiple ways (see Higgins, 1996; Trope, 1986). For example, in testing the hypothesis, "Is my friend a nice guy?", one can construe the behavior of teasing an acquaintance as friendly banter, although the behavior may reflect a cruel streak. However, one could not use evidence relating to the intelligence to determine the acquaintance's friendliness because it is not applicable to the focal hypothesis, nor could one use unambiguously cruel behaviors to confirm one's hypothesis because they cannot be interpreted as friendly.

Error-Cost Moderators

It was suggested earlier that false rejection of a positive hypothesis is subjectively costly because it implies a loss of opportunities. In some cases, however, the opposite errors may be associated with such losses. For example, if one conceives of the hypothesis as reflecting a changeable attribute, then false acceptance of the positive hypothesis (e.g., "I am a good squash player") may lead to ignoring negative feedback that would enable one to improve the attribute in question. In fact, it has been shown that the implicit beliefs one holds about the changeability of an attribute affect the interpretation of failure feedback. Specifically, those who believe that attributes are changeable react to failure feedback in an instrumental fashion, presumably because they interpret the feedback as indicating that there is a weakness to overcome. Conversely, those who believe those attributes to be unchangeable react quite differently, essentially giving up because they believe the failure feedback to be indicative of an unimprovable deficiency (see Dweck et al., 1993, for a review).

In addition, it is possible that changeability beliefs may act directly on the affective impact of information, thereby decreasing the motivation to seek out positives and avoid negatives. Direct evidence for this was found in a study by Gervey and Trope (1995), in which beliefs about the changeability of attributes were manipulated. In their study, positivity bias was eliminated when information pertained to changeable attributes, but was relatively strong when the information pertained to unchangeable attributes. Moreover, measures of affect were consistent with this pattern of results, suggesting that changeability beliefs moderate the affective impact of information.

Individual differences in outcome focus may also moderate the positivity bias. Higgins (1987, 1996b) suggested a distinction between individuals with a positive versus a negative outcome focus. People with a positive outcome focus tend to frame events in terms of the presence or absence of positive outcomes, whereas people with a negative outcome focus tend to frame events in terms of the presence or absence of negative outcomes. For instance, a person with a positive outcome focus will view weekends as a time for pleasant activities and weekdays as a time for unpleasant activities. A person with a negative outcome focus will view weekends in terms of the absence of unpleasant duties and weekdays in terms of their presence. Individuals with a negative outcome focus are likely to frame hypotheses in negative terms more than individuals with a positive outcome focus. Because the negative hypothesis is focal for negatively focused people, the cost associated with failing to detect it looms larger for them, compared with people with a positive outcome focus. Thus, although hypothesis testing by positive outcome-focus people may be primarily designed to detect desired possibilities, hypothesis testing by negative outcome-focus people may be primarily designed to detect undesired possibilities.

CONCLUSIONS AND IMPLICATIONS

This concluding section examines the notions of accuracy and bias from the perspective of the pragmatic hypothesis-testing model. Then it reexamines the controversy introduced at the outset of the chapter: Is wishful thinking a precondition for mental health or an indicator of pathology? Finally, it discusses some implications of the notions of subjectivity and pragmatism, which are incorporated in our model.

Accuracy and Bias

Wishful thinking is viewed as a product of normal hypothesis testing, which is subjective and pragmatic. According to our model, hypothesis testing is always motivated by the desire to be accurate (i.e., to avoid error). The concern with avoiding errors is pragmatic because error costs are personal; they are defined within the specific situation in which the hypothesis is tested. Moreover, because there are two possible errors with two independent costs, the person is naturally "biased" in being more careful to avoid the more costly of these. Because falsely rejecting a positive hypothesis is often more costly than falsely accepting it, the system is often "biased" toward accepting positive hypotheses.

The term *bias* is used here to indicate uneven consideration of the two errors, rather than a deviation from a normative model. It is important to acknowledge that, in most areas, there is no normative model stipulating "appropriate" error costs and the thresholds associated with them. Consequently, there is no basis to assume that one set of acceptance–rejection thresholds is more correct, or "normative," than the other. Moreover, even when normative thresholds exist, they are not necessarily symmetrical. In science, for example, the criteria for accepting a hypothesis are much more stringent than for rejecting it. The judicial system is also deliberately biased toward more lenient rejection of the "guilty" hypothesis than for accepting it—bias designed to reflect social norms and values. Both systems are biased, yet neither is considered "inaccurate." In the same way, bias is not believed to be the polar opposite of accuracy in the lay hypothesis-testing system. Instead, accuracy and bias are independent constructs.

Wishful Thinking and Mental Health

Taylor and Brown (1988) refuted the idea that wishful thinking is a hallmark of pathology. Instead, they suggested that it is a precondition of mental health. Moreover, they argued that some amount of reality distortion is psychologically adaptive, and therefore, a "reality-distorting mechanism" was evolutionarily selected.

Our model certainly disagrees with the view of wishful thinking as an indicator of pathology. As has been shown, it is likely to be part of normal hypothesis testing. This chapter does not fully embrace Taylor and Brown's (1988) idea of a system that is specifically designed to produce positive distortions of reality. Instead, according to this analysis, wishful thinking is a by-product of the system, rather than its goal. Reality distortion is not built into the model to make people less susceptible to distress and depression, and thereby to provide a better evolutionary fit. Instead, the system is adaptive in that it is sensitive to the person's concerns, be they emotional, practical, interpersonal, and so on. In that sense, the system does not grant emotional costs any priority over other concerns, nor does it view the effect of positivity on the system as bypassing the normal hypothesis-testing process.

Some Consequences of Subjectivity

The cognitive mechanisms of hypothesis testing are subjective. Choosing the focal hypothesis and selecting evidence are contingent on subjective expectancies, and the interpretation of evidence heavily relies on the subjective construal of its meaning, rather than reflects "the objective reality." Moreover, subjectivity is inevitable, and there is no normative criterion for distinguishing normal from pathological degrees of subjectivity. There appears to be no qualitative difference between normal "disambiguation" of evidence and pathological "reality distortion." Rather, the distinction between normal and distorting subjective construals appears to be a matter of degree and social norms.

Subjectivity and pragmatism imply that one's conclusions are likely to appear wrong or biased to another person, who interprets the evidence differently and assumes different error costs. In addition, people rarely think of their own views and conclusions as subjectively construed and their interests as distinct from those of others. Instead, they assume that they depict reality "as it really is," and that others share their concerns (Griffin & Ross, 1991). Consequently, they often infer that a view or conclusion that deviates from their own is "biased," "distorted," or "mistaken."

Considering the subjectivity of the construal and decision processes, little agreement is likely to be found between people who share the same situation. Even such obvious questions as identifying actions and behaviors (e.g., was his behavior aggressive, assertive, or friendly?) appear to yield little agreement. One can expect that evaluations (e.g., is he a trustworthy person?) and judgments of relative importance (e.g., is taking the test worth the risk?) will yield even less agreement.

It may be that, in many instances, the label *positivity bias,* or *wishful thinking,* reflects an outside view that ignores the subjectivity component. What appears biased and distorted to one person may seem justified and internally coherent to another (see Kruglanski, 1989; Schwarz, 1994). Lacking any normative criteria for weighing costs or distinguishing between legitimate disambiguation of evidence and "reality distortion," there is no normative basis for favoring one subjective interpretation over another. Therefore, it may be that positivity bias and wishful thinking are merely an "outsider's perspective" on an otherwise normal hypothesis-testing process.

REFERENCES

Alicke, M. D. (1985). Global self-evaluation as determined by the desirability and controllability of trait adjectives. *Journal of Personality and Social Psychology, 49,* 1621–1630.

Andersen, S. M., Spielman, L. A., & Bargh, J. A. (1992). Future-event schemas and certainty about the future: Automaticity in depressives' future-event predictions. *Journal of Personality and Social Psychology, 63,* 711–723.

Anderson, C. A. (1983). Imagination and expectation: The effect of imagining behavioral scripts on personal intentions. *Journal of Personality and Social Psychology, 45,* 293–305.

Asch, S. E. (1946). Forming impressions of personality. *Journal of Abnormal and Social Psychology, 59,* 177–181.

Bradley, G. W. (1978). Self-serving biases in the attributional process: A reexamination of the fact or fiction question. *Journal of Personality and Social Psychology, 36,* 56–71.

Brehm, J. W., & Cohen, A. R. (1962). *Explorations in cognitive dissonance.* New York: Wiley.

Brown, J. D. (1986). Evaluations of self and others: Self-enhancement biases in social judgments. *Social Cognition, 4,* 353–376.

Bruner, J. S., & Postman, L. (1947). Emotional selectivity in perception and reaction. *Journal of Personality, 16,* 69–77.

Campbell, J. D. (1986). Similarity and uniqueness: The effects of attribution type, relevance, and individual differences in self-esteem and depression. *Journal of Personality and Social Psychology, 50,* 281–294.

Campbell, J. D., & Fairey, P. J. (1985). Effects of self-esteem on hypothetical explanations and verbalization of expectancies on future performance. *Journal of Personality and Social Psychology, 48,* 1097–1111.

Comer, R., & Laird, J. D. (1975). Choosing to suffer as a consequence of expecting to suffer: Why do people do it? *Journal of Personality and Social Psychology, 35,* 459–477.

Crocker, J. (1982). Biased questions in judgment of covariation studies. *Personality and Social Psychology Bulletin, 8,* 214–220.

Darley, J. M., & Gross, P. H. (1983). A hypothesis-confirming bias in labeling effects. *Journal of Personality and Social Psychology, 44,* 20–33.

Ditto, P. H., & Lopez, D. F. (1992). Motivated skepticism: Use of differential decision criteria for preferred and nonpreferred conclusions. *Journal of Personality and Social Psychology, 63,* 568–584.

Dweck, C. A., Hong, Y., & Chiu, C. (1993). Implicit theories: Individual differences in the likelihood and meaning of dispositional inference. *Personality and Social Psychology Bulletin, 19,* 644–656.

Erdelyi, H. M. (1974). A new look at the new look: Perceptual defense and vigilance. *Psychological Review, 81,* 1–25.

Festinger, L. (1957). *A theory of cognitive dissonance.* Evanston, IL: Row, Peterson.

Festinger, L., & Carlsmith, J. M. (1959). Cognitive consequences of forced compliance. *Journal of Abnormal and Social Psychology, 58,* 203–210.

Fischhoff, B., & Beyth-Marom, R. (1983). Hypothesis evaluation from a Bayesian perspective. *Psychological Review, 90,* 239–260.

Fiske, S. T., & Taylor, S. E. (1984). *Social cognition.* Reading, MA: Addison-Wesley.

Frey, D. (1986). Recent research on selective exposure to information. In L. Berkowitz (Ed.), *Advances in experimental social psychology* (Vol. 19, pp. 41–80). New York: Academic Press.

Friedrich, J. (1993). Primary error detection and minimization (PEDMIN) strategies in social cognition: A reinterpretation of confirmation bias phenomena. *Psychological Review, 100,* 298–319.

Gerard, H. B., & White, G. L. (1983). Post-decisional reevaluation of choice alternatives. *Personality and Social Psychology Bulletin, 9,* 364–369.

Gervey, B., & Trope, Y. (1995, June). *The moderating role of changeability in information-search strategies.* Poster presented at the 7th annual convention of the American Psychological Society, New York.

Gilbert, D. (1991). How mental systems believe. *American Psychologist, 46,* 107–119.

Greenwald, A. G. (1980). The totalitarian ego: Fabrication and revision of personal history. *American Psychologist, 35,* 603–618.

Gregory, W. L., Cialdini, R. B., & Carpenter, K. M. (1982). Self-relevant scenarios as mediators of likelihood estimates and compliance: Does imagining make it so? *Journal of Personality and Social Psychology, 43,* 89–99.

Griffin, D. W., & Ross, L. (1991). Subjective construal, social inference, and human misunderstanding. In M. Zanna (Ed.), *Advances in experimental social psychology* (Vol. 24, 319–359). New York: Academic Press.

Heider, F. (1958). *The psychology of interpersonal relations.* New York: Wiley.

Higgins, F. T. (1987). Self discrepancy: A theory relating self and affect. *Psychological Review, 94,* 319–340.

Higgins, E. T. (1996a). Ideals, oughts, and regulatory outcome focus: Relating affect and motivation to distinct pains and pleasures. In P. M. Gollwitzer & J. A. Bargh (Eds.), *Action science: Linking cognition and motivation to behavior.* New York: Guilford.

Higgins, E. T. (1996b). Knowledge activation: Accessibility, applicability and salience. In E. T. Higgins & A. W. Kruglanski (Eds.), *Social psychology: Handbook of basic principles.* New York: Guilford.

Higgins, E. T., & King, G. A. (1981). Accessibility of social constructs: Information-processing consequences of individual and contextual variability. In N. Cantor & J. F. Kihlstrom (Eds.), *Personality, cognition, and social interaction* (pp. 69–122). Hillsdale, NJ: Lawrence Erlbaum Associates.

Isen, A. M. (1984). Toward understanding the role of affect in cognition. In R. S. Wyer & T. K. Srull (Eds.), *Handbook of social cognition* (Vol 3, pp. 179–236). Hillsdale, NJ: Lawrence Erlbaum Associates.

Jahoda, M. (1958). *Current concepts of positive mental health.* New York: Basic Books.

Jones, E. E., & Davis, K. E. (1965). From acts to dispositions: The attributional process in person perception. In L. Berkowitz (Ed.), *Advances in experimental social psychology* (Vol. 2, pp. 219–266). New York: Academic Press.

Jones, E. E., & Nisbett, R. E. (1972). The actor and the observer: Divergent perceptions of causality. In E. E. Jones, D. E. Kanouse, H. H. Kelley, R. E. Nisbett, S. Valins, & B. Weiner (Eds.), *Attribution: Perceiving the causes of behavior* (pp. 79–94). Morristown, NJ: General Learning Press.

Jourard, S. M., & Landesman, T. (1980). *Healthy personality: An approach from the viewpoint of humanistic psychology* (4th ed.). New York: Macmillan.

Kelley, G. A. (1955). *A theory of personality: The psychology of personal constructs*. New York: W. W. Norton.

Koehler, D. J. (1991). Explanation, imagination, and confidence in judgment. *Psychological Bulletin, 110,* 499–519.

Kruglanski, A. W. (1989). *Lay epistemics and human knowledge*. New York: Plenum.

Kunda, Z. (1987). Motivated inference: Self-serving generation and evaluation of causal theories. *Journal of Personality and Social Psychology, 53,* 636–647.

Kunda, Z. (1990). The case for motivated reasoning. *Psychological Bulletin, 108,* 480–498.

Langer, E. J. (1975). The illusion of control. *Journal of Personality and Social Psychology, 32,* 311–328.

Lazarus, R. S. (1983). The costs and benefits of denial. In S. Breznitz (Ed.), *Denial of stress* (pp. 1–30). New York: International Universities Press.

Lewinsohn, P. M., Mischel, W., Chaplin, W., & Barton, R. (1980). Social competence and depression: The role of illusory self-perceptions. *Journal of Abnormal Psychology, 89,* 203–212.

Liberman, A., & Chaiken, S. (1992). Defensive processing of personally relevant health messages. *Personality and Social Psychology Bulletin, 18,* 669–679.

Markus, H., & Nurius, P. (1986). Possible selves. *American Psychologist, 41,* 954–969.

Matlin, M. W., & Strang, D. J. (1978). *The pollyanna principle: Selectivity in language, memory and thought.* Cambridge, MA: Schenkman.

Miller, D. T., & Ross, M. (1975). Self-serving biases in the attribution of causality: Fact or fiction? *Psychological Bulletin, 82,* 213–225.

Nisbett, R. E., & Ross, L. (1980). *Human inference: Strategies and shortcomings of social judgment.* Engelwood Cliffs, NJ: Prentice-Hall.

Perdue, C. W., Dovidio, J. F., Gurtman, M. B., & Tyler, R. B. (1990). Us and them: Social categorization and the process of intergroup bias. *Journal of Personality and Social Psychology, 59,* 475–486.

Pyszczynski, T. A., & Greenberg, J. (1987). Toward an integration of cognitive and motivational perspectives in social inference: A biased hypothesis-testing model. In L. Berkowitz (Ed.), *Advances in experimental social psychology* (Vol. 20, pp. 297–334). New York: Academic Press.

Pyszczynski, T. A., Greenberg, J., & Holt, K. (1985). Maintaining consistency between self-serving beliefs and available data: A bias in information evaluation. *Personality and Social Psychology Bulletin, 11,* 179–190.

Quattrone, G. A., & Tversky, A. (1984). Causal versus diagnostic contingencies: On self-deception and on the voter's illusion. *Journal of Personality and Social Psychology, 46,* 237–248.

Rosenthal, R. (1969). Interpersonal expectations: Effects of the experimenter's hypothesis. In R. Rosenthal & R. L. Rosnow (Eds.), *Artifact in behavioral research* (pp. 181–277). New York: Academic Press.

Rosenthal, R. (1985). From unconscious experimenter bias to teacher expectancy effects. In J. B. Dusek, V. C. Hall, & W. J. Meyer (Eds.), *Teacher expectancies* (pp. 37–65). Hillsdale, NJ: Lawrence Erlbaum Associates.

Rosenthal, R., & Jacobson, L. (1968). *Pygmalion in the classroom: Teacher expectation and pupil's intellectual development.* New York: Holt, Rhinehart & Winston.

Rosenthal, R., & Fode, K. L. (1963). Three experiments in experimenter bias. *Psychological Reports, 12,* 491–511.

Ross, L. (1977). The intuitive psychologist and his shortcomings: Distortions in the attributional process. In L. Berkowitz (Ed.), *Advances in experimental social psychology* (Vol. 10, pp. 174–221). New York: Academic Press.

Ross, M., & Fletcher, G. J. O. (1985). Attribution and social perception. In G. J. Lindzey & E. Aronson (Eds.), *The handbook of social psychology* (3rd ed., pp. 73–122). Reading, MA: Addison-Wesley.

Sackheim, H. A., & Gur, R. C. (1977). Self-deception, self-confrontation, and consciousness. In G. Schwartz & D. Shapiro (Eds.), *Consciousness and self-regulation* (pp. 139–197). New York: Plenum.

Sanitioso, R., Kunda, Z., & Fong, G. (1990). Motivated recruitment of autobiographical memories. *Journal of Personality and Social Psychology, 59,* 229–241.

Schwarz, N. (1994). Judgment in social context: Biases, shortcomings, and the logic of conversation. In M. P. Zanna (Ed.), *Advances in experimental social psychology* (Vol. 26, pp. 123–161). New York: Academic Press.

Sherman, S. J., Skov, R. B., Hervitz, E. F., & Stock, C. B. (1981). The effects of explaining hypothetical future events: From possibility to probability to actuality and beyond. *Journal of Experimental Social Psychology, 17,* 142–158.

Snyder, M., & Swann, W. B., Jr. (1978). Hypothesis-testing processes in social interaction. *Journal of Personality and Social Psychology, 36,* 1202–1212.

Snyder, M., & Uranowitz, S. W. (1978). Reconstructing the past: Some cognitive consequences of person perception. *Journal of Personality and Social Psychology, 36,* 941–950.

Svenson, O. (1981). Are we all less risky and more skillful than our fellow drivers? *Acta Psychologica, 47,* 143–148.

Tajfel, H., & Turner, J. C. (1986). The social identity of intergroup behavior. In S. Worchel & W. Austin (Eds.), *Psychology of inter-group relations* (pp. 7–24). Chicago: Nelson-Hall.

Taylor, S. E. (1991). Asymmetrical effects of positive and negative events: The mobilization-minimization hypothesis. *Psychological Bulletin, 110,* 67–85.

Taylor, S. E., & Brown, J. D. (1988). Illusion and well-being: A social psychological perspective on mental health. *Psychological Bulletin, 110,* 67–83.

Taylor, S. E., & Kouvumaki, J. H. (1976). The perception of self and others: Acquaintanceship, affect and actor-observer differences. *Journal of Personality and Social Psychology, 33,* 403–408.

Trope, Y. (1986). Identification and inferential processes in dispositional attribution. *Psychological Review, 93,* 239–257.

Trope, Y., Cohen, O., & Alfieri, T. (1991). Behavior identification as a mediator of dispositional inference. *Journal of Personality and Social Psychology, 61,* 873–883.

Trope, Y., & Liberman, A. (1993). The use of trait conceptions to identify other people's behavior and draw inferences about their personalities. *Personality and Social Psychology Bulletin, 19,* 553–562.

Trope, Y., & Liberman, A. (1996). Social hypothesis testing: Cognitive and motivational mechanisms. In E. T. Higgins & A. W. Kruglanski (Eds.), *Social psychology: Handbook of basic principles.* New York: Guilford.

Tversky, A., & Kahneman, D. (1981). The framing of decisions and the psychology of choice. *Science, 211,* 453–458.

Weinstein, N. D. (1980). Unrealistic optimism about future life events. *Journal of Personality and Social Psychology, 39,* 806–820.

Weinstein, N. D. (1982). Unrealistic optimism about susceptibility to health problems. *Journal of Behavioral Medicine, 5,* 441–460.

Wyer, R. S., & Frey, D. (1983). The effects of feedback about self and others on the recall and judgments of feedback-relevant information. *Journal of Experimental Social Psychology, 19,* 540–559.

6

Identifying the Origin of Mental Experience

Marcia K. Johnson

The relationship among our perceptions, memories, knowledge, beliefs, and expectations on the one hand and reality on the other hand is one of the most intriguing questions in cognitive psychology (e.g., Johnson, 1988; Johnson & Raye, 1981; Johnson & Sherman, 1990). The evidence that this relationship is complex comes from a myriad of events in our everyday lives, from clinical, behavioral, and neurological observations, and is reflected in classic themes in art and literature. We sometimes forget whether we only thought about doing something or actually did it; we forget information was derived from fiction and recount it later as fact; authors unwittingly plagiarize; eyewitnesses disagree markedly on the details of a crime soon thereafter; couples disagree years later on the details of their first date; an interviewer remembers more weaknesses than strengths of a job candidate whose clothes, gender, or skin color are different from the norm for that job; an adult may remember childhood abuse that did not occur (e.g., see Johnson, Hashtroudi, & Lindsay, 1993; Loftus, 1993; Ross, in press; Wilson & Brekke, 1994).

Clinical observations of delusions and hallucinations associated with psychopathology provide striking examples of mental experiences divorced from reality that severely disrupt an individual's ability to function. As a result of certain types of organic brain disease, patients may deny one of their own limbs belongs to them or recount bizarre tales as events they actually experienced (Johnson, 1988, 1991a; Moscovitch, 1989; Stuss, Alexander, Lieberman, & Levine, 1978). Novels and movies sometimes compellingly depict a world in which dreams and reality are indistinguishable, or in which it is impossible to decide among various individuals' accounts of an event (the film *Rashomon*). The cumulative effect of all these examples might be that memory bears little relation to reality and is not to be trusted. However, this conclusion would reflect a naive constructivism that no more represents the nature of memory than does naive realism (Johnson, 1983). Errors of memory give clues, just as do errors of perception, about how memory works, including how it works when it is accurate.

My collaborators and I have argued that various errors and distortions of memory can be usefully understood within a framework for characterizing how memories are established, consolidated or maintained over time, accessed, and evaluated—the source-monitoring framework (e.g., Johnson, 1988; Johnson et al., 1993). This framework is an extension of the reality-monitoring model proposed by Johnson and Raye (1981) and draws on the multiple-entry, modular (MEM) cognitive architecture proposed by Johnson and colleagues (Johnson, 1983, 1991a, 1991b, 1992; Johnson & Chalfonte, 1994; Johnson & Hirst, 1993; Johnson & Multhaup, 1992).

According to this framework, the elements of perceptual experience (e.g., identified objects, their locations, colors, etc.) and reflective experience (e.g., ideas, plans) are encoded and bound together as a consequence of perception and reflection (e.g., Johnson, 1992). "Events" are constructed and remembered according to the background knowledge or schemas active at the time and the task agenda (e.g., Bartlett, 1932; Bransford & Johnson, 1973; Schank & Abelson, 1977). These constructed "accounts"—constructed products (Bransford & Johnson, 1973) or mental models (Johnson-Laird, 1983) of comprehension, interpretation, and problem solving—are subsequently rehearsed and narratized (Nelson, 1993; Spence, 1982). They are activated only if appropriate cues are available (e.g., McGeoch, 1932; Tulving & Thomson, 1973). Based on their phenomenal properties and relation to other memories, knowledge, and beliefs, they are evaluated (or monitored) and may be taken to be veridical memories according to criteria that change based on current conditions (e.g., the task, importance of errors, time, motivation, etc.; Johnson, Hashtroudi, & Lindsay, 1993; Johnson & Raye, 1981).

Within this framework, errors and distortions of memory can arise (a) from factors operating as memory records are first established; (b) during an intervening interval; (c) at the time when memory records are subsequently accessed; and (d) when they are evaluated. The first three of these divisions are sometimes called *encoding, storage* (retention, consolidation), and *retrieval*; the last, *evaluation* (or monitoring), is often not explicitly considered at all. The next section describes the MEM cognitive architecture—a framework for characterizing cognitive processes underlying learning and memory. With this background in mind, the section returns to the issue of how individuals evaluate and discriminate the origin of information while remembering and considers conditions that affect source accuracy.

A MULTIPLE-ENTRY, MODULAR MEMORY SYSTEM

According to a multiple-entry, modular (MEM) memory system, memory is produced by perception and reflection; that is, it is the record of both perceptual and reflective activity (Johnson, 1983; see also Kolers & Roediger, 1984). MEM is an attempt to specify the types of perceptual and reflective component subprocesses needed for the wide range of memory phenomena illustrated in people's thought and behavior. The MEM architecture organizes these component processes into four functional subsystems, as shown in Fig. 6.1. The subsystems normally interact in any complex task but are proposed to be modular in the sense that they can engage in some functions without reference to other subsystems. The perceptual subsystems, P-1 and P-2, process and record information that is largely the consequence of perceptual processes. The reflective subsystems, R-1 and R-2, process and record information that is the consequence of internally generated processes, such as imaging and planning, that may occur independently of external stimuli. P-1 processes act on information that is typically not the focus of phenomenal awareness (e.g., cues that allow one to anticipate the trajectory of a moving object). P-2 processes act on a phenomenal world of objects and events. The reflective subsystems, R-1 and R-2, are generative; they allow one to manipulate information and memories (e.g., through imagining, retrieving, predicting, and comparing), and are driven by goals called *agendas*. The difference between R-1 and R-2 processes could be described as tactical versus strategic, or habitual versus deliberate; R-2 and P-2 typically operate on more complex data structures than do R-1 and P-1, respectively.

The P-1 subsystem is composed of processes of locating, resolving, tracking, and extracting. As examples, *locating* includes processes involved in visual capture of attention as well as auditory locating processes (e.g., Weiskrantz, 1986; Yantis & Johnson, 1990); *resolving* includes processes for defining basic perceptual units (e.g., edges [Marr, 1982], geons [Biederman, 1987], or deriving structural descriptions [Riddoch & Humphreys, 1987; Schacter, 1992]); *tracking* includes processes involved in following a moving stimulus (e.g., with stimulus-guided eye movements; Kowler & Martins, 1982); and *extracting* includes processes involved in extracting invariants, such as texture gradients and flow patterns (Gibson, 1950).

The P-2 subsystem includes the component processes of placing, identifying, examining, and structuring. As examples, *placing* includes processes that represent the relation of objects to each other (Mishkin, Ungerleider, & Macko, 1983), *identifying* includes processes that assign stimuli to meaningful categories (e.g., Biederman, 1987), *examining* in-

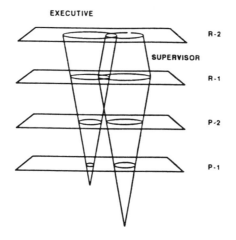

(a)

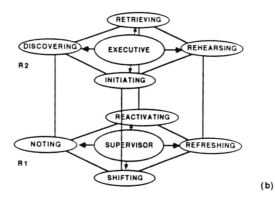

(b)

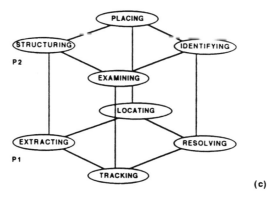

(c)

FIG. 6.1

cludes processes (often driven by learned perceptual schemes) that guide the order of perceptual inspection of a stimulus array (e.g., Hochberg, 1970), and *structuring* includes processes that parse temporally extended stimuli into "syntactic" units (e.g., the syntax of one's language, patterns of familiar movements, or melodic structures from notes; Fodor, Bever, & Garrett, 1974; Krumhansl, 1990). As is apparent from these examples, perceptual component processes in MEM cumulate the products of prior experience. Thus, perception, especially P-2 processing, includes meaningful responses to meaningful stimuli.

Reflection allows one to go beyond the immediate consequences (both direct and associative) of stimulus-evoked activation. Whereas perception is exogenously generated cognition, reflection is endogenously generated cognition. Reflective processes are what give people the sense that they are taking an active role in their thought and behavior. This idea of active control is often assigned to a central executive in cognitive theories (e.g., Baddeley, 1992). In MEM, there is no central executive. Rather, reflection is guided by agendas, any one of which serves as a virtual executive while it is active (cf. Dennett, 1991). For convenience of reference, in Fig. 6.1, the collection of possible R-1 agendas is denoted *supervisor* and the collection of possible R-2 agendas is denoted *executive*. It is important for agendas to be represented separately in the two reflective subsystems because their interaction provides a mechanism for (a) control and monitoring of complex thought and action, (b) self-observation and self-control, and (c) certain forms of consciousness (see Johnson & Reeder, in press, for a more extended discussion of MEM and consciousness). Agendas (both well learned and ad hoc) recruit various reflective and perceptual processes in the service of specific goals and motives.

The component processes of R-1 are *refreshing, reactivating, shifting,* and *noting. Refreshing* prolongs activation of already active perceptual and reflective representations. For example, refreshing of targets likely occurs when the signal indicates which subset of items in a complex display are to be reported (Sperling, 1960). *Reactivating* brings inactive

---

FIG. 6.1. (a) A multiple-entry, modular (MEM) memory system, consisting of two reflective subsystems, R-1 and R-2, and two perceptual subsystems, P-1 and P-2. Reflective and perceptual subsystems can interact through control and monitoring processes (supervisor and executive processes of R-1 and R-2, respectively), which have relatively greater access to and control over reflective than perceptual subsystems. (b) Component subprocesses of R-1 and R-2. (c) Component subprocesses of P-1 and P-2. From Johnson, M. K., in *Mental Imagery* (p. 4) by R. G. Kunzendorf, 1991b, New York: Plenum. Copyright 1991 by Plenum. Adapted by permission.

representations back into an active state. For example, reactivating occurs when a specific task agenda (e.g., the goal to organize and learn a list) is combined with a current cue to activate relevant prior information (e.g., seeing *dog* in a list reminds one that *cat* was previously on the list). *Shifting* involves changing a current activation pattern in combination with a task agenda or cues (e.g., shifting from thinking of a dog's tail to thinking of a dog's ears in an imagery task; Kosslyn, 1980). *Noting* involves identifying relations within current activation patterns (e.g., noting that cats and dogs are both animals, or noting that a dog's ears are pointed).

The component processes of R-2 are *rehearsing, retrieving, initiating,* and *discovering.* These are analogous to R-1 processes, but are more extended and sometimes require iterations that are initiated or controlled by endogenously generated cues. For example, *rehearsing* requires recycling back to representations to keep them active. Hence, rehearsing requires that some representation be kept active of the number of items to be rehearsed, or the interval since a particular item was last rehearsed (e.g., Baddeley, 1986). *Retrieving* requires the self-generation of cues when the task agenda and immediately available cues are not sufficient to activate the desired representation (e.g., Reiser, 1986). For example, if the task agenda to recall List A and the experimenter-provided cue *vegetable* are not enough to produce reactivation of a target item, one might cue oneself with questions: Were there any green vegetables on the list? Any unusual vegetables? Similarly, *initiating* involves shifts in how active information is considered. These shifts are generated by cues that were endogenously generated to solve a task problem. For example, in the tumor-radiation problem (Duncker, 1945; Gick & Holyoak, 1980), the subject might initiate a shift from thinking about how to destroy the tumor to how not to damage the patient's flesh by listing all the potential problems in the situation. *Discovering* involves finding relations that are not immediately present in a given activation pattern, but that require some mediating idea that is self-generated, perhaps by some algorithm or strategy (Gentner, 1988). For example, in looking for a way to relate two stories, one might try to characterize the theme of each at the most general level and then look for matching ideas.

The activity of any of these component processes generates changes in memory (i.e., records or representations). Subsequent activities directed at these representations (reactivating, noting, etc.) also generate changes in memory. Changes in memory can be expressed in behavior (e.g., seeing something more easily under degraded conditions that was seen before; Jacoby & Dallas, 1981) or phenomenal experiences, such as remembering an autobiographical event (e.g., Johnson, Foley, Suengas,

& Raye, 1988) or knowing a fact (Collins & Quillian, 1969). For example, memory representations in P-1 and P-2, including representation of concepts representing the identity of objects, are likely responsible for many cases of priming (e.g., DeSchepper & Treisman, 1996; Dunn & Kirsner, 1988; Jacoby & Dallas, 1981; Tulving & Schacter, 1990) and perceptual learning (Cohen & Squire, 1980; Nissen & Bullemer, 1987). Face recognition may be based largely on memory representations in P-2, but is sometimes augmented with memory of cognitive operations provided by R-1 or R-2 (e.g., noting a face looks like Uncle Bob). Recall of categorized lists may be largely based on representations generated by organizational activity of R-1, and recall of complex stories is more likely based on representations generated by R-2 activity. Of course, processes from all subsystems may be operating in any particular situation.

The term *representation* does not imply that a memory consists of information represented by a single node or by a single, unified trace. It is assumed in MEM that memories are distributed among the processing circuits that were in effect when they were established. Furthermore, some features may be recorded, but not bound together, or some bound features may fail to be activated under some task conditions that could be activated under others. Likewise, features may be activated in new combinations that would give rise to source errors. Evidence for these assumptions is considered in later sections of this chapter.

Various breakdowns in cognition and memory occur when any one or any combination of these component processes are disrupted through distraction, stress, drugs, psychopathology, or brain damage (e.g., Johnson, 1983; Johnson & Hirst, 1993). For example, perceptual phenomena such as blindsight or agnosias could occur from selective disruptions in perceptual processes, or in the interactions between perceptual and reflective processes (Johnson & Reeder, in press). Deficits in complex learning and problem solving might occur if R-2 processes were disrupted (Johnson & Hirst, 1993). Disruptions in consciousness would arise from disruptions in transactions between subsystems (Johnson & Reeder, in press). This chapter is particularly concerned with how breakdowns might occur in an individual's ability to identify the origin of memories.

The component processes of MEM are described in terms of a mid-level vocabulary. The proposed processes are polymorphic, each representing a class of similar operations performed on different data types (Johnson & Hirst, 1993; Johnson & Reeder, in press). Thus, for example, the same term is applied to similar operations that occur in different sensory modalities. It is proposed here that the component processes of MEM represent different transactions among brain regions or circuits of activity (Johnson, 1992; Johnson & Chalfonte, 1994). Because these component processes are interactions among regions, they can be disrupted in more than one way. Because different circuits are dedicated to different versions of a process (e.g., refreshing auditory/verbal information would involve a different circuit than refreshing visual/pictorial information), considerable specificity of disruption from highly localized brain lesions would be expected. Some of the specific brain regions that are implicated in MEM's processing circuits are considered after reviewing behavioral evidence regarding source-monitoring processes.

SOURCE MONITORING

Our investigations of source monitoring and reality monitoring are directed at clarifying underlying mechanisms that allow people, despite the potential for confusion illustrated in the introductory paragraph, to manage to operate in the real world rather well, both as individuals and in a sociocultural context (Johnson, in press; Johnson & Reeder, in press; Johnson et al., 1993). When we began this research in the 1970s (Johnson, 1977; Johnson, Taylor, & Raye, 1977), we confronted two critical problems that affected the approach. The first was that perception and reflection (inference, imagination, etc.) are normally so intertwined it is hard to say where one ends and the other begins (e.g., Bartlett, 1932; Bransford & Johnson, 1973). How, then, could the memory representations generated by perception and reflection be compared and the mechanisms that are important for discriminating between them investigated? The second problem was that memory is both constructive (at encoding) and reconstructive (at recall). How could one know, in any particular situation, whether source misattributions reflected confusions of the records of prior constructions with records of prior perceptions, or whether source misattributions reflected confusions of new constructions with records of prior perceptions? Of course, based on an understanding of memory as both constructive and reconstructive, both types of source confusions were expected to occur under appropriate circumstances, but it was important to be able to say which type the subjects were producing. This led to the development of experimental paradigms that addressed both these problems by starting with clear, rather than ambiguous, events occurring at specified points in time.

Although perception and reflection are intertwined, the relative proportions of each, across situations, vary along a continuum. Thus, we started with the two ends of the continuum of information that people acquire: information that is derived primarily from external events (e.g., pictures or words we presented) and information that is the result of internally generated cognitive operations (e.g., images or words the subjects generated). If we could clarify the conditions under which (and thus the mechanisms by which) these two are distinguished in memory, we would be able to extend the analysis to understanding the more difficult to investigate, intermediate cases, in which the representation of a single event consists of a complex mixture of perception and imagination. Similarly, if we controlled when the perceived and imagined events took place, rather than leaving the imagination up to the spontaneous mental activity of the subject, as was done in most earlier studies (e.g., Deese, 1959; Johnson, Bransford, & Solomon, 1973), we would know that subjects were confusing past imaginations with past perceptions.

The processes of distinguishing externally and internally generated information is referred to as *reality monitoring*. However, reality monitoring is just one subset of the larger problem of identifying the origin and veridicality of perceptions, memories, knowledge, and beliefs, which is called *source monitoring* (Johnson, 1988). In addition to discriminating between information from primarily internal versus external sources, source monitoring includes distinguishing among different types of internally generated information (e.g., what one thought from what one said), distinguishing among different external sources (e.g., what one heard on the news from what one heard a colleague speculate at the office), as well as identifying other contextual attributes of an event (e.g., where and when it occurred, its color, etc.).[1] Because the mechanisms of reality monitoring should be clearer if compared to other types of source monitoring, such comparisons have been an ongoing part of the strategy for exploring the mechanisms by which memories become distorted (e.g., Foley, Johnson, & Raye, 1983; Raye & Johnson, 1980; see also Johnson, 1988) and, by extension, the mechanisms by which knowledge and beliefs become distorted (Johnson, 1988).

Our approach to understanding source monitoring is based on two propositions. First, mental experiences from different sources differ on average in their phenomenal qualities. Second, distinguishing between or among sources is potentially a two-factor attributional process: The first typically is a quick decision based on phenomenal qualities of a

---

[1]The term *source* is used as a general way of referring to those aspects of experience that have variously been called origin, circumstances, or context in addition to source (e.g., Spencer & Raz, 1995). Source information, like context, is generally distinguished from "content" or "item" information. Thus, if you see a series of words, the semantic meaning of each is presumed to be the content, and aspects—such as color, typeface, location, voice, general environmental details, mood, state of mind, and so forth—are presumed to constitute the context or source information. To some extent, the distinction between content and context (source) is artificial because it should depend on the goals of the subject. However, it has heuristic value, hence it is used here.

mental experience, and the second usually is a slower process that was initially called *extended reasoning*. Extended reasoning included retrieval processes, judgments based on other supporting or disconfirming knowledge or memories, assumptions about how memory works, and so forth. These two types of processes are now thought of as governed by R-1 and R-2 agendas, respectively, and thus they are referred to as *heuristic* (or R-1) and *strategic* (or R-2), following Chaiken's (Chaiken, Lieberman, & Eagly, 1989) terminology for processes involved in evaluating persuasive messages (Johnson et al., 1993).

Qualitative Characteristics of Memories and Judgment Processes

Among the most important attributes of memories that make them "episodic" or identify their origin are perceptual information (e.g., sound, color), contextual information (spatial and temporal), information about cognitive operations (imagining, retrieving, inferring), semantic information, and affective information. The heuristic decision processes used to distinguish source capitalize on average differences in these attributes among memories from various sources. For example, compared with internally generated memories, externally generated memories typically have more sensory/perceptual and spatial/temporal information, and their semantic information tends to be more detailed and less abstract. Also, memory records information not only about the consequence of mental activity, but about the mental activities as well; this record of cognitive operations tends to be more available for imaginal than for perceptual processes (i.e., perception is typically somewhat more automatic than imaginal processes). If two classes of memories (e.g., internally and externally derived) tend to differ in these ways, even if their distributions overlap on some or all qualities, they generally could be discriminated, although errors would sometimes occur. Errors should be related to predictable deviations from the average distributions (e.g., people who are good imagers should have more difficulty than poor imagers distinguishing whether they perceived or imagined a picture of an object, and they do; Johnson, Raye, Wang, & Taylor, 1979).

Many source-monitoring decisions are made rapidly or heuristically on the basis of qualitative characteristics of activated memories. For example, one might attribute a memory to perception based on the amount or vividness of perceptual detail in the memory. Or one might attribute a memory of a statement to the newspaper because the memory includes the information that it was on the front page. In these cases, there may be little awareness of the source-judgment process, but a judgment process has, nevertheless, occurred. At other times, a more systematic or deliberative decision may be made requiring the retrieval of additional information or an inferential, strategic reasoning process. For example, trying to remember who proposed an idea in a meeting might include retrieving other information about what each person is currently working on, and therefore who was the more likely candidate. Of course, any additional information that is retrieved is potentially subjected to a heuristic check, and can become the cue for further strategic retrieval.

Both heuristic and strategic processes require setting criteria for making a judgment and procedures for comparing activated information to the criteria. For example, if the amount of contextual detail exceeds X, the heuristic evaluation is that the event was probably perceived. Similarly, some threshold, Y, for the degree of consistency between the target memory and additionally retrieved knowledge or information must be exceeded for a strategic evaluation that an event was perceived. Which judgment processes are used in any given situation should be affected by the relative distributions of memory characteristics and higher level agendas that might change the need (threshold) to be accurate (e.g., the cost of a mistake), or might change the relative weights given to different memory characteristics (e.g., affective information and perceptual information). For example, criteria are likely to be more lax in a casual conversation with a friend (e.g., recalling the source of gossip) than in a professional meeting (e.g., recalling the source of scientific data).

Errors and Deficits in Source Monitoring

Given this basic characterization of source monitoring, it is clear that errors may be introduced in a number of specific ways.

Factors Operating When Target Memories Are Encoded

Feature Binding. Accuracy of source monitoring varies as a function of the quality of the underlying information in memory. That is, a complex event memory depends on the binding of various features of experience together into a cohesive representation, such that when one aspect is activated other aspects are as well (Johnson, 1992). Incidental binding of some features occurs as a consequence of perceptual processing (e.g., item and location; Hasher & Zacks, 1979), but such incidental binding is less likely to support recall than recognition (Chalfonte & Johnson, 1995). The binding of other features (e.g., color and item) appears to profit from intentional processing even for recognition (Chalfonte & Johnson, 1996). Color and location are the types of attributes necessary for identifying the origin of item information.

What are the processes that produce binding among the features of memories? According to MEM, some binding among features may occur as a consequence of coactivation during perceptual processing alone, but binding is affected by reflective processes as well (Johnson, 1992; Johnson & Chalfonte, 1994). For example, feature binding between a person, Bill, and the color of his shirt is more likely to occur if the idea or image of Bill and his shirt color are *refreshed* or *reactivated* together than if they are not. Similarly, binding between Bill's voice and the semantic content of what he says is more likely to occur if those two features (voice and content) are *refreshed* or *reactivated* together. Binding is also augmented by more organizational reflective processes, such as *noting* that Bill's shirt and pants do not match. Consistent with this, when subjects are distracted during an initial experience—by being required to do a secondary task that interferes with their ability to engage in reflective operations for processing the target material—their later source accuracy is reduced (Craik, 1983; Craik & Byrd, 1982; Jacoby, Woloshyn, & Kelley, 1989).

Among the factors that can affect the nature and quality of feature binding, perhaps one of the most intriguing is emotion. Under some circumstances, emotion can disrupt the encoding of perceptual information and/or the binding of perceptual information to content (Hashtroudi, Johnson, Vnek, & Ferguson, 1994; Suengas & Johnson, 1988). For example, in a recent series of studies (Johnson, Nolde, & De Leonardis, 1996, subjects listened to a tape of two people speaking. The speakers made various statements that varied in emotion (as rated by other subjects): Congress should pass a law prohibiting prayer in the classroom; I support the death penalty; I have an intense fear of flying; There is too much violence on TV; Interracial relationships do not bother me; I can speak two languages fluently; The Sistine Chapel is in Rome. In the actual experiment, the subjects' focus was varied while they were listening to the speakers. In one condition, subjects were told the investigators were interested in people's ability to perceive other people's emotions; in another condition, subjects were told the investigators were interested in the degree to which they agreed with what was being said. After a 10-minute retention interval, subjects took a surprise memory test. The results were quite clear. Relative to focusing on how the speaker felt, when subjects focused on how they felt, they had higher old–new recognition, but lower source-accuracy scores. Also, in the self-focus condition, there tended to be a negative correlation between rated emotion of the statements and source accuracy. Subjects were less accurate on the more emotion-evoking statements. These findings suggest that attention (i.e., *refreshing, retrieving, noting,* etc.) to one's own emotional reactions may occur at the expense of attention (i.e., *refreshing, retrieving, noting,* etc.) to other aspects of events that are critical for later identifying the origin of remembered information.

The Discriminability of Sources.   Even if various memory attributes are bound into complex event memories, the likelihood of later misattributing memories from one source to another is related to the similarity of the memories from the two sources. That is, the nature of the encoding operations (perceptual and reflective cognitive operations engaged, semantic schemas recruited, etc.) determines the potential for later discriminability of memories from various sources. For example, Lindsay, Johnson, and Kwon (1991) showed that the more semantically similar the topics addressed by two speakers were, the more likely subjects were to later confuse what one speaker said with what another said.

Perceptual similarity is critical as well. Ferguson, Hashtroudi, and Johnson (1992) showed that the more similar two speakers were, the more likely subjects were to confuse what each had said. Johnson et al. (1979) varied the number of times subjects saw various pictures and the number of times they imagined each of the pictures. Subsequently, subjects were asked to indicate how many times they had seen a picture. Frequency judgments of good imagers were more influenced by the number of times they had imagined a picture than were frequency judgments of poor imagers. This outcome is consistent with the idea that the degree of perceptual information in memories for perceived and imagined objects was more similar for the good imagers than for the poor imagers (see also Dobson & Markham, 1993; Markham & Hynes, 1993).

Likewise, the type of cognitive operations engaged can create records that are more or less discriminable for events of various classes. For example, Durso and Johnson's (1980) subjects saw some concepts represented as pictures and some as words. During presentation of the concepts, some subjects rated the time it would take for an artist to draw the pictures or to draw pictures the subjects imagined for the word items. Other subjects gave a function for each item (e.g., knife–cut). Durso and Johnson suggested that the subjects in the function task would be likely to spontaneously generate images of the items referred to by words as they answered the function questions. These spontaneously generated images would have less salient cognitive operations than the intentionally constructed images of subjects in the artist time judgment task. Because the difference between the cognitive operations information in the records of perceived and imagined events should be less clear for the function than the artist time group, the function group should later be more likely to claim they had seen pictures of items presented as words. The results were consistent with this prediction. Subjects were three times as likely to falsely claim they had seen pictures of word items in the function than in the artist time judgment condition (see also Rabinowitz, 1989; Finke, Johnson, & Shyi, 1988). Similarly, Dodson and Johnson (1996; Experiment 2) showed that the more similar the cognitive operations performed on two classes of items were, the more likely they were to be later confused (see also Johnson, De Leonardis, Hashtroudi, & Ferguson, 1995; Lindsay & Johnson, 1991).

Factors Operating Before or After Target Events

Not only do the component cognitive processes engaged initially affect source monitoring, but what happens before and after an event can have a marked effect on the accuracy of one's memory for that event. For example, reactivating content information can increase the chances that it is remembered later (Hogan & Kintsch, 1971; Landauer & Bjork, 1978). There is not direct evidence regarding reactivation and memory for source, and such studies are very much needed. However, there is some evidence from studies of subjects' ratings of the phenomenal characteristics of their memories. Suengas and Johnson (1988) had subjects participate in or imagine participating in various simulated autobiographical events, such as wrapping a package, meeting someone, or having coffee and cookies. Subjects actually engaged in some activities or were asked to imagine engaging in others, guided by a script. Later, subjects filled out a memory characteristics questionnaire (MCQ) designed to assess various qualitative characteristics of their memories (e.g., How well do you remember the spatial arrangement of objects? How well do you remember how you felt at the time?). Generally, the ratings on characteristics such as visual clarity and contextual detail are higher for perceived than for imagined events (see also Hashtroudi, Johnson, & Chrosniak, 1990). Suengas and Johnson also investigated the impact on MCQ ratings of having subjects think about events after they happened. They found that, if people do not think about events, visual details and other characteristics tend to be less accessible over time. If people do think about events, visual and other details tend to be maintained. They also found that the effect of thinking about imagined events was about the same as thinking about perceived events. This finding suggests that if people selectively reactivate imaginations, memories for those imaginations could begin to rival in vividness perceived events from the same time frame. Thus, depending on what is reactivated, thinking about events could preserve: (a) veridical memories of actual events, (b) the vividness of memories of imagined events, or (c) the vividness of the imagined embellishments of either actual or imagined events. That is, depending on what representations cognitive operations such as *reac-*

tivating and *retrieving* are applied to, they can act to consolidate and maintain veridical or nonveridical memories, knowledge, and beliefs.

In addition to considering the kinds of rumination and rehearsal (thinking and talking) individuals do about an event after the fact, along with any associated imagining, it is also important to consider the other types of events that might intervene between the time of the initial event and its attempted recall. Has the individual heard or read other accounts? Seen pictures? Seen related movies or read related novels? All of these intervening events (and, in fact, prior events as well) are potential sources of memories that can become candidates for confusion with the original event. Particularly intriguing is the status of information generated in dreams. Although most dreams seem extremely short-lived, evidence suggests that the information persists longer than one might expect (Johnson, Kahan, & Raye, 1984), and thus one's own dreams provide elements that may subsequently be cued and confused with actual events.

Elements or features from prior or subsequent events can recombine with elements of a target event to create false memories. For example, Henkel and Franklin (in press) had subjects see some pictures and imagine others. Subjects were more likely to later claim they had seen an imagined item (e.g., a lollipop) if they had seen a presented picture that shared some features with the imagined item (e.g., a magnifying glass). Thus, attributes of perceptually experienced events can increase the chances of believing that one has perceived other events that one has only imagined. A subsequent study (Henkel & Franklin, 1995) showed an intriguing cross-modal effect. Subjects who heard a dog barking and, at another point, imagined seeing a dog were more likely later to believe they had actually seen a dog than were subjects who had twice imagined seeing a dog. More generally, source confusions as a consequence of recombinations of perceived elements of stimuli can occur (Reinitz, Lammers, & Cochran, 1992). That is, subjects may recognize various elements, but not accurately remember which events were the source of the elements (i.e., to which other elements these were bound), and thus falsely attribute the recombined elements to a single event.

Factors Operating During the Access and Monitoring of Memories

Finally, distortions in memory can be introduced by factors occurring at the time an individual uses or draws on memory records. First, consider that accurate source attribution depends on the successful revival of information that could specify source. What would disrupt revival of such information? Any mismatch between encoding and testing conditions reduces the chances for successful revival of potentially useful source-specifying information (e.g., Tulving & Thomson, 1973). If cue conditions are not sufficient to revive perceptual, contextual, affective, semantic, or cognitive operations information that can help specify the origin of a memory or belief, then clearly source monitoring will suffer. A mismatch could happen because external cues are not appropriate (e.g., a change in environment; Godden & Baddeley, 1975), or because internal cues, such as mood, are not appropriate (Eich & Metcalfe, 1989).

Even if appropriate cues are present, certain conditions may interfere with source monitoring. Such interference can come from distraction, stress, depression, and drug-induced effects. Consider the case where an individual is asked to monitor the origin of information while performing another, unrelated task (Jacoby et al., 1989; Zaragoza & Lane, 1994). A secondary task may induce source confusions in a number of ways: It may interfere with (a) the activation of attribute information, (b) *noting* the relevance of attribute information to a source-monitoring agenda, or (c) the *retrieval* of additional confirming or disconfirming evidence. If the revived information is not specific enough, if the individual's agenda does not call for explicit source monitoring, or if the secondary task is sufficiently demanding, people may be induced to make source judgments on the basis of familiarity (e.g., Jacoby et al., 1989). As is discussed next, all source attributions (even those based on familiarity; see Dodson & Johnson, 1996) occur in the context of agenda-controlled criteria.

Because source judgments are attributions about the origins of memories, knowledge, and beliefs, they are always made in the context of evaluative criteria. Is this evidence sufficient to conclude that this mental experience arose because of a specific past experience (attributing a memory to a past event)? Is this evidence sufficient to conclude that this knowledge has a basis in fact (e.g., read in a reputable source, based on direct experience, etc.)? Is this evidence sufficient to conclude that this belief is reasonable given what I know or remember? Thus, there is a hierarchy of reality monitoring, whereby truth at the level of belief depends on veridicality at the level of knowledge, which depends on veridicality at the level of episodic events. That is, reasonable beliefs depend on accurate knowledge, which depends on veridical event memories. The criteria applied at any of these levels are not fixed, but change with circumstances. The level of evidence one feels one needs in order to say they remember, know, or believe depends on many factors, including the active agenda, social context, cost of mistakes, and amount of distraction.

Several experiments demonstrate the effects of shifts in criteria in source monitoring, depending on test conditions. For example, Dodson and Johnson (1993) had subjects look at a series of pictures of unrelated complex scenes. Subjects then read short passages describing scenes, some of which had been previously shown as pictures, but most of which had not. Later, subjects were given verbal cues that referred to pictured and/or read scenes and new scenes. Subjects were asked to indicate which scenes had been shown as pictures and which had not, and then to indicate which had been described in a passage and which had not. Replicating a result previously reported by Intraub and Hoffman (1992), Dodson and Johnson found a high rate of source errors: Subjects frequently claimed to have seen pictures for scenes that had only been described. Like Intraub and Hoffman, Dodson and Johnson attributed these false recognitions to reality-monitoring failures. Presumably, subjects imagined scenes while they read about them and later mistook their imagined scenes for pictured scenes.

However, in a second condition, Dodson and Johnson asked subjects to indicate for each test item whether they had seen it as a picture, read it as a description, both seen and read it, or neither. With this relatively subtle change in test instructions, the false recognitions were greatly reduced. The second type of test apparently tightened the subjects' criteria for attributing a memory to a perceived picture. When subjects explicitly considered whether a memory was derived from a picture or narrative, they evidently looked more carefully at the level of perceptual detail in the memory, or looked more carefully for evidence of the types of cognitive operations that generated the memory (e.g., imagining, reading). Any increase in the amount of perceptual detail required as evidence that a remembered item was actually perceived would decrease the number of false recognitions of imagined scenes. Similar reductions of source confusion with a change in test conditions have been reported in eyewitness testimony (Lindsay & Johnson, 1989; Zaragoza & Lane, 1994) and false fame (Multhaup, 1995) paradigms (see also Hasher & Griffin, 1978; Raye, Johnson, & Taylor, 1980).

Some errors in reality monitoring are introduced at the time of remembering not because of disrupted retrieval or inappropriate criteria, but because the individual has a poor knowledge base. For example, certain memories might be quite vivid, say the memory of a spaceship that occurred in a dream. Before a child has acquired a working knowledge about dreams, it might be extremely difficult not to attribute such a recollection to memory for a real event.

Individuals do not have to forget the actual source to misattribute information to another source. For example, in an eyewitness study, subjects do not have to forget that they read certain information to mistakenly believe that they also saw it as part of the original event (Dodson & Johnson, 1993; Lindsay & Johnson, 1989; Zaragoza & Lane,

1994). They can believe that they both saw it and read about it later (see also Fiedler et al., 1995). In fact, there may be certain circumstances in which one's confidence that they saw something is actually increased by their recollection that they "also" heard it described by someone else.

As discussed earlier, source confusions often arise because information is misattributed to perception that was filled in by inferences, schemas, or knowledge-driven constructive processes engaged as events are processed, comprehended, and responded to in everyday activities and similarly engaged reconstructively as events are subsequently remembered. Typically these generations are assumed or believed to be true at the time they occur (regardless of whether they are in fact). Resulting reality-monitoring errors may often escape people's awareness because construction and reconstruction is a ubiquitous aspect of perceiving, comprehending, and remembering. However, it is important to emphasize that people may later attribute to reality or be influenced by information that they initially knew was imagined, fictional, or dubious (Durso & Johnson, 1980; Finke et al., 1988). For example, Fiedler et al. (1995) found that subjects might answer a question about a previously seen video correctly and then later falsely recognize information that had been presupposed by the same misleading question they had answered correctly. Subjects can know they are reading fiction and later have their attitudes influenced by what they read (Gerrig & Prentice, 1991). They can also know that an idea came from their own dream initially, but later claim they heard it from someone else (Johnson et al., 1984), or be told information is false and yet later be influenced by it (Gilbert, Tafarodi, & Malone, 1993). That is, what people remember, know, or believe may incorporate information from waking imagination, dreams, conversations with known liars, novels, TV programs, movies, and so forth— from sources that people understood at the time did not represent a true state of affairs.

Source accuracy is also affected by one's motivation to be accurate, including one's assessment of the effort involved and the costs of mistakes. For example, memories and beliefs that enhance self-esteem are often examined less carefully than those that do not. In short, reality monitoring can be thought of as a case in which one is persuading oneself, hence the factors that operate in any persuasion situation should operate in reality monitoring (cf. Eagly & Chaiken, 1993).

Finally, at all stages, source memory is affected by the social context. At encoding, social dynamics may determine how events are interpreted to begin with. Other people affect which cognitive agendas are operating, which in turn determine which aspects of experience are refreshed, noted, and bound into cohesive or complex event representations. During any retention interval, social interaction is one of the most important contexts for rehearsal and rumination about past events (e.g., Nelson, 1993), and one of the most likely sources of information that potentially might be confused with information derived from the original event. To a great extent, the interest and social support of others determines which memories, knowledge, and beliefs are worth preserving and which are likely to be embellished. Social factors operate during remembering. For example, remembered social interactions can be taken as evidence for the veridicality of one's own memories (e.g., Johnson et al., 1988). Remembering often takes place interactively in discussions where people come to agree on what happened (Edwards & Middleton, 1986a, 1986b; Edwards, Potter, & Middleton, 1992). Perhaps most important, the social context helps establish the evidence criteria used (Is this a casual conversation or a discussion with important consequences?), and provides support for or challenges to what one has remembered, asserted as fact, or offered as reasonable belief. Social processes and institutional, cultural mechanisms (investigative news reporting, courts, educational practices) can either support or work against accurate reality monitoring (Johnson, in press).

Summary of the Source-Monitoring Framework

Three broad classes of source monitoring have been distinguished (Johnson, 1988; Johnson & Sherman, 1990): Reality-testing processes evaluate the origin of current perceptions; reality-monitoring processes evaluate the origin of memories, knowledge, and beliefs; and reality-checking processes evaluate the reasonableness or probability of anticipated or imagined futures. All are carried out by R-1, heuristic judgment processes applied to the evidence at hand (e.g., vividness of the mental experience, the ease with which a future can be imagined) and R-2, systematic processes that search out other relevant evidence and evaluate it (e.g., noting a tail on an object to confirm it is a dog; retrieving one's qualifications for a hoped-for job). Everyone experiences errors in reality testing, monitoring, and checking, but severe, chronic breakdowns produce hallucinations and delusions that can profoundly disrupt an individual's ability to function.

Based on the source-monitoring framework, the following are some of the factors that can lead to false memories, and false beliefs in general, and that can produce hallucinations, confabulations, and delusions, especially if several factors operate in combination (Johnson, 1988, 1991a, 1991b): (a) Interpretive, inferential, and constructive processes in understanding add information based on prior knowledge. Furthermore, the schemas used may be partially or wholly constructed from self-generated and not necessarily veridical information. (b) Complex perceptions, event memories, knowledge, or beliefs require the binding together of various features of experience; inappropriate agendas, stress, distraction, drugs, and brain damage can disrupt these binding processes. (c) Because perceptual information is an especially important cue in reality monitoring, the perceptual characteristics of phenomenal experience (including imagined events or real anomalous perceptual experiences, such as seeing floaters) tend to compel belief regardless of their origin. (d) Rehearsal (rumination, talking about) inflates estimates of the frequency of events, increases vividness and elaboration of imagined information, and embeds imagined events and ideas in a network of other events, beliefs, or emotions. This vividness and embeddedness may be taken as evidence that the memory or belief is veridical. (e) Anything that decreases reflective control (e.g., dreams, hypnosis) should make events more likely to be taken for real or beliefs more compelling or persuasive. This occurs either because current perceptual experience (or ideas) or activated records of perceptual information (or ideas) dominate phenomenal experience when reflective activity is "turned off," or because the experience (or memory) of reflective control is a primary cue that information is originating from within (the "unbidden" seems to come from without). (f) Inappropriate criteria, such as applying a low standard of evidence for an idea or memory one finds comforting or that fits with an active agenda or a favored hypothesis, induces reality-monitoring failures. (g) Individual differences account for some of the variability in source monitoring. For example, individuals differ in habitual attitudes, such as their modes of dealing with ambiguity or how willing they are to trust first impressions. Johnson (1991b) further suggested there may be individuals who rely primarily on R-1 processes (experiential types) and others who rely primarily on R-2 processes (instrumental types); they might show different patterns of reality-monitoring failures. For example, experiential individuals may be more persuaded by perceptual detail (use R-1 heuristics), whereas instrumental individuals may be more persuaded by whether something seems plausible (use R-2 strategies). Each type of decision rule, if unchecked by the other, can lead to error. (h) Reality monitoring is a skill. Adopting a critical attitude toward one's memories and beliefs may not be spontaneous, but may require some education and practice (e.g., see also Gilbert, 1991). (i) Accurate reality monitoring depends, to some extent, on the availability of alternative interpretations for mental experiences, especially feelings. An individual who thinks that some physical symptoms could arise from a hormone imbalance will develop a different set of hypotheses to test than an individual who only considers an invasion of his or her body by aliens. Social and cultural contexts are especially important, and can either support false beliefs or help correct them. In short, false memories and beliefs that are severe enough to be called confabulations and delusions can result from intense and unusual perceptual experiences, inappropriate weighting of various qualities of mental experience, selective interpretation or rehearsal, selective confirming of hypotheses, loss in control over reflection, lax criteria induced by low motivation, stress, distraction or drugs, poor coping skills or lack of alternative hypotheses for dealing with potentially dysfunctional cognitions and emotions, social isolation, or dysfunctional social support for delusional ideas.

Using Source Monitoring to Frame and Explore Other Issues

There are a number of cognitive, social, clinical, developmental, and neuropsychological research areas where identifying the origin of mental experiences is a critical component. Thus, the source-monitoring framework might productively be brought to bear and might be further developed in return. Among these are: hindsight bias, impact of fiction on beliefs, development and maintenance of stereotypes, attribution of ideas (e.g., cryptomnesia, gender/race bias), spread of rumor, development of appearance–reality distinction and understanding of mental states such as dreams and imagination, hallucinations, and multiple-personality disorder. Consider two research areas that illustrate a productive intersection between interests and concepts arising from the study of source monitoring and the study of other issues: suggestibility effects (in eyewitness memory, interviewing child witnesses and therapy-assisted adult recovery of repressed memories) and cognitive deficits associated with aging.

Suggestibility. There are several areas in which false memories and beliefs resulting from reality-monitoring failures have been of particular interest recently. The source-monitoring framework has been used to investigate and characterize suggestibility effects in eyewitness testimony (Lindsay, 1993; Zaragoza & Lane, 1994). For example, Zaragoza and Lane compared the effects of introducing misleading information in the context of asking subjects questions (e.g., "When the man looked at his wristwatch before opening the door, did he appear anxious?") or in the context of a descriptive narrative ("When the man looked at his wristwatch before opening the door, he appeared very anxious"). They found that subjects were more likely to claim to have seen the wristwatch (which was not, in fact, in the original event) in the question than in the narrative condition. Zaragoza and Lane concluded that the way the misinformation was introduced influenced the qualitative characteristics of the memories for the suggested items, not memory for the occurrence of the information per se. They suggested that the questions induced the subjects to actively retrieve and reconstruct the original event, and then imagine the suggested information as part of their construction of the original event.

In part prompted by pressing questions about the veridicality of child testimony in sexual abuse cases, researchers have attempted to assess the accuracy of children's memory for complex events, including their susceptibility to suggestion (Ceci & Bruck, 1993; Goodman, Hirschman, Hepps, & Rudy, 1991). In a particularly striking example of fabricated memories resulting from suggestion, Ceci, Crotteau Huffman, Smith, and Loftus (1994) asked children to think about some events that had happened to them and some events that had never happened (e.g., "Did you ever get your hand caught in a mousetrap and have to go to the hospital to get if off?"). Children were asked about these real and fictional events once a week for several weeks. At the last session, children were asked to tell which events really happened and to describe them. A number of children claimed they remembered the false events (although they had denied them initially), and gave considerable detail about them. Furthermore, the detail appeared to develop with rehearsals of the events (see also Suengas & Johnson, 1988).

Subsequently, Ceci, Loftus, Leichtman, and Bruck (1994) conducted a similar study, but told children the fictional events actually happened and asked them to create a visual picture of the events in their head. Children were asked to visualize the events and to describe them approximately once a week for 12 weeks. At the last session, a new interviewer told the children that the other interviewer had made some mistakes, and that some of the events had never really happened. Children made more "false assents" on the last session than they had initially. Most children were more likely to say that fictional neutral events and fictional positive events had happened than that fictional negative events had happened. Ceci and colleagues also showed videotapes of children from this and the previous experiment to clinicians and researchers, who could not discriminate accounts of real and fictional events above chance (cf. Johnson & Suengas, 1989).

Ceci et al. pointed out that, with repetition, the children's accounts became increasingly detailed, coherent, and vivid, much as Johnson (1988) suggested that delusions develop with rehearsal. As in the case of delusions, some children evidently developed the conviction that the fictional events had actually happened. As Ceci et al. emphasized, transcripts of therapists and investigators who work with children in child abuse cases indicate that these adults sometimes use techniques that could induce later reality-monitoring failures in the children. Perhaps the worst of these are encouraging children to imagine events and re-peatedly questioning them in a leading manner, which suggests the types of answers or information expected.

The source-monitoring framework has also been used to explain how false memories might arise from therapeutic practices used to help pa-tients recover repressed memories (Belli & Loftus, 1994; Lindsay & Read, 1994). For example, to help patients remember forgotten events, some therapists (a) question patients under hypnosis, (b) encourage patients to believe that dreams reflect real events or use dreams to cue the recall of real events, (c) use guided imagery, (d) encourage patients to join abuse survivor support groups in which they hear many accounts of abuse, and (e) assign self-help books that include statements such as, "If you think you were abused and your life shows the symptoms, then you were" (Bass & Davis, 1988, p. 22). In a recent survey (Poole, Lindsay, Memon, & Bull, 1995), 7% of the licensed therapists who responded reported using at least one of these techniques, although there was also considerable disagreement about the advisability of a number of them. Regardless of whether these techniques sometimes result in recovery of accurate forgotten memories, it is clear that they encourage clients to (a) develop abuse schemas for interpreting the memories, emotions, and physical symptoms they do have; (b) vividly and repeatedly imagine events they are not sure happened; (c) adopt very lax criteria for generat-ing ideas about what might have happened and for evaluating the veri-dicality of memories and beliefs; and (d) encourage them to give great weight to emotion as a cue to veridicality. All of these factors, along with the authority and social support of the therapist, would be expected to promote reality-monitoring errors. Thus, these practices should be used cautiously, if at all (Belli & Loftus, 1994; Lindsay & Read, 1994; Loftus, 1993; Poole et al., 1995).

One question of both theoretical and practical concern is, who is most "at risk" from potentially suggestive therapeutic practices, or from sto-ries of child abuse in the media, novels, and movies? Does education inoculate some individuals better than others against induced false memories and beliefs? Undoubtedly there are some patients who have not been abused who would not come to believe they were even after many months of suggestive practices. However, there may be others who have not been abused who might relatively easily develop false memories or false beliefs about abuse.[2] Similarly, not all subjects show source confusions in laboratory studies of either simple, neutral mate-

---

[2]Suggestibility of some individuals is not an argument against responsible discussions of child abuse any more than hypochondria is an argument against responsible health information.

rials, such as perceived and imagined pictures, nor of autobiographical recall of suggested events. There may be correlations among some measures of source-monitoring confusions and individuals' scores on measures assessing social conformity, suggestibility, hypnotic responsiveness, and the degree to which they are vivid imagers or "fantasy-prone" (e.g., Wilson & Barber, 1983). Also, studies of individual differences might be a way to test the idea that developing false memories and beliefs is aided by, but does not depend on, vivid imagery; compelling interpretive experiences may be sufficient as well (Johnson, 1988).

Aging and Source Monitoring.   Aging does not appear to produce uniform deficits in cognitive tasks, but rather disrupts some types more than others. For example, event memory appears to be more disrupted than does the kind of memory that underlies priming on implicit tasks (Light, 1991). As indicated by the earlier discussion of the source-monitoring framework, a memory for an event is the outcome of many factors operating at encoding, during the retention interval, and while the individual is remembering. Thus, accounting for age differences in event memory means specifying which of these factors is more likely than others to show changes with age.

As a beginning, it appears that age-related deficits in memory for source (context) tend to be greater than age-related deficits in memory for content (for a review and meta-analysis, see Spencer & Raz, 1995). For example, Ferguson et al. (1992) found that, even when younger and older adults were equated on old–new recognition, older adults were poorer at identifying which of two similar speakers had said particular words (also see Light, 1991; Schacter, Kaszniak, Kihlstrom, & Valdiserri, 1991). The cognitive mechanisms of age-related differences in memory for context are not completely understood (e.g., Spencer & Raz, 1995), but the source-monitoring framework provides guidelines for approaching the question systematically.

First, one might expect that some age differences are related to efficacy of binding processes during initial encoding. This hypothesis has been explored by Chalfonte and Johnson (1995, 1996). Chalfonte and Johnson pointed out that many studies of aging and context/source memory do not separate potential deficits in encoding features from potential deficits in binding features together. They tested these two factors separately and found that, relative to young adults, elderly subjects had a greater recognition memory deficit on the feature of location, but not a greater deficit on the feature of color. Thus, these two attributes do not appear to show a uniform disruption with age. However, Chalfonte and Johnson also found that elderly subjects had deficits binding either location or color to content. De Leonardis (1996) had subjects perform specific cognitive operations (orienting tasks) on words said by two speakers. Then subjects were asked to identify either the speaker or the cognitive operation engaged for each item. De Leonardis found that elderly adults showed equal deficits relative to young adults on both identification tasks. In general, such findings point to the necessity of comparing source deficits in more detail and distinguishing between feature encoding and binding deficits, both of which may be produced by aging.

In addition to potential differences in the efficacy of binding processes in younger and older adults, there may be differences in the aspects of experiences they reactivate and retrieve (i.e., ruminate and talk about) later. For example, Hashtroudi, Johnson, Vnek, and Ferguson (1994) had pairs of subjects act in a short play (Phase 1), think about it afterward (Phase 2), and then attempt to identify who said which lines on a surprise source-monitoring test (Phase 3). Older adults were less accurate than younger adults at source monitoring in Phase 3, if they had been instructed to think about how they had felt during the play or if they had been simply instructed to think about the play with no particular focus suggested in Phase 2. In contrast, when subjects were instructed to think about factual aspects of the play (e.g., what people said), older adults and younger adults did not differ significantly in their ability to discriminate their lines from the other actors. Therefore, at least some age-related deficits in source monitoring may reflect differences in what interests older and younger individuals, and thus what they think about (i.e., what receives reflective processing).

Older and younger adults may also apply different criteria in making source attributions. Available evidence suggests that older adults, like younger adults, show improved source accuracy when test conditions are changed from encouraging familiarity-based responding to making more stringent analyses of source-specifying characteristics of memories (Multhaup, 1995; Multhaup, De Leonardis, Johnson, Brown, & Hashtroudi, 1996). At the same time, there is some evidence that older adults may differentially weight different dimensions. For example, in one study, the correlation between subjects' rating of the perceptual clarity of their memories and their certainty in the accuracy of their memories was approximately the same for older and younger adults, whereas the correlation between subjects' ratings of the amount of emotion in their memories and their certainty in the accuracy of their memories was higher for older than for younger adults (Hashtroudi, Johnson, & Chrosniak; cited in Johnson & Multhaup, 1992). This finding suggests that, under some circumstances, older adults may give greater weight to emotional than to more factual information in evaluating the veridicality of memories. These and other potential age-related differences in how memories are rehearsed and evaluated await further study.

Although it is clear that some age-related deficits in source memory are related to age-related differences in what individuals focus on either at encoding, during the retention interval, or at test, this is likely not the whole problem. When encoding processes are more controlled, older adults still show deficits for bound feature information (Chalfonte & Johnson, 1996; De Leonardis, 1996), which appear to be greater the more similar the sources to be discriminated (Ferguson et al., 1992). Furthermore, when older individuals are engaged in a cognitive task that does not induce binding of content and perceptual features, they appear to suffer a disproportionate deficit from the addition of the cognitive task (Johnson, De Leonardis, et al., 1995). The extent to which age-related deficits reflect incidental binding deficits or deficits in more reflectively guided binding processes remains to be sorted out.

One potential benefit from a more detailed understanding of age-related changes in source memory is that aging is also associated with certain changes in brain structures, and thus might help clarify the neuropsychology of source monitoring. Two types of findings are particularly relevant: Older adults show evidence of neuropathology (e.g., cell loss, amyloid plaques, granulovacuolar degeneration) in the hippocampal system (Ivy, MacLeod, Petit, & Markus, 1992). In addition, physiological and behavioral studies suggest that the frontal cortex is particularly sensitive to the effects of aging (Albert & Kaplan, 1980; Gerard & Weisberg, 1986; Haug et al., 1983; Kemper, 1984; McEntree & Crook, 1990; Woodruff, 1982). Some evidence that age-related declines in source monitoring are associated with deficits in frontal lobe functioning were provided by Craik, Morris, Morris, and Loewen (1990). They found that older subjects' ability to identify whether a fact was learned in the experiment or outside the experiment was negatively correlated with perseverative errors on the Wisconsin Card Sort Test (WCST) and positively with performance on a verbal fluency test (two standard neuropsychological tests used to assess frontal function). However, Johnson et al. (1995) did not find a significant correlation between either older subjects' WCST or fluency tests and subjects' scores on a source test that asked them to identify who had said particular words. Given the complexity of attributes that go into making up source (i.e., that make up an event or episode) and the lack of precision of frontal tests, variations in outcomes should not be too surprising. Nevertheless, as is discussed next, it is quite plausible that some of the source-monitoring deficit associated with aging could arise from dysfunction of hippocampal and frontal systems.

BRAIN MECHANISMS OF SOURCE MEMORY

Current conceptions about the neural mechanisms underlying memory for source come primarily from studies of brain-damaged patients who show marked failures of source monitoring of various types (e.g., amnesics, frontal patients, Capgras' patients, and anosognosia patients). The cumulative evidence from these strikingly different patient populations points to two brain regions that are critical for creating, providing access to, and monitoring memory for events: the medial-temporal region, particularly the hippocampal system, and the prefrontal cortex.

Medial-Temporal Regions and Source Memory

The role of the medial-temporal brain areas, and especially the hippocampus, in memory for events has been well documented (e.g., Milner, 1970; Squire, 1983, 1987). Although the specific cognitive processes mediated by the hippocampal system that account for event memory are not entirely clear, this region appears to be critical for two types of functions: feature binding and reactivating. These functions are undoubtedly interrelated, but for ease of discussion are considered separately.

The Hippocampal System and Feature Binding. Several investigators have proposed that medial-temporal brain areas, especially the hippocampal system, play a central role in binding features together into complex eventlike memories (e.g., Cohen & Eichenbaum, 1993; Johnson & Chalfonte, 1994; Metcalfe, Cottrell, & Mencl, 1992). These ideas are similar to earlier theories of amnesia, which proposed that amnesics have deficits in context memory (Hirst, 1982; Mayes, 1988). Evidence regarding the context-deficit hypothesis has been equivocal because of (a) methodological issues regarding how it should be tested (e.g., see Chalfonte, Verfaellie, Johnson, & Reiss, in press), and (b) the suggestion that only amnesics with frontal damage in addition to medial-temporal damage show contextual deficits that are larger than their deficits on memory for the semantic content of items (Shimamura & Squire, 1987). However, it is increasingly clear that both content and contextual (or source) deficits can come about in more than one way, and thus a model that attributes content memory to the hippocampus and context (or source) memory to the frontal lobes is an oversimplification (Johnson et al., 1993). Consequently, this section considers the roles that both medial-temporal and frontal regions might play in establishing, retaining, reviving, and evaluating memories for events (i.e., memories that have phenomenal attributes of source).

Recent studies by Chalfonte et al. (in press) and Kroll, Knight, Metcalfe, Wolf, and Tulving (in press) illustrate the possible role of the hippocampal system in feature binding. Chalfonte et al. showed subjects a 7×7 array with pictures in some, but not all, locations. Subsequently, subjects were given an old–new recognition test for which items had been present, or a recognition test that required them to identify both an item and its correct location. Amnesics with presumed hippocampal system damage, but not Korsakoff's amnesics, tended to show a disproportionate deficit in their memory for the locations of items relative to their memory for the items. Chalfonte et al. proposed that the hippocampal system is involved in coding the feature of location, as well as in the incidental binding of item and location (cf. O'Keefe & Nadel, 1978). They further proposed that the hippocampus is part of a circuit along with other medial-temporal areas, including diencephalic regions, which operates in the binding of features in general—hence the general similarity of the deficits from amnesias of various etiologies and the extra memory deficit that patients with hippocampal damage seem to show.

Other evidence implicating the hippocampus in binding has recently been reported by Kroll et al. (1996). Kroll et al. showed subjects two-syllable words (Experiment 1) and tested recognition memory. Subjects were more likely to have false alarms to re-paired elements of stimuli than to completely new items, suggesting features were remembered, but their connections were not. Furthermore, this effect was exaggerated in left-hippocampal subjects relative to right-hippocampal subjects or normal controls. A second experiment using drawings of faces found false recognitions of re-pairings of elements to be higher than normal controls in both left- and right-hemisphere-damaged patients. Kroll et al. suggested that the hippocampus plays a critical role in "binding of informational elements into coherent, separately accessible, long-term engrams" (p. 194). Kroll et al.'s idea of binding is similar to the perceptual binding we have proposed—a binding process that can be set in motion by purely perceptual processes resulting from a single exposure (Johnson, 1992; Johnson & Chalfonte, 1994). However, we postulate that binding is also augmented when perceptual records are the target of further reflective processing. Both types of binding—perceptual and reflective—may be hippocampally dependent and time limited (see also Rovee-Collier, 1990).

The Hippocampus and Reactivating.   Johnson and Hirst (1991, 1993; see also Johnson & Chalfonte, 1994) suggested that the hippocampus is part of a neural circuit that underlies the component process of *reactivating*. Reactivating is distinguished from *refreshing*, *rehearsing*, and *retrieving* in the typical time frame and activation levels of the target representation over which the various component processes are presumed to operate, and the degree of cuing required. As described in a previous section, *refreshing* and *rehearsing* operate on information that is currently in a state of relatively high activation, whereas *reactivating* and *retrieving* operate on information that is in an inactive state (or functionally a low state of activation). This means that *refreshing* and *rehearsing* typically operate during and shortly after a stimulus occurs, whereas *reactivating* and *retrieving* typically operate somewhat later.

However, what is critical for whether reactivating (rather than refreshing or rehearsing) occurs is whether the stimulus is a target of current perceptual or reflective processing, not whether it is physically present in the environment. For example, reactivation might occur when a subject reads a sentence that cues the recollection of a related point from an earlier paragraph on the same page. In this case, the reactivated item is available in the immediate environment, but not cognitively present until it is reactivated. Reactivating is accomplished as an R-1 process via current cues (in combination with current agendas), whereas retrieving (R-2) requires additional reflective input, such as self-generated cues or a recall strategy (e.g., let me try to recall what else I've read by this author).

From the MEM perspective, reactivations are a central mechanism of memory consolidation and, along with organizational processes (i.e., *shifting, noting, initiating, discovering*), largely determine whether memories will, on later occasions, be accessible via *reactivation* and *retrieval* (e.g., Johnson, 1992). Representations that do not undergo such reactivations may persist in the memory system, and perhaps be manifested in thought and behavior (e.g., Eich, 1984; DeSchepper & Treisman, 1996), or perhaps yield familiarity responses if encountered again. Nevertheless, they will not become part of one's autobiographical repertoire of event memories (Nelson, 1993) or stock of voluntarily accessible knowledge (e.g., Hogan & Kintsch, 1971; Landauer & Bjork, 1978). Thus, at least some of the profound effects of medial-temporal brain damage on acquiring new factual or autobiographical memories could be accounted for by a deficit in the component process of *reactivating* (Johnson & Chalfonte, 1994; Johnson & Hirst, 1991). The activation of information via more complex, strategic *retrieving* is dependent on frontal systems of the brain (Johnson, 1990; Schacter, 1987; Shimamura, Janowsky, & Squire, 1991). Similar to the distinction between *reactivating* and *retrieving* based on the MEM framework, Moscovitch (1992) suggested a distinction between associative (cue-driven) and strategic retrieval, the former mediated by the hippocampal system and the latter mediated by the frontal system.

Frontal Regions and Source Memory

There is general consensus about the types of activities that frontal systems are critical for: planning, self-regulation, maintenance of non-automatic cognitive or behavioral set, sustained mental activity, and organization of events (Daigneault, Braun, & Whitaker, 1992; Stuss & Benson, 1986). Several important theoretical ideas about the cognitive mechanisms underlying these activities have also been proposed, including Baddeley's (1986) working memory, Goldman-Rakic's (1987) representational memory, Norman and Shallice's (1986) Supervisory Attentional System, and Stuss' (1991) reflectiveness system. These constructs can be organized by the MEM architecture to provide a unifying model of frontal functions expressed in terms of a set of component cognitive processes with memory outcomes.

For example, consider Goldman-Rakic's (1987) model of prefrontal cortex (PFC) functions (see also Daigneault et al., 1992; Weinberger, 1993). According to Goldman-Rakic, the PFC keeps representations (either perceptual or symbolic) in an active state so that they can modulate behavior. This allows behavior to be guided in the absence of current external stimuli. Furthermore, there is no central executive or unitary processor (see also Johnson & Reeder, in press), but rather multiple specialized processes identified with various prefrontal subdivisions that are dedicated to particular informational domains (Goldman-Rakic, 1995). Goldman-Rakic likened these specialized processors to a "working memory" (Baddeley, 1986). Similarly, Fuster (1995) suggested that the PFC performs the function of working memory, plus maintains a "preparatory set." There are a number of lines of evidence for this view; in particular, cortical neurons in PFC remain active after the offset of a stimulus (Goldman-Rakic, 1987; Fuster, 1989). The constructs of *working memory* or a *maintained representation* correspond in MEM to processes that maintain activation of target records through *refreshing* or *rehearsing*. The construct of *preparatory set* (Fuster) or *active schema* (Shallice) correspond to *agendas*. Presumably, different component processes in the reflective subsystems of MEM are associated with activation in PFC. Furthermore, the different cognitive processes postulated in MEM are realized via different circuits depending on the intra- and extrafrontal regions that are also recruited as part of a particular circuit. Because the PFC has connections with many other brain regions, it could perform the variety of functions required by R-1 and R-2 subsystems (e.g., see also Desimone & Duncan, 1995). Also, PFC functions can be usefully discussed with the mid-level concepts proposed in MEM. That is, the PFC appears to receive information to which meaning has already been imparted (e.g., after the P-2 process of *identifying* has created a representation), and to intend behavior at the level of complex acts (e.g., "chair") and not specific movements (move tongue and lips; cf. Weinberger, 1993).

Other functions typically attributed to the PFC, in addition to maintaining information in an active state (e.g., deciding, planning, sequencing, self-control, and consciousness), have been described in terms of MEM as well. For example, Johnson and Reeder (in press) proposed that self-control arises from one reflective subsystem monitoring and controlling the other (e.g., R-1 by R-2).

The component processes in MEM's reflective subsystems should not be thought of as "in" the PFC, but rather as transactions between different frontal areas or between frontal regions and extrafrontal brain regions (e.g., temporal, parietal). For example, a circuit involving the occipital-parietal regions appears to be involved in the perceptual representation of spatial relations among meaningful objects (e.g., *identifying* and *placing*; Kolb & Whishaw, 1990). It is suggested here that various regions of the PFC are required for *refreshing, rehearsing, reactivating,* or *retrieving* such representations. Similarly, other regions of the PFC are required for *shifting, initiating, noting,* or *discovering* spatial relationships between spatially represented objects. In fact, one region of the PFC may take the representations held active by another region of the PFC and make comparisons among them via *noting* and *shifting* processes. This would constitute the type of transaction between R-1 and R-2 that Johnson and Reeder described in more detail. Finally, all such transactions are presumably guided by agendas (e.g., Furster's "prepatory set" or Shallice's "schemas") that are also active in areas of the PFC. Other regions of the PFC and other brain areas (e.g., temporal) would be involved in circuits for *refreshing, rehearsing, reactivating,* or *retrieving* representations of, say, verbal information, and yet others would be required for *shifting, initiating, noting,* or *discovering* symbolic relations among the representations of verbal information.

Furthermore, the agendas that recruit component cognitive processes in MEM are activated and maintained, in part, by emotional/motivational factors, which are served by limbic-hypothalamic circuits projecting to the orbital PFC. The motoric actions initiated as a consequence of the outcomes of perceptual and reflective processes recruited in the service of agendas are mediated by projections to the motor cortex (Kolb & Whishaw, 1990; Weinberger, 1993). Clearly, the hippocampal system participates in some, but not all, of these circuits. For example, we postulated that the hippocampus participates with PFC in *reactivation* circuits, by which ongoing agendas combine with other current cues (both external and internal) to revive bound feature combinations that people experience as event memories (i.e., that people attribute to a particular source; Johnson & Chalfonte, 1994; Johnson & Hirst, 1991).

In MEM, self-consciousness, self-control, and other such recursive instances of monitoring and control (e.g., awareness of awareness) are achieved by transactions between R-1 and R-2 subsystems. One possibility is that R-1 and R-2 processes are associated with the right and left PFC, respectively. This distinction fits the common characterization of right-hemisphere processes as more heuristic and holistic and left-hemisphere processes as more systematic, analytic, and planful. This could also account for certain disruptions of consciousness that occur when the two hemispheres are disconnected (Springer & Deutsch, 1985) because many aspects of consciousness require R-1/R-2 transactions (Johnson & Reeder, in press). However, an interesting alternative is that R-1 and R-2 functions are both represented in both hemispheres, but disproportionately so (e.g., Kolb & Whishaw, 1990). That is, the right hemisphere typically may be relatively more dedicated to R-1 functions and the left relatively more to R-2 functions. Variations in the balance may account for certain individual differences in which types of information are processed holistically and which analytically.

Considering the cognitive architecture depicted in MEM, it is easy to see why the frontal lobes have been clinically implicated in so many aspects of cognition, personality, and behavior, including problem solving and memory, regulation of thought, emotion and action, and consciousness (e.g., Stuss & Benson, 1986). This is because the R-1 and R-2 reflective component processes that sustain, revive, and organize information, and the learned agendas that recruit these processes in the service of motivationally significant goals, underlie all functionally adaptive learned thought and behavior.

The fact that no single, relatively small region of the PFC can be identified with a single executive controlling all frontal functions accounts for why so-called "frontal tests" are not always correlated with each other nor with performance on a particular experimental task, such as source monitoring. For example, Moscovitch, Osimani, Wortzman, and Freedman (1990) reported a frontal patient who was impaired on a verbal fluency (FAS) test, but not on the Wisconsin Card Sort Test (see also Parkin, Yeomans, & Bindschaedler, 1994). Frontal tests have been clinically useful despite this lack of precision in what they measure. They are complex enough to involve several processes (e.g., WCST), any one of which might be disrupted by frontal damage (e.g., motivation, maintenance of set, ability to refresh or rehearse outcomes, etc.). In addition, patients' lesions are often large enough to encompass the more limited functions that certain frontal tasks assess (e.g., FAS).

With this characterization of frontal function in mind, it is easy to see that frontal lobe damage might produce deficits in source monitoring for any one (or more) of a variety of reasons (Johnson, 1991a). Frontal deficits could disrupt reflectively promoted binding by disrupting consolidation, which would normally result from *reactivating* and *retrieving*. Frontal deficits could also disrupt the ability to hold alternative representations active by *refreshing* and *noting* relations between them. Comparing representations is essential for discovering contradictions that could lead one to reject information that otherwise seems compelling (e.g., on the basis of its clarity of perceptual detail). Frontal damage could disrupt the ability to strategically *retrieve* additional confirming or disconfirming evidence—again, evidence that would be critical for evaluating other evidence pointing to a particular source. Furthermore, frontal damage could produce changes in motivation that might induce lax source-monitoring criteria (e.g., lack of concern with inconsistency). Insofar as frontal deficits disrupt interactions between R-1 and R-2, access to records of cognition operations might be disrupted, making it more difficult to identify oneself as the origin of remembered information.

Consistent with this picture of multiple mechanisms for disrupting source monitoring, clinical cases of disrupted source monitoring are extremely variable in their characteristics. Cases vary in the frequency of confabulation, how mundane or bizarre the confabulations are, and how long the period of confabulation lasts (e.g., Johnson, 1991a; Kopelman, 1987). They have been attributed to various types of "executive" disorders, including deficits in ability to self-monitor and indifference (e.g., Kapur & Coughlan, 1980; Stuss et al., 1978). The more severe and longer lasting forms of confabulation appear to be associated with large lesions that disrupt both the medial-basal forebrain and frontal cognitive systems. Less severe, more transient confabulation appears to result from lesions limited to basal forebrain or orbital-frontal cortex. However, "The precise location and extent of frontal damage necessary for the development of the executive systems deficits specific or sufficient for the emergence of spontaneous confabulation are not known" (Fischer, Alexander, D'Esposito, & Otto, 1995, p. 27).

In trying to link brain regions to complex behavior like confabulation, part of the problem (as this analysis of source monitoring makes clear) is that there is no single, simple cognitive factor producing confabulation and delusions. For example, Johnson, O'Connor, and Cantor (1995) explored cognitive deficits underlying confabulation of a patient, GS, following an anterior communicating artery aneurysm that produced frontal damage. We compared GS with three nonconfabulating frontal patients matched for age, education, and neuropsychological measures of memory and frontal deficits, and with three age- and education-matched control subjects. Like frontal controls, GS underestimated temporal durations and showed poor source memory (speaker identification). What distinguished GS from the frontal controls was that his deficit in autobiographical recall was even greater than theirs, and his recall of laboratory-induced memories for imagined events was more detailed. We suggested that any one factor (e.g., deficits in source memory, deficits in ability to recall autobiographical memory, and propensity toward detailed imaginations) alone might not produce confabulation, but an interaction among these tendencies could disrupt a patient's ability to discriminate fact from fantasy.

The study of GS also highlights another important fact: All the patients had frontal damage, but only GS showed a clinically significant degree of confabulation. That is, not all "frontal syndrome" patients confabulate (Stuss & Benson, 1986). Standard diagnostic tests for frontal symptoms alone do not differentiate between frontal patients who confabulate and those who do not. In addition, although GS and the frontal controls were matched on neuropsychological tests of memory and attention/executive function, they were not matched on location of lesion. A given neuropsychological profile is only a rough index of associated brain damage. All three frontal controls had evidence of left frontal lesions on computerized tomography (CT) scan, whereas GS's CT scan revealed bilateral frontal lesions. Thus, it is tempting to attribute GS's confabulation to right frontal lesions. However, confabulation has been observed in patients with left frontal damage (e.g., DeLuca & Cicerone, 1991; Kapur & Coughlan, 1980), as well as those with right or bilateral damage (e.g., Joseph, 1986; Moscovitch, 1989). Hence, right frontal damage does not appear to be a necessary condition for confabulation (see also Fischer et al., 1995).

An intriguing possibility is that GS's poor autobiographical recall was related to the damage to his right PFC (Tulving, Kapur, Craik, Moscovitch, & Houle, 1994). Tulving et al. reviewed available published studies, and noted that right frontal damage seems to be correlated with deficits in retrieval (whereas left frontal damage seems to be correlated with encoding deficits). Johnson, O'Connor, and Cantor (1995) suggested that any detailed apparent memory (whether real or invented) might stand out against a background of impoverished autobiographical recall. Bilateral frontal damage may then disrupt the R-1/R-2 interactions necessary for critically evaluating activated information or holding it active while other confirming and/or disconfirming evidence is retrieved.

Although confabulation does not appear to result from right frontal damage alone, right-hemisphere damage is often associated with various forms of confabulation or deficits in reality monitoring (e.g., anosognosia accompanying hemiopia or hemiplegia). For example, consider *Capgras syndrome*, in which a patient believes that a person, usually someone close, has been replaced by someone similar—a double or impostor. The patient will say that the "impostor" looks like the "replaced" person, but the patient claims to know the "impostor" is not that person. Although initially thought to be a symptom associated with functional psychopathology, more recently, case descriptions and theoretical analyses have emphasized the possible organic basis of Capgras syndrome.

Ellis and Young (1990) pointed out that a Capgras patient seems to "recognize" the double as like the target person, but not to have the appropriate associated affect that is normally part of the familiarity response to a known person. They suggested that Capgras results from damage or disconnection within a neurological pathway signaling either emotional significance or familiarity. Ellis and Young also suggested that deficits in a face-recognition system combine with a tendency toward persecutory delusions to generate the Capgras delusion. That is, patients "mistake a change in themselves for a change in others (i.e., because altered affective reactions make people seem strange, they must have been 'replaced')." An anomalous perceptual experience combines with an incorrect interpretation (see also Johnson, 1988; Maher, 1974). Thus, Ellis and Young posited that a disordered face-detection system is combined with a disordered self-analysis or judgment system (Benson & Stuss, 1990) to produce the delusion. In MEM, the face-detection system would be a subdomain of the P-1 and P-2 subsystems (e.g., involving the component process of identifying), and the judgment system would reflect R-1 and R-2 processing. Consistent with Ellis and Young's analysis, Capgras patients score poorly on unfamiliar face recognition or matching, and Capgras delusion is associated with right temporal damage compounded with superimposed frontal dysfunction (Cutting, 1990; Ellis & Young, 1990; Joseph, 1986).

Finally, consider a case recently described by Kopelman, Guinan, and Lewis (1995). Their patient, WM, is a woman with the delusion that she has a relationship with a famous orchestral conductor (she was diagnosed with De Clerambault's syndrome secondary to schizophrenia). WM believes the relationship began many years before when they saw each other at a fruit-picking farm in East Anglia. According to her, they exchanged no words then, but he subsequently followed her to London and another town, but then stopped pursuing her. She believes they will be married someday, writes to him regularly, and believes they experience each other's thoughts. Unfortunately, Kopelman et al. could not get a scan for this patient, but she scored normally on IQ tests and, notably, on tests of frontal lobe function (e.g., FAS, cognitive estimates, card sorting). Kopelman et al. suggested that, although these delusions might superficially resemble confabulation associated with organic damage, they may arise somewhat differently. Confabulations often represent a "process of disorganized, out-of-context, and incoherent retrieval of past memories," whereas delusional memories may arise from a "predisposition to interpret the external world in particular ways, contingent upon underlying affective or cognitive factors. . . . " (p. 75). Kopelman et al. suggested that frontal deficits are responsible for decontextualized and incoherent memories, but not for "slippage" in interpretive schemas. However, as Ellis and Young's account of Capgras patients suggested, they too appear to have some "slippage" in interpretive schemas.

Interestingly, although WM scored at the 92nd percentile on recognition memory for words, she scored at only the 23rd percentile on recognition memory for faces. This poor recognition of faces is quite interesting (cf. Ellis & Young, 1990). It suggests that WM might have seen someone in East Anglia who resembled the conductor, exchanged what she took to be (or which were) meaningful looks with that person, and begun a rich fantasy about subsequent events. Similarly, she could have subsequently "recognized" the conductor in other faces, supporting the belief that he was showing an interest in her by following her. Clearly, poor face recognition alone would not be enough to support an elaborate delusion, but delusional thinking might well have taken "advantage" of the opportunity presented by poor face recognition (cf. Maher, 1974; Maher & Ross, 1984, for discussion of the idea that delusions sometimes arise around anomolous perceptual experiences).[3]

Nevertheless, as Kopelman et al. (1995) suggested, there is an important distinction between disordered memories and beliefs that arise because of organically caused deficits in memory and cognition (e.g., a deficit in strategic retrieving, an inability to prolong activation via refreshing) and disordered memories and beliefs that arise because of deficient use of intact mechanisms. These nonorganic deficiencies can come about for many reasons, including skewed schemas resulting from ignorance of facts and social support for bizarre beliefs. Both Kopelman et al. and Ellis and Young illustrated the potential value of combining cognitive neuropsychology and what Ellis and de Pauw (1994) called *cognitive neuropsychiatry,* in which biological, cognitive, motivational, and social factors are all taken into account in understanding a pattern of symptoms. This same multilevel approach should be productive in considering the complete range of situations in which issues of source mon-

---

[3]Another interesting possibility is that WM is a case of a fantasy-prone personality (Wilson & Barber, 1983).

itoring arise, including eyewitness testimony; children's accounts of abuse; adult recovery of childhood memories; and hallucinations, delusions, and confabulations associated with psychopathology or organic causes.

Degrees of Frontal Deficits

Whether organically, psychodynamically, or socially based, confabulations, delusions, and other clinically significant reality-monitoring failures may reflect frontal dysfunction, but we might differentiate the type of frontal dysfunction by "degree" (analogous to burns). The most serious types of frontal deficits are "third degree." These arise from organically based disruptions in the underlying circuits that support certain cognitive activities. For example, lesions in some areas of the frontal lobes may disrupt the ability to hold verbal information online (i.e., *refresh* or *rehearse* it). Lesions in other prefrontal areas may disrupt the ability to shift to new ways of looking at a stimulus, or to new agendas or schemas.

However, lesions are not necessary—there are other ways to disrupt such "frontal" activities. If neurologically intact subjects are given a second, distracting task, such as monitoring an auditory sequence for combinations of odd digits (Craik, 1983) or performing a finger-tapping task (Moscovitch & Umilta, 1991), they will find it difficult to engage in reflective activities such as *refreshing, rehearsing, shifting,* and *noting.* Presumably, other conditions of distraction, such as depression or emotional stress, have similar disruptive consequences (e.g., Hasher & Zacks, 1979). In these nonlesion cases, there is a deficit in appropriate frontal processing as a secondary consequence of other factors—a second-degree frontal deficit.

Finally, consider cases in which people do not engage in reflective processing because they do not know how (e.g., children have to learn mnemonic techniques), do not know that it is appropriate, are not in the habit of doing so, or because they are not motivated to do so. These cases might be thought of as first-degree frontal deficits. In short, there are a number of ways to shut down or attenuate reflective activity.

Frontal Deficits of Different Degrees May Interact

Considering that there may be different degrees of frontal dysfunction highlights the possibility of considering the interaction of deficits of different degrees. For example, a lesion-induced third-degree deficit may produce different patterns depending on whether the patient has premorbid first-degree deficits. Furthermore, we would not expect frontal deficits of any degree necessarily to be general. For example, circumscribed frontal lesions may cause third-degree deficits in processing verbal, but not visual, information or vice versa. Certain types of distraction are more likely to produce second-degree deficits on some tasks than on others. An individual may be in the habit of dealing reflectively with job-related information, but not personal interactions or vice versa (i.e., first-degree reflective deficits may be evident in some areas, but not others). Hence, we should find premorbid individual characteristics affecting how the consequences of frontal damage are manifested (e.g., O'Connor, Walbridge, Sandson, & Alexander, 1995). Such interactions may help account for the great variability in thought and behavior patterns shown by patients with frontal damage, as well as patients under stress or in a depressed state.

FINAL REMARKS

To survive, a cognitive system that takes in information from the external world and generates information itself has to have mechanisms for distinguishing the origin of information. This chapter gives an overview of the approach my colleagues and I have developed for exploring how such discriminations are accomplished. We call this approach the *source-monitoring framework,* but perhaps we should call it the *source framework* because it includes more than a focus on the evaluative phase of remembering. It also includes proposals about the conditions for establishing complex event memories in the first place, and an emphasis on prior and subsequent events and mental processes (e.g., rumination), which can affect the likelihood that memories and beliefs will be veridical. We believe this approach can provide a framework for understanding the particular ways that source monitoring may be vulnerable to organic brain damage, social and cultural factors, and dysfunctional cognitive activities. Converging evidence from many investigators conducting controlled laboratory studies of cognitive and social processes, along with case studies and group studies of patients from various clinical populations, is moving us closer to an appreciation of the complex dynamics involved in attributing mental experiences to sources. Furthermore, although the source-monitoring framework has been most frequently applied to understanding memories for events and, to a lesser extent, attitudes or beliefs, an appropriately expanded source-monitoring framework should also be useful for investigating the processes involved in evaluating ongoing perception (reality testing; e.g., Perky, 1910) and future plans and expectations (reality checking; e.g., Johnson & Sherman, 1990).

With respect to event memory, we have attempted to specify the mechanisms by which event memories are established, maintained, revived, and evaluated. We have described these mechanisms in terms of a general cognitive architecture, MEM, which proposes a mid-level vocabulary for conceptualizing perceptual and reflective processes. Thus, we attempted to characterize relevant factors both in terms of the class of information that might be involved (e.g., a high level of perceptual detail) and the processes that might be involved (e.g., perceptual detail maintained through *reactivating* or perceptual detail embellished through *reactivating, shifting,* and *noting*). It provides a conceptual structure for generating experiments (e.g., investigating potential age-related differences in source memory, or suggestibility effects in eyewitness testimony or autobiographical memory). Furthermore, MEM component processes can be related to brain circuits involving structures such as the hippocampal and frontal systems, and processes such as binding and executive control, which appear to be central for identifying the sources of mental experiences.

Our goal is to clarify source memory without underestimating the complexity of the problem. For example, it is most natural to think of deficits or disruption as reducing or eliminating a particular type of cognitive activity. But it is important to remember that a cognitive deficit does not necessarily just leave a blank in the stream of consciousness where that cognitive process might otherwise have been. Deficits in processes may have a secondary effect of increasing other processes. If one's ability to remember past events is disrupted, one might ruminate or elaborate on what one does remember. If one's ability to anticipate and plan for future action is disrupted, one might obsess over current perceptions and thoughts. Furthermore, what one does think about then creates the background knowledge, beliefs, and schemas that "capture" new incoming information—selecting among elements, generating one interpretation over another, and perhaps triggering reactivation and retrieval of related thoughts.

Whether normal or disrupted, cognitive activity is embedded in motivational, social, and cultural contexts. Source monitoring accompanies all this cognitive activity, sometimes with conscious awareness and sometimes as part of the natural, ongoing use of available perceptual and memorial information—sometimes accurately, sometimes resulting in minor inaccuracies, and sometimes in serious distortions or extreme delusions. Because much can be learned about a process from looking at "normal" errors, or more serious errors that arise when the processes break down, research efforts tend to focus on producing and/or explaining errors and distortions. Nevertheless, we should not lose sight of the fact that the study of source monitoring reveals how processes work that generally allow people to accurately identify the origin of mental experiences, and to be appropriately cautious when information seems equivocal.

ACKNOWLEDGMENTS

Preparation of this chapter was supported by NIA grant AG09253. I would like to thank Linda Henkel and Carol Raye for helpful comments on an earlier draft.

REFERENCES

Albert, M. S., & Kaplan, E. (1980). Organic implications of neuropsychological deficits in the elderly. In L. W. Poon, J. L. Fozard, L. S. Cermak, D. Arenberg, & L. W. Thompson (Eds.), *New directions in memory and aging: Proceedings of the George A. Talland Memorial Conference* (pp. 403–432). Hillsdale, NJ: Lawrence Erlbaum Associates.

Baddeley, A. (1986). *Working memory: Oxford Psychology Series No 11.* New York: Oxford University Press.

Baddeley, A. (1992). Working memory: The interface between memory and cognition. *Journal of Cognitive Neuroscience, 4,* 281–288.

Bartlett, F. C. (1932). *Remembering: A study in experimental and social psychology.* Cambridge, MA: Cambridge University Press.

Bass, E., & Davis, L. (1988). *The courage to heal: A guide for women survivors of child sexual abuse.* New York: Harper & Row.

Belli, R., & Loftus, E. (1994). Recovered memories of childhood abuse: A source monitoring perspective. In S. J. Lynn & J. W. Rhue (Eds.), *Dissociation: Clinical and theoretical perspectives* (pp. 415–433). New York: Guilford.

Benson, D. F., & Stuss, D. T. (1990). Frontal lobe influences on delusions: A clinical perspective. *Schizophrenia Bulletin, 16,* 403–411.

Biederman, I. (1987). Recognition by components: A theory of human image understanding. *Psychological Review, 94,* 115–147.

Bransford, J. D., & Johnson, M. K. (1973). Considerations of some problems of comprehension. In W. Chase (Ed.), *Visual information processing* (pp. 383–438). New York: Academic Press.

Ceci, S. J., & Bruck, M. (1993). Suggestibility of the child witness: A historical review and synthesis. *Psychological Bulletin, 113*(3), 403–439.

Ceci, S. J., Crotteau Huffman, M. L., Smith, E., & Loftus, E. F. (1994). Repeatedly thinking about a non-event: Source misattributions among preschoolers. *Consciousness and Cognition, 3*(3/4), 388–407.

Ceci, S. J., Loftus, E., Leichtman, M., & Bruck, M. (1994). The possible role of source misattributions in the creation of false beliefs among preschoolers. *International Journal of Clinical and Experimental Hypnosis, 42*(4), 304–320.

Chaiken, S., Lieberman, A., & Eagly, A. H. (1989). Heuristic and systematic information processing within and beyond the persuasion context. In J. S. Uleman & J. A. Bargh (Eds.), *Unintended thought* (pp. 212–252). New York: Guilford.

Chalfonte, B., Verfaellie, M., Johnson, M. K., & Reiss, L. (in press). Spatial location memory in amnesia: Binding item and location information under incidental and intentional encoding conditions. *Memory.*

Chalfonte, B. L., & Johnson, M. K. (1996). Feature memory and binding in young and older adults. *Memory & Cognition, 24*, 403–416.

Chalfonte, B. L., & Johnson, M. K. (1995). *Adult age differences in location memory and binding, recognition and recall under incidental and intentional encoding conditions*. Unpublished manuscript.

Cohen, N. J., & Eichenbaum, H. (1993). *Memory, amnesia, and the hippocampal system*. Cambridge, MA: MIT Press.

Cohen, N. J., & Squire, L. R. (1980). Preserved learning and retention of pattern-analyzing skill in amnesia: Dissociation of knowing how and knowing that. *Science, 210*, 207–210.

Collins, A. M., & Quillian, M. R. (1969). Retrieval time from semantic memory. *Journal of Verbal Learning and Verbal Behavior, 8*, 240–248.

Craik, F. I. M. (1983). On the transfer of information from temporary to permanent memory. *Philosophical Transaction of the Royal Society of London, B302*, 341–359.

Craik, F. I. M. (1986). A functional account of age differences in memory. In F. Klix & H. Hagendorf (Eds.), *Human memory and cognitive capabilities: Mechanisms and performances* (pp. 409–422). New York: Elsevier.

Craik, F. I. M., & Byrd, M. (1982). Aging and cognitive deficits: The role of attentional resources. In F. I. M. Craik & S. E. Trehub (Eds.), *Aging and cognitive processes* (pp. 191–211). New York: Plenum.

Craik, F. I. M., Morris, L. W., Morris, R. G., & Loewen, E. R. (1990). Relations between source amnesia and frontal lobe functioning in older adults. *Psychology and Aging, 5*, 148–151.

Cutting, J. (1990). *The right cerebral hemisphere and psychiatric disorders*. Oxford: Oxford University Press.

Daigneault, S., Braun, C. M. J., & Whitaker, H. A. (1992). An empirical test of two opposing theoretical models of prefrontal function. *Brain and Cognition, 19*, 48–71.

Deese, J. (1959). On the prediction of occurrence of particular verbal intrusions in immediate recall. *Journal of Experimental Psychology, 58*, 17–22.

De Leonardis, D. M. (1996). *Aging and source monitoring: The relation between cognitive operations and perceptual information*. Unpublished doctoral dissertation, George Washington University, Washington, DC.

DeLuca, J., & Cicerone, K. D. (1991). Confabulation following aneurysm of the anterior communicating artery. *Cortex, 27*, 417–423.

Dennett, D. C. (1991). *Consciousness explained*. Boston: Little, Brown.

DeSchepper, B., & Treisman, A. (1996). Visual memory for novel shapes: Implicit coding without attention. *Journal of Experimental Psychology: Learning, Memory and Cognition, 22*, 1–21.

Desimone, R., & Duncan, J. (1995). Neural mechanisms of selective visual attention. *Annual Review of Neuroscience, 18*, 193–222.

Dobson, M., & Markham, R. (1993). Imagery ability and source monitoring: Implications for eyewitness memory. *British Journal of Psychology, 32*, 111–118.

Dodson, C. S., & Johnson, M. K. (1993). The rate of false source attributions depends on how questions are asked. *American Journal of Psychology, 106*(4), 541–557.

Dodson, C. S., & Johnson, M. K. (1996). Some problems with the process dissociation approach to memory. *Journal of Experimental Psychology: General, 125*, 181–194.

Duncker, K. (1945). On problem solving. *Psychological Monographs, 58*, (5, Whole No. 270, 1–112).

Dunn, J. C., & Kirsner, K. (1988). Discovering functionally independent mental processes: The principle of reversed association. *Psychological Review, 95*, 91–101.

Durso, F. T., & Johnson, M. K. (1980). The effects of orienting tasks on recognition, recall, and modality confusion of pictures and words. *Journal of Verbal Learning and Verbal Behavior, 19,* 416–429.

Eagly, A., & Chaiken, S. (1993). *The psychology of attitudes.* New York: Harcourt Brace.

Edwards, D., & Middleton, D. (1986a). Joint remembering: Constructing an account of shared experience through conversational discourse. *Discourse Processes, 9,* 423–459.

Edwards, D., & Middleton, D. (1986b). Text for memory: Joint recall with a scribe. *Human Learning, 5,* 125–138.

Edwards, D., Potter, J., & Middleton, D. (1992). Toward a discursive psychology of remembering. *The Psychologist, 5,* 441–446.

Eich, E. (1984). Memory for unattended events: Remembering with and without awareness. *Memory and Cognition, 12,* 105–111.

Eich, E., & Metcalfe, J. (1989). Mood dependent memory for internal versus external events. *Journal of Experimental Psychology: Learning, Memory, and Cognition, 15,* 443–455.

Ellis, H. D., & Young, A. W. (1988). *Human cognitive neuropsychology.* Hillsdale, NJ: Lawrence Erlbaum Associates.

Ellis, H. D., & Young, A. W. (1990). Accounting for delusional misidentifications. *British Journal of Psychiatry, 157,* 239–248.

Ellis, H. D., & de Pauw, K. W. (1994). The cognitive neuropsychiatric origins of the Capgras delusion. In A. S. David & J. C. Cutting (Eds.), *The neuropsychology of schizophrenia* (pp. 317–335). Hove, England: Lawrence Erlbaum Associates.

Ferguson, S., Hashtroudi, S., & Johnson, M. K. (1992). Age differences in using source-relevant cues. *Psychology and Aging, 7,* 443–452.

Fiedler, K., Walther, E., Armbruster, T., Fay, D., Kuntz, H., & Naumann, U. (1995). *Do you really know what you have seen? Intrusion errors and presupposition effect in construction memory.* Unpublished manuscript.

Finke, R. A., Johnson, M. K., & Shyi, G. C. W. (1988). Memory confusions for real and imagined completions of symmetrical visual patterns. *Memory & Cognition, 16,* 133–137.

Fischer, R. S., Alexander, M. P., D'Esposito, M., & Otto, R. (1995). Neuropsychological and neuroanatomical correlates of confabulation. *Journal of Clinical and Experimental Neuropsychology, 17*(1), 20–28.

Fodor, J. A., Bever, T. G., & Garrett, M. F. (1974). *The psychology of language: An introduction to psycholinguistics and generative grammar.* New York: McGraw-Hill.

Foley, M. A., Johnson, M. K., & Raye, C. L. (1983). Age-related changes in confusion between memories for thoughts and memories for speech. *Child Development, 54,* 51–60.

Fuster, J. M. (1989). *The prefrontal cortex.* New York: Raven Press.

Fuster, J. M. (1995, March). *Temporal processing.* Paper presented at the New York Academy of Sciences workshop on Structure and Functions of the Human Prefrontal Cortex, New York.

Gentner, D. (1988). Analogical inference and analogical access. In A. Prieditis (Ed.), *Analogica* (pp. 63–88). San Mateo, CA: Kaufmann.

Gerard, G., & Weisberg, L. A. (1986). MRI periventricular lesions in adults. *Neurology, 36,* 998–1001.

Gerrig, R. J., & Prentice, D. A. (1991). The representation of fictional information. *Psychological Science, 2,* 336–340.

Gibson, J. J. (1950). *The perception of the visual world.* Boston: Houghton-Mifflin.

Gick, M., & Holyoak, K. (1980). Analogical problem solving. *Cognitive Psychology, 12,* 306–355.

Gilbert, D. T. (1991). How mental systems believe. *American Psychologist, 46,* 107–119.

Gilbert, D. T., Tafarodi, R. W., & Malone, P. S. (1993). You can't not believe everything you read. *Journal of Personality and Social Psychology, 65,* 221–233.

Godden, D. R., & Baddeley, A. D. (1975). Context-dependent memory in two natural environments: On land and underwater. *British Journal of Psychology, 66,* 325–331.

Goldman-Rakic, P. S. (1987). Circuitry of primate prefrontal cortex and regulation of behavior by representational memory. In F. Plum (Ed.), *Handbook of physiology: The nervous system.* Bethesda, MD: American Physiological Society.

Goodman, G. S., Hirschman, J. E., Hepps, D., & Rudy, L. (1991). Children's memory for stressful events. *Merrill-Palmer Quarterly, 37,* 109–157.

Hasher, L., & Griffin, M. (1978). Reconstructive and reproductive processes in memory. *Journal of Experimental Psychology: Human Learning and Memory, 4,* 318–330.

Hasher, L., & Zacks, R. T. (1979). Automatic and effortful processes in memory. *Journal of Experimental Psychology: General, 108,* 356–388.

Hashtroudi, S., Johnson, M. K., & Chrosniak, L. D. (1990). Aging and qualitative characteristics of memories for perceived and imagined complex events. *Psychology and Aging, 5,* 119–126.

Hashtroudi, S., Johnson, M. K., Vnek, N., & Ferguson, S. A. (1994). Aging and the effects of affective and factual focus on source monitoring and recall. *Psychology and Aging, 9*(1), 160–170.

Haug, H., Barmwater, U., Eggers, R., Fischer, D., Kuhl, S., & Sass, N. L. (1983). Anatomical changes in the aging brain: Morphometric analysis of the human prosencephalon. In J. Cervos-Navarro & H. I. Sakander (Eds.), *Brain aging: Neuropathology and neuropharmacology* (Vol. 21, pp. 1–12). New York: Raven.

Henkel, L., & Franklin, N. (1995, November). *Reality monitoring across modalities.* Paper presented at the 36th annual meeting of the Psychonomic Society, Los Angeles, CA.

Henkel, L., & Franklin, N. (in press). How to inflate a basketball: Reality monitoring for physically similar and conceptually related objects. *Memory & Cognition.*

Hirst, W. (1982). The amnesic syndrome: Descriptions and explanations. *Psychological Bulletin, 91,* 435–460.

Hochberg, J. E. (1970). Attention, organization, and consciousness. In D. I. Mostofsky (Ed.), *Attention: Contemporary theory and analysis* (pp. 99–124). New York: Appleton-Century-Crofts.

Hochberg, J. E. (1978). *Perception* (2nd ed.). Englewood Cliffs, NJ: Prentice-Hall.

Hogan, R. M., & Kintsch, W. (1971). Differential effects of study and test trials on long-term recognition and recall. *Journal of Verbal Learning and Verbal Behavior, 10,* 562–567.

Intraub, H., & Hoffman, J. E. (1992). Reading and visual memory: Remembering scenes that were never seen. *American Journal of Psychology, 105,* 101–114.

Ivy, G. O., MacLeod, C. M., Petit, T. L., & Markus, E. J. (1992). A physiological framework for perceptual and cognitive changes in aging. In F. I. M. Craik & T. A. Salthouse (Eds.), *The handbook of aging and cognition* (pp. 273–314). Hillsdale, NJ: Lawrence Erlbaum Associates.

Jacoby, L. L., & Dallas, M. (1981). On the relationship between autobiographical memory and perceptual learning. *Journal of Experimental Psychology: General, 110*(3), 306–340.

Jacoby, L. L., Woloshyn, V., & Kelley, C. M. (1989). Becoming famous without being recognized: Unconscious influences of memory produced by dividing attention. *Journal of Experimental Psychology: General, 118*(2), 115–125.

Johnson, M. K. (1977). What is being counted none the less? In I. M. Birnbaum & E. S. Parker (Eds.), *Alcohol and human memory* (pp. 43–57). Hillsdale, NJ: Lawrence Erlbaum Associates.

Johnson, M. K. (1983). A multiple-entry, modular memory system. *The Psychology of Learning and Motivation: Advances in Research and Theory, 17,* 81–123.

Johnson, M. K. (1988). Discriminating the origin of information. In T. F. Oltmanns & B. A. Maher (Eds.), *Delusional beliefs* (pp. 34–65). New York: Wiley.

Johnson, M. K. (1990). Functional forms of human memory. In J. L. McGaugh, N. M. Weinberger, & G. Lynch (Eds.), *Brain organization and memory: Cells, systems and circuits* (pp. 106–134). New York: Oxford University Press.

Johnson, M. K. (1991a). Reality monitoring: Evidence from confabulation in organic brain disease patients. In G. P. Prigatano & D. L. Schacter (Eds.), *Awareness of deficit after brain injury: Clinical and theoretical issues* (pp. 176–197). New York: Oxford University Press.

Johnson, M. K. (1991b). Reflection, reality monitoring and the self. In R. G. Kunzendorf (Ed.), *Mental imagery: Proceedings of the eleventh annual conference of the American Association for the Study of Mental Imagery* (pp. 3–16). New York: Plenum.

Johnson, M. K. (1992). MEM: Mechanisms of recollection. *Journal of Cognitive Neuroscience, 4,* 268–280.

Johnson, M. K. (in press). Fact, fantasy, and public policy. In D. Herrmann, C. McEvoy, C. Hertzog, P. Hertel, & M. K. Johnson (Eds.), *Basic and applied memory research: Theory in context.* Mahwah, NJ: Lawrence Erlbaum Associates.

Johnson, M. K., Bransford, J. D., & Solomon, S. K. (1973). Memory for tacit implications of sentences. *Journal of Experimental Psychology, 98,* 203–205.

Johnson, M. K., & Chalfonte, B. L. (1994). Binding complex memories: The role of reactivation and the hippocampus. In D. L. Schacter & E. Tulving (Eds.), *Memory systems 1994* (pp. 311–350). Cambridge, MA: MIT Press.

Johnson, M. K., De Leonardis, D., Hashtroudi, S., & Ferguson, S. (1995). Aging and single versus multiple cues in source monitoring. *Psychology and Aging, 10,* 507–517.

Johnson, M. K., Foley, M. A., Suengas, A. G., & Raye, C. L. (1988). Phenomenal characteristics of memories for perceived and imagined autobiographical events. *Journal of Experimental Psychology: General, 117,* 371–376.

Johnson, M. K., Hashtroudi, S., & Lindsay, D. S. (1993). Source monitoring. *Psychological Bulletin, 114*(1), 3–28.

Johnson, M. K., & Hirst, W. (1991). Processing subsystems of memory. In R. G. Lister & H. J. Weingartner (Eds.), *Perspectives on cognitive neuroscience* (pp. 197–217). New York: Oxford University Press.

Johnson, M. K., & Hirst, W. (1993). MEM: Memory subsystems as processes. In A. F. Collins, S. E. Gathercole, M. A. Conway, & P. E. Morris (Eds.), *Theories of memory* (pp. 241–286). Hove, England: Lawrence Erlbaum Associates.

Johnson, M. K., Kahan, T. L., & Raye, C. L. (1984). Dreams and reality monitoring. *Journal of Experimental Psychology: General,* 329–344.

Johnson, M. K., & Multhaup, K. S. (1992). Emotion and MEM. In S.-A. Christianson (Ed.), *The handbook of emotion and memory: Current research and theory* (pp. 33–66). Hillsdale, NJ: Lawrence Erlbaum Associates.

Johnson, M. K., Nolde, S. F., & De Leonardis, D. M. (1996). Emotional focus and source monitoring. *Journal of Memory and Language, 35,* 135–156.

Johnson, M. K., O'Connor, M., & Cantor, J. (1995). *Confabulation, memory deficits, and frontal dysfunction.* Manuscript submitted for publication.

Johnson, M. K., & Raye, C. L. (1981). Reality monitoring. *Psychological Review, 88,* 67–85.

Johnson, M. K., Raye, C. L., Wang, A. Y., & Taylor, T. H. (1979). Fact and fantasy: The roles of accuracy and variability in confusing imaginations with perceptual experiences. *Journal of Experimental Psychology: Human Learning and Memory, 5,* 229–240.

Johnson, M. K., & Reeder, J. A. (in press). Consciousness as meta-processing. In J. D. Cohen & J. W. Schooler (Eds.), *Scientific approaches to consciousness.* Mahwah, NJ: Lawrence Erlbaum Associates.

Johnson, M. K., & Sherman, S. J. (1990). Constructing and reconstructing the past and the future in the present. In E. T. Higgins & R. M. Sorrentino (Eds.), *Handbook of motivation and cognition: Foundations of social behavior* (pp. 482–526). New York: Guilford.

Johnson, M. K., & Suengas, A. G. (1989). Reality monitoring judgments of other people's memories. *Bulletin of the Psychonomic Society, 27,* 107–110.

Johnson, M. K., Taylor, T. H., & Raye, C. L. (1977). Fact and fantasy: The effects of internally generating events on the apparent frequency of externally generated events. *Memory and Cognition, 5,* 116–122.

Johnson-Laird, P. N. (1983). *Mental models.* Cambridge, MA: Harvard University Press.

Joseph, R. (1986). Confabulation and delusional denial: Frontal lobe and lateralized influences. *Journal of Clinical Psychology, 45,* 507–520.

Kapur, N., & Coughlan, A. K. (1980). Confabulation and frontal lobe dysfunction. *Journal of Neurology, Neurosurgery, & Psychiatry, 43,* 461–463.

Kemper, T. (1984). Neuroanatomical and neuropathological changes in normal aging and in dementia. In M. L. Albert (Ed.), *Clinical neurology of aging* (pp. 9–52). New York: Oxford University Press.

Kolers, P. A., & Roediger, H. L. (1984). Procedures of mind. *Journal of Verbal Learning and Verbal Behavior, 23,* 425–449.

Kolb, B., & Whishaw, I. (1990). *Fundamentals of human neuropsychology.* New York: Freeman.

Kopelman, M. D. (1987). Two types of confabulation. *Journal of Neurology and Neurosurgical Psychiatry, 50,* 1482–1487.

Kopelman, M. D., Guinan, E. M., & Lewis, P. D. R. (1995). Delusional memory, confabulation, and frontal lobe dysfunction: A case study in De Clerambault's syndrome. *Neurocase, 1,* 71–77.

Kosslyn, S. M. (1980). *Image and mind.* Cambridge, MA: Harvard University Press.

Kowler, E., & Martins, A. J. (1982). Eye movements of preschool children. *Science, 215,* 997–999.

Kroll, N. E. A., Knight, R. T., Metcalfe, J., Wolf, E. S., & Tulving, E. (1996). Consolidation failure as a source of memory illusions. *Journal of Memory and Language, 35,* 176–196.

Krumhansl, C. L. (1990). *Cognitive foundations of musical pitch.* New York: Oxford University Press.

Landauer, T. K., & Bjork, R. A. (1978). Optimum rehearsal patterns and name learning. In M. M. Gruneberg, P. E. Morris, & R. N. Sykes (Eds.), *Practical aspects of memory* (pp. 625–632). New York: Academic Press.

Light, L. L. (1991). Memory and aging: Four hypotheses in search of data. *Annual Review of Psychology, 42,* 333–376.

Lindsay, D. S. (1993). Eyewitness suggestibility. *Current Directions in Psychological Science, 2*(3), 86–89.

Lindsay, D. S. (1994). Memory source monitoring and eyewitness testimony. In D. F. Ross, J. D. Read, & M. P. Toglia (Eds.), *Adult eyewitness testimony: Current trends and developments* (pp. 27–55). New York: Cambridge University Press.

Lindsay, D. S., & Johnson, M. K. (1989). The eyewitness suggestibility effect and memory for source. *Memory & Cognition, 17,* 349–358.

Lindsay, D. S., & Johnson, M. K. (1991). Recognition memory and source monitoring. *Bulletin of the Psychonomic Society, 29,* 203–205.

Lindsay, D. S., Johnson, M. K., & Kwon, P. (1991). Developmental changes in memory source monitoring. *Journal of Experimental Child Psychology, 52,* 297–318.

Lindsay, D. S., & Read, J. D. (1994). Psychotherapy and memories of childhood sexual abuse. *Applied Cognitive Psychology, 8,* 281–338.

Loftus, E. (1993). The reality of repressed memories. *American Psychologist, 48*(5), 518–537.

Maher, B. (1974). Delusional thinking and perceptual disorder. *Journal of Individual Psychology, 30,* 98–113.

Maher, B., & Ross, J. S. (1984). Delusions. In H. E. Adams, & P. B. Sutker (Eds.), *Comprehensive handbook of psychopathology* (pp. 383–409). New York: Plenum Press.

Markham, R., & Hynes, L. (1993). The effect of vividness of imagery on reality monitoring. *Journal of Mental Imagery, 17*, 159–170.

Marr, D. (1982). *Vision.* San Francisco: Freeman.

Mayes, A. R. (1988). *Human organic memory disorders.* New York: Cambridge University Press.

McEntree, W. J., & Crook, T. H. (1990). Age associated memory impairment: A role for catecholamine. *Neuropsychology, 40*, 526–530.

McGeoch, J. A. (1932). Forgetting and the law of disuse. *Psychological Review, 39*, 352–370.

Metcalfe, J., Cottrell, G. W., & Mencl, W. E. (1992). Cognitive binding: A computational-modeling analysis of a distinction between implicit and explicit memory. *Journal of Cognitive Neuroscience, 4*, 289–298.

Milner, B. (1970). Memory and the medial temporal regions of the brain. In K. H. Pribram & D. E. Broadbent (Eds.), *Biology of memory* (pp. 29–50). New York: Academic Press.

Mishkin, M., Ungerleider, L. G., & Macko, K. A. (1983). Object vision and spatial vision: Two central pathways. *Trends in Neuroscience, 6*, 414–417.

Moscovitch, M. (1989). Confabulation and the frontal systems: Strategic versus associative retrieval in neuropsychological theories of memory. In I. H. L. Roediger & F. I. M. Craik (Eds.), *Varieties of memory and consciousness: Essays in honour of Endel Tulving* (pp. 133–160). Hillsdale, NJ: Lawrence Erlbaum Associates.

Moscovitch, M. (1992). Memory and working-with-memory: A component process model based on modules and central systems. *Journal of Cognitive Neuroscience, 4*, 257–267.

Moscovitch, M., Osimani, A., Wortzman, G., & Freedman, M. (1990). The dorsomedial nucleus of the thalamus, frontal-lobe function, and memory—A case report. *Journal of Clinical and Experimental Neuropsychology, 12*, 87.

Moscovitch, M., & Umilta, C. (1991). Conscious and nonconscious aspects of memory: A neuropsychological framework of modules and control systems. In R. G. Lister & H. J. Weingartner (Eds.), *Perspectives on cognitive neuroscience* (pp. 229–266). New York: Oxford University Press.

Multhaup, K. S. (1995). Aging, source, and decision criteria: When false fame errors do and do not occur. *Psychology and Aging, 10*, 492–497.

Multhaup, K. S., De Leonardis, D. M., Johnson, M. K., Brown, A. M., & Hashtroudi, S. (1996, April). *Source memory and eyewitness suggestibility in older adults.* Paper presented at the Sixth Biennial Cognitive Aging Conference, Atlanta, GA.

Nelson, K. (1993). The psychological and social origins of autobiographical memory. *Psychological Science, 4*, 7–14.

Nissen, M. J., & Bullemer, P. (1987). Attentional requirements of learning: Evidence from performance measures. *Cognitive Psychology, 19*, 1–32.

Norman, D. A., & Shallice, T. (1986). Attention to action: Willed and automatic control of behavior. In R. J. Davidson, G. E. Schwartz, & D. Shapiro (Eds.), *Consciousness and self-regulation* (Vol. 4, pp. 1–18). New York: Plenum.

O'Connor, M., Walbridge, M., Sandson, T., & Alexander, M. A. (1995). *Neuropsychological analysis of Capgras syndrome.* Manuscript submitted for publication.

O'Keefe, J., & Nadel, L. (1978). *The hippocampus as a cognitive map.* Oxford, England: Clarendon.

Parkin, A., Yeomans, J., & Bindschaedler, C. (1994). Further characterization of the executive memory impairment following frontal lobe lesions. *Brain and Cognition, 26*, 23–42.

Perky, C. W. (1910). An experimental study of imagination. *American Journal of Psychology, 21*, 422–452.

Poole, D. A., Lindsay, D. S., Memon, A., & Bull, R. (1995). Psychotherapy and the recovery of memories of childhood sexual abuse: U.S. and British practitioner's opinions, practices, and experiences. *Journal of Consulting and Clinical Psychology, 63*, 426–437.

Rabinowitz, J. C. (1989). Judgments of origin and generation effects: Comparisons between young and elderly adults. *Psychology and Aging, 4,* 259–268.

Raye, C. L., & Johnson, M. K. (1980). Reality monitoring vs. discriminating between external sources of memories. *Bulletin of the Psychonomic Society, 15,* 405–408.

Raye, C. L., Johnson, M. K., & Taylor, T. H. (1980). Is there something special about memory for internally generated information? *Memory & Cognition, 8,* 141–148.

Reinitz, M., Lammers, W., & Cochran, B. (1992). Memory-conjunction errors: Miscombination of stored stimulus features can produce illusions of memory. *Memory and Cognition, 20*(1), 1–11.

Reiser, B. J. (1986). The encoding and retrieval of memories of real-world experiences. In J. A. Galambos, R. P. Abelson, & J. B. Black (Eds.), *Knowledge structures* (pp. 71–99). Hillsdale, NJ: Lawrence Erlbaum Associates.

Riddoch, M. J., & Humphreys, G. W. (1987). Visual object processing in optic aphasia: A case of semantic access agnosia. *Cognitive Neuropsychology, 4,* 131–186.

Ross, M. (in press). Validating memories. In N. L. Stein, P. A. Ornstein, B. Tversky, & C. Brainerd (Eds.), *Memory for everyday and emotional events.* Mahwah, NJ: Lawrence Erlbaum Associates.

Rovee-Collier, C. (1990). The "memory system" of prelinguistic infants. In A. Diamond (Ed.), *The development and neural bases of higher cognitive functions* (Vol. 608, pp. 517–542). New York: New York Academy of Sciences.

Schacter, D. L. (1987). Memory, amnesia, and frontal lobe dysfunction. *Psychobiology, 15,* 21–36.

Schacter, D. L. (1992). Priming and multiple memory systems: Perceptual mechanisms of implicit memory. *Journal of Cognitive Neuroscience, 4,* 244–256.

Schacter, D. L., Kaszniak, A. W., Kihlstrom, J. F., & Valdiserri, M. (1991). The relation between source memory and aging. *Psychology and Aging, 6,* 559–568.

Schank, R. C., & Abelson, R. P. (1977). *Scripts, plans, goals, and understanding: An inquiry into human knowledge structures.* Hillsdale, NJ: Lawrence Erlbaum Associates.

Shimamura, A. P., Janowsky, J. S., & Squire, L. R. (1991). What is the role of frontal lobe damage in memory disorders? In H. S. Levin, H. M. Eisenberg, & A. L. Benton (Eds.), *Frontal lobe function and disorder* (pp. 173–195). New York: Oxford University Press.

Shimamura, A. P., & Squire, L. R. (1987). A neuropsychological study of fact memory and source amnesia. *Journal of Experimental Psychology: Learning, Memory, and Cognition, 13,* 464–473.

Spence, D. P. (1982). *Narrative truth and historical context: Meaning and interpretation in psychoanalysis.* New York: Norton.

Spencer, W. D., & Raz, N. (1995). Differential effects of aging on memory for content and context: A meta-analysis. *Psychology and Aging, 10,* 527–539.

Sperling, G. (1960). The information available in brief visual presentations. *Psychological Monographs, 74,* 1–29.

Springer, S., & Deutsch, G. (1985). *Left brain, right brain* (rev. ed.). New York: Freeman.

Squire, L. R. (1983). The hippocampus and the neuropsychology of memory. In W. Seifert (Ed.), *Neurobiology of the hippocampus* (pp. 491–511). New York: Academic Press.

Squire, L. R. (1987). *Memory and brain.* New York: Oxford University Press.

Stuss, D. T. (1991). Self, awareness and the frontal lobes: A neuropsychological perspective. In J. Strauss & G. R. Goethals (Eds.), *The self: Interdisciplinary approaches* (pp. 255–278). New York: Springer-Verlag.

Stuss, D. T., Alexander, M. P., Lieberman, A., & Levine, H. (1978). An extraordinary form of confabulation. *Neurology, 28,* 1166–1172.

Stuss, D. T., & Benson, D. F. (1986). *The frontal lobes.* New York: Raven.

Suengas, A. G., & Johnson, M. K. (1988). Qualitative effects of rehearsal on memories for perceived and imagined complex events. *Journal of Experimental Psychology: General, 117,* 377–389.

Tulving, E., Kapur, S., Craik, F., Moscovitch, M., & Houle, S. (1994). Hemispheric encoding/retrieval asymmetry in episodic memory: Positron emission tomography findings. *Proceedings of the National Academy of Sciences of the United States of America, 91,* 2016–2020.

Tulving, E., & Schacter, D. L. (1990). Priming and human memory systems. *Science, 247,* 301–306.

Tulving, E., & Thomson, D. M. (1973). Encoding specificity and retrieval processes in episodic memory. *Psychological Review, 80,* 352–373.

Weinberger, D. (1993). A connectionist approach to the prefrontal cortex. *Journal of Neuropsychiatry, 5,* 241–253.

Weiskrantz, L. (1986). *Blindsight.* Oxford, England: Clarendon.

Wilson, S. C., & Barber, T. X. (1983). The fantasy-prone personality: Implications for understanding imagery, hypnosis, and parapsychological phenomena. In A. A. Sheikh (Ed.), *Imagery: Current theory, research and application* (pp. 340–387). New York: Wiley.

Wilson, T. D., & Brekke, N. (1994). Mental contamination and mental correction: Unwanted influences. *Psychological Bulletin, 116,* 117–142.

Woodruff, D. S. (1982). Advances in the psychophysiology of aging. In F. I. M. Craik & S. Trehub (Eds.), *Aging and cognitive processes* (pp. 29–53). New York: Plenum.

Yantis, S., & Johnson, D. N. (1990). Mechanisms of attentional priority. *Journal of Experimental Psychology: Human Perception and Performance, 16,* 812–825.

Zaragoza, M. S., & Lane, S. M. (1994). Source misattributions and the suggestibility of eyewitness memory. *Journal of Experimental Psychology: Learning, Memory and Cognition, 20*(4), 934–945.

Zaragoza, M. S., & Muench, J. (1989, November). *Source confusion following exposure to misleading postevent information.* Paper presented at the 30th annual meeting of the Psychonomics Society, Atlanta, GA.

7

How Can We Be Sure? Using Truth Criteria to Validate Memories

Michael Ross
Tara K. MacDonald

Because memory is fallible, people sometimes report divergent recollections of the same events. Most people have recalled an incident with what they presumed to be complete accuracy, only to discover that another person recalls it differently. When presented with such discrepancies, people may attempt to evaluate the accuracy of each memory. Occasionally, these assessments have significant implications. Jury members may base their judgments of guilt or innocence on whether the plaintiff's or defendant's testimony is more compelling. At other times, assessments of memories' accuracy are less consequential; a husband and wife might debate whether they saw *The Way We Were* of *The Exorcist* on their first date 20 years ago.

What criteria do people use to appraise the accuracy of recollections? The standards may differ, depending on whether people attempt to establish if a person is lying or inadvertently misremembering an event. In some situations, people try to discern whether another person is telling the truth or purposefully lying. In other contexts, individuals examine whether they or others might be inadvertently misremembering an event. Jurors may well consider whether a witness is lying, but a wife is more likely to view her husband as forgetful, rather than deceitful, when his memory of their first date differs from hers.

In this chapter, we focus on inadvertent misremembering. We first discuss the recollection process and why people recall events differently. Second, we examine truth criteria—standards that individuals use to validate their own and other people's memories. Finally, we consider whether these criteria are reliable indicators of memory accuracy. The current debate over the accuracy of recovered memories is used as context for evaluating the usefulness of truth criteria.

THE RECOLLECTION PROCESS

To analyze the recollection process, it is convenient, albeit an oversimplification, to divide the act of remembering into three distinct stages: encoding, retrieval, and reporting of a memory.

Encoding

Suppose you try to remember a scene from a cocktail party. Your internal representation of the gathering is neither a precise copy of the event nor identical to other people's representations of the same affair. You are unlikely to reconstruct the party exactly as it happened because you failed to encode all aspects of the scene. In most everyday contexts, there is simply too much occurring in the environment for a person to take note of everything. Also, what you perceived would depend on your outlook, both physically (vantage point, lighting, etc.) and psychologically (e.g., your emotional state; see Stein, Trabasso, & Liwag, 1994). Third, it is unlikely that you transferred everything that you observed from short-term to long-term memory (people's names, clothing, etc.). Finally, your preexisting knowledge (e.g., of party manners or of people's personalities and relationships) would affect what you see and how you interpret and understand events (Bransford & Franks, 1971; Bruner & Goodman, 1947; Mead, 1929/1964; Spiro, 1977). Thus, every party-goer observes and encodes a somewhat different party (cf. Hastorf & Cantril, 1954).

Retrieval

Just as internal representations are not normally exact copies of external events, so, too, recollective experiences are not necessarily precise reproductions of the initial, internal representations in long-term memory. Both encoding and retrieval processes contribute to differences between recollections and initial representations. People's original encoding of events varies in strength and quality, depending, for example, on the importance and distinctiveness of the event. As a result, individuals forget some episodes more rapidly than others (Brewer, 1988, 1992; Johnson, Hashtroudi, & Lindsay, 1993; Moscovitch & Craik, 1976; Spiro, 1977).

During retrieval, people's current knowledge and beliefs influence their recollective experiences. Memories consistent with people's present knowledge are often more accessible than memories containing contradictory information. People also tend to interpret ambiguous memories as congruent with their current knowledge (Anderson & Pichert, 1978; Bartlett, 1932; Cantor & Mischel, 1977; Hastie, 1981; Markus, 1977; Mischel, Ebbesen, & Zeiss, 1976; Ross, 1989; Schank & Abelson, 1977; Snyder & Uranowitz, 1978; Spence, 1982; Taylor & Crocker, 1981). When individuals are unable to recall relevant information, they may guess at the past, using their present knowledge as a guide for inferring what must have occurred (Bellezza & Bower, 1981).

In addition, people's motivation for engaging in recall affects their retrieval of memories (Kunda, 1990; Ross & Buehler, 1994). Similar to present knowledge, people's goals and motives can influence the recollective experience by altering what individuals remember and how they interpret that information (Kunda, 1990; Ross & Buehler, 1994). For example, Santioso, Kunda, and Fong (1990) induced individuals to believe that extroversion is superior to introversion or vice versa. Later, individuals who favored extroversion more readily recalled engaging in extroverted behaviors than did those who preferred introversion.

Reporting

People's goals and motives also affect how they choose to describe their recollective experience to others. Even when people are not deliberately lying, they might not report an event exactly as they remember it. Sometimes people edit memories, leaving out or simplifying details so as not to bore or confuse their audience (Brown & Levinson, 1978; Cansler & Stiles, 1981; DePaulo & Coleman, 1986; Turnbull, 1992). At other times, rememberers alter their recollections to entertain or impress their listeners (Ross & Holmberg, 1990). Stories sometimes seem to take on a life of their own through repeated telling. There is research evidence that errors in earlier recollections tend to persist in subsequent reproductions (Neisser & Harsch, 1992; Roediger & McDermott, 1995; Loftus, 1988). Along these lines, a grandfather of the second author reminisces about how he could eat prodigious amounts of food as a young man and still remain thin. One story concerns the great number of pork chops he once devoured in a single sitting. Family members maintain that the number he allegedly consumed has increased over the years. Likely, even he no longer knows how many he actually ate.

In summary, people's memories are not carbon copies of the original episodes. Fortunately, people typically do not need to recall events exactly. Does it really matter how many pork chops grandpa ate so many years ago? It is more important that he has a story he likes telling and that his family enjoys hearing.

VALIDATING MEMORIES

Individuals often feel little need to verify their own or other people's accounts. Rather than subjecting their memories to extensive evaluation, individuals usually accept them uncritically (Ross, in press). Even people who recognize that their memory of an episode conflicts with someone else's tend to assume the validity of their own accounts (Ross, Karr, & Buehler, 1992). A belief in the accuracy of many of one's own recollections is probably important to mental well-being. People's sense of their identity is intricately bound to their personal memories.

In Western culture, individuals also assume the truthfulness of other people's accounts. Grice (1975) suggested that, in everyday conversation, listeners typically presume that others tell the truth. Social psychologists have reported dozens of experiments on the "correspondence bias" that indicate that people tend to accept another's behavior and words at face value (Gilbert & Malone, 1995). Even research participants who are informed that a speaker may deceive them are disposed to believe him or her (DePaulo, Stone, & Lassiter, 1985; Fleming, Darley, Hilton, & Kojetin, 1990; Krauss, 1981).

Occasionally, however, people are motivated to assess how accurately a recollection depicts some earlier occurrence. When people's memories conflict, rememberers and their audiences may be prompted to evaluate the accuracy of each recollection. People may also try to verify recollections that seem vague, incomplete, or unusual. People's tendency to seek verification presumably varies with the importance of accurate recall: Individuals may be more inclined to document memories in legal than in social contexts.

Suppose individuals are motivated to assess the truth of either their own or someone else's personal memory. How might they do so? If feasible, they may seek external verification of a memory. Dates, times, and other details of people's stories can sometimes be checked. The possibility of such verification is often lacking for personal memories, however, and people are forced to seek other standards for evaluating recollections. Research has revealed eight general criteria that people use to assess their own and other people's memories (Ross, in press). We will next describe these truth criteria and examine their validity.

TRUTH CRITERIA

Memory Qualities

People can assess the accuracy of memories by examining qualities of the recollections. A number of researchers have found that genuine memories are different from fantasized events or erroneous recollections. Actual memories contain more perceptual and contextual details, more information about subjective emotional states, as well as less information about cognitive operations than do fantasized episodes (Johnson, 1988; Johnson, Foley, Suengas, & Raye, 1988; Johnson et al., 1993; Johnson & Raye, 1981; Steller, 1988; Undeutsch, 1988). Schooler, Gerhard, and Loftus (1986) contrasted participants' verbal descriptions of an object they had seen to their descriptions of an object that had merely been suggested to them in a questionnaire. Genuine memories of the object contained more information about its sensory attributes. In contrast, suggested memories contained more references to cognitive processes, more references to why the object might have been present, and more verbal hedges. Dunning and Stern (1994) presented participants with a videotape of a theft, and subsequently asked them to identify the culprit from a photo lineup. Participants who made accurate identifications tended to report making their judgments through automatic processes (e.g., that the face of the thief just "popped out"). Participants who made inaccurate identifications were more likely to describe making their decisions on the basis of cognitive strategies (e.g., the process of elimination).

People are at least somewhat aware of the qualities that characterize genuine memories (e.g., Dunning & Stern, 1994, Study 5; Johnson et al., 1988, 1993; Schooler et al., 1986). Despite this intuitive knowledge, observers tend to differentiate genuine from false memories at only slightly above chance levels. Researchers have attempted to increase accuracy by training observers to distinguish genuine from false memories. Such efforts have met with limited success. Researchers have compared "enlightened" observers, who are explicitly told which cues to consider when making judgments, to "naive" observers, who are left to their own devices. The two groups do not differ when making assessments about genuine memories. When making judgments about false or suggested memories, enlightened observers tend to outperform naive observers at a level that is statistically significant, but not spectacular. Dunning and Stern (1994, Study 5) and Schooler et al. (1986, Experiment 4) found that enlightened observers were 10% more accurate than naive observers. Although useful, memory qualities do not appear to provide a definitive basis for evaluating the accuracy of recollections. The studies that compared the performance of enlightened to naive assessors all involved evaluations of other people's memories. It would be interesting to examine whether enlightened rememberers would more accurately judge the accuracy of their own recollections.

Memorability of Events

Individuals can examine the nature of the recalled event to assess the accuracy of a memory. People deem some events to be more memorable than others. Researchers who have examined people's ability to predict whether they will remember experimental stimuli report fairly high levels of predictive success (Brewer, 1996). These data suggest that people's theories of the memorableness of events may be reasonably accurate.

It is not always easy to specify which events will be retained, however. Certain episodes are memorable because they occur at a particular time or in a context that gives them special meaning. The same event may be memorable for some people and forgettable for others. For example, the two authors of this chapter apparently first met 4 years ago when the second author (Tara), a candidate for graduate school, was interviewed by the first author, a professor. Tara, on the one hand, can remember the interview in detail, or at least she thinks she can. She can recall vivid details of the conversation, where and when the interview took place, and especially a slip she made during the conversation that caused her a considerable amount of postinterview consternation. Mike, on the other hand, can recall nothing of the interview—not even the glaring error that Tara supposedly made.

Why might this be so? For Tara, the interview was a significant event that could potentially have a large impact on her career. In contrast, the interview was much less important to Mike. Consequently, Tara was probably more attentive to her words and actions during the interview than Mike. Also, Tara thought about the interview at length afterward, regretting her error. Thus, she probably devoted more study time to the interview than Mike. Tara has experienced only a few interviews of this type; she remembers each of these interviews as a distinct episode. For Mike, the interview was one of many with potential graduate students, so he might hold a generic memory for interviews with incoming students. As a result, he would find it difficult to recall the specific details of any particular interview (Neisser, 1981).

The interview, if it occurred, aroused considerably more anxiety in Tara than in Mike. There has been a great deal of research examining whether emotional arousal, particularly stress, enhances or decreases long-term memory of events. In a comprehensive review of the literature, Christianson (1992) found that arousal generally facilitated recall of the central aspects of events, but decreased accuracy for recall of peripheral details. However, the distinction between central and peripheral details is not always clear-cut, especially for real-world events. Perhaps people's intuitions incorporate the various factors that influence the memorability of events. This cannot be ascertained on the basis of available evidence. Further research on the issue is warranted.

Internal Consistency

It is often supposed that genuine memories are internally consistent (e.g., Johnson et al., 1993; Ross et al., 1992). Incoherence and internal contradiction seem to be good reasons for denying the reality of recollections. Ross et al. (1992) asked rememberers and their audiences to assess the accuracy of memories and explain their judgments. About 90% of rememberers and 50% of their audiences invoked an internal consistency criterion as one justification for their validity judgments.

Not all social observers agree, however, that internal consistency is a hallmark of valid memories. Well-told stories are coherent, but real life may not be: "Reality never makes sense. . . . Fiction has unity, fiction has style. Facts possess neither. In the raw, existence is always one damn thing after another. . . . " (Huxley, 1955, p. 9). Along these same lines, Steller (1988) suggested that false testimonies tend to be more coherent than true testimonies. Mead (1929/1964) noted that life is disorderly, but argued that people normally impose organization while recollecting the past.

In summary, the internal consistency criterion may have contradictory implications. On the one hand, incoherence and internal contradiction seem to provide a basis for rejecting the reality of recollections. On the other hand, high coherence may also render memories suspect. It is difficult to establish a priori where the cutoff points are: When is a memory sufficiently (in)coherent to be a believable depiction of an episode in a person's life?

Reliability

Assessors can consider whether a memory remains consistent over time, judging reliable memories to be more valid than recollections that change. Reliability does not guarantee validity, however. A person could describe an event incorrectly the first time and then continue to report it in the same false manner on subsequent occasions. (Neisser & Harsch, 1992; Roediger & McDermott, 1995; Schooler et al., 1988). However, it may seem that low reliability is strong evidence of a lack of validity. But what does low reliability invalidate? The first report? Later reports? All reports? Baddeley and Wilson (1986) interpreted a lack of reliability as evidence that their brain-injured patients confabulated their initial reports (and perhaps their subsequent descriptions) of an episode. In contrast, Neisser and Harsch (1992) did not question the first report of memories when later accounts were contradictory. Instead, they used the recall interval as a basis for assuming the validity of the first recall and the falsity of the second. Finally, Fivush (1993) found that low reliability does not necessarily invalidate any reports. She asked preschool children to recount the same episodes over a series of interviews. The children were markedly inconsistent: Only 10% of the information they recalled about an event on the second interview overlapped with what they recalled about that same episode on the first interview. Unreliability did not signal inaccuracy, however. About 90% of what the children recalled was deemed accurate by their parents.[1]

Congruence with Other Knowledge

Individuals may examine a memory to determine if the details agree with their previous experiences and general knowledge. Individuals frequently invoke this knowledge criterion to evaluate the accuracy of their own and other people's memories (Johnson et al., 1993; Ross et al., 1992; Steller, 1988; Undeutsch, 1988). The value of this standard depends primarily on the accuracy of the assessor's knowledge. At best, the usefulness of testing a memory against everyday knowledge is one-sided. People may be able to reject some reports as false (although they could be mistaken if their knowledge is fallacious), but they cannot know with certainty that a report is true simply because it is consistent with their everyday knowledge.

Consensus

Suppose that you and a family member have conflicting memories about a gathering that you both attended. You could assess whose memory is more accurate by surveying other people's recollections of the event. The consensus criterion is often applied in legal settings to evaluate the accounts of various witnesses. In simulated trials, mock jurors are more convinced by corroborated testimony than by unsubstantiated testimony (Duggan et al., 1989).

Consensus is no guarantee of accuracy, however. Agreement provides convincing evidence only if the observations are independent.

---

[1]We do not presume the accuracy of the parental reports.

When people share the same perspectives, they may be misled by agreement. In previous eras, people with similar vantage points and background knowledge believed that the sun rotated around a flat earth. Along the same lines, Platt (1980) observed that consensus among family members about events in their lives is no guarantee of validity. Family members may hold norms and values that differ from those evidenced by their neighbors or members of other socioeconomic classes.

Agreement is a particularly pernicious standard when people achieve it through selective consensus seeking. To bolster their beliefs in their memories, people can judiciously search out others who will affirm their recollections. Newman and Baumeister (1996) observed that people who report that they were abducted by aliens often join support groups or attend conferences where they share their experiences with others who suppose that they, too, were abductees. Such contact may increase people's faith in the accuracy of their abduction memories. Similarly, avoidance of contrary opinions may prevent people from reevaluating their memories and beliefs. In their book *When Prophecy Fails*, Festinger, Riecken, and Schachter (1956) described members of a doomsday group. These individuals believed that the leader of their cult was in contact with aliens who predicted the end of the world. Group members maintained increasingly exclusive contact with each other as their prophecies failed and their beliefs were ridiculed by outsiders.

Context of Recall

People use the circumstances in which the recall occurs as a basis for evaluating memories. Recollections reported in some contexts seem more believable than the same memories recounted in different contexts. We will concentrate on two contextual factors that have received considerable research attention from psychologists: the effects of leading questions and the effects of hypnosis on the accuracy of recall.

Interrogators may inadvertently lead people to fabricate their pasts. Rememberers sometimes alter their accounts of events when interrogators and therapists ask leading questions (Loftus, 1993; Ofshe, 1992). Compared with older children and adults, younger children appear to be particularly inclined to report false memories in response to leading questions (Ceci & Bruck, 1993; Poole, 1995). On the basis of such evidence, some psychologists have concluded that spontaneous recall is often more valid than recall that occurs in response to extensive probing (e.g., Ceci & Bruck, 1993; Loftus, 1993).

However, open-ended recall is not necessarily more accurate than recall prompted by questioning. Younger children tend to need questions and cues to provide detailed accounts of past events, even relatively recent episodes (Fivush, 1993). Moreover, contrary to the usual concern regarding leading questions, some authorities advocate their use in special circumstances. MacFarlane (1985) argued that leading questions help investigators gather accurate information from child witnesses in sexual abuse cases. Leading questions may encourage accurate reporting if witnesses remember an event well, but are reluctant to disclose it because of embarrassment, fear, and so forth.

There has also been much controversy about the accuracy of memories that are elicited through hypnosis. Early enthusiasm for the value of hypnosis has been replaced by growing skepticism. After reviewing studies examining the accuracy of hypnotically refreshed memory, Kihlstrom (in press) concluded that hypnosis may sometimes increase people's vulnerability to leading questions and reduce their ability to distinguish fantasy from reality. Newman and Baumeister (1996) came to the same conclusions in a review of memories of alien abductions that were generated under hypnosis.

There is little doubt that recall is affected by context. But once again, it is difficult to draw definitive conclusions about the conditions that promote accurate recall. In both research and real life, we ask rememberers questions because they do not necessarily provide us with the information we are looking for in their open-ended recall. Questions can inform as well as mislead. Hypnosis, too, is a double-edged sword. It facilitates the recall of both valid and false memories (Dywan & Bowers, 1983). Extensive probing and hypnosis provide reason to be concerned about the accuracy of memories, but are not sufficient bases for rejecting memories.

Source Characteristics

People sometimes base their judgments of memories on characteristics of the rememberer. Psychologists have investigated a number of traits that may predict accuracy of recall, including the rememberer's age, gender, expertise, character, and confidence in the accuracy of the recall. Do such source characteristics provide convincing evidence of the validity of memories?

Age has perhaps received more research attention than any other characteristic of rememberers. Psychologists studying eyewitness testimony have been particularly concerned with the accuracy of children's memories. There has been a lively debate concerning whether the testimony of young children is more or less trustworthy than that of adults. An emerging consensus seems to be that children are often quite accurate in their reports of the past, but that they are more susceptible than adults to leading questions (Ceci & Bruck, 1993; Poole, 1995).

Individuals at the other end of the age spectrum have also received close research scrutiny. There is a stereotype in Western culture that older people evidence a decline in memory ability (e.g., McFarland, Ross, & Giltrow, 1992; Rothbaum, 1983). The research evidence suggests that older people do experience increased difficulty remembering some types of information under some conditions. For example, older adults are less accurate at remembering contextual and sensoriperceptual information than younger adults (Burke & Light, 1981; Hashtroudi, Johnson, & Chrosniak, 1989). Other research has found little difference between older and younger adults in automatic aspects of information processing (e.g., familiarity judgments). However, older people are less able to engage in more effortful conscious processing (e.g., judgments about context; Craik & Byrd, 1982). In summary, the relationship between age and memory is sufficiently complex to defy sweeping generalizations.

Some psychologists have proposed that gender predicts the accuracy of people's recollections in certain content domains. William Stern, the originator of experimental research on eyewitness testimony, commented on the credibility of female witnesses in child sexual abuse cases. Accepting the cultural beliefs of his day, Stern deemed women to be untrustworthy witnesses in sexual abuse cases (Undeutsch, 1988). Stereotypes have changed, and people today would likely reject Stern's claims.

Surveys of the memory literature provide little evidence of gender differences in the accuracy of recall. Maccoby and Jacklin's (1974) review indicated that traditional tests of memory have generally failed to show systematic gender differences, although verbal memory may be better in females than in males. The research summarized by Maccoby and Jacklin was conducted primarily with children. Evidence from the adult memory literature is sparse. Tests for gender differences are typically not reported in published studies of memory (Ross & Holmberg, 1990). Researchers in the gerontology area have been somewhat more interested in gender differences in accuracy of recall, but the data are mixed (Ross & Holmberg, 1990). Some researchers report evidence favoring one or the other gender, and many report no differences.

Regardless of whether there are gender differences in the accuracy of recall, gender does influence people's assessments of the credibility of some memories. For example, Ross and Holmberg (1990) asked husbands and wives to evaluate the accuracy of each other's memories for various events in their relationship, such as their first date together. Both spouses rated the wives' memories as more accurate. Because Ross and Holmberg were unable to assess the validity of the couples' memories, it is unclear whether spouses' assessments reflected their experiences, gender stereotypes, or both.

Women may exhibit better memories for family histories if they possess greater expertise than men in the area of social relationships. Experts in domains such as chess, physics, and soccer possess detailed cognitive schemata that facilitate superior memory in their area of expertise (Charness, 1988). Conceivably, women may develop a more articulated and complex understanding of relationships than do men. Observations that can be related to such a well-differentiated memory structure are more likely to be recalled.

People also use their assessments of a rememberer's character as indicators of credibility (Undeutsch, 1988). Some individuals are deemed more trustworthy or believable than others. It may be useful to take these personal characteristics into account when deciding whether someone is lying. It is less likely that character is linked to misremembering episodes. Everyone inadvertently misremembers some episodes, and everyone also reports events accurately.

Besides considering rememberers' traits, audiences can scrutinize rememberers' behaviors for clues concerning the accuracy of their recollections. Rememberers' apparent confidence in their memories is a particularly important cue for observers. The higher the confidence, the more faith observers have in the memories (Ross, in press). Is confidence a compelling cue? The evidence is mixed: Some researchers report a strong relation (e.g., Brewer, 1988, 1996), and others report either no relation or a weak association (e.g., Neisser & Harsch, 1992; Wells, Lindsay, & Fergusson, 1979) between rememberers' confidence and the accuracy of their recall. In a meta-analysis of 35 studies of eyewitness testimony, Bothwell, Deffenbacher, and Brigham (1987) found that the average correlation between confidence and accuracy of face recognition was .25. The authors noted that the relationship between confidence and accuracy is higher under moderate arousal than under conditions of high arousal.

In summary, the evidence linking source characteristics to the accuracy of recall is mixed. Most attributes seem to provide, at best, moderate predictability. Even the facilitating effects of expertise are limited to certain constellations of stimuli. For example, the memory advantage of master chess players disappears when chess pieces are placed randomly on the board (Chase & Simon, 1973).

USING THE TRUTH CRITERIA

The truth criteria have considerable face validity, but offer no guarantee of success. If people apply these standards systematically and impartially, the criteria, singly or in combination, fail to provide a definitive basis for accepting or rejecting a specific recollection. Moreover, individuals do not tend to use these standards systematically. Rather, they focus on some criteria and ignore others (Ross & Newby, 1996). Sometimes a selective focus is dictated by circumstances. For example, consensus information may be unavailable or perhaps less readily obtainable than internal consistency or knowledge congruence information. At other times, people evoke standards that support their preferred position; they argue for the accuracy of specific memories by stressing the importance of criteria that support the validity of a recollection (e.g., memory quality) and deemphasizing standards (e.g., consensus) that would raise doubts. As is shown next, the selective use of truth criteria is well illustrated in the debate over recovered memories of abuse.

Truth Criteria and the Recovered Memories Controversy

In recent years, increasing numbers of adults have recovered memories of childhood abuse. They describe forgetting the abuse for long periods of time, and then remembering it. The recollection often surfaces in the context of therapy. Psychologists are currently debating whether memories of traumatic events such as abuse can be repressed and then recovered, and, if so, whether the recovered memories are likely to be accurate (e.g., Bowers & Farvolden, 1996; Kihlstrom, in press; Loftus, 1993; Spiegel & Scheflin, 1994).[2] The controversy extends beyond the psychological community. In the United States, judges are grappling with whether the scientific evidence for repression is sufficient to justify the introduction of recovered memories as evidence in criminal trials. As an example, here is Judge Hilary Caplan's assessment: "The court in no way is judging [the plaintiffs'] credibility, but their recollection. That did not meet the test of scientific reliability. . . . No empirical studies verify the existence of repressed memory. There is no way to test the validity of these memories" ("Recovered Memory Claim Denied," 1995, p. 9).

Although many psychologists and psychiatrists would applaud this judge's conclusion, many others would not (Bowers & Farvolden, 1996; Kihlstrom, in press). Clinicians often argue that it is difficult, perhaps impossible, to study repression using the standard scientific tools of

---

[2]To clarify, the controversy does not concern whether child abuse occurs with distressing frequency. It does. Nor does the controversy concern all memories for abuse. Rather, the debate concerns the validity of memories that have been forgotten (repressed) and that subsequently "surface" years later, often while the rememberer is in therapy.

experimental psychologists, and that the clinical evidence in favor of repression is strong (Bowers & Farvolden, 1996; Terr, 1994). Some advocates of repression assert that recovered memories are almost always accurate (e.g., Terr, 1994). Other advocates hold that recovered memories can be true or false (Bowers & Farvolden, 1996).

We are not prepared to reject the possibility of recovered memories of abuse. In everyday life, people often forget something (e.g., a name, a shopping list) and subsequently recall it accurately. Such reminiscence effects have also been revealed in laboratory studies of list learning (Brown, 1923; Madigan, 1976). Of course, there are large differences between forgetting a name for a relatively short time and not remembering for many years repeated instances of sexual abuse. Nonetheless, the reminiscence phenomenon suggests that people could potentially recall forgotten aspects of their distant pasts. However, there is no reason to suppose that such recall is inevitably accurate. Similar to other memories, recovered memories are susceptible to suggestion, misinterpretation, and so forth.

If one adopts the conservative view that some recovered memories are genuine and some are false, one is then left with the issue of deciding which are which. In this sense, the problem is no different from determining the truth or falsity of other memories. The difficulty of the decision is exacerbated, however, by the long gap in time between the alleged event and the recovery of the memory of that event. With increasing time, the feasibility of obtaining external verification, such as physical evidence of abuse, decreases. It thus becomes necessary to rely on truth criteria to establish the truth or falsity of recovered memories. What can truth criteria reveal about the validity of these recollections?

Some (although by no means all) recovered memories of abuse are reported with considerable sensory, perceptual, and emotional vividness. Such memory qualities provide rememberers and their audiences with seemingly powerful evidence that the abuse occurred. Vivid memories can be misleading, however. In particular, people may mistake the source of their recollections, confusing an episode they read, saw, heard about, or imagined for an episode that they experienced (Johnson, 1988; Loftus, 1993; Newman & Baumeister, 1996; Ross, in press). As noted earlier, memory qualities do not provide a definitive basis for distinguishing false memories from genuine recollections.

The context of the recall may provide evidence of the validity of abuse memories. Many therapists suppose that repressed memories of childhood trauma cause psychological problems, such as depression and eating disorders. In the context of therapy, clinicians who hold this belief may probe their clients' memories for evidence of repressed abuse (Kihlstrom, in press). These therapists may implicitly or explicitly suggest to their patients that they were victimized by childhood sexual abuse. Also, that many (although by no means all) memories of abuse are recovered under hypnosis further complicates the issue. With the right hypnotherapist, some patients are led to recall past lives or alien abductions (Bowers & Farvolden, 1996; Kihlstrom, in press; Newman & Baumeister, 1996). If, as is presumed, such memories are false, then why not be skeptical about abuse memories that are generated in similar circumstances?

Many lay people and therapists would reject this pessimistic conclusion about the impact of hypnosis on recall. Lay people may use the fact that abuse memories are recovered under hypnosis as support for the validity of the recollections. There is widespread belief that hypnosis helps people unlock memories from their past (Loftus & Loftus, 1980; Yapko, 1992). Also, one can agree that incompetent or misguided therapists can misuse hypnosis to yield false memories, while arguing that well-qualified therapists can use hypnosis to enhance accurate recall. Indeed, the research evidence shows that hypnosis can facilitate the recall of genuine as well as false memories (Dywan & Bowers, 1983).

The knowledge congruence criterion may be particularly applicable to recovered memories of abuse. It is now a common belief among psychologists and lay people that childhood trauma, such as sexual abuse, can decrease psychological well-being later in life. Adults who experience problems of adjustment may seek therapy or read self-help books, where they encounter the theory that childhood abuse and its repression may explain their current distress. They may then disregard other possible sources of their difficulties. They may also overestimate the strength of the connection between childhood abuse and subsequent mental health. Not all victims of child abuse experience psychological problems in adulthood (Bowers & Farvolden, 1996).

A review of the abuse literature suggests the importance of the social consensus criterion. In many cases, the alleged perpetrators maintain their innocence, reacting to the accusations of abuse with apparent surprise and outrage. Although there are often no witnesses to the alleged abuse, the supposed perpetrators and victims can still gain backing from others. Individuals can choose their audiences selectively, avoiding those who do not validate their memories. Thousands of parents who have been accused of abuse have joined the False Memory Syndrome Foundation, whose meetings and newsletters reinforce parents' beliefs in their own innocence. People who come to believe that they were abused as children may withdraw from their families, which prevents those who are charged with abuse from challenging these accusations (Kihlstrom, in press). Indeed, therapists sometimes encourage their clients to avoid contact with those who do not support the memories of abuse. Spiegel and Scheflin (1994) cited a case where parents of a patient successfully sued a therapist for instructing the patient to break contact with her parents if they did not accept her memory of abuse.

As this brief review indicates, the recovered memory domain provides a testing ground for various truth criteria. The evidence suggests that people use the standards selectively, and that the criteria do not provide a definitive basis for establishing the validity of specific recollections.

ON DISTINGUISHING FACT FROM FICTION
IN EVERYDAY LIFE

There is little evidence that people typically walk around entirely confused or misguided about their pasts. How do people function effectively in everyday life if they lack the tools to differentiate fact from fiction? There are several answers to this question. First, most people lead structured, repetitive lives. Individuals can readily construct at least the gist of many past experiences because the episodes are repeated and do not differ greatly from current events.

Also, as Mead (1929/1964) noted, individuals' constructions of the past are rule-governed, and usually not flights of fantasy. People's portrayals of previous episodes are constrained by other past occurrences, present events, and projections of future lines of action. Mead's analysis of the "implied objective past" is illustrative. Behavioral realities of the present lead one to conclude that certain events must have happened in the past. For example, if one is in an office in the psychology building, one must have arisen from bed and transported oneself to the university. Individuals are confident of their own or other people's memories to the extent that the recollections connect in a believable way to memories of other previous episodes and to present realities.

As well, fact and fiction often coexist in autobiographical memory. Many recollections are both true and false, as Neisser (1981) documented in his analysis of John Dean's memory. Fortunately, it does not normally matter that people tend to blend fact and fiction. Although John Dean exaggerated his own importance and misreported dates, times, as well as other particulars, he did get many important details correct. He managed to present the gist of his conversations with President Nixon. Generally, it serves people's purposes well to recall the gist or theme of past episodes. To return to an earlier example, the theme of Tara's grandfather's story is that he used to overeat without gaining weight. The pork chop tale is simply an amusing anecdote that serves to illustrate his thesis. Most of the time, people are probably fortunate not to have the equivalent of an airplane's black box in their heads. Psychologically, it is often to their advantage to use and adapt the past for their current purposes.

This same flexibility can pose a challenge, however, to individuals interested in assessing the validity of people's memories. The truth criteria that individuals standardly employ are useful, but not definitive, standards. Sometimes people simply cannot know which of two contrasting accounts of the past is valid, or whether both are partially accurate. The truth criteria help individuals make educated guesses, and that is often the best they can do when external verification of the recollections is impossible. However, people can improve the quality of their inferences by using the criteria in an even-handed fashion. Individuals are most likely to deceive themselves when they selectively employ the standards to justify their preferred views of reality.

ACKNOWLEDGMENTS

Preparation of this chapter was supported by a research grant and a doctoral fellowship from the Social Sciences and Humanities Research Council of Canada.

REFERENCES

Anderson, R. C., & Pichert, J. W. (1978). Recall of previously unrecallable information following a shift in perspective. *Journal of Verbal Learning and Verbal Behavior, 17*, 1–12.

Baddeley, A., & Wilson, B. (1986). Amnesia, autobiographical memory, and confabulation. In D. C. Rubin (Ed.), *Autobiographical memory* (pp. 225–252). New York: Cambridge University Press.

Bartlett, F. C. (1932). *Remembering: A study in experimental and social psychology.* London: Cambridge University Press.

Bellezza, F. S., & Bower, G. H. (1981). Person stereotypes and memory for people. *Journal of Personality and Social Psychology, 41*, 856–865.

Bothwell, R., Deffenbacher, K., & Brigham, J. (1987). Correlation of eyewitness accuracy and confidence: Optimality hypothesis revised. *Journal of Applied Psychology, 72*, 691–695.

Bowers, K. S., & Farvolden, P. (1996). Revisiting a century-old Freudian slip—from suggestion disavowed to the truth repressed. *Psychological Bulletin, 119*, 355–380.

Bransford, J. D., & Franks, J. J. (1971). The abstraction of linguistic ideas. *Cognitive Psychology, 2*, 331–350.

Brewer, W. F. (1988). Memory for randomly sampled autobiographical events. In U. Neisser & E. Winograd (Eds.), *Remembering reconsidered: Ecological and traditional approaches to the study of memory* (pp. 21–90). New York: Cambridge University Press.

Brewer, W. F. (1992). The theoretical and empirical status of the flashbulb memory hypothesis. In E. Winograd & U. Neisser (Eds.), *Affect and accuracy in recall: Studies of "flashbulb" memories* (pp. 274–305). New York: Cambridge University Press.

Brewer, W. F. (1996). What is recollective memory? In D. C. Rubin (Ed.), *Remembering our past: Studies in autobiographical memory* (pp. 19–66). Cambridge, England: Cambridge University Press.

Brown, P., & Levinson, S. (1978). Universals in language use: Politeness phenomena. In E. Goody (Ed.), *Question and politeness* (pp. 56–310). Cambridge, England: Cambridge University Press.

Brown, W. (1923). To what extent is memory measured by a single recall? *Journal of Experimental Psychology, 6,* 337–382.

Bruner, J. S., & Goodman, C. C. (1947). Value and need as organizing factors in perception. *Journal of Abnormal and Social Psychology, 42,* 33–44.

Burke, D. M., & Light, L. L. (1981). Memory and aging: The role of retrieval processes. *Psychological Bulletin, 90,* 513–546.

Cansler, D., & Stiles, W. (1981). Relative status and interpersonal presumptuousness. *Journal of Experimental Social Psychology, 17,* 459–471.

Cantor, N., & Mischel, W. (1977). Traits as prototypes: Effects on recognition memory. *Journal of Personality and Social Psychology, 35,* 38–48.

Ceci, S. J., & Bruck, M. (1993). Suggestibility of the child witness: A historical review and synthesis. *Psychological Bulletin, 11,* 403–439.

Chase, W. G., & Simon, H. A. (1973). Perception in chess. *Cognitive Psychology, 4,* 55–81.

Charness, N. (1988). Expertise in chess, music, and physics: A cognitive perspective. In L. Obler & D. Fein (Eds.), *The exceptional brain* (pp. 399–426). New York: Guilford.

Christianson, S. (1992). *The handbook of emotion and memory: Research and theory.* Hillsdale, NJ: Lawrence Erlbaum Associates.

Craik, F. I. M., & Byrd, M. (1982). Aging and cognitive deficits: The role of attentional resources. In F. I. M. Craik & S. Trehub (Eds.), *Aging and cognitive processes* (pp. 95–112). New York: Plenum.

DePaulo, B., & Coleman, L. (1986). Talking to children, foreigners, and retarded adults. *Journal of Personality and Social Psychology, 51,* 945–959.

DePaulo, B. M., Stone, J. I., & Lassiter, G. D. (1985). Deceiving and detecting deceit. In B. R. Schlenker (Ed.), *The self and social life* (pp. 323–370). New York: McGraw-Hill.

Duggan, L. M. III, Aubrey, M., Doherty, E., Isquith, P., Levine, M., & Scheiner, J. (1989). The credibility of children as witnesses in a simulated child sexual abuse trial. In S. J. Ceci, D. F. Ross, & M. P. Toglia (Eds.), *Perspectives on children's testimony* (pp. 71–99). New York: Springer-Verlag.

Dunning, D., & Stern, L. B. (1994). Distinguishing accurate from inaccurate eyewitness identifications via inquiries about decision processes. *Journal of Personality and Social Psychology, 67,* 818–835.

Dywan, J., & Bowers, K. S. (1983). The use of hypnosis to enhance recall. *Science, 222,* 184–185.

Festinger, L., Riecken, H. W., & Schachter, S. (1956). *When prophecy fails.* Minneapolis: University of Minnesota Press.

Fivush, R. (1993). Developmental perspectives on autobiographical recall. In G. S. Goodman & B. L. Bottoms (Eds.), *Child victims, child witnesses* (pp. 1–24). New York: Guilford.

Fleming, J. H., Darley, J. M., Hilton, J. L., & Kojetin, B. A. (1990). Multiple audience problem: A strategic communication perspective on social perception. *Journal of Personality and Social Psychology, 58,* 593–609.

Gilbert, D. T., & Malone, P. S. (1995). The correspondence bias. *Psychological Bulletin, 117,* 21–38.

Grice, H. P. (1975). Logic and conversation. In P. Cole & J. Morgan (Eds.), *Syntax and semantics: Vol. 3. Speech acts* (pp. 41–58). New York: Academic Press.

Hashtroudi, S., Johnson, M. K., & Chrosniak, L. D. (1989). Aging and source monitoring. *Psychology and Aging, 4,* 106–112.

Hastie, R. (1981). Schematic principles in human memory. In E. T. Higgins, C. P. Herman, & M. P. Zanna (Eds.), *The Ontario Symposium: Vol. 1. Social cognition* (pp. 39–88). Hillsdale, NJ: Lawrence Erlbaum Associates.

Hastorf, A., & Cantril, H. (1954). They saw a game: A case study. *Journal of Abnormal and Social Psychology, 57,* 315–320.

Huxley, A. (1955). *The genius and the goddess.* New York: Harper.

Johnson, M. K. (1988). Reality monitoring: An experimental phenomenological approach. *Journal of Experimental Psychology: General, 117,* 390–394.

Johnson, M. K., Foley, M. A., Suengas, A. G., & Raye, C. L. (1988). Phenomenal characteristics of memories for perceived and imagined autobiographical events. *Journal of Experimental Psychology: General, 117,* 371–376.

Johnson, M. K., Hashtroudi, S., & Lindsay, D. S. (1993). Source monitoring. *Psychological Bulletin, 114,* 3–28.

Johnson, M. K., & Raye, C. L. (1981). Reality monitoring. *Psychological Review, 88,* 67–85.

Kihlstrom, J. F. (in press). Exhumed memory. In S. J. Lynn & N. P. Spanos (Eds.), *Truth in memory.* New York: Guilford.

Krauss, R. M. (1981). Impression formation, impression management, and nonverbal behaviors. In E. T. Higgins, C. P. Herman, & M. P. Zanna (Eds.), *The Ontario Symposium: Vol. 1. Social cognition* (pp. 323–341). Hillsdale, NJ: Lawrence Erlbaum Associates.

Kunda, Z. (1990). The case for motivated reasoning. *Psychological Bulletin, 108,* 480–498.

Loftus, E. F. (1993). The reality of repressed memories. *American Psychologist, 48,* 518–537.

Loftus, E. F., & Loftus, G. R. (1980). On the permanence of stored information in the human brain. *American Psychologist, 35,* 409–420.

Maccoby, E. E., & Jacklin, C. N. (1974). *The psychology of sex differences.* Stanford, CA: Stanford University Press.

MacFarlane, K. (1985). Diagnostic evaluations and the use of videotapes in child sexual abuse cases. *Miami Law Review, 40,* 135–155.

Madigan, S. A. (1976). Reminiscence and item recovery in free recall. *Memory and Cognition, 4,* 233–236.

Markus, H. (1977). Self-schemata and processing information about the self. *Journal of Personality and Social Psychology, 35,* 63–78.

McFarland, C., Ross, M., & Giltrow, M. (1992). Biased recollections in older adults: The role of implicit theories of aging. *Journal of Personality and Social Psychology, 62,* 837–850.

Mead, G. H. (1964). The nature of the past. In A. J. Reck (Ed.), *Selective writings: George Herbert Mead* (pp. 345–354). Chicago: University of Chicago Press. (Original work published 1929)

Mischel, W., Ebbesen, E. B., & Zeiss, A. M. (1976). Determinants of selective memory about the self. *Journal of Consulting and Clinical Psychology, 1,* 92–103.

Moscovitch, M., & Craik, F. I. M. (1976). Depth of processing, retrieval cues, and uniqueness of encoding as factors in recall. *Journal of Verbal Learning and Verbal Behavior, 15,* 447–468.

Neisser, U. (1981). John Dean's memory: A case study. *Cognition, 9,* 1–22.

Neisser, U., & Harsch, N. (1992). Phantom flashbulbs: False recollections of hearing the news about Challenger. In E. Winograd & U. Neisser (Eds.), *Affect and accuracy in recall: Studies of "flashbulb" memories* (pp. 9–31). New York: Cambridge University Press.

Newman, L. S., & Baumeister, R. F. (1996). Toward an explanation of the UFO abduction phenomenon: Hypnotic elaboration, extraterrestrial sadomasochism, and spurious memories. *Psychological Inquiry, 7,* 99–126.

Ofshe, R. J. (1992). Inadvertent hypnosis during interrogation: False confession due to dissociative state; misidentified multiple personality, and the satanic cult hypothesis. *International Journal of Clinical and Experimental Hypnosis, 40,* 125–156.

Platt, S. (1980). On establishing the validity of "objective" data: Can we rely on cross-interview agreement? *Psychological Medicine, 10,* 573–581.

Poole, D. A. (1995, May). Repeated questioning and the child witness: A reevaluation. In F. J. Morrison (Chair), *Children's memory: Implications for testimony.* Symposium conducted at the 67th annual meeting of the Midwestern Psychological Association, Chicago, Illinois.

Recovered memory claim denied in sex abuse case. (1995, June). *False Memory Foundation Newsletter, 4,* 9. (Original citation: *The Baltimore Sun,* May 6, 1995)

Roediger, H. L. III, & McDermott, K. B. (1995). Creating false memories: Remembering words not presented in lists. *Journal of Experimental Psychology: Learning, Memory, and Cognition, 21,* 803–814.

Ross, M. (1989). Relation of implicit theories to the construction of personal histories. *Psychological Review, 96,* 341–357.

Ross, M. (in press). Validating memories. In N. L. Stein, P. A. Ornstein, B. Tversky, & C. Brainerd (Eds.), *Memory for everyday and emotional events.* Mahwah, NJ: Lawrence Erlbaum Associates.

Ross, M., & Buehler, R. (1994). Creative remembering. In U. Neisser & R. Fivush (Eds.), *The remembering self* (pp. 205–235). New York: Cambridge University Press.

Ross, M., & Holmberg, D. (1990). Recounting the past: Gender differences in the recall of events in the history of a close relationship. In J. M. Olson & M. P. Zanna (Eds.), *The Ontario Symposium: Vol. 6. Self-inference processes* (pp. 135–152). Hillsdale, NJ: Lawrence Erlbaum Associates.

Ross, M., Karr, J. W., & Buehler, R. (1992). *Assessing the accuracy of conflicting autobiographical memories.* Unpublished manuscript, University of Waterloo, Ontario, Canada.

Ross, M., & Newby, I. R. (1996). Distinguishing memory from fantasy. *Psychological Inquiry, 7,* 173–177.

Rothbaum, F. (1983). Aging and age stereotypes. *Social Cognition, 2,* 171–184.

Santioso, R., Kunda, Z., & Fong, G. T. (1990). Motivated recruitment of autobiographical memories. *Journal of Personality and Social Psychology, 59,* 229–241.

Schank, R. C., & Abelson, R. P. (1977). *Scripts, plans, goals and understanding.* Hillsdale, NJ: Lawrence Erlbaum Associates.

Schooler, J. W., Foster, A. F., & Loftus, E. F. (1988). Some deleterious consequences of the act of recollection. *Memory & Cognition, 16,* 243–251.

Schooler, J. W., Gerhard, D., & Loftus, E. F. (1986). Qualities of the unreal. *Journal of Personality and Social Psychology, 12,* 171–181.

Snyder, M., & Uranowitz, S. M. (1978). Reconstructing the past: Some cognitive consequences of person perception. *Journal of Personality and Social Psychology, 36,* 941–950.

Spence, D. P. (1982). *Narrative truth and historical truth: Meaning and interpretation in psychoanalysis.* New York: Norton.

Spiegel, D., & Scheflin, A. W. (1994). Dissociated or fabricated? Psychiatric aspects of repressed memory in criminal and civil cases. *International Journal of Clinical and Experimental Hypnosis, 42,* 411–432.

Spiro, R. J. (1977). Remembering information from text: Theoretical and empirical issues concerning the "state of schema" reconstruction hypothesis. In R. C. Anderson, R. J. Spiro, & W. E. Montague (Eds.), *Schooling and the acquisition of knowledge* (pp. 137–165). Hillsdale, NJ: Lawrence Erlbaum Associates.

Stein, N. L., Trabasso, T., & Liwag, M. (1994). The rashomon phenomenon: Personal frames and future oriented appraisals in memory for emotional events. In M. Haith (Ed.), *Future-oriented processes* (pp. 409–435). Chicago: University of Chicago Press.

Steller, M. (1988). Recent developments in statement analysis. In J. C. Yuille (Ed.), *Credibility assessment* (pp. 135–154). The Netherlands: Kluwer.

Stern, W. (1910). Abstracts of lectures on the psychology of testimony and on the study of individuality. *American Journal of Psychology, 21,* 270–282.

Taylor, S. E., & Crocker, J. (1981). Schematic bases of social information processing. In E. T. Higgins, C. P. Herman, & M. P. Zanna (Eds.), *The Ontario Symposium: Vol. 1. Social cognition* (pp. 89–134). Hillsdale, NJ: Lawrence Erlbaum Associates.

Terr, L. (1994). *Unchained memories.* New York: Basic Books.

Turnbull, W. (1992). A conversation approach to explanation, with emphasis on politeness and accounting. In M. L. McLaughlin, M. J. Cody, & S. J. Read (Eds.), *Explaining one's self to others: Reason-giving in a social context* (pp. 105–129). Hillsdale, NJ: Lawrence Erlbaum Associates.

Undeutsch, U. (1988). The development of statement reality analysis. In J. C. Yuille (Ed.), *Credibility assessment* (pp. 101–120). The Netherlands: Kluwer.

Wells, G. L., Lindsay, R. C., & Fergusson, T. J. (1979). Accuracy, confidence, and juror perceptions in eyewitness identification. *Journal of Applied Psychology, 64,* 440–448.

Yapko, M. D. (1992). *Suggestions of abuse.* New York: Simon & Schuster.

8

The Single-Mindedness and Isolation of Dreams

Allan Rechtschaffen

The most noted psychological properties of dreams—their bizarreness and their meaningfulness or symbolic value—are neither unique to nor even remarkably distinctive of dreaming. Studies of large dream samples (Snyder, Karacan, Tharp, & Scott, 1968; Dorus, Dorus, & Rechtschaffen, 1971) reveal that relatively few dreams are very bizarre, which suggests that dreams have a reputation for bizarreness because bizarre dreams are most recalled and savored. Also, artists or even common daydreamers can create images and plots as wild as the strangest dreams. Meaningfulness is certainly not restricted to dreams. Most waking thought or behavior can be interpreted, correctly or incorrectly, as having a significance beyond immediate appearances. Indeed, one of Freud's major ideas was to identify the similarities between the psychopathology of everyday life and the psychopathology of everynight life.

The intent here is not to begrudge the attention to bizarreness and meaning; many dreams are more bizarre and symbolic than most waking thought. Rather, this chapter contrasts this attention to the scant notice given to another psychological property, which may be more distinctive of dreaming and in some ways more remarkable. I call this property the *single-mindedness* of dreams. This chapter lays no claim to its discovery; as we shall see, implicitly people accept it so well that they notice with surprise only the rare exceptions. My thoughts about single-mindedness come mostly from observations of my own dreams.

By "single-mindedness" of dreams, I mean the strong tendency for a single train of related thoughts and images to persist over extended periods without disruption or competition from other simultaneous thoughts

This chapter is reprinted from *Sleep, 1,* pp. 97–109. Copyright © 1978, *Sleep.* Reprinted with permission.

and images. It may never be determined whether more than one thought or image can occupy a mind at once. How can one hope to distinguish simultaneous thoughts from thoughts separated by indiscriminably short intervals? Nevertheless, in spontaneous waking mentation, there is, at the very least, such a rapid fluctuation of thoughts and images that phenomenologically they may be considered simultaneous. By comparison, several features of dreams reveal their relative single-mindedness.[1]

NONREFLECTIVENESS

Waking consciousness generally contains at least two prevalent streams. One stream contains "voluntary" mental productions, thoughts and images that "pop" into people's head, and sense impressions. The other is a reflective or evaluative stream, which seemingly monitors the first and places it in some perspective. The reflective stream seems to judge whether the thoughts or images are integral to the mental task of the moment or irrelevant intrusions from a separate part of the mind— whether the thoughts are deliberate, voluntary mental productions, or spontaneous, uncontrolled thoughts—or whether the images come from the external world or from within.

In dreams, the reflective stream of consciousness is drastically attenuated. While people dream, they are usually unaware that they are lying in bed, unaware that the images before them are hallucinatory, and unaware that they are dreaming. In one study from our laboratory (Zimmerman, 1970), subjects were asked, upon being awakened from rapid eye movement (REM) periods, whether they had been aware during the dream that they were lying in bed, and whether they had been aware that they were observing the contents of their own minds rather than the "real world." The answers to both questions were "no" approximately 90% of the time.[2] My own opinion, although I could not prove it, is that even these figures overestimate reflectiveness in dreams, which is exaggerated by poor recall, a failure to fully comprehend the questions during nocturnal awakenings, and a confusion between the dream experience and mental experiences during the process of awakening.

More recently, two subjects selected from a larger pool of subjects

---

[1]Unless specified otherwise, this chapter refers to *manifest* dream content only.

[2]The prevalence of nonreflectiveness contrasts interestingly with the paucity of bizarreness in the REM reports of Zimmerman's subjects. Independent judges made ratings of how distorted or fantastic the dream content was on a scale of 1–6, with the lower score indicating the most distortion. For a group of 16 "light sleepers," the mean distortion rating was only 4.59; for the 16 "deep sleepers," the mean rating was only 4.69. Clearly, nonreflectiveness was much more of a characteristic feature of the dream mentation than bizarreness.

were studied. These subjects were chosen because they were bright, verbally articulate, awakened quickly, and reported dream content in great detail. In only 4 (2.4%) of 168 REM period awakenings that yielded dream recall did these two subjects report any awareness that they were dreaming during the dream.[3] Even in these four reports, the reflective awareness was only obtained for portions of the dream, and was not continuous for the entire dream experience.

The failure to recognize a dream as a dream while it is in progress is rather remarkable; it defies the rules of reinforcement and discrimination learning. How many times could people have avoided the agony of bad dreams had they realized it was "only a dream" at the time? How many times have people awakened from a dream and recognized immediately that it was "only a dream"? Despite these dream–reality discriminations, and despite the reinforcement people get for making the discrimination, people seem almost entirely incapable of making the discrimination while they are dreaming.

Although the previous data indicate a massive failure of reflective awareness during dreaming, the distinction from waking mentation is certainly not absolute. Fragmentary dreamlike experiences that lack reflective awareness do occur during wakefulness (Foulkes & Fleisher, 1975; Foulkes & Scott, 1973; Foulkes & Vogel, 1965), although at a substantially lower rate than during nocturnal dreaming. In the study of Foulkes and Fleisher, approximately 15% of reports of spontaneous mentation elicited from awake subjects would unambiguously fit our concept of nonreflectiveness because the subjects reported that they were not controlling their thoughts, that they were unaware of being in the laboratory, and that the mentation was hallucinatory. In an additional 22% of the waking reports, subjects were nonreflective in the sense of having lost awareness of being in the laboratory, but the mentation was nonhallucinatory (i.e., the subjects were "lost in thought"), and the subjects may or may not have been controlling their thoughts. (Volitional control, at least phenomenologically, immediately implies reflectiveness—i.e., one part of the mind tells another part where to go, observes its progress, and corrects its deviations.)

Not only is the incidence of nonreflectiveness much lower during wakefulness than during nocturnal dreaming, but the Foulkes and Fleisher report also indicates that waking nonreflectiveness tends to be momentary and interspersed with reflective evaluation. The extended periods of nonreflectiveness that characterize most dreaming is rarely achieved during wakefulness.

It is incorrect to imply that cognitive activity per se is absent from dreams. Molinari and Foulkes (1969) have shown that much dream activ-

---

[3]I am grateful to Donald L. Bliwise for collecting these data.

ity is in the nature of judging, comparing, evaluating, and so on. For the most part, however, such cognitive activities are part of the prevailing dream story, not a separate stream of reflective consciousness that tells people that it is "only a story."

Almost any mention of the nonreflectiveness of dreams is quickly protested by a report of a dream or several dreams in which the sleeper was aware that he or she was dreaming and sometimes able to control the dream content. Such dreams do occur—they are called *lucid dreams*—and some people have them more than others. The occurrence of a lucid dream is usually greeted with surprise, and sometimes delight, which shows how well people implicitly accept the more characteristic nonreflectiveness of dreams.

The infrequency of lucid dreams is illustrated by our own frustrated attempt to study them in the laboratory simultaneously with physiological monitoring. Frequently, we obtain subjects for sleep and dream studies by placing an advertisement in the university's student newspaper. Usually about 100 persons respond to such an advertisement. To obtain a sample of lucid dreamers, we advertised for "subjects who *regularly* know they are dreaming *while* they are dreaming." Only four persons responded to this advertisement. Interviews with the four indicated that two of them had misunderstood the advertisement and were not really lucid dreamers. The remaining two were studied for two nights each in the laboratory, where one produced six REM dream reports and the other produced seven. In only one of the reports of each of these subjects was there some indication of lucidity; in both cases, this consisted of fragmentary points of awareness that they were dreaming, rather than a pervasive awareness of dreaming throughout the dream.

It has often been asked why people occasionally have lucid dreams. It is a peculiar question. The question should be, why are not all dreams lucid, as is most of conscious experience? Yet occasional lucidity in dreams is useful as a demonstration of what most dreams are not. Only when we can see the possibility of the lucid dream do we fully realize what a massively nonreflective state dreaming usually is—what a truly distinctive psychological experience it is. In fact, there is no other single state short of severe and chronic psychosis in which there is such a persistent, massive, regular loss of reflectiveness. Herein may lie the most distinctive psychological characteristic of dreaming. People can all have peculiar thoughts and images dozens of times a day, and these may symbolically reflect motivational forces of which people are not aware. This is like dreaming. But it is only during dreaming that most people regularly lose so completely the road map of their own consciousness.

One might argue that perhaps too much has been made of nonreflectiveness in dreams—that the paucity of reflective awareness in dreams is simply secondary to the hallucinatory quality of the dreams. Because dreams cannot be differentiated from sense impressions of external reality, there may be no more reason to reflect on their reality status than there is to reflect on the reality of the tables and chairs that surround one during wakefulness. One could argue that, during wakefulness, although the capacity of reflective evaluation is more or less continuously present, people typically do not conduct epistemological discussions with themselves, on a manifestly conscious level, about the reality of the tables and chairs that impinge on their sense organs. Such arguments propose that, once the hallucinatory quality of the dream is accepted, perhaps one should not expect to find in it any more reflective evaluation of what is real and unreal than is consciously experienced in wakefulness.

The previous arguments would be perfectly acceptable if dreams contained only tables, chairs, and other similarly mundane articles that required no critical evaluation. But at times dreams do contain images that, had they occurred during wakefulness, would have caused the individual to reflect very seriously on their origins. For example, I recently dreamed that my father, who has been dead for many years, engaged me in conversation. My "understanding" in the dream was that he had returned from a place where dead souls rest to discuss a matter with me. In the dream, I was, for a passing moment, puzzled that he had been able to return from the dead, but I had no doubt that it had happened. We had a warm, quiet talk in an atmosphere of peace and calm. At no point did I question whether it was a dream or a hallucination. To me it was happening. Had the same events transpired during wakefulness, I would have reflected very, very seriously on the origins of the experience. The point is that dreams lack reflective awareness even when their contents would ordinarily inspire very active, conscious, critical reflection during wakefulness.

In view of the previous considerations, the issue could well be turned around. Instead of asking whether the nonreflectiveness of the dream is secondary to its hallucinatory quality, one could ask whether dream images are hallucinatory because of their nonreflectiveness. Perhaps what would otherwise amount to only self-generated images, clearly recognized as such during wakefulness, become hallucinations in dreams because people are unable to reflectively evaluate them while they are in that state.

Perhaps this is a silly discourse. As some might argue, if non-reflectiveness is intrinsic to the definition of a hallucination, then it is meaningless to question whether the nonreflectiveness is causal to the hallucination. I think there is a legitimate substantive issue at stake. If one suspends preconceptions of what is or is not intrinsic to hallucinations, one may admit that there are images, like those experienced under psychoactive drugs, that have such sensory intensity that one cannot reject their reality on the basis of the sensory image alone. Yet a knowledge of context may cause one to question the reality. One may know that one is drugged and that one may be "seeing things," or one may speculate, "That can't be a real horse in my bathtub." Apparently there are conscious domains in which one may hallucinate in a sensory sense, and yet retain an intellectual reflectiveness. Because dreams are not such a state, it is indeed legitimate to wonder whether dream hallucinations are not secondary to dream single-mindedness.

These considerations add up to a "passive" view of dreaming, inasmuch as they suggest that the hallucinatory images that appear in dreams may derive more from the removal of the restraints of reflective awareness than from the "power" of the intruding images and thoughts.

LACK OF IMAGINATION

A second reason for thinking of dreams as single-minded is that, relative to waking thought, they are largely lacking in imagination. This may seem a rather foolish statement to make about dreams, which are often considered among the most imaginative of human productions. However, we do not refer to the fanciful, complicated, novel characteristics of some dreams, which generally cause people to think of them as imaginative. Rather, this refers now to imagination in the sense as the capacity to conjure up images and thoughts that may occupy consciousness simultaneously or near simultaneously with another stream of thoughts and images. For example, as I write this chapter, I am sitting at my desk confronted with a pad of yellow paper, the words I have just written on it, and, in the periphery, an assortment of pens, coffee cups, and so on. At the same time that this reality dominates my visual imagery, I can see in my "mind's eye" a much more pleasant scene of a tennis court, a party, or almost anything else I choose. Dreams seem to be different. When I dream of one scene, very rarely do I simultaneously imagine another scene. If, for example, I dream of sitting at my desk writing this chapter, I would not in the dream be simultaneously imagining a tennis court.

The issue of dream imagination has not been systematically studied in our laboratory. However, from the thousands of dream reports I have heard, my strong impression is that nonimaginativeness is characteristic of the dreams of others, not just my own. We systematically inquired about this dimension of imagination in the two intelligent, articulate, good dream recallers mentioned earlier. In only 22 (or 13.3%) of 168

REM period awakenings with dream recall did these subjects report "thinking about something" above and beyond an immediate participation in the dream events. Even in most of these instances, the thoughts proved to be about the passing dream events, rather than different topics. In only two (or 1.2%) of the awakenings was there any report of "seeing something else" in the dream—something that was not immediately part and parcel of the dream events.

Sometimes one may experience alternative versions of a single dream theme. I have occasionally found myself in a dream sequence that seemed to be moving toward an undesirable outcome and then apparently "trying" some alternative version of the prior sequence. But these alternatives seemed to occur sequentially one at a time. For example, it was very different from that familiar situation of wakefulness, where one is listening to a speaker and his "mind is somewhere else." By comparison, I cannot remember a dream report that took the form, "Well I was dreaming of such and such, but as I was dreaming this I was imagining a different scene that was completely unrelated."

THEMATIC COHERENCE

The third line of evidence for the single-mindedness of dreams is their thematic coherence. Dreams tend to take the form of a story; events and scenes follow each other historically. The history is sometimes unusual, and the story may take unexpected turns or be punctuated with somewhat discordant intrusions. Nevertheless, there is a definite chronological march of thematically connected material, which probably proceeds without significant detours for longer periods of time than most spontaneous waking thought. The tendency for dreams to tell one story at a time contributes phenomenologically to a picture of single-mindedness. Perhaps the single-mindedness of thematic coherence is possible because attenuated reflectiveness and imagination prevent interruption by competing thought streams.

POOR RECALL

A fourth argument for the single-mindedness of dreams is more speculative than the preceding three because it requires a major inference from the phenomenological data, rather than phenomenological data per se. Nevertheless, it is a major phenomenon that is consistent with the general view developed here. This phenomenon is people's terribly poor memory for dreams.

Memory for dreams is so poor that, up until 25 years ago, it was generally believed that dreams were relatively rare, capriciously occurring events. It was believed that, although some people had a dream almost every night, many dreamed only once a week, once a month, or even less frequently. Then the discoveries of REM sleep and its association with dreams (Aserinsky & Kleitman, 1953; Dement & Kleitman, 1957) changed this view. It is now known that human adults have about four REM periods a night, and that they can recall dreams on about 80%–90% of awakenings from REM periods. Dream recall drops off precipitously as awakenings are delayed beyond the end of the REM period (Wolpert & Trosman, 1958). Although mental activity is reported less frequently on awakenings from non-REM sleep, and although the non-REM reports tend to be more conceptual and thoughtlike than REM dreams, on occasion full-blown, bona fide dreams are also reported on non-REM awakenings (Foulkes, 1962; Rechtschaffen, Verdone, & Wheaton, 1963). Taking all the evidence together, it now appears that most people forget three or more dreams, or over an hour's worth of dreaming, each night. Considering that dreams are personally relevant and sometimes dramatic, this represents truly massive forgetting.

Massive forgetting is not restricted to dreams; it tends to occur whenever a set to remember is lacking. Apart from particularly dramatic events and items that one deliberately sets out to store in memory, the majority of waking experience is lost forever. An average person probably had about a thousand minutes of waking consciousness yesterday. How many of them could that person relate now? Probably not too many; he or she did not see a need at the time to commit these experiences to memory. There is a world of difference in the memory for what people read casually and what they read with the specific intention of retrieving it for an examination.

It can now be speculatively inferred that one reason for the massive forgetting of dreams is that the conditions that limit dreaming consciousness to a single thought stream also limit the capacity to simul taneously adopt a set for remembering that thought stream (i.e., typically people cannot or do not say to themselves during the dream, "I must remember this"). This limitation is certainly not absolute, as witnessed by the fact that some dreams are remembered and by the often noted increase in dream recall when psychotherapy increases the motivation for dream recall. Also, it is doubtful whether the limited capacity for adopting a memory set is entirely responsible for poor dream recall. Some of the dramatic events that must have transpired in unrecalled dreams, had they occurred during wakefulness, would certainly be well recalled with or without a set for remembering them. Nevertheless, the fact of poor recall for dreams, when they are followed immediately by sleep, is consistent with the phenomenological observations on the single-mindedness of dreams.

I do not want to say more to convince you of the single-mindedness of dreams. After all, I have proposed it as a major, relatively distinctive, immediately apparent phenomenological characteristic of dreams, not a subtle nuance. If one cannot agree the next time one awakens from a dream that the dream was single-minded, then the concept has little merit. Assuming for the time being, however, that dreams are single-minded, one may consider some of the implications.

DREAM ISOLATION

Another way to describe the single-mindedness of dreams would be to say that dream consciousness, at least on a manifest level, is isolated from other systems of consciousness (i.e., reflection, voluntary control, other images, etc.). This isolation may be just one manifestation of a more generalized isolation of dream consciousness—not only from other systems of consciousness, but from stimulus input, autonomic activity, organismic state, and motor output as well. There is insufficient space here to develop the theme of generalized dream isolation comprehensively. However, a few examples, although somewhat selective, help identify the position.

Everyone knows that dream content is connected to other variables (e.g., it is affected by presleep and contemporaneous stimuli, and is correlated with organismic state and motor output). However, the main point, is that these connections are by and large quite weak (i.e., dream consciousness is relatively isolated from these variables).[4]

The presleep experiences of the first night in a sleep laboratory certainly affect the thoughts and feelings of the new subject. Nevertheless, only about one third of the dreams during the first night have manifest content unambiguously related to the laboratory situation (Dement, Kahn, & Roffwarg, 1965). Because dreams are largely visual, one might expect visual stimuli to strongly affect dream content. However, Rechtschaffen and Foulkes (1965) could not find a single clear instance of incorporation into the dream of stimulus objects presented in front of subjects sleeping with their eyes taped open. Dement and Wolpert (1958) found that presentations of tones, light flashes, and sprays of cold water during REM periods produced incorporation in only 9%, 24%, and 47% of subsequent dream reports, respectively. Even a shock to the wrist delivered at an intensity known to produce a cortical response

---

[4]A similar point of view was expressed and documented in greater detail by Foulkes (1966).

resulted in direct incorporations on only about one fifth of the presentations and indirect incorporations (including any reference to the laboratory situation) on about one third of the presentations (Koulack, 1969). Thus, the limited effect of external stimuli cannot be explained by their failure to enter the central nervous system.

Some of the incorporation percentages reported earlier and elsewhere in the literature may appear reasonably substantial at first glance, but other considerations attenuate their significance. First, relatively powerful stimuli were used. The new laboratory situation would almost certainly have been in the minds of subjects if they had stayed awake, yet it entered into only one third of the dreams. A spray of cold water would certainly enter the consciousness of awake subjects, but was incorporated into dreams less than half the time. Second, the mere incidence of incorporation overestimates the effect on total dream content. A stimulus might appear in dreams on 50% of presentations, but this does not mean that half the dream content was determined by the stimulus. Usually the incorporations appear only momentarily in the dream; considerably less than half the total dream content is attributable to the stimulus. Third, when external stimuli are incorporated, they tend to be absorbed into the prevailing dream, rather than start a new theme determined primarily by the stimulus. In his or her enthusiasm for showing some understanding of how images are formed, the dream researcher frequently refers to the statistically significant effects of presleep and contemporaneous stimuli. What frequently gets lost in this enthusiasm is an overall appreciation of how little of the totality of dream content can be accounted for by such external factors.

Apart from their well-known relationship to the REM state, dreams also appear to be relatively isolated from the organismic condition of the dreamer. Dream content generally correlates rather poorly with autonomic variables (Rechtschaffen, 1973). Of 15 dream reports collected from three subjects who completely restricted their fluid intake for 24 hours, only 5 contained elements that might have been related to thirst (Dement & Wolpert, 1958). Full or partial erections were reported in 95% of REM periods by Fisher, Gross, and Zuch (1965) and in 80% of REM periods by Karacan, Goodenough, Shapiro, and Starker (1966). In contrast, manifestly sexual interactions have been reported to occur in only 12% of the dreams of male subjects (Hall & Van de Castle, 1966). How often would one expect young adult males to have erections during wakefulness without concurrent sexual thoughts? Not only do nonsexual dreams occur in the presence of physiological sexual arousal, but sexual dreams may occur in the absence of physiological sexual arousal. Money (1960) found that quadriplegic patients with spinal cord transections, which precluded genital-pelvic sensations, could have dreams with orgasmic imagery.

Although there is some correspondence between dream imagery and muscle activity in some subjects (Gardner, Grossman, Roffwarg, & Weiner, 1975; Wolpert, 1960), the overriding feature of dreams is the extent to which vigorous dream imagery is accompanied by little or no motor output. In one sense, this is a banal point. Of course, there must be a restriction of motor output during sleep, otherwise people would not sleep very much. For that reason, the spinal inhibition of motor outflow during REM sleep (Pompeiano, 1967) makes functional sense. However, dream imagery is selectively weak in inducing motor responses. Despite the general low level of motor activity during sleep and the specific motor inhibition of REM sleep, subjects can remain motorically quite responsive to external stimuli during sleep. For example, it is not difficult to awaken a subject from a REM period simply by calling his or her name in a moderate voice over an intercom. By contrast, consider some of the amazing, sometimes terrifying dreams that people have slept through. Dream images are simply poor stimuli for producing motor responses, which may be one more example of the generalized isolation of the dream.

THEORETICAL IMPLICATIONS

Some of the theoretical questions raised by dream isolation are considered in this section. First, is dream isolation epiphenomenal to physiological characteristics of sleep, or does it serve specific functions? For example, might dream isolation help protect sleep against central nervous system arousal or dream consciousness? (This is essentially an extrapolation from Freudian dream theory—i.e., if dreams protect sleep, then isolated dreams might protect sleep that much better.) Might dream isolation facilitate certain psychological processes? For example, problems might be best ventilated or worked through when the mind is relatively unencumbered by recent stimuli, external stimuli, cognizance of organismic state, proprioceptive feedback, intruding thoughts, or the restraints of critical reflection.

Second, how is dream isolation related to other dream characteristics? Do bizarre thoughts, symbolic representations, and hallucinations occur passively in dreams because reflectiveness and anchors to internal and external stimuli are attenuated? Conversely, is there an independent drive for the expression of dream thoughts, images, and symbols that isolation functions to facilitate? Or are both the expression and isolation part of a single process, such as the suspension of ego control?

Third, what does dream isolation imply for the psychophysiology of dreaming? One implication is that the relationship of dream content to autonomic and motoric activity is destined to be limited. The occurrence of dreaming per se is, of course, correlated with autonomic (e.g., cardio-respiratory irregularity) and motor patterns (tonic inhibition of head and neck muscles, combined with generalized muscle twitching). However, these correlations seem to depend on the relationship of both the physi-ological and psychological variables to the REM state because the rela-tionships between the two sets of variables within a state are not very strong (Rechtschaffen, 1973). The expectation of correlations within states derives from models of vigorous interaction among central, mo-tor, and autonomic events during wakefulness. In contrast, dream isola-tion suggests that the best physiological correlates of dreaming might ultimately be found in a brain activity (or a peripheral manifestation of it) that does not interact strongly with conventional autonomic and mo-tor variables. In addition, dream isolation suggests that his brain activity would be relatively little affected by recent events, external stimuli, or general organismic condition, and would be relatively unrelated to those brain activities that are involved in volitional, reflective, critical thought. As a corollary to the last point, the identification of brain processes that are not associated with dreaming could help in the search for those that are involved in volitional, reflective, critical thought.[5]

Fourth, if dreams are indeed relatively isolated from recent stimuli, systemic state, and other thought systems, where in the world does dream content come from? There are several possibilities, each of which has been considered in one or another of the major theories of dream content. In fact, these theories may be viewed not so much as integrative statements of what is clearly known about dream formation, but more as struggles to explain generally obvious, if not explicitly stated, facts of dream isolation. Theories of dream content would not be needed if it was readily attributable to recent events, external stimuli, organismic state, and the familiar thought systems of wakefulness.

One interpretation of the origin of dream content in the face of dream isolation is that both are the products of the "disorganized" activity of the brain during sleep. This is the one interpretation we would be most strongly inclined to reject. If there is any isomorphism between mental

---

[5]This discussion is, of course, fraught with implicit assumptions about causal directions between dream experience and physiological events. As elaborated elsewhere (Recht-schaffen, 1975) this issue of causal direction cannot be resolved empirically, but theoretical assumptions about it can help organize old facts and generate new ones.

experience and brain activity, then one could hardly infer a disorganized brain from dream content because dream content is not especially disorganized. As indicated earlier, dreams frequently take the form of definite stories. There is neither the kaleidoscope of unrelated images nor the cacophony of isolated thoughts and words that one might expect in truly disorganized consciousness. Waking consciousness, with its rapid juxtaposition of sensations, thoughts, wanderings, and reflections, probably comes closer to the hypothetical disorganized mind than does the dream. Perhaps one of the best arguments for both dream organization and dream isolation is the recurring dream. It seems most unlikely that disorganized brain activity could produce the same dream over intervals of days, weeks, or longer. The reappearance of dreams over long intervals of very eventful waking life suggests how isolated from that waking life dreams may be.

A more popular explanation of the origins of dream content in the face of dream isolation is that the isolation is only apparent—that connections between manifest dream content and its origins have to be disguised. Otherwise threatening mental elements could not be discharged, or the discharge would awaken the dreamer. Of course, this kind of explanation is a cornerstone of Freudian dream theory and many of its variants. This theory has already encompassed some of the phenomena of isolation, such as the blocking of motor discharge. Given the agile theoretical concepts of unconscious forces, repression, withdrawal of ego cathexis, psychological transformation (the dream work), and secondary elaboration, it would probably not be difficult to develop theoretical explanations of all the phenomena of dream isolation.

Another popular theory of dream content is that it emerges from a reservoir of psychological activity that has a lower threshold of release during sleep than during wakefulness, and therefore seems disconnected from waking consciousness and the variables that affect it. The nature of the reservoir varies from theory to theory (e.g., infantile wishes, repressed memories, racial unconsciousness, genetically preprogrammed ideas).

In contrast to reservoir theories, the dream may be seen as a new, original, creative product. From this perspective, dream isolation and the relative freedom from stimuli, reflective evaluation, and old thought systems that it implies may provide favorable or even obligatory conditions for such creation.

As the previously stated possibilities suggest, the theoretical reconciliation of dream origin and dream isolation does not present much of a problem. The major problem, as always, is the task of agreeing on empirical referents for the theoretical terms, generating testable predictions from them, and doing well-controlled research that yields reliable results.

POSTSCRIPT

The concept of dream isolation is in one sense a peculiar duck. Usually, a phenomenon is understood by its relationships to other phenomena. Dream isolation emphasizes a lack of relationship between dream consciousness and other phenomena. How then can it help one's understanding of dreams? The answer is that a lack of relationship is evidence about relationships. It reveals what the phenomenon *is not*. The facts of dream isolation are not just statements of ignorance. They are statements about the nature of our beast. They may also be signals that we are still a long way from knowing the forces that make our beast tick.

SUMMARY

Dreams are described as *single-minded,* meaning that they tend to be unaccompanied by other, simultaneous streams of thought and imagery. Four manifestations of single-mindedness were discussed in this chapter: (a) absence of a reflective awareness that one is dreaming while the dream is in progress, (b) absence of alternative images and thoughts while attending to the primary dream content, (c) tendency for dream content to stay on a single thematic track, and (d) absence of a set to remember the dream while it is in progress. This isolation of dream content from other thought systems is then considered as but one manifestation of a more generalized relative isolation of dream content, which includes isolation from presleep stimuli, contemporaneous stimuli, organismic state, and autonomic and motor activity. Some of the implications of dream isolation for dream psychophysiology and theories of dreaming are outlined.

ACKNOWLEDGMENTS

This chapter is an expansion of a talk presented at the meeting of the Association for the Psychophysiological Study of Sleep, Edinburgh, Scotland, July 1975. It was supported by grants MH-4151 and MH-18428 from the National Institutes of Health.

REFERENCES

Aserinsky, E., & Kleitman, N. (1953). Regularly occurring periods of eye motility, and concomitant phenomena, during sleep. *Science, 118,* 273–274.

Dement, W., Kahn, E., & Roffwarg, H. P. (1965). The influence of the laboratory situation on the dreams of the experimental subject. *Journal of Nervous and Mental Disease, 140,* 119–131.

216

Dement, W., & Kleitman, N. (1957). The relation of eye movements during sleep to dream activity: An objective method for the study of dreaming. *Journal of Experimental Psychology, 53,* 339–346.

Dement, W., & Wolpert, E. A. (1958). The relation of eye movements, body motility, and external stimuli to dream content. *Journal of Experimental Psychology, 55,* 543–553.

Dorus, E., Dorus, W., & Rechtschaffen, A. (1971). The incidence of novelty in dreams. *Archives of General Psychiatry, 25,* 364–368.

Fisher, C., Gross, J., & Zuch, J. (1965). Cycle of penile erection synchronous with dreaming (REM) sleep. *Archives of General Psychiatry, 12,* 29–45.

Foulkes, D. (1962). Dream reports from different stages of sleep. *Journal of Abnormal Psychology, 65,* 14–25.

Foulkes, D. (1966). *The psychology of sleep.* New York: Scribner's.

Foulkes, D., & Fleisher, S. (1975). Mental activity in relaxed wakefulness. *Journal of Abnormal Psychology, 84,* 66–75.

Foulkes, D., & Scott, E. (1973). An above-zero waking baseline for the incidence of momentarily hallucinatory mentation. In M. H. Chase, W. C. Stern, & P. L. Walter (Eds.), *Sleep research* (Vol. 2, p. 108). Los Angeles, CA: Brain Information Service/Brain Research Institute, UCLA.

Foulkes, D., & Vogel, G. (1965). Mental activity at sleep onset. *Journal of Abnormal Psychology, 70,* 231–243.

Gardner, R., Grossman, W. I., Roffwarg, H. P., & Weiner, H. (1975). The relationship of small limb movements during REM sleep to dreamed limb action. *Psychosomatic Medicine, 37,* 147–159.

Hall, C. S., & Van de Castle, R. L. (1966). *The content analysis of dreams.* New York: Appleton-Century-Crofts.

Karacan, I., Goodenough, D. R., Shapiro, A., & Starker, S. (1966). Erection cycle during sleep in relation to dream anxiety. *Archives of General Psychiatry, 15,* 183–189.

Koulack, D. (1969). Effects of somatosensory stimulation on dream content. *Archives of General Psychiatry, 20,* 718–725.

Molinari, S., & Foulkes, D. (1969). Tonic and phasic events during sleep: Psychological correlates and implications. *Perceptual and Motor Skills* (Suppl. 1-V29), 343–367.

Money, J. (1960). Phantom orgasm in the dreams of paraplegic men and women. *Archives of General Psychiatry, 3,* 373–382.

Pompeiano, O. (1967). The neurophysiological mechanisms of the postural and motor events during desynchronized sleep. In S. Kety, E. V. Evarts, & H. L. Williams (Eds.), *Sleep and altered states of conscious* (pp. 351–423). Baltimore: Williams & Wilkins.

Rechtschaffen, A. (1973). The psychophysiology of mental activity during sleep. In F. J. McGuigan & R. A. Schoonover (Eds.), *The psychophysiology of thinking* (pp. 153–205). New York: Academic Press.

Rechtschaffen, A. (1975). Scientific method in the study of altered states of consciousness with illustrations from sleep and dream research. In The Drug Abuse Council Inc. (Eds.), *Altered states of consciousness, current views and research problems* (pp. 135–191). Washington, DC: Smithsonian Institution Press.

Rechtschaffen, A., & Foulkes, D. (1965). Effect of visual stimuli on dream content. *Perceptual and Motor Skills, 20,* 1149–1160.

Rechtschaffen, A., Verdone, P., & Wheaton, J. (1963). Reports of mental activity during sleep. *Canadian Psychiatric Association Journal, 8,* 409–414.

Snyder, F., Karacan, I., Tharp, V. K., & Scott, J. (1968). Phenomenology of REMs dreaming. *Psychophysiology, 4,* 375.

Wolpert, E. A. (1960). Studies in psychophysiology of dreams: II. An electromyographic study of dreaming. *Archives of General Psychiatry, 2,* 231–241.

Wolpert, E. A., & Trosman, H. (1958). Studies in psychophysiology of dreams: I. Experimental evocation of sequential dream episodes. *Archives of Neurological Psychiatry, 79,* 603–606.

Zimmerman, W. B. (1970). Sleep mentation and auditory awakening thresholds. *Psychophysiology, 6,* 540–549.

Postscript, 1995

Allan Rechtschaffen

Since the original publication of this chapter, more recent data, reading, and thought have expanded thoughts about the mediation of nonreflectiveness in dreams.

Among the most important empirical findings about dreams in recent years are the results of Foulkes and his associates on developmental changes in dreaming (Foulkes, 1982). They showed that dreams are rare and fragmentary in very young children, and do not begin to approach adult dreams in length and complexity until about ages 7–9. The emergence of adultlike dreams in children is correlated with the development of their visuospatial skills. Also, dreaming is rare in certain neurological patients, frequently those with visuospatial impairments (e.g., Doricchi & Violani, 1992; Jus et al., 1973; Murri et al., 1992). These facts emphasize that dreaming is a relatively high-level cognitive activity, which makes the loss of reflective awareness in dreams even more remarkable. Except for relatively rare lucid dreams, people do not know they are dreaming while they are dreaming. The use of advanced cognitive skills in dream construction supports our earlier contention that this loss of reflective awareness (i.e., the monitoring of one's own conscious processes) is not simply a consequence of disorganized brain functioning. This loss is a specific failure of one's normal waking ability to distinguish the part of one's own minds that comes from accurate sense perception from the part one makes up oneself.

The loss of reflective awareness is most apparent in dreams because there is so much highly organized, sometimes bizarre, conscious material that is not appreciated as internally generated. However, the loss of reflective awareness is probably not limited to dreaming, but may be characteristic of sleep as a whole. Although people are immediately aware of having been asleep when they awaken in the morning or during brief arousals, generally they are not aware of being asleep while in that state. Even in the reports of relatively realistic, drifting thoughts about contemporary concerns that are often elicited on awakenings from non-REM sleep, there is rarely any recognition that these thoughts are being generated during sleep or even that one is lying in bed during the night.

In the years since the original paper was prepared, cognitive psychologists have shown increased interest in the mechanisms by which people normally differentiate reality from internally generated thoughts and images. A leader in this area, Johnson (1991) proposed that one way the differentiation is made is by comparing the phenomenal characteristics of the perceptions and thoughts: ". . . memories for perceived and imagined events differ in average value along a number of dimensions. Memories originating in perception typically have more perceptual information (e.g., color, sound), contextual time and place information, and more meaningful detail . . . " (p. 181). Surely the failure to recognize dreams as "unreal" cannot derive from an absence of dream–reality differences on these dimensions. Dreams are not recognized as unreal, although they provide little contextual time or place information, auditory detail is scarce (often people "get the message" of what someone said without actually hearing the words), and visual qualities tend toward color desaturation and loss of background detail (Rechtschaffen & Buchignani, 1992). Johnson also proposed that internally generated productions may be detected by reason (e.g., they don't fit known facts). However, dreams are so completely nonreflective that rarely is there any indication of such evaluative thought while the dream is in progress. The failure to recognize the dream as imaginary is not attributable to its phenomenological characteristics. Rather, some specific faculty for distinguishing reality from imagination is not working.

Are there other models of a failed reflective faculty that can put some meat on the bare bones of this contention? Although analogies between dreaming and psychosis go back at least to Plato and are still underlined in contemporary psychoanalytic thought, psychotic hallucinations and delusions are not particularly good models of what goes on in dreaming. Psychotic hallucinations are mostly auditory (voices), whereas dream imagery is mostly visual. Psychotic delusions and hallucinations are relatively circumscribed distortions of reality often related to the patient's conflicts; the remainder of conscious experience may be entirely realistic. In the dream, all is unreal; none of it corresponds to the reality of the moment. Toxic or senile deleriums are not good models of dream consciousness either. Dreams are much more organized, and they rarely display the pervasive confusion and attendant anxiety of delerium. Rather, the best models of dreamlike lapses of reality testing may be in the confabulations of certain brain-injured patients. In a good neurological model of dream nonreflectiveness, while awake, patients should, show the same failures to distinguish reality and imagination that they regularly show during sleep. Such models could identify loci of brain activities that discriminate between reality and imagination.

The best model of dreamlike waking activity has been the patients with anterior cingulectomies (Whitty & Lewin, 1957). These patients were minimally confused, aware of having undergone surgery, and fully oriented for place and person. Yet their internally generated thoughts and images assumed such clarity and vividness that the patients had difficulty distinguishing them from reality. For example, one patient described scenes of having tea with his wife or of friends coming to talk to him as "a sort of waking dream. . . . My thoughts seem to be out of control, they go off on their own—so vivid" (p. 73). Another patient spoke of having been visited by a brother and his wife, even though he had had no visitors. The patient was aware that he had imagined this visit, but emphasized its vividness. Because the postsurgical "waking dream" phenomenon lasted only several days before subsiding, Whitty and Lewin suggested that it may have been the effect of a discharging lesion, rather than an interruption of fixed anatomical pathways. They further suggested that the injury potentials may have discharged through anatomical links to the medial-temporal lobe. This appears to be a viable anatomical model of dream generation. Buchsbaum et al. (1989) reported that glucose metabolic rate of the human cingulate gyrus was higher during REM sleep than during wakefulness, and Maquet et al. (1990) reported the same for the left anterior and middle temporal cortex. However, the cingulectomy patients may have been better models for dream generation than for lapses of reflection because they worked at making the distinction between dream and reality, and remained skeptical of their dream productions (e.g., "I'm not sure the half the time if I just thought it or it really happened" [p. 73]).

A better model for lapses in reflection may be the confabulations of patients with frontal lobe injury. *Confabulation* has been variously defined. It is spoken of here in the sense described by Johnson (1991): ". . . false statements that are not made to deceive, are typically more coherent than thoughts produced during delerium, and do not reflect underlying psychopathology" (p. 187). Stuss, Alexander, Lieberman, and Levine (1978) described "an extraordinary form of confabulation" in frontal lobe injury that was "spontaneous, impulsive, and self-propagating, often based on inappropriate environmental stimuli" (p. 1166). The confabulations of one patient were described as "reminiscent of the loosening of spatial, temporal, and logical relationships experienced in dreams" (p. 1168). Unlike the cingulectomy patients, the frontal lobe patients showed no doubts about the veracity of their confabulations.

Both Johnson and Stuss et al. reviewed additional reports from other investigators, which supported an important role for the frontal lobes in reality testing.

These results suggest that decreases in frontal lobe activity could be responsible for decreased self-monitoring during sleep. This suggestion is supported by a greater decrease of human glucose metabolic rate during non-REM sleep in the frontal lobes than in the temporal or occipital lobes (Buchsbaum et al., 1989). In a similar vein, Madsen et al. (1991) reported that, in human REM sleep, cerebral blood flow was decreased in inferior frontal regions while it was increased in the associative visual cortex. But all is not well with the hypothesis because Jus et al. (1973) found a remarkable decrease of dream reports on REM awakenings in lobotomized schizophrenic patients compared with well-matched schizophrenic controls. It is difficult to argue that decreased frontal lobe activity may be responsible for the nonreflectiveness of dreams if decreased frontal lobe input precludes the occurrence of dreaming altogether. Of course, it remains possible that, in intact persons, different frontal lobe circuits participate in dream generation and reflective awareness; in lobotomized patients, both functions might be knocked out. Nevertheless, the need to reconcile an apparent contradiction emphasizes the tentative quality of our hypothesis.

The unrealistic wanderings of people's minds may serve a purpose. They might reflect the "idling" of a brain that cannot easily accelerate from a dead stop or the heuristic scanning of memory banks and associations. In any event, it is obviously advantageous to distinguish them from reality while people are awake. But why should the mechanisms for making these discriminations be suspended during sleep while other mechanisms, such as those used for image and story construction, are maintained? This can only be answered speculatively. Sleep might rest the critical faculties used for thinking logically, separating fact and fantasy, and resisting lazy lapses into the latter. This possibility is challenged by the absence of any evidence that "mental work" increases the need for sleep. A second possibility is that reflective consciousness may be incompatible with sleep. Imagine trying to fall asleep or stay asleep while critically evaluating your conscious productions and their relationships to the events of the preceding day. In fact, it is the inability to suspend such critical thought that many insomniacs describe as the major impediment to their sleep. As Foulkes (1985) suggested, it may be "a necessary part of the experience we call 'sleep' that we lose a directive and reflective self. You can't fall asleep, or be asleep, if your waking self is still regulating and reflecting upon your conscious mental state" (p. 42).

In summary, our more recent thoughts about nonreflectiveness during sleep in general and dreams in particular suggest that it reflects the suspension of a specific faculty for differentiating reality from imagination, that this faculty is potentially traceable to specific brain activities, that the frontal lobes are a candidate site for such activities, and that the suspension of these activities may be permissive for sleep.

REFERENCES TO POSTSCRIPT 1995

Buchsbaum, M. S., Gillin, J. C., Wu, J., Hazlett, E., Sicottee, M., & Dupont, R. M. (1989). Regional cerebral glucose metabolic rate in human sleep assessed by positron emission tomography. *Life Sciences, 45,* 1349–1356.

Doricchi, F., & Violani, C. (1992). Dream recall in brain-damaged patients: A contribution to the neuropsychology of dreaming through a review of the literature. In J. S. Antrobus & M. Bertini (Eds.), *The Neuropsychology of sleep and dreaming* (pp. 99–140). Hillsdale, NJ: Lawrence Erlbaum Associates.

Foulkes, D. (1982). *Children's dreams: Longitudinal studies.* New York: Wiley.

Foulkes, D. (1985). *Dreaming: A cognitive-psychological analysis.* Hillsdale, NJ: Lawrence Erlbaum Associates.

Johnson, M. J. (1991). Reality monitoring: Evidence from confabulation in organic brain disease patients. In G. P. Prigatano & D. L. Schacter (Eds.), *Awareness of deficit after brain injury* (pp. 176–197). New York: Oxford.

Jus, A., Jus, K., Villenueve, A., Pires, A., Lachance, R., Fortier, J., & Villaneuve, R. (1973). Studies on dream recall in chronic schizophrenic patients after prefrontal lobotomy. *Biological Psychiatry, 6,* 275–293.

Madsen, P. L., Holm, S., Vorstrup, S., Friberg, L., Lassen, N. A., & Wildschoidtz, G. (1991). Human regional cerebral blood flow during rapid eye-movement sleep. *Journal of Cerebral Blood Flow and Metabolism, 11,* 502–507.

Maquet, P., Dive, D., Salmon, E., Sadzot, B., Franco, G., Poirrer, R., von Frenckell, R., & Franck, G. (1990). Cerebral glucose utilization during sleep—wake cycle in man determined by positron emission tomography and [18F]2-flouro-2-deoxy-D-glucose method. *Brain Research, 513,* 136–143.

Murri, L., Bonanni, E., Stafanini, A., Goldstein, A., Navona, C., & Denoth, F. (1992). Neurological approaches to the dream problem. In J. S. Antrobus & M. Bertini (Eds.), *The neuropsychology of sleep and dreaming* (pp. 87–98). Hillsdale, NJ: Lawrence Erlbaum Associates.

Rechtschaffen, A., & Buchignani, C. (1992). The visual appearance of dreams. In J. S. Antrobus, & M. Bertini (Eds.), *The neuropsychology of sleep and dreaming* (pp. 143–155). Hillsdale, NJ: Lawrence Erlbaum Associates.

Stuss, D. T., Alexander, M. P., Lieberman, A., & Levine, (1978). An extraordinary form of confabulation. *Neurology, 28,* 1166–1172.

Whitty, C. W. M., & Lewin, W. (1957). Vivid day-dreaming: An unusual form of confusion following anterior cigulectomy. *Brain, 80,* 72–76.

9

Denial, Anxiety, and Information Processing

Hasida Ben-Zur
Shlomo Breznitz

Recent years have witnessed a growing interest in the conceptualization and research of the defense mechanism termed *denial*, its manifestations, and its functions (e.g., Breznitz, 1983a; Cramer, 1991; Dorpat, 1985). However, the specific ways in which this mechanism enables people to not see, not hear, not think, and, in general, not process information that has the potential to induce anxiety and worry have yet to be outlined.

This chapter starts with a general description of several approaches dealing with variants of information rejection, focusing on how people avoid processing threats originating in the external world. This type of coping with threatening reality is assumed to depend on the way the human mind can reconcile conflicting pieces of data. Findings from anxiety and denial studies, together with information-processing principles, are combined to lay a basis for several types of operations that can prevent the meaning of threatening information from reaching consciousness. These operations can be investigated by using cognitive tasks that require subjects to deal with negative input. The use of such tasks may overcome the basic problems inherent in research on denial.

VARIANTS OF INFORMATION REJECTION

Freud (1926/1956) was the first to propose that denial represents an intrapsychic mechanism that operates unconsciously to banish anxiety and other unpleasant feelings from the human mind. Following Freud, most studies on *denial* defined it as the negation of something in word or act (e.g., Goldberg, 1983; Lazarus, 1983). For example, Weisman and

225

Hackett (1961) and Dimsdale and Hackett (1982) saw denial as the repudiation of meaning to allay unpleasant affects, whereas Plutchik, Kellerman, and Conte (1979) defined *denial* as the lack of awareness of certain events, experiences, or feelings that would be painful to acknowledge.

In earlier writings, denial was treated as one specific defense mechanism out of the many defenses. It was sometimes claimed to be a primitive mechanism at the lower levels of adaptation (Vaillant, 1977) that creates social difficulties and obstructs conflict resolution (see Heilbrun, 1984). However, the concept evolved and several frameworks were offered to better understand the functions it may serve. Thus, Breznitz (1983b) described seven kinds of denial according to what is being denied: denial of information, threatening information, personal relevance, urgency, vulnerability/responsibility, affect, and affect relevance. These seven types of denial are stages in the same process; the person may engage in each, depending on the intensity, probability, and imminence of the threat or danger. Such a scheme offers a solution to the problem of the conflicting duality in the evaluation of the denial mechanism. On the one hand, denial can be seen as a primitive defense mechanism used sometimes by people in psychotic states when it is applied to the total information, thereby representing a maximum distortion of reality. On the other hand, it can be envisioned as part of the day-to-day coping process, characterizing the reactions of normal individuals, who may deal with a stressful encounter by denying only certain aspects of the threatening reality. Thus, a person may acknowledge the fact that smoking is unhealthy in principle, but will offer all kinds of excuses to better deny the hazards of smoking to him or her personally (denial of personal relevance) at the present time (denial of urgency).

Another type of differentiation was suggested by Cramer (1991), who presented two forms of denial, according to the operations employed. One group of operations is related to the perceptual system, warding off reality through not seeing, avoidance, or distortion of perception. The other group of operations occurs on the cognitive level, involving the construction of personal fantasies.

The theoretical considerations discussed previously imply that denial is a complex mechanism with a variety of manifestations that go beyond a simple negation. Moreover, psychological theory and research have offered other types of related mechanisms, the functions and operations of which are sometimes akin to those of denial. The psychological literature shows that denial is but one of the many mechanisms presumably used by humans in their everyday transactions with reality. It can be related to at least three different theoretical constructs each evolving within a specific framework: defense mechanisms derived from psychoanalytic theory, coping strategies developed in stress theory and re-

search, and self-deception tactics from the evolution theory of deception. This chapter mentions the basic arguments of each approach, de-
lineating its main similarities and differences from denial.

Psychoanalytic Theory

Traditionally, denial belongs with a long list of defenses aimed at protecting the person from real or imagined threats, conflicts, and frustra-
tions. It has been claimed to share with other defense mechanisms, such
as repression, projection, and rationalization, the capacity to defend
against anxiety and guilt that originate in instinctual impulses and external prohibitions (see Cramer, 1991). To fulfill this function, all defenses
distort reality and operate unconsciously (Hall & Lindzey, 1970).

How would denial be distinguished from the various other forms of
psychological defense, such as repression, rationalization, or projection?
Fisher and Fisher (1993) categorized the defenses into five clusters, with
denial, repression, and reaction formation being grouped together under the label of *reversal* (i.e., they are based on shutting out or denying
threats). Because denial means negation, in principle it could be the
negation of an impulse, feeling or thought, or external reality (Lazarus,
1983). However, in the psychoanalytical literature, denial is seen as focused on external reality, whereas impulses and motives (internal demands) are dealt with by repression. Thus, in denial, the information
may not get in at all, or may get in and get lost before it is deeply
processed. The threatening stimulus may be registered, but the registration is only partial (Spence, 1983), or the processing of the threatening
stimulus stops and attention is directed elsewhere (Dorpat, 1985).

It has recently been claimed that denial functions not only ward off
external reality, but also avoid internal stimuli, such as memories, which
are preconscious (Cramer, 1991). The present authors argue that, to
avoid conceptual confusion, denial should be used strictly when the
negation of external input is taking place. Thoughts and memories are
prevented from reaching consciousness through the working of repression.

Coping Strategies

Within the context of coping theory and research, a new type of construct evolved—namely, cognitive avoidance (Krohne, 1993), exemplified by the mental disengagement strategy (Carver, Scheier, &
Weintraub, 1989) and the cognitive style of blunting (Miller, 1989).
Avoidance strategies, together with the defense mechanisms, are considered components of the palliative coping mode first introduced by

Lazarus (1966) and later termed *emotion-focused coping* (Lazarus & Folkman, 1984). The prime function of this mode of coping is to reduce or moderate both the negative emotions and the physiological arousal associated with stress without changing the objective situation.

Avoidance strategies characterize individuals who are intolerant of emotional arousal, as opposed to those who are vigilant, sensitizers, or monitors, and who tend toward intolerance of uncertainty (see Krohne, 1993). This property of avoidance strategies is embedded in the original function of denial as outlined earlier. However, mechanisms of cognitive avoidance may differ from denial in that they are not necessarily operating unconsciously, and that they may entail less reality distortion. Thus, attempts to mentally disengage oneself from threatening information imply control over cognitive processes when behavioral disengagement is not possible, and include alternative activities such as daydreaming, sleep, and so on. Denial, in contrast, means the refusal to believe that the stressor exists, or to act as if it were not real. Still, according to self-rating measures (Carver et al., 1989), the association between reported use of denial and mental disengagement strategies is sometimes positive and substantial. This may suggest, however, that the measurement of defenses by self-report measures is problematic.

The previously mentioned research also raises the more general issue of the nature of the relationship between defenses and other mechanisms of coping. It seems that a debate exists concerning the origin of the defenses in relation to coping and adaptation in general. On the one hand, the defenses can be seen as the more basic mechanisms used to deal with instinctual conflicts, with coping strategies emerging from them. On the other hand, it was argued that the defenses may have developed from mechanisms of coping and adaptation (see Cramer, 1991).

Self-Deception

Within the framework of evolutionary theory and the sociobiological perspective, the concept of self-deception is discussed and interpreted along the lines of the broader phenomenon of deception. It is claimed to be basically aimed at obtaining more resources for the individual animal and human being. Thus, self-deception has the primary adaptive function of making humans better deceivers (Krebs, Denton, & Higgins, 1988; Trivers, 1985) by hiding from the deceived the signs of self-knowledge that may give the deception away. According to Gur and Sackeim (1979), the self-deception mechanism involves the maintenance of two simultaneously contradicting beliefs held on different levels of consciousness, and a motivated act determines which belief is not subject to awareness. Krebs et al. (1988) added the need for intention as part of the process, suggesting that an unconscious process must intend to deceive a conscious one.

Among the self-deception mechanisms mentioned are such phenomena as beneffectance (the tendency to present oneself as being both beneficial and effective), exaggeration (of beneficial outcomes), and perceptual defense (Trivers, 1985), the latter not easily distinguished from denial. Such mechanisms also include cognitive biases that are (a) self-serving, (b) enhancing and protecting of individuals' self-esteem, (c) impressive to others, and, in general (d) aiding individuals in their social interactions. The extra adaptive value of these mechanisms seems to come from the same origin as the one proposed for denial: It is claimed that it is adaptive to distort the truth when it hurts and when acknowledging it may make the individual less fit than a misconception or a self-delusion (Krebs et al., 1988). Thus, although self-deception may have originated in deception, current theory assigns it a function of defense.

Advantages and Disadvantages
of Information Rejection

Are denial or denial-like processes adaptive? The answer to such a question would depend on certain characteristics of the stressful encounter. In early psychoanalytic research, denial and the other defenses were considered mechanisms, the use of which demands energy and interferes with the person's healthy way of coping with reality. More recently, positive views have been expressed in regard to psychological defense. According to Fisher and Fisher (1993), because people cannot avoid great catastrophes such as death and loss, "it is presumed that existence is manageable only if self-deceptive and pretense-based fictions are cultivated. . . . To maintain a sense that the world is a reasonable place, average, normal persons are diversely required to deny what they know . . ." (p. 171). Thus, denial, as well as other defenses, are assumed to be normal, if not indispensable, psychological devices that facilitate people's day-to-day functioning. As already mentioned, Krebs et al. (1988) went further, suggesting that it is adaptive to distort reality when acknowledging the truth makes one less fit than believing a lie. It seems that denial may take its place among the many types of biases regarding the self, such as self-deception (Krebs et al., 1988) and positive illusions (Taylor & Brown, 1988).

Nevertheless, it should be pointed out that denial-like processes acquire a positive value only with reference to the characteristics of the threat and the time frame in which it occurs (Lazarus, 1983). Denying the threat or its consequences is a way of coping with the negative effects of stress on physiological arousal, subjective feelings, and task performance without solving the problem or reducing objective danger. Thus, denial may have some positive value if the person cannot do anything to change the objective reality and if short-term effectiveness is considered (see Suls & Fletcher, 1985). Lazarus (1983) also believed that it may give the person time to mobilize resources, although this aspect of denial was questioned by Haan (1977).

When something can be done to reduce or avoid future danger, the use of denial-like processes can be hazardous to one's health or life. For instance, Lazarus (1983) cited research results suggesting that denial may lead to delay in seeking medical help. Furthermore, Janis (1983; Janis & Mann, 1977) showed that denial may lead to faulty decision making based on biased information preferences. These findings emphasize the importance of studying the cognitive mechanisms of denial. A more thorough understanding of how denial operates can be useful in situations where communication of threatening information is expected to lead to protective action.

Summary

The common basis of most of the psychological mechanisms presented here seems to be both their purpose and mode of operation. They are aimed at defending persons against anxiety, emotional arousal, or other unpleasant thoughts and feelings. They perform this function by utilizing the brain's ability to sustain contradictory information on different levels of consciousness.

COGNITIVE BACKGROUND OF DEFENSE

Although current theories of stress and coping incorporate denial as one of the many types of human coping strategies (e.g., Carver et al., 1989; Lazarus, 1966), the ways in which it operates are not yet clarified. It seems, however, that in current approaches to self-deception and defense, these constructs are seen to evolve from biased information processing. This idea is not far from Freud's notions concerning defense mechanisms. For example, Erdelyi and Goldberg (1979) discussed Freud's psychoanalytic theory as a cognitive approach, with reality misperceived, misremembered, or misconstrued for the purpose of defense. Krebs et al. (1988) mentioned types of self-serving and self-centered cognitive biases, with ego-enhancing motives and defense being one possible "hot" source for these biases.

Thus, considering the defense mechanism of repression, Erdelyi and Goldberg suggested a processing-bias model, in which information processing is biased (selective, tendentious) in input regions (e.g., eye-fixation strategies, biased encoding, and rehearsal) and output regions (e.g., biased retrieval and reporting strategies). Such bias can occur along the entire cognitive domain, and it may become stronger when dealing with interpretations rather than facts and occurrences. Thus, people can avoid frightening reality by changing the focus of attention, and can escape painful meanings by biased sampling of context, which will lead to nonthreatening interpretations of dangerous stimuli.

The interesting question, in this regard, is how do the defenses operate, or how does the system know that it should avoid painful stimuli, prefer one favorable memory over another, not retrieve painful memories, and so on? In other words, how does the system know that it should not know?

In the case of denial, one way to explain this paradoxical state is to assume that only part of the information is registered, which then sets this defense mechanism into operation. This "leakage" orients the person toward avoidance of the dangerous aspects of the environment. However, because partial information gets in, it can sometimes, together with the person's own fantasies, produce a reality that is more terrifying than actual reality (Spence, 1983). In the same vein, in Dorpat's (1985) hypothesis, a preconscious appraisal of danger or trauma is the first stage of the denial process, leading to painful affect, which in turn is followed by cognitive arrest and then screening behavior. This approach assumes that the painful affect leads to focal attention turned toward something else, and to the unconscious rejection and destroying of the cause of the painful affect. Cognitive arrest is then followed by ideas, fantasies, or affects that are used by the person to fill in the gaps brought about by the previous stage. In this process, attention plays a major role—focal attention being diverted from the disturbing stimulus to something else.

Thus, the paradox of denial is solved by assuming that perception is a multistage process, and that stimuli can be registered without being consciously perceived. Hence, threatening information may be apprehended on one level of awareness but not on another (see Epstein, 1994, and the discussion further on), or semantic processing may be blocked so that the full meaning of the threat is prevented from becoming conscious. Assuming that appraisal of threat can be done automatically by comparing present stimuli with an existing database (Breznitz, 1990a), the assessment of the resemblance between the current stimulus array and past, emotionally disturbing memory enables the system to immediately block further processing.

There is neurological evidence of the brain's ability to maintain in parallel conflicting evidence. It comes from research on the brain hemispheres that suggests that the two hemispheres mediate different types of experiences or knowledge (see Krebs et al., 1988). However, even if one assumes that the right, nonverbal hemisphere has priority in data processing, the nature of the mechanism that enables it to stop data from being processed by the left, verbal hemisphere is not really known. Perhaps the right hemisphere is better at detecting emotionally loaded input, and therefore can accomplish the cognitive arrest described earlier.

Cognitive Research of Defense

Defense mechanisms have been assessed in the past by various types of questionnaires, interviews, projective and semiprojective tests, and reviews of longitudinal behaviors (see reviews by Cramer, 1991; Fisher & Fisher, 1993). The main problem in using direct verbal measures of defense is that the functioning of the defenses is assumed to be unconscious, and therefore it is doubtful that people can give valid answers to questions in this particular domain. The less intrusive measures, such as the use of TAT (Cramer, 1991), are problematic because of their reliance on scoring categories and raters' judgments.

The theoretical conceptualizations presented here suggest an alternative way to investigate. If a person uses denial to ward off anxiety evoked by disturbing (i.e., emotional) stimuli, the processing of such stimuli should be found incomplete, biased, and shallow. In the past, tasks such as word-association tests and memory of events were used to study repression (see Erdelyi & Goldberg, 1979). The study of perceptual defense (i.e., the tendency of subjects to resist perceiving anxiety-evoking stimuli) attempted to show the effects of emotional stimuli on unconscious perception, although several mechanisms, such as familiarity and report bias, were offered as alternative explanations (Neisser, 1967). Other versions of this research strategy are based on percept-genetic theory. These versions consist of presentations of pictures for short durations that become longer on each presentation, with the subjects describing what they saw each time (Cramer, 1991). The notion behind such tasks is that the perceptual process will replicate the stages of defense during normal development.

The report problem embedded in such methodologies was overcome by using either nonverbal behavior or cognitive tasks, which are less dependent on direct report of perceptions and sensations. Luborsky, Blinder, and Schimek (1965) showed that repressors' eyes tend to roam around dangerous (i.e., sexual) zones in a picture, but not to focus on these zones. Spence (1983) found that repressors tend to avoid looking or searching for information about themselves, even if such information is available in the room and they have access to it. These studies were conducted with people categorized as repressors, but their results support the idea that denial may be related to biased information processing. Findings from the domain of anxiety research also support this idea.

Cognitive Performance and Anxiety

If denial functions to ward off anxiety and other unpleasant feelings, then research done on the relationship between anxiety and cognitive performance may be highly relevant to understanding how denial operates. Certainly if one assumes that one reason for heightened anxiety is a failure of the defensive mechanism, then anxiety research can be viewed as dealing with the opposite pole of denial and other defenses.

Past research on the relationship between cognitive functioning and anxiety focused on the quality of performance by high- and low-anxious individuals, tapping the processing capacity aspects of the anxious individual (see Eysenck, MacLeod, & Mathews, 1987). An alternative approach is content-based, and relies on the assumption that individuals high and low on anxiety will differ in their reactions to threatening stimuli.

Two major lines of research can be discerned. The first concerns the studies carried out on the immediate perceptual and attentional processes in relation to threatening and nonthreatening stimuli. Thus, MacLeod, Mathews, and Tata (1986) found that patients with diagnosed anxiety reacted faster to a probe when it replaced either a social or a physical threat word, without regard to whether it was presented on attended or unattended channel; a low-anxiety normal group reacted faster when it replaced a neutral word. This type of finding suggests that the processing of threats by anxious people is preattentive (or automatic). It was also found that when subjects were asked to name the color of threatening words (a variant of the Stroop test), anxious subjects showed a slowing effect, as compared with controls (see Mogg, Mathews, & Weinman, 1989). Thus, anxiety affects the way threats are processed; this way of processing will, in turn, affect anxiety, as well as other behavioral and physiological aspects.

The second line of research is concerned with ambiguous stimuli that can be interpreted as neutral or threatening. Eysenck et al. (1987) reported that high-anxious (trait) subjects produced more threat-related interpretations to homophones having two meanings than low-anxious subjects. However, the relation to state anxiety was low and marginally significant. Mathews, Richards, and Eysenck (1989) reported similar results with clinically anxious and recovering subjects.

It is difficult to interpret these results in terms of situational effects; it could be suggested that high-anxious subjects have greater familiarity with threat interpretations because of past experience. Another possibility is that the presentation of a homophone activates the two meanings automatically, but a preattentive bias among high-anxious people selects the threatening meaning. Thus, anxious individuals are prone to interpret ambiguity in an alarming manner. Because ambiguous events are common in everyday life, such an interpretive bias may be involved in maintaining anxiety states.

Most of the significant associations reported between anxiety and attentional, or interpretive, bias are found for clinically mood-disordered patients who are contrasted with normal control subjects (see MacLeod & Mathews, 1988). These groups differ on both state and trait emotions. To differentiate between these two possible antecedents of differential performance, high trait-anxiety and low trait-anxiety students performed on the probe-detection paradigm of MacLeod at al. (1986) twice: Twelve weeks before an end-of-year examination and the week before the examination. Subjects were tested with two kinds of threat words: related (*foolish, failure*) and unrelated (*lonely, painful*) to the examination. Also, their state anxiety and depression were measured each time. Low trait-anxiety individuals detected the probe faster when it appeared in the opposite area to the threat stimulus, whereas high trait-anxiety individuals were fastest in detecting probes in the same area as the threat. One week before exam, the increase in state anxiety in both groups was related to different attentional changes: High trait-anxiety subjects directed attention toward the area in which examination-related words appeared, whereas the opposite effect was observed for low trait-anxiety subjects. Thus, attentional bias is associated with some interactive function involving both trait and state anxiety.

So far, the research has dealt with biased perception or attention in anxiety. In an experiment designed to assess memory for threat words, Mogg, Mathews, and Weinman (1987) did not find evidence for better recall or recognition of these words by anxious subjects. In contrast, an opposite trend was observed, with the suggestion that anxious subjects may voluntarily avoid elaborative processing of threatening stimuli.

In another study, the question of whether a mood-congruent memory bias exists in anxiety was tested by both implicit (word-completion) and explicit (cued-recall) memory tests (Mathews, Mogg, May, & Eysenck, 1989). High-anxiety, recovered, and normal control subjects were presented with two out of three sets of stimulus words containing positive, neutral, and threatening (physical and social) items. They were first asked to imagine a scene involving them and the word, and then to rate the words on an unpleasant–pleasant continuum. Following the rating tasks, they were given cued-recall (explicit memory) and word-completion (implicit memory) tests. No differences were found between the groups on cued recall. On the word-completion test, which included primed and unprimed words, anxious subjects generated more threat completions (in comparison with nonthreatening words) than recovered or control subjects. The relationship between the implicit and explicit memory biases was near zero. The implication of these results is that the threat value of information has different consequences for high-anxiety or normal subjects' memory representations. Although intended retrieval strategies may obscure the type of elaboration of threats, implicit memory tests may be more appropriate for investigating the representation of threatening information in memory.

Summary

Concerning the cognitive performance of anxious individuals, Mathews (1993) concluded that high-anxious individuals are more prone to perceive threats at the early stages of encoding and registering information, but they may sometimes avoid further processing of the threatening cues at later stages. This conclusion can be further elaborated for deniars, who may be less prone to process information at first stages, and who may also, or because of that, process information less elaborately and less efficiently in later stages as well.

CURRENT EMPIRICAL ASSESSMENTS OF DENIAL

Self-Reference Tasks

Two types of paper-and-pencil tasks were designed in recent years to measure defenses. One was proposed by Heilbrun (1984), who presented subjects with four tasks, each requiring the evaluation of their own personality characteristics in such a way that four types of defenses (i.e., projection, repression, rationalization, and denial) could be inferred. Thus, subjects were presented with behavioral adjectives (favorable, neutral, or unfavorable) and asked to judge each as more or less characteristic of themselves, using their peers as a standard. To measure denial, the list was presented again, with emphasis on the possible arbitrary nature of such choices. Subjects were asked to denote which of the original decisions had been arbitrary. The denial score included the number of times subjects said that a negative disclaimed trait involved an arbitrary decision. This type of measure is problematic on two counts. First, it deals with threats to self-esteem—the type of information that is discussed in relation to repression. Second, it assumes that subjects are denying on the first presentation of adjectives, but not on the second one.

The second type of measure asked people to evaluate the personal likelihood or risk of various threats (Weinstein, 1982), or to indicate the chance (between 0%–100%) of encountering a negative event in comparison with the general population (Ben-Zur, Breznitz, & Hashmonay, 1993; Breznitz, 1990b; Hashmonay, 1989) or their peers (Zakay, 1983). Weinstein (1982, 1987) found a tendency to self-rate chances of encountering various health problems as lower in comparison with the general population—a phenomenon he called *unrealistic optimism;* Zakay (1983) reported that subjects' estimations of positive and negative events were biased: They assessed a negative event as something that is more likely to happen to others and a positive event as more likely to happen to themselves. Hashmonay (1989) investigated the use of denial among Type A and Type B individuals as measured by the Jenkins Activity Survey (JAS; Jenkins, Zyzanski, & Rosenman, 1979), with a chances questionnaire (denial of personal relevance) composed of negative and positive health- and achievement-related events. The subjects rated their chances of experiencing each event in relation to some fictional value that "characterizes" the whole population. Denial was measured by the extent to which subjects rated their chances as lower than those of the general population. Type As denied their chances of failure more than their chances of illness when compared with Type Bs. These results suggest that Type As may use denial of failure more often, and this tendency is instrumental in their struggle for success (see Ben-Zur et al., 1993).

Like others, we found a general tendency in our subjects to underestimate their chances of suffering a negative event. In accordance with Butler and Mathews (1983, 1987), we also found that high-anxiety people rate their chances of getting hurt as higher than low-anxious people (Ben-Zur et al., 1993). This result adds to the validity of the chances estimation method as tapping denial-like processes, assuming that high-anxious people are less successful in defending themselves against aversive events.

In a recent study done in our laboratory, 40 male and 40 female subjects completed the chances questionnaire. In accordance with Weidner and Collins (1993) regarding gender differences in coping, claiming men to be more avoidant than women, we also found that male students underestimated their chances of getting hurt more than female students. This finding lends further support to the measuring of denial by self-reference tasks.

The previously described tasks, although measuring denial by indirect methods, still suffer because verbal assessments are required. Thus, subjects may be at least partially aware that rating their chances as lower or higher is reflective of their personality. Task performance is less obtrusive by far, producing objective measurements such as reaction times and errors.

Perceptual and Memory Tasks

As described earlier, the Stroop test was used to demonstrate anxiety processes. Giles and Cairns (1989) investigated denial versus habituation to violence in Northern Ireland by using a variant of the Stroop test. Of three types of groups—Northern Irish, English living in Northern Ireland, or English living in England—the English living in Ireland took more time to read the color of violent words (vs. neutral) than either the other two groups that did not differ among themselves. Thus, there was no indication of denial in Northern Ireland students, and perhaps they habituated to the situation of continued violence.

Hashmonay (1989) investigated the use of denial among Type A and Type B individuals. Subjects were tested on the Stroop test with boards presenting either health- or achievement-related positive, negative, or neutral words, as well as unrelated neutral words. Following the Stroop test, subjects were asked to perform a rating task for half of the negative, positive, and neutral words of each domain (a male–female rating task that leads to a superficial processing of meaning); they were then tested on a surprise recognition test.

Analysis of the Stroop test results show that Type A men performed faster on achievement-related words when compared with neutral words, whereas Type A women showed the opposite effect. Type A men also remembered the positive achievement-related words less than the positive health-related words; the opposite was found for Type A women. In light of the interactions with gender, these results should be viewed with caution. They suggest that denial in relation to achievement may characterize Type A men when tested on task performance.

Summary

The empirical research concerning cognitive measures and denial is still at its outset. A theoretical framework is needed to direct the choice of cognitive tasks and measures for denial research.

DENIAL AND COGNITIVE FUNCTIONING:
PROPOSED OPERATIONS

Current psychological research is characterized by an information-processing approach to human cognitive functioning (see Eysenck, 1993; Lachman, Lachman, & Butterfield, 1979; Neisser, 1967; Reed, 1988). According to this approach, information is processed by several systems (e.g., attention, perception) that transform it in various ways. In addition, top–down processes, guided by past experience and expectations, are assumed to affect perceptions and cognitions.

On the input side, processing can be characterized along several dimensions. Thus, it has been claimed that there are levels of processing inputs (Craik & Lockhart, 1972); the deeper the processing of information is, the more likely it is to be retained and remembered. Another notion concerns serial and parallel processes. Processes can be envisaged to occur simultaneously if, for example, one assumes that one is attentive and conscious while the others are automatic (e.g., Ben-Zur, 1989; Hasher & Zacks, 1979; Posner & Snyder, 1975).

On the output side, retrieval seems to depend on cues. Implicit memory tests show that certain memory items can be retrieved even if they are not accessible under direct, conscious attempts at remembering (see Eysenck, 1993).

The idea that cognitive functioning is multidimensional or a multiprocess goes back to Freud and his theory of personality (see Epstein, 1994; Neisser, 1967). Indeed, Freud was the first to make a distinction between primary and secondary processing—the first controlled by the id to create mental images of objects that can relieve tension, and the second related to the operations of the ego, being actually utilized in realistic thinking (Hall & Lindzey, 1970). This scheme initiated the study of various types of dichotomies in almost all cognitive domains, such as the preattentive and attentive, the automatic and controlled, or the intuitive and rational, to mention only a few.

An information-processing approach to denial needs to assume the following: (a) Information processing is composed of several stages, (b) cognitive controls can influence processing at each stage, and (c) emotional arousal can, in principle, affect the operation of cognitive controls.

It is further assumed that the use of denial for coping with threatening information entails cognitive processes that minimize the chances that the full meaning of the threat will reach consciousness. The following are suggestions for several operations that may indicate the work of denial. Following Cramer (1991), we distinguish between early and late stages in the processing of threatening stimuli: the first related to perception and attention, and the second related to memory. However, it is assumed that memory deficits indicative of denial result from inter-ference during the encoding stage, rather than problems in retrieval.

In the early stages of processing, cues implying danger are detected by preattentive processes and may affect further processing in the fol-lowing ways.

Shallow Processing

Following levels of processing notions, it is assumed that attention can be directed toward those aspects of the stimulus that do not convey threatening meaning to the individual. Thus, the tendency to process the physical aspects of the information (i.e., sound, visual forms, colors, location) will be stronger than the tendency to process the semantic aspects (i.e., meaning).

The Stroop test can be used to study denial. Previous research sug-gests that anxious subjects perform more slowly in color naming when the colored stimuli are negative words (see Mathews, 1993). It can be assumed that subjects who tend to deny threatening stimuli will per-form faster in color naming when the color stimuli are negative words versus positive or neutral words, or, at the same rate, when compared with anxious subjects. Denial here is made possible by attending to the physical aspects of the stimulus. Good performance on the Stroop test is presumably based on the ability to reject unrelated information either by not processing it or by inhibiting its output.

Segmentation

Denial can also be indicated in the early stages of processing in opera-tions in which attention is drawn toward specific details, rather than the whole. Such operations will result in meaning being lost or not appre-hended. Perceptual tasks such as letter detection in visual search can help establish this type of process. Thus, a person who tends to deny threats may be able to detect letters in negative words without paying much attention to their meaning.

Partial Meaning

There are cases where meaning cannot be disregarded for successful functioning. However, it still may be possible to deny threats by attend-ing to less threatening meanings or contents. Thus, ambiguous words are a good example because they may possess both negative and neutral (or positive) meaning. Testing the apprehension of meaning of such words can be done by testing the type of association that is given to each, testing the type of stimulus that is activated following them, or using the listening and writing test of Eysenck et al. (1987). Because anxious subjects typically show higher sensitization to negative meaning in this type of test, it may be that denial leads to preference of the neutral meaning. This type of operation may also lead to distortion of meaning when conditions favor one meaning over another.

Blocking

In its most extreme form, under conditions of grave threat or danger, denial may result in stopping processing altogether. This is an extreme case, and may be exemplified by perseveration of responses in word associations (Breznitz, 1983c). Thus, the subject stops reacting to the stimulus and produces an unrelated association that is repeated again and again. However, this type of behavior is rare, and probably characterizes psychotic states or extreme levels of situational anxiety.

Retrieval Blocks and Errors

Denial may also be indicated in later stages of processing, by such manifestations as not being able to remember information or retrieving incorrect or alternative information instead of the actual information.

Problems at the retrieval stage are indicative of processing that was done automatically without being consciously apprehended, or that was shallow and fragmented. However, this type of operation is more difficult to measure and is not easily differentiated from repression. Also, it was found that anxious subjects exhibit problems in retrieving negative information from memory (Mathews, 1993). This means that inability to retrieve information may be problematic because of emotional processes during both input and output. Thus, memory tests must be clearly constructed so they can distinguish between anxiety, repression, and denial operations.

REFERENCES

Ben-Zur, H. (1989). Automatic and directed search processes in solving simple semantic memory problems. *Memory & Cognition, 17*(5), 617–626.

Ben-Zur, H., Breznitz, S., & Hashmonay, R. (1993). Type-A behavior pattern and denial of failure-related information. In H. W. Krohne (Ed.), *Attention and avoidance: Strategies in coping with aversiveness* (pp. 171–190). Seattle: Hogrefe & Huber.

Breznitz, S. (Ed.). (1983a). *The denial of stress.* New York: International Universities Press.

Breznitz, S. (1983b). The seven kinds of denial. In S. Breznitz (Ed.), *The denial of stress* (pp. 257–280). New York: International Universities Press.

Breznitz, S. (1983c). Anticipatory stress and denial. In S. Breznitz (Ed.), *The denial of stress* (pp. 225–255). New York: International Universities Press.

Breznitz, S. (1990a). Theory-based stress measurement? Not yet. *Psychological Inquiry, 1,* 17–19.

Breznitz, S. (1990b). *Enhancing performance under stress by information about its expected duration.* (Final Tech. Rep. to ARI Contract No. DAJA-86-C-0048). Haifa, Israel: University of Haifa Press.

Butler, G., & Mathews, A. (1983). Cognitive processes in anxiety. *Advances in Behaviour Research and Therapy, 5,* 51–62.

Butler, G., & Mathews, A. (1987). Anticipatory anxiety and risk perception. *Cognitive Therapy and Research, 11,* 551–565.

Carver, C. S., Scheier, M. F., & Weintraub, J. K. (1989). Assessing coping strategies: A theoretically based approach. *Journal of Personality and Social Psychology, 56,* 267–283.

Craik, F. I. M., & Lockhart, R. S. (1972). Levels of processing: A framework for memory research. *Journal of Verbal Learning and Verbal Behavior, 11,* 671–684.

Cramer, P. (1991). *The development of defense mechanisms: Theory, research, and assessment.* New York: Springer-Verlag.

Dimsdale, J. E., & Hackett, T. P. (1982). Effect of denial on cardiac health and psychological assessment. *American Journal of Psychiatry, 139,* 1477–1480.

Dorpat, T. L. (1985). *Denial and defense in the therapeutic situation.* New York: Aronson.

Epstein, S. (1994). Integration of the cognitive and the psychodynamic unconscious. *American Psychologist, 49,* 709–724.

Erdelyi, M. H., & Goldberg, B. (1979). Let's not sweep repression under the rug: Toward a cognitive psychology of repression. In J. F. Kihlstrom & F. J. Evans (Eds.), *Functional disorders of memory* (pp. 355–402). Hillsdale, NJ: Lawrence Erlbaum Associates.

Eysenck, M. W. (1993). *Principles of cognitive psychology,* Hillsdale, NJ: Lawrence Erlbaum Associates.

Eysenck, M. W., MacLeod, C., & Mathews, A. (1987). Cognitive functioning and anxiety. *Psychological Research, 49,* 189–195.

Fisher, S., & Fisher, R. L. (1993). *The psychology of adaptation to absurdity: Tactics of make-believe.* Hillsdale, NJ: Lawrence Erlbaum Associates.

Freud, S. (1956). Inhibitions, symptoms and anxiety. In J. Strachey (Ed.), *The standard edition of the complete psychological works of Sigmund Freud* (Vol. 20). London: Hogarth. (Original work published 1926)

Giles, M., & Cairns, E. (1989). Colour naming of violence-related words in Northern Ireland. *British Journal of Clinical Psychology, 28,* 87–88.

Goldberg, L. (1983). The concept and mechanisms of denial: A selective overview. In S. Breznitz (Ed.), *The denial of stress* (pp. 83–95). New York: International Universities Press.

Gur, R. C., & Sackeim, H. A. (1979). Self-deception: A concept in search of a phenomenon. *Journal of Personality and Social Psychology, 4,* 147–169.

Haan, N. (1977). *Coping and defending: Processes of self-environment organization.* New York: Academic Press.

Hall, C. S., & Lindzey, G. (1970). *Theories of personality* (2nd ed.). New York: Wiley.

Hasher, L., & Zacks, R. T. (1979). Automatic and effortful processes in memory. *Journal of Experimental Psychology: General, 108,* 356–388.

Hashmonay, R. (1989). *The use of differential denial by individuals characterized by Type A behavior pattern.* Unpublished master's thesis, Tel Aviv University.

Heilbrun, A. B., Jr. (1984). Cognitive defenses and life stress: An information-processing analysis. *Psychological Reports, 54,* 3–17.

Janis, I. L. (1983). Preventing pathological denial by means of stress inoculation. In S. Breznitz (Ed.), *The denial of stress* (pp. 35–76). New York: International Universities Press.

Janis, I. L., & Mann, L. (1977). *Decision making: A Psychological analysis of conflict, choice and commitment*. New York: The Free Press.

Jenkins, C. D., Zyzanski, S. J., & Rosenman, R. H. (1979). *Jenkins activity survey*. New York: Psychological Corporation.

Krebs, D., Denton, K., & Higgins, N. C. (1988). On the evolution of self-knowledge and self-deception. In K. B. MacDonald (Ed.), *Sociobiological perspectives on human development* (pp. 103–139). New York: Springer-Verlag.

Krohne, H. W. (1993). Vigilance and cognitive avoidance as concepts in coping research. In H. W. Krohne (Ed.), *Attention and avoidance: Strategies in coping with aversiveness* (pp. 19–50). Seattle: Hogrefe & Huber.

Lachman, R., Lachman, J. L., & Butterfield, E. C. (1979). *Cognitive psychology and information processing*. Hillsdale, NJ: Lawrence Erlbaum Associates.

Lazarus, R. S. (1966). *Psychological stress and the coping process*. New York: McGraw-Hill.

Lazarus, R. S. (1983). The costs and benefits of denial. In S. Breznitz (Ed.), *The denial of stress* (pp. 1–30). New York: International Universities Press.

Lazarus, R. S., & Folkman, S. (1984). *Stress, appraisal, and coping*. New York: Springer.

Luborsky, L., Blinder, B., & Schimek, J. (1965). Looking, recalling and GSR as a function of defense. *Journal of Abnormal Psychology, 70,* 270–280.

MacLeod, C., & Mathews, A. (1988). Anxiety and the allocation of attention to threat. *The Quarterly Journal of Experimental Psychology, 40A,* 653–670.

MacLeod, C., Mathews, A., & Tata, P. (1986). Attentional bias in emotional disorders. *Journal of Abnormal Psychology, 95,* 15–20.

Mathews, M. (1993). Attention and memory for threat in anxiety. In H. W. Krohne (Ed.), *Attention and avoidance: Strategies in coping with aversiveness* (pp. 119–135). Seattle: Hogrefe & Huber.

Mathews, M., Mogg, K., May, J., & Eysenck, M. W. (1989). Implicit and explicit memory bias in anxiety. *Journal of Abnormal Psychology, 98,* 236–240.

Mathews, A., Richards, A., & Eysenck, M. W. (1989). Interpretation of homophones related to threat in anxiety states. *Journal of Abnormal Psychology, 98,* 31–34.

Miller, S. M. (1989). Cognitive informational styles in the process of coping with threat and frustration. *Advances in Behaviour Research and Therapy, 11,* 223–234.

Mogg, K., Mathews, A., & Weinman, J. (1987). Memory bias in clinical anxiety. *Journal of Abnormal Psychology, 96,* 94–98.

Mogg, K., Mathews, A., & Weinman, J. (1989). Selective processing of threat cues in anxiety states: A replication. *Behaviour Research and Therapy, 27,* 317–323.

Neisser, U. (1967). *Cognitive psychology*. New York: Appleton-Century-Crofts.

Plutchik, R., Kellerman, H., & Conte, H. R. (1979). A structural theory of ego defenses and emotions. In C. E. Izard (Ed.), *Emotions in personality and psychopathology* (pp. 229–257). New York: Plenum.

Posner, M. I., & Snyder, C. R. R. (1975). Attention and cognitive control. In R. L. Solso (Ed.), *Information processing and cognition: The Loyola symposium* (pp. 55–85). Hillsdale, NJ: Lawrence Erlbaum Associates.

Reed, S. K. (1988). *Cognition: Theory and application* (2nd ed.). Monterey, CA: Brooks/Cole.

Spence, D. P. (1983). The paradox of denial. In S. Breznitz (Ed.), *The denial of stress* (pp. 103–123). New York: International Universities Press.

Suls, J., & Fletcher, B. (1985). The relative efficacy of avoidant and nonavoidant coping strategies: A meta-analysis. *Health Psychology, 4,* 249–288.

Taylor, S. E., & Brown, J. D. (1988). Illusion and well-being: A social psychological perspective on mental health. *Psychological Bulletin, 103*(2), 193–210.

Trivers, R. (1985). *Social evolution*. Menlo Park, CA: Benjamin/Cummings.

Weidner, G., & Collins, R. L. (1993). Gender, coping, and health. In H. W. Krohne (Ed.),

Attention and avoidance: Strategies in coping with aversiveness (pp. 19–50). Seattle: Hogrefe & Huber.

Weisman, A., & Hackett, T. P. (1961). Predilection to death: Death and dying as a psychiatric problem. *Psychosomatic Medicine, 23,* 232–256.

Weinstein, N. D. (1982). Unrealistic optimism about susceptibility to health problems. *Journal of Behavioral Medicine, 5,* 441–460.

Weinstein, N. D. (1987). Unrealistic optimism about susceptibility to health problems: Conclusions from a community-wide sample. *Journal of Behavioral Medicine, 10,* 481–500.

Zakay, D. (1983). The relationship between the probability assessor and the outcomes of an event as a determiner of subjective probability. *Acta Psychologica, 53,* 271–280.

Vaillant, G. E. (1977). *Adaptation to life.* Boston: Little, Brown.

10

Imposture Syndromes:
A Clinical View

Lloyd A. Wells

Impostors are notorious in great literature and art. One thinks of Thomas Chatterton and Boris Godunov. They are not unknown in history: A wonderful section of Paris is named after St. Germain des Près. In the psychiatric literature, however, they receive little consideration, especially in recent years. Work continues to be done on syndromes of imposture (Gediman, 1985, 1986; Kets de Vries, 1990; King & Ford, 1988; Spivak, Rodin, & Sutherland, 1994), but it is sparse. Nevertheless, imposture is ubiquitous, and impostors have much to teach us.

Imposture has previously been defined as "the attempt to make others believe that one is someone other than himself or herself or fills a role for which he is not in fact qualified" (Wells, 1986, p. 588). Syndromes of imposture have fascinated psychiatrists since Johannes Weyer, the "father" of psychiatry, described such a patient whom he actually allowed to live with his family so that he could study her in depth.

In this chapter, I attempt to describe some clinical impostors whom I have known and to describe the relationship of some of these syndromes to developmental factors. The general public is probably most familiar with the syndrome of the "great impostor"—someone who passes him or herself off as someone else; who functions at a profession (or series of professions) for which he or she is not, in fact, qualified; or who inherits money under a false identity. A classic case was described by Abraham (1935). Abraham's patient had considerable success as an impostor before and after World War I, but stopped his imposture after marrying a much older woman. Abraham viewed imposture as a syndrome that derived from oedipal pathology. The exploits of the late Frederick Demarra in this country, and George Psalmonogar's efforts to establish himself as the representative of Formosa to Great Britain in the past, are examples of the syndrome.

Many psychoanalysts have been peripherally interested in imposture: Most, with Abraham (1935) and Greenacre (1958a, 1958b), have viewed it as oedipal pathology. I would maintain, however, that the syndrome is multifaceted, and often represents the failure of various adaptive mechanisms, often having its roots in play and transitional relatedness. Several cases that illustrate the types of imposture syndromes commonly seen in clinical practice are presented herein.

IMPOSTURE FOR GAIN[1]

Roger Tichborne was born of an English father and a French mother. His early years were spent in France, and French was his first language. With the death of his young cousin, it became apparent that Roger would be heir to the barony of Tichborne. His mother opposed the boy's moving to England, or even visiting, until, when Roger was 16, his uncle died. He was allowed to accompany his father to the funeral, with the promise to his mother that he would return immediately. Instead, he was enrolled at an English school, where he stayed for 3 years, with minimal contact with his reportedly infuriated mother. The mother apparently attempted a rapprochement with her son around the issue of an arranged marriage, but this, too, he refused. After a brief army career, Roger Tichborne made a trip to South America and was lost at sea.

His guilt-ridden mother was unable to accept the fact of his death—with that of the rest of the crew and passengers on his ship. Having moved to her son's English estate, she advertised widely for news of him, and made payments to several sailors who made trips to the estate to acknowledge that they had, indeed, seen Roger. She advertised worldwide for news of her son, which was soon forthcoming. A man from Walla Walla, Australia, claimed to be her son and, with the help of a retired servant of the family, learned details of the estate and family. In fact, this man was Arthur Orton, an obese English butcher. He later confessed that he had never known, or indeed heard of, Roger Tichborne until he had seen the advertisement placed by Lady Tichborne. He claimed that he was Roger Tichborne initially on a dare from a friend. Immediately before his planned meeting with Lady Tichborne, he alleged that he was ill, so that lady Tichborne came to visit him as he lay in bed in his darkened hotel room. This visit was not entirely satisfactory; Orton "remembered" the grandfather Roger

---

[1]The cases on imposture for gain, Munchausen's syndrome, hoaxes, literary imposture, transvestism, anorexia nervosa, circumscribed or limited imposture, imposture by proxy, and garden-variety imposture are taken from "Varieties of Imposture" by L. A. Wells, 1986, *Perspectives in Biology and Medicine, 29*, pp. 588–610. Copyright ©1986 by University of Chicago Press. Reprinted by permission.

Tichborne had never met, recalled attending a school he had not attended, and recalled a childhood illness Tichborne had not had. Nevertheless, the guilty Lady Tichborne was satisfied, rationalizing that her son was confused and "as if in a dream." She welcomed Orton and his wife and children, and was extremely generous to them.

Orton's next step was to sue the current Tichborne heir, Sir Alfred Tichborne. He zealously talked to people who had known Roger Tichborne, then went to meet Roger's old friends, "remembering" old times with them. As a result, at the trial, Arthur Orton had over 100 witnesses willing to swear that he was Roger Tichborne. The trial actually seemed to be going in Orton's favor, until his own vanity compelled him to testify personally, which was not necessary. Despite the diligent imposture that he had achieved to that point, Orton's performance as a witness at the trial was ludicrous. He was unable to recall a single detail of his childhood, and could not remember his college, his mother's maiden name, any details of the Tichborne estate, the French language, and details of Tichborne's relationship with his fiancée. The fact that the claimant had the initials "A.O." tattooed on his arm, furthermore, did not help his case. The case was not only judged for Sir Alfred Tichborne; Arthur Orton was indicted, convicted, and sentenced to 14 years imprisonment. Orton served 10 years in prison, confessed and published his imposture, and died, in poverty, 14 years after he was released from prison. An impostor to the end, his coffin is inscribed, "Sir Robert Charles Doughty Tichborne."

Imposture for gain, well illustrated by the case of Arthur Orton, is a common form of imposture described in the daily newspaper and seen, from time to time, by forensic psychiatrist. But it does not come to psychiatric attention frequently outside the forensic setting. The pure sociopath pretending to be someone else for his or her own gain may get away with it, but the seeds of the true impostor's self-destruction are often implanted in the imposture. In Orton's case, for example, the legal proceedings appeared to be in his favor until, without any necessity to do so, he insisted on testifying personally and made an utter fool of himself. He ended up being sentenced to prison, and he confessed to the crime. All of this happened despite his previous ability to convince many people that he was, in fact, Roger Tichborne. His coffin states that he is Roger Tichborne. It is not uncommon for impostors to confess, but to insist at death that they really are the person they had claimed to be.

MUNCHAUSEN'S SYNDROME

A 32-year-old man presented with a chief complaint of weight loss of 2 years' duration. He was 6' 1" and weighed 118 pounds at the time of admission. He stated that he had had a pancreatic insulinoma removed, and that he had had two further abdominal surgeries. The examining physician sent for records of these previous interventions, writing to the physicians and hospitals listed by the patient. He stated that his most recent diagnosis had been Crohn's disease, following multiple biopsies.

On examination, he was a frail-appearing man with two healed abdominal incisions. Physical examination was otherwise unremarkable. On mental status examination, he was pleasant, cooperative, and medically knowledgeable, and he used a considerable amount of intellectualization. He did not seem anxious about his illness, and joked about it in a nondefensive manner. There was no evidence of affective or thought disorder, and there was no apparent cognitive impairment.

He was anemic and had copious diarrhea and gross hematuria. Stools were markedly positive for phenolphthalein. A syringe was found in his room. When confronted with his physicians' suspicions, he was bland and unconcerned. He readily agreed to speak with a psychiatrist, but offered little in the interview. The next day, he left the hospital.

Two months later, one of the physicians who had been involved in his case received a telephone call from a woman who said that she was the patient's wife. She stated that he had just returned home from the hospital—although he had, in fact, left 2 months previously—and she had questions regarding the inoperable, metastatic malignant illness that the patient alleged had been diagnosed, as well as about the experimental chemotherapy he said he was receiving.

This case is illustrative of many features of this baffling syndrome. The secondary gain in the disorder is sometimes apparent, but it is never as clear as that in imposture for gain, for example. The patient's feigned illness can, however, become the cornerstone of his or her life. Sadomasochistic issues are usually quite obvious. This patient put himself through all sorts of painful self-inflicted procedures, but also tormented his wife with his stories about a fatal outcome.

An implicit relationship of Munchausen's syndrome with other forms of imposture has been provided by Spiro (1968). Specifically, the author provided a case study of a man who had Munchausen's syndrome, and who also impersonated physicians, lawyers, and private detectives while drinking in various bars. In this case, the impostor often was successful in impersonating his chosen role, but at the end of the evening he sometimes confessed. Such "confessions" sometimes prompted physical violence against the patient. Components of the syndrome enumerated by Spiro included imposture, flight, masochism, a sense of control reinforced by control of the "illness," hostility, and a reworking of conflict. The patient I described demonstrated many of these characteristics, including imposture, flight, hostility (toward his wife), and masochism.

Medical imposture takes many forms besides Munchausen's syndrome and Munchausen's by proxy (Spivak & Rodin, 1994). In addition to these, there is frank, conscious malingering. There are gray areas, as well. Although "compensation neurosis" is nowhere to be found in official nosologies, it is a common entity with conscious and unconscious components. Somatization disorder (Briquet's syndrome) is not associated with conscious manufacture of the somatic complaints, but several patients with this disorder have talked to me of conscious exaggeration and dramatization of their symptoms.

HOAXES

An unhappy young woman whose boyfriend had left her for another girlfriend submitted to the newspaper an elaborate account of her "small wedding" to the man in question right after he had left on a lengthy vacation. His friends were surprised when they read the account of the "wedding," but knew he had dated the young woman in the past. His current girlfriend read the account and was hurt and very angry at him. When he returned from his vacation, he was bewildered by many wedding gifts, letters, and an angry message of rejection from his girlfriend. Again, in the case of the woman who placed the marriage description in the newspaper, one sees imposture, hostility, mastery of conflict, and much secondary gain.

LITERARY IMPOSTURE

Literary imposture can be of several types. George Eliot, for example, was a woman writing under a man's name because she felt it would be impossible to publish her work as a woman. Here, there is no apparent psychopathology. Several writers, particularly writers of popular novels in the 20th century, have written under two or more names for the purpose of reducing income tax. Such action probably qualifies as a mild form of imposture for gain.

Other modern writers who have had serious literary reputations at stake have chosen to publish light fiction under pseudonyms. Here, there is no psychopathology. Would Graham Greene not be given more consideration as a major novelist had he published his spy stories under a pseudonym?

McPherson and Chatterton both perpetrated more notorious literary hoaxes. The role of possible psychopathology in their specific hoaxes is unclear. It is interesting to speculate, however, about a possible link of creativity with some of these impostures. Many painters and actors apparently have perpetrated hoaxes. The dynamics of this phenomenon are unclear and variable, but the link of creativity with imposture is worth exploring. Klotz (1992) reviewed fascinating hoaxes and imposture in medicine and science (see Kaplan, 1987, for further reading).

TRANSVESTISM

A 38-year-old man presented for psychiatric evaluation with this chief complaint: "Have you fellows done much research on transvestism in the last few years?" At or before the age of 4, the patient enjoyed dressing in his older sister's clothes; at about age 7, he began stealing women's clothes from clotheslines. As a young adolescent, he fantasized about dressing as a girl, dating a boy, and then "fooling" him; he did this on five occasions.

He joined the navy and was discharged 6 years later after being discovered in female dress during a short liberty. Two additional arrests in the large city in which he lived also occurred. Although his own sexual activities were entirely heterosexual, it was necessary for him to wear female clothing while having intercourse. His desire for sexual activity was extremely low, his fantasies centered around "passing" as a woman and also becoming a woman via a sex change operation.

As an adolescent and young man, the patient planned his cross-dressing experiences with the deliberate intention of producing sexual excitement. As he aged, however, he obtained less sexual gratification from these episodes, but instead found them calming and pacifying. He cross-dressed much more frequently when under stress or when working extra hard.

The patient's mother was from a prominent, well-educated family. Several of her siblings and close relatives were well known in the legal, clerical, and medical professions. She married a self-educated man who became successful in a trade; he was several rungs beneath her on the social ladder. She verbally berated the husband on a daily basis, and occasionally hit him with her fists, according to the recollection of the patient and his older sister. This sister, almost 2 years older than the patient, was bright and attractive with many friends during childhood and adolescence. She received a master's degree and is successful in her work.

As a child, the patient always did poorly in school, with low grades and frequent comments by his teachers that he did not "live up to his potential." When he was tested for the first time, as an adult, it became apparent that he had moderately severe dyslexia. His mother punished him for his poor school performance by limiting his social opportunities, and, allegedly to embarrass him, dressed him in girls' clothing.

The patient had many areas of success. He was a popular and successful amateur athlete. His navy service was as an aviator, and he was much decorated for extraordinary bravery in combat and rescue operations. He married and brought up a very successful son with no apparent sexual deviations. He became a successful business executive despite his dyslexia and relatively poor academic background. He was held in great esteem by his community, where he headed several fund drives and civic organizations.

He had one other area of imposture besides transvestism. He purchased clerical clothes and, while away from home, often posed as a priest. He made a "clergy" sign for his car, which was often prominently displayed when he parked in no-parking zones (with good results, according to the patient). He enjoyed wearing a raincoat and sitting in waiting areas. When a person nearby would tell an off-color story, the patient would wait almost until the punch line, then unbutton his coat and apologetically state that he was a clergyman.

In most of his activities, this patient was relentlessly hard-driving. He pushed himself hard, and expected no less of his colleagues and those who worked for him. He refused to allow himself to meet any dependency needs. While dressed as a woman, he felt more compassionate and allowed himself to feel weak and dependent. Thus, his cross-dressing provided him with his only opportunity for relaxation. As time went on, he derived less sexual gratification from his cross-dressing and participated in it primarily as a means to relieve stress.

Although transvestism is usually not discussed in commentaries on imposture, it seems to be clearly a syndrome of imposture. In this case, a man, usually, is attempting to pass as a woman. Although most impostors are well aware of their imposture, transvestites often perform an imposture with themselves as subjects and objects: They try to convince themselves that they are woman as well, or at least that they are *like* women (Ovesey & Person, 1973). While "passing" as women, they describe a feeling state of femininity, or their own version of femininity. The case presented here is interesting in that the patient displayed many other forms of imposture besides dressing as a woman.

Identity diffusion, which is comparable to that found in people with "as-if" personalities, has been described in transsexuals, but not in transvestites. In this patient, however, there was clearly a partially resolved identity diffusion, which became apparent in the transference. Person and Ovesey (1978) commented on transvestites' lack of tenderness as well as their obsessiveness. This patient was quite obsessive, but he was capable of great tenderness. For decades, however, he was subjectively unable to feel any tenderness except when he was dressed as a woman. It was only in late middle age that he was able to achieve this at other times. The patient's sexual drive was very low, which was also compatible with Person and Ovesey's findings. They also speculated on the role of clothes as both successor transitional objects and fetishistic defenses against incest.

In her writing about transvestism, Greenacre (1958a, 1958b) stressed the preservation of infantile objects through the cross-dressing, and thought it protected the patient against severe identity diffusion. She also commented that many transvestites have a fascination for amputated body parts. This patient frequently discussed his abhorrence of a colleague with an artificial arm, which intrigued him. The patient also enjoyed removing his full set of false teeth at public functions for the shock value.

Abraham (1935) described the fantasy of the body as phallus, and Lewin (1933) wrote about the role of this phenomenon in various paraphilias. Although the patient described did not have such a fantasy, other transvestites interviewed by the author have reported it. Segal (1965) described the role of transvestism as both impulse and defense against harsh superego strictures, and Socarides (1970) speculated that the disorder is associated with suffering and unconscious conflict, similar to other perversions.

The case presented is of transvestism, but other paraphilias also have many aspects of imposture. For example, there are many elements of imposture in sadomasochism. Overtly sadomasochistic sexual practices often contain elements of imposture in both "victim" and "victimizer."[2] Most people who engage in this type of sexual behavior are, at various times, willing to play sadistic or masochist roles. Just as the transvestite patient discussed earlier splits masculine and feminine personality characteristics into extreme, mutually incompatible roles, the sadomasochist splits dominance–submission and independence–dependence personality characteristics. The sadomasochistic sexual encounter often involves a fantasized or manufactured incident that provokes the "punishment." Often both partners are admittedly acting roles in an agreed-on drama they have scripted together. Finally, this type of behavior allows people who are often quite impaired to imagine that they are totally dominant and in control of the lives of others, or, alternatively, that they serve a perfect human being. The highly ritualized playacting involved in such encounters can also protect the people from some of the vicissitudes of true intimacy.

---

[2]This section on paraphilias is taken from "Varieties of Imposture" by L. A. Wells, 1986, *Perspectives in Biology and Medicine, 29*, pp. 588–610. Copyright ©1986 by University of Chicago Press. Reprinted by permission.

Litman and Swearingen (1972) wrote about some of these phenomena, finding that sadomasochists are able to dramatize their often drab lives, as well as erotize helplessness and overcome it. They see such behavior as allowing them some capacity for relationships and transcendence. Each person in such a dyad, however, is just a part object for the other. Finally, as in other types of imposture, the apparent situation is not the real one. In fact, it is the masochistic partner who is usually in control of the duration and severity of pain during the sadomasochistic encounter.

ANOREXIA NERVOSA

Case 1

The patient was a 25-year-old married, childless professional who was referred because of recurrent anorexia nervosa. Eight years previously, she had been hospitalized for this disorder and had a good outcome. Body image remained distorted, and eating patterns remained odd, but she stopped vomiting and was able to maintain her weight.

At age 23, she married a man with whom she had had a long-standing sexual relationship and about whom she had great ambivalence. Despite a university education, he was chronically unemployed, holding menial jobs for a few weeks and then quitting. He also had recurrent legal problems because of writing bad checks. Two months after the marriage and 5 days after the hospitalization of her grandfather for a myocardial infarction, the patient noted an increased preoccupation with food. Over the next 2 months, other features of anorexia nervosa with bulimia and vomiting emerged. She developed a markedly abnormal body image, feeling she was very fat albeit realizing that this perception was invalid. She lost 26% of her body weight. When she presented for psychiatric assessment, she was 5' 6" and weighed 86 pounds. She exercised for more than 2 hours daily, ate popcorn voluminously, and had developed amenorrhea and a great reduction in her sexual drive. Her mother and father were both obese. Her father was also an alcoholic, and had been flirtatious and sexually provocative with the patient on many occasions. Her mother-in-law was grossly obese and very preoccupied by the patient's thinness. Indeed, she sent bakery products 200 miles through the mail twice each week to the patient. The patient met *DSM–III* criteria for anorexia nervosa, and also had bulimia and vomiting.

This patient was involved in several impostures of varying magnitudes. When driving alone, she fantasized that she was an actress and performed several roles in the car. At other times, she fantasized that she was another person, often a male. At parties, she tended to eat voluminously. When friends would comment enviously that she seemed able to eat well without gaining weight, she would laugh and say, "That's because I have anorexia nervosa with bulimia and vomiting." She reveled in the fact that she presented this truth in such a manner that her friends would laugh and not suspect her of having the syndrome that she did, indeed, have. More seriously, this highly intelligent young woman, who dropped out of college after 1 year, obtained the forged credentials of a master's degree. She used these to obtain employment and apparently performed her job very well, earning the highest possible merit raise 3 years consecutively.

Case 2

A 26-year-old woman presented with a 4-year history of moderately well-controlled anorexia nervosa. She was the only daughter of a wealthy and powerful businessman who drank excessively and, from her description, had many sociopathic traits. He and the patient's mother desperately wanted the patient to have a career in the arts; she had taken extensive music, painting, and elocution lessons from early childhood. However, at age 20, the patient left home and moved to California. There, she said, she had been making inroads into the entertainment industry, working in several choruses, singing a few solos, acting small parts in films, and touring in summer stock playing major roles. Her parents called the physician several times. It was apparent that they, too, believed this account of her professional life.

The patient declined the recommended treatment for her illness, and contacted a friend to take her home. When the friend, a middle-aged woman, arrived, she asked to speak with the physician. He spoke with her after receiving permission from the patient. The friend asked if the patient had "been snowing you with all that bull," and gave a very different account of the patient's life. Apparently, the patient had gone to Hollywood to become an entertainer, but was unable to find employment. She drifted into some rather seamy part-time jobs, including one in a sexually oriented massage parlor, where she met her friend. This middle-aged woman became quite protective of the patient in a maternal, rather than a sexual, way, and persuaded her to become her roommate. She helped her find work in a clothing factory, which the patient had done for 18 months prior to her psychiatric evaluation.

A variant of imposture in relation to the anorexia nervosa syndrome was also seen by the author. A hysteroid 19-year-old adolescent female who had attained psychiatric attention after a series of spectacular suicide gestures was featured in the newspaper as a heroic, recovering anorectic. She, in fact, had never had any features of this syndrome, but had known several patients who did have it.

These cases of anorexia nervosa are clearly accompanied by imposture syndromes. Although many clinicians who care for anorectic patients, often in states of semistarvation, are struck by their apparent poverty of creative thought and imaginative fantasy, this is far from the case in many patients, if not most (Wells, 1982). Volkan (1965) described his "little man" phenomenon in a case of anorexia nervosa. In this phenomenon, a person is aware of a "little being" inside him or herself that comments on or is responsible for many of the person's activities. This phenomenon is related to some of the findings in dissociative disorders, which is discussed later.

Story (1976) wrote about the role of impersonation in patients with anorexia nervosa. According to him, these patients caricature a perfect mother and attempt to create a perfect inner being. Critchley (1979c) addressed body image in relation to syndromes that are certainly related to imposture. For example, he has written on the significance of tattoos. He has also described the "Miss Havisham" syndrome, in which people (usually women) seem to become arrested at a certain age in terms of their dress, attempted appearance, and actions.

CIRCUMSCRIBED OR LIMITED IMPOSTURE

A 37-year-old married physician, father of four, was a successful and respected medical specialist. He was the only boy in a family of four children, and had had an intense and ambivalent bond with his mother from an early age. He presented for psychiatric evaluation with symptoms of mild depression and anhedonia.

When he was a child, his mother had had very high expectations for the patient, and had urged him to become a surgeon from at least age 5. When he decided to become a surgeon at age 8, she began to urge him to become chairman of a major department. He graduated from medical school and discovered that another medical specialty interested him most. He completed residency training in this specialty, and became successful in practice. However, he was unable ever to tell his mother about this career change.

During his mother's infrequent visits to his home, which was several hundred miles from hers, the patient and his family maintained the charade that he was a surgeon. When he returned from work, he would tell anecdotes about the day's operations, mistakes of surgical colleagues, and promising surgical research he was doing. When he was

35, he told his mother that he had become chairman of the department of surgery.

In other respects, his life was a model of probity. He was distressed by the imposture and felt exceedingly guilty about it, but maintained that telling his mother the truth would be so distressing to her that "she would be destroyed." He was also completely unable to express any anger directed toward his mother. This patient had felt controlled by his mother from an early age. He felt that she had made great sacrifices for him and, as a result, that it was his duty to please her. However, his attempt to "please" her, rooted as it was in his profound ambivalence, led to superficiality in their contacts, and emotional and indeed physical separation. In this imposture, the patient portrayed his mother's version of what should be his own ego ideal, but the unconscious hostility also served to effect psychological separation. The parody of her wish allowed him to separate and individuate, and thus served to emancipate him from his mother, which presumably did not please her. The dynamics of this case are implicit.

IMPOSTURE BY PROXY

Perhaps the most malevolent form of imposture is imposture by proxy, in which a person or couple fosters or directly implements a form of imposture in another person, often a child. This imposture by proxy often involves medical or sexual imposture. Three cases are described.

Case 1

A 34-year-old registered nurse brought her 8-year-old child, who had juvenile-onset diabetes mellitus, to a pediatric unit for severe hypoglycemic episodes on three occasions over a 4-month period. The child adamantly denied any tampering with his usual insulin dose, and extensive work up for insulin antibodies was negative. On the final admission, a tired pediatric resident, lacking in tact, asked the mother if she had been injecting extra insulin. The mother tearfully admitted that she had indeed been doing this for reasons unknown to her.

Case 2

A 3-year-old child was referred for evaluation of chronic, severe diarrhea that had led to episodic hypokalemia. An extensive gastroenterologic work up was negative, and phenolphthalein was found in stool samples. The child's parents admitted that they had been giving the child large amounts of laxatives. They were in the process of suing one hospital to which the child had been admitted.

Case 3

A 4-year-old boy was referred for psychiatric evaluation by the director of his nursery school because she feared "he may be a homosexual." At nursery school, this boy appeared to be very delicate, and preferred to play with little girls rather than little boys. He had been overheard asking girls if he could have articles of their clothing. On two occasions, he came to school wearing dresses. When queried about this, he told the teacher that he always wore dresses at home. His father refused to participate in the evaluation, insisting that nothing was wrong with his son. The mother showed *la belle indifférence* to the situation, readily admitting that she dressed her son as a girl because she thought he appeared very "cute" when she did this. She had hoped for a girl during her pregnancy, and was pleased that her son appeared to be so feminine. She felt that most men were "harsh and nasty" and wanted to prevent this occurrence in her boy.

The "use" of a child to meet parental needs is unfortunately commonplace, and the role of a child as parental scapegoat is also relatively common. However, with the child either the bad repository of the parent's unacceptable self or the conduit of the parent's disguised and unacceptable wishes, the overt destructiveness of imposture by proxy is direct and is usually viewed as appalling. The reader is referred to Schreier and Libow's (1993) book for further elucidation of this puzzling syndrome.

GARDEN-VARIETY IMPOSTURE

Case

The patient was a 26-year-old woman who asked for psychotherapy because of chronic dysphoria. She was the older of two children—the only girl. Her mother was perceived as a rather narcissistic woman who needed her daughter to meet her own needs. The patient attempted to meet her mother's expectations. As a result, she hid many "unpleasant" aspects of her life from her mother. These included failing in professional school and an induced abortion.

From her earliest memories, the patient held a secret belief, unshared until her therapy, that she was "special" and "chosen" to accomplish some great event. She had many fantasies of this nature over the years. In her adult daydreams, she visualized her "special" self as a beautiful young child.

In her work, she was upwardly mobile. She chose jobs primarily based on the opportunity for professional advancement. However, she obtained the jobs by what she viewed as a form of imposture: She would convince the potential employer that the job, which per se held relatively little interest for her, was what she had hoped to do for many years. Despite her record of frequent job changes, she was almost always convincing.

Impostures of this variety are viewed as fun and are engaged in by many healthy people. Costume parties and similar events allow people to enjoy the transitory phenomenon of imposture without any of its drawbacks. In the case discussed, a relatively healthy young woman who had the "little man" phenomenon of Volkan (1965) used her "imposture" adaptively. This "internalized special child" helped with creativity, self-esteem, and flexibility.

MULTIPLE-PERSONALITY DISORDER AND DISSOCIATION

Case 1

This patient was studied extensively because she was in psychoanalytic treatment, now in its fifth year. Most patients with multiple-personality disorder or dissociative disorders have not been treated with this modality, and none has been treated psychoanalytically for so long.

The patient is in her early 30s—a single mother of a young teenage son. She was initially referred by her son's pediatrician because of his behavior problems, which, over the years, have been extreme. Initially, she seemed to be a pleasant, rather dim-witted, well-meaning young woman. She described a rather idyllic childhood as the daughter of well-off parents, her father quite well known in his professional field. She had a well-paying job that she disliked, but excelled at, and she had a few friends, most of whom were rather hedonistic. She disclosed little about her social life, but I thought from her references and my inferences that she was rather promiscuous, and that she enjoyed parties a lot, but tried to do the best for her son. I provided her with some education about raising children and with occasional supportive therapy. I often became inexplicably sleepy during her therapy hours, and often could not reconstruct them. I chalked this up to the fact that she seemed rather boring and not very bright.

Rather abruptly, a change occurred. One day, Mary brought in some writing she had found at home that had frightened her very much. It started out in her own hand and progressed to that of a much more immature hand with a series of childhood thoughts. Over time, Mary told me about a very different childhood, replete with physical abuse from her father. She particularly remembered a beating at age 4, in which she had first "left" her body, initially seeing her mother grow ever more distant in a tunnel, and then hovering above her body, realizing that she was hurt, but not feeling pain. She also remembered many episodes of highly aberrant and intrusive behavior on the mother's part, as well as being the victim of sexual assault and fellatio by her paternal grandfather when she was 9. She had had a persistent fantasy that someone would realize what was going on and take her out of the family, and she had discussions with what seemed to be "God," who kept her from suicide. She had developed a full-fledged dissociative system, which continued to evolve over a great many years. The system subsumed a number of "rules," which had been imposed in her childhood belief to keep her from being killed. The first of these had to do with never directly telling anyone what was going on. The second was that she was completely responsible for what was going on, with the corollary that she could learn, if she were sufficiently observant, "never to make the same mistake twice," and thus to stop what was going on. The second rule and its corollary gave her an immense sense of control in a situation that, of course, she could not control.

In dissociated states, she told me four times of a long-lasting sexual relationship with her father, which persisted until she was at least 18 and perhaps into adult life. In nondissociated states, she did not acknowledge this situation, although she admitted that she was flooded with intrusive thoughts and even hallucinations of a possible sexual relationship with her father: "I just don't think that could have happened: He loved me." She had a great deal of illogic about love: "If people love you, what they do to you is really different than what it might seem." Like other patients with this disorder, she was profoundly ambivalent about her father.

Mary had many positive sequelae from her defensive system. These included an extraordinarily precise, virtually photographic, memory. This seemed ironic in the context of "sending away" so many bad memories, but it was highly adaptive in many regards. She developed a profound, completely idiosyncratic ethical sense and a morality that was based on not inflicting harm and not being manipulative. The third underpinning of this moral sense was the primacy of trust, which, of course, was highly problematic because she did not know what the primal truth was. In my view, her immense creativity was a direct result of her intelligence coupled with her dissociative system. She was also able to amuse herself in solitary pursuits (e.g., chess games played in her head against herself, and a mathematical game that involved music she composed in her head). She was also able to perform extremely well in emergency situations. Small wonder that the patient has been loathe to give up her dissociative system. Bliss (1986) described a similar patient and other adaptive features of the syndrome.

However, Mary's system was a great detriment to her. Mary played the role of "ditz," which kept people from being too intrusive, but which also led virtually everyone to assume she was dim-witted. In fact, her Wechsler Intelligence Scale (WIS) provides a full-scale IQ of just under 140. She was profoundly isolated from others, to the extent that she studied them "so that I can act as if I am a human being." She often doubted that she was truly human. Finally, the system kept her from realizing what was "true," leading to a profound sense of "badness," even evil, given the primacy to truth in her moral system. Mary viewed the disorder as metaphor, rather than reification. The most similar case I have found is Pierre Janet's "Madeleine"—now about 100 years old— and not more current, lurid accounts.

Although Mary's case is notable for its dissimulation, she enjoyed participating in impostures, and often did this for fun. As a young woman, these impostures would take the form of going to a bar, finding a man, and convincing him that she was a famous person. She would pretend to be endlessly fascinated by the man, and would get several ways to reach him and then never contact him again. She had a fear of and fascination with losing all identity, as well. She was often preoccupied by the life of a wandering bag lady, finding it, in many ways, attractive, but only if she had choice and control over where, when, and how long to be one.

Her son also enjoyed imposture, although he knew nothing of his mother's. He often pretended and convinced others that his father was a notorious felon or a famous scientist. When in danger of being expelled from school for habitual truancy, he convinced a savvy principal that his mother had severe alcoholism and that he was leaving school to go home and check on her sobriety. (The principal lectured Mary about the "appalling" effects of her drinking, although she did not have a drinking problem. To keep her son in school, she was complicit with this imposture).

Mary loathed most holidays because she had very unhappy memories. Her favorite holiday, by far, was Halloween. Each year she celebrated it, planning weeks in advance what she would wear and who she would "be." She often roamed the streets in strange apparel on Halloween night, often into the small hours of the morning. She enjoyed answering her door to trick-or-treaters in her strange garb, acting the role fully even as she handed out candy. Mary once said, "I am a series of performances, and I only value what lies between the performances."

Case 2

Ariadne was a 5-year-old girl who was admitted because of suicidal ideation and an attempt, in which she ran into the street hoping to be hit by a car. In the course of her evaluation, it was apparent that much of her play was hypersexual. Otherwise, however, she seemed to be a happy little girl. She was bright, read very well for her age, and was socially adept. She often said that she had not really wanted to die, but had been "mad" at her mother.

Her mother told us early in Ariadne's hospitalization that she herself had multiple-personality disorder. She displayed this very dramatically at every possible occasion, often switching into pseudoinfantile language. She insisted that she had been sexually abused by her father, her mother, three of her brothers, two bishops, seven priests, and four deacons, as well as by her three husbands. She also insisted that Ariadne had been sexually abused by the third of these husbands. Several investigations by the Department of Social Services had resulted in no positive findings. Nevertheless, Ariadne did show hypersexualized behavior and signs of posttraumatic stress, with severe nightmares, much crying out in her sleep, and a marked startle response. The name of the third husband was David. When a boy named David was admitted to the unit, Ariadne said, "See, that must be the one who abused me." Observation of the mother and Ariadne together demonstrated the mother's sexual fondling of her daughter. The child was placed in foster care and thrived. Within a year, there was no evidence of posttraumatic stress.

Case 3

Susan was an 18-year-old adolescent in treatment for mild depression and mild bulimia nervosa. Raised by caring parents, she was moderately unhappy with them, especially their moderately conservative political views. She wanted a revolution so that the poor would be empowered. Over a couple of years, she continued to be unhappy, but performed moderately well academically and socially. She was a voracious student of television talk shows, and often talked of the plight of people she had seen on these programs. She had no evidence of posttraumatic stress or dissociation.

During one session, she talked of a dream she had had in which a former babysitter and she had been doing "something uncomfortable."

Over the next couple of sessions, she found herself "wondering" whether this babysitter might have involved herself with the patient in sexual games. This was subsequently not discussed further in the therapy.

The patient went to college and went to an eating disorders therapist, who was relatively untrained. She apparently told her the same dream/hypothesis. Over several sessions, this was discussed, and the patient (and therapist) became convinced that, at age 3, the patient and her two sisters had been sexually abused by the babysitter, and that this was, in fact, the cause of all her problems. The therapist threatened to report me to the Board of Medical Examiners for not having reported Susan's "memory" of "horrific abuse," although, to date, she has not done so. She used "memory-enhancement" techniques throughout the treatment.

Interviews with both of the patient's siblings were prominent for bewilderment on their part. They had no recollection of any sexual games with the babysitter in question, whom they remembered well. The patient and her therapist went to the police, who conducted an investigation. After interviewing many other children whom the babysitter had cared for over the years, the police found the case to be completely negative. These widely disparate cases of imposture syndromes have been encountered in a clinical practice that does not specialize in such syndromes. Imposture is there to be found if one looks for it.

Three cases of putative multiple-personality disorder with severe dissociation have been presented, illustrating the difficulties and complexity of this diagnosis. Multiple-personality disorder has been described, under various names, for many centuries. It fascinated psychiatrists of the late 19th and early 20th centuries. It has always been a rare disorder, although its adherents now claim that it is very common. I think the second and third cases may demonstrate why it is very "common."

The first case, in my view, demonstrates true multiple-personality disorder. Mary walks out of the pages of Pierre Janet. She has a subtle disorder, well hidden from most observers and, much of the time, from herself. It took me a long time to realize what was going on in her psyche. At best, my realization has been an extremely crude approximation.

The second case is, of course, a case of imposture by proxy. I do not believe that the patient's mother has multiple-personality disorder, as she claims, but she is clearly a very destructive force in her child's life. The effects of a single, borderline parent on a child have not been well delineated, but may have something to do with subsequent syndromes of "true" imposture.

Mary, the patient in Case 1, termed the type of dissociative disorder described in Case 3 the "Oprah Variant." She pointed out to me that the scores of people with alleged multiple-personality disorders who publicize their alleged degradation on television talk shows "have something very bad, but not what they say it is." (Indeed, one of her greatest fears is that she will "turn out to be" such a variant.)

The patient in Case 3 did not have multiple-personality disorder or anything akin to it. She had some moderate symptoms of dysphoria, with occasional bulimic episodes, in the context of a maturation identity disorder at the end of adolescence. Working with a zealous and poorly trained therapist, she manufactured an episode of sexual abuse, and the therapist suggested to her repeatedly that "other personalities" dealt with it, which is why the patient did not remember it very well. I suppose this could be viewed as a form of imposture by proxy on the therapist's part. On the patient's part, it became pure simulation, with potentially tragic results.

What of Mary, in Case 1? Here we have an imposture syndrome, I believe, that relies on conscious and unconscious dissimulation, rather than simulation. Mary did not want the nature of her psychological organization to be discovered, and she erected enormous barriers against such discovery. This phenomenon is further discussed later.

These cases raise very interesting questions. The first is, what leads a person to become an impostor—to pretend to be, attempt to be, or perhaps become someone he or she is not? In writing about imposture, it is necessary to consider its relationship to borderline personality disorder and dissociative disorders.

BORDERLINE DISORDERS

What does it mean to be *borderline*? The term is ill-chosen, and its clinical meaning varies considerably. As defined in the fourth edition of the *Diagnostic and Statistical Manual of Mental Disorders*, of course, *borderline* consists of

> a pervasive pattern of instability of interpersonal relationships, self-image, and affects, and marked impulsivity . . . as indicated by five (or more) of the following:
> 1. frantic efforts to avoid real or imagined abandonment . . .
> 2. a pattern of unstable and intense interpersonal relationships characterized by alternating between extremes of idealization and devaluation
> 3. identity disturbance . . .

4. impulsivity in at least two areas that are potentially self-damaging . . .
5. recurrent suicidal behavior, gestures, or threats, or self-mutilating behavior
6. affective instability . . .
7. chronic feeling of emptiness
8. inappropriate, intense anger or difficulty controlling anger . . .
9. transient, stress-related paranoid ideation or severe dissociative symptoms. (American Psychiatric Association, 1994, p. 654)

This approach fails to capture the human drama and experience of the borderline condition, which is perhaps better depicted in literature and films than in diagnostic and statistical manuals. As Davis and Akiskal (1986) commented, the borderline syndrome is heterogeneous with links to and that overlap with the schizophrenias, affective disorders, and various organic states as well. In its "pure" form, it may well be related to childhood object loss. A shifting sense of personal identity, a perceived absence of personal identity, and a personal identity in flux because of affective instability are hallmarks of the condition. The need for these people to absorb components of identity from their surroundings, even extending to their clothes (Seeman, 1978), is very common. To me, after 20 years of studying the syndrome, the most salient features are the affective instability, the profound issues with identity, and the use of both projective identification and many types of splitting—vertical, horizontal, and dyadic. Vertical and horizontal splitting are mental phenomena, whereas dyadic splitting occurs in interactions and can be observed.

In projective identification, there is a dyadic defensive operation. One person sends the projective identification into the world, but, for them to be effective for that person, another person must receive them. As Catherall (1991) pointed out, the recipient of projective identifications is, to some extent, a willing recipient albeit, usually, on an unconscious basis. The acceptance of the projective identification rewards the borderline person with a reinforcement that he or she is, indeed, real, and it gives some sense, however transient, of who he or she really is. (In my view, this is also a major component of the dynamic of romantic love.)

In dyadic splitting, the borderline person, using projective identification, finds potential good people and identifies with them. He also projects his own "bad self" on others, and they become a rogue's gallery in his eyes. This defense, also dyadic, causes hospital staffs, in particular, to become confused and embroiled in all sorts of intrigue. The "good" people work hard on behalf of the patient and attempt to rescue him or her from the consequences of his or her own actions, whereas the "bad" people magnify every peccadillo into something monstrous. The patient usually is, as he or she asserts, treated unfairly, and a treatment impasse often occurs.

Behaviorally, these patients are exciting and engaging. One senses that they *live* more than others, although they usually describe a sense of internal emptiness that is pervasive and extremely discouraging to them. They often do not feel real, and they test their lack of reality with such maneuvers as delicate self-cutting. The sight of their own blood and the pain experienced can actually have a calming effect on them. They lead lives of stable instability: There is predictability in the chaos, somehow. They are dramatic, very unhappy people.

A great many of the impostors I have known meet criteria for the diagnosis of borderline personality disorder. Is this an incidental finding, or are imposture syndromes etiologically related to borderline disorders? There is virtually no research on this question. In my own view, there is considerable overlap between syndromes of imposture and borderline personality disorder. First, members of both groups show a high level of creativity, although it is often flawed creativity. Second, rage is predominant in both groups. Third, drama and conflict are found in both groups. Fourth, an identity disorder is evident in both groups. Fifth, the defenses of dyadic splitting and projective identification are found in virtually all borderline patients; all the impostors I have known use projective identification while many use dyadic splitting as well.

Although borderline personality disorder does not make a person an impostor, there is a sense in borderline patients—true impostors or not—that they are, in fact, impostors of a sort (i.e., strangers to the human race, pretending, and trying to fit in). Perhaps people's rage at borderline patients has something to do with the fact that all humans have this dilemma, to greater or lesser degrees. The borderline syndrome is a continuum, and all people are placed somewhere on it. This is true for imposture as well.

DISSOCIATION

What of dissociation and the variety of imposture syndromes? Although many impostors do not dissociate, I believe that many do. Dissociation is a very primitive defense, perhaps one of the few shared with other animals. Rabbits about to be devoured have the same expression as human beings who are dissociating. Essentially, dissociation is the ability to distance oneself mentally from what is happening and to become unaware of it.

The syndromes of dissociation include fugue states, posessioniform states, multiple personality (dissociative identity disorder), other amnestic states, and unusual, culture-bound syndromes such as *amok*. Dissociation is often experienced (and observed) in the context of ongoing abuse, especially in childhood. But it also occurs in creative people who have not apparently been abused. Many children with persistent imaginary companions have the ability to dissociate.

Because dissociative disorders are linked with pathology, there is an unfortunate tendency to think that dissociation is somehow very bad. As with other defenses, however, it has adaptive and maladaptive features (the case of Mary demonstrates both). The splitting off of components of the mind, conscious and unconscious, which occurs in dissociation, is also on a continuum. Most human beings who drive cars have had the experience of "spacing out" and driving safely for several miles without conscious recollection of it. This is garden-variety dissociation. Other types become progressively more pathological. The case of Mary demonstrates this phenomenon very well.

As with some aspects of the borderline condition, dissociators also seem to have a high level of creativity, although, again, it may be an autistic creativity essentially unshared with, and even actively hidden from, the world. The cases of dissociation presented, and especially that of Mary, show some of the primary characteristics of these disorders and their unusual relationship to imposture. For some of these patients—and certainly for Mary—time is experienced, subjectively, very differently than it is by most people. Mary often discussed, philosophically, the construct of time, which she saw as a human construct that was largely irrelevant and probably unreal. Time is experienced in unusual ways by many people with syndromes of imposture (e.g., see Critchley, 1979b for a discussion of Miss Havisham). There may be a link between borderline personality disorder and at least some dissociative states (Gunderson & Sabo, 1993). A high prevalence of childhood abuse, especially sexual abuse, has been demonstrated in both disorders. Many patients with dissociative disorders meet formal criteria for borderline disorder as well.

Benner and Joscelyne (1984) argued that multiple-personality disorder is not a hysterical state, as it has been viewed classically, but is, in fact, a form of borderline personality disorder. The authors reviewed the various conceptions of splitting by Fairbairn, Kohut, and Kernberg, with particular attention to Kohut's concept of horizontal and vertical splitting and Kernberg's view that the function of splitting is the separation of certain introjects, identification, and self- and object representation. Using Winnicott's schema of boundary formation through oscillation, with *I* and *not me* forming an oscillating boundary through multiple projections and identification, they pointed out that this process is thwarted by traumatization. The authors argued that multiple personality is a borderline state because of the similarities in these of splitting by patients with the two disorders. In addition, Searles and others described highly developed and distinct ego states in some borderline patients who do not formally qualify for a diagnosis of multiple personality disorder.

In a nonblind approach using several rating instruments, Horevitz and Braun (1984) reviewed 93 cases of multiple-personality disorder using records. There were not sufficient data to diagnose 60 of these patients as borderline or not. Of the remaining 33, for whom there were sufficient data, 23 formally qualified for a concomitant diagnosis of borderline personality disorder. Thus, the prevalence of borderline disorder was very high (almost 70%), but not ubiquitous. The authors pointed out that these finding argue against the assertion that multiple-personality (or other dissociative) states merely represent a subtype of borderline personality disorder.

Although the treatment concerns of borderline patients and those with severe dissociative disorders may be quite similar, with a long and often stormy course and many problems with transference and countertransference, there does seem to be clinical evidence that they are not always the same disorder. In fact, I would, contend that the "Oprah" variant of multiple-personality disorder, which is exhibitionistic and not related to dissimulation, is a variant of borderline personality disorder. In contrast, classical cases such as Mary's, which are much more rare and difficult to discern, are more hysterical in nature.

Dince's (1977) article on partial dissociation links the borderline state to dissociation. Dince commented on the way many borderline patients can "expel" certain material from consciousness—in ways ranging from purposeful to preconscious. He asserted that borderline patients are able to volitionally set dissociative capacities in motion. Relying on denial (and perhaps other primitive defenses), the borderline patient has semiautomatic responses to "highly charged aggressive or sexual-aggressive affect." As he wrote, "the dissociated self, the not-me, has to be triggered and to take over in order to do that which would evoke fearful guilt and shame in the original, hated self" (p. 340).

Fast (1974) wrote a fascinating article on multiple identities in borderline personality organization. In contrast to the many discussions in the literature on defenses and defensive constructs, this article shows some of the relationships between imposture and the borderline state. Fast described a nonclinical population of 13 high-achieving people with borderline tendencies. She noted the painful sense of an absence of self or even any central organization. These people, without having multiple personality disorder, did have a sense of several disparate identities. These people were unfortunate in many ways. But all reported a sense, which Fast called "exhilarating," that they could *be* anything. Fast suggested that these patients can create roles and characters that become invested with a great deal of energy and, perhaps, some autonomy.

Bram Stoker, the author of *Dracula,* also wrote a book about imposture (Stoker, 1910). Raines, Raines, and Singer (1994) described Dracula as the epitome of a borderline patient. In an interesting study, Ludwig (1994) correlated high levels of productive creativity (published fiction) with a higher prevalence than expected of affective disorders, panic disorders, drug abuse, anxiety disorders, and eating disorders. There was also a higher prevalence of sexual abuse in the childhood of these creative women.

In Briquet's syndrome, which is related to disorders of imposture, there is a significant association of a history of abuse and current dissociation (Pribor, Yutzy, Dean, & Wetzel, 1993). Goodwin (1988) described a person with Munchausen's syndrome who had a history of severe abuse in childhood. Indeed, she viewed her patient's Munchausen's syndrome as part of an overall dissociative disorder. Several other reports link Munchausen's syndrome with severe childhood abuse.

TOWARD A THEORY OF IMPOSTURE

The various syndromes of imposture, their perpetrators, the hoaxes that are performed, and the impostors, especially, are full of irony. One of the major ironies is the strange convergence of both simulation and dissimulation in these persons. Even as they simulate an intentionally false complete or partial identity, many impostors are dissimulating— acting "normal" to hide certain things about themselves.

The great impostors, of course, are masters of simulation, but there is often dissimulation as well. For example, Mary represents a patient who generally dissimulated well enough to keep her true clinical picture hidden from her psychiatrist for many years, from the rest of the world, and, most of the time, from herself. At the same time, she was not a mean impostor, and was able to successfully carry out many good simulations.

It seems that simulation and dissimulation are flip sides of the same coin, and that both must be considered in attempting to formulate any theory of imposture. Imposture is a disparate group of behaviors, and some readers might protest that the different categories described here have little in common. However, there are many features in common to most of the variants described in this chapter (see Gediman, 1985, for a discussion of imposture and its wide-ranging dynamics).

The clinical theories of imposture are primarily psychoanalytic and still have considerable value for the practicing clinician. The old analysts, of course, thought that impostors had problems with their mothers. Many do. Greenson's (1968) thoughts about disidentifying with the mother seems relevant to the anorectic patients described, who separate from their mothers through mimicry and rage. The same concepts are applicable to the transvestite patient and perhaps to other forms of sexual imposture as well. Uncertainty with masculinity related to a strong identification with the mother, in early development, should proceed to disidentification. If this is imperfectly achieved, the result is envy of the mother and a split-off self-representation of her, which is, of course, a borderline phenomenon, as Khan (1962) delineated.

Helene Deutsch had a career-long interest in impostors and imposture, perhaps starting with her article on pathological lying (Deutsch, 1982, p. 385). In that article, she described a girl with *pseudologia fantastica* in the context of attempted sexual abuse. Her conclusions are worth quoting:

> Thus, pseudology appears in situations in which the maturing individual is confronted by vigorous real demands for liberation from the past. Memory traces of experiences that really occurred are once more activated, and are joined to already powerfully operative transference trends. Thus, wish-fantasies assume the character of real experience and, for a time, relieve the individual of the obligations of real life from which . . . he would still like to withdraw. . . . In case of major, sustained pseudology that determines a person's whole life, the attempt at liberation will have failed; and the neurosis will have stabilized in that form. The not-yet-analyzed figure of the confidence trickster probably belongs to this type. In this, there seem to be far-reaching analogies to the myth-creating forces. . . .

In the context of this article, I am struck that the only case of *pseudologia fantastica* I have seen in a child was in a teenage girl who had been horrifically abused, as legally documented, as a young child, and who had a "secretive mode" of self (Copolillo, Horton, & Haller, 1981).

In 1933, Wiersma, contributed an excellent article on pathological lying in patients considered to have been impostors. Wiersma was struck by these patients' narcissism and self-absorption. He also noted many similarities between imposture and the creative play of children. Virtually all the clinical variants of imposture syndromes, with the possible exception of imposture for gain, show serious problems with identity constructs, marked ambivalence toward the mother, and the use of projective identification. Splitting is often found as well.

I have argued previously (Wells, 1986) that most impostures are efforts at reparation and adaptation, however bizarre they may seem. The theories of Subbotsky (1993) may be heuristic in this regard. *Magical repair*, a concept well developed by Karush and Ovesey (1961), is a thrust of many imposture syndromes. According to Karush and Ovesey, efforts at magical repair are pre-oedipal, and are sometimes activated by failures or major challenges in adult life. Activation of early mechanisms brings up the entire concept of play (Nagera, 1969). However desperate they may be, there is a playful aspect to imposture; the imposture itself, however serious at some levels, is a game at others. Ekstein and Friedman (1957) contrasted playing, playacting, and acting out, which may form a continuum.

The compulsive and driven nature of many acts of imposture warrants comment. Many impostors have obsessive natures, and many impostures are obsessive–compulsive, even if this is not their major character style. In a paper relating caricature to obsessiveness, Rosen (1963) viewed *caricature* as a reenactment of trauma, and described *obsessions* as "grotesque parodies without laughter" and *compulsions* as "ritual travesties without fun." The imposture, viewed this way, can achieve the dimension of an artificially induced drive, such as alcoholism. (Indeed, alcohol use is significant for many impostors. Several of the patients described in this chapter found themselves more involved in imposture when mildly intoxicated.) Spiro (1968) described an association between alcoholism and Munchausen's syndrome. The loss of control found in alcoholism is also found in many impostors, but in a different manner. Whatever one thinks of this view of caricature, many impostures certainly achieve the dimensions of grotesque parodies and ritual travesties.

Possible etiologic factors related to patients' families also need to be considered. Besdine's (1968) classic article on "Jocasta mothering" discussed the effect of mothering such as a child would receive from the mother and wife of Oedipus. These mothers, according to Besdine, have an enormous affect hunger; as a result, they have extremely close relationships with the (male) children, often to the exclusion of the spouse, if he is present at all. These children often grow up to be very creative and also very narcissistic, according to Besdine. In my view, this is a clinically observable phenomenon, and many male impostors describe this kind of relationship with their mothers.

Bergler (1944) described the primary dynamic of imposture as representing a pre-oedipal revenge against the mother; Deutsch (1955) asserted that the mothers of impostors overstimulate them orally with concomitant narcissism, inability to tolerate delay of gratification, and primitive defenses. However risible some of the classic views of imposture may seem, it is clear that maternal and familial factors influence impostors. I have previously proposed (Wells, 1986) that compulsive wanderers, people with limited impostures, and those with factitious disorders are often searching for a mother; those with sexual impostures are both becoming and defeating their mothers. I suggested that anorectic impostors were refusing to become their mothers, and that great impostors are simultaneously making the effort to please and punish their mothers.

Family members of many impostors play a role in perpetrating the imposture. Transvestites' wives and girlfriends often help them "dress"; sadomasochistic impostors often have permanent partners; and even in imposture for gain, the victim often unconsciously colludes with the impostor. Lady Tichborne, needing her son, found him in Arthur Orton.

I do not pretend to have a heuristic model for imposture, which is an individual, maladaptive (usually), and creative act. Every imposture is different, and every impostor is unique. In understanding imposture, however, it behooves one to think of the classic analytical view, the concept of play, creativity, borderline states, and dissociation. *Pseudologia fantastica* has similar, multifaceted features (King & Ford, 1988) and is related to imposture.

Few impostors seek treatment, although some certainly do. However, it is rare, for impostors to seek treatment for imposture per se. It is unknown whether the dynamics of impostors who seek treatment and those who do not are similar. Certainly, in many who seek treatment, there is a confused childhood pattern of overstimulation along with rejection or implied rejection.

Play receives insufficient attention in efforts to understand developmental anomalies in adults. Although often severely pathological, imposture almost always has a component of play. Among others, Deutsch (1955) delineated a relationship between imposture and play, likening it to young children's play. Simmel (1926) pointed out that playing allows children to temporarily adopt adult roles—often powerful ones. He mentioned the role of the physician as an example.

What of the impostor's creativity? Perpetrating a successful imposture is not the same as writing a great book or painting a great picture, although there are similarities. Barchilon (1973) wrote of "integrating the impossible," which is just what impostors do, as the function of creative activity. Indeed, the ranks of reported impostors seem to be overrepresented with artists, writers, and actors. Greenacre (1958a, 1958b) wrote about this possible relationship, making the interesting point that, early in their careers, many artists and writers believe they are impostors. (In the case of Mary, this was such an intrusive and controlling belief that she had to carry with her proof of her profession because, at work, she would become overwhelmed with the belief that she was an impostor.) In his fascinating essay on self-portraits, Critchley (1979a) demonstrated that a great many self-portraits are, in fact, impostures of a sort. Often artists paint mirror images of themselves, and these frequently are not very good depictions of the artists' actual appearances. In a study of artists, Dudek (1968) noted their rich associations, primary process thinking, and "ready access to affects." Most of the impostors described herein have rich associations, much primary process thinking, but less ready access to affects. If creativity is, in part, regression in the service of the ego, imposture represents a variant that may be conceptualized as regression in the service of parts of the ego, with sometimes maladaptive results. The artist creates art while the impostor becomes art.

Such splits occur, of course, in borderline patients. The processes of denial, dissociation, and partial dissociation maintain these splits in part–object relations, which may be necessary for imposture. When the dissociation is extreme, one sees the kind of imposture that features dissimulation more than simulation, as demonstrated by the case of Mary. When the dissociation is less extreme, one sees most of the other variants of imposture described. When the dissociation is volitional and controllable, one finds the kind of imposture that gains money or revenge.

Inherent throughout this chapter is the concept that imposture can be partially adaptive. It may be thought of, too, as an adaptive process gone awry. Grinker (1961) asserted that imposture is a form of mastery. Abraham (1935) believed that imposture made the impostor feel worthy and, perhaps, lovable. Through the repetition compulsion, the impostor, now able to feel lovable, went about repetitively proving that he was not lovable. Stoker (1910), the author of *Dracula*, believed that there were sociological roots of imposture, but that the excitement of the imposture made impostors feel good.

Deutsch (1955) wrote that, "The world is crowded with 'as if' personalities, and even more so with impostors and pretenders. Ever since I became interested in the impostor, he pursues me everywhere. I find him among my friends and acquaintances, as well as in myself" (p. 503). To maintain their ego ideal, most people engage in small simulations to others and significant dissimulations to themselves. The impostor, with multiple ego ideals, acts them out. Rarely does he or she stop at success.

REFERENCES

Abraham, K. (1935). The history of an impostor in the light of psychoanalytic knowledge. *Psychoanalytic Quarterly, 4*, 570–587.

American Psychiatric Association. (1994). *Diagnostic and Statistical Manual* (4th ed., Rev.). Washington, DC: Author.

Barchilon, J. (1973). Pleasure, mockery and creative integrations: Their relationships to childhood knowledge, a learning deficit and the literature of the absurd. *International Journal of Psychoanalysis, 54*, 19–34.

Benner, D. G., & Joscelyne, B. (1984). Multiple personality as a borderline disorder. *The Journal of Nervous and Mental Disease, 172*, 98–104.

Bergler, E. (1944). Psychopathology of impostors. *Journal of Criminal Psychopathology, 5*, 695–714.

Besdine, M. (1968). The Jocasta complex, mothering and genius. *Psychoanalytic Review, 55*, 259–276, 574–600.

Bliss, E. L. (1986). *Multiple personality, allied disorders and hypnosis.* New York: Oxford University Press.

Catherall, D. R. (1991). Aggression and projective identification in the treatment of victims. *Psychotherapy, 28*, 145–149.

Coppolillo, H. P., Horton, P. C., & Haller, L. (1981). Secrets and the secretive mode. *Journal of the American Academy of Child Psychiatry, 20*, 71–83.

Critchley, M. (1979a). Ecce homo: Observations upon self-portraiture. In M. Critchley (Ed.), *The divine banquet of the brain and other essays* (pp. 121–129). New York: Raven.

Critchley, M. (1979b). The Miss Havisham syndrome. In M. Critchley (Ed.), *The divine banquet of the brain and other essays* (pp. 136–140). New York: Raven.

Critchley, M. (1979c). Tattooed ladies, tattooed men. In M. Critchley (Ed.), *The divine banquet of the brain and other essays* (pp. 141–148). New York: Raven.

Davis, G. C., & Akiskal, H. S. (1986). Descriptive, biological and theoretical aspects of borderline personality disorder. *Hospital and Community Psychiatry, 37*, 685–692.

Deutsch, H. (1955). The impostor: Contribution to ego psychology of a type of psychopath. *Psychoanalytic Quarterly, 24*, 483–505.

Deutsch, H. (1982). On the pathological lie (pseudologia phantastica). *Journal of the American Academy of Psychoanalysis, 10*, 369–386.

Dince, P. R. (1977). Partial dissociation as encountered in the borderline patient. *Journal of the American Academy of Psychoanalysis, 5*, 327–345.

Dudek, S. K. (1968). Regression and creativity: A comparison of the Rorschach records of successful vs. unsuccessful painters and writers. *Journal of Nervous and Mental Diseases, 147*, 535–546.

Ekstein, R., & Friedman, S. W. (1957). The function of acting out, play action and play acting in the psychotherapeutic process. *Journal of the American Psychoanalytical Association, 5*, 581–629.

Fast, I. (1974). Multiple identities in borderline personality organization. *British Journal of Medical Psychology, 47*, 291–300.

Gediman, H. K. (1985). Imposture, inauthenticity, and feeling fraudulent. *Journal of the American Psychoanalytic Association, 33*, 911–935.

Gediman, H. K. (1986). The plight of the imposturous candidate: Learning amidst the pressures and pulls of power in the institute. *Psychoanalytic Inquiry, 6*, 67–91.

Goodwin, J. (1988). Munchausen's syndrome as a dissociative disorder. *Dissociation, 1*, 54–60.

Greenacre, P. (1958a). The impostor. *Psychoanalytic Quarterly, 27*, 359–382.

Greenacre, P. (1958b). The relation of the impostor to the artist. *Psychoanalytic Study of the Child, 13,* 521–540.

Greenson, R. R. (1968). Dis-identifying from mother: Its special importance for the boy. *International Journal of Psychoanalysis, 49,* 370–374.

Grinker, R. R., Jr. (1961). Imposture as a form of mastery. *Archives of General Psychiatry, 5,* 449–452.

Gunderson, J. G., & Sabo, A. N. (1993). The phenomenological and conceptual interface between borderline personality disorder and PTSD. *American Journal of Psychiatry, 150,* 19–27.

Horevitz, R. P., & Braun, B. G. (1984). Are multiple personalities borderline? An analysis of 33 cases. *Psychiatric Clinics of North America, 7,* 69–87.

Kaplan, L. J. (1987). *The family romance of the impostor-poet Thomas Chatterton.* New York: Atheneum.

Karush, A., & Ovesey, L. (1961). Unconscious mechanisms of magical repair. *Archives of General Psychiatry, 5,* 55–69.

Kets de Vries, M. F. (1990). The impostor syndrome: Developmental and societal issues. *Human Relations, 43,* 667–686.

Khan, M. M. R. (1962). The role of polymorph-perverse body-experiences and object-relations in ego-integration. *British Journal of Medical Psychology, 35,* 245–261.

King, B. H., & Ford, C. V. (1988). Pseudologia fantastica. *Acta Psychiatrica Scandinavica, 77,* 1–6.

Klotz, I. M. (1992). Munchausen syndrome: Hoaxes, parodies, and tall tales in science and medicine. *Perspectives in Biology and Medicine, 36,* 139–154.

Lewin, B. D. (1933). The body as phallus. *Psychoanalytic Quarterly, 2,* 24–47.

Litman, R. E., & Swearingen, C. (1972). Bondage and suicide. *Archives of General Psychiatry, 27,* 80.

Ludwig, A. M. (1994). Mental illness and creative activity in female writers. *American Journal of Psychiatry, 151,* 1650–1656.

Nagera, H. (1969). The imaginary companion: Its significance for ego development and conflict solution. *Psychoanalytic Study of the Child,* 165–196.

Ovesey, L., & Person, E. (1973). Gender identity and sexual psychopathology in men: A psychodynamic analysis of homosexuality, transsexualism, and transvestism. *Journal of the American Academy of Psychoanalysis, 1,* 53–72.

Person, E., & Ovesey, L. (1978). Transvestism: New perspectives. *Journal of the American Academy of Psychoanalysis, 6,* 301–323.

Pribor, E. F., Yutzy, S. H., Dean, J. T., & Wetzel, R. D. (1993). Briquet's syndrome, dissociation, and abuse. *American Journal of Psychiatry, 150,* 1507–1511.

Raines, J. M., Raines, L. C., & Singer, M. (1994). Dracula: Disorders of the self and borderline personality organization. *Psychiatry Clinics of North America, 17,* 811–826.

Rosen, V. H. (1963). Variants of comic caricature and their relationship to obsessive-compulsive phenomena. *Journal of the American Psychoanalytic Association, 11,* 704–724.

Schreier, H. A., & Libow, J. A. (1993). *Hurting for love: Munchausen by proxy syndrome.* New York: Guilford.

Seeman, M. V. (1978). Am I what I wear? Identity conflicts in borderline patients. *Canadian Psychiatric Association Journal, 23,* 579–582.

Segal, M. M. (1965). Transvestism as an impulse and as a defense. *International Journal of Psychoanalysis, 46,* 209–217.

Simmel, E. (1926). The "doctor-game," illness and the profession of medicine. *International Journal of Psychoanalysis, 7,* 470–483.

Socarides, C. W. (1970). A psychoanalytic study of the desire for sexual transformation ("transsexualism"): The plaster-of-paris man. *International Journal of Psychoanalysis, 51,* 341–349.

Spiro, H. R. (1968). Chronic factitious illness: Munchausen's syndrome. *Archives of General Psychiatry, 18,* 569–579.

Spivak, H., & Rodin, G. (1994). The psychology of factitious disorders: A reconsideration. *Psychosomatics, 35,* 25–34.

Stengel, E. (1939). Studies on the psychopathology of compulsive wandering. *British Journal of Medical Psychology, 18,* 250–254.

Stoker, B. (1910). *Famous impostors.* New York: Sturgic & Walter.

Story, I. (1976). Caricature and impersonating the other: Observations from the psychotherapy of anorexia nervosa. *Psychiatry, 39,* 176–188.

Subbotsky, E. V. (1993). *Foundations of the mind: Children's understanding of reality.* Cambridge, MA: Harvard University Press.

Volkan, V. (1965). The observation of the "little man" phenomenon in a case of anorexia nervosa. *British Journal of Medical Psychology, 38,* 299–311.

Wells, L. A. (1986). Varieties of imposture. *Perspectives in Biology and Medicine, 29,* 588–610.

Wells, L. A. (1982). The need for an other in anorexia nervosa: Separation, part objects, and transitional objects. *Psychiatric Annals, 12,* 325–330.

Wiersma, D. (1993). On pathological lying. *Character and Personality, 2,* 48–61.

11

Neuropsychology of Self-Deception: The Case of Prosopagnosia

Israel Nachson

THE VARIETY OF PROSOPAGNOSIC MANIFESTATIONS

Prosopagnosia ("not knowing faces" in Greek) is a rare neurological syndrome that consists of inability to recognize familiar faces in the absence of severe intellectual, sensory, or cognitive impairment. Apparently, it is the result of a failure to extract physiognomic invariants or associated semantic memories (Damasio, Damasio, & Tranel, 1990; Young, 1988). The term *prosopagnosia* was coined by Bodamer in 1947, although earlier reports (e.g., by Wigan in 1844, Charcot in 1888, and Wilbrand in 1892) of patients showing this syndrome had appeared in the literature before (see Ellis, 1989).

Usually, prosopagnosic patients know they are looking at a face and they can name its parts, yet they cannot tell whose face it is. According to Damasio, Damasio, and Van Hoesen (1982), this is an example of the inability to perceive individuality within a class of objects. In his literature search, Ellis (1989) found only two cases of patients who did not recognize facial stimuli *qua faces* (Sacks, 1987; Wilbrand, 1892). However, reports of these cases should be considered with caution because they are based on informal clinical observations without experimental corroboration.

Agnetti, Carreras, Pinna, and Rosati (1978) provided a first-hand report by a patient, BP, who was telling how he suddenly could not recognize familiar faces: "I was sitting at the table with my father, my brother and his wife . . . suddenly . . . they looked unfamiliar . . . I could see the different parts of their faces, but I could not associate those faces with known persons" (p. 51).

Newcombe, Mehta, and De Haan (1994) told the story of a man who was standing next to a family friend whom he had known all his life, without any experience of familiarity. Upon learning of the incidence, his father reacted strongly to this apparent discourtesy. Shortly afterward, he saw a man walking toward him. "Mindful of my father's recent forceful comments, I decided to play it safe. As we passed, I said 'good morning, Sir.' My father said later that I had never addressed him as politely before or since" (p. 108). Another patient tells: "At the club I saw someone strange staring at me, and asked the steward who it was. You'll laugh at me: I had been looking at myself in the mirror" (Pallis, 1955, p. 219).

COMPONENTIAL RECOGNITION OF FACES

The personal stories quoted previously make it clear that prosopagnosic patients cannot recognize familiar faces when perceived configurationally, as a whole (see Levine & Calvanio, 1989). Correct recognitions, or guesses, may appear only when the patients perceive them componentially, feature by feature (Davidoff, 1988; Nardelli, Coccia, Fiaschi, Terzian, & Rizzuto, 1982; Young, Humphreys, Riddoch, Hellawell, & De Haan, 1994). Pallis' (1955) patient, AH, admits: "I can see the eyes, nose and mouth quite clearly, but they just don't add up. They all seem chalked in, like a blackboard . . . the hair may help a lot, or if there is a moustache" (p. 219).

Whiteley and Warrington's (1977) patient, QL, who could not recognize his family members, the medical staff with whom he had daily encounters, and his reflection in the mirror, could readily describe the appearance of Prince Charles: "Larger face than father, with long hair, side parting, nose quite pronounced but not remarkably so, usually smiling" (p. 397).

Bodamer's (1947) patient, A, emphasizes the importance of paraphernalia in guessing a person's identity: "I don't recognize people by their faces, but by the paraphernalia, not the facial structure. With you (the doctor), I see the size first of all, then the glasses, then the rest" (Ellis & Florence, 1990, p. 93).

Componential, or piecemeal, strategy of face recognition is considered less efficient than the normal, configurational strategy (Carey, 1981; Carey & Diamond, 1977; Frith, Stevens, Johnson, Owens, & Crow, 1983; Rhodes, Brake, & Atkinson, 1993; Sergent, 1988a), and it is adversely affected by contextual changes (Damasio et al., 1990). It is characteristic of young children (Carey, 1981; Carey & Diamond, 1977), and it appears in perception of inverted faces and in performance on other difficult face-recognition tasks, where configurational processing is disrupted (Carey, 1978, 1981; Endo, 1986; Phillips & Rawls, 1979; Sergent, 1984; Yin, 1969).

Despite the similarities in performance between young children and subjects watching inverted faces on the one hand and prosopagnosic patients on the other hand, they differ from each other in a meaningful way. The former, who cannot use configurational strategy, fall back on the less efficient, componential strategy to *recognize* faces. By contrast, the latter use the componential strategy (i.e., by relying on specific facial features or on typical paraphernalia) to tell whose face they are associated with. That means that they recognize the features or objects, and *remember* whom they belong to, without actually recognizing the face they are looking at. This might be the reason that contextual changes in feature presentation reduce the incidence of face recognition (see Damasio et al., 1990).

Face recognition based on componential analysis is an inferential process, as is evident by the report by Etcoff, Freeman, and Cave's (1991) patient, LH: "I see the Third Reich insignia, the swastika, so it must be Hitler . . . you wouldn't be mean enough to show me an underling like Goebles" (p. 29). Occasionally, such inferences might lead to mistaken identifications. Sergent and Villemure's (1989) patient, BM, mistook her neurosurgeon for Ronald Reagan because both had dark hair. Judging from the background of the picture, she reasoned that "this is Washington, the White House, . . . so it must be the President, that's Ronald Reagan" (p. 985).

Conceivably, a mistaken inference may account for Sacks' (1987) patient, Dr. P, who, looking for his hat, "reached out his hand and took hold of his wife's head, tried to lift it off, to put it on. He had apparently mistaken his wife for a hat!" (p. 11).

SPECIFICITY OF FACE RECOGNITION

A question has arisen as to whether face recognition involves special cognitive and neuropsychological processing (see Nachson, 1995). One way to demonstrate specificity of face recognition is by exposing double dissociations of prosopagnosia from other visual syndromes. However, the existence of these dissociations is a controversial issue. Some authors (Blanc-Garin, 1986; Damasio et al., 1982; Davidoff & Landis, 1990) believe that prosopagnosia is associated with a general impairment of "contextual evocation," whereas others (Ellis & Young, 1989; McNeil & Warrington, 1993; Young, 1988; see also Benton, 1990; Farah, 1990, 1994b) argue that it constitutes a specific impairment of face recognition.

Clinical evidence is equivocal. As Young (1988) pointed out, some pros-opagnosic patients indeed suffer from impairments in recognition of nonfacial stimuli, such as food items, abstract symbols, animals, and cars (Blanc-Garin, 1984, 1986; Bornstein, 1963; Damasio & Damasio, 1986; Damasio et al., 1982; De Renzi, Scotti & Spinnler, 1969; Lhermitte, Chaine, Escourelle, Ducarne, & Pillon, 1972; MacRae & Trolle, 1956; Newcombe, 1979; Pallis, 1955), or in covert recognition of familiar faces, cars, and flowers (De Haan, Young, & Newcombe, 1991). However, other patients have face-specific impairments (Assal, Favre, & Anderes, 1984; Bruyer & Velge, 1981; Bruyer et al., 1983; De Renzi, 1986a; De Renzi, Faglioni, Grossi, & Nichelli, 1991; Tzavaras, Hecaén, & Le Bras, 1970).

The most telling evidence for the specificity of face recognition, how-ever, seems to come from cases of agnosia without prosopagnosia (Assal et al., 1984; Behrmann, Moscovitch, & Winocour, 1994; Bornstein, 1963; Bornstein, Sroka, & Munitz, 1969; McCarthy & Warrington, 1986; Rumi-ati, Humphreys, Riddoch, & Bateman, 1994). Feinberg, Schindler, Ochoa, Kwan, and Farah (1994) reported seven cases of associative visu-al agnosia with pure alexia, without prosopagnosia. Ebata, Ogawa, Tan-aka, Mizuno, and Yoshida (1991) similarly observed a case of *meta-morphosia* (apparent reduction in size of a given hemiface) without prosopagnosia. Finally, Sergent and Signoret (1992b) conducted a pos-itron emission tomography (PET) study showing that face and object processing are dissociable functions that presumably involve different neural structures. Although there is a fair amount of agreement as to what constitutes prosopagnosia, the issue of its anatomical substrate is controversial.

ANATOMICAL SUBSTRATE OF PROSOPAGNOSIA

Bilateral Lesions

Postmortem analyses; visual field studies; data obtained from comput-erized tomography (CT) and PET; nuclear magnetic resonance (NMR) results; and observations of patients with cerebral hemispherectomies, callosal surgeries, and amnesic syndromes have all demonstrated that prosopagnosia is linked to bilateral occipitotemporal lesions involving mainly the lingual and fusiform gyri (Bauer, 1984; Bruyer et al., 1983; Damasio & Damasio, 1983, 1986; Damasio et al., 1982; Damasio, Dam-asio, & Tranel, 1986; Damasio, Tranel, & Damasio, 1990a; Hecaén, 1981; Nardelli et al., 1982; Sergent, 1995). More recently, Ettlin et al. (1992) studied 54 right-handed patients with sequential unilateral brain dam-age. When the patients first sustained right-hemisphere damage, they showed left visual neglect, but no prosopagnosia. Only when they sub-sequently sustained left-hemisphere damage did they show prosopag-nosic symptomatology. These anatomical data are consistent with new PET findings (Sergent, Ohta, & MacDonald, 1992) showing that face recognition involves the right lingual, fusiform, and parahippocampal gyri, as well as the bilateral anterior temporal cortex. Sergent (1988a) believed that both hemispheres are similarly able to process configura-tional facial stimuli, although they are attuned to different physical as-pects of the faces.

Unilateral Lesions

However, Damasio and colleagues (Damasio et al., 1982, 1986) noted that, although each hemisphere learns, recognizes, and recalls faces (albeit in a strategically different manner), the right hemisphere is more efficient than the left, and that unilateral right-hemisphere lesions can cause transient impairment in face recognition. A number of authors (Campbell, Landis, & Regard, 1986; De Renzi, 1986a, 1986b; De Renzi, Perani, Carlesimo, Silveri, & Fazio, 1994; Habib, 1986; Hecaén & An-gelergues, 1962; Landis, Cummings, Christen, Bogen, & Imhof, 1986; Landis, Regard, Bliestle, & Kleihues, 1988; Levy, 1980; Meadows, 1974; Rapcsak, Polster, Comer, & Rubens, 1994; Renault, Signoret, Debruille, Breton, & Bolgert, 1989; Sergent & Signoret, 1992b; Sergent & Villemure, 1989; Whiteley & Warrington, 1977) indeed reported cases of prosopag-nosia due to unilateral right-hemisphere damage. In a recent review of about 150 cases of prosopagnosia, not a single patient was found to have suffered from left-hemisphere damage (Sergent, 1995; but see Goldberg & Barr, 1991). However, De Renzi et al. (1994) reviewed 27 cases with neuroimaging evidence and three cases with surgical evidence, all show-ing a link between prosopagnosia and right-hemisphere damage. Ben-ton (1990) argued that prosopagnosia can be produced by right-hemi-sphere damage alone because normal face recognition depends on the integrity of the right inferior occipitotemporal area, where visual infor-mation is conceivably transmitted to the mesial and inferior temporal regions on its way to the memory storage.

   Therefore, although it is true that the mechanism for face recognition is bilateral, "the crucial lesion that produces disability, like the lesion of aphasia in right handed persons, is unilateral" (Benton, 1990, p. 493). This conclusion is corroborated by the performance of three split-brain patients whose left but not right hemispheres showed marked deficits in face perception (Gazzaniga & Smylie, 1983). Other neurological syn-dromes involving difficulties in face perception are also associated with right-hemisphere dysfunctions (e.g., Bowers, Bauer, Coslett, & Heilman, 1985; De Renzi, Bonacini, & Faglioni, 1989; De Renzi, Faglioni, & Spinnler, 1968; Flude, Ellis, & Kay, 1989; Malone, Morris, Kay, & Levin, 1982; Newcombe, De Haan, Ross, & Young, 1989; Ross, 1980; Young, De Haan, Newcombe, & Hay, 1990; Young, Flude, Hay, & Ellis, 1993).

Roles of the Left and Right Hemispheres in Face Recognition

In the final analysis, however, it seems that the disagreements between the "bilateralists" and the "unilateralists" is more a matter of emphasis than of an irreconcilable division of opinions. There seems to be unanimous agreement that prosopagnosia is usually linked to bilateral lesions, although the right hemisphere plays a more important role than the left in producing this syndrome. It appears that, although both hemispheres can process facial stimuli, the right hemisphere is better in constructing facial representations, perhaps due to its greater sensitivity to critical physical characteristics (Sergent, 1988a; Young, Hay, & McWeeny, 1985). This conclusion is in line with data showing left visual field (right-hemisphere) advantage (in terms of accuracy and reaction time) by normal adults for face recognition (Anderson & Parkin, 1985; Cohen-Levine & Koch-Weser, 1982; Hatta, 1979; Hay, 1981; Hilliard, 1973; Jones, 1979; Klein, Moscovitch, & Vigna, 1976; Rizzolatti, Umilta, & Berlucchi, 1971; St. John, 1981; Young et al., 1985; Young Hay, McWeeny, & Ellis, 1985; but see Puschel & Zaidel, 1994), which also appears among infants and young children (De Schonen & Mathivet, 1990; Marcel & Rajan, 1975; Reynolds & Jeeves, 1978).

However, examination of same–different judgments of faces presented in the left or right visual field revealed that, depending on the experimental condition, face recognition can be mediated by either the left or right hemisphere (Hillger & Koenig, 1991). Specifically, left visual field (right-hemisphere) advantage was found for face identification (*same* condition), and right visual field (left-hemisphere) advantage was found for face discrimination (*different* condition). Similar notions about the link between hemispheric dominance for facial recognition and task demands have been suggested by Sergent (1985), Sergent and Bindra (1981), and Bruyer and Stroot (1984).

Other authors have suggested that the predominance of a given hemisphere for face processing varies with the processing stage (Sergent, 1982a, 1982b, 1988a, 1988b). In particular, it was suggested that familiarization with given faces involves hemispheric shifts (Ross & Turkewitz, 1982). Ross-Kossak and Turkewitz (1984) believed that ". . .there are three levels of processing facial information, beginning with a relatively primitive type of right hemisphere processing, progressing to an analytic mode of left hemisphere processing, and culminating in a more advanced and integrated type of right hemisphere processing" (p. 476).

According to Rhodes' (1985) model, however, face recognition begins with visuospatial processing mainly by the right hemisphere, and ends with processing of semantic information and retrieval of names mainly by the left hemisphere. Within a different framework, Rotenberg and Elizur (1992) came to the same conclusion, assuming that input processing in the right hemisphere proceeds unconsciously and gains conscious awareness only upon reaching the left hemisphere.

COVERT RECOGNITION OF FACES

Prosopagnosic patients—who cannot tell a person by the face—are nonetheless able to tell who the person is by nonfacial clues, such as voice, gait, smell, jewelry, environmental context, hairstyle, posture, movement, physiognomic features, and clothes (e.g., Bornstein et al., 1969; Bruyer et al., 1983; Cohn, Neumann, & Wood, 1977; De Renzi et al., 1991; Etcoff, Freeman, & Cave, 1991; Suttleworth, Syring, & Allen, 1982). Correct guesses are possible perhaps because the context in which a given face is being perceived allows the entertainment of only a limited number of identity hypotheses (Damasio, Tranel, & Damasio, 1990a).

Three explanations may account for the failure to visually identify other persons' faces: perceptual deficit, impairment in the memory storage for faces, and difficulties in retrieval of faces from memory. Clearly, prosopagnosic patients who can tell that a face is a face, and not another object, do not have perceptual problems at the basic structural level. Evidence of covert recognition of familiar faces seems to show that, at least for some patients, the syndrome involves impairment in retrieval, and not in storage of facial representations.

The Guilty Knowledge Technique

The story of covert face recognition by prosopagnosic patients began with Bauer's (1984) creative idea to apply the guilty knowledge technique (GKT), which is used for lie detection, to the study of face recognition. The GKT is based on Lykken's (1959, 1960) psychophysiological technique for detecting guilt. It consists of questions regarding specific aspects of a given event that are assumed to be known to the person familiar with that event. Each question is given a number of alternative answers (with equivalent arousal values), one of which is correct (relevant). The knowledgeable person is expected to show larger electrodermal, cardiovascular, and other physiological responses to the presentation of the relevant than of the irrelevant items (Ben-Shakhar & Furedy, 1990). Electrodermal responsivity is considered one of the best psychophysiological indices for detecting information under the GKT (Waid, Wilson, & Orne, 1981). The robustness of this technique may be demonstrated by Ben-Shakhar and Gati's (1987) finding of larger electrodermal responses to the presentation of the relevant face than of the irrelevant faces, even when one or two features of the relevant face are either ommitted or replaced. It has been suggested that the relevant item has a "signal value" that produces stronger orienting responses than the irrelevant items (Elaad & Ben-Shakhar, 1989; Gati & Ben-Shakhar, 1990; Lykken, 1974). Under these conditions, responsivity to the relevant items does not require their conscious identification (Bauer & Verfaellie, 1992).

Adopting this technique, Bauer (1984) presented a prosopagnosic patient, LE, with pictures of famous faces and faces of the patient's family members. Each face was presented together with five names, one of which was the correct name. The patient's task was to match the faces with their correct names. Correct identification of famous faces was obtained for only 20% of the faces. However, maximal skin conductance responsivity was found for 60% of the correct face–name matches. The respective figures for the faces of family members were 25% and 62.5%. Face-recognition deficit was specific for familiar faces, as evident by the fact that the patient could match unfamiliar faces on Benton and Van Allen's (1973) Face Recognition Test. Similar findings have subsequently been reported by Bauer (1986), Bauer and Verfaellie (1988), Tranel and Damasio (1985), and Tranel, Damasio, and Damasio (1988). Covert recognition of subliminally presented faces by normal subjects was recently uncovered by Ellis, Young, and Koenken (1993), who detected higher peak amplitudes of skin conductance responses (SCRs) in recognizing familiar than unfamiliar faces, which was similar to that found in recognizing supraliminally presented faces. Finally, using P300 as an index of covert recognition, Renault et al. (1989) found that its latency varied with face familiarity.

It should be pointed out that a major difference in the use of the GKT technique for detection of deception and for tapping implicit recognition is subjects' motivation. In the former case, the suspects try to conceal the relevant information, whereas in the latter case, the subjects try to identify the explicitly unrecognizable stimuli.

Behavioral Indices of Covert Face Recognition

The physiological findings of covert face recognition are buttressed by behavioral data. Rizzo, Hurtig, and Damasio (1987) demonstrated differential eye movements by prosopagnosic patients in watching familiar and unfamiliar faces. De Haan and colleagues (De Haan, Young, & Newcombe, 1987a, 1987b, 1991; Young & De Haan, 1988; Young, Hellawell, & De Haan, 1988) tested a prosopagnosic patient, PH, who showed no overt recognition of faces, but revealed effects of covert recognition by demonstrating normal influences of familiarity in face-recognition tasks involving matching, learning, and interference. For example, in one experiment, PH was presented with pairs of faces—half were familiar to him and half were unfamiliar. His task was to tell whether the two members of a pair belonged to the same or different persons. Similar to normal controls, he was faster at matching familiar than unfamiliar faces. Like normals, his matching was based on internal, rather than external, features (but see Davidoff, Mathews, & Newcombe, 1986). When deriving the occupation of famous pop stars and politicians from their faces, reaction time (RT) was longer when the name–face pair was incongruent (the two members of a pair were drawn from different occupation categories) than when they were congruent with each other.

Similarly, when PH had to make forced-choice decisions between correct and incorrect alternative names for familiar faces, his RT was shorter for the correct names. Finally, in learning pairs of faces and names or occupations, he was better when the pairs were true than when they were untrue. Other prosopagnosic patients and normal subjects have shown similar savings on face–name relearning tasks (Bruyer et al., 1983; Wallace & Farah, 1992). Greve and Bauer (1990) presented a prosopagnosic patient with a series of unfamiliar faces, followed by a forced-choice recognition test ("which of the two faces did you see?"). The patient preferred the target faces, without any indication of overt recognition. Another prosopagnosic patient similarly demonstrated enhancement of performance of face-recognition tasks through indirect memories. For example, paired associate learning was faster for true than for untrue face–name pairs (Sergent & Poncet, 1990). However, it should be pointed out that covert recognition demonstrated by prosopagnosic patients is apparent in laboratory situations only. In everyday life, these patients do not show signs of covert face recognition (Young, 1994a).

Models of Covert Face Recognition

Two Pathways Model.   Bauer's (1984) account for the phenomenon of covert recognition is based on the assumption that there are two visual pathways from the limbic system to the visual cortex, ventral and dorsal, which are associated with overt and covert recognition, respectively. When the ventral pathway is impaired and the dorsal pathway is intact, covert recognition without overt recognition appears. That is because the ventral pathway is linked to object and face identification ("what"), whereas the dorsal pathway is linked to spatial location and direction of attention ("where"); see De Haan, Bauer, and Greve (1992). The opposite condition—where only the dorsal pathway is impaired—is believed to be associated with Capgras delusion (i.e., that familiar persons, objects, and locations have been replaced by impersonating doubles; Ellis & de Paun, 1994).

Therefore, lack of overt recognition with covert responsivity seems to demonstrate that the perceptual recognition system is intact, but its output fails to reach conscious awareness due to impairment in the transmission system. Sergent and Poncet (1990) speculate that the impaired connection between representations and memory might be due to a heightened threshold of activation of information that underlies conscious recognition, which might be due, in turn, to reduced effectiveness of the synaptic transmission. This view is shared by students of covert recognition from both physiological and behavioral perspectives (Bauer, 1984; Young & De Haan, 1988).

Interactive Models. New alternative interactive models suggest, that in cases of prosopagnosia, the face-recognition system indeed malfunctions as a consequence of which overt recognition is lost. However, its residual functioning can still evoke covert recognition presumably because it is more sensitive than overt recognition to the residual, low-quality functioning of the damaged system (Farah, 1994a; Farah, O'Reilly, & Vecera, 1993; Van Gulick, 1994; Wallace & Farah, 1992). One of these models, the Interactive Activation Model (Burton, Young, Bruce, Johnston, & Ellis, 1991; Young & De Haan, 1988) accounts for implicit face recognition in terms of Bruce and Young's (1986) face recognition model. According to this model, once a facial stimulus is structurally encoded, it is processed by a *face recognition unit* (FRU) which, by comparing it to stored templates, discriminates between it and other familiar or unfamiliar faces. The FRU activates the *person identity node* (PIN), which allows access to semantic information about the person whose face is being observed, and provides access to the *name generator* that enables identification of the person by name. Whenever the activation from the (intact) FRU to the PIN is too weak to raise the activation of the latter above threshold, covert face recognition with the absence of overt recognition appears. Empirical support for this model was recently provided by Diamond, Valentine, Mayes, and Sandel (1994).

The interactive models seem to be more parsimonious than other models because they do not postulate different forms of prosopagnosia as due to differential malfunctions at various stages of the face-recognition process. Instead, they are based on the assumption that both overt and covert recognitions are subserved by a single process (for similar controversies concerning other perceptual and memory functions, see Nachson, 1995; Schacter, 1992). The feasibility of the single-process hypothesis was recently demonstrated by Farah and her colleagues (Farah, 1994a; Farah et al., 1993; for evaluations and criticisms of Farah's approach, see Farah, 1994a) by using a simulated connectionist model of a damaged face-recognition system. However, Young and De Haan (1990) argued that it is unlikely that the covert recognition shown by their patient, PH, could have been produced by a degraded perceptual system because he had shown similar priming effects for faces and names. On a more general level, Farah (1994a) admitted that one may argue that computer models can only demonstrate the sufficiency of a theory, and not its empirical truth, whereas the alternative models are empirically grounded. Indeed, the compatibility of Farah's (1994a) model with neurophysiological processes has been questioned (Davidoff & Renault, 1994; Diederich, 1994; Van Hezewijk & De Haan, 1994; but see Farah's [1994a] answers). Therefore, despite its parsimonious qualities, it is doubtful whether Farah's model can provide an adequate explanation of face perception in general, and of covert recognition in prosopagnosia in particular. These and other reservations seem to justify Van Hezewijk and De Haan's (1994) conclusion that the interactive approach "must drop its pretense of being a completely independent alternative conceptual framework. It cannot be much more than an 'implementational theory' of cognitive (dys)function, complementary to competence theories" (p. 86).

The Heterogenous Nature of Prosopagnosia

Covert recognition of faces is not a universal feature of prosopagnosia. In many cases, failure to overtly recognize familiar faces is not accompanied by covert recognition (Bauer, 1986; Campbell & De Haan, 1994; De Haan & Campbell, 1991; De Haan et al., 1992; Humphreys et al., 1992; Newcombe, Young, & De Haan, 1989; Sergent & Villemure, 1989; Young & Ellis, 1989; Young et al., 1994). Therefore, prosopagnosia is not a unitary syndrome. Without covert recognition, prosopagnosia may not be conceived of in terms of dissociation between the intact perceptual and visual systems, but rather in terms of impairment in the perceptual system (Newcombe et al., 1989).

The heterogenous nature of prosopagnosia was detected long ago (e.g., Beyn & Knyazeva, 1962). More recently, it was eloquently demonstrated by Sergent and Signoret (1992a, 1992b), who found three patients with different right-hemisphere damages that were linked to somewhat different face-recognition deficits. Pertinent behavioral data have led Bruyer (1991) and Young et al. (1994) to a similar conclusion. The latter compared performance of two prosopagnosic patients, PH and HJA, on imaging tasks. PH's performance was impaired, but HJA showed preserved imagery for single faces when making feature-by-feature comparisons between imaged faces. The authors concluded that prosopagnosia has a multistage causation, and that the specific deficit depends on the particular stage damaged. Comparison of two other patients, PH and BD, led to the same conclusion. PH demonstrated some degree of covert recognition, but BD could not tell people from faces, names, and voices (see Hanley, Young, & Pearson, 1989). Therefore, Young and De Haan (1992) reasoned that the impairment in the recognition system was deeper for the latter than for the former patient.

In a recent review, Young (1994b) compared the performance of three prosopagnosic patients—NR, PH, and MS—who seemed to have suffered from a degradation of FRUs, a damage to the outputs of the otherwise intact FRUs, and an impairment of inputs transmitted to the FRUs, respectively. According to Young (1994b), these findings reflect a hierarchy of possible loci of impairments, whereby MS's impairment affected an early stage of the perceptual system, PH's deficit affected a later stage, and NR's dysfunction affected an interim stage. Different prosopagnosic symptoms are thus associated with deficits in different levels of the face-recognition process (Damasio, 1985; De Haan et al., 1992; Schweich & Bruyer, 1993).

Apperceptive and Associative Prosopagnosias

The idea that agnosias may be subcategorized into "apperceptive" (perceptual) and "associative" (mnesic) dates back to Lissauer (1890). *Apperception* means object identification by piecing together sensory impressions into a perceptual whole; *association* means identification of specific objects as members of generic categories by matching and linking them to previous experience (Bauer, 1986; Warrington, 1982). As Goldberg and Barr (1991) pointed out, physical object identification involves processing of features or attributes that are specific to the object, whereas associative (semantic) object identification involves processing features that are common across many objects. Accordingly, unlike object identification, *face recognition* is, by definition, a task of physical identification because its purpose is to identify one specific person as being different from another.

In line with Lissauer's (1890) reasoning, Hecaén (1981) differentiated between two kinds of prosopagnosia: one that is due to input deficit and the other that is due to disconnection of input from stored representations. Similar distinctions between perceptual and mnesic deficits have been made by others (De Renzi, 1986a; De Renzi et al., 1991; Ellis, 1986; Hay & Young, 1982; Hecaén & Angelergues, 1962; Meadows, 1974). Perceptual and amnesic (associative) prosopagnosias have both been linked to bilateral damages (to the inferior occipitotemporal visual association cortices and the anterior temporal regions, respectively; Damasio, Tranel, & Damasio, 1990b). However, Goldberg and Barr (1991) maintained that the two syndromes can be differentially linked to unilateral right- and left-hemisphere lesions, respectively. Moreover, the former, but not the latter, type of agnosia is accompanied by unawareness of the deficit.

COVERT RECOGNITION, CONSCIOUS AWARENESS, AND SELF-DECEPTION

Clearly, covert recognition cannot be associated with apperceptive prosopagnosia because the former implies a loss of awareness of the facial representations in memory without a breakdown of the perceptual system. As a literature survey shows, all but two patients (Sacks, 1987; Wilbrand, 1892) know that a face is a face, but do not know to whom it belongs. In more general terms, prosopagnosia may be conceived of as an example of an impairment in the recognition of a previously well-known, specific member of a given visual class, even as the recognition of the class is not impaired (Damasio & Damasio, 1983). Indeed, perception of unfamiliar faces and recognition of familiar faces are dissociated from each other (Benton, 1990; Benton & Van Allen, 1972; Malone et al., 1982; see also Parry, Young, Saul, & Moss, 1991; Rizzo et al., 1987; Tranel et al., 1988; Warrington & James, 1967). Thus, the latter, but not the former, involves episodic memory (which is mediated by semantic, verbal encoding), is affected by context and view, is obligatory and automatic, and is more efficient from internal than from external features (Young & Bruce, 1991).

Prosopagnosia and Anosognosia

Covert recognition implies that prosopagnosic patients who cannot consciously (overtly) recognize familiar faces, but are able to unconsciously (covertly) recognize them, are unaware of their residual ability. In this respect, covert recognition is distinguishable from similar anosognosic phenomena. The term *anosognosia* refers to unawareness of neurological deficits that may accompany a variety of neurological syndromes, such as hemiplegia, Anton's syndrome, amnesic syndromes, hemianopia, amnesia, head injury, alexia, and aphasia (Babinski, 1914; Bruyer, 1991; McGlynn & Schacter, 1989; Schacter, 1990).

In their comprehensive review, McGlynn and Schacter (1989) pointed out that:

> a significant number of patients are entirely unaware of their deficits: Some amnesic patients claim that their memory is perfectly normal, aphasic patients frequently do not know that their linguistic productions lack coherence and meaning, and hemiplegic patients often do not realize, and sometimes deny, that they have a motor impairment. Yet these same deficits are all too apparent to others and have a profound effect on afflicted patients' everyday lives. (p. 144)

However, unlike anosognosic patients—who are totally unaware of and therefore deny the existence of their respective deficits—prosopagnosic patients, who profess inability to recognize familiar faces, are unaware of their residual ability to covertly respond to them. Therefore, the denial is not of the deficit, but of the residual capability. There exists ample evidence showing that prosopagnosic patients are indeed explicitly aware of their deficit. A typical case is described by Bodamer (1947):

> Apart from the eyes, I see the face blurred. I don't see that which marks out a face. I don't see a particular expression of a face, my eye always goes to the most striking part of the face, and with living people I find the eye the most striking expression. When I see the eye of a face, I go from there to the other parts of the face. But when I look for that which is special about the face, I don't find it. (cited in Ellis & Florence, 1990, pp. 92–93)

Young, De Haan, and Newcombe (1990) described a rare case of a prosopagnosic patient, SP, who was specifically anosognosic about her face-recognition deficit, but fully aware of her other impairments (poor memory, hemiplegia, and hemianopia). But this case is atypical. Prosopagnosia also differs from other neurological syndromes that involve loss of awareness. As Damasio and Damasio (1983) pointed out, prosopagnosia differs from visual object agnosia, in that the former involves a deficit in recognizing a given member of a recognizable class of objects, whereas the latter involves a deficit in recognizing the entire class.

Prosopagnosia and Blindsight

As a syndrome characterized by unawareness of the residual capability, prosopagnosia shares some features with another neurological syndrome—blindsight. *Blindsight* refers to a visual field defect that results from a partial destruction or dennervation of the striate cortex (see Poppel, Held, & Frost, 1973; Weiskrantz, Warrington, Sanders, & Marshall,

1974). Blindsight patients are consciously blind to visual stimuli presented in parts of the visual field that are linked to the damaged cortical area. Some patients, however, can detect stimulus location, movement direction and velocity, and size (Cowey & Stoerig, 1992; Stoerig, 1987; Stoerig & Cowey, 1989a, 1989b; Weiskrantz, 1980, 1986, 1987, 1989; Weiskrantz et al., 1974). As Cowey and Stoerig (1992) pointed out, "these far-ranging residual visual capacities can be demonstrated even though the patients assert that they do not see anything in the field defects and are surprised when their often excellent performance is pointed out to them" (p. 11).

A strikingly similar phenomenon was demonstrated by Feinberg (1985) with a normal subject who received hypnotic suggestion that one of his eyes was blind. When that eye was covered, the subject maintained that he did not see anything. Subsequently, the subject wore polarized glasses that were perpendicularly polarized with respect to each other. The subject was led to believe that they were protective sunglasses. Numbers and words were then presented to the subject in such a way that some could be perceived by one eye and others by the other eye. Thus, some of the stimuli could be perceived only by the eye that had been suggested to be blind. Data analysis showed, however, that the visual stimuli were identified about equally well from the two eyes. This case clearly demonstrates covert recognition, which is associated with neither neurological syndromes nor with "perceptual defense" or unconsciously motivated denial for the protection of ego integrity. Furthermore, the reversibility of hypnotic suggestibility seems to indicate that the dissociation between unconscious and conscious systems is functional (similar cases of accurate discriminations of visual stimuli by hypnotically "blind" subjects have been reported by Sackeim, Nordlie, and Gur [1979]).

Despite the similarities, prosopagnosia and blindsight differ from each other: The former involves awareness that the object perceived is a face and that covert recognition may be revealed even when patients fail to perform above chance level on some forced-choice discrimination tasks, whereas the latter is characterized by unawareness of any visual stimulus despite patients' discriminations above chance level (De Haan, Young, & Newcombe, 1987a; Humphreys et al., 1992).

Motivational Aspects

Prosopagnosia shares with other neurological syndromes a common feature—namely, conscious unawareness of some aspects of the deficit. Therefore, the question may arise as to whether theories of conscious unawareness also apply to covert face recognition in prosopagnosia.

Theoretical accounts of the anosognosic syndromes were critically reviewed by McGlynn and Schacter (1989). The theories range from a variety of neuroanatomical, psychodynamic, and motivational theories through Schacter's (1989) own cognitive theory. Theories regarding neuroanatomical substrates of covert recognition in prosopagnosia were discussed earlier. However, the relevance of the motivational and dynamic theories to prosopagnosia should be briefly addressed. As McGlynn and Schacter (1989) pointed out, these theories account for anosognosia in terms of denial of illness, which helps defend the ego against the adverse effects of anxiety and stress, thus contributing to the person's adaptation and well-being. McGlynn and Schacter leveled seven criticisms against these theories. Two of these referred to the specificity of anosognosia (which does not make sense if denial is supposed to protect the person against the effects of all serious deficits) and to the link between lesion site and unawareness (which is unaccountable for in motivational or dynamic terms).

These criticisms are also applicable to prosopagnosia. However, an additional point may be raised regarding prosopagnosia and blindsight, where the patients do not deny the existence of a deficit, but are unaware of their residual functioning capabilities. It appears that, in these two syndromes, patients' well-being could be enhanced by acknowledging, rather than denying, their ability to recognize stimuli under certain conditions. Denial of the residual capabilities in these cases would therefore be counterproductive as a defense mechanism, and, as such, should have been abandoned.

Nachson, Myslobodsky, and Bentin (1995), recently observed a case of a woman, EY, who insisted that she could not recognize familiar faces, but in fact showed normal, overt recognition of faces of famous people and family members (as well as normal magnetic resonance imaging [MRI]). A dynamic explanation could possibly be suitable for this case.

Explicit and Implicit Knowledge

It seems that Schacter, McAndrews, and Moscovitch's (1988) descriptive model, which was originally developed to account for implicit–explicit dissociations, is comprehensive enough to account for both anosognosic deficits and prosopagnosic symptoms, despite their differences. The model, Dissociable Interactions and Conscious Experience (DICE), was originally formulated in general terms, but was subsequently adapted for face recognition by De Haan et al. (1992). According to the adapted model, overt recognition of faces is distinguishable from the face-processing module. Modular output does not reach consciousness until it activates a conscious awareness system (CAS), which presumably involves the frontal and inferior temporal lobes (Schacter, 1989; but see Farah, 1994c). Once a CAS has been activated, knowledge is explicit. However, when the face-recognition module is dissociated from CAS, there is no conscious awareness of the face, although knowledge can still be expressed through verbal, motor, and other bodily responses. In that case, face recognition is implicit. Thus, both overt and covert face recognition result from different outputs of the same processing module. As Schacter (1989) pointed out, this model is in line with various conceptions of the modularity of the mind (e.g., Fodor, 1983; Gardner, 1983; Gazzaniga, 1985), which view modular information processing as domain specific (for a discussion of the specificity of face recognition, see Nachson, 1995). Schacter's (1989) CAS therefore serves as a gate to consciousness—so that whatever passes through this gate reaches consciousness, is explicitly acknowledged, and can reach the executive system, whereas whatever does not pass through the system cannot gain conscious awareness, although it can certainly affect verbal and motor responses implicitly.

According to the DICE model, implicit knowledge, in the absence of explicit knowledge, is due to a dissociation between modular processes and the conscious awareness system (for criticism of the concepts of DICE and CAS, see Dennett, 1991; Farah, 1994c). As shown previously, this dissociation can be either structural or functional. In either case, the dissociation does not depend on any specific content of the modular system. Therefore, in a given case (e.g., in anosognosic syndromes), it may be manifested by denial of a defective cognitive function, whereas in another case (e.g., in blindsight and prosopagnosia), it can be manifested by a denial of a residual cognitive capability. However, the dynamics of the development and maintenance of the various dissociations need further elaboration.

Deception and Self-Deception

Regardless of etiology and dynamics, all the implicit–explicit dissociations may be conceived of as instances of self-deception: The afflicted persons consciously believe that they are either capable or incapable of performing a given task, whereas in fact the opposite is true. The essence of self-deception is unawareness of one's mode of functioning. Once a person intentionally tries to foster in another person a belief that he or she considers false, it is a case of outright deception, rather than self-deception (Zuckerman, De Paulo, & Rosenthal, 1981). Self-deception is considered paradoxical, as it implies that the same individual has contradictory beliefs or mental states (Sackeim, 1988). Accordingly, the criterion for self-deception entails that two contradictory mental contents or beliefs occur simultaneously in an individual who is not aware of one of them. The operation that determines which mental state or belief is and which is not subject to awareness is unconsciously motivated by the wish to achieve a high self-esteem, while denying contradictory evidence (Sackeim, 1988; Sackeim & Gur, 1978). However, as shown previously, the motivational aspect of the definition of self-deception is not applicable to neurological syndromes.

Within the neuropsychological framework, self-deception may be conceptualized in terms of dissociations between two or more cognitive systems.[1] In the case of deception, it is assumed that the central and autonomic nervous systems are functionally dissociated from each other, so that even when the deceiving suspects are consciously and intentionally telling lies, their autonomous responses, which are not under conscious control, may respond differentially when the suspects tell lies and when they answer truthfully. As a centrally controlled process (which involves conscious awareness, perceptual and memory mediation, as well as intention and verbalization), deception is not a modular process. Therefore, it cannot be conceptualized within the DICE model, which postulates dissociations between modular and central systems.

By contrast, self-deception may involve modular processes. Although similar dissociations have been observed across different anosognosic syndromes, experimental tasks, types of information, and perceptual and cognitive processes, all syndromes are domain specific in the sense that impaired access to consciousness is limited to the affected domain (Schacter, 1989). Thus, patients suffering from memory defects may deny the existence of the defect, but still be quite alert to their difficulties in performing cognitive or motor functions that do not involve memory processes. Likewise, prosopagnosic patients who covertly recognize familiar faces without overt awareness may be quite accurate in describing other disabilities. Therefore, self-deception in prosopagnosia may be

---

[1]Conceptualization of some neurological syndromes (such as aphasia, agnosia, and apraxia) in terms of dissociations between intact anatomical loci was forcefully advocated over 30 years ago by Geschwind (1965a, 1965b). Specifically, he distinguished between cortical syndromes due to lesions in the grey matter and conduction syndromes due to lesions in the white matter. The latter involve structural disconnections of neural pathways that disrupt the normal transmission of input from one brain area to another. Effects of structural disconnections are most conspicuous in cases of commissurotomy, where the two cerebral hemispheres are surgically disconnected from each other by severing the corpus callosum that connects them (e.g., Gazzaniga, 1970; Sperry, 1982; Zaidel, 1983). Anosognosic syndromes are also linked to structural brain damage (see McGlynn & Schacter, 1989). By contrast, the concept of self-deception does not entail a structural disconnection between anatomical areas, but rather a functional dissociation between cognitive functions. Self-deception in some neurological syndromes, in terms of limited access to certain kinds of information, was postulated by Lockard and Mateer (1988).

conceptualized within the DICE model in terms of a dissociation between a (largely modular) face-recognition system and the (central) conscious awareness system.

Although covert recognition in prosopagnosia is conceivable in terms of self-deception, it clearly differs from self-deception in everyday life: Unlike the latter, the former is not associated with unrealistic dreams and fantasies that help people overcome difficulties, or inflate self-esteem (see Sackeim, 1988; Solomon, 1993). On the contrary, it involves lack of awareness of some functioning cognitive capabilities. Self-deception in covert (face) recognition by prosopagnosic patients also differs from dynamically driven self-deception in that, unlike the latter, the former does not play a role in purposeful blocking of overt recognition (see Greenwald, 1988). Therefore, prosopagnosia stands out as an unusual phenomenon among other neurological syndromes with covert functions, as well as among cases of self-deception in nonpathological populations. Given the uniqueness of the human face and the specificity of face-recognition processes (see Nachson, 1995), this conclusion comes as no surprise.

ACKNOWLEDGMENT

The author thanks Michael Myslobodsky and Uri Hadar for their helpful comments on an earlier draft of this chapter.

REFERENCES

Agnetti, V., Carreras, M., Pinna, L., & Rosati, G. (1978). Ictal prosopagnosia and epileptogenic damage of the dominant hemisphere: A case history. *Cortex, 14*, 50–57.

Anderson, E., & Parkin, A. J. (1985). On the nature of the left visual field advantage for faces. *Cortex, 21*, 453–459.

Assal, G., Favre, C., & Anderes, J. O. (1984). Non-reconnaissance d'animaux familiers chez un paysan: Zoo-agnosie ou prosopagnosie pour les animaux [Non-recognition of familiar animals by a farmer: Zoo-agnosia or prosopagnosia for animals]. *Revue Neurologique, 140*, 580–584.

Babinski, M. J. (1914). Contribution a l'etude des troubles mentaux dans l'hemisplegie organique cerebrale (Anosognosie) [Contribution of studies on mental disorders in cerebral organic hemiplegia (anosognosia)]. *Revue Neurologique, 12*, 845–847.

Bauer, R. M. (1984). Autonomic recognition of names and faces in prosopagnosia: A neuropsychological application of the Guilty Knowledge Test. *Neuropsychologia, 22*, 457–469.

Bauer, R. M. (1986). The cognitive psychophysiology of prosopagnosia. In H. D. Ellis, M. A. Jeeves, F. Newcombe, & A. Young (Eds.), *Aspects of face processing* (pp. 253–272). Dordrecht: Nijhoff.

Bauer, R. M., & Verfaellie, M. (1988). Electrodermal discrimination of familiar but not unfamiliar faces in prosopagnosia. *Brain and Cognition, 8*, 240–252.

Bauer, R. M., & Verfaellie, M. (1992). Memory dissociations: A cognitive psychophysiology perspective. In L. R. Squire & N. Butters (Eds.), *Neuropsychology of memory* (pp. 58–71). New York: Guilford.

Behrmann, M., Moscovitch, M., & Winocour, G. (1994). Mental imagery without visual perception of objects: Evidence from a patient with visual agnosia. *Journal of Experimental Psychology: Human Perception and Performance, 20,* 1068–1087.

Ben-Shakhar, G., & Furedy, J. J. (1990). *Theories and applications in the detection of deception: A psychophysiological and international perspective.* New York: Springer-Verlag.

Ben-Shakhar, G., & Gati, I. (1987). Common and distinctive features of verbal and pictorial stimuli as determinants of psychophysiological responsivity. *Journal of Experimental Psychology: General, 116,* 91–105.

Benton, A. (1990). Facial recognition 1990. *Cortex, 26,* 491–499.

Benton, A., & Van Allen, M. W. (1972). Prosopagnosia and facial discrimination. *Journal of the Neurological Sciences, 15,* 167–172.

Benton, A. L., & Van Allen, M. W. (1973). *Test of facial recognition* (Neurosurgery Center Publication 287). Ames, IA: University of Iowa Press.

Beyn, E. S., & Knyazeva, G. R. (1962). The problem of prosopagnosia. *Journal of Neurology, Neurosurgery, and Psychiatry, 25,* 154–158.

Blanc-Garin, J. (1984). Perception des visages et reconnaissance de la physiognomie dans l'agnosie des visages [Face perception and recognition of physiognamy in face agnosia]. *L'Annee Psychologique, 84,* 573–598.

Blanc-Garin, J. (1986). Faces and non-faces in prosopagnosic patients. In H. D. Ellis, M. A. Jeeves, F. Newcombe, & A. Young (Eds.), *Aspects of face processing* (pp. 273–278). Dordrecht: Nijhoff.

Bodamer, J. (1947). Die Prosop-Agnosie (Die Agnosie des physiognomieerkennens) [Prosopagnosia (Agnosia of the recognition of physiognomy)]. *Archiv für Psychiatrie und Nervenkrankeheiten, 179,* 6–53.

Bornstein, B. (1963). Prosopagnosia. In L. Halpern (Ed.), *Problems of dynamic neurology* (pp. 283–318). Jerusalem: Hadassah Medical School.

Bornstein, B., Sroka, H., & Munitz, H. (1969). Prosopagnosia with animal face agnosia. *Cortex, 5,* 164–169.

Bowers, D., Bauer, R. M., Coslett, H. B., & Heilman, K. M. (1985). Processing of faces by patients with unilateral hemisphere lesions: I. Dissociation between judgments of facial affect and facial identity. *Brain and Cognition, 4,* 258–272.

Bruce, V., & Young, A. W. (1986). Understanding face recognition. *British Journal of Psychology, 77,* 305–327.

Bruyer, R. (1991). Covert face recognition in prosopagnosia: A review. *Brain and Cognition, 15,* 223–235.

Bruyer, R., Laterre, C., Seron, X., Feyereisen, P., Stypstein, E., Pierrard, E., & Rectem, D. (1983). A case of prosopagnosia with some preserved covert remembrance of familiar faces. *Brain and Cognition, 2,* 257–284.

Bruyer, R., & Stroot, C. (1984). Lateral differences in face processing: Task and modality effects. *Cortex, 20,* 377–390.

Bruyer, R., & Velge, V. (1981). Lesions cerebrale unilaterale et trouble de la perception des visages: Specifite du deficit? [Unilateral cerebral lesions in disorders of face perception: Is the deficit specific?]. *Acta Neurologica Belgica, 81,* 321–332.

Burton, A. M., Young, A. W., Bruce, V., Johnston, R. A., & Ellis, A. W. (1991). Understanding covert recognition. *Cognition, 39,* 129–166.

Campbell, R., & De Haan, E. (1994). Developmental prosopagnosia: A functional analysis and implications for remediation. In M. J. Riddoch & G. W. Humphreys (Eds.), *Cogni-*

tive neuropsychology and cognitive rehabilitation (pp. 77–101). Hove: Lawrence Erlbaum Associates.

Campbell, R., Landis, T., & Regard, M. (1986). Face recognition and lipreading. *Brain, 109*, 509–521.

Carey, S. (1978). A case study: Face recognition. In E. Walker (Ed.), *Explorations in the biology of language* (pp. 175–201). Hassocks, Sussex: Harvester.

Carey, S. (1981). The development of face perception. In G. Davies, H. D. Ellis, & J. Shepherd (Eds.), *Perceiving and remembering faces* (pp. 9–38). London: Academic Press.

Carey, S., & Diamond, R. (1977). From piecemeal to configurational representation of faces. *Science, 195*, 312–314.

Cohen-Levine, S., & Koch-Weser, M. P. (1982). Right hemisphere superiority in the recognition of famous faces. *Brain and Language, 1*, 10–22.

Cohn, R., Neumann, M. A., & Wood, D. H. (1977). Prosopagnosia: A clinicopathological study. *Annals of Neurology, 1*, 177–182.

Cowey, A., & Stoerig, P. (1992). Reflections on blindsight. In A. D. Milner & M. D. Rugg (Eds.), *The neuropsychology of consciousness* (pp. 11–32). London: Academic Press.

Damasio, A. R. (1985). Prosopagnosia. *Trends in Neuroscience, 8*, 132–135.

Damasio, A. R., & Damasio, H. (1983). Localization in lesions in achromatopsia and prosopagnosia. In A. Kertesz (Ed.), *Localization in neuropsychology* (pp. 417–428). New York: Academic Press.

Damasio, A. R., & Damasio, H. (1986). The anatomical substrate of prosopagnosia. In R. Bruyer (Ed.), *The neuropsychology of face perception and facial expression* (pp. 31–38). Hillsdale, NJ: Lawrence Erlbaum Associates.

Damasio, A. R., Damasio, H., & Tranel, D. (1986). Prosopagnosia: Anatomic and physiologic aspects. In H. D. Ellis, J. A. Jeeves, F. Newcombe, & A. Young (Eds.), *Aspects of face processing* (pp. 268–272). Dordrecht: Nijhoff.

Damasio, A. R., Damasio, H., & Tranel, D. (1990). Impairments of visual recognition as clues to the processes of memory. In G. M. Edelman, W. E. Gall, & W. M. Cowan (Eds.), *Signal and sense: Local and global order in perceptual maps* (pp. 451–473). New York: Wiley-Liss.

Damasio, A. R., Damasio, H., & Van Hoesen, G. W. (1982). Prosopagnosia: Anatomic basis and behavioral mechanisms. *Neurology, 32*, 331–341.

Damasio, A. R., Tranel, D., & Damasio, H. (1990a). Face agnosia and the neural substrates of memory. *Annual Review of Neuroscience, 13*, 89–109.

Damasio, A. R., Tranel, D., & Damasio, H. (1990b). Varieties of face agnosia: Different neuropsychological profiles and neural substrates. *Journal of Clinical and Experimental Neuropsychology, 12*, 66.

Davidoff, J. (1988). Prosopagnosia: A disorder of rapid spatial integration. In G. Denes, C. Semenza, & P. Bisiach (Eds.), *Perspectives on cognitive neuropsychology* (pp. 297–309). Hove: Lawrence Erlbaum Associates.

Davidoff, J., & Landis, T. (1990). Recognition of unfamiliar faces in prosopagnosia. *Neuropsychologia, 28*, 1143–1161.

Davidoff, J., Mathews, & Newcombe, F. (1986). Observations on a case of prosopagnosia. In H. D. Ellis, M. A. Jeeves, F. Newcombe, & A. Young (Eds.), *Aspects of face processing* (pp. 279–290). Dordrecht: Nijhoff.

Davidoff, J., & Renault, B. (1994). Further advantages of abandoning the locality assumption in face recognition. *Behavioral and Brain Sciences, 17*, 68.

De Haan, E. H. F., Bauer, R. M., & Greve, K. W. (1992). Behavioral and physiological evidence for covert face recognition in a prosopagnosic patient. *Cortex, 28*, 77–95.

De Haan, E. H. F., & Campbell, R. (1991). A fifteen year following-up of a case of developmental prosopagnosia. *Cortex, 27*, 489–509.

De Haan, E. H. F., Young, A. W., & Newcombe, F. (1987a). Face recognition without awareness. *Cognitive Neuropsychology, 4*, 385–415.

De Haan, E. H. F., Young, A. W., & Newcombe, F. (1987b). Faces interfere with name classification in a prosopagnosic patient. *Cortex, 23*, 309–316.

De Haan, E. H. F., Young, A. W., & Newcombe, F. (1991). Covert and overt recognition in prosopagnosia. *Brain, 114*, 2575–2591.

De Renzi, E. (1986a). Current issues on prosopagnosia. In H. D. Ellis, J. A. Jeeves, F. Newcombe, & A. Young (Eds.), *Aspects of face processing* (pp. 243–252). Dordrecht: Nijhoff.

De Renzi, E. (1986b). Prosopagnosia in two patients with CT scan: Evidence of damage confined to the right hemisphere. *Neuropsychologia, 24*, 385–389.

De Renzi, E., Bonacini, M. G., & Faglioni, P. (1989). Right posterior brain-damaged patients are poor at assessing the age of a face. *Neuropsychologia, 27*, 839–848.

De Renzi, E., Faglioni, P., Grossi, D., & Nichelli, P. (1991). Apperceptive and associative forms of prosopagnosia. *Cortex, 27*, 213–221.

De Renzi, E., Faglioni, P., & Spinnler, H. (1968). The performance of patients with unilateral brain damage on face recognition tasks. *Cortex, 4*, 17–34.

De Renzi, E., Perani, D., Carlesimo, G. A., Silveri, M. C., & Fazio, F. (1994). Prosopagnosia can be associated with damage confined to the right hemisphere—an MR and PET study and a review of the literature. *Neuropsychologia, 32*, 893–902.

De Renzi, E., Scotti, G., & Spinnler, H. (1969). Perceptual and dissociative disorders of visual recognition. *Neurology, 19*, 634–642.

De Schonen, S., & Mathivet, E. (1990). Hemispheric asymmetry in a face discrimination task in infants. *Child Development, 61*, 1192–1205.

Dennett, D. C. (1991). *Consciousness explained*. Boston: Little, Brown.

Diamond, B. J., Valentine, T., Mayes, A. R., & Sandel, M. E. (1994). Evidence of covert recognition in a prosopagnosic patient. *Cortex, 30*, 377–394.

Diederich, J. (1994). Neurocomputing and modularity. *Behavioral and Brain Sciences, 17*, 68–69.

Ebata, S., Ogawa, M., Tanaka, Y., Mizuno, Y., & Yoshida, M. (1991). Apparent reduction in the size of one side of the face associated with a small retrosplenial hemorrhage. *Journal of Neurology, Neurosurgery, and Psychiatry, 54*, 68–70.

Elaad, E., & Ben-Shakhar, G. (1989). Effects of motivation and verbal response type on psychophysiological detection of information. *Psychophysiology, 26*, 442–451.

Ellis, H. D. (1986). Disorders of face recognition. In K. Poeck, J. J. Freund, & H. Ganshirt (Eds.), *Neurology* (pp. 179–187). Berlin: Springer-Verlag.

Ellis, H. D. (1989). Prosopagnosia. In A. F. Bennett & K. M. McConkey (Eds.), *Cognition in individual and social contexts* (pp. 593–602). Amsterdam: Elsevier.

Ellis, H. D., & de Paun, K. W. (1994). The cognitive neuropsychiatric origins of the Capgras delusion. In A. S. David & J. C. Cutting (Eds.), *The neuropsychology of schizophrenia* (pp. 317–334). Hillsdale, NJ: Lawrence Erlbaum Associates.

Ellis, H. D., & Florence, M. (1990). Bodamers's (1947) paper on prosopagnosia. *Cognitive Neuropsychology, 7*, 81–105.

Ellis, H. D., & Young, A. W. (1989). Are faces special? In A. W. Young & H. D. Ellis (Eds.), *Handbook of research on face processing* (pp. 1–26). Amsterdam: North-Holland.

Ellis, H. D., Young, A. W., & Koenken, G. (1993). Covert face recognition without prosopagnosia. *Behavioural Neurology, 6*, 27–32.

Endo, M. (1986). Perception of upside-down faces: An analysis from the viewpoint of cue saliency. In H. D. Ellis, M. A. Jeeves, F. Newcombe, & A. Young (Eds.), *Aspects of face processing* (pp. 53–60). Dordrecht: Nijhoff.

Etcoff, N. L., Freeman, R., & Cave, K. R. (1991). Can we lose memories of faces? Content specificity and awareness in a prosopagnosic. *Journal of Cognitive Neuroscience, 3*, 25–41.

Ettlin, T. M., Beckson, M., Benson, D. F., Langfitt, J. T., Amos, E. C., & Pineda, G. S. (1992). Prosopagnosia: A bihemispheric disorder. *Cortex, 28*, 129–134.

Farah, M. J. (1990). *Visual agnosia: Disorders of object recognition and what they tell us about normal vision.* Cambridge, MA: MIT Press.

Farah, M. J. (1994a). Neuropsychological inference with an interactive brain: A critique of the "locality" assumption. *Behavioral and Brain Sciences, 17*, 43–104.

Farah, M. J. (1994b). Specialization within visual object recognition: Clues from prosopagnosia and alexia. In M. J. Farah & G. Ratcliff (Eds.), *The neuropsychology of high-level vision: Collected tutorial essays* (pp. 133–146). Hillsdale, NJ: Lawrence Erlbaum Associates.

Farah, M. J. (1994c). Visual perception and visual awareness after brain damage: A tutorial review. In C. Umilta & M. Moscovitch (Eds.), *Attention and performance: XV. Information processing* (pp. 37–76). Cambridge, MA: MIT Press.

Farah, M. J., O'Reilly, R. C., & Vecera, S. P. (1993). Dissociated overt and covert recognition as an emergent property of a lesioned neural network. *Psychological Review, 100*, 571–588.

Feinberg, I. M. (1985). *The principle of the supplementation in describing psychotic phenomena.* Unpublished study.

Feinberg, T. E., Schindler, R. J., Ochoa, E., Kwan, P. C., & Farah, M. J. (1994). Associative visual agnosia and alexia without prosopagnosia. *Cortex, 30*, 395–412.

Flude, B. M., Ellis, A. W., & Kay, J. (1989). Face processing and name retrieval in an anomic aphasic: Names are stored separately from semantic information about familiar people. *Brain and Cognition, 11*, 60–72.

Fodor, J. (1983). *The modularity of the mind.* Cambridge, MA: MIT Press.

Frith, C. D., Stevens, M., Johnson, E. C., Owens, D. G. C., & Crow, T. J. (1983). Integration of schematic faces and other complex objects in schizophrenia. *Journal of Nervous and Mental Disease, 171*, 34–39.

Gardner, H. (1983). *Frames of mind.* New York: Basic Books.

Gati, I., & Ben-Shakhar, G. (1990). Novelty and significance in orienting and habituation: A feature-matching approach. *Journal of Experimental Psychology: General, 119*, 251–263.

Gazzaniga, M. S. (1970). *The bisected brain.* New York: Appleton-Century-Crofts.

Gazzaniga, M. S. (1985). *The social brain.* New York: Basic Books.

Gazzaniga, M. S., & Smylie, C. S. (1983). Facial recognition and brain asymmetries: Clues to underlying mechanisms. *Annals of Neurology, 13*, 536–540.

Geschwind, N. (1965a). Disconnection syndromes in animals and man, part I. *Brain, 88*, 237–294.

Geschwind, N. (1965b). Disconnection syndromes in animals and man, part II. *Brain, 88*, 585–644.

Goldberg, E., & Barr, W. B. (1991). Three possible mechanisms of unawareness of deficit. In G. P. Prigatano & D. L. Schacter (Eds.), *Awareness of deficit after brain injury* (pp. 152–175). New York: Oxford University Press.

Greenwald, A. G. (1988). Knowledge and self-deception. In J. S. Lockard & D. L. Paulhus (Eds.), *Self-deception: An adaptive mechanism?* (pp. 113–131). Englewood-Cliffs, NJ: Prentice-Hall.

Greve, K. W., & Bauer, R. M. (1990). Implicit learning of new faces in prosopagnosia: An application of the mere-exposure paradigm. *Neuropsychology, 1*, 1035–1041.

Habib, M. (1986). Visual hypoemotionality and prosopagnosia associated with right temporal lobe isolation. *Neuropsychologia, 24*, 577–582.

Hanley, J. R., Young, A. W., & Pearson, N. A. (1989). Defective recognition of familiar people. *Cognitive Neuropsychology, 6*, 179–210.

Hatta, T. (1979). Perceptual and memory components of facial recognition task in normal subjects. *Memoirs of Osaka Kyoiku University, 27*, 223–229.

Hay, D. C. (1981). Asymmetries in face processing: Evidence for a right hemisphere perceptual advantage. *Quarterly Journal of Experimental Psychology, 33A*, 267–274.

Hay, D. C., & Young, A. W. (1982). The human face. In A. W. Ellis (Ed.), *Normality and pathology in cognitive functions* (pp. 173–202). London: Academic Press.

Hecaén, H. (1981). The neuropsychology of face recognition. In G. Davies, H. Ellis, & J. Shepherd (Eds.), *Perceiving and remembering faces* (pp. 39–54). London: Academic Press.

Hecaén, H., & Angelergues, R. (1962). Agnosia for faces (prosopagnosia). *Archives of Neurology, 7*, 92–100.

Hillger, L. A., & Koenig, O. (1991). Separable mechanisms in face processing: Evidence form hemispheric specialization. *Journal of Cognitive Neuroscience, 3*, 1–58.

Hilliard, R. D. (1973). Hemispheric laterality effects on a facial recognition task in normal subjects. *Cortex, 9*, 246–258.

Humphreys, G. W., Troscianko, T., Riddoch, M. J., Boucart, M., Donnelly, N., & Harding, F. A. (1992). Covert processing in different visual recognition systems. In A. D. Milner & M. D. Rugg (Eds.), *The neuropsychology of consciousness* (pp. 39–68). London: Academic Press.

Jones, B. (1979). Lateral asymmetry in testing long-term memory for faces. *Cortex, 15*, 183–186.

Klein, D., Moscovitch, M., & Vigna, C. (1976). Attentional mechanisms and perceptual asymmetries in tachistoscopic recognition of words and faces. *Neuropsychologia, 14*, 55–66.

Landis, T., Cummings, J. L., Christen, L., Bogen, J. E., & Imhof, H.-G. (1986). Are unilateral right posterior cerebral lesions sufficient to cause prosopagnosia? Clinical and radiological findings in six additional patients. *Cortex, 22*, 243–252.

Landis, T., Regard, M., Bliestle, A., & Kleihues, P. (1988). Prosopagnosia and agnosia for noncanonial views. *Brain, 111*, 1287–1297.

Levine, D. N., & Calvanio, R. (1989). Prosopagnosia: A defect in visual configural processing. *Brain and Cognition, 10*, 149–170.

Levy, J. (1980). Cerebral asymmetry and the psychology of man. In M. C. Wittrock (Ed.), *The brain and psychology* (pp. 245–319). New York: Academic Press.

Lhermitte, F., Chaine, F., Escourelle, R., Ducarne, B., & Pillon, B. (1972). Etude anatomoclinique d'un cas de prosopagnosia [Anatomoclinical study of a case of prosopagnosia]. *Revue Neurologique, 126*, 329–346.

Lissauer, H. (1890). Ein Fall von Seelenblindheit nebst einem Beitrage zur Theorie derselben [A case of mental blindness with a theoretical contribution]. *Archiv für Psychiatrie und Nervenkrankheit, 21*, 222–270.

Lockard, J. S., & Mateer, C. A. (1988). Neural bases of self-deception. In J. S. Lockard & D. L. Paulhus (Eds.), *Self-deception: An adaptive mechanism?* (pp. 23–39). Englewood Cliffs, NJ: Prentice-Hall.

Lykken, D. T. (1959). The GSR in the detection of guilt. *Journal of Applied Psychology, 43*, 385–388.

Lykken, D. T. (1960). The validity of the guilty knowledge technique: The effects of faking. *Journal of Applied Psychology, 44*, 258–262.

Lykken, D. T. (1974). Psychology and the lie detection industry. *American Psychologist, 29*, 725–739.

MacRae, D., & Trolle, E. (1956). The defect of function in visual agnosia. *Brain, 79*, 94–110.

Malone, D. R., Morris, H. H., Kay, M. C., & Levin, H. S. (1982). Prosopagnosia: A double dissociation between the recognition of familiar and unfamiliar faces. *Journal of Neurology, Neurosurgery, and Psychiatry, 45,* 820–822.

Marcel, T., & Rajan, P. (1975). Lateral specialization for recognition of words and faces in good and poor readers. *Neuropsychologia, 13,* 489–497.

McCarthy, R. A., & Warrington, E. K. (1986). Visual associative agnosia: A clinical-anatomical study of a single case. *Journal of Neurology, Neurosurgery, and Psychiatry, 49,* 1233–1240.

McGlynn, S. M., & Schacter, D. L. (1989). Unawareness of deficits in neuropsychological syndromes. *Journal of Clinical and Experimental Neuropsychology, 11,* 143–205.

McNeil, J. E., & Warrington, E. K. (1993). Prosopagnosia: A face-specific disorder. *The Quarterly Journal of Experimental Psychology, 46A,* 1–10.

Meadows, J. C. (1974). The anatomical basis of prosopagnosia. *Journal of Neurology, Neurosurgery and Psychiatry, 37,* 489–501.

Nachson, I. (1995). On the modularity of face recognition: The riddle of domain specificity. *Journal of Clinical and Experimental Neuropsychology, 17,* 256–275.

Nachson, I., Myslobodsky, M., & Bentin, S. (1995). *False prosopagnosia: A case study.* Unpublished data.

Nardelli, E., Coccia, B. G., Fiaschi, A., Terzian, H., & Rizzuto, N. (1982). Prosopagnosia: Report of four cases. *European Neurology, 21,* 289–297.

Newcombe, F. (1979). The processing of visual information in prosopagnosia and acquired dyslexia: Functional versus physiological interpretation. In D. J. Oborne, M. M. Grunberg, & J. R. Eiser (Eds.), *Research in psychology and medicine: Vol. 1. Physical aspects: Pain, stress, diagnosis and organic damage* (pp. 315–322). London: Academic Press.

Newcombe, F., De Haan, E. H. F., Ross, J., & Young, A. W. (1989). Face processing, laterality and contrast sensitivity. *Neuropsychologia, 27,* 523–538.

Newcombe, F., Mehta, Z., & De Haan, E. H. F. (1994). Category specificity in visual recognition. In M. J. Farah & G. Ratcliff (Eds.), *The neuropsychology of high-level vision: Collected tutorial essays* (pp. 103–132). Hillsdale, NJ: Lawrence Erlbaum Associates.

Newcombe, F., Young, A. W., & De Haan, E. H. F. (1989). Prosopagnosia and object agnosia without covert recognition. *Neuropsychologia, 27,* 179–191.

Pallis, C. A. (1955). Impaired identification of faces and places with agnosia for colours: Report of a case due to cerebral embolism. *Journal of Neurology, Neurosurgery and Psychiatry, 18,* 218–224.

Parry, F. M., Young, A. W., Saul, J. S. M., & Moss, A. (1991). Dissociable face processing impairments after brain injury. *Journal of Clinical and Experimental Neuropsychology, 13,* 545–558.

Phillips, R. J., & Rawls, R. E. (1979). Recognition of upright and inverted faces: A correlational study. *Perception, 8,* 577–583.

Poppel, E., Held, R., & Frost, D. (1973). Residual visual function after brain wounds involving the central visual pathways in man. *Nature, 243,* 295–296.

Puschel, J., & Zaidel, E. (1994). The Benton-Van Allen faces: A lateralized tachistoscopic study. *Neuropsychologia, 32,* 357–367.

Rapcsak, S. Z., Polster, M. R., Comer, J. F., & Rubens, B. (1994). False recognition and misidentification of faces following right hemisphere damage. *Cortex, 30,* 565–584.

Renault, B., Signoret, J.-L., Debruille, B., Breton, F., & Bolgert, F. (1989). Brain potentials reveal covert facial recognition in prosopagnosia. *Neuropsychologia, 27,* 905–912.

Reynolds, D. McQ., & Jeeves, M. A. (1978). A developmental study of hemisphere specialization for recognition of faces in normal subjects. *Cortex, 14,* 511–520.

Rhodes, G. (1985). Lateralized processes in face recognition. *British Journal of Psychology, 76,* 249–271.

Rhodes, G., Brake, S., & Atkinson, A. P. (1993). What's lost in inverted faces? *Cognition, 22,* 19–41.

Rizzo, M., Hurtig, M., & Damasio, A. R. (1987). The role of scanpaths in facial recognition and learning. *Annals of Neurology, 22,* 41–45.

Rizzolatti, G., Umilta, C., & Berlucchi, G. (1971). Opposite superiorities of the right and left cerebral hemispheres in discriminative reaction time to physiognomical and alphabetical material. *Brain, 94,* 431–442.

Ross, E. D. (1980). Sensory-specific and fractional disorders of recent memory in man: 1. Isolated loss of visual recent memory. *Archives of Neurology, 37,* 193–200.

Ross, P., & Turkewitz, G. (1982). Changes in hemispheric advantage in processing facial information with increasing stimulus familiarization. *Cortex, 18,* 489–499.

Ross-Kossak, P., & Turkewitz, G. (1984). Relationship between changes in hemispheric advantage during familiarization to faces and proficiency in facial recognition. *Neuropsychologia, 22,* 471–477.

Rotenberg, V. S., & Elizur, A. (1992). The interactions between left and right hemispheres and the problem of the psychological defense mechanisms. *Dynamic Psychiatry, 25,* 306–315.

Rumiati, R. I., Humphreys, G. W., Riddoch, M. J., & Bateman, A. (1994). Visual object agnosia without prosopagnosia or alexia: Evidence for hierarchical theories of visual recognition. *Visual Cognition, 1,* 181–225.

Sackeim, H. A. (1988). Self-deception: A synthesis. In J. S. Lockard & D. L. Paulhus (Eds.), *Self-deception: An adaptive mechanisms?* (pp. 146–165). Englewood Cliffs, NJ: Prentice-Hall.

Sackeim, H. A., & Gur, R. C. (1978). Self-deception self-confrontation, and consciousness. In G. E. Schwartz & D. Shapiro (Eds.), *Consciousness and self-regulation: Advances in research* (Vol. 2, pp. 139–197). New York: Plenum.

Sackeim, H. A., Nordlie, J. W., & Gur, R. C. (1979). A model of hysterical and hypnotic blindness: Cognition, motivation, and awareness. *Journal of Abnormal Psychology, 88,* 474–489.

Sacks, O. (1987). *The man who mistook his wife for a hat.* New York: Harper & Row.

Schacter, D. L. (1989). On the relation between memory and consciousness: Dissociable interactions and conscious experience. In H. L. Roediger III & F. I. M. Craik (Eds.), *Varieties of memory and consciousness* (pp. 355–389). Hillsdale, NJ: Lawrence Erlbaum Associates.

Schacter, D. L. (1990). Toward a cognitive neuropsychology of awareness: Implicit knowledge and anosognosia. *Journal of Clinical and Experimental Neuropsychology, 12,* 155–178.

Schacter, D. L. (1992). Understanding implicit memory: A cognitive neuroscience approach. *American Psychologist, 47,* 559–569.

Schacter, D. L., McAndrews, M. P., & Moscovitch, M. (1988). Access to consciousness: Dissociations between implicit and explicit knowledge in neurological syndromes. In L. Weiskrantz (Ed.), *Thought without language* (pp. 242–278). New York: Oxford University Press.

Schweich, M., & Bruyer, R. (1993). Heterogeneity in the cognitive manifestations of prosopagnosia: The study of a group of single cases. *Cognitive Neuropsychology, 10,* 529–547.

Sergent, J. (1982a). About face: Left hemisphere involvement in processing physiognomics. *Journal of Experimental Psychology: Human Perception and Performance, 8,* 1–14.

Sergent, J. (1982b). The cerebral balance of power: Confrontation or cooperation? *Journal of Experimental Psychology: Human Perception and Performance, 8,* 253–272.

Sergent, J. (1984). An investigation into component and configural processes underlying face perception. *British Journal of Psychology, 75,* 221–242.

Sergent, J. (1985). Influence of task and input factors on hemispheric involvement in face processing. *Journal of Experimental Psychology: Human Perception and Performance, 11,* 846–861.

Sergent, J. (1988a). Face perception: Underlying processes and hemispheric contribution. In G. Denes, C. Semenza, & P. Bisiachi (Eds.), *Perspectives on cognitive neuropsychology* (pp. 271–295). Hillsdale, NJ: Lawrence Erlbaum Associates.

Sergent, J. (1988b). Face perception and the right hemisphere. In L. Weiskrantz (Ed.), *Thought without language* (pp. 108–131). Oxford, England: Clarendon.

Sergent, J. (1995). Visualizing the working cerebral hemispheres. In F. L. Kitterle (Ed.), *Hemispheric communication: Mechanisms and models* (pp. 189–210). Hillsdale, NJ: Lawrence Erlbaum Associates.

Sergent, J., & Bindra, D. (1981). Differential hemispheric processing of faces: Methodological considerations and reinterpretations. *Psychological Bulletin, 89,* 541–554.

Sergent, J., Ohta, S., & MacDonald, B. (1992). Functional neuroanatomy of face and object processing. *Brain, 115,* 15–36.

Sergent, J., & Poncet, M. (1990). From covert to overt recognition of faces in a prosopagnosic patient. *Brain, 113,* 989–1004.

Sergent, J., & Signoret, J.-L. (1992a). Implicit access to knowledge derived from unrecognized faces in prosopagnosia. *Cerebral Cortex, 2,* 389–400.

Sergent, J., & Signoret, J.-L. (1992b). Varieties of functional deficits in prosopagnosia. *Cerebral Cortex, 2,* 375–388.

Sergent, J., & Villemure, J.-G. (1989). Prosopagnosia in a right hemispherectomized patient. *Brain, 112,* 975–995.

Solomon, R. C. (1993). What a tangled web: Deception and self-deception in philosophy. In M. Lewis & C. Sarni (Eds.), *Lying and deception in everyday life* (pp. 3–59). New York: Guilford.

Sperry, R. (1982). Some effects of disconnecting the cerebral hemispheres. *Science, 217,* 1223–1226.

St. John, R. C. (1981). Lateral asymmetry in face perception. *Canadian Journal of Psychology, 35,* 213–223.

Stoerig, P. (1987). Chromaticity and achromaticity: Evidence of a functional differentiation in visual field defects. *Brain, 110,* 869–886.

Stoerig, P., & Cowey, A. (1989a). Residual target detection as a function of stimulus size. *Brain, 112,* 1123–1139.

Stoerig, P., & Cowey, A. (1989b). Wavelength sensitivity in blindsight. *Nature, 342,* 916–918.

Suttleworth, E. C., Jr., Syring, V., & Allen, N. (1982). Further observations on the nature of prosopagnosia. *Brain and Cognition, 1,* 307–322.

Tranel, D., & Damasio, A. R. (1985). Knowledge without awareness: An autonomic index of facial recognition by prosopagnosics. *Science, 228,* 1453–1454.

Tranel, D., Damasio, A. R., & Damasio, H. (1988). Intact recognition of facial expression, gender, and age in patients with impaired recognition of face identity. *Neurology, 38,* 690–696.

Tzavaras, A., Hecaén, H., & Le Bras, H. (1970). Le probleme de la specifite du deficit de la reconnaissance du visage humain lors des lesions hemispheriques unilaterales [The problem of deficit specificity in human face recognition due to unilateral hemispheric lesions]. *Neuropsychologia, 8,* 403–416.

Van Gulick, R. (1994). Prosopagnosia, conscious awareness and the interactive brain. *Behavioral and Brain Sciences, 17,* 84–85.

Van Hezewijk, R., & De Haan, E. H. F. (1994). The symbolic brain or the invisible hand? *Behavioral and Brain Sciences, 17,* 85–86.

Waid, W. M., Wilson, S. K., & Orne, M. T. (1981). Cross-modal physiological effects of electrodermal lability in the detection of deception. *Journal of Personality and Social Psychology, 40,* 1118–1125.

Wallace, M. A., & Farah, M. J. (1992). Savings in relearning of face-name associations as evidence for "covert recognition" in prosopagnosia. *Journal of Cognitive Neuroscience, 4,* 150–159.

Warrington, E. K. (1982). Neuropsychological studies of object recognition. *Philosophical Transactions of the Royal Society of London (Biology), 298,* 16–33.

Warrington, E. K., & James, M. (1967). An experimental investigation of facial recognition in patients with unilateral cerebral lesions. *Cortex, 3,* 317–326.

Weiskrantz, L. (1980). Varieties of residual experience. *Quarterly Journal of Experimental Psychology, 32,* 365–386.

Weiskrantz, L. (1986). *Blindsight: A case study and implications.* New York: Oxford University Press.

Weiskrantz, L. (1987). Residual vision in scotoma: A follow-up study of "form" discrimination. *Brain, 110,* 77–92.

Weiskrantz, L. (1989). Blindsight. In H. Goodglass & A. R. Damasio (Eds.), *Handbook of neuropsychology* (pp. 375–385). Amsterdam: Elsevier.

Weiskrantz, L., Warrington, E. K., Sanders, M. D., & Marshall, J. (1974). Visual capacity in the hemianopic field following a restricted occipital ablation. *Brain, 97,* 709–728.

Whiteley, A. M., & Warrington, E. K. (1977). Prosopagnosia: A clinical, psychological, and anatomical study of three patients. *Journal of Neurology, Neurosurgery and Psychiatry, 40,* 395–403.

Wilbrand, H. (1892). Ein Fall von Seelenblindheit und Hemianopsie mit Sections Befund [A case of mental blindness and hemianopia with post mortem findings]. *Deutche Zeitschrift für Nervenheilkunde, 2,* 361–387.

Yin, R. K. (1969). Looking at upside-down faces. *Journal of Experimental Psychology, 81,* 141–145.

Young, A. W. (1988). Functional organization of visual recognition. In L. Weiskrantz (Ed.), *Thought without language* (pp. 78–107). Oxford, England: Clarendon.

Young, A. W. (1994a). Conscious and non-conscious recognition of familiar faces. In C. Umilta & M. Moscovitch (Eds.), *Attention and performance: XV. Information processing* (pp. 153–178). Cambridge, England: Cambridge University Press.

Young, A. W. (1994b). Covert recognition. In M. J. Farah & G. Ratcliff (Eds.), *The neuropsychology of high-level vision* (pp. 331–358). Hillsdale, NJ: Lawrence Erlbaum Associates.

Young, A. W., & Bruce, V. (1991). Perceptual categories and the computation of "Grandmother." *European Journal of Cognitive Psychology, 3,* 5–49.

Young, A. W., & De Haan, E. H. F. (1988). Boundaries of covert recognition in prosopagnosia. *Cognitive Neuropsychology, 5,* 317–336.

Young, A. W., & De Haan, E. H. F. (1990). Impairments of visual awareness. *Mind and Language, 5,* 29–48.

Young, A. W., & De Haan, E. H. F. (1992). Face recognition and awareness after brain injury. In A. D. Milner & M. D. Rugg (Eds.), *The neuropsychology of consciousness* (pp. 69–90). London: Academic Press.

Young, A. W., De Haan, E. H. F., & Newcombe, F. (1990). Unawareness of impaired face recognition. *Brain and Cognition, 14,* 1–18.

Young, A. W., & Ellis, H. D. (1989). Childhood prosopagnosia. *Brain and Cognition, 9,* 16–47.

Young, A. W., Flude, B. M., Hay, D. C., & Ellis, A. W. (1993). Impaired discrimination of familiar from unfamiliar faces. *Cortex, 29,* 65–75.

Young, A. W., Hay, D. C., & McWeeny, K. H. (1985). Right cerebral hemisphere superiority for constructing facial representations. *Neuropsychologia, 23,* 195–202.

Young, A. W., Hay, D. C., McWeeny, K. H., & Ellis, A. W. (1985). Familiarity decisions for faces presented to the left and right cerebral hemispheres. *Brain and Cognition, 4*, 439–450.

Young, A. W., Hellawell, D., & De Haan, E. H. F. (1988). Cross domain semantic priming in normal subjects and a prosopagnosic patient. *Quarterly Journal of Experimental Psychology, 40A*, 561–580.

Young, A. W., Humphreys, G. W., Riddoch, M. J., Hellawell, D. J., & De Haan, E. H. F. (1994). Recognition impairments and face imagery. *Neuropsychologia, 32*, 693–702.

Zaidel, E. (1983). Disconnection syndrome as a model for laterality effects in the normal brain. In J. B. Hellige (Ed.), *Cerebral hemisphere asymmetry* (pp. 95–151). New York: Praeger.

Zuckerman, M., De Paulo, B. M., & Rosenthal, R. (1981). Verbal and nonverbal communication of deception. *Advances in Experimental Social Psychology, 14*, 1–59.

12

Mnemopoesis: Memories That Wish Themselves to Be Recalled?

Leslie Hicks
Michael S. Myslobodsky

> That man must be tremendously ignorant: he answers every question that is put to him.
> —Voltaire, *Dictionnaire Philosophique: Annales*

Everyone is guilty of occasional inaccuracy in recalling past events. Some distortions are purposeful; when they are also implausible, inadequate, or grotesque, the person is said to be afflicted by *pseudologia phantastica*. Another category of incongruous stories is designated as *delusional*. These are false convictions not corrected by experience or reason; when encountered in the context of a major psychiatric malady, they are often disguised (Linn, 1967).

A different class of fictitious accounts is designated as confabulation. Roget's *International Thesaurus* lists *Confabulation* as a synonym of words denoting misrepresentation, exaggeration, fabrication, and so on. That is pretty close to what the literature suggests they are—conversational fables. But these are not fables to fool others for gain, as is true for *pseudologia phantastica*, in which individuals actually remember the real plot behind the fabricated version. Confabulators do not remember the true story.

In contrast to delusional patients, confabulators show responses that are less organized and more accidental, that undergo no intellectual processing, and that are never disguised (Beck, Beck, Levitt, & Molish, 1961). Although delusional and confabulatory narratives may both defy logic, delusional patients resist criticism, whereas patients with "fantastic" confabulations are simply indifferent to contradictions and common sense. When challenged, confabulating patients do not stand firm behind their account. If anything, they are only too happy to admit errors when their condition begins to improve (Talland, 1961).

When are such inaccuracies precipitated? Who are the susceptible individuals? What is the relationship among confabulations, memory deficit, and states of consciousness? These questions have been with us for a long time. Although an understanding of mental functions is undergoing constant revision, the history of confabulations conceived of as part of memory dysfunction is somewhat less glorious. Rarely has such an important phenomenon managed to stay so poorly researched for so long. In the past two decades, confabulation was entered only about 90 times as a key word—a surprisingly modest bibliographic increment for such a robust category of amnestic disorders.

QUESTIONING THE DEFINITIONS

Before proceeding further, it would be helpful to examine some major terms in the area. Early on, *confabulations* were conceived of as false memories (Kraepelin, 1919). E. Bleuler (1950) took grave exception to the view that confabulations are a form of "memory hallucinations which fill in memory gaps" (p. 143). Instead, he likened such fabrications to *pseudologia phantastica*—in the sense of a hysteriform wish-formation manipulated by external pressures. Yet the Kraepelinian view appeared to be more appealing, and was supported by authoritative statements years later that confabulations were indeed maneuvers for filling in gaps in a failing memory (e.g., Wyke & Warrington, 1960), or that they represented "the production of incorrect information . . . " (Stuss & Benson, 1983, p. 122). Kraepelin's definition implies the activity of a brain "controller" that *monitors* the deficit and then *seizes* any random story to fill in the memory gap. Neither Bleuler's nor Kraepelin's assumptions have been formally tested. What is known is that confabulations are present in alcoholics with severe memory disorders and in demented patients in whom such a self-monitoring controller is hardly present.

Still, confabulated responses do not necessarily require the presence of such a devastating depletion of memory as encountered in patients with Korsakoff's syndrome. Even when such damage is obvious, some amnesics may not manifest confabulations at all (M. Johnson, 1991; Stuss, Alexander, Liberman, & Levine, 1978). Also, individuals with confabulations may have normal-range performance in formal memory tests (Kapur & Coughlan, 1980; Stuss, Alexander, Lieberman, & Levine, et al., 1978). Talland (1961) noted that Korsakoff felt that amnesia was not a *sine qua non* for confabulation. According to Joslyn, Grundvig, and Chamberlain (1978), confabulators and nonconfabulators did not differ in overall memory functioning as assessed by the Wechsler Memory Scale (WMS; Wechsler, 1981). Gainotti (1975) asserted: "no evident parallelism can be found between confabulations and memory loss" (p. 105). If formal memory loss is not an obligatory condition for all forms of confabulated responses, confabulations may be more appropriately classified, along with reduplications, as *paramnesic disorders* (McCarthy & Warrington, 1990).

Bleuler (1950) was doubtful that such memory falsifications occurred in conditions of clouded consciousness with impaired capacity to self-criticism, and described as a counterexample a personal case in which a successful salesman recounted stories of his fantastic adventures. Berlyne (1972) saw confabulations as the "falsification of memory occurring *in a clear consciousness in association with organically derived amnesia*" (p. 38; italics added). This definition was tailored to fit the fabrications seen in Korsakoff's patients. However, it did not specify how "clear" this clear consciousness should be. Consciousness is a multicomponent condition. It is composed of perception, attention, emotions, monitoring of the self, and the state of others. Its level is frequently difficult to characterize with satisfactory precision. Furthermore, careful observations are needed to ensure that not even a slight measure of cloudy consciousness is present. That could be a tough task in psychopathology, where "clouding may be so mild as to be unrecognized as such" (Slater & Roth, 1969). One of the chief signs of the presence of a "reflective stream of consciousness" is the capacity to judge whether thoughts or images are related to a current cognitive process or represent an alien product—an uncontrolled intrusion into an otherwise normal mentation (Rechtshaffen, 1978). Apparently some consciousness deficiencies may be the main reason that confabulations are not recognized by the patient as self-generated fibs, and, therefore, are seldom referenced to reality.

CONDITIONS OF CONFABULATIONS

The Role of Self-Monitoring

Berlyne's (1972) definition did not explain whether the diagnosis of confabulation should be applied when organic background and clear consciousness are ruled out. This invites amendments to the definition that could legitimize the term in a variety of maladies. Fisher (1989) broadened the territory of confabulations by suggesting that amnesics who act as if their recall is adequate are, in many respects, similar to the cortically deaf or blind who behave as if they see and hear. The common denominator of all such conditions is that patients are unaware of their deficit, have poor insight into their condition, and may be frankly anosognosic.

Most striking are the cases in which the confabulated material includes items related to the patient's major disability. Thus, centrally blind patients may react to questions regarding their home environment with instant confabulations ("confabulatory pseudorecognitions") that are so plausible that they have to be validated against accounts of family members (Critchley, 1979; Weinstein & Kahn, 1959). Unawareness or denial of blindness in the Anton syndrome is coupled with confabulations. One of Critchley's (1979) patients with central blindness, when asked to describe the appearance of a dress worn by a woman in his office, did so without hesitation. The woman was not even present in his office. A patient of Talland (1961), a woman in her 70s with a wizened, bent body, when asked what she would like to do when she left the hospital, responded that she would like to go out to dances on Saturday nights. Some of these responses, however playful, are consistent with the presence of implicit knowledge. As an example, a patient in the Mt. Sinai Hospital in New York, described by Weinstein and Kahn (1959), insisted that he was a resident of a rest home in Florida, but referred to it as "Mt. Cyanide Rest Home." Geschwind (1982), who drew attention to this episode, observed that this pun on the name of the hospital could not be produced unless the patient had this information implicitly.

The necessity of reduced self-monitoring that would lead to confabulated recall is also emphasized by others (Mercer, Wapner, Gardner, & Benson, 1977; Shapiro, Alexander, Gardner, & Mercer, 1981). According to Fisher (1989), reduced self-monitoring is the major trigger of confabulated responses: "The subject cannot say 'I don't know' if he is unaware of his deficit. . . . 'I don't know' represents a relatively preserved intellect" (p. 128). Because some normal individuals experience difficulty admitting incomplete knowledge or sheer ignorance, one might think that they, too, should not be immune to confabulation. This turns out to be true, although such confabulations appear in the form of "momentary," yet plausible, intrusions or elaborations that surface when the recollections of tested events are imperfect (Kopelman, 1987).

The Role of Affective Background

Other noncognitive modulators of memory processes operate through altering the state of drives, mood, and the degree of emotional tension. Confabulations frequently develop against the looming affective background, which may or may not be accounted for by the self. For example, themes with a strong affective charge (e.g., a wartime experience) are more likely to appear as a perseverative confabulated item (Mercer et al., 1977). Some writers have argued that confabulated responses have distinct positive, motivational dimensions, and are associated with the nature of patients' problems (Weinstein, 1987; Weinstein & Kahn, 1959). They are reminiscent of magical solutions to difficult intra- or interpersonal problems exported from the past, or to delusions that arise in situations that demand vigorous self-assertion. For Weinstein and Kahn (1959), confabulations represent coping or adapting to the stress inflicted by awareness of individual incompetence. Gainotti (1975) supported this idea by demonstrating that patients with a premorbid pattern of denial of illness, who have a need for prestige in interpersonal relations, are more likely to confabulate than patients who do not have these traits.

There are problems involved when tension is nominated as an essential ingredient of a process leading to confabulated responses. It seems to operate only, or chiefly, for certain types of fabrications (e.g., "confabulations of denial"; Gainotti, 1975), which are distinguished by their content (because they "seem to play a function of avoiding the catastrophic reaction") and their resistance to corrections. However, these "confabulations of denial" have more features of delusions and elaborations on the theme of the patients' anosognosia. Also, according to Weinstein and Kahn (1959), patients with "complete explicit denial" appear to be lacking in anxiety and tension, and manifest little confabulated responses outside the content of denial. It is not certain whether demented patients deal with unappreciated and unresolved emotional conflict by producing confabulated response. It is clear that, in both normal individuals and patients, confabulations may be catalyzed by such emotional pressure as the (perceived) need to come up with a recall. The more a patient believes an answer should be given, the more likely it is that confabulations will appear (Mercer et al., 1977). This burden to respond might be loosely defined as the *guru situation* (i.e., an obligation to provide a satisfactory reply no matter what).

Confabulations as Legitimized Distortions

Confabulators avoid engaging in fabrications that can be flagrantly disconfirmed. In this respect, they seem to share some motives for a frank lie ("honest lying"; Moscovitch, 1989) in order to appeal to an interlocutor, or to avoid creating an awkward or embarrassing social situation. These falsifications result from memory problems for which emotions and the sociocultural background provide a magnificent escape rationale. Confabulating patients retain an awareness of their ability to fabricate and recruit defense mechanisms that protect the self from the distress associated with discovery of these distortions. For example, questions pertaining to shared knowledge, or those that require a more precise response, such as "Who won the Super Bowl last year?" may yield a typical normal "don't know" response from patients with frank confabulations (Dalla Barba, Cipolotti, & Denes, 1989; Mercer et al., 1977). Thus, the ease with which a patient may plunge into the realm of "legitimate lies" or the illusion of knowledge of the reported event likens confabulations to the "positive illusion" of Taylor (1989). For Taylor, people who maintain an overly optimistic assessment of their situations or knowledge are better adjusted to their circumstances and, more specifically, are better prepared to control stressful events. It is believed that people suffering from depression frequently exhibit less positive illusions, which, for the majority of the normal population, serve as a buffer against the harsh impact of reality (Taylor, 1989). A repetitive admission of ignorance in the self-depreciating depressive patient who often responds "I don't know" is incompatible with confabulation. Such a definition implies that inaccuracies that are not punctuated by skeptical disclaimers may be suspected of being confabulated responses. The longer a patient takes to answer a question, the less likely he or she is to confabulate, suggesting that the ability to monitor one's answer improves the accuracy of responses (Mercer et al., 1977).

Material of Confabulations

As the previous accounts imply, the material of confabulations is harvested from current life events, social relationships, and sources of personal identity (Weinstein & Lyerly, 1968). These arise in response to questions that may be legitimately ornamented. The patient's penchant for confabulation can be encouraged. For example, a question asked in an animated tone—"Do you remember that trip by night through the African jungle, when natives attacked the train?"—elicited a confabulated recollection in a Korsakoff patient. Later, the interviewer challenged the story: "Did you *really* remember taking such a train trip?" The characteristic answer was, "Well I suppose I must have taken it, because you said I did, and you are a doctor" (Kinsbourne, 1989). This anecdote suggests that confabulations can be elicited by prompted recall and blossom in the atmosphere of legitimized fictitious accounts. Readiness to confabulate can be encouraged or sanctioned by a sympathetic listener. Patients readily respond to a subtle smile, a gaze, nods of approval, and so on, all of which represent normative regulation. Confabulations in patients with Anton syndrome have been known to be frequently provoked by suggestion (Critchley, 1979). It was noticed that individuals with learning disabilities and low IQ (under 80), too, confabulate more readily and are more susceptible to "leading questions" (Clare & Gudjonsson, 1993). In lay language, this implies a highly permissible (trusting) attitude to events that normally would not pass the gate of cognitive assessment.

Memory researchers have difficulty monitoring the number of errors of recollections made in the psychological laboratory. The majority of tests that tap into the phenomenon of confabulations do not discuss the reliability of verification standards. Within academic psychology, autobiographical memory is often assessed through the use of tests that examine a patient's ability to accurately reproduce the wording of a standard story. Yet predictions based on error rates in memorization tasks may not be automatically translated to tasks relating to personal recall of autobiographical data (Ross, 1991).

The content of recalled material is often classified along the lines of its origin (i.e., as either elicited or volunteered by the patient). Indeed, although the terms *confabulation* and *confabulated responses* are frequently used interchangeably, confabulations are designated as either spontaneous or provoked. Cummings (1985) asserted that "Confabulation is closely related to amnesia and indicates the production of *incorrect answers in response to questions*" (p. 36; italics added). Later in his text, he redefined *confabulations* as *"spontaneous* untruths occurring in patients with amnesia" (p. 163; italics added). The word *spontaneous* originates from *spoute*, which is Latin for "done by one's free will, voluntarily." One might argue that if confabulations are only volunteered, rather than elicited, products (triggered by an explicit question) of some cues intrinsic to the procedure, they hardly differ, on the criterion of spontaneity, from the lies of *pseudologia phantastica*.

If, on the contrary, no confabulation is ever genuinely willful, then the reference to their spontaneity is confusing. That does not mean that this subdivision is not helpful in the clinical context. Berlyne's (1972) taxonomy follows Bonhoeffer (1904) in its strong emphasis on the differences between the two. Fleeting intrusions ("momentary confabulations"), occasionally recorded in normals, are attributed to the category of *provoked confabulations*. The latter are thought of as different from the florid "spontaneous" confabulations of amnesic patients. Only these "real" confabulations are believed to achieve "fantastic" proportions. They are thought of as pathological phenomena (Berlyne, 1972; M. Kopelman, 1987).

However, the degree of ornamentation of intrusions (elaborations?) is not an unambiguous sign of spontaneous, "pathological" responses. Kopelman (1987) felt that healthy subjects in his study might have responded with more florid confabulations if they were tested at longer retention intervals. His observations pose this more general question: What degree of alien experience must be integrated into memory to be regarded as a fabricated recall? The accurate answer to this question is not available because constant updating of memory and reinterpretation of past experience is a normal process (Ross & MacDonald, chap. 7, this volume). Even information that conflicts rather blatantly with originally formed representations may be successfully incorporated (Loftus, 1979). That is why Talland (1961) felt that the verisimilitude of confabulations is often a relative category. He frequently reserved the term *confabulation* for real-world distortions, whereas more fantastic and incongruous materials were treated separately under the heading of *fabrications* (Talland, 1961). Apparently, the latter category of fabrications of a personal nature might be more accurately, and less pejoratively, designated as *mnemopoetic accounts*, or *mnemopoesis* (from Greek *mnemon*, pertaining to memory, and *poietes*, concerned with creation).

AN INTEGRATION OF FINDINGS
WITH NEUROANATOMY

Confabulations are associated with organic brain damage. Although they are encountered following anterior cingulectomy (Whitty & Lewin, 1960) and damage to the basal ganglia (Damasio, Graff-Radford, Eslinger, Damasio, & Kassell, 1985), they are notably frequent companions of frontal lobe lesions (Berlyne, 1972; Fischer, Alexander, D'Esposito, & Otto, 1995; Joseph, 1986; Kapur, 1988; Kapur & Coughlan, 1980; M. Kopelman, 1987; Moscovitch, 1989; Stuss et al., 1978; see, however, Dalla Barba, 1993; Kern, Van Gorp, Cummings, Brown, & Osato, 1992). Even when confabulations develop following damage to other locations, such as right cerebral infarction (Wapner, Hamby, & Gardner, 1981), frontal atrophy appears to be an important complementary factor (Levine & Grek, 1984). Janowsky, Shimamura, Kritchevsky, and Squire (1989) obtained deficits in verbal fluency and a reduced score in the Wisconsin Card Sorting Test, but found no memory deficit associated with frontal impairment. Confabulations are frequently reported in patients with infarctions in the area of the distribution of the anterior communicating artery. The neuropathological lesions in such cases vary. Most commonly they involve the basal forebrain as well as the frontal lobe (the "dual-lesion" hypothesis; see also DeLuca & Diamond, 1995, for a review). If no single, specific brain lesion is sufficient to account for confabulations, what makes a frontal deficit an important factor in false recollection even in cases with no formal memory loss?

There are numerous cognitive functions whose control is attributed to the frontal lobe (e.g., planning and sequencing of actions, inhibiting irrelevant responses, and self-monitoring, particularly in the social setting; Fuster, 1984; Stuss & Benson, 1984). Moscovitch (1989) described frontal patients as individuals who "haphazardly combine information from disparate events, jumble their sequence, and essentially accept as veridical whatever the ecphoric process delivers to consciousness" (p. 155). A possible scenario of excessive vulnerability to confabulations following frontal lesion may be attributed to the activity of the temporo-parietal cortex, unopposed by prefrontal inhibitory circuits. An appealing rationale for such an attribution stems from the belief of Denny-Brown and Chambers (1956)—that "the behavioral organization represented by the cerebral cortex is arranged to serve two general types of reaction to the environment, the one a series of positive tropisms, the other a series of negative tropisms" (p. 106). The first they termed an *approach reaction* (linked to frontal deficit), the other a *withdrawal* or *avoiding reaction* (linked to parietal deficit). Lhermitte, Pillon, and Serdaru (1986) noticed that frontal lobe patients manifest an unusual dependence on social and physical environmental cues. These patients imitate the examiner's gestures and manipulate any physical objects within their reach, although these objects are completely irrelevant to the social circumstances. These "imitation" and "utilization behaviors" were defined as the *environmental dependency syndrome* (Lhermitte, 1986).

Based on the foregoing, it is tempting to liken the process of search in the mnemonic field to the manual "grasp" of objects appearing in the visual field. This metaphor alludes to the frontal lobe patient's inability to resist fleeting associations in the realm of memory, be they trivial or fictitious.

CONFABULATIONS AS "RECALL INDUCTION"

How the search in the mnemonic field is conducted and what is recalled are determined by input requirements. Consider that the strategy of a search, or rather the allocation of address in the mnemonic field, is initiated by the type of question (input assignment) being asked. It is thus similar to the process of identification and classification of perceptual material. According to MacKay (1991), an effective guidance by incoming stimuli could conceivably be achieved by either of the following solutions:

> The one extreme would be to install a bank of "feature-filters" covering the whole range of possible inputs, so that each input became internally identifiable by the distribution of excitation, and appropriate logical networks could be installed to set up an appropriate state of readiness for each distribution. The other extreme would be to install a single *self-adjusting imitator of the input or some transform of the input, and allow it to fumble its way into balance with each input change under the guidance of the comparator or error indicator.* . . . Suffice it here to say that whereas the first is wasteful of equipment unless all combinations of inputs are equally likely, the second is

wasteful of time unless most combinations of input are highly unlikely. The best solution would seem to lie in a combination of the two principles. . . . (p. 95; italics added)

According to these solutions, the question "Who wrote the poem 'Excelsior'?" initiates a search for a precise input-receptor congruity in a reasonably simple address of the mnemonic field. Such a search is executed by dedicated filters or channels ("expert systems" in computer parlance) that permit no gross inaccuracies, and that are destined either to locate the desired match or elicit a normal "don't know" answer. Assuming that the complexity of memory traces is represented by a system of elaborately shaped receptors, the accuracy of recall would be determined by a reasonably snug fit between the mental image and its stored representation. In this case, "don't know" acknowledges a no-match input-receptor condition. However, there are other categories of questions that are not expected to provide a tight input-stored information congruity. These are more likely to elicit confabulatory circumlocutions.

Thus, the answer to the question, "Who were your favorite writers in high school?", may be excusably imprecise, and influenced and distorted by expectations of peers, family members, self-esteem, ambitions, current state of emotions, and so on. It may require leaning on the "internal adaptive matching" of MacKay (1991). Such inaccuracies might also suggest that, normally, an imperfect input-receptor fit is well tolerated by perfectly clear consciousness, and under certain circumstances a recall may feature contents of an infinite number of "memory receptors" with different degrees of relevance to input. In a way, nonselective input accommodation acts as if there is a measure of *induction* of the input-receptor fit—in other words, when a number of solutions of various degrees of credibility are *actively* fitted for a recall. Unlike the previous straightforward strategy of memory retrieval, which is rapid, automated, and tolerates no ambiguities or "stupidities"—as Moscovitch and Umilta (1990) would have defined it—the fit-induction procedure must seem infinitely more liberal or "imaginative," so to speak.

However imprecise, this "imaginative" process of match location could be a biological norm. It must have been preserved by "natural selection" not to provide a precise recall, but for its ability to recruit the whole richness of available material under the pressure of needs (i.e., the goals, expectancies, and purpose of Tolman, 1932). After all, adaptation to reality "is not directly given in perception or remembering but is an attribution that is the outcome of judgment processes" (M. Johnson, 1991, p. 180). Perhaps the process of induced fit must be facilitated when reality monitoring is deficient, even in the absence of blatant memory failure (M. Johnson, 1991). It is tempting to posit that such fit-induction strategies are particularly activated following a frontal deficit in the presence of parietal disinhibition, which increases the affinity to random associations (M. Johnson, chap. 6, this volume; Moscovitch, 1989). By violating input requirements, fit-induction creates confusion, thereby contributing to mnemopoesis.

A word of disclaimer is in order at this point. The notion of "induced fit" is borrowed from molecular biology, whereby receptors are postulated to *actively* modify their conformation such as to fit a ligand (Koshland, 1976). Its export to the realm of memory is not intended to emphasize the biological universality of the mechanism. It is simply meant to illustrate a situation in which a significant degree of flexibility of receptors in various layers of the mnemonic field admits misfits, and irrelevant or fictitious elements are permitted to intrude and become selected as credible items of recall. It does not give, nor was it intended to provide, real insight into the molecular machinery involved. Such a process may easily be conceived of as strictly synaptical and network-based in nature, when the loss of the property to use selectively stored information ("adaptive filtering"; Miller, Li, & Desimone, 1991) leads to a plurality of recall options. Yet the intuitive advantage of this metaphor seems obvious when one examines the blatant inaccuracies of "updated" autobiographical recollection described by Ross and MacDonald (chap. 7, this volume) in normal individuals. This metaphor may be helpful in understanding the "exhaustive serial search" strategy of Sternberg (1966), in that the necessity of repeated trials of different degrees of match in the entire relevant memory file could be conceivably based on the mechanisms of induced fit.

CONFABULATIONS IN PSYCHOPATHOLOGY

Among other conditions, confabulations might be expected to bloom in schizophrenia. The latter is a malady in which physiological dysfunction of the prefrontal cortex seems to be present (Berman & Weinberger, 1990). Also, during the 1980s and 1990s, a number of investigators have advanced the problem of memory limitations in schizophrenia, including difficulties in access and/or retrieval of items from semantic memory in response to contextual cues (e.g., Calev, Korin, Kugelmass, & Lerer, 1987; Cutting, 1985; Gold, Randolph, Carpenter, Goldberg, & Weinberger, 1992; Goldberg et al., 1993; Goldberg, Weinberger, Pliskin, Berman, & Podd, 1989; Kwapil, Hegley, Chapman, & Chapman, 1990; Manschreck et al., 1988; Murchie & Weckowicz, 1980; Robertson & Taylor, 1985; Saykin et al., 1991; Sengel & Lovallo, 1983). Perhaps the puzzling autobiographical memory failure in some patients who underestimate their age by several years, or even by more than two decades, is among the most extraordinary deficits (Goldberg et al., 1988; Stevens, Crow, Bowman, & Coles, 1978). One might only wonder why then confabulations are not encountered in schizophrenia.

One difficulty in examining falsities in recollection is that schizophrenia is associated with a primary language disorder and reduced language comprehension (Cutting & Murphy, 1988; Rieberg & Vetter, 1994; Silverberg-Shalev, Gordon, Bentin, & Aronson, 1981). Thus, a poor showing in recall of long paragraphs alone would have been impeachable if taken as a reliable index of confabulation. True, Joslyn et al. (1978) noted that chronic schizophrenic patients manifest embellishments on the Memory-for-Design Test almost twice as frequently as controls. However, it is not clear how these embellishments are related to bona fide (verbal) confabulations. Myslobodsky, Goldberg, Johnson, Hicks, and Weinberger (1992) reported that schizophrenic patients are singularly ineffective in lip-reading simple 3- to 6-word cliché sentences. In contrast to normals, some schizophrenic patients propose completely irrelevant guesses even when some words are recognized (lip-read) correctly. This was particularly surprising because the same patients manifested normal sensitivity to the "blend illusion" of McGurk and MacDonald (1976), and were fully competent in lip-reading isolated words. Lip-reading is somewhat akin to the Stroop effect in that it requires an inhibition of diverse plausible, but erroneous matches. The plausibility selection may go wrong in the case of difficulties with response inhibition caused by frontal lobe deficiency. However, this suggestion could not explain why such a disinhibitory effect happens nor the relevance of these inaccuracies to confabulations.

The neuronal machinery responsible for lip-reading was shown to be lateralized to the left hemisphere and appears to be impaired following left posterior hemisphere lesion (Campbell, Landis, & Regard, 1986). Campbell et al. described an interesting double dissociation of lip-reading from the ability to discriminate facial features. One of their two nonaphasic patients with occipito-temporal ischemic infarction lost susceptibility to the "blend illusion" (McGurk & MacDonald, 1976), but competently matched expressions across pictures of the lower face. The other patient showed the converse impairment, developing prosopagnosia following right-hemisphere lesion, but appearing to be a competent lip reader. Thus, it is uncertain whether a poor showing in lip-reading is at all relevant to frontal lobe deficit in schizophrenia.

Lip-reading of sentences is not an easy task; word boundaries are far more difficult to identify in a lip-read than in a voiced sentence. It may be compared to a task with degraded input (akin to one that requires coping with blurred signals or reduced time of exposure). Perhaps lip-reading could be likened to the so-called "echoic illusion" (Skinner, 1957), which is based on a tendency to "identify" short sentences that are deliberately illegible. Operationally, the effect is elicited when a subject is asked to identify recurrent low-intensity tape-recorded speech sounds, or sounds recorded against a noisy background that emulate fragments of natural speech as if heard through a wall. A normal subject perceives that something was being said and responds with items that bear little formal relation with the "echoic stimuli."

It was speculated earlier that the mnemonic search with such input requirements should facilitate the rate of mismatch by the mechanism of induced fit. The latter would be the more activated the more a subject experienced difficulty in relating information about external cues (words) in the visual modality to memory representations of the stock of overlearned sentence material encoded and stored as auditory material. The failure to reach the contextual matrix that permits a precise match of articulatory features could force a patient to continue the search. The multiplicity of potentially matched representations provided by such a search could make the patient more "permeable" to chancy choices and false positives, the verity of which is determined by current needs, delusions, or random memory traces. Schizophrenic patients are recognized as giving excessive weight to the study of details (Cutting, 1985). This deficit is further aggravated by their poor impulse control and impulsivity in Gestalt formation. Being incapable of integrating word items into more semantically complex units, they might use successive unintegrated preparatory steps in stimulus processing (Shakow, 1963), which is contrary to the beneficial tactics that require sacrificing a fragment of the message in the interest of grasping the sentence's whole idea.

Some elaborations are likely to be catalyzed by delusions. These are difficult to tell apart from confabulations without a special analysis. The delusional load was particularly difficult to trace in short responses. Thus, it is conceivable that delusion, too, could have rendered a patient incompetent at mastering a complex Gestalt. As pointed out by Fleminger (1992), delusions have authority over perceptions by casting a background of expectations. This background acts as a surrogate of familiarity when a search for congruity between a target stimulus and its stored image fails, thereby legitimizing the low probability guesses. It is not known what a patient makes of lip-reading.

Finally, one cannot conclude without admitting the possible contribution of emotional tension to improbable responses to lip-read sentences. Anxiety is known to hinder memory performance. It upsets retrieval in particular, causing what is frequently designated as the "effort paradox"

(Ross, 1991). Smith (1975) pointed out that emotional tension or anxiety impedes an acquisition of visual information by suppressing the source of nonvisual knowledge:

> In any situation where an individual is anxious, or unsure of himself, or has experienced an unhappy succession of "failures", his behavior exhibits an inevitable consequence—he demands far more information before he makes a decision. His very hesitance aggravates his difficulties, regardless of the material he is reading or his underlying reading abilities. The more anxious he is, the less likely he is to rely on nonvisual information. . . . Where the relaxed individual sees order, tenseness creates visual confusion. (p. 357)

This description is a reasonable scenario for embellishment or frank confabulations. In general, schizophrenics are sensitive to disapproval (Arieti, 1955; Rodnick & Garmezy, 1957) and loss of self-respect (Haskins, 1931), thus they might experience pressure to come up with any solution other than "don't know." It is uncertain whether, and to what extent, emotional tension contributed to inaccuracies during lip-reading. The autonomic measures of arousal were not monitored in that study, nor were patients' self-reports solicited. However, it has been noticed elsewhere (Myslobodsky et al., 1992) that schizophrenic patients were occasionally alarmed by their patent inadequacy in lip-reading of sentences. Still, unlike numerous other tasks of laboratory neuropsychology, deficient lip-reading is hardly perceived as psychologically damaging, and thus a less likely contributor to implausible responses than the variables discussed earlier.

EPILOGUE

Confabulation is a fortunate term. It continues to enjoy widespread usage. Yet the purist in the field will surely notice that its definitions are vague and tolerantly employed with regard to any inaccuracy of reproduction of target materials, verbal and visual alike. Perhaps the latter tendency should, indeed, be resisted. One stipulation of the term is imposed by its etymology (*com* - together + *fabulari* - colloquy, in Latin). The latter underscores two important features of the phenomenon—its being a product of verbal communication and its being an elicited response in its process. In other words, *all* confabulations are provoked speech phenomena to the extent that they are motivated by the presence of the listener. In a way, they represent a true "language for others" and, unlike day dreams, are unthinkable without an audience. The listener's interest or his or her presence is as important for eliciting a colorful story as for eliciting symptomatology in patients with *pseudologia phantastica*, or imposture. Only in the most advanced stages of senile dementia does the speaker take little account of the presence of the interlocutor and engage in "egocentric speech" (De Ajuriaguerra & Tissot, 1975).

One might be hesitant to follow Bender, Curran, and Schilder (1956) in categorizing the enrichment items elicited in a variety of visual tests (e.g., Joslyn et al., 1978; Kern et al., 1992), fabulized responses to the inkblots (Rapaport et al., 1968), or unintentional actions "incongruous to patients' history, background, and present situation" (Dalla Barba, 1993, p. 2) as *confabulations*. Although the elaboration errors on recall of geometric forms are more frequently encountered among confabulators (Joslyn et al., 1978), a special conceptual context is needed to unify falsities in different modalities. In a similar vein, redundant elements that might conceivably enrich a half-forgotten deftness also do not classify as confabulations. When somebody tells that a smell of wine makes him or her think of a summer night, it may be a case of synesthesia, rather than confabulation.

The lack of a universally accepted and discrete definition of confabulational items on phenomenological or clinical grounds calls for the establishment of partitions between different grades of confabulations, such as intrusions, elaborations, and mnemopoesis. *Intrusions* could be defined as alien elements in otherwise semantically congruous and sequentially contiguous recall. A single word might be conceived of as the minimal item of intrusions—hence a unit of confabulations. Thus, alien syllables that lead to word alterations must be seen as either spoonerisms or neologisms, but not intrusions.

Elaborations would represent a more significant lexical departure from the target material (imagined or tested). To qualify for elaborations, the contextual integrity of the target submitted for recall should not be mutilated. One must be confident that a patient has no formal language disorder because intrusions may be confused with the stereotypic perseverations ("contaminations") of demented patients, whereas elaborations could bear a superficial likeness to the intricate circumlocutions of aphasics searching for the elusive term (De Ajuriaguerra & Tissot, 1975).

Mnemopoesis could be defined as elaborations that lose contact with the context of target materials; they may acquire declarative features, and thus grow to the level of expressive, nonpragmatic narratives. The latter could conflict with personal experience or the social status of a patient, and/or might be grossly misplaced chronologically. Clearly, unlike inaccuracies in the form of intrusions and elaborations, which may be embedded in normal recall, frank mnemopoesis is hardly a normal phenomenon.

This classification requires that the term *confabulation* be used sparingly. As an example, a letter added to the left portion of a word by a patient with hemineglect could hardly be defined as of confabulational origin (Chatterjee, 1995). How such a response is different from intrusion errors to acoustically or visually presented verbal material, or a wild story of a trip to the neighboring country by a Korsakoff's patient, remains uncertain. Further, this subdivision does not settle the issue of whether the various forms of "incorrect information" represent several overlapping, but dissimilar classes, or whether there is a continuum between momentary, simple, provoked intrusions and more elaborate confabulations, with ornate mnemopoesis representing the high end of the disorder's spectrum. Nor does this classification deal explicitly with the issue of reactive versus spontaneous confabulations. The temptation to add the dimension of reactivity-spontaneity (Berlyne, 1972) could be attributed to the fact that some items (e.g., intrusions) are difficult to recognize unless they are specifically looked for in the course of formal neuropsychological testing. In this respect, they may be designated as *elicited*. Likewise, elaborations and mnemopoesis may either be elicited in a similar paradigm or represent a spontaneous event (i.e., encouraged by a less structured situation [e.g., a nod or a sympathetic smile of the interviewer could do the job]). This departs from Berlyne's (1972) principle of partitioning, which considers evoked versus spontaneous dichotomy as synonymous to thematical diversity of the confabulated items.

In summary, in view of the foregoing, *confabulations* could be defined as verbalizations containing various degrees of distortions of the target material (submitted in the course of a trial or implied), propelled by a handicapping situation (deficient mnemonic functions, a state of discomfort or anxiety with a reduced level of self-monitoring) and unusual avidity to irrelevant associations in the realm of memory akin to the environmental dependency syndrome.

ACKNOWLEDGMENTS

This chapter profited from several valuable discussions we had with colleagues who called many important references to our attention. For that we wish to thank R. Karniol, A. Martin, M. Moscovitch, B. Ross, and M. Ross who read earlier versions of this chapter. Ms. C. Ocampo helped with typing the manuscript.

REFERENCES

Arieti, S. (1955). *Interpretation of schizophrenia.* New York: Brunner.
Beck, S. J., Beck, A. G., Levitt, E. E., & Molish, H. B. (1961). *Rorschach's test: Basic processes* (3rd ed.). New York: Grune & Stratton.

Bender, L., Curran, F., & Schilder, P. (1956). Organization of memory traces in the Korsakoff syndrome. *Archives of Neurology & Psychiatry, 39*, 482–487.

Berlyne, D. E. (1954). Knowledge and stimulus-response psychology. *Psychological Review, 61*, 245–254.

Berlyne, N. (1972). Confabulation. *British Journal of Psychiatry, 120*, 31–39.

Berman, K. F., & Weinberger, D. R. (1990). The prefrontal cortex in schizophrenia and other neuropsychiatric diseases: In vivo physiological correlates of cognitive diseases. *Progress in Brain Research, 85*, 521–537.

Bleuler, E. (1950). *Dementia praecox or the group of Schizophrenias.* New York: International University Press.

Bonhoeffer, K. (1904). Der Korsakowsche Symptomenkompler in seinen Beziehungen zu den verschiedenen Krankheitsformen. [The Korsakoff's syndrome in its relationships to different forms of illness]. *Allgemeine Zeitung Psychiatrie, 16*, 744–752.

Calev, A., Korin, Y., Kugelmass, S., & Lerer, B. (1987). Performance of chronic schizophrenics on matched word and design recall tasks. *Biological Psychiatry, 22*, 699–709.

Calev, A., Venables, P. H., & Monk, A. F. (1983). Evidence for distinct verbal memory pathologies in severely and mildly disturbed schizophrenics. *Schizophrenia Bulletin, 9*, 247.

Campbell, R. T., Landis, T., & Regard, M. (1986). Face recognition and lip-reading: A neurological dissociation. *Brain, 109*, 509–521.

Chatterjee, A. (1995). Cross-over, completion and confabulation in unilateral spatial neglect. *Brain, 118*, 455–465.

Cholden, L. (1956). Observations on psychotherapy of schizophrenia. In F. Fromm-Reichmann & J. L. Moreno (Eds.), *Progress in psychotherapy* (pp. 239–247). New York: Grune & Stratton.

Clare, I. C., & Gudjonsson, G. H. (1993). Interrogative suggestibility, confabulation, and acquiescence in people with mild learning disabilities (mental handicap): Implications for reliability during police interrogations. *British Journal of Clinical Psychology, 32*, 295–301.

Critchley, M. (1979). Modes of reaction to central blindness. *The divine banquet of the brain* (pp. 156–162). New York: Raven.

Cummings, J. L. (1985). *Clinical neuropsychiatry.* Orlando, FL: Grune & Stratton.

Cutting, J. (1985). *The psychology of schizophrenia.* London: Churchill.

Cutting, J., & Murphy, D. (1988). Schizophrenic thought disorder: A psychological and organic perspective. *British Journal of Psychiatry, 152*, 310–319.

Dalla Barba, G. (1993). Confabulation: Knowledge and recollective experience. *Cognitive Neuropsychology, 10*, 1–20.

Dalla Barba, G., Cipolotti, L., & Denes, G. (1990). Autobiographical memory loss and confabulation in Korsakoff's syndrome: A case report. *Cortex, 26*, 525–534.

Damasio, A. R., Graff-Radford, N. R., Eslinger, P. J., Damasio, H., & Kassell, N. (1985). Amnesia following basal forebrain lesions. *Archives of Neurology, 42*, 263–271.

De Ajuriaguerra, V., & Tissot, R. (1975). Some aspects of language in various forms of senile dementia (Comparisons with language in children). In E. H. Lenneberg & E. Lenneberg (Eds.), *Foundations of language development* (Vol. 2, pp. 323–339). New York: Academic Press.

DeLuca, J., & Diamond, B. J. (1995). Aneurysm of the anterior communicating artery: A review of neuroanatomical and neuropsychological sequelae. *Journal of Clinical and Experimental Neuropsychology, 17*, 100–121.

Denny-Brown, D., & Chambers, R. A. (1956). The parietal lobe and behavior. *Association for Research in Nervous and Mental Disease, 36*, 35–117.

Fischer, R. S., Alexander, M. P., D'Esposito, M. D., & Otto, R. (1995). Neuropsychological and neuroanatomical correlates of confabulation. *Journal of Clinical and Experimental Psychology, 17,* 20–28.

Fisher, C. M. (1989). Neurologic fragments: II. Remarks on anosognosia, confabulation, memory, and other topics; and an appendix on self-observation. *Neurology, 39,* 127–132.

Fleminger, S. (1992). Seeing is believing: The role of "preconscious" perceptual processing in delusional misidentification. *British Journal of Psychiatry, 160,* 293–303.

Fuster, J. M. (1984). The prefrontal cortex and temporal integration. In A. Peters & E. G. Jones (Eds.), *Cerebral cortex: Association and auditory cortices* (Vol. 4, pp. 151–177). New York: Plenum.

Gainotti, G. (1975). Confabulation of denial in senile dementia. *Psychiatria Clinica, 8,* 899–908.

Geschwind, N. (1982). Disorders of attention: A frontier in neuropsychology. *Philosophical Transactions of the Royal Society (London), B298,* 173–185.

Gold, J. M., Randolph, C., Carpenter, C. J., Goldberg, T. E., & Weinberger, D. R. (1992). The performance of patients with schizophrenia on the Wechsler Memory Scale–Revised. *Clinical Neuropsychology, 6,* 367–373.

Goldberg, T. E., Kleinman, J. E., Daniel, D. G., Myslobodsky, M. S., Ragland, J., & Weinberger, D. R. (1988). Dementia praecox revisited. Age disorientation, mental status, and ventricular enlargement. *British Journal of Psychiatry, 153,* 187–190.

Goldberg, T., Torrey, E. F., Gold, J. M., Ragland, J. D., Bigelow, L. B., & Weinberger, D. R. (1993). Learning and memory in monozygotic twins discordant for schizophrenia. *Psychological Medicine, 23,* 71–85.

Goldberg, T., Weinberger, D. R., Pliskin, N. H., Berman, K. B., & Podd, M. H. (1989). Recall memory deficit in schizophrenia. *Schizophrenia Research, 2,* 251–257.

Haskins, R. G. (1931). Dementia praecox: A simplified formulation. *Journal of the American Medical Association, 96,* 1209–1212.

Janowsky, J. S., Shimamura, A. P., Kritchevsky, M., & Squire, L. (1989). Cognitive impairment following frontal lobe damage and its relevance to human amnesia. *Behavioural Neuroscience, 103,* 548–560.

Johnson, F. M., Hicks, L., Goldberg, T., & Myslobodsky, M. S. (1988). Sex differences in lipreading. *Bulletin of the Psychonometric Society, 26,* 106–108.

Johnson, M. K. (1991). Reality monitoring: Evidence from confabulation in organic brain disease patients. In G. P. Prigatano & D. L. Schachter (Eds.), *Awareness of deficit after brain injury: Clinical and theoretical issues* (pp. 177–197). New York: Oxford University Press.

Joseph, R. (1986). Confabulation and delusional denial: Frontal lobe and lateralised influences. *Journal of Clinical Psychology, 42,* 507–520.

Joslyn, D., Grundvig, J. L., & Chamberlain, C. J. (1978). Predicting confabulation from the Graham-Kendall Memory-for-Design test. *Journal of Consulting and Clinical Psychology, 46,* 181–182.

Kapur, N. (1988). *Memory disorders in clinical practice.* London: Butterworths.

Kapur, N., & Coughlan, A. K. (1980). Confabulation and frontal lobe dysfunction. *Journal of Neurology, Neurosurgery, & Psychiatry, 43,* 461–463.

Kern, R. S., Van Gorp, W. G., Cummings, J. L., Brown, W. S., & Osato, S. S. (1992). Confabulation in Alzheimer's disease. *Brain & Cognition, 19,* 172–182.

Kinsbourne, M. (1989). The boundaries of episodic remembering: Comments on the second section. In H. I. Roediger & F. I. M. Craik (Eds.), *Varieties of memory & consciousness* (pp. 179–187). Hillsdale, NJ: Lawrence Erlbaum Associates.

Kopelman, M. D. (1987). Two types of confabulation. *Journal of Neurology, Neurosurgery, & Psychiatry, 50,* 1482–1487.

Koshland, D. E. (1976). The evolution of function in enzymes. *Federation Proceedings, 35,* 2104–2111.

Kraepelin, E. (1919). *Dementia praecox.* Chicago, IL: Chicago Medical Books.

Kwapil, T. R., Hegley, D. C., Chapman, L. J., & Chapman, J. P. (1990). Facilitation of word recognition by semantic priming in schizophrenia. *Journal of Abnormal Psychology, 99,* 215–221.

Levine, D. N., & Grek, A. (1984). The anatomic basis of delusions after right cerebral infarction. *Neurology, 34,* 577–582.

Lhermitte, F. (1986). Human autonomy and the frontal lobes: II. Patient behavior in complex and social situations. The "environmental dependency syndrome." *Annals of Neurology, 19,* 335–343.

Lhermitte, F., Pillon, B., & Serdaru, M. (1986). Human autonomy and the frontal lobes: I. Imitation and utilization behavior: A neuropsychological study of 75 patients. *Annals of Neurology, 19,* 326–334.

Linn, L. (1967). Clinical manifestations of psychiatric disorders. In A. M. Freedman & H. I. Kaplan (Eds.), *Comprehensive textbook of psychiatry* (p. 553). Baltimore: Waverly.

Loftus, E. T. (1979). Reactions to blatantly contradictory information. *Memory & Cognition, 7,* 368–379.

MacDonald, J., & McGurk, H. (1978). Visual influences on speech perception processes. *Perception & Psychophysics, 24,* 253–257.

MacKay, D. M. (1991). *Behind the eye.* Cambridge, MA: Basil Blackwell.

Manschreck, T. C., Maher, B. A., Milavetz, J. J., Ames, D., Weisstein, C. C., & Schneyer, M. L. (1988). Semantic priming in thought disordered schizophrenic patients. *Schizophrenia Research, 1,* 61–66.

McCarthy, R. A., & Warrington, E. K. (1990). *Cognitive neuropsychology: A clinical introduction.* San Diego: Academic Press.

McGurk, H., & MacDonald, J. (1976). Hearing lips and seeing voices. *Nature, 264,* 746–748.

Mercer, B., Wapner, W., Gardner, H., & Benson, D. F. (1977). A study of confabulation. *Archives of Neurology, 34,* 429–433.

Miller, E. D., Li, L., & Desimone, R. (1991). A neural mechanism for working and recognition memory in inferior temporal cortex. *Science, 254,* 1337.

Moscovitch, M. (1989). Confabulation and the frontal systems: Strategic versus associated retrieval in neuropsychological theories of memory. In H. I. Roediger & F. I. M. Craik (Eds.), *Varieties of memory and consciousness* (pp. 133–160). Hillsdale, NJ: Lawrence Erlbaum Associates.

Moscovitch, M., & Umilta, C. (1990). Modularity and neuropsychology: Modules and central processes in attention and memory. In M. Schwartz (Ed.), *Modular deficits in Alzheimer's-type dementia* (pp. 2–59). Cambridge, MA: MIT Press.

Myslobodsky, M. S. (1988). Petit mal status as a paradigm of the functional anatomy of awareness. In M. S. Myslobodsky & A. F. Mirsky (Eds.), *Elements of petit mal epilepsy* (pp. 71–104). New York: Lang.

Myslobodsky, M. S., Goldberg, T., Johnson, F., Hicks, L. H., & Weinberger, D. R. (1992). Lip-reading in patients with schizophrenia. *Journal of Nervous and Mental Diseases, 180,* 168–171.

Rechtschaffen, A. (1978). The single-mindedness and isolation of dreams. *Sleep, 1,* 97–109.

Rieberg, R. W., & Vetter, H. (1994). The problem of language and thought in schizophrenia: A review. *Journal of Psycholinguistic Research, 23,* 149–195.

Robertson, G., & Taylor, P. S. (1985). Some cognitive correlates of schizophrenic illness. *Psychological Bulletin, 15,* 81–98.

Rodnick, E. H., & Garmezy, N. (1957). An experimental approach to the study of motivation in schizophrenia. In M. R. Jones (Ed.), *Nebraska symposium on motivation* (pp. 109–184). Lincoln, NE: University of Nebraska Press.

Ross, B. M. (1991). *Remembering the personal past. Descriptions of autobiographical memory.* New York: Oxford University Press.

Saykin, A. J., Gur, R. C., Gur, R. E., Mozley, P. D., Mozley, L. H., Resnick, S. M., et al. (1991). Neuropsychological function in schizophrenia: Selective impairment in memory and learning. *Archives of General Psychiatry, 48,* 618–624.

Sengel, R. A., & Lovallo, W. R. (1983). Effects of cueing on immediate and recent memory in schizophrenics. *Journal of Nervous & Mental Disease, 171,* 426–430.

Shakow, D. (1963). Psychological deficit in schizophrenia. *Behavioural Science, 8,* 275–305.

Shapiro, B. E., Alexander, M. P., Gardner, H., & Mercer, B. (1981). Mechanism confabulation. *Neurology, 31,* 1070–1076.

Silverberg-Shalev, R., Gordon, H. W., Bentin, S., & Aronson, A. (1981). Selective language deterioration in chronic schizophrenia. *Journal of Neurology, Neurosurgery, & Psychiatry, 44,* 547–551.

Skinner, B. F. (1957). *Verbal behaviour.* Englewood Cliffs, NJ: Prentice-Hall.

Slater, E., & Roth, M. (1969). *Clinical psychiatry* (3rd ed.). London: Bailliere Tindall & Cassell.

Smith, F. (1975). The relation between spoken and written language. In E. H. Lenneberg & E. Lenneberg (Eds.), *Foundations of language development* (Vol. 2, pp. 347–360). New York: Academic Press.

Sternberg, S. (1966). High-speed scanning in human memory. *Science, 153,* 652–654.

Stevens, M., Crow, T. J., Bowman, M., & Coles, E. C. (1978). Age disorientation in chronic schizophrenia: A constant prevalence of 25% in a mental hospital population? *British Journal of Psychiatry, 133,* 130–136.

Stuss, D. T., Alexander, M. P., Lieberman, A., & Levine, H. (1978). An extraordinary form of confabulation. *Neurology, 28,* 1166–1172.

Stuss, D. T., & Benson, D. F. (1983). Emotional concomitants of psychosurgery. In K. M. Heilman & P. Satz (Eds.), *Neuropsychology of human emotion* (pp. 111–140). New York: Guilford.

Stuss, D. T., & Benson, D. F. (1984). Neuropsychological studies of the frontal lobes. *Psychological Bulletin, 95,* 3–28.

Talland, G. A. (1961). Confabulation in the Wernicke-Korsakoff syndrome. *Journal of Nervous & Mental Disease, 132,* 361–381.

Taylor, S. (1989). *Positive illusions. Creative self-deception and the healthy mind.* New York: Basic Books.

Tolman, E. E. (1932). *Purposive behavior in animals and men.* New York: Century.

Wapner, W., Hamby, S., & Gardner, H. (1981). The role of the right hemisphere in the apprehension of complex linguistic materials. *Brain and Language, 14,* 15–33.

Wechsler, D. (1981). *WAIS–R manual.* New York: The Psychological Corporation.

Weinstein, E. A. (1987). The functions of confabulation. *Psychiatry, 50,* 88–89.

Weinstein, E. A., & Kahn, R. L. (1959). Symbolic reorganization in brain injuries. In S. Arieti (Ed.), *American handbook of psychiatry* (Vol. 1, pp. 965–981). New York: Basic Books.

Weinstein, E. A., Kahn, R. L., & Malitz, S. (1955). Confabulation as a social process. *Psychiatry, 19,* 383–396.

Weinstein, E. A., & Lyerly, O. G. (1968). Confabulation in severe brain injury cases. *Archives of General Psychiatry, 18,* 348–354.

Whitty, C. W. M., & Lewin, W. (1960). A Korsakoff syndrome in the post-cingulectomy confusional state. *Brain, 83,* 648–653.

Wyke, M., & Warrington, E. (1960). An experimental analysis of confabulation in a case of Korsakoff's syndrome using a tachistoscopic method. *Journal of Neurology, Neurosurgery, & Psychiatry, 23,* 327–333.

13

Phantom Limb Phenomena and Their Neural Mechanism

Marshall Devor

A "sensory ghost" is in each of us. It is part and parcel of the certainty that a unique "self" resides somewhere behind our eyes—the self of conscious awareness. As asserted by Descartes, awareness may be the only thing of which we can be entirely confident. An inseparable part of the feeling of self is the feeling of body schema. I can feel my body as a liminal sensory presence whenever I pay attention to it. Likewise, if someone touches me or if I suffer a burn, I have no doubt that what was touched or burned was a part of my body, of me. Like most people, I will deny that *I am* my body. More or less at will I can focus on some body part, or ignore it. Even when some spot cries out in pain, it is possible to direct attention elsewhere. Indeed, focusing attention away from a painful part is one of the fundamental strategies available for coping with chronic pain. Individuals skilled and practiced at this can perform feats that amaze and enthrall: reclining on a bed of nails, walking on fire, piercing themselves with sharp swords, and so forth (Melzack & Wall 1982).

Despite the feeling that I am not my body, I cannot conjure myself without one. Even during focused introspection, or on those rare occasions when I feel myself rising out of my body so that I can almost look back and see myself (the so-called "out-of-body experience") I am not a disembodied energy, but a form with arms (or wings) and legs. The feeling of a body schema is concrete, like the feeling of self itself. It is so much so that introspectively, I am sure that if I woke up tomorrow morning and one of my arms were gone, I would immediately feel its absence. I imagine that the feeling would be like the absence of the third arm that I never had. However, I also know that this prediction would be dead wrong. In actual fact, nearly all adults who have suffered amputation of an arm or a leg, for whatever reason, continue to feel the limb as if it were still present. This feeling of a limb that is objectively gone is called *phantom limb* sensation. Its underlying mechanism, expressed in as reductionist of terms as possible at present, is the subject of this chapter.

Descriptions by amputees usually stress the astonishing reality of the phantom limb. The phantom is as much a part of their body as any of their remaining limbs. This paradox is without a doubt one of the most bewildering and enduring mysteries of all of medical science. In the words of Ambroise Paré (1552/1649), "Verily it is a thing wondrous strange and prodigious, and which will scarse be credited unlesse by such as have seene with their eyes and heard with their eares, the patients who have many moneths after the cutting away of the Legge, greviously complained that they felt exceeding great paine of the Leg so cut off." What is the feeling of body, the "sensory ghost," if, when a part is cut away, the whole continues to be felt?

It should not be concluded that a complete body schema is an irrevocable part of the feeling of self. Many (although not all) individuals who were born without a limb, or who suffered amputation at a very young age, do not feel the missing limb's presence. More dramatic still are patients who have suffered certain forms of injury to the posterior parietal cortex, usually as a result of a stroke. Such individuals sometimes report that their leg is gone, despite that their body, including the leg, is physically intact (somatosensory hemineglect syndrome). More than that, they may insist that someone else's leg is lying in their bed with them and demand that it be taken away immediately. Even sight of the leg attached to their body is not enough to banish the clear feeling that the limb is not a part of them.

The perception of a body schema is clearly something that occurs in the brain. However, there is an intimate relationship between that schema and the actual body. Amputation, and the emergence of "phantom limb sensation," is one of those rare events in which the normal fusion of the two is disrupted. As such, the phenomenon provides an extraordinary window onto the normal relationship between the physical body and conscious experience—an opportunity to investigate, with the tools of modern neuroscience, the problem of body and mind. In this chapter, I try to show that phantom limb sensation can largely be understood in terms of currently known neurophysiological processes. There is nothing supernatural about phantoms, and they do not require extraordinary or mystical explanations.

PHANTOM LIMB EXPERIENCE

There are an estimated half-million amputees living in the United States and a proportionately larger number in the rest of the world. Virtually all of these millions of individuals feel a phantom limb. Although there is a considerable amount of individual variability in the sensation, the basic features are predictable. Phantoms occur regardless of whether the individual was aware of the phenomenon before amputation, whether the amputation was long expected or sudden and violent, and without regard to the personality or emotional makeup of the individual (Sherman, Devor, Casey Jones, Katz, & Marbach, 1996). From time to time, authors have proposed that phantoms are a reflection of frank psychopathology (e.g., Exalt, Randall, & Morris, 1947), or at least failure to emotionally accept the handicap (Szasz, 1957). Although these inferences are not altogether unreasonable, given the colorful and often ghoulish folklore that has developed over the centuries concerning phantom limb sensation, the psychometric data firmly discredit them (Sherman et al., 1996).

A typical story, dating from the mid-19th century, tells of a recent amputee who felt an awful crawling sensation in his phantom leg. This was explained to his satisfaction when a friend went and retrieved the discarded extremity, and found that it was infested by maggots. A related story comes from Scandinavian folklore of a man who had a terrible burning pain in his phantom arm. The amputated arm had in fact been cremated. The solution to the burning pain, so goes the yarn, was to have the ashes scattered in an ice-cold lake. In classical literature, phantom limb sensation is often portrayed as the best possible proof of the existence of the eternal soul. Maybe so.

In today's world, it should go without saying that the fate of the amputated limb can have no direct effect on the sensory experience of the amputee. However, the drama of the amputation event and the fear and mystery of the attendant phantom experience no doubt provide fertile ground for anchoring and encouraging deeply held beliefs and superstitions. There is also little doubt that the occasional amputee might find entertainment value in spinning ghostly yarns—and what better basis for a good story to gain added color through repetition. Finally, amputation does not protect one from mental illness. Indeed, the disruption in life plans occasioned by handicap, and phantom limb pain when it occurs, sometimes triggers depression and other reactive psychological difficulties. If one is to learn anything concrete about the neural processes responsible for phantom limb sensation, it is important to focus on its typical and reliable manifestations, and not be led too far astray by the bizarre. Fortunately, there is a large literature on the subject, with many descriptions by individuals from all cultures and walks of life spanning many years (e.g., Cronholm, 1951; Jensen & Rasmussen, 1994; W. Livingston, 1938; Melzack, 1989; Sherman et al. 1996; Siegfried & Zimmerman, 1981). Each phantom is as individual as the person who feels it. Like the Platonic "table," however, this individuality does not contradict discussion of phantom limb sensation in general.

The Quality of Phantom Limb Sensation and Phantom Limb Pain

Many amputees report that there was no time after their amputation that they did not feel their missing limb as still present. That means that it was either present before the amputation, or that it came on within the time of postsurgical anaesthesia or postraumatic shock/pain (i.e., within a matter of hours). There are many stories of relieved patients awaking in the mistaken belief that the surgeon had decided against amputating the leg after all, or of trying to step out of bed onto a leg that was not there.

The quality of the sensation nearly always changes over time: capriciously from hour to hour and day to day, and also in a much slower, fairly regular time sequence characterized mostly by fading. At its peak, say during the first few months postamputation, the limb is typically full sized and attached to the stump in a natural way like a normal limb. Its position varies from individual to individual. For example, the phantom arm may feel as if it is hanging naturally to the side, or as if it is suspended outstretched or flexed to the front, the side, or above the head. It may also be in a strained position, twisted behind the back in an arm lock, for example. In this case, it is likely to feel as if someone were holding your intact arm in that position—that is, desperately cramped and painful. This sensation may last for weeks or months.

Descriptions of phantoms recall paraesthesias: tingling, crawling, pins and needles, pulsating, glowing, warm, and so on (i.e., not unlike the sensation of a leg that has "gone to sleep"). Such nonpainful phantoms are usually welcomed, especially because they feel so much a part of the body. When the individual is wearing a prosthesis, particularly if it is seen, the phantom tends to enter and fill the prosthesis, giving the sensation of walking on a natural leg. Sometimes, however, the sensation is less benign. There may be a sense of cramping, or the limb may feel as if it is being stabbed by a knife, burned with a torch, shocked electrically, or twisted in a vice. Pains such as these, which are "referred" into the phantom limb (i.e., that are felt as if they are coming from the phantom limb), are called *phantom limb pains*.

Phantom limb pain is very common during the first weeks after amputation, but tends to fade with the passing months. Most classical texts report categorically that 5% or less of amputees have chronic phantom limb pain. These are individuals who demand frequent medical attention either because their pain is particularly severe or because they have difficulty living with the pain for other reasons. In 1984, Sherman, Sherman, and Parker published the results of a large survey in which they asked thousands of amputees from among American military veterans to report on their phantom sensations. The large majority, nearly 80%, reported that they have significant phantom limb pain for at least several days every month. Many had tried various treatments offered by their physicians. Unlike these physicians, most eventually came to realize that this was an exercise in futility (Sherman, Sherman, & Gal, 1980). Since 1984, most reports on the incidence of phantom limb pain have given figures in the range of 50%–80%, rather than the classical 5% figure. This startling jump almost certainly reflects the obtuseness of the earlier means of evaluation, rather than a sudden change in the natural history of postamputation phantoms over the past decade.

In discussing phantom limb pain, it is important to distinguish between pain felt in the phantom limb and pain felt in the stump. The amputation stump is fully innervated tissue like any other in the body, and it has been subjected to severe trauma. Any number of processes— from inflammation to neuromas to a tight fitting prosthesis—can cause pain here. This is stump pain. Only if the pain is felt *in the phantom* is it phantom limb pain. Stimuli in the stump, particularly ones affecting stump neuromas, sometimes cause pain to be felt in the phantom. This is properly termed *phantom limb pain*, although it is triggered by a known stimulus to the stump and does not arise spontaneously.

Other Body Parts and Phantoms Without Amputation

Although amputation of arms or legs virtually always elicits phantom sensation, loss of other parts may also do so, if less frequently. Thus, there are reports of phantom breast, phantom penis (sometimes flaccid, sometimes erect), phantom rectum, and phantom nose. Some of these phenomena are surprisingly common. Some 30% of women who have undergone mastectomy, for example, report feeling a phantom breast (Sherman et al., 1996; Weinstein, 1969). In general, the incidence of both phantom sensation and phantom pain is proportional to the innervation density of the lost body part and the size of its representation in central homunculi (e.g., Weinstein, 1969). The primary trigger of phantom limb sensation is loss of neural continuity from the extremity to the central nervous system (CNS). Thus, blocking of the innervation of a limb by injury to its peripheral nerves or associated dorsal roots consistently yields phantom sensation, with or without phantom pain, even though the limb itself remains physically attached. A common cause of this condition is avulsion of cervicothoracic dorsal roots from the spinal cord by massive hyperextension of the arm (brachial plexus avulsion). This is an occasional result of motorcycle accidents. The outcome is a limp, anaesthetic arm, and a phantom that is frequently excruciatingly painful (Wynn-Parry, 1980). When not viewed by the patient, the felt position of the (phantom) arm is unrelated to the position of the real arm. For example, the real arm may be lifted to the side while the phantom arm remains at the patient's side. Spinal cord injury with paralysis is another common example of phantom sensation without amputation (e.g., Weinstein, 1969). Many patients feel the presence of part or all of the lower part of their body, although stimuli there, no matter how strong, are not felt. The position of this phantom body does not necessarily correspond to that of the real body.

Movement, Kinesthesia, and Interaction with the Surroundings

In a fraction of amputees, the phantom limb moves naturally. A phantom arm, for example, may swing at the side with each stride. This feeling is enhanced when the phantom takes up residence within the prosthesis. Sometimes there is also a sense of voluntary movement of the limb, and even of the individual fingers.

The ghostly nature of the phantom is illustrated in interactions with the surroundings. Amputees with a phantom arm extended to the side prefer to turn sideways as they pass through a doorway to avoid having their phantom pass through the jamb. A phantom thrust "through" a tabletop comes out the other side. In at least one report, however, the phantom telescoped inward the moment the tip of the stump contacted the tabletop. The tendency of phantoms to merge with prostheses was mentioned earlier. This is even more spectacular when the body part is still present. For example, Prof. R. Melzack described a young athlete who was paralyzed with a high cervical spinal cord break (R. Melzack, personal communication). When lying on his back, this young man was plagued by the feeling of his (phantom) legs making bicycling movements in the air above his body. This phantom exercise was exhausting. Melzack's solution to this problem was to position a mirror so that the man could see his (real) legs. The mere sight of them caused the phantom legs to merge with the real legs and come to rest.

Changes with Time and Exacerbating Factors

As noted, the clarity of phantom limbs tends to fade over the first 6–12 months postamputation. This follows a characteristic pattern. First, the proximal limb (forearm, thigh) loses its salience so that the hand (or foot) feels more and more like it is floating disconnected from the stump. Next, the missing forearm foreshortens and the phantom hand (or foot) "telescopes" in, toward the stump, leaving the phantom palm and fingers emerging directly from the stump, or even within it. Interestingly, telescoping sometimes reverses itself transiently, so that the phantom regains its original length and shape. This has been reported as a sequel to spinal and epidural anaesthesia (Carrie & Glynn, 1986) and after the injection of hypertonic saline into the intervertebral space (Feinstein, Luce, & Langton, 1954).

A long list of other factors have been reported that can change the quality of phantom limb sensation and, in particular, exacerbate phantom pain. The more frequently reported ones include: touch, pressure and inflammation in the stump, cold weather, urination, defecation, ejaculation, coughing, yawning, anxiety, and emotional stress. Interestingly, a preponderance of these items appear to bare a relationship to autonomic nervous system function. This unexpected correlation is discussed in detail later.

It has long been held that infants born without a limb, or children who suffered amputation at a very early age, do not feel a phantom limb. However, patient investigation has yielded several dozen reports of phantoms in children with congenitally absent limbs (Vetter & Weinstein, 1967). Although there are few reliable data on the incidence of this phenomenon, it appears to be far below the nearly 100% incidence reported in adult amputees—probably under 20% for amputations at less than 2 years of age. By 6 years of age, the values approach those of adults (Simmel, 1962b; Weinstein, 1969). In terms of quality, these phantoms resemble those reported by adult amputees, although pain is rare.

A potential criticism of this work is that most of the subjects were children when queried, and might have been more suggestible and hence less reliable witnesses than adults. However, Saadah and Melzack (1994) recently surveyed intelligent, alert adults (mean age 24 years) who had been born without a limb. Of 75 respondents (55 due to thalidomide, 20 "idiopathic") 7 (11%) reported that they had experienced phantom limb sensation at some time in their life. Four of the seven were interviewed. In each case, the phantom appeared to be triggered by trauma or surgery to the residual malformed limb ($n = 3$) or stump ($n = 1$). None reported pain, although one described occasional intense itching in her phantom foot.

A "Typical" Case History

Phantom limb sensation in any given individual is a unique variation on the theme just traced. To round out the picture, it is worthwhile to consider an actual case. The following description is from Livingston (1938). He reported on a man, age 54, whose right hand was caught in a machine from which it could not be extricated for several minutes:

> A few hours later the mangled hand and forearm were amputated about 5 cm. below the elbow. He did not suffer an unexpected amount of pain during the month required for the healing of the surgical wound. When he left the hospital, at the end of six weeks, he was conscious of a "deep,

heavy pain" in the top of the right shoulder. In the next few weeks this pain became gradually eased, but in the same interval he became increasingly aware of the absent hand. It felt as if it were in a cupped position, tipped slightly toward the ulnar side. He was not able to move any of the fingers. At times he would feel "cramps" in a finger or in the whole hand associated with a "smarting, tingling sensation." When the stump was exposed to cool air the forearm would feel "icy cold." This sensation rarely involved the phantom hand, which was more commonly the seat of a burning sense of heat, "as if it were held too close to a hot stove." He complained of "shooting pains" in various parts of the hand, but his chief complaint was of a sense of "terrible" tension, "as if the muscles were set and the skin too tight." When this sensation was most intense the sweat would pour from the axilla so as to soak his shirt and sleeve. In times of emotional excitement he could be diverted so as to forget his pain momentarily, but there was a peculiarly unbearable quality in it that prevented him from reading or doing any sedentary task. Although the pain was described as being worse during the day, his sleep was fitful and he stated that he was "worn out" with pain.

The stump was well constructed and of normal color. It was cold to palpation and extremely hyperaesthetic. He seemed to tolerate light touch less well than a firm grasp of the stump. At each end of a curved scar across the cubital fossa was a definitely localized point of special tenderness which had been called a neuroma. Similar neuromas had been excised previously from other areas, without relieving the pain. When these sensitive spots were touched the patient would jerk away and complain of a shock-like pain which required several minutes to subside. He constantly guarded the stump with his other hand and was of the impression that this guarding continued even during his sleep. Motion at the shoulder and elbow was restricted, and the muscles were weak. When one flexed the elbow sharply there was precipitated a clonic jerking of the stump which he could not control. There was a tendency for the jerking to come on spontaneously. He was seen to rub the stump gently with his other hand at times. He explained that rubbing the stump seemed to alter the character of the pain in some fashion, but he was not sure that it was diminished materially by the action. When a sphygmomanometer cuff on the upper part of the arm was inflated just sufficiently to cut off the arterial circulation, he reported a definite relief from the pain. In addition, he reported that the feeling of tension in the phantom hand was distinctly less. When the pressure was released the stump flushed normally, and the sensitiveness returned within a few seconds. (p. 355–356)

NEURAL MECHANISMS

In discussing the origins of phantom limb sensation, including phantom limb pain, most authors express one of three convictions: that phantoms (a) arise in the periphery, especially in the amputation stump; (b) arise in the central nervous system (CNS), particularly the spinal cord; and (c) are akin to hallucinations, and arise in the psyche. By considering the clinical phenomenology reviewed earlier, in the light of recent neuro-physiological data obtained from animal experimentation I try to show that each of these three plays a role. The neural activity underlying phantom limb sensation appears to originate primarily at abnormal sites of neural discharge in the periphery and, to a certain extent, in the CNS. These signals are amplified by central sensitizing mechanisms triggered by the nerve injury, and by the abnormal discharge itself. The composite signal drives a high-order cell assembly whose activity defines conscious sensation of the limb. It is the properties of this central representation that determine the shape of the phantom percept, whereas the lower level drive determines its intensity and sensory quality. Although all three levels play a role, the primacy and ready accessibility of peripheral nervous system (PNS) processes recommend them as the best targets for therapeutic intervention. One previously ignored PNS structure—the dorsal root ganglion (DRG)—appears to make a particularly important contribution to phantom limb pain, and should be exploited in the design of future therapeutic trials.

Where Is Sensation?

Perception of a limb (i.e., the "somatosensory psyche") is a consequence of activity of neurons in one or more CNS representations of the body (homunculi). Following Melzack (1989), this assembly of cells is referred to here as the "neural matrix of conscious sensation." Where are these neurons?

Direct electrical stimulation of the arm representation in the primary somatosensory cortex evokes a sensation felt in the arm, not one felt in the head (Penfield & Rasmussen, 1955). Likewise, in amputees, such stimulation evokes phantom limb sensation (Woolsey, Theodore, Erickson, & Gilson, 1979). However, the fact that primary cortical stimulation evokes recognizable sensation does not mean that the neural matrix of conscious sensation resides there. Sensation could reside in a subsequent, higher order neural map, or it could be distributed in several cortical and/or subcortical regions that function in parallel. The same can be said of brain regions that drive the primary somatosensory cortex. Local stimulation of the ventrobasal thalamus also evokes sensation of the limb, as does stimulation of the dorsal column nuclei and the dorsal horn of the spinal cord (e.g., Davis, Tasker, Kiss, Hutchinson, & Dostrovsky, 1995).

Moving into the periphery does not change the analysis. Stimulation of sensory endings in the skin evokes sensation not because consciousness resides in the skin, but because it ultimately evokes conscious sensory experience in the brain. The necessary conclusion is that understanding phantom sensation amounts to identifying those sources of neural excitation, active in amputees, that are most directly responsible for shaping the activity of the neural matrix of conscious sensation.

The perceptual body schema unquestionably resides in the brain (Melzack, 1989). Setting off on a flight of fancy, imagine a disembodied brain, soaking in a nutrient bath on a laboratory bench, still alive and awake. Without a retina, the individual inside probably experiences the room lights as out. However, that should not prevent his or her conjuring up detailed and colorful visual images, or "experiencing" light when an electrical probe is applied to the optic nerve or visual cortex.

How would such individuals experience their bodies. One possibility would be the "absence" of body—the somatosensory equivalent of visual blackness. Alternatively, they may experience a "phantom" body, equivalent to the visual dream. In either event, electrical stimulation of the spinal cord, or the somatosensory thalamus or cortex, should trigger an overriding sensory experience—the somatosensory equivalent of stimulation-elicited light. The neural matrix of conscious sensation may have some intrinsic activity, but normally it is filled with content (activated) by afferent input originating from below. "Peripheral stimuli are the blood the sensory ghost must drink in order to be awakened to its phantom existence" (Gallinek, 1940).

In an intact limb, "from below" generally means sensory receptors of peripheral nerve endings. In the case of amputation, the skin and deep limb tissues are gone. However, it cannot be concluded that the residual phantom sensation must be generated autonomously at the highest levels of perceiving. One needs first to consider all of the potential ectopic sources that lie between the missing limb and the neural matrix of conscious sensation.

PNS SOURCES OF NEURAL ACTIVITY UNDERLYING PHANTOM LIMB SENSATION

Laboratory investigations over the past decade or two (reviewed in Devor, 1994) have provided a wealth of information on potential sources of abnormal impulse initiation between the skin and the cortex. The cellular mechanisms responsible for this activity are also coming to be understood—information that will be essential in the development of more effective therapies (Devor, Lomazov, & Matzner, 1994). Much of this information has come from animal models of nerve injury. As is to be expected, the data derived from such models are more useful for investigating the parameters and mechanisms of the abnormal firing process than for asking questions about resultant sensation. However, the correlation between abnormal neural activity in animal preparations and sensations experienced by human amputees is so striking as to strongly imply that this activity indeed underlies phantom limb sensation in man. In the few instances where abnormal neural firing has been studied experimentally in human amputees, the conclusions from the animal work have been largely confirmed.

Abnormal Discharge Originating in Nerve End Neuromas

Mechanosensitivity of Neuromas. The cell body of primary sensory neurons resides in the (paraspinal) DRGs and not in the limb itself. Therefore, limb amputation leaves a proximal nerve stump still connected to the DRG, the spinal roots, and the spinal cord. When the cut end of the nerve attempts to regenerate, but cannot because its target tissue (the amputated limb) is gone, a nerve end neuroma forms. When nerves are cut, neuromas always form. Despite many attempts, nobody has found a way to stop the abortive effort of the axon stump to regenerate. The question is only whether the neuroma that forms will be a source of paraesthesias and pain.

It has been obvious since ancient times that pressing on a nerve end neuroma often evokes paraesthesias and pain (Tinel sign). Direct recordings from neuromas in experimental animals has confirmed that ectopic discharge is indeed generated in neuromas during the application of mechanical force (see Fig. 13.1; Devor, 1994; Wall & Gutnick, 1974), and this has been confirmed in humans including amputees with phantom limb (Nordin, Nystrom, Wallin, & Hagbarth, 1984; Nystrom & Hagbarth, 1981). The relation of this evoked discharge to phantom sensation is straightforward. Pressure on the ends of stump nerves generates stump pain. Pressure on neuromas of nerves that used to serve the missing limb triggers or exacerbates phantom limb pain (Henderson & Smyth, 1948; Kugelberg, 1946; Livingston, 1945; Souques-Poisot, 1905; Sunderland, 1978). Each burst of evoked ectopic discharge generated by percussion of the neuroma triggers a corresponding burst of phantom pain (Nystrom & Hagbarth, 1981).

The additional sensation evoked by pressing on neuromas is, of course, distinguishable as a superimposed sensation (Henderson & Smyth, 1948). The preexisting background phantom derives from ongoing activity originating at various abnormal sources. The mechanosensitivity of neuroma endings, however, may contribute to this background. Potential causes of pressure internal to the stump include

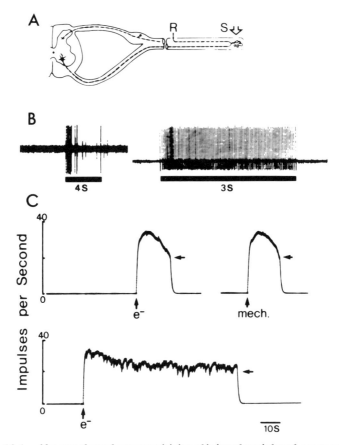

FIG. 13.1.   Abnormal mechanosensitivity of injured peripheral nerve axons.
(A) Recordings were made from sensory axons (R) in chronically injured rat
sciatic nerve (see Devor, 1994). (B) Many fibers responded to sustained displacement at the injury site (S) with a rapidly (left) or slowly adapting (right)
impulse discharge. (C) Some fibers responded with a prolonged discharge
burst that long outlasted the momentary stimulus applied (electrical [e] or
mechanical [mech.], Devor, Lomazov, & Matzner, 1994).

adhesions, oedema, and muscle spasm. It is presumably on this basis
that the reduction of stump muscle spasm reduces phantom limb pain
(Sherman & Arena, 1992). External to the stump are obvious factors such
as pressure from a poorly fitting prosthesis.

Mechanosensitivity is a normal property of some types of sensory
endings in skin, muscle, and so on. Axons at midnerve are not mechanosensitive. If they were, then pressing on one's median nerve with a
fingertip would evoke paraesthesias in the medial part of one's hand.
This does not occur normally, but would if the nerve had been chron-

ically injured at that site. Because much of the abnormal discharge associated with phantom limb pain originates at such abnormal (i.e., ectopic) sites, it is referred to here as *ectopic firing*, or *ectopia*.

Ectopic mechanosensitivity is a property of the individual injured axon. It does not require axonal aggregates. When large numbers of axons become trapped within the bulk nerve end, an easily palpable neuroma is detectable. However, there may also be profuse, chaotic sprouting into the surrounding tissue. The consequent formation of disseminated microneuromas may present as general tissue sensitivity, and thus not be recognized as a neuroma at all. The development of ectopic mechanosensitivity is not a trivial process. The emergence of mechanosensitivity at ectopic midnerve neuroma sites requires a fairly complex alteration of the local electrical membrane properties of the injured nerve fibers. The specifics of synthesis, transport, and membrane incorporation of the proteins required to generate mechanosensitivity have only begun to be investigated (Devor, 1994; Devor et al., 1994).

Spontaneous Ectopia in Neuromas.   Sensory fibers in nerve end neuromas and disseminated microneuromas often have spontaneous impulse discharge unrelated to any discernible stimuli (Fig. 13.2; Devor, 1994; Wall & Gutnick, 1974). The underlying physiology is closely related to mechanosensitivity, but is not identical to it. Thus, not all spontaneously active axons are mechanosensitive, and not all mechanosensitive axons fire spontaneously. Spontaneous firing is expected to evoke an ongoing phantom sensation. The quality of the phantom— tingling or cramping, stabbing or burning, tonic or paroxysmal—must be related to the particular population of afferent fibers that happen to be firing spontaneously (e.g., low threshold mechanoreceptors versus nociceptors) and to their dynamics. Electric shocks activate all afferent types simultaneously. Such activity occurring as a spontaneous paroxysm of ectopia is expected to feel electric shocklike.

A point frequently raised to undermine the role of neuroma pathophysiology in phantom pain is that neuromas take a long time to develop, whereas phantoms often appear "immediately" (hours or days). This argument reveals a fundamental misunderstanding of the functional properties of injured afferents. It is true that the massive tangle of sprouts described by pathologists takes weeks or months to form. However, spontaneous firing begins immediately on axonal division ("injury discharge") and, in some axons at least, never fades. Massive spontaneous firing is present within 3 days (Baik-Han, Kim, & Chung, 1990; Devor, 1994; Devor & Bernstein, 1982). Mechanosensitivity emerges within hours (Koschorke, Meyer, Tillman, & Campbell, 1991; Michaelis, Blenk, Jänig, & Vogel, 1995). The biological process responsible for neu-

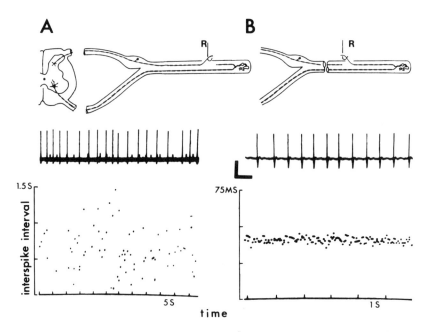

FIG. 13.2. Spontaneous ectopic discharge is generated in chronically injured sensory neurons (Devor, 1994). Alternative sources are the DRG (A)
and the nerve injury site (B). The dot displays below the sample spike trains
illustrate two of the most common firing patterns: slow irregular (left—the
most common pattern in DRGs) and rapid rhythmic, with highly regular
intervals between consecutive impulses (right—the most common pattern
in neuromas).

roma ectopia appears to be related to axonal endbulb formation, which
is rapid, rather than to the slower formation of a swollen bulk nerve
end neuroma (Fried, Govrin-Lippmann, Rosenthal, Ellisman, & Devor,
1991).

Other Sensitivities. Phantom sensation is variable from individual to individual, and often changes over time. So, too, with the degree
and pattern of spontaneous and evoked neuroma firing. Moreover,
both are influenced by a range of similar factors. For example, neuroma
firing is often accelerated by sympathetic stimulation (specifically, nor-
adrenaline released from postganglionic sympathetic endings in the
neuroma) and by circulating adrenaline. In both cases, the adrenergic
agonist appears to act on alpha-adrenoreceptors in afferent endings in
the neuroma (Devor, 1994). The expected sensory correlates—exacerbation of phantom pain during sympathetic activation caused by emotional
stress, increased abdominal pressure (e.g., coughing), autonomic func-

tion, and so on—were noted earlier. Interestingly, urination, defecation, and ejaculation, which involve activation of autonomic efferents in the lumbosacral region exclusively, exacerbate phantom leg pain, but not phantom arm pain (Haber, 1956). As expected, direct injection of adrenergic agonists into neuromas evokes intense phantom pain in human amputees (Chabal, Jacobson, Russell, & Burchiel, 1992).

Neuroma endings may also develop sensitivity to a variety of other internal and external stimuli. For example, some classes of neuroma afferents (e.g., nociceptors) are sensitive to inflammatory mediators (e.g., prostaglandins) that may be present in the stump (Devor, White, Goetzl, & Levine, 1992); many are also sensitive to ischemia and anoxia (Korenman & Devor, 1981). This is presumably the reason that decreased blood flow in the residual limb frequently triggers burning phantom pain (Sherman & Arena, 1992). One of the unexpected ectopic sensitivities of unmyelinated neuroma afferents is to cold (Matzner & Devor, 1987). This accounts for pain exacerbation during cold weather in patients living in northern climates, and for the soothing effect of stump socks and other methods of warming the stump (Engkvist, Wahren, Wallin, Torebjork, & Nystrom, 1985). The list of sensitivities of neuroma endings identified to date is already long (Devor, 1994), but is unlikely complete. In effect, any depolarizing stimulus probably activates neuroma endings.

Interindividual Variability. The experience of phantom limb sensation and pain is unique to the individual amputee. This includes the quality and intensity of ongoing pain, and peculiarities in the specific stimuli that exacerbate it. At least three factors associated with abnormal neural discharge probably contribute to interindividual variability:

1. The amount of ectopia generated in neuromas depends on which nerve is involved, where it was cut, and how it interacts with surround tissue in the stump. There are also intrinsic differences in the likelihood that a given functional class of afferent will develop ectopic sensitivity and ectopic spontaneous firing. These are *excitability* variables associated with the injured sensory neuron itself (Devor, 1994).
2. The degree of neuroma activity also depends on the presence of exacerbating stimuli. Is there local inflammation? Is there good tissue oxygenation? What is the temperature outside?
3. There is good evidence from animal preparations for a constitutional, genetically inherited predisposition for painful versus quiescent nerve injuries (Devor, 1994).

Selective breeding has proved that it is possible to generate strains of animals that consistently show high or, alternatively, low levels of neuropathic symptomatology following a uniform nerve injury (Devor & Raber, 1990). Genetic predisposition may account for the elevated probability that, if one neuroma is a source of pain, others in the same individual will also be painful (Henderson & Smyth, 1948; White & Sweet, 1969). A priori, it is not unreasonable to expect that a particularly painful neuroma is "the luck of the draw," and that reamputation will deal a new hand of cards. Unfortunately, this logic does not usually apply in practice. Excision of painful neuromas is almost always followed by the development of a new painful neuroma (Sunderland, 1978; White & Sweet, 1969). The implication is that there is an intrinsic, individual predisposition to neuropathic pain in man as in animals (Devor & Raber, 1990; Mailis & Wade, 1994).

Failure of Treatments Aimed at Particular Exacerbating Factors.   I stress the *multiplicity* of factors that determine spontaneous neuroma firing, the large variety of exacerbating conditions, and the fact that these vary from individual to individual and from time to time. Illegal parking will often elicit a traffic fine, but consistently feeding the meter will not protect you from a speeding citation. Likewise, removal of a particular type of exacerbating stimulus (e.g., by sympatholysis) may affect the annoyance of phantom pain during micturation, but it is unlikely to have a decisive effect on the overall level of pain. The multiplicity of independent exacerbating factors is a likely explanation of the failure of so many treatment modalities (Sherman et al., 1980).

Failure of Neuroma Excision and Reamputation.   As noted, neuroma ectopia develops rapidly. Therefore, excision of neuromas, or reamputation at a higher level, is not expected to provide more than temporary relief, except in those selected cases in which a particular exacerbating stimulus, usually mechanical, was dominant. The original, constitutionally determined pathophysiology responsible for spontaneous neuroma firing simply reestablishes itself. Indeed, pain is often more severe after reamputation because the original level of nerve injury is closer to the DRG, and because additional, proximal nerve tributaries are now involved.

Is Ectopic Discharge Originating in Neuromas a Major Source of the Neural Activity That Generates Phantom Limb Sensation and Phantom Limb Pain?   This question should be easily answered. As noted earlier, mechanical, chemical, and electrical stimulation of neuromas evokes sensation referred into the phantom. However, to establish the role of neuromas in creating the baseline phantom, one needs to know whether silencing the relevant nerves with a diagnostic local anesthetic block well central to the stump (e.g., brachial or lumbar plexus block) causes the phantom and its pain to vanish. Unfortunately, the published literature provides distressingly little guidance on this issue. There are three common sources of confusion:

1. One needs assurance that the diagnostic block was complete. Specifically, one needs to know that the Tinel sign evoked from the major stump neuromas is gone. For large nerve trunks, complete block is notoriously hard to accomplish. There can be no doubt that pain resulting from percussion of a neuroma indeed reflects ectopic impulses originating in the neuroma. The question mark is only with respect to *spontaneous* phantom pain. Unfortunately, this information is rarely provided.

2. If the phantom "persists" despite complete block of stump nerves, one needs to know if this is the original phantom or a new, qualitatively different one. Nerve block in *intact* limbs consistently yields a phantom sensation if the block is complete (Melzack & Bromage, 1973; Simmel, 1962a). This is most commonly experienced with dental anesthesia. The lip may be totally insensitive, but one does not feel a "hole" in one's face. Rather, there is a "numb" sensation—usually of a swollen lip. *This is a phantom.* The source of neural activity underlying such so-called "normal phantoms" is presumably central to the block, perhaps the DRG. Alternatively, they may result from the release of spinal neurons from ongoing inhibition due to normal low threshold afferent input (Wall, 1981). Indeed, such disinhibition could contribute to true amputation phantoms, although probably not to phantom pain, because "normal phantoms" are never painful. The diagnosing physician needs to determine whether, in the presence of nerve block, the patient is feeling a "normal phantom" or his original idiosyncratic phantom.

3. Local anesthetics cannot be relied on to block the propagation of nerve impulses for more than a few tens of minutes. Recovery from the block is signaled by return of the Tinel sign. As a practical matter, pain relief sometimes long outlasts the expected duration of the block. A possible reason is movement of the local anesthetic to the source of ectopic firing. The process of impulse generation is far more sensitive to local anesthetics than that of impulse propagation (Devor, Wall & Catalan, 1992; Devor et al., 1994). Nerve blocks, even if repeated many times, cannot be expected to produce long-lasting relief. Nonetheless, many authors register as "failures" trials in which one or a few blocks failed to cure pain. Their conclusion that the neuroma cannot be a prime source

of pain is patently absurd. If the pain stopped even for a few minutes during the block, this is good evidence of a peripheral source. The provision of lasting relief requires development of ways to eliminate ectopia on a long-term basis.

Given the unsatisfactory state of the clinical literature on this issue, I have made a point of probing clinicians experienced with phantom limb, always stressing the three sources of confusion noted previously. Most whom I have consulted believe that phantom limb sensation and pain are temporarily stopped by nerve block, or at least substantially reduced, in at least 90% of amputees. Part of the residual 10% remain in question because of uncertainties as to the completeness of the block. Nonetheless, it is widely believed that, occasionally, phantom pain persists despite satisfactory block. This kind of informal survey, even when supported by corresponding declarations in textbooks, is admittedly unsatisfactory in the extreme—quantitative data are needed. In their absence, however, the figure of less than 10% serves as a starting point in considering more central sources of ectopia.

Ectopia Originating in the Dorsal Root Ganglion

Ectopia Originating in DRGs—Animal Studies.   Animal experimentation has shown that DRGs associated with an injured nerve are a second major source of spontaneous ectopic discharge (Fig. 13.2; Burchiel, 1984; Kajander, Wakisaka, & Bennett, 1992; Wall & Devor, 1983). Indeed, even in the absence of nerve injury, a low level of ongoing activity is generated in the DRG. This may form the basis for the "normal phantom" experienced during nerve block in intact limbs. Indeed, part of the normal sensation of the body at rest may derive from this source. In the presence of nerve injury, recordings of ectopic firing from dorsal root axons central to the DRG show that both the neuroma and the DRG make a significant contribution. Individual axons may show a dual source (Kirk, 1974; Wall & Devor, 1983).

Just as in the neuroma, ectopic activity originating with axotomized DRGs is exacerbated by mechanical, physical (e.g., temperature), chemical, and metabolic variables (Devor, 1994). Sympathetic efferent activity and circulating adrenaline, for example, affect DRG ectopia much as they do neuroma ectopia (Devor, Janig, & Michaelis, 1994).

Ectopia Originating in DRGs—Human Studies.   DRG ectopia has not been sought specifically in neurographic recordings in humans. However, while recording from nerves central to a neuroma in patients with phantoms, Nystrom and Hagbarth (1981) noted that anesthetic block of the neuroma eliminated the Tinel response, but failed to eliminate much of the ongoing nerve activity. It is likely that this persistent activity originated in the DRG and propagated outward to the recording electrode.

Another specific indication of DRG involvement in phantom limb sensation comes from studies by Feinstein et al. (1954), who injected hypertonic (6%) saline into the interspinous tissue in normal volunteers. This stimulus evoked transient pain in the corresponding dermatome. Identical stimulation in amputees rapidly (within seconds) evoked a natural painful phantom limb sensation, and "filled out" phantoms that had faded with time postamputation and become incomplete. In animal preparations, axons do not fire on topical application of 6% saline. However, DRG neurons do (Devor, unpublished data). Feinstein et al. were probably activating the DRG nearest to their injection needle. The exacerbation of the phantom was often followed by its disappearance for a time—an effect expected from the postactivation refractoriness of DRG neurons (perhaps due to prolonged activity-dependent afterhyperpolarization; Amir & Devor, 1996). Interspinous injection of procaine caused phantom pain and paresthesias to decrease in intensity, although they did not usually disappear completely. Combined suppression of ectopia from several neighboring DRGs and associated neuromas is probably necessary to completely silence the phantom.

Amplification and Cross-Excitation in DRGs.   Ectopia in the DRG can amplify afferent signals that originate in stump neuromas and in normal sensory endings in the stump. One such amplification process is evoked DRG after discharge. A DRG neuron that is silent, but on the threshold of firing, might be nudged into a firing mode by spike activity arising in the stump (Devor, 1994). A second such amplification process is DRG cross-excitation. It has recently been established that activity in one population of DRG neurons tends to depolarize and excite neighboring neurons that share the same ganglion (Devor & Wall, 1990). Exacerbation of DRG ectopia by sympathetic efferent activity was noted earlier (Devor et al., 1994). The net effect of these amplification processes is to augment the impulse barrage flooding the CNS.

If phantom limb sensation were generated within DRGs or within neuromas and DRGs, nerve block would not stop it. Thus, among the phantoms that are legitimately spared by nerve block, some, and perhaps all, probably have a DRG component. To date, the DRG has rarely, if ever, been excluded as a possible source of the ectopic discharge underlying phantom limb sensation. For this reason, it is impossible to estimate in what proportion of cases, in which the neuroma is not essential, a CNS source needs to be invoked.

CNS SOURCES OF THE ECTOPIA UNDERLYING PHANTOM LIMB SENSATION

Why Doesn't Dorsal Rhizotomy or Ganglionectomy Work?

There have been many attempts to eliminate neuropathic pain, including painful phantoms, by surgical interruption of the dorsal roots (dorsal rhizotomy) or excision of the DRGs. Both types of surgery almost always provide relief for a short time, but pain returns after weeks or months despite maintained, total anesthesia of the stump and elimination of the Tinel sign ("anaesthesia dolourosa"; White & Sweet, 1969). Thus, as a practical matter, rhizotomy is ineffective except when the expected lifetime of the patient is short. Investigators who favor CNS models of phantom limb pain point out that if abnormal impulse activity associated with neuromas, DRGs, or any other PNS source were responsible for the pain, rhizotomy or ganglionectomy should provide definitive relief.

Compelling as this argument appears at first glance, it is misleading. Indeed, the mere fact that rhizotomy usually does relieve phantom pain for a time constitutes *prima facie* evidence for a peripheral source of the underlying ectopia. The question is, why does pain return? In intact limbs, even when it is beyond doubt that a painful source is in peripheral tissue, deafferentation rarely provides lasting relief. Sure enough, rhizotomy eliminates pain derived from the peripheral tissue. However, this original pain is replaced by a new pain—"deafferentation pain"— triggered by the rhizotomy. It is the eventual emergence of deafferentation pain that renders rhizotomy and ganglionectomy ineffective clinical strategies. Deafferentation pain is a separate phenomenon whose emergence cannot be taken as evidence that the original pain source lay within the CNS.

If phantom limb pain were generated primarily in the CNS, rhizotomy should not relieve it even temporarily. Stretching credulity somewhat, it could be argued that the central generator of phantom pain is somehow suppressed by rhizotomy, and that is emerges once again when this suppression fades (diaschisis). In principle, it should be possible to detect whether a postrhizotomy phantom is or is not a novel sensory event. Specifically, if the phantom derived from ectopia in the neuroma and DRG, its sensory details (burning, shooting, etc.) would probably change following rhizotomy. If the postrhizotomy phantom were qualitatively identical to the original phantom, this would hint at a CNS source. Unfortunately, such detailed sensory analysis is rarely reported. Moreover, even if it were, it would not necessarily be conclusive. At least some aspects of sensory quality are determined high in the

CNS, within the neural matrix of conscious sensation. Latent CNS percepts might be kindled equally well by afferent drive from the neuroma/DRG and the spinal cord.

Abnormal Discharge Originating in the CNS

The Dorsal Horn of the Spinal Cord.   Dorsal rhizotomy may trigger elevated spontaneous firing in the dorsal horn, including activity with an unusually bursting pattern. Neural activity of this sort, which has been documented in both animals and humans, is thought to contribute to deafferentation pain (Loeser & Ward, 1967; Loeser, Ward, & White, 1968). Similar activity also occurs following nerve injury, and thus it may contribute to postamputation phantom sensation. In the latter case, however, it is necessary to exclude the possibility that the increased central activity is not simply secondary to peripheral activation (Sotgiu, Biella, & Riva, 1994).

Traumatic avulsion of dorsal roots, in the absence of amputation, triggers some of the most severe cases of phantom limb pain (Wynn-Parry, 1980). An often effective remedy, at least for a time, is destruction of the dorsal horn by means of dorsal root entry zone (DREZ) surgery (Nashold & Ostdahl, 1979). This implies that ectopic firing in the deafferented dorsal horn is a primary source of pain in these patients. The DREZ operation may also be useful for postamputation pain (Saris, Iacono, & Nashold, 1988). However, this is consistent with a PNS origin of the underlying ectopia, as well as an intrinsic spinal origin.

Supraspinal Representations: Phantom Body Pain in Paraplegics.   An often cited piece of evidence in favor of ectopic sources in supraspinal CNS structures is the existence of "phantom body" sensation in patients with (clinically) complete spinal cord transection (Melzack, 1989). Although the reality of this phenomenon is not in question, its relevance to postamputation phantoms remains tenuous. The reason is the same as that concerning dorsal rhizotomy. Even in those rare cases in which an amputation phantom preceded the spinal cord injury (Bors, 1951), it is generally impossible to know whether one is dealing with persistence of the original phantom or its replacement by a new one. In general, phantom sensation in paraplegics lacks the clarity and immediacy of amputation phantoms (Weinstein, 1969).

Anterolateral cordotomy (transection of the anterolateral white matter of the spinal cord) usually eliminates phantom pain in amputees for a time. Pain returns within 6 months in about 50% of cases, however, and within 3 years in 80% of cases (Siegfried & Cetinalp, 1981; White & Sweet, 1969). As for cordotomy in the treatment of pain in general, the return of phantom pain reflects either the emergence of a new phantom of central origin or the uncovering of an alternative spinal conduction pathway.

Elevated bursty neural activity has been reported in the somatosensory thalamus (ventrobasal complex) and cortex following nerve injury, dorsal rhizotomy, and spinal cord injury, both in animals and humans (Albe-Fessard & Lombard, 1983; Dougherty & Lenz, 1994; Guilbaud, 1991; Lenz et al., 1987; Lombard, Nashold, & Pelissier, 1983). Such discharge might underlie phantoms of supraspinal origin. Infrequently, supraspinal lesions along the central somatosensory conduction pathways have been shown to trigger phantom limb pain. For example, Baron and Maier (1995) recently reported on a patient with a traumatic medullary infarction located along the spinobulbothalamic tract on the left side. In addition, the right leg was amputated. Phantom limb pain was present, and it was exacerbated by stimuli applied to the stump. Epidural block eliminated the stump sensitivity, but the phantom persisted. Perhaps its origin was at the site of infarction.

Electrical stimulation of the cortical limb representation in amputees can evoke phantom sensation, including pain (Woolsey et al., 1979). Likewise, there have been several reports of sudden relief from phantom pain following surgical lesions of the somatosensory cortex, or spontaneous infarction (Appenzeller & Bicknell, 1969; Woolsey et al., 1979; Yarnitzky, Barron, & Bental, 1988). This observation suggests either a subcortical ectopic source, or one intrinsic to the affected cortex. In principle, abnormal firing subserving phantom limb sensation might arise anywhere along the somatosensory projection pathway, including within the neural matrix of conscious sensation itself.

CNS NEUROPLASTICITY

Central Sensitization Triggered by Noxious Input

Ectopic discharge from neuromas and DRGs probably contributes to phantom limb pain in two different ways. Most obvious, it directly drives central transmission neurons, and hence evokes sensation. There is also a second, indirect mode. Specifically, it is now known that C-fiber input from peripheral tissue can trigger a unique spinal hyperreactivity state called *central sensitization* (Devor et al., 1991; Woolf, 1992). In the presence of central sensitization, sensory input in myelinated $A\beta$ afferents, that normally evokes touch sensation, is felt as pain (secondary hyperalgesia; Campbell, Raja, Meyer, & MacKinnon, 1988; Hardy, Wolf, & Goodell, 1952; LaMotte, Shain, Simone, & Tsai, 1991; Torebjork, Lundberg, & LaMotte, 1992). Ectopic nociceptive input from injured nerve branches can likewise trigger central sensitization (Gracely, Lynch, & Bennett, 1992).

Fortunately, central sensitization has only a short half life, fading within 1 or a few hours (Gracely et al., 1992; Koltzenburg, Torebjork, & Wahren, 1994). For this reason, the secondary hyperalgesia triggered by acute injuries only briefly outlasts the instigating peripheral noxious drive. Unfortunately, in the presence of a continued nociceptive input, such as from neuroma or DRG ectopia, central sensitization can apparently be maintained (refreshed) indefinitely. In an intact limb, this occasions an extended zone of ongoing pain and (secondary) hyperalgesia (Gracely et al., 1992). After amputation, the expected outcome is pain amplification, with phantom limb pain aroused by ectopic Aβ activity, as well as Aδ and C ectopia. In addition, central sensitization could yield (secondary) hyperalgesia on the stump (Jensen & Rasmussen, 1994).

Long-Term CNS Changes Following Nerve Injury

Peripheral nerve injury triggers a number of persistent CNS amplification processes over and above the noxious input-mediated central sensitization just discussed (Devor, 1988). The mechanism and clinical relevance of these effects, however, are uncertain. It is now well established that nerve injury induces substantial metabolic change in primary afferent neurons in the DRG after transection of peripheral axons. For example, in DRG neurons, the synthesis of some proteins is upregulated, whereas that of others is downregulated (e.g., Hokfelt, Zhang, & Wiesenfeld-Hallin, 1994). Similarly, changes in gene expression occur in postsynaptic sensory neurons in the spinal cord (Dubner & Ruda, 1992). There are a number of correlated, and perhaps consequential, functional (synaptic) changes in the CNS. These include the collapse of presynaptic inhibition (Wall & Devor, 1981) and functional rewiring, including the expansion of somatosensory receptive fields (Devor & Wall, 1981).

It is widely assumed that one or more of these functional changes contribute to some aspects of chronic neuropathic pain conditions, probably including phantom limb pain, but the precise links remain tenuous and speculative. For example, it has been proposed that, in the course of synaptic rewiring, low threshold afferents come to be functionally connected to ascending spinal projections neurons that signal pain (Devor, 1988). Another speculation is that the rapid neural discharge generated by the acutely injured peripheral tissue brings about the excitotoxic death of inhibitory interneurons in the spinal cord (Dubner & Ruda, 1992; Seltzer, Beilin, Ginzburg, Paran, & Shimko, 1991; Wilcox, 1991), and hence a hyperexcitable, disinhibited spinal cord. If this is so, then by preemptively blocking the acute "injury discharge" associated with the amputation surgery, the later development of chronic pain might be prevented. There is some suggestive evidence to this effect in animal preparations (Coderre, Katz, Vaccarino, & Melzack, 1993; Coderre & Melzack, 1985, 1987; Dennis & Melzack, 1979; Gonzales-Darder, Barbera, & Abellan, 1986; Katz, Vaccarino, Coderre, & Melzack, 1991; Seltzer et al. 1991), but only two relevant studies concerning human amputees (Bach, Noreng, & Tjellden, 1988; Jahangiri, Bradley, Jayatunga, & Dark, 1994). In both, extensive local anesthetic block of limb afferentation before amputation led to a lower than expected incidence of phantom pain on follow-up. Unfortunately, however, both studies suffered from too small a sample size and too short a follow-up time.

"Centralization" of Phantom Limb Pain and "Pain Memories"

There is a long and firmly held belief in the clinical literature that chronic neuropathic pain, including phantom limb pain, may begin in the periphery, but eventually "burns its way" into the CNS and becomes independent of peripheral sources ("centralization"). The fact that peripheral injury and injury-related sensory signals may alter central gene expression has given new impetus to this idea. The belief in centralization has several clinical underpinnings, but none is very reliable. For example, it is often pointed out that pains not resolved early tend to be refractory to later treatment. A moment of reflection shows this argument to be circular. After all, those pains that are intrinsically refractory are the very ones most likely to persist despite multiple treatments and the passage of time.

Other cited evidence of centralization is the reported sensation in phantom limbs of preamputation details, such as rings, bunions, focal pains, and so on (Cronholm, 1951; Haber, 1956; Henderson & Smyth, 1948; Katz & Melzack, 1990; Parkes, 1973). Similarly, the position of the phantom is thought to frequently reflect the last position of the limb prior to amputation. Unfortunately, it is difficult to know whether these anecdotes reflect specific sensations, prompting by the attending physician, or memories aroused, say, by similar sensations associated with stump neuromas or ectopic DRG activity ("anchoring"). The same problem holds for phantoms that "persist" despite dorsal rhizotomy or spinal transection. As noted earlier, these events trigger (new) deafferentation and central pains that could be rationalized by the patient and his or her physician as continuation of an old pain that is in fact gone. Controlled, prospective studies are needed. Jensen, Krebs, Nielsen, and Rasmussen (1985) made the first effort in this direction. In their cohort, virtually all of the patients had limb pain prior to amputation. Immediately after amputation, phantom pain resembled the preamputation pain in location and character in only one third of the patients; after 2 years, in only 10%. Sudden traumatic amputation of previously healthy limbs does not appear to yield results very different from amputation after extended periods of pain (Carlen, Wall, Nadvorna, & Steinbach, 1978; Sherman & Sherman, 1985), but this matter has not been studied in a sufficiently systematic manner.

In most amputees, nerve or spinal block transiently suppresses phantom pain. This indicates that the generator does not become independent of the periphery even when the pain has lasted for years. A similar conclusion can be drawn from studies of chronic nonphantom pain in humans and animals. For example, a patient described by Gracely et al. (1992) had a localized scar that proved to be the primary source of a long-standing neuropathic pain. This source triggered Aβ a touch-mediated hyperalgesia over a large part of the limb, presumably as a result of central sensitization. Within seconds or minutes of local anesthetic block of the primary ectopic source, the widespread tenderness disappeared; it returned immediately as the block wore off. Likewise, despite years of prior arthritic pain, total hip replacement surgery generally provides rapid relief, with no sign of pain having been centralized.

Amputation Distorts Central Somatosensory Maps— A Possible Basis for Telescoping of Phantom Limbs

As described earlier, the shape and position of phantoms usually change with time, often in an orderly sequence. First, the proximal limb (arm, thigh) tends to fade. Later, the perceived location of the distal limb (hand, foot) "telescopes" inward toward the stump. This process is usually complete within the first year or two postamputation. Such alterations have their counterpart in late changes in PNS ectopia (Devor, 1994), retrograde death of axotomized and deafferented neurons, and observed changes in the shape of central somatosensory maps over time.

Retrograde Degeneration of Neurons Following Nerve Injury. In neonates, transection of the peripheral branch of a sensory neuron rapidly leads to the death of the neuron. This "retrograde cell death" undoubtedly contributes to the relative scarcity and indistinct nature of phantom limbs in individuals with congenitally absent limbs, or juvenile amputations as noted previously. Sensory neurons in adult DRGs are far less sensitive to axonal transection. However, in time, a proportion of chronically axotomized DRG neurons do die (e.g., Devor, Govrin-Lippmann, Frank, & Raber, 1985). Their gradual attrition may well play a role in the late fading of phantoms. Neurons that have died cannot contribute to the ectopic discharge generated in stump neuromas and DRGs. Interestingly, retrograde cell death can sweep transsynaptically back into the CNS. Thus, beginning many months after the injury, there may be substantial atrophy in the dorsal horn due to retrograde transynaptic loss of deafferented spinal neurons. Indeed, there are several reports of atrophy in the cortical representation of the missing limb in long-term amputees (Campbell, 1905; Dougherty & Lenz, 1994; Woolsey et al., 1979). This reflects retrograde atrophy across several synapses.

The Shape of Central Somatosensory Maps.   The shape of central somatosensory maps (homunculi) reflects the density of sensory innervation of the corresponding tissues and the accuracy (resolution) of sensory discrimination, and not the actual or perceived shape of the limb. For example, the fingers and lips are overrepresented in proportion to their contribution to body surface area, whereas the abdomen and thorax are underrepresented (Penfield & Rasmussen, 1955). This principle, which is also seen in CNS visual and auditory maps, has long been presumed to reflect genetic preprogramming coupled with fine tuning by the environment during a critical period of early life.

Recent evidence indicates that in the somatosensory system, in contrast to other sensory systems, central maps may remain labile into adulthood. For example, when nerves of the hind limb are severed acutely, cells in the corresponding part of the spinal map cease responding to stimulation of the skin. However, some time later, they regain response, now to stimulation of neighboring, still innervated skin of the thigh and lower back (Fig. 13.3; Devor & Wall, 1981). In effect, the thigh/back representation has spread into the former foot area. Corresponding adjustments in the shape of somatosensory maps are expressed at the level of the dorsal column nuclei, the thalamus, and the somatosensory cortex in animals and humans (Devor, 1988; Kaas, Merzenich, & Killackey, 1982; Yang et al., 1994).

There are two expected sensory consequences of such map reorganization. First, spatial resolution on the stump (e.g., as measured by two-point discrimination) should improve. This is because a much larger proportion of the central maps is now devoted to the (proximal) skin of the stump. This phenomenon is well known in human amputees (Haber, 1955; Teuber, Krieger, & Bender, 1949; Weinstein, 1969). The second expected consequence is that, in amputees, stimulation of the thigh (stump) and lower back should provoke sensation felt in the phantom foot, and stimulation of the forearm, chest wall, and chin should provoke sensation referred to the phantom arm. Indeed, both of these pat-

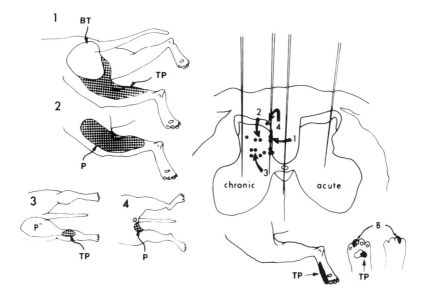

FIG. 13.3.   Reorganization of a CNS somatosensory map following nerve injury. Neurons in the medial part of the lower lumbar dorsal horn normally
map the distal part of the foot. That is, cells in this part of the spinal body
representation respond to stimulation of a toe, or a small patch of skin on
the foot (sketches on the lower right; B—response to light brushing of skin,
T—touch, P—pressure). All such responses are silenced immediately on
acute transection of the nerves serving the foot (sciatic and saphenous
nerves). However, days to weeks later, these same cells begin to respond to
the nearest adjacent skin (i.e., the calf, thigh, and lower back; sketches on
the left). This functional "rewiring" and map reorganization occur in the
CNS, not in the periphery (Devor & Wall, 1981).

terns of reference have also been well described in human amputees
(Cronholm, 1951; Howe, 1983; Katz & Melzack, 1987; Ramachandran,
Stewart, & Rogers-Ramachandran, 1992). If such functional remapping
occurs in the modality domain, as it does in the spatial domain, one
consequence might be persistent pain in response to light touch. Indeed, it has recently been reported that the extent of cortical remapping
in amputees correlates well with phantom pain sensation (Flor et al.,
1995). The cortical change is most likely a simple reflection of spinal
central sensitization due to intense ectopic activity in the periphery.
However, it also might be causal.

Central Maps and Distortion of the Body Schema.   Imagine
that the somatosensory homunculus in the dorsal horn, or one in the
primary somatosensory cortex, constituted the neural matrix of con-

scious sensation. In that case, its internal layout would reflect the way the body was felt. As the thigh/back expanded onto the foot area, the foot would fade from the perceived body schema and the thigh/back would expand. Likewise, in upper limb amputees, the phantom hand would fade and the chest/chin would inflate. These changes should take weeks to months at most. In fact, distortions of these sorts in the body schema are not described by amputees. Rather, as noted, stimulation of the thigh/back comes to be referred *into* the phantom foot in this time frame, and stimulation of the forearm/chest/chin comes to be referred into the phantom hand. Both foot and hand retain their natural shape, size, and salience in the body schema, although the proximal limb fades. This is direct evidence that the neural matrix of conscious sensation is not coterminus with the dorsal horn body map or with the primary cortical body maps.

However, within the time frame of (many) months, distortions of the perceived body schema do commonly occur. Inward telescoping of the distal extremity is the prime example. Likewise, as noted, when loss of limb occurred prenatally or at a young age, the body schema usually does not include the missing part. Such alterations in the body schema imply that, in time, the internal layout of the neural matrix of conscious sensation becomes distorted. Indeed, this lability may prove to be the handle with which the seat of (somatosensory) consciousness, the "sensory ghost", might ultimately be located. Specifically, in amputees whose phantom hand has telescoped, one might search for a central map in which the hand representation has drifted toward the representation of the stump. Modern imaging techniques, such as functional MRI or magnetoencephalography (MEG), might already have sufficient spatial resolution to make such a search feasible.

SUMMARY AND PERSPECTIVE

Imagine for the moment that a CNS map of the body has been discovered, in which the limb representation telescoped inward toward the stump in exactly the manner of telescoping of the perceived phantom. Further imagine that a focal injury within this region of grey matter, in otherwise intact individuals, leads to elimination of the corresponding part from the perceptual body schema (i.e., leads to the syndrome of somatosensory neglect noted earlier). Together, these two observations would constitute powerful evidence that the area in question is an integral part of the neural matrix of conscious sensation—the very haunt of the "somatosensory ghost". Such a discovery would not answer the deepest questions concerning mind–body relations. For example, it would tell little about the nature of the neural circuit operations that constitute conscious awareness; it would tell little about how somatosensory perception is bound with the other senses, with memory, and with motor programs; and it would tell little about how such concepts as will, anticipation, and fear are represented in the electrical and chemical fabric of the brain. However, it would give a jumping-off point for asking such questions, a rare means of getting out of the philosopher's chair, and stepping up to the research bench.

The neural circuit just posited *is* the somatosensory self. By the hypothesis layed out in this chapter, impulse firing of, say, primary sensory neurons in the lower lumbar DRGs triggers activity in cells in this circuit that represent the foot. This gives rise to a sensation of "foot." If the foot is present and the primary sensory neurons that innervate it are activated in the normal way at their sensory transducer endings, the somatosensory self will have received a true report and the resulting sensation of "foot" will correspond to objective reality. However, as has been seen, these DRG neurons can also fire abnormally, irrespective of whether the foot is actually present. The consequent sensation of a (phantom) foot no longer corresponds to objective reality. Perceptually, however, it is no less real. The self has been "deceived" by ectopia.

Telescoping, and related changes in the perceptual map including somatosensory neglect, constitute an entirely different kind of sensory "deception". The full body schema represents the form as it was meant to be, evolutionarily and developmentally, even if it no longer is that way due to injury or amputation. The telescoped body schema and the body schema in which a limb is blanked out by somatosensory hemineglect represent somatic forms that do not exist and never did. Indeed, the objective body may be delivering to the neural matrix of conscious sensation true sensory information about a healthy, existing limb, but that cannot be processed normally because of the CNS change. The distortion in this case, the "deceit," occurs not in the lumbar DRGs, but at the level of the neural matrix of conscious sensation. Thus, phantom limb phenomena reveal two fundamentally different forms of "deceit" in the mind–body relation.

ACKNOWLEDGMENTS

The author's research on pathophysiological processes underlying phantom limb pain is supported primarily by grants from the U.S.–Israel Binational Science Foundation (BSF), the Israel Ministry of Science and Arts, the Israel Science Foundation, the German–Israel Foundation for Research and Development (GIF), and the Hebrew University Center for

Research on Pain. This chapter is derived from chapter 2 of *Phantom Pain*, edited by R. A. Sherman, M. Devor, D. E. Casey Jones, J. Katz, and J. J. Marbach, Plenum, New York, 1996, in press.

REFERENCES

Albe-Fessard, D., & Lombard, M. C. (1983). Use of an animal model to evaluate the origin of and the protection against deafferentation pain. *Advances in Pain Research, 5,* 691–700.

Amir, R., & Devor, M. (1996). Spike-evoked suppression and burst patterning in dorsal root ganglion neurons.

Appenzeller, O., & Bicknell, J. M. (1969). Effects of nervous system lesions on phantom experience in amputees. *Neurology, 19,* 141–146.

Bach, S., Noreng, M. F., & Tjellden, N. U. (1988). Phantom limb pain in amputees during the first 12 months following limb amputation, after preoperative lumbar epidural blockade. *Pain, 33,* 297–301.

Baik-Han, E. J., Kim, K. J., & Chung, J. M. (1990). Prolonged ongoing discharges of sensory nerves as recorded in isolated nerves in the rat. *Journal of Neuroscience Research, 27,* 219–227.

Baron, R., & Maier, C. (1995). Phantom limb pain: Are cutaneous nociceptors and spino-thalamic neurons involved in the signalling and maintenance of spontaneous and touch-evoked pain? A case report. *Pain, 60,* 223–228.

Bors, E. (1951). Phantom limbs in patients with spinal cord injury. *Archives of Neurology and Psychiatry, 66,* 610–631.

Burchiel, K. J. (1984). Spontaneous impulse generation in normal and denervated dorsal root ganglia: Sensitivity to alpha-adrenergic stimulation and hypoxia. *Experimental Neurology, 85,* 257–273.

Campbell, A. W. (1905). *Histological studies on the localization of cerebral function.* Cambridge, England: Cambridge University Press.

Campbell, J. N., Raja, S. N., Meyer, R. A., & MacKinnon, S. E. (1988). Myelinated afferents signal the hyperalgesia associated with nerve injury. *Pain, 32,* 89–94.

Carlen, P. L., Wall, P. D., Nadvorna, H., & Steinbach, T. (1978). Phantom limbs and related phenomena in recent traumatic amputations. *Neurology, 28,* 211–217.

Carrie, L. E. S., & Glynn, C. J. (1986). Phantom limb pain and epidural anesthesia for cesarian section. *Anesthesiology, 65,* 220–221.

Chabal, C., Jacobson, L., Russell, L. C., & Burchiel, K. J. (1992). Pain responses to perineuromal injection of normal saline, epinephrine, and lidocaine in humans. *Pain, 49,* 9–12.

Coderre, T. J., Katz, J., Vaccarino, A. L., & Melzack, R. (1993). Contribution of central neuroplasticity to pathological pain: Review of clinical and experimental evidence. *Pain, 52,* 259–285.

Coderre, T. J., & Melzack, R. (1985). Increased pain sensitivity following heat injury involves a central mechanism. *Behavioral Brain Research, 15,* 259–262.

Coderre, T. J., & Melzack, R. (1987). Cutaneous hyperalgesia: Contributions of the peripheral and central nervous systems to the increase in pain sensitivity after injury. *Brain Research, 404,* 95–106.

Cronholm, B. (1951). Phantom limb in amputees. *Acta Psychiatrica Neurologica Scandanavica* (Suppl. 72), 76–310.

Davis, K. D., Tasker, R. R., Kiss, Z. H. T., Hutchinson, W. D., & Dostrovsky, J. O. (1995). Visceral pain evoked by thalamic microstimulation in humans. *NeuroReport, 6,* 369–374.

Dennis, S. G., & Melzack, R. (1979). Self-mutilation after dorsal rhizotomy in rats: Effects of prior pain and pattern of root lesions. *Experimental Neurology, 65*, 412–421.

Devor, M. (1988). Central changes mediating neuropathic pain. In R. Dubner, G. F. Gebhart, & M. R. Bond (Eds.), *Pain research and clinical management* (Vol. 3, pp. 114–128). Amsterdam: Elsevier.

Devor, M. (1994). The pathophysiology of damaged peripheral nerve. In P. D. Wall & R. Melzack (Eds.), *Textbook of pain* (3rd ed., pp. 79–100). London: Churchill-Livingstone.

Devor, M., Basbaum, A. I., Bennett, G. J., Blumberg, H., Campbell, J. N., Dembowsky, K. P., Guilbaud, G., Janig, W., Koltzenburg, M., Levine, J. D., Otten, U. H., & Portenoy, R. K. (1991). Mechanisms of neuropathic pain following peripheral injury. In A. I. Basbaum & J.-M. Besson (Eds.). *Towards a new pharmacotherapy of pain* (pp. 417–440). Chichester, England: Dahlem Konferenzen, Wiley.

Devor, M., & Bernstein, J. J. (1982). Abnormal impulse generation in neuromas: Electrophysiology and ultrastructure. In J. Ochoa & W. Culp (Eds.), *Abnormal nerves and muscles as impulse generators* (pp. 363–380). Oxford, England: Oxford University Press.

Devor, M., Govrin-Lippmann, R., Frank, I., & Raber, P. (1985). Proliferation of primary sensory neurons in adult rat DRG and the kinetics of retrograde cell loss after sciatic nerve section. *Somatosensory Research, 3*, 139–167.

Devor, M., Janig, W., & Michaelis, M. (1994). Modulation of activity in dorsal root ganglion (DRG) neurons by sympathetic activation in nerve-injured rats. *Journal of Neurophysiology, 71*, 38–47.

Devor, M., Lomazov, P., & Matzner, O. (1994). Na$^+$ channel accumulation in injured axons as a substrate for neuropathic pain. In J. Boivie, P. Hansson, & U. Lindblom (Eds.), *Touch, temperature and pain in health and disease, Wenner-Gren Center Foundation Symposia* (pp. 207–230). Seattle WA: IASP Press.

Devor, M., & Raber, P. (1990). Heritability of symptoms in an animal model of neuropathic pain. *Pain, 42*, 51–67.

Devor, M., & Wall, P. D. (1981). Plasticity in the spinal cord sensory map following peripheral nerve injury in rats. *Journal of Neuroscience, 1*, 679–684.

Devor, M., & Wall, P. D. (1990). Cross excitation among dorsal root ganglion neurons in nerve injured and intact rats. *Journal of Neurophysiology, 64*, 1733–1746.

Devor, M., Wall, P. D., & Catalan, N. (1992). Systemic lidocaine silences ectopic neuroma and DRG discharge without blocking nerve conduction. *Pain, 48*, 261–268.

Devor, M., White, D. M., Goetzl, E. J., & Levine, J. D. (1992). Eicosanoids, but not tachykinins, excite C-fiber endings in rat sciatic nerve-end neuromas. *NeuroReport, 3*, 21–24.

Dougherty, P. M., & Lenz, F. A. (1994). Plasticity of the somatosensory system following neural injury. In J. Boivie, P. Hansson, & U. Lindblom (Eds.), *Touch, temperature and pain in health and disease, Wenner-Gren Center Foundation Symposia* (pp. 439–460). Seattle: IASP Press.

Dubner, R., & Ruda, M. (1992). Activity-dependent neuronal plasticity following tissue injury and inflammation. *Trends in Neuroscience, 15*, 96–103.

Engkvist, O., Wahren, L. K., Wallin, E., Torebjork, E., & Nystrom, B. (1985). Effects of regional intravenous guanethidine block in posttraumatic cold intolerance in hand amputees. *Journal of Hand Surgery, 10*, 145–150.

Ewalt, J. R., Randall, G. C., & Morris, H. (1947). The phantom limb. *Psychosomatic Medicine, 9*, 118–123.

Feinstein, B., Luce, J. C., & Langton, J. N. K. (1954). The influence of phantom limbs. In P. Klopseg & P. Wilson (Eds.), *Human limbs and their substitutes* (pp. 79–138). New York: McGraw-Hill.

Flor, H., Elbert, T., Knecht, S., Wienbruch, C., Pantev, C., Birbaumer, N., Larbig, W., &

Taub, E. (1995). Phantom-limb pain as a perceptual correlate of cortical reorganization following arm amputation. *Nature, 375*, 482–484.

Fried, K., Govrin-Lippmann, R., Rosenthal, F., Ellisman, M. H., & Devor, M. (1991). Ultrastructure of afferent axon endings in a neuroma. *Journal of Neurocytology, 20*, 682–701.

Gallinek, A. (1940). The phantom limb. Its origin and its relationship to the hallucinations of psychotic states. *American Journal of Psychiatry, 96*, 413–422.

Gonzales-Darder, J. M., Barbera, J., & Abellan, M. J. (1986). Effect of prior anaesthesia on autotomy following sciatic transection in rats. *Pain, 24*, 87–91.

Gracely, R. H., Lynch, S. A., & Bennett, G. J. (1992). Painful neuropathy: Altered central processing maintained dynamically by peripheral input. *Pain, 51*, 175–194.

Guilbaud, G. (1991). Neuronal responsivity at supra-spinal levels (ventrobasal thalamus complex and SM1 cortex) in a rat model of mononeuropathy. In J. M. Besson & G. Guilbaud (Eds.), *Lesions of primary afferent fibers as a tool for the study of clinical pain* (pp. 219–232). Amsterdam: Excerpta Medica.

Haber, W. B. (1955). Effects of loss of limb on sensory function. *Journal of Psychology, 40*, 115–123.

Haber, W. B. (1956). Observations on phantom limb phenomena. *Archives of Neurology and Psychiatry, 75*, 624–636.

Hardy, J. D., Wolf, H. G., & Goodell, H. (1952). *Pain sensations and reactions.* Baltimore: William & Wilkins.

Henderson, W. R., & Smyth, G. E. (1948). Phantom limbs. *Journal of Neurology, Neurosurgery and Psychiatry, 11*, 88–112.

Hokfelt, T., Zhang, X., & Wiesenfeld-Hallin, Z. (1994). Messenger plasticity in primary sensory neurons following axotomy and its functional implications. *Trends in Neuroscience, 17*, 22–30.

Howe, J. F. (1983). Phantom limb pain—a re-afferentation syndrome. *Pain, 15*, 101–107.

Jahangiri, M., Bradley, J. W. P., Jayatunga, A. P., & Dark, C. H. (1994). Prevention of phantom pain after major lower limb amputation by epidural infusion of diamorphine, clonidine and bupivicaine. *Annals of the Royal College of Surgeons (England), 76*, 324–326.

Jensen, T. S., Krebs, B., Nielsen, J., & Rasmussen, P. (1985). Immediate and long-term phantom pain in amputees: Incidence, clinical characteristics and relationship to pre-amputation pain. *Pain, 21*, 268–278.

Jensen, T. S., & Rasmussen, P. (1994). Phantom pain and other phenomena after amputation. In P. D. Wall & R. Melzack (Eds.), *Textbook of pain* (3rd ed., pp. 651–665). London: Churchill.

Kaas, J. H., Merzenich, M. M., & Killackey, H. P. (1982). The reorganization of somatosensory cortex following peripheral nerve damage in adult and developing mammals. *Annual Review of Neuroscience, 6*, 325–356.

Kajander, K. C., Wakisaka, S., & Bennett, G. J. (1992). Spontaneous discharge originates in the dorsal root ganglion at the onset of a painful peripheral neuropathy in the rat. *Neuroscience Letters, 138*, 225–228.

Katz, J., & Melzack, R. (1987). Referred sensation in chronic pain patients. *Pain, 28*, 51–59.

Katz, J., & Melzack, R. (1990). Pain "memories" in phantom limbs: Review and clinical observations. *Pain, 43*, 319–336.

Katz, J., Vaccarino, A. L., Coderre, T. J., & Melzack, R. (1991). Injury prior to neurectomy alters the pattern of autotomy in rats: Behavioral evidence of central neural plasticity. *Anaesthesiology, 75*, 876–883.

Kirk, E. J. (1974). Impulses in dorsal spinal nerve rootlets in cats and rabbits arising from dorsal root ganglia isolated from the periphery. *Journal of Comparative Neurology, 2*, 165–176.

Koltzenburg, M., Torebjork, H. E., & Wahren, L. K. (1994). Nociceptor modulated central sensitization causes mechanical hyperalgesia in acute chemogenic and chronic neuropathic pain. *Brain, 117,* 579–591.

Korenman, E. M. D., & Devor, M. (1981). Ectopic adrenergic sensitivity in damaged peripheral nerve axons in the rat. *Experimental Neurology, 72,* 63–81.

Koschorke, G. M., Meyer, R. A., Tillman, D. B., & Campbell, J. N. (1991). Ectopic excitability of injured nerves in monkey: Entrained responses to vibratory stimuli. *Journal of Neurophysiology, 65,* 693–701.

Kugelberg, E. (1946). "Injury activity" and "trigger zones" in human nerves. *Brain, 69,* 310–324.

LaMotte, R. H., Shain, D., Simone, D. A., & Tsai, E. -F. (1991). Neurogenic hyper-algesia: Psychophysical studies of underlying mechanisms. *Journal of Neurophysiology, 66,* 190–211.

Lenz, F. A., Tasker, R. R., Dostrovsky, J. O., Kwan, H. C., Gorecki, J., Hirayama, T., & Murphy, J. T. (1987). Abnormal single-unit activity recorded in the somato-sensory thalamus of a quadraplegic patient with central pain. *Pain, 31,* 225–236.

Livingston, K. E. (1945). The phantom limb syndrome: A discussion of the role of major peripheral nerve neuromas. *Journal of Neurosurgery, 2,* 251–255.

Livingston, W. K. (1938). Fantom limb pain. *Archives of Surgery, 37,* 353–370.

Loeser, J. D., & Ward, A. A. (1967). Some effects of deafferentation on neurons of the cat spinal cord. *Archives of Neurology (Chicago), 17,* 629–636.

Loeser, J. D., Ward, A. A., & White, L. E. (1968). Chronic deafferentation of human spinal cord neurons. *Journal of Neurosurgery, 29,* 48–50.

Lombard, M. C., Nashold, B. S., & Pelissier, T. (1983). Thalamic recordings in rats with hyperalgesia. *Advanced Pain Research, 5,* 767–772.

Mailis, A., & Wade, J. (1994). Profile of caucasian females with possible genetic predisposition to reflex sympathetic dystrophy: A pilot study. *Clinical Journal of Pain, 10,* 210–217.

Matzner, O., & Devor, M. (1987). Contrasting thermal sensitivity of spontaneously active A- and C-fibers in experimental nerve-end neuromas. *Pain, 30,* 373–384.

Melzack, R. (1989). Phantom limbs, the self and the brain. *Canadian Psychology, 30,* 1–16.

Melzack, R., & Bromage, P. R. (1973). Experimental phantom limbs. *Experimental Neurology, 39,* 261–269.

Melzack, R., & Wall, P. D. (1982). *The challenge of pain.* New York: Basic Books.

Michaelis, M., Blenk, K.-H., Jänig, W., & Vogel, C. (1995). Development of spontaneous activity and mechano-sensitivity in axotomized nerve fibers during the first hours after nerve transection in rats. *Journal of Neurophysiology, 74,* 1020–1027.

Nashold, B. S., & Ostdahl, R. H. (1979). Dorsal root entry zone lesions for pain relief. *Journal of Neurosurgery, 51,* 59–69.

Nordin, M., Nystrom, B., Wallin, U., & Hagbarth, K.-E. (1984). Ectopic sensory discharges and paresthesiae in patients with disorders of peripheral nerves, dorsal roots and dorsal columns. *Pain, 20,* 231–245.

Nystrom, B., & Hagbarth, K. E. (1981). Microelectrode recording from transected nerves in amputees with phantom limb pain. *Neuroscience Letters, 27,* 211–216.

Onofrio, B. M., & Campa, H. K. (1972). Evaluation of rhizotomy: Review of 12 years' experience. *Journal of Neurosurgery, 36,* 751–755.

Pare', A. (1649). The works of that famous chirurgian, Ambrose Parey (T. Johnson, Trans.). (p. 773). London: Cotes. (Original work published 1552).

Parkes, C. M. (1973). Factors determining the persistence of phantom pain in the amputee. *Journal of Psychosomatic Research, 17,* 97–108.

Penfield, W., & Rasmussen, T. (1955). *The cerebral cortex of man.* New York: Macmillan.

Ramachandran, V. S., Stewart, M., & Rogers-Ramachandran, D. C. (1992). Perceptual correlates of massive cortical reorganization. *NeuroReport, 3*, 583–586.

Saadah, E. S. M., & Melzack, R. (1994). Phantom limb experience in congenital limb-deficient adults. *Cortex, 30*, 479–485.

Saris, S. C., Iacono, R. P., & Nashold, B. S., Jr. (1988). Successful treatment of phantom pain with dorsal root entry zone coagulation. *Applied Neurophysiology, 51*, 188–197.

Seltzer, Z., Beilin, B. Z., Ginzburg, R., Paran, Y., & Shimko, T. (1991). The role of injury discharge in the induction of neuropathic pain behavior in rats. *Pain, 46*, 327–336.

Sherman, R. A., & Arena, J. G. (1992). Phantom limb pain: Mechanisms, incidence and treatment. *Clinical Review of Physical Medicine, 4*, 1–26.

Sherman, R. A., Devor, M., Casey Jones, D. E., Katz, J., & Marbach, J. J. (1996). *Phantom pain.* New York: Plenum.

Sherman, R. A., & Sherman, C. J. (1985). A comparison of phantom sensations among amputees whose amputations were of civilian and military origin. *Pain, 21*, 91–97.

Sherman, R. A., Sherman, C. J., & Gall, N. G. (1980). A survey of current phantom limb pain treatment in the United States. *Pain, 8*, 85–99.

Sherman, R. A., Sherman, C. J., & Parker, L. (1984). Chronic phantom and stump pain among American veterans: Results of a survey. *Pain, 18*, 83–95.

Siegfried, J., & Cetinalp, E. (1981). Neurosurgical treatment of phantom limb pain: A survey of methods. In J. Siegfried & M. Zimmerman (Eds.), *Phantom and stump pain* (pp. 148–155). Berlin: Springer-Verlag.

Siegfried, J., & Zimmerman, M. (Eds.). (1981). *Phantom and stump pain.* Berlin: Springer-Verlag.

Simmel, M. L. (1962a). The reality of phantom sensations. *Social Research, 29*, 337–356.

Simmel, M. L. (1962b). Phantom experiences following amputation in childhood. *Journal of Neurology, Neurosurgery and Psychiatry, 25*, 69–78.

Sotgiu, M. L., Biella, G., & Riva, L. (1994). A study of early ongoing activity in dorsal horn units following sciatic nerve constriction. *NeuroReport, 5*, 2609–2612.

Souques-Poisot, A. (1905). Origine peripherique des hallucinations des membres amputes. *Review of Neurology (Paris), 13*, 1112–1116.

Sunderland, S. (1978). *Nerves and nerve injuries.* Baltimore: Williams & Wilkins.

Szasz, T. S. (1957). *Pain and pleasure: A study of bodily feeling.* New York: Basic Books.

Teuber, H.-L., Krieger, H. P., & Bender, M. B. (1949). Reorganization of sensory function in amputation stumps: Two-point discrimination. *Federation Proceedings, 8*, 156.

Torebjork, H. E., Lundberg, L. E. R., & LaMotte, R. H. (1992). Central changes in processing of mechanoreceptive input in capsaicin-induced secondary hyperalgesia in humans. *Journal of Physiology, 448*, 765–780.

Vetter, R. J., & Weinstein, S. (1967). The history of the phantom in congenitally absent limbs. *Neuropsychologia, 5*, 335–338.

Wall, P. D. (1981). On the origin of pain associated with amputation. In J. Siegfried & M. Zimmerman (Eds.), *Phantom and stump pain* (pp. 2–14). Berlin: Springer-Verlag.

Wall, P. D., & Devor, M. (1981). The effect of peripheral nerve injury on dorsal root potentials and on the transmission of afferent signals into the spinal cord. *Brain Research, 209*, 95–111.

Wall, P. D., & Devor, M. (1983). Sensory afferent impulses originate from dorsal root ganglia as well as from the periphery in normal and nerve-injured rats. *Pain, 17*, 321–339.

Wall, P. D., & Gutnick, M. (1974). Properties of afferent nerve impulses originating from a neuroma. *Nature (London), 248*, 740–743.

Weinstein, S. (1969). Neuropsychology of the phantom. In A. L. Benton (Ed.), *Contributions to clinical neuropsychology* (pp. 73–110). Chicago: Aldine.

White, J. C., & Sweet, W. H. (1969). *Pain and the neurosurgeon.* Springfield, IL: Thomas.

Wilcox, G. L. (1991). Excitatory neurotransmitters and pain. In M. R. Bond, J. E. Charlton, & C. J. Woolf (Eds.), *Proceedings of the 5th World Congress on Pain* (pp. 263–276). Amsterdam: Elsevier.

Woolf, C. J. (1992). Excitability changes in central neurons following peripheral damage. In W. D. Willis, Jr. (Ed.), *Hyperalgesia and allodynia* (pp. 221–243). New York: Raven.

Woolsey, C. N., Theodore, M. D., Erickson, C., & Gilson, W. E. (1979). Localization in somatic sensory and motor areas of human cerebral cortex as determined by direct recording of evoked potentials and electrical stimulation. *Journal of Neurosurgery, 51,* 476–506.

Wynn-Parry, C. B. (1980). Pain in avulsion lesions of the brachial plexus. *Pain, 9,* 41–53.

Yang, T. T., Gallen, C. C., Ramachandran, V. S., Cobb, S., Schwartz, B. J., & Bloom, F. E. (1994). Noninvasive detection of cerebral plasticity in adult human somatosensory cortex. *NeuroReport, 5,* 701–704.

Yarnitzky, D., Barron, S. A., & Bental, E. (1988). Disappearance of phantom pain after focal brain infarction. *Pain, 32,* 285–287.

Awareness Salvaged by Cunning: Rehabilitation by Deception in Audiovisual Neglect

Michael S. Myslobodsky

The ease with which any sector of extracorporal space is explored is determined by a concerted effort of a host of systems—perceptual, motor, attentional, volitional, and mnemonic—as well as the agenda of needs, drives, and emotions. They all determine whether one has "spatial competence" (i.e., the ability to handle specific spatial tasks in a way more efficient than if they were handled by other control systems). The competence of the system monitoring space around us becomes apparent in its breakdown. One such condition is known as *unilateral spatial neglect* (USN). In this case, competence is measured by the residual capacity for regulation, which could be defined in most general terms as a property of achieving normal function by abnormal means. Complete loss of regulation is direct proof of this control system's uniqueness.

USN represents a good example of what happens when such regulations are lost. It is associated with lesions in numerous brain sites on the right and left side of the brain (parietal, frontal, cingulate, thalamic, striatal, and reticular) emerging separately or in various combinations. Yet commonly the syndrome of loss of visuospatial competence in right-handed individuals is particularly severe and lasting following right parietal injury. That is why, until very recently, USN was portrayed as the syndrome of visual neglect, operationally defined as a reduced ability or complete failure to orient, recall, and respond to cues in the contralesional (left) hemispace (Bisiach, 1988; Bisiach & Vallar, 1988; Critchley, 1953; De Renzi, 1982; Mesulam, 1981; Weinstein & Friedland, 1977). Consequently, visual neglect has been most vigorously explored.

The common neurological practice to quantify the magnitude of USN deficit is to ask a patient to read a sentence or a long word, bisect

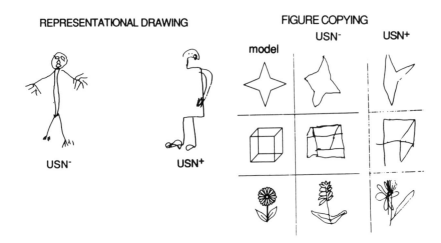

FIG. 14.1. USN$^+$ is commonly established and quantified by asking a patient to bisect horizontal lines, check specified targets in a target-cancellation form, make a simple drawing from memory ("representational drawing"), or copy a picture ("figure copying"). Note that in a USN-positive (USN$^+$) case, there are signs of deficient performance on the left. USN is frequently, although not exclusively, the syndrome of right-brain injury. It may be associated with lesions of numerous brain sites (parietal, frontal, cingulate, thalamic, striatal, reticular), appearing separately or in combination. The present example is that of a patient with USN (USN$^+$) following right-hemithalamic lesion described by Weisz, Oksenberg, Soroker, and Myslobodsky (1995). A USN-negative (USN$^-$) patient had left hemithalamic lesion.

horizontal lines, copy a picture, make a simple drawing from memory, check specified targets in target-cancellation forms, and so on (Fig. 14.1). Yet USN is not confined to the limitations of vision. Some patients may also manifest tactile extinction (De Renzi, Faglioni, & Scotti, 1970; Schwartz, Marchok, Kreinick, & Flynn, 1979); others show increased vibrotactile reaction times (Pierson-Savage, Bradshaw, Bradshaw, & Nettleton, 1988), loss of position sense in the left hand (Newcombe, Ratclif, & Damasio, 1987), olfactory extinction (Bellas, Novelly, Eskenazi, & Wasserstein, 1988), distorted mental representation of the world (Bisiach, Luzzatti, & Perani, 1979), or difficulties answering questions coming from the contralesional side (Battersby, Bender, Pollack, & Kahn, 1956; De Renzi, Gentilini, & Barbieri, 1989; Heilman & Valenstein, 1979).

However, there may be different clusters of symptoms and their dissociations from one another (Umilta, 1995). Some patients experience loss of pain and discomfort in the absence of analgesia (i.e., "asymboly for pain"; Schilder & Stengel, 1931), flattened affect and difficulty in recognizing emotion in faces (Watson, Velnstein, & Heilman, 1981), and perplexing psychopathology, such as fantastic confusional states (Critchley, 1979). The syndrome may also result in a decreased volition to move contralesionally and a failure to monitor one's limitations. Still another striking feature is patients' oblivion to being robbed by the malady of half of their extrapersonal space. That is, USN patients may try to walk despite their paralysis, remain unsure of their body image, and may not recognize their limbs as their own (asomatognosia; Weinstein & Friedland, 1977). Moreover, they sometimes exhibit dissociative symptoms, such as delusional personification, disapproval, or frank hatred of paretic extremities (misoplegia; Critchley, 1979). This spectrum of symptoms can be conceived of as a breakdown of the system monitoring awareness of personal and peripersonal space and reality testing, leading to extreme self-deception. The tendency to draw from memory only half of a common picture (Fig. 14.1) indicates that the patients' loss of spatial competence is accompanied by fading of their insight and ability to judge their own performance. Some patients with asomatognosia manifest profound indifference to or minimization of their deficit, as well as euphoria, ironic comments on their condition, or outright denial of the disorder (anosognosia; Gainotti, 1972, 1983). The tendency of patients to cover up their faux pas may be amazing in its absurdity and is akin to what Geschwind (1982) designated as the *propagation of error.*

Thus, USN represents a complex "cognitive inability" (Robertson & Marshall, 1993) in orientation, attention, volition, memory, and action, as well as the lost capacity of patients to see through other minds (i.e., to compare the state of their perception to that of others, and to modify their behavior on the basis of their own introspection). As such, USN deserves to be scrutinized as a neurological model of conditions manifesting signs of self-deception.

THE CASE OF MR. B

Humans are highly visual creatures; their brain devotes immense resources to visual processing. The diagnosis of USN is made on the basis of the disregard of visual stimuli arriving from one side of extracorporal space, typically the contralesional side. Limited efforts have been made in the analysis of auditory inattention. This disorder is no less dramatic. The present chapter explores what makes an individual lose control of peripersonal space, based chiefly on the example of audiovisual hemineglect.

The finding that USN may be associated with auditory neglect is, of course, nothing new. "You know my wife accused me of ignoring her. . . . She was on my left talking to me and I didn't even answer her," confided Mr. B (Case 24179) to his doctor, some time after his puzzling inattention to auditory stimuli originating from the left side of his periperonal space somewhat abated (Battersby et al., 1956, p. 87). A similar question coming from the right would have been answered matter of factly.

Mr. B was a typical case of USN. At the dinner table, he was unaware of a plate on his left, and thus placed his left forearm into it. He did not cover the left side of the body with a blanket. His drawing of a daisy had the petals completely missing on the left; he read only the right portion of phrases; and after scrutinizing pictures, he was able to recall only the details depicted on the right side. Why did he also fail to respond to the question coming from the left? Did he hear the question, but brush aside its relevance? Was Mr. B locked in the "tacit knowing" of the world that he was no longer able to share? The answers to these questions are not simple. Our concept of the brain assumes that it is an avid collector and updater of information. When a malady hinders an account of the world, the brain is said to have lost this capacity. Yet there is an inverse process that actually prevents irrelevant information from troubling the centers. For example, one does not normally monitor one's heart beats or gastrointestinal motility; when one does, such information may disrupt cognition. An unusual illusion was shared by Reid (1813/1970), who misperceived his heart beats for a "knock" at the door and was even compelled to open a door to a "visitor." Thus, it is clear that the brain must devote a share of its activity to protecting itself from excessive stimulation (MacKay, 1991), and that such gating could be overwhelming in a syndrome like USN.

Another difficulty is associated with the fact that awareness can be decomposed into numerous components (e.g., corporal awareness, extracorporal awareness, volitional awareness, motivational awareness, mnemonic awareness, etc.), such that a feeling of profound perceptual nothingness, with no awareness of the "shrinking" of extracorporal space, could be a specific self-deception, manifested in one domain but not in the other. That is why perceptual experience in USN and awareness of this experience could conceivably dissociate. In such a rare condition as Anton's syndrome, a blind patient insists that he or she sees perfectly well and fabricates a detailed account of what is in front of him or her. USN is possibly an example of an ailment that exposes varied components of consciousness mentioned earlier (see also Myslobodsky, 1988).

Still another problem is anatomical in nature. The auditory system is a fine tool that is capable of resolving the location of stimuli with great precision. A schematic in Fig. 14.2 gives a highly simplified overview of the auditory pathway as being composed of six relay stations. Acoustic messages are processed by the cochlear nucleus; its compact ventral and

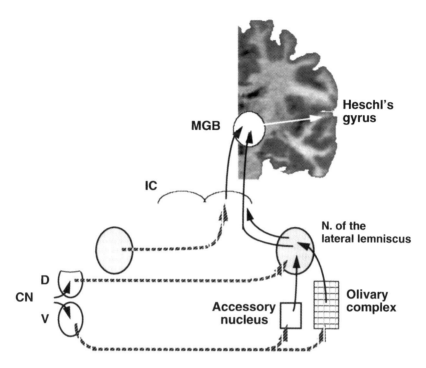

FIG. 14.2.   A highly simplified diagram of the auditory pathway composed of six relay stations. Abbreviations: CN, cochlear nucleus; D, dorsal; MGB, medial geniculate body; V, ventral; IC, inferior colliculi.

serpentlike dorsal parts are visible in the floor of the lateral recess of the IV ventricle. The ventral part is the site of origin of the ventral tract, which then progresses to the olivary complex on both sides. The latter is thus capable of comparing stimuli arriving from both ears. Similar analysis is further conducted in the accessory nucleus. The axons of the dorsal cochlear nucleus make up the dorsal auditory tract, which crosses to the opposite side and synapses on neurons of the nucleus of the lateral lemniscus. This is yet another station in which precise binaural interaction takes place. The axons, leaving the olivary complex and the nucleus of the lateral lemniscus, proceed both ipsilaterally and contralaterally. The next stations are the inferior colliculi, the medial geniculate, and, finally, the primary auditory cortex in the temporal lobe (Webster & Garey, 1990). Thus, even assuming that sensory input to the right hemisphere is grossly disordered (Denny-Brown, Meyer, & Horenstein, 1952), verbal information could still find its way, via the direct and/or subordinate ipsilateral pathway, to the left hemisphere.

NORMAL BRAIN-EVOKED POTENTIALS WITH NO
AWARENESS OF ENVIRONMENTAL EVENTS

The perceptually deficient system in patients with USN continues to register sensory signals as certified by the analysis of event-related potentials. For all we know, they are easily registered in patients with USN (Vallar, Bottini, Sterzi, Passerini, & Rusconi, 1991; Vallar, Sandroni, Rusconi, & Barbieri, 1991), as well as USN laboratory models (Feeney & Wier, 1979). Figure 14.3 exemplifies our own case of virtually normal visual-evoked potentials in a patient with USN. It demonstrates that the major positive component (P100) to monocular stimuli (reversing checkerboard patterns) appears identically over the left and right hemispheres. Only occasionally were there recordings of somewhat delayed P100 to stimuli delivered to the ipsilesional eye. However, this dysfunction is of a peripheral nature, and could be attributed to prechiasmatic abnormalities caused by carotid occlusive disease.[1]

A similar bilateral registration of sensory stimuli continues in slow-wave sleep. Weisz, Oksenberg, Soroker, and Myslobodsky (1995) recorded EEG during midafternoon sleep in two patients with unilateral hemorrhagic infarction in the thalamus. One patient had signs of reduced attention in contralesional space following right lateral thalamic lesion. The other patient's infarction was centered in the left posterior-ventrolateral thalamus with no signs of USN. In both cases, waking and midafternoon sleep records showed symmetric resting EEG at C_3 and C_4. In contrast, monaural sounds (clicks) elicited bilaterally symmetrical K-complexes only in the second patient. In the first patient with the right thalamic lesion, both left- and right-ear clicks failed to elicit K-complexes in the right cerebral hemisphere, whereas normal K-complexes continued to appear at C_3 as well as F_z. In neither patient did the frequency of evoked K-complexes depend on the side of stimulated ear. Similarly, in USN patients with unilateral infarction of the right hemisphere, both left- and right-ear clicks elicited K-complexes of identical amplitude at F_z. These results indicate that patients' receiving sensory stations operate normally and are receiving sensory input. Perhaps in a manner similar to conversion patients, USN patients "withdraw" from sensory experience and are not concerned with not experiencing external stimuli.

---

[1]To prove this attribution, visual-evoked potentials were retested following the so-called "photostress" (i.e., monocular preexposure to bright flickering lights; Servin, Tour, & Kershaw, 1967). Further delays of P100 on retest or a delay of originally normal potentials were obtained and interpreted—after Domman, Shargrough, and Whisnat (1982)—as suggesting that delayed P100 was associated with a metabolic deficit due to reduced flow in the ophthalmic artery.

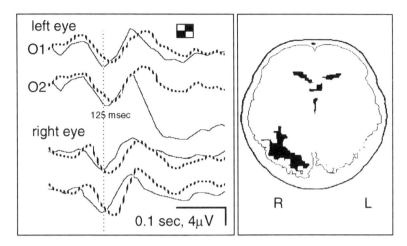

FIG. 14.3. Averaged visual-evoked potentials (200 responses) to reversing checkerboard patterns in a patient with USN and right-hemisphere damage confirmed by a CT scan (patient's right is on the viewer's left). Visual acuity of a patient is refracted to 20/20. Recordings were conducted from the left and right occiput (O_1, O_2). Midfrontal electrode at F_z served as a reference. The reversing black and white patterns (luminance measured 16 cd/m² and 1 cd/m² for white and black squares, respectively; each square made up 63' of arc of the visual angle) are delivered monocularly. Note practically identical P100 over the right and left hemispheres. Dotted VEP traces represent the effects of "photostress" (see footnote on p. 368).

One could now ask whether this sensory information has any significance for cognition. If it does, what is it and why has the content and operations in the sensory channels been dissociated from Mr. B's conscious awareness? If it does not, why is it so robustly present in the sensory cortex and not dissipated by ongoing activity? Specifically, why were his wife's messages not transferred for semantic analysis? Conceivably, one might posit that when a stimulus arrives from the left ear, it is cross-validated by information coming via the "stronger," crossed pathway from the right side. When this cross-validation is degraded (e.g., when bilateral synchrony is disrupted), as might be the case in USN, the validity of left-ear (right-hemisphere) information is maintained by the implicit awareness of the presence of left-hemispace-relevant information on the right. If such information is not available, an auditory input is rejected by central processors.

The possibility suggested here is that, due to a strong intersensory bias and, specifically, a coupling between auditory and visual systems (Schankweiler, 1961), such rejection of stimuli—and thus auditory neglect—develops in the context of visual inattention (DeRenzi, 1982).

When sensory inputs are spatially separated, perception of their spatial location, as well as the information they carry, is increasingly affected by personal preferences, specific instructions, and previous experience. The observer may remain unaware of the discrepancy, as well as the reason for their biased percepts. This phenomenon is especially striking when vision and audition are placed in a spatial conflict, where sight takes precedence over sound. Normally, spatial attention is facilitated when eyes are fixated in the direction of the relevant ear during dichotic listening tasks (Gopher, 1973; Reisberg, Scheiber, & Potemken, 1981). The effect does not occur in a situation of monaural listening (Gopher, 1973). Furthermore, in a binaural selective-listening task, human subjects either maximize or reduce their performance by looking in the direction of the relevant or irrelevant inputs, respectively (Reisberg et al., 1981). This reflects a tendency, described a century ago (see Blauert, 1983, for review), for auditory and visual events to merge spatially when the directionality of an auditory stimulus is established by selecting a visual target identified with the sound. Even when the visual system provides a blatantly misleading cue, people still tend to hear in the direction they see. As Blauert (1983) put it: "What the subject sees during sound presentation, and where the subject sees it, are factors determining the position of the auditory event" (p. 193). In other words, the interdependence of the two modalities may often be judgmental in nature. Blauert referred to Stratton's (1887) experience, in which eyeglasses that turned the visual world upside down inverted the auditory events in the visual field.

The precedence of vision over audition underlies a compelling illusion known as *ventriloquism*. The term *ventriloquism* comes from the Latin words *venter* ('belly') and *loquor* ('to speak'). The celebrated art of speaking with slightly parted lips and a different voice frequency creates an impression of one's voice being thrown to a distant spot in visual space. The brain has an image of how the stimulus generating the sounds should look and chooses a visual location that will bring the perceptual world into register. Unwittingly, observers are led by this single most plausible solution while staring at the dummy object (a loudspeaker or a puppet), rather than at the vocalizer's mouth. Having limited skill in the art myself, I was able to entertain my students by opening a lecture on the effect with an improvised monologue of the famous puppet, Kermit the Frog. The belief that this attribution is correct is exceptionally strong, occuring as if no compensatory mechanism exists to deal with misaligned sensory stimuli. As Stein and Meredith (1993) observed:

At one time or another almost all of us have been charmed by the skill of an effective ventriloquist. You don't quite suspend your belief that wooden heads can't talk, and you always know which one is the dummy and which one is not, but because the dummy's lips, eyes, and head are moving and the ventriloquist's aren't, you experience the voice as coming from the dummy. This entertainer's trick actually says more about the audience than the performer, because the experience is due less to his capability to throw his voice, than to the dominance of some sensory cues over the perception of others. (p. 3)

Why is attention so easily focused on the dummy? Why does the audience make such an unrealistic attribution? Presumably, the enhanced level of arousal associated with the performance leads to the unusual narrowing of attention and its being focused on the most startling item, leaving out all peripheral details. One example of such constricted attention can be found in the so-called "weapon focus" (Kramer, Buckhout, & Eugenio, 1990; Loftus, Loftus, & Meso, 1987)—when a witness of a violent crime remembers the threatening weapon, rather than the face or dress of the assailant. This narrow focus of attention is likely to channel the attribution of auditory speech to the site of a remotely plausible visual event. Examples of such intersensory bias, in which vision deceives other senses, are abundant and accompany people from infancy. It is worth recalling that, in normal human infants, the tendency of both modalities to merge spatially exists minutes after birth (Wertheimer, 1961). Infants orient both their head and mouth toward their mothers' voice and nipple. Bourre (1993) wrote that foods' expected visual characteristics determine their gastronomic properties, such that people do not fully taste mint unless the liquid is green, do not taste black currant unless the candy is purple, do not taste lemon cake unless it is yellow, and so on.

The channeling effect of vision may possibly be at work in USN as well. In early descriptions of parietal neglect, Denny-Brown (1956) observed that the effect of the "withdrawal" of a hand from tactual stimuli may be facilitated by vision. This observation suggests that reducing the impact of vision would alleviate the tendency to "withdraw" (i.e., reduce the symptomatology of USN). Luria's (1959) patient with disturbed alignment of handwriting following bilateral lesion did better when asked to close his eyes. Another patient with right parieto-occipital lesion (von Dongen & Drooglever-Fortuyn, 1968) also showed improved graphic ability when asked to draw with his eyes closed. Cubelli, Nichelli, Bonito, De Tanti, and Inzaghi (1991) observed a patient with right-hemisphere lesion and left-hemispatial neglect who showed an exaggerated preference for the left side of the piano keyboard when blindfolded.

LOSS OF HEARING BY THE EYES: TRADING OFF SPACE FOR ACCURACY

In patients with USN, the boundaries of the ignored space may be determined by gaze direction and trunk orientation (Bisiach & Vallar, 1988; Bradshaw, Nettelton, Pierson, Wilson, & Nathan, 1987). The tendency is so powerful that one has to provide a patient with a cue in the neglected space to convince him or her that something relevant may possibly appear there. By diverting attentional resources to the right, one's vision unwittingly creates a paradigm of deception (i.e., an expectation that all that is bound to happen must happen on the right). That is why De Renzi et al. (1970) cautioned that studies of multimodal neglect may be easily confounded by difficulties in establishing the extent of the contribution of involuntary changes of gaze and posture. With this admonition in mind, one would typically tend to unconfound the effects of visual input, say, by blindfolding a patient (e.g., Pierson et al., 1988). But would it not be more prudent to exploit the existing spatial incompetence of patients by further deceiving them that what they expect to happen will happen in their attended space? Operationally, such intentional confounding of auditory perception could be achieved by creating spatial disparity using a dummy loudspeaker. The question posed by such a design is whether previously ignored stimuli would be admitted to consciousness by deliberately introducing the rational for allesthesia. Normally, when a dummy loudspeaker is located either on the left or right of a subject, while sound is actually being delivered antero-posteriorily, the listener is easily deceived as to the actual source of the sound (Pierson, Bradshaw, & Nettleton, 1983). Paradoxically, this might suggest that the process opposite to the one that determines the ventriloquist illusion underlies the deficit in patients with USN. That is, USN patients ignore auditory stimuli because such stimuli originate from the side of no visual regard. Even if discerned, such messages could be trivialized and regarded as carrying very little increment in information and looked for on the right.

If the perceptual salience of the auditory signal during combined audiovisual perception is primarily determined on the basis of visual anchors, and the meaning is derived from combinations and comparisons of both inputs, one would expect to be able to ameliorate auditory neglect by leading a patient to believe that contralesional sounds origi-

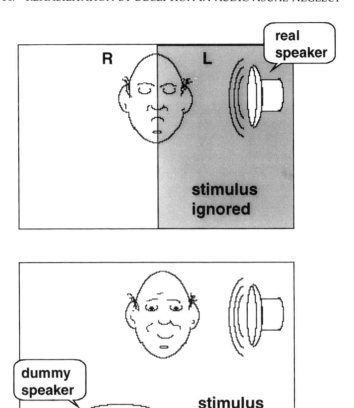

FIG. 14.4. Schematic diagram of experimental setting for eliciting the ventriloquist effect. A real speaker was located at 90° to the left of the subject. A fictitious source of auditory stimuli (a "dummy speaker") was visible in front of the subject at 40°–45° to the right off the midline (see Calamaro, Soroker, & Myslobodsky, 1995).

nate on the homolesional side. Calamaro, Soroker, and Myslobodsky (1995) have shown precisely that. They asked six USN patients following right-hemisphere lesion to detect and identify consonant–vowel (CV) syllables presented by concealed loudspeakers on the left and right sides. Having documented a reliable auditory inattention on the left side, they retested the patients with a fictitious source of sound (a "dummy loudspeaker") positioned in the attended (right) visual space (Fig. 14.4). These conditions caused a vigorous responding to sounds delivered in the contralesional space.

The message to take home is that neglected sensory events are actually processed to a sufficiently high level so as to permit an attribution of perceptual state to an extracorporal event on the right. An individual who is capable of forming a simple context-related hypothesis becomes more aware of his or her own state of mind within the limits of attributions formed. This then certainly is not a complete recovery of awareness. The ability to hear sounds translated from contralesional to ipsilesional space is a form of induced "alloacusis" (Diamond & Bender, 1965). In other words, an improvement experienced in the presence of a dummy speaker is bought at the price of confusion regarding the real source of the sounds. However, gross deception as to the source of stimuli appears to contribute to awareness of their presence. Notice that the trick of salubrious deception is reminiscent of similar effects in conversion disorder, when, by trickery, patients also can be made to perceive stimuli that otherwise they claim eluded them.

SYNTHETIC PERCEPTION AND EXPERIENCE-RELATED MISIDENTIFICATION OF EVENTS

Helmholtz (1877/1954) described perception as analytic or synthetic. The user of analytic strategies identifies details or components of complex sensory events. Some analysis is so bizarre as to intrude into the perceptual territory of neighboring senses and identify properties that do not objectively exist. They smell colors, hear taste, experience volume of letters, and taste shapes (Cystowic, 1989). This rather unusual effect is designated as *synesthesia*. An eminent psychiatrist, Eugene Bleuler was a synesthete himself (see Marks, 1978, for review). By contrast, the synthetic strategy combines isolated sensory events into a unified percept—a blend.

A newborn baby assembles such blends by following the mother's face with his or her eyes, juxtaposing the facial features with the smell of her skin, taste of her milk, sounds of her voice, and resistance of her body to touch and grasp. Like a monkey who tends to "use her hands as an extension of her eyes" (Humphrey, 1970), the neonate "packages" perceptual data together with visual experience, voluntary prehension, and palpatory exploration. An intermodal processing of tactual and visual, visual and buccal, and tactile and auditory spaces becomes coordinated as early as 3–9 months of neonatal life (Piaget, 1969). Helmholtz alluded to smell and taste that frequently "unite to form a single whole: Using our tongues constantly, we are scarcely aware that the peculiar character of many articles of food and drink, as vinegar or wine, depends also upon the sensation of smell, their vapours entering the back part of the nose through the gullet" (p. 63). The role of vision and visual imagery is important in making tactual localization and haptic estimates (Gibson, 1966). In the perception of space, vision predominates haptic touch. When normal subjects are given two similar objects of identical weight but different size, a smaller one is perceived as heavier. This phenomenon is known as *the size–weight illusion.* Surprisingly, schizophrenic patients showed striking insensitivity to the illusion, thereby accurately discriminating between weights (Feigenberg, 1971, 1974).

The synergism between visual and auditory sensations are particularly common (Driver & Spence, 1994; Spelke, 1979). Infants seem capable of spontaneous "metaphorical" audiovisual matching (e.g., identifying the relevance of an ascending tone to an upward-pointing arrow, and a descending tone to an arrow pointing down; Wagner, Winner, Cichetti, & Gardner, 1981). They can also compare the intensity of sounds with the view and direction of a car (Walker-Andrews & Lennon, 1985). The audiovisual components of such intertwined stimuli are not necessarily equivalent ("symmetrical") in their ability to activate exogenous orienting (Spence & Driver, 1995). With time and experience, each component could possibly elicit more complex percepts than those caused by the physical properties of such stimuli (e.g., by their spatial confugartion, order, spectrum, and intensity). Visual localization is not influenced by auditory displacement. A symmetric effect would have been deadly for the ventriloquist illusion.

Helmholtz argued in his "Physiological Optics" that the perception of the world of forms is composed of visual sensations modulated by experience and memory. *Merriam-Webster's* definition capitalizes on this point by defining *perceptions* as "physical sensation as interpreted in the light of experience; the integration of sensory impressions of events in the external world . . . derived from past experience and serving as a basis for or as verified by further meaningful [expectant] action." The ventriloquist effect is an eloquent example of a process driven by perceptual appearance of the stimulation scenario. By presenting a specific article (a dummy speaker), one apparently calls into action expectations and motivated behavior, as well as a specialized system for encoding nonspatial (configurational) features of visual stimuli. Everyone learns, and then accepts as axiomatic, that a sound heard in the visual presence of a loudspeaker is most likely to originate from the loudspeaker, rather than from any other source. Perhaps this inference was made by a patient who proved to be dead wrong, but salvaged previously ignored input.

"Why are the goal posts behind the line at the end of the fields? In the game of Rugby the goal posts are right at the end," asked Queen Elizabeth, when attending a football game at the University of Maryland in 1957. This question, as well as other items of small talk in the Queen's Box, appeared almost verbatim in *Life Magazine* on December 12, 1957. None, with the exception of the Governor of Maryland and President of the University of Maryland, heard this. No reporter was permitted in the Queen's vicinity. Yet this conversation was seen through a high-powered telescope by an expert speechreader located 200 yards from the Queen's Box (Jeffers & Barley, 1971).

Making sense of speech movement so accurately and rapidly requires a high degree of skill. The majority of people may experience difficulty in picking up even standard cliché sentences when their topic is unpredictable. Yet the stimuli of visual speech, although not a viable medium for communication, appear to be ecologically valid when combined with auditory speech (Massaro, 1987, 1989). Thus, viewing the articulatory movements of a speaker appears to enhance intelligibility of conversational speech. Speech-reading was found to be particularly useful in the presence of noise, which is detrimental to receiving cues of place of articulation, as opposed to nasality and voicing, which are easy to hear but impossible to see (Miller & Nicely, 1955). Accordingly, under conditions of loss of specific phonoacoustic information, lip-reading may act as a complementary aid to hearing (Sumby & Pollack, 1954; Summerfield, 1979). One might wonder whether the principle of complement is upheld when auditory and visual stimuli are spatially separated. Specifically, one might wonder whether inferential cues as to manner of articulation in attended (ipsilesional) space would help a patient with auditory neglect to mentally reconstruct a syllable voiced in the ignored (contralesional) space.

The straightforward separation of audiovisual (AV) stimuli is complicated by the fact, demonstrated earlier, that the presence of a TV monitor in the attended space would cause a person to attribute sounds to the direction of visual regard (i.e., create the "ventriloquist illusion"), thereby confounding results. Thus, an independent contribution of lip-reading in the attended field could possibly be shown through the delivery of conflicting auditory and visual information. Such a mismatch would either increase the number of errors (Dodd, 1977) or elicit a qualitatively different effect, such as the synthesis of both inputs. We took advantage of the "blend illusion" of McGurk and MacDonald (1976), which is elicited when conflicting consonant–vowel (CV) syllables are presented in

376

the auditory and visual modalities. For example, the combination of video [*ga*] with audio [*ba*] yields a percept of [*da*] (i.e., a blend of the seen and heard inputs). The failure to discern discrepant AV inputs is a natural phenomenon, and the blend percept occurs with no awareness of conflict in the majority of the normal population (McGurk & Mac-Donald, 1976). This illusion is a sensitive instrument. It may be disrupted when acoustical categorization of verbal stimuli ("voice-onset-time") appears slightly before discernible lip movements occur. This dissociation may have contributed to the feeling of incongruity of video and auditory inputs, and an unusual resistance to blending in native Hebrew-speaking subjects (Aloufy, Lapidot, & Myslobodsky, 1996). Thus, the susceptibility of USN patients to the illusion would prove that a fairly high degree of phonological processing is taking place in the ignored space.

Soroker, Calamaro, and Myslobodsky (1995) examined susceptibility to this illusion in seven patients with clinically detectable visual neglect following right-hemisphere damage. All had signs of auditory neglect, as confirmed by the inferior identification of syllables delivered through a loudspeaker on the left side. Figure 14.5 illustrates the principle of testing, whereby sounds were delivered in the contralesional space, and the TV monitor—displaying the face of the speaker—was positioned in ipsilesional space. As expected, bimodal stimulation increased the identification of sounds in patients from 25% to 66%, compared with 58% to 81% in controls.

To ascertain the contribution of visual (articulatory) profiles in perceptual gain, these data were reprocessed as a function of response category (i.e., illusory blends, nonillusory biased responses, and omissions). The blends were predominantly composed of true fusions and combinations. In both groups, fusions were obtained when front consonants were heard, whereas back consonants were lip-read. In contrast, lip-read front consonants heard together with back consonants (e.g., video /*b*/, /*f*/) with acoustic /*k*/, /*g*/, /*h*/, /*t*/ yielded "combinations" (/*bka*/, /*bha*/, /*bga*/, /*pha*/, /*fta*/) in 64.7% of such conflicting pairs.

Thus, USN patients were susceptible to the blend illusion at the level of normal controls, and differed in the number of nonillusory items and omissions. This experience confirms that auditory information in the "ignored space" is processed to the required level and properly matched to the co-processed visual information on the right. Predictably, maximal accuracy was achieved when auditory and visual stimuli were concordant and salient (e.g., /*b,p,m*/). When conflicting bilabial (auditory) and velar (visual) stimuli were administered, the pathological attention gradient must have prompted selection of a visual articulatory configuration, whereas the ventriloquist effect should have offered recovery of

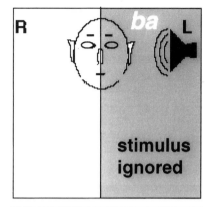

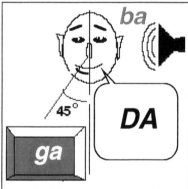

FIG. 14.5. Experimental setting for eliciting the McGurk effect. The source of syllabic sounds was located at 90° to the left of the subject. A TV monitor for lip-reading of conflicting syllables was visible at 40°–45° to the right off the midline.

the bilabial sounds. USN patients answered with labio-dental (/fa/), alveolar (/ta/, /da/), and nasal (/na/) syllables, thereby indicating the production of a synthetic illusory compromise based on preconscious categorization of both inputs, rather than on mere mislocalization of auditory percepts to the right, as is the case in the ventriloquist illusion.

It has yet to be elucidated whether perceptual misattribution of syllabic sounds affected by nonspeech visual items in the visual space (i.e., the ventriloquist effect) and AV integration of auditory and visual speech (the "McGurk effect") are based on dissimilar processes, or whether they reflect different operational aspects of the same innate multimodal neuronal device. The fact that the ventriloquist illusion apparently serves as a reliable vehicle for the blend illusion is consistent with the possibility that the multimodal neuronal net processes both kinds of information. This is achieved by augmenting output in case of spatial disparity, rather than discarding one of the noncongruent inputs. The ethological advantage of such a template is in its ability to be utilized either as a computational map solely for spatial orientation, or to provide visuospatial coordinates that can take into account the place and manner of articulation of auditory stimuli for linguistically relevant distinctions, and thus reconstruct the indissoluble whole.

RELATING THE VENTRILOQUIST EFFECT
TO NEUROPHYSIOLOGY: MULTIMODAL
INPUT PROCESSING

One might further ask, What is this map? Where does the compounded percept occur? How is it made? What is its substrate? It has long been postulated that USN represents deficient processing of multimodal input, which leads to a breakdown of the coherent picture of extracorporal space, thereby causing the "amorphosynthesis" of Denny-Brown (Denny-Brown, 1956; Denny-Brown, Meyer, & Horenstein, 1952). As mentioned previously, the most frequent correlate of USN is an injury to the parietal lobe. The parietal lobe is a region chiefly responsible for promulgation of behavior dominated by the sense of vision. It is composed of several divisions that are involved in the crossmodality mapping of extrapersonal signals. It provides the layout of the world with personal reference information used for orientation and spatial guidance of somatic movements. Some neurons in the parietal lobe are known to readily respond to visual stimuli when the latter are relevant to the somatic coordinate system (see Hyvärinen, 1982, for a review). In the monkey, Cortical Area $2v$ responds to both proprioceptive and optokinetic visual stimuli. Its neurons represent a system performing the permutation of the visual modality into a coordinate system of somatic, auditory, and vestibular modalities. The additive or interactive validation of stimuli is fundamental to establishing how relevant the cue is to bodily functions and behavior. Some neurons in Area 5 of monkeys appear to be insensitive to environmental stimuli other than those that were relevant in the context of motivated projection of the arm to the target (Mountcastle, Lynch, Georgopolous, Sakata, & Acuna, 1975).

The breakdown of multimodal maps cannot be attributed solely to parietal lobe dysfunction. A number of cells in the frontal eye field show presaccadic activity that is equally strong irrespective of whether the saccades were made to the visual or auditory targets (Bruce & Goldberg, 1985). The temporal lobe, too, has complex multimodal functions, and conceivably may handle such audiovisual maps. In primates, some visual neurons in the inferotemporal cortex have bilateral receptive fields.

According to Seltzer and Pandya (1994), the superior temporal polysensory (STP) cortex receives input from the parietal cortex along its length; mid-STP cortex (Areas TPO-2 and -3) has input from the inferior caudal parietal lobule, whereas caudal STP cortex (Area TPO-4) has afferent connections with the lower bank of the intraparietal sulcus and medial parietal lobe. The multisensory neurons, driven both by auditory and visual stimuli, can be encountered in a vast number of cortical regions implicated in spatial control and its breakdown in USN, such as the visual cortex, caudal inferior parietal lobule, temporo-parietal cortex, caudal superior temporal gyrus, frontal cortex, striatum, and superior colliculi (e.g., Benevento, Fallon, Davis, & Rezak, 1977; Bental, Dafny, & Feldman, 1968; Buser & Imbert, 1961; Gordon, 1972; Jung, Kornhuber, & da Fonseca, 1963; Meredith & Stein, 1986; Stein & Meredith, 1993; Suzuki & Azuma, 1977).

The multimodal net of a different category consists of neurons that respond during a co-activation of visual and auditory inputs, in particular during their spatial merger. These neurons are rather appropriate candidates for providing the layout of the world, such that sounds can "send" the retina precisely to its source and aid in achieving a somatomotor interaction with what is seen. Hubel, Henson, Rupert, and Galambos (1959) were apparently the first to record such "attention units" in the auditory cortex of the cat, which could be driven by auditory stimuli only when the cat turned his gaze to the source of sound. Similar neurons that have an advanced ability to resolve the source of a sound, especially of naturally strong modulated sounds, and compare their direction with that of visual stimuli were also recorded in the occipito-parietal area of cats and monkeys (Leinonen, Hyvärinen, & Sovijarvi, 1980; Morrell, 1972; Spinelli, Starr, & Barrett, 1968), as well as in the superior colliculus of a variety of animals (e.g., Harris, 1986; Stein & Meredith, 1993; Wickelgren, 1971).

The ease with which neglected auditory input is recovered in the presence of a fictitious cue in homolesional space unambiguously implicates supramodal facilities of the left hemisphere, which are known to be involved in neglect recovery (Pantano et al., 1991). The left hemisphere must have both categories of audiovisual neurons. Both are genuinely supramodal. Yet the first type seems more likely to provide a neural substrate for such phenomena as the effect of enhancement of subjective brightness of visual stimuli delivered synchronously with sounds (Wilkinson, Price, London, & Stein, 1993). By contrast, the network based on the second variety of multimodal "attention neurons" is perhaps more fitting for the transmutations of activities in the auditory somatotopic space into the "egocentric" coordinates, including the audiovisual synthesis underlying the ventriloquist effect. It has been proposed that the multisensory interdependence needed for audiovisual mapping of extracorporal space is disrupted in USN, due to the ipsilesional shift of the "egocentric" coordinates (Vallar et al., 1991; Ventre, Flandrin, & Jeannerod, 1984).

The multimodal neurons have lent the supramodal maps an air of actuality. As long as such neurons were present, the maps ceased to be merely convenient (and possibly imaginary) ways of explaining behavior. Clearly, the functions of these cells are not rigidly determined, and may be animated by a dummy target. Our findings emphasize that, within the object-centered system of processing, awareness is easily regained when the maps are re-registered, even if with imperfect alignment.

It is of note that neglected audition was reclaimed when input visual cue originated at a location more than 100° away from it (i.e., in the patently noncorresponding point of the visual space). It looks as if the functions of the map are more determined by the character of the template than by the precise properties of the input. It would not be surprising if any position of the fictitious source in the attended visual field would be actively fitted to appear as a credible source of syllabic sounds, thereby suggesting that in reality these two modalities do not need to map onto each other perfectly.

Which "map" decides that this input is relevant, and how does it do the job so easily? Would it perform more selectively if offered an array of locations of a fictitious source? Would it need training to achieve a better fit? We do not know the answers to these questions. What one might infer from this experience is that the audiovisual cross-referencing leading to the ventriloquist illusion is computed by neurons with rather large receptive fields, such as neurons in the superior colliculus (Stein & Meredith, 1993) and/or lateral intraparietal area (Robinson, Goldberg, & Stanton, 1978), which explains why they tolerate such imprecise alignment (Stein & Meredith, 1993). Moreover, these neurons have potentialities in excess of what the cross-modal mapping requires. Stein and Meredith (1993) speculated that the evolutionary significance of large receptive fields in multisensory structures is in "offsetting the disruptive influences that small misalignments of sensory organs would have on multisensory register" (p. 156).

Battersby et al. (1956) pondered why some of their patients manifested asymmetries in their response to sound localization. They hypothesized that some modalities are more crucial for spatial perception than others. They maintained that vision is "probably the most important spatial and distant receptor possessed by primates. Hence, when visual function on one side is disrupted by cerebral damage, and mental confusion and disorientation are also present, the signs of spatial 'inattention' tend to appear" (p. 90). During one of his last testing sessions, Battersby's patient, Mr. B, mused while taking the phrase-reading test: "The last time I read these things (the phrases), I would start at the left and jump all the way to the right" (Battersby et al., 1956, p. 87). Conceivably, his hearing used to make a crude leap to the right as well, thereby missing the sounds of speech.

THE NEURONAL ANATOMY OF THE VENTRILOQUIST EFFECT

The neuroanatomical components and location of the network contributing to USN and its amelioration remain elusive. Their complexity must be staggering. As Garey (1990) pointed out, "the number of routes for visual information to take between the retina and the visual cortex is miriad" (p. 968). The parietal cortices have reciprocal connections with more than 60 brain structures (Hyvärinen, 1982). In addition, a number of brain regions mentioned earlier (e.g., the extrastriate cortex, superior colliculi, basal ganglia, thalamus, prefrontal cortex, and superior temporal cortex) could potentially establish functional interrelations for mediating cross-modal integration in the visual space. Only a few such structures and pathways are sampled in Fig. 14.6.[2] Among them, the superior colliculi (SC) and striatum have a special place.

The colliculi neurons have long been recognized to participate in orientation to signals in the visual panorama (see Yeomans & Tehovnik, 1988, for a review). They were mentioned previously to deal with cross-modal information and its translation into the map of motor action in space (Stein & Meredith, 1993). Hess (1981) argued that the SC are the major control station for head and body turning tendencies and a chief instrument of the "visual grasp reflex." Their removal (Schneider, 1969; Sprague & Meikle, 1965) or targeted lesions of multimodal deeper colliculi layers (Casagrande, Harting, Hall, & Diamond, 1972) are associated with a profound experimental unilateral attention deficit with unimpaired vision, akin to USN, in humans. The role of SC in audiovisual integration that occurs in the context of orienting reflex is thus undeniable, although what actually happens there can only be stated in such vague metaphors as coordination, association, and mapping. Figure 14.6a highlights the fact that colliculi neurons depend on input from the posterior cortex, which is overwhelmingly homolateral (Sprague,

---

[2]Most of what is known regarding changes in brain morphology following injury originates from comparative studies in subprimates, including lower mammals. Thus, these results must be interpreted with due regard to significant differences between species.

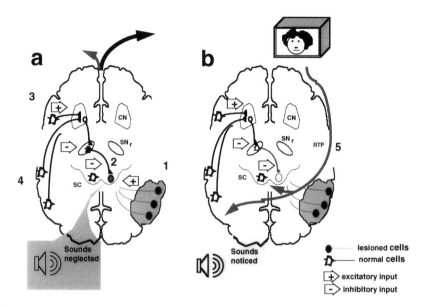

FIG. 14.6. Schematic diagram of pathways assumed to contribute to USN (a) as well as (b) to the salubrious effect of deception (the ventriloquist effect). (a) Effects of neocortical lesion on the double-inhibitory loop through the basal ganglia (McHaffie, Norita, Dunning, & Stein, 1993): (1) Parietal cortex damage that reduces activity of tectal cells and degrades their directional asymmetry to contralesional input; (2) Inhibitory nigrotectal projections; (3) Fronto-striatal excitatory projections; (4) Posterior (visual and parietal) cortico-striatal pathways. b. By exhibiting a dummy speaker in the attended space, one is capable of activating contralesional tectal cells via RTP (5), as well as the left parietal cortex. The event expected to follow a scenario opposite to that pictured in (a): (i) enhanced activity of the left parietal cortex; (ii) enhanced excitability of GABAergic striatal neurons; (iii) reduced firing of SN_r neurons; and (iv) relative disinhibition of ipsilesional colliculus. Consistent with Redgrave, Westby, and Dean (1993), Fig. 14.6b assumes ipsilaterally projected pathways as responding to visual stimuli, whereas contralaterally projected pathways as responding to auditory stimulation. Abbreviations: CN = caudate nucleus; SC = superior colliculus, SN_r = substantia nigra, pars reticulata; RTP = retinotectal projections.

1966) and excitatory (Ogasawara, McHaffie, & Stein, 1984). Thus, they respond with depressed excitability following right parietal damage. USN can then be pictured (Fig. 14.6a) as the net effect of parietal damage and reduced collicular activity deprived of excitatory corticotectal input (1).

The striato-nigro-tectal pathway (2) is still another component of the network, and was given a central place in Fig. 14.6. An active inhibition of tectospinal activity by the cortico-strio-tectal pathway may be an important component of USN. It should be recalled that the ipsilesional colliculus was thought to become handicapped, not only due to the loss of excitatory corticotectal input, but also by the unmitigated inhibitory barrage coming from its contralesional counterpart, chiefly via the crossed nigrotectal pathway (Wallace, Rosenquist, & Sprague, 1989, 1990). Originally, it was shown that a cat rendered persistently hemianopic by an extensive unilateral lesion of the posterior cortex appears to restore spontaneous visual orientation following intercollicular section or damage inflicted to the contralesional colliculus (Sprague, 1966). This paradoxical recovery, now widely known as the "Sprague effect," was attributed to the inhibitory interconnections between the neighboring colliculi (Sprague, 1966). It appeared, however, that such inhibition is provided by nigrotectal neurons converging on deep lamina tectospinal neurons. The disruption of fibers coming from a small area in the contralesional rostro-lateral substantia nigra pars reticulata (SN_r) is capable of restoring spontaneous scanning in the unattended space (i.e., the Sprague effect; Wallace et al., 1990).

Whether the ventriloquist illusion can be understood in terms of normalized function within the neuronal network assumed to underlie USN (i.e., deficient ipsilesional corticotectal input along with hyperactive contralesional nigrotectal projections) remains uncertain. At first glance, this effect is controlled by external informative visual stimuli, and thus must depend on the spared sensory apparatus in the left hemisphere. However, the essential feature of such visual stimuli is that they carry an obligatory auditory component. Such a component could not be assumed otherwise than through representational knowledge of such an audiovisual association. The ability of the assumed audiovisual properties of the stimuli to guide behaviors in the absence of an auditory component coming from the same direction is a characteristic attributable to the prefrontal system (Goldman-Rakic, 1987).

Another problem is visual attention to a dummy speaker. In itself, a cue in the attended space could only sharpen visual neglect by activating the retinotectal input (5), which is chiefly contralateral (Weisz, Balázc, & Adám, 1994) and terminates in deep collicular layers (Beckstead & Frankfurter, 1983). The parietal cortex is connected to prefrontal cortex by a system of reciprocal connections. Both cortices are united by a more complex indirect network via the thalamus and/or hippocampus and cingulate (see Goldman-Rakic, 1987, for a review). These pathways cannot be utilized with the premorbid efficacy for the transmission and processing of visuospatial information in the right hemisphere following its injury. Exhibiting a dummy speaker on the right could then possibly activate an alternative fronto-parietal traffic (Fig. 14.6a, 3) of impulses in the left hemisphere replacing the lost right parieto-tectal input. The increased left prefrontal activity would tend to increase striatal output, thereby decreasing the firing of nigro-tectal afferents. A similar effect could conceivably be achieved through axons from the visual cortex (4), which terminate in the striatum (Alheid, Heimer, & Switzer, 1990). In keeping with Wallace et al. (1990), Fig. 14.6b attributes the effect to the axons from SN_r. These are known to project to both the ipsilateral and contralateral SC (its intermediate and deep gray; Giolli, Blanks, Torigoe, & Williams, 1985; Parent, Mackey, Smith, & Boucher, 1983). Only contralateral input was shown (Fig. 14.6) because ipsilesional GABAergic inhibitory nigrotectal input is ineffective, when lesioned, in restoring visuomotor orientation in the unattended space (i.e., the Sprague effect; Ciaramitaro, Rosenquist, & Wallace, 1993). Thus, the contralesional colliculi cells would be relatively disinhibited compared with ipsilesional neurons, thereby determining the directionality of recovered behavior. Figure 14.6b suggests that the chain of events leading to sound perception in the presence of the dummy speaker is composed of (a) elevated cortico-striatal activity, (b) enhanced excitability of GABAergic striatal neurons, (c) reduced firing of SN_r cells, and (d) relative disinhibition of ipsilesional colliculus. Auditory input, given synchronously with the visual, must function in activating multimodal cells in deep collicular layers, thereby leading to the recovery of earlier unattended sounds, albeit, in the presence of a strong bias of visual attention to the right. The proposed possibility that retinoextrastriate pathways in the left hemisphere take on the functions of the missing visuotectal projections on the right must remain hypothetical until the whole picture of remodeling connections in the damaged network will be better understood and include its other components, in particular the medial pulvinar and hippocampal cells.

AWARENESS SALVAGED BY DECEPTION

It is a truism, of both popular and academic psychology, that a number of variables (e.g., attitudes, cognitive style, personality characteristics, social pressure, etc.) may enhance or distort perception, and thus spatial competence. The "stimulus" may be inferred from the patient's response in the past, as a phenomenological theorist suggested (Wylie, 1968). A priori, theoretical considerations have thus made plausible the idea that processing in the neglected space in patients with USN must also depend on the perception of relevance arising from the circumstances surrounding the task in the attended space. Thus, the question of clinical utility of deception for USN rehabilitation cannot be resolved correctly outside specific environmental situations. In fact, the present experiment conducted in a highly structured laboratory condition cannot predict improved performance in a real-life situation, in which a multitude of relevant and irrelevant cues appear simultaneously in several modalities. Yet an improvement is certainly useful. Consider a question posed by Stewart (1982)—of whether a surviving superior colliculus establishes maladaptive connections when its counterpart has been removed. In the domain of the capacity of regulation, the answer to the question is certainly in the negative when an animal is seen solving a visuospatial puzzle. Nonetheless, miswired circuits would do an effective job when an animal just needs to be informed of a presence of a visual stimulus.

The fact that relevance worked to salvage information delivered in the ignored space indicates that the information was available implicitly. In this respect, the present evidence adds to a number of other neuropsychological and psychophysiological findings of "knowledge without awareness" obtained in USN and other conditions (e.g., Bauer & Verfaellie, 1988; Marshall & Halligan, 1988; Tranel & Damasio, 1985; Volpe, Ledoux, & Gazzaniga, 1979). The susceptibility to the ventriloquial effect and blending illusion supports this principle. Also, it affirms that one's responses to environmental stimuli are frequently determined by what one is compelled to believe they are, rather than by what one experiences (also see Driver & Spence, 1994). As Marcel Proust mused: "The evidence of senses is also an operation of the mind, in which conviction creates the evidence" (cited in Critchley, 1986, p. 238). What appears important is not the physical parameters of the stimulus, but the way the patient sees it as a part of the environment. Our experience emphasizes the fact that auditory neglect may be modulated by the tendency of the patient to hear the world in the context of the references of his or her beliefs. Krech (1932) summarized this point in a handsome dictum: "Rabbits smell what they expect, not what they sniff."

Although the ventriloquist effect was not intended as a means of USN therapy, it was important to this end because its exploration afforded a glimpse of rehabilitation by "deception." One should bear in mind that the extreme openness of a patient to the illusion suggests a relationship between perception and the innate properties of the neuronal net. Thus, it could be a stable effect, although such variables as influencability, compliance, conformity, or attitude change could possibly modulate its magnitude.

It was mentioned earlier that, in normal human infants, the tendency of both modalities to merge spatially exists within minutes after birth (Wertheimer, 1961), such that infants orient both their head and mouth in the direction of the voice and nipple of their mother. In addition, bottle-fed neonates easily learn to cope with spatial disparity by turning their eyes toward the voice and looking for a face while their mouths orient in the opposite direction in reaching for the bottle (Alegria & Noirot, 1978). This example illustrates that a flagrant deception of the senses may be an instrument of survival. The recovery of auditory neglect, even in the form of "alloacusis," is a particularly striking demonstration that awareness (or rather an increment in spatial competence) may be bought at the price of deception. Perhaps it is fitting to conclude that "a capacity for self-deception is accordingly a suggestive diagnostic sign of a conscious organism" (Johnson-Laird, 1983, p. 476). Nature worked to select minds that opt to be wrong about the organization of the extracorporal world, rather than to completely lose a good half of it.

ACKNOWLEDGMENTS

This work was supported, in part, by the Israel Academy of Sciences grant to MSM. The author wishes to express his appreciation to S. Aloufy, N. Calamaro, A. Oksenberg, M. Lapidot, C. Serfati, N. Soroker, and J. Weisz for time and efforts invested in testing patients and control participants. Thanks are due to U. Hadar, M. Lapidot, and I. Nachsohn for their comments on an earlier version of this chapter.

REFERENCES

Alegria, J., & Noirot, E. (1978). Neonate orientation behavior towards human voice. *International Journal of Behavioral Development, 1,* 291–312.

Alheid, G. F., Heimer, L., & Switzer, R. C. (1990). Basal ganglia. In G. Paxinos (Ed.), *The human nervous system* (pp. 483–582). San Diego: Academic Press.

Aloufy, S., Lapidot, M., & Myslobodsky, M. (1996). Differences in susceptibility to the "blending illusion" among native Hebrew and English speakers. *Brain and Language, 53,* 51–57.

Battersby, W. S., Bender, M. B., Pollack, M., & Kahn, R. L. (1956). Unilateral "spatial agnosia" (inattention). *Brain, 79,* 68–93.

Bauer, R. M., & Verfaellie, M. (1988). Electrodermal discrimination of familiar but not unfamiliar faces in prosopagnosia. *Brain and Cognition, 8,* 240–252.

Beckstead, R. M., & Frankfurter, A. (1983). A direct projection from the retina to the intermediate gray layer of the superior colliculus demonstrated by anterograde transport of horseradish peroxidase in monkey, cat and rat. *Experimental Brain Research, 52,* 261–268.

Bellas, D. H., Novelly, R. A., Eskenazi, B., & Wasserstein, J. (1988). Unilateral displacement of the olfactory sense. *Cortex, 24,* 267–275.

Benevento, L. A., Fallon, J., Davis, B. J., & Rezak, M. (1977). Auditory-visual interaction in single cells in the cortex of the superior temporal sulcus and orbital cortex of the macaque monkey. *Experimental Neurology, 57,* 849–872.

Bental, E., Dafny, N., & Feldman, S. (1968). Convergence of auditory and visual stimuli on single cells in the primary visual cortex of unanesthetized unrestrained cats. *Experimental Neurology, 20,* 341–351.

Bisiach, E. (1988). The (haunted) brain and consciousness. In A. J. Marsel & E. Bisiach (Eds.), *Consciousness in contemporary science* (pp. 101–120). Oxford, England: Oxford University Press.

Bisiach, E., Luzzatti, C., & Perani, D. (1979). Unilateral neglect, representational schemata and consciousness. *Brain, 101,* 609–618.

Bisiach, E., & Vallar, G. (1988). Hemineglect in humans. In F. Boller & J. Grafman (Eds.), *Handbook of neuropsychology* (Vol. 1, pp. 195–225). Amsterdam: Elsevier.

Blauert, J. (1983). *Spatial hearing. The psychophysics of human sound localization.* Cambridge, MA: MIT Press.

Bourre, J.-M. (1993). *Brainfood.* Boston: Little, Brown.

Bradshaw, J. L., Nettelton, N. C., Pierson, J. M., Wilson, L., & Nathan, G. (1987). Coordinates of extracorporal space. In M. Jeannerod (Ed.), *Neurophysiological and neuropsychological aspects of spatial neglect* (pp. 41–67). Amsterdam: North-Holland.

Bruce, C. J., & Goldberg, M. E. (1985). Primate frontal eye fields: I. Single neurons discharging before saccades. *Journal of Neurophysiology, 53,* 603–635.

Buser, P., & Imbert, M. (1961). Sensory projections to the motor cortex in cats: A microelectrode study. In W. A. Rosenblith (Ed.), *Sensory communication* (pp. 597–626). New York: MIT Press/Wiley.

Calamaro, N., Soroker, N., & Myslobodsky, M. S. (1995). False recovery from auditory hemineglect produced by source misattribution of auditory stimuli (the Ventriloquist effect). *Restorative Neurology & Neurosciences, 7,* 151–156.

Casagrande, V. A., Harting, J. K., Hall, W. C., & Diamond, I. T. (1972). Superior colliculus in the tree shrew: A structural and functional subdivision into superficial and deep layers. *Science, 177,* 444–447.

Ciaramitaro, V., Rosenquist, A. C., & Wallace, S. F. (1993). Lesions of the substantia nigra ipsilateral to a visual cortical lesion fail to restore visual orientation behavior in the cat. *Society of Neurosciences, Abstracts, 19,* 766.

Critchley, M. (1953). *The parietal lobes.* London: Edward Arnold.

Critchley, M. (1979). *The divine banquet of the brain and other essays.* New York: Raven.

Critchley, M. (1986). *The citadel of the senses and other essays.* New York: Raven.

Cubelli, R., Nichelli, P., Bonito, V., De Tanti, A., & Inzaghi, M. G. (1991). Different patterns of dissociation in unilateral neglect. *Brain and Cognition, 15,* 139–159.

Cystowic, R. E. (1989). *Synesthesia: A union of the senses.* New York: Springer-Verlag.

Denny-Brown, D. (1956). Positive and negative aspects of cerebral cortical functions. *North Carolina Medical Journal, 17,* 295–303.

Denny-Brown, D., Meyer, J. S., & Horenstein, G. (1952). The significance of perceptual rivalry resulting from parietal lesion. *Brain, 75,* 433–471.

De Renzi, E. (1982). *Disorders of space exploration and cognition.* Chichester, England: Wiley.

De Renzi, E., Faglioni, P., & Scotti, G. (1970). Hemispheric contribution to exploration of space through the visual and tactile modality. *Cortex, 6,* 191–203.

De Renzi, E., Gentilini, M., & Barbieri, C. (1989). Auditory neglect. *Journal of Neurology, Neurosurgery and Psychiatry, 52,* 613–617.

Diamond, S. P., & Bender, M. B. (1965). An auditory extinction and alloacusis. *Transactions of American Neurological Association, 90,* 154–157.

Dodd, B. (1977). The role of vision in the perception of speech. *Perception, 6,* 31–40.

Domman, G. A., Shargrough, F. W., & Whisnat, J. P. (1982). Carotid occlusive disease. Effect of bright light on visual evoked response. *Archives of Neurology,* 687–689.

Driver, J., & Spence, C. J. (1994). Spatial synergies between auditory and visual attention. In C. Umiltà & M. Moscovitch (Eds.), *Attention and performance XIV* (pp. 311–331). Hillsdale, NJ: Lawrence Erlbaum Associates.

Feeney, D. M., & Wier, C. S. (1979). Sensory neglect after lesions of substantia nigra or lateral hypothalamus: Differential severity and recovery function. *Brain Research, 178,* 329–346.

Feigenberg, I. (1971). Probability prognosis and schizophrenia. *Soviet Science Review, 2,* 119–123.

Feigenberg, I. (1974). Schizophrenia and probability prediction. *Soviet Psychology, 12,* 3–22.

Garey, L. J. (1990). Visual system. In G. Paxinos (Ed.), *The nervous system* (pp. 945–977). San Diego: Academic Press.

Gainotti, G. (1972). Emotional behavior and hemispheric side of lesion. *Cortex, 8,* 41–55.

Gainotti, G. (1983). Laterality of affect: The emotional behavior of right- and left-brain-damaged patients. In M. Myslobodsky (Ed.), *Hemisyndromes. Psychiatry, neurology, psychobiology* (pp. 175–192). New York: Academic Press.

Geschwind, N. (1982). Disorders of attention: A frontier in neuropsychology. *Philosophical Transections of the Royal Society (London), B298,* 173–185.

Gibson, J. J. (1966). *The senses considered as perceptual systems.* Boston: Houghton Mifflin.

Giolli, R. A., Blanks, R. H. I., Torigoe, Y., & Williams, D. D. (1985). Projections of medial terminal accessory nuclei, and substantia nigra of rabbit and rat as studied by retrograde axonal transport of horseradish peroxidase. *Journal of Comparative Neurology, 232,* 99–116.

Goldman-Rakic, P. S. (1987). Circuitry of primate prefrontal cortex and regulation of behavior by representational knowledge. In F. Plum & V. Mountcastle (Eds.), *Handbook of physiology* (Vol. 5, pp. 373–417). Washington, DC: American Physiological Society.

Gopher, D. (1973). Eye-movements patterns in selective listening tasks of focused attention. *Perception and Psychophysics, 14,* 259–264.

Gordon, B. (1972). The superior colliculus of the brain. *Scientific American, 227,* 72–83.

Graybiel, A. (1978). Organization of the nigrotectal connection: An experimental tracer study in the cat. *Brain Research, 143,* 339–348.

Guiton, D., Crommelinck, M., & Roucoux, A. (1980). Stimulation of the superior colliculus in the alert cat: I. Eye movements and neck EMG activity evoked when the head is restrained. *Experimental Brain Research, 39,* 63–73.

Harris, W. A. (1986, March). Learned topography: The eye instructs the ear. *Trends in Neurosciences,* pp. 84–86.

Heilman, K. M., & Valenstein, E. (1979). Mechanisms underlying hemispatial neglect. *Annals of Neurology, 5,* 166–170.

Helmholtz, H. (1954). *On the sensation of tone as a physiological basis for the theory of music.* New York: Dover. (Original work published 1877).

Hess, W. R. (1981). In K. Akert (Trans.), *Biological order and brain organization: Selected works of W. R. Hess* (pp. 269–304). New York: Springer-Verlag.

Hubel, D. H., Henson, C. O., Rupert, A., & Galambos, R. (1959). "Attention" units in auditory cortex. *Science, 129,* 1279–1280.

Humphrey, N. K. (1970). What the frog's eye tells the monkey's brain. *Brain, Behavior and Evolution, 3,* 324–337.

Hyvärinen, J. (1982). Posterior parietal lobe of the primate brain. *Physiological Review, 61,* 1060–1129.

Jeffers, J., & Barley, M. (1971). *Speechreading (lipreading).* Springfield, IL: Thomas.

Johnson-Laird, P. N. (1983). *Mental models. Towards a cognitive science of language, inference, and consciousness.* Cambridge, MA: Harvard University Press.

Jung, R., Kornhuber, H. H., & da Fonseca, J. S. (1963). Multisensory convergence on cortical neurons: Neuronal effects of visual, acoustic and vestibular stimuli in the superior convolutions of the cat's cortex. In G. Moruzzi, A. Fessard, & H. H. Jasper (Eds.), *Brain Mechanisms: Vol. 1, Progress in brain research* (pp. 207–240). Amsterdam: Elsevier.

Kramer, T. H., Buckhout, R., & Eugenio, P. (1990). Weapon focus, arousal, and eyewitness memory: Attention must be payed. *Law and Human Behavior, 14,* 167–184.

Krech, D. (1932). "Hypothesis" in the rat. *Psychological Review, 39,* 516–532.

Leinonen, L., Hyvärinen, J., & Sovijarvi, A. R. A. (1980). Functional properties of neurons in the temporo-parietal association cortex of awake monkey. *Experimental Brain Research, 39,* 203– 215.

Loftus, E. F., Loftus, G. R., & Meso, J. (1987). Some facts about "Weapon Focus." *Law and Human Behavior, 11,* 55–62.

Luria, A. (1959). Disorders of "simultaneous perception" in a case of bilateral occipito-parietal brain injury. *Brain, 82,* 437–449.

MacKay, D. M. (1991). *Behind the eye.* Cambridge, MA: Basil Blackwell.

McGurk, H., & MacDonald, J. (1976). Hearing lips and seeing voices. *Nature, 264,* 746–748.

Marks, L. E. (1978). *The unity of the senses. Interrelations among the modalities.* New York: Academic Press.

Marshall, J. C., & Halligan, P. W. (1988). Blindsight and insight in visuo-spatial neglect. *Nature, 336,* 766–767.

Massaro, D. W. (1989). Multiple book review of speech perception by ear and eye: A paradigm for psychological inquiry. *Behavioral and Brain Sciences, 12,* 741–794.

Massaro, D. W. (1987). *Speech perception by ear and eye.* Hillsdale, NJ: Lawrence Erlbaum Associates.

McHaffie, J. G., Norita, M., Dunning, D. D., & Stein, B. E. (1993). Corticotectal relationships: Direct and "indirect" corticotectal pathways. *Progress in Brain Research, 95,* 139–150.

Meredith, M. A., & Stein, B. E. (1986). Visual, auditory, and somatosensory convergence on cells in superior colliculus results in multisensory integration. *Journal of Neurophysiology, 56,* 640–662.

Mesulam, M.-M. (1981). A cortical network for direct attention and unilateral neglect. *Annals of Neurology, 10,* 309–325.

Miller, J. L., & Nicely, P. E. (1955). An analysis of perceptual confusions among some English consonants. *Journal of Acoustic Society of America, 27,* 338–352.

Morrell, F. (1972). Visual system's view of acoustic space. *Nature, 238,* 44–46.

Mountcastle, V. B., Lynch, J. C., Georgopolous, A., Sakata, H., & Acuna, C. (1975). Posterior parietal association cortex of the monkey: Command functions for operations within extrapersonal space. *Journal of Neurophysiology, 38,* 871–908.

Newcombe, F., Ratclif, G., & Damasio, H. (1987). Dissociable visual and spatial impairments following right posterior cerebral lesions: Clinical, neuropsychological and anatomical evidence. *Neuropsychologia, 25,* 149–161.

Ogasawara, K., McHaffie, J. G., & Stein, B. E. (1984). Two visual corticotectal systems in cat. *Journal of Neurophysiology, 52,* 1226–1245.

Pantano, P., Guariglia, C., Juduca, A., Lenzi, G. L., Fieschi, C., & Pizzamiglio, L. (1991). Cerebral blood flow patterns in the rehabilitation of visuo-spatial neglect. *Journal of Cerebral Blood Flow and Metabolism, 11,* (Suppl. 2), S383.

Parent, A., Mackey, A., Smith, Y., & Boucher, R. (1983). The output organization of the substantia nigra in primate as revealed by retrograde double labeling method. *Brain Research Bulletin, 10,* 529–537.

Piaget, J. (1969). *The mechanisms of perception.* London: Routledge & Kegan Paul.

Pierson, J. M., Bradshaw, J. L., & Nettleton, N. C. (1983). Head and body space to left and right, from and rear: I. Unidirectional competitive auditory stimulation. *Neuropsychologia, 21,* 463–473.

Pierson-Savage, J. M., Bradshaw, J. L., Bradshaw, J. A., & Nettleton, N. C. (1988). Vibrotactile reaction times in unilateral neglect. The effects of hand location, rehabilitation and eyes open/closed. *Brain, 111,* 1531–1545.

Redgrave, P., Westby, G. W. M., & Dean, P. (1993). Functional architecture of rodent superior colliculus. *Progress in Brain Research, 95,* 69–77.

Reid, T. (1970). *An inquiry into the human mind.* Chicago: University of Chicago Press. (Original work published 1813)

Reisberg, D., Scheiber, R., & Potemken, L. (1981). Eye position and the control of auditory attention. *Journal of Experimental Psychology, 7,* 318–323.

Robertson, I. H., & Marshall, J. C. (Eds.). (1993). *Unilateral neglect: Clinical and experimental studies.* Hillsdale, NJ: Lawrence Erlbaum Associates.

Robinson, D. L., Goldberg, M. E., & Stanton, G. B. (1978). Parietal association cortex in the primate: Sensory mechanisms and behavioral modulations. *Journal of Neurophysiology, 41,* 910–932.

Schankweiler, D. P. (1961). Performance of brain-damaged patients on two tests of sound localization. *Journal of Comparative and Physiological Psychology, 54,* 375–381.

Schilder, P., & Stengel, E. (1931). Asymbolia for pain. *Archives of Neurology and Psychiatry, 25,* 598–600.

Schneider, G. E. (1969). Two visual systems. *Science, 163,* 895–902.

Schwartz, A. S., Marchok, P. L., Kreinick, C. J., & Flynn, R. E. (1979). The asymmetric lateralization of tactile extinction in patients with unilateral cerebral dysfunction. *Brain, 102,* 669–684.

Seltzer, B., & Pandya, D. N. (1994). Parietal, temporal, and occipital projections to cortex of the superior temporal sulcus in the rhesus-monkey. A retrograde tracer study. *Journal of Comparative Neurology, 343,* 445–463.

Servin, S. L., Tour, R. L., & Kershaw, R. H. (1967). Macular function and the photostress test. *Archives of Ophthalmology, 77,* 2–7.

Soroker, N., Calamaro, N., & Myslobodsky, M. (1995). McGurk illusion to bilateral administration of sensory stimuli in patients with hemispatial neglect. *Neuropsychologia, 33,* 461–470.

Spelke, E. S. (1979). Perceiving bimodally specified events in infancy. *Developmental Psychology, 15,* 626–636.

Spence, C. J., & Driver, J. (1996). Audiovisual links in endogenous spatial attention. *Journal of Experimental Psychology: Human Perception and Performance, 22,* 1005–1030.

Spinelli, D. N., Starr, A., & Barrett, T. W. (1968). Auditory specificity in unit recordings from cat's visual cortex. *Experimental Neurology, 22,* 75–84.

Sprague, J. M. (1966). Interaction of cortex and superior colliculus in mediation of visually guided behavior in the cat. *Science, 153,* 1544–1547.

Sprague, J. M., & Meikle, T. H., Jr. (1965). The role of the superior colliculus in visually-guided behavior. *Experimental Neurology, 11,* 115–146.

Stein, B. E., & Meredith, M. A. (1993). *The merging of the senses.* Cambridge, MA: MIT Press.

Stewart, O. (1982). Assessing the functional significance of lesion-induced neonatal plasticity. *International Review of Neurobiology, 23,* 197–253.

Sumby, W. H., & Pollack, J. (1954). Visual contribution to speech intelligibility in noise. *Journal of Acoustic Society of America, 26,* 212–215.

Summerfield, A. Q. (1979). Use of visual information for phonemic perception. *Phonetica, 36,* 314–331.

Suzuki, H., & Azuma, M. (1977). Prefrontal neuronal activity during gazing at a light spot in the monkey. *Brain Research, 126,* 495–508.

Tranel, D., & Damasio, A. R. (1985). Knowledge without awareness: An autonomic index of facial recognition in patients with unilateral cerebral lesions. *Science, 228,*1453–1454.

Umilta, C. (1995). Domain-specific forms of neglect. *Journal of Clinical and Experimental Neuropsychology, 17,* 209–219.

Vallar, G., Bottini, G., Sterzi, R., Passerini, D., & Rusconi, M. L. (1991). Hemianesthesia, sensory neglect, and defective access to conscious experience. *Neurology, 41,* 650–652.

Vallar, G., Sandroni, P., Rusconi, M. L., & Barbieri, S. (1991). Hemianopia, hemianesthesia, and spatial neglect: A study with evoked potentials. *Neurology, 41,* 1918–1922.

Ventre, J., Flandrin, J. M., & Jeannerod, M. (1984). In search for the egocentric reference. A neuropsychological hypothesis. *Neuropsychologia, 22,* 797–806.

Volpe, B. T., Ledoux, J. E., & Gazzaniga, M. S. (1979). Information processing of visual stimuli in an "extinguished" filed. *Nature, 282,* 722–724.

von Dongen, H. R., & Drooglever Fortuyn, J. (1968). Drawing with closed eyes. *Journal of Neurology, Neurosurgery and Psychiatry, 71,* 275–280.

Walker-Andrews, A. S., & Lennon, A. M. (1985). Auditory-visual perception of changing distance in human infants. *Child Development, 56,* 544–548.

Wallace, S. F., Rosenquist, A. C., & Sprague, J. M. (1989). Recovery from cortical blindness mediated by destruction of nontectotectal fibers in the comissure of the superior colliculus in the cat. *Journal of Comparative Neurology, 282,* 429–450.

Wallace, S. F., Rosenquist, A. C., & Sprague, J. M. (1990). Ibotenic acid lesions of the lateral substantia nigra restore visual orientation behavior in the hemianopic cat. *Journal of Comparative Neurology, 296,* 222–252.

Watson, R. T., Velnstein, E., & Heilman, K. M. (1981). Thalamic neglect. Possible role of the medial thalamus and nucleus reticularis in behavior. *Annals of Neurology, 38,* 501–506.

Webster, W. R., & Garey, L. J. (1990). Auditory system. In G. Paxinos (Ed.), *The human nervous system* (pp. 889–944). San Diego, CA: Academic Press.

Weinstein, E. A., & Friedland, R. P. (1977). *Hemi-inattention and hemisphere specialization.* New York: Raven.

Weisz, J., Balázc, L., & Adám, G. (1994). The effect of monocular viewing on heartbeat discrimination. *Psychophysiology, 31,* 370–374.

Weisz, J., Oksenberg, A., Soroker, N., & Myslobodsky, M. S. (1995). Effects of hemithalamic damage on K-complexes evoked by monoaural stimuli during midafternoon sleep. *Electroencephalography & Clinical Neurophysiology, 94,* 148–150.

Wertheimer, M. (1961). Psychomotor coordination of auditory and visual space at birth. *Science, 134,* 692.

Wickelgren, B. G. (1971). Superior colliculus: Some receptive filed properties of bimodally receptive cells. *Science, 173,* 69–71.

Wilkinson, L. K., Price, D. D., London, N., & Stein, B. E. (1993). Multisensory integration influences perception of visual intensity. *Society for Neurosciences (Abstracts), 19,* 738.

Wylie, R. C. (1968). The present status of self theory. In E. F. Borgatta & W. W. Lambert (Eds.), *Handbook of personality theory and research* (pp. 728–787) Chicago: Rand McNally.

Yeomans, J. S., & Tehovnik, E. J. (1988). Turning responses evoked by stimulation of visuomotor pathways. *Brain Research Reviews, 13,* 235–258.

Author Index

Note: Page numbers followed by n refer to footnotes.

A

Abellan, M. J., 350, *358*
Abelson, R. P., 134, *179*, 183, *200*
Abraham, K., 245, 246, 252, 272, *273*
Ackerman, D., 14, *19*
Acuna, C., 379, *390*
Adàm, G., 384, *392*
Agassi, J., 25, 26, 27, 31, 33, 34, 35, 37, 39, 43, 45, 47, 48, *49*
Agassi, J. B., 31, *50*
Agnetti, V., 277, *295*
Akiskal, H. S., 264, *273*
Aks, D.J., 99, *101*
Albe-Fessard, D., 348, *356*
Albert, M. S., 158, *172*
Alegria, J., 387, *387*
Alexander, M. A., 170, *178*
Alexander, M. P., 133, 165, 166, *174, 179*, 221, 223, 308, 310, 314, *323, 326*
Alfieri, T., 116, *130*
Alheid, G. F., 385, *387*
Alicke, M. D., 106, *127*
Allen, N., 283, *303*
Allport, F. H., 58, *70*
Aloufy, S., 377, *387*
Alric, V., 5, *19*
American College Dictionary, *100*
American Psychiatric Association, 264, *273*
Ames, A. J., 80, 93, *100*
Ames, D., 317, *325*
Amir, R., 345, *356*
Amos, E. C., *299*
Anderes, J. O., 280, *295*

Andersen, S. M., 123, *127*
Anderson, C. A., 113, *127*
Anderson, E., 282, *295*
Anderson, R. C., 183, *197*
Angelergues, R., 281, 289, *300*
Appenzeller, O., 348, *356*
Arena, J. G., 338, 341, *360*
Arieti, S., 320, *322*
Armbruster, T., 150, *174*
Aronson, A., 318, *326*
Asch, S. E., 8, *19, 127*
Aserinsky, E., 210, *216*
Assad, J. A., 93, *100*
Assal, G., 280, *295*
Atkinson, A. P., 278, *302*
Attneave, F., 78, *100*
Aubrey, M., *198*
Azuma, M., 380, *391*

B

Babinski, M. J., 290, *295*
Bach, S., 350, *356*
Bacon, F., 35, *50*
Baddeley, A. D., 137, 138, 148, 162, *172, 175*, 188, *197*
Baik-Han, E. J., 339, *356*
Baker, R. A., *19*
Balàzc, L., 384, *392*
Banaji, M. R., 66, *70*
Banton, T., 85, 98, *100*
Barber, T. X., 156, 168, *180*
Barbera, J., 350, *358*
Barbieri, C., 364, *388*
Barbieri, S., 368, *392*
Barchilon, J., 271, *273*
Bargh, J. A., 123, *127*

Barley, M., 376, *389*
Barmwater, U., 158, *175*
Baron, R., 348, *356*
Barr, W. B., 281, 288, 289, *299*
Barrett, T. W., 380, *391*
Barron, S. A., 348, *361*
Bartlett, F. C., 134, 140, *172, 183, 197*
Barton, R., 106, *129*
Basbaum, A. I., 348, *357*
Bass, E., 155, *172*
Bateman, A., 280, *302*
Battersby, W. S., 364, 366, 381, 382, *387*
Bauer, R. M., 280, 281, 283, 284, 285, 286, 287,
    288, 292, *295, 296, 297, 299, 386, 387*
Baumeister, R. F., 189, 190, 194, 195, *199*
Baumgartner, G., 85, *102*
Beck, A. G., 307, *322*
Beck, S. J., 307, *322*
Beckett, P. A., 82, *100*
Beckson, M., *299*
Beckstead, R. M., 384, *387*
Behrmann, M., 280, *296*
Beilin, B. Z., 349, 350, *360*
Bellas, D. H., 364, *387*
Bellezza, F. S., 183, *197*
Belli, R., 155, *172*
Bender, L., 321, *323*
Bender, M. B., 352, *360*, 364, 366, 374, 381, 382,
    387, 388
Benedetti, F., 87, *100*
Benevento, L. A., 380, *387*
Bénézech, M., 5, *19*
Benner, D. G., 266, *273*
Bennett, G. J., 344, 348, 349, *357, 358*
Ben-Shakhar, G., 284, *296, 298, 299*
Benson, D. F., 162, 164, 166, 167, *172, 179, 299,*
    308, 310, 311, 312, 314, *325, 326*
Bental, E., 348, *361*, 380, *387*
Bentin, S., 292, *301*, 318, *326*
Benton, A., 279, 281, 284, 289, *296*
Ben-Zur, H., 236, 238, *240*
Bergler, E., 270, *273*
Berlucchi, G., 282, *302*
Berlyne, D. E., 313, 314, 321, *323*
Berlyne, N., 309, *323*
Berman, K. B., 317, *324*
Berman, K. F., 317, *323*
Bernal, J. D., 43, *50*
Bernstein, I. H., 97, 98, *101*
Bernstein, J. J., 339, *357*
Berry, J. W., 96, *102*
Besdine, M., 270, *273*
Betin, S., *326*
Bever, T. G., 137, *174*
Beyn, E. S., 287, *296*
Beyth-Marom, R., *128*

Bicknell, J. M., 348, *356*
Biederman, I., 135, *172*
Biella, G., 347, *360*
Bigelow, L. B., *324*
Bindra, D., 282, *303*
Bindschaedler, C., 164, *178*
Birbaumer, N., 353, *357*
Bisiach, E., 363, 364, 372, *388*
Bjork, R. A., 146, 161, *177*
Blanc-Garin, J., 279, 280, *296*
Blanks, R. H. I., 385, *389*
Blauert, J., 370, *388*
Blenk, K.-H., 339, *359*
Bleuler, E., 308, 309, *323*
Bliestle, A., 281, *300*
Blinder, B., 233, *242*
Bliss, E. L., 17, *19*, 260, *273*
Block, R. A., 95, *103*
Bloom, F. E., 352, *361*
Blumberg, H., 348, *357*
Bodamer, J., 277, 278, 290, *296*
Bogen, J. E., 281, *300*
Bolgert, F., 281, 284, *301*
Bonacini, M. G., *298*
Bonanni, E., 219, *223*
Bonhoeffer, K., 313, *323*
Bonito, V., 371, *388*
Bornstein, B., 280, 283, *296*
Bors, E., 347, *356*
Bothwell, R., 192, *197*
Bottini, G., 368, 381, *392*
Boucart, M., 287, 291, *300*
Boucher, R., 385, *390*
Bourre, J.-M., 371, *388*
Bower, G. H., 183, *197*
Bowers, D., 281, *296*
Bowers, K. S., 190, 193, 194, 195, *197, 198*
Bowman, M., 318, *326*
Bradley, G. W., 106, *127*
Bradley, J. W. P., 350, *358*
Bradshaw, J. A., 364, 372, *390*
Bradshaw, J. L., 364, 372, *388, 390*
Brake, S., 278, *302*
Bransford, J. D., 134, 140, 141, *172, 176, 197*
Braun, B. G., 267, *274*
Braun, C. M. J., 162, *173*
Brehm, J. W., 109, *127*
Brekke, N., 133, *180*
Breton, F., 281, 284, *301*
Brewer, W. F., 182, 186, 192, *197, 198*
Breznitz, S., 225, 226, 231, 236, 240, *240, 241*
Bridgeman, B., 92, *102*
Brigham, J., 192, *197*
Broadbent, D. E., *70*
Broddick, O. A., 94, *100*
Bromage, P. R., 343, *359*

Brown, A. M., 157, *178*
Brown, J. D., 105, 106, 108, 111, 126, *127, 130,*
	229, *242*
Brown, P., 183, *198*
Brown, W. S., *198,* 314, 321, *324*
Browne, C. T., 58, *70*
Bruan, B. G., *274*
Bruce, C. J., 379, *388*
Bruce, V., 286, 289, *296, 304*
Bruck, M., 154, *172,* 189, 190, *198*
Bruner, J. S., 3, 6, 7, *19,* 94, *100,* 105, 109, 111,
	127, 182, *198*
Brunswick, E., 98, *100*
Bruyer, R., 280, 282, 283, 285, 288, 290, *296, 302*
Buchignani, C., 220, *223*
Buchsbaum, M. S., 221, 222, *223*
Buckhout, R., 371, *390*
Buehler, R., 183, 184, 187, 188, *200*
Bull, R., 155, *178*
Bullemer, P., 139, *178*
Burchiel, K. J., 341, 344, *356*
Burke, D. M., 191, *198*
Burton, A. M., 286, *296*
Buser, P., 380, *388*
Butler, G., 236, *241*
Butterfield, E. C., 238, *242*
Byrd, M., 144, *173,* 191, *198*

C

Cairns, E., 237, *241*
Calamaro, N., 16, *20,* 373, 377, *388, 391*
Calev, A., 317, *323*
Calvanio, R., 278, *300*
Campa, H. K., *359*
Campbell, A. W., 352, *356*
Campbell, J. D., 106, 113, *127*
Campbell, J. N., 339, 348, *356, 357, 359*
Campbell, R. T., 281, 287, *296, 297,* 318, *323*
Cansler, D., 183, *198*
Cantor, J., 165, 166, *176*
Cantor, N., 183, *198*
Cantril, H., 182, *199*
Carey, S., 278, 279, *297*
Carlen, P. L., 351, *356*
Carlesimo, G. A., 281, *298*
Carlsmith, J. M., 108, *128*
Carpenter, C. J., 317, *324*
Carpenter, K. M., 114, *128*
Carr, H., 98, *100*
Carreras, M., 277, *295*
Carrie, L. E. S., 333, *356*
Carver, C. S., 227, 228, 230, *241*
Casagrande, V. A., 382, *388*
Casey Jones, D. E., 329, 331, *360*
Catalan, N., 343, *357*
Catherall, D. R., 264, *273*

Cave, K. R., 279, 283, *299*
Ceci, S. J., 11, *19,* 154, *172,* 189, 190, *198*
Cetinalp, E., 347, *360*
Chabal, C., 341, *356*
Chaiken, S., 111, 121, *129,* 142, 150, *172, 174*
Chaine, F., 280, *300*
Chalfonte, B. L., 134, 139, 143, 144, 156, 158,
	159, 160, 161, 164, *172, 173, 176*
Chamberlain, C. J., 308, 318, 321, *324*
Chambers, R. A., 315, *323*
Chaplin, W., 106, *129*
Chapman, J. P., 317, *325*
Chapman, L. J., 317, *325*
Charness, N., 192, *198*
Chase, W. G., 192, *198*
Chatterjee, A., 321, *323*
Chiu, C., 107, *128*
Cholden, L., *323*
Christen, L., 281, *300*
Christianson, S., 187, *198*
Chrosnaik, L. D., 146, 157, *175,* 191, *199*
Chung, J. M., 339, *356*
Cialdini, R. B., 114, *128*
Ciaramitaro, V., 385, *388*
Cicerone, K. D., 166, *173*
Cipolotti, L., 312, *323*
Claparède, E., 65, *70*
Clare, I. C., 312, *323*
Clark, B., 97, *100*
Cobb, S., 352, *361*
Coccia, B. G., 278, *301*
Cochran, B., 14, *179*
Coderre, T. J., 350, *356, 358*
Cohen, A. R., 109, *127*
Cohen, N. J., 139, 159, *173*
Cohen, O., 116, *130*
Cohen-Levine, S., 282, *297*
Cohn, R., 283, *297*
Coleman, L., 183, *198*
Coles, E. C., 318, *326*
Collins, A. M., 139, *173*
Collins, J. F., 88, *101*
Collins, R. L., 236, *242*
Comer, J. F., 281, *301*
Comer, R., 108, 109, *127*
Condorcet, M., 38, *50*
Conte, H. R., 226, *242*
Coppolillo, H. P., 269, *273*
Coren, S., 73, 75, 77, 88, 92, 96, 98, 99, *100, 101,*
	102
Coslett, H. B., 281, *296*
Cottrell, G. W., 159, *178*
Coughlan, A. K., 165, 166, *177,* 308, 314, *324*
Cowey, A., 291, *297, 303*
Craik, F. I. M., 144, 158, 166, 169, *173, 180,* 182,
	191, *198, 199,* 238, *241*

Cramer, P., 225, 226, 227, 228, 232, 238, *241*
Critchley, M., 10, 12, *19*, 255, 266, 272, *273*, 310, 312, *323*, 363, 365, 386, *388*
Crocker, J., 107, *127*, 183, *201*
Crommelinck, M., *389*
Cronholm, B., 329, 350, 353, *356*
Crook, T. H., 158, *178*
Crotteau Huffman, M. L., 154, *172*
Crow, T. J., 278, *299*, 318, *326*
Cubelli, R., 371, *388*
Cummings, J. L., 281, *300*, 313, 314, 321, *323, 324*
Curran, F., 321, *323*
Cutting, J., 167, *173*, 317, 318, 319, *323*
Cystowic, R. E., 374, *388*

D

Dafny, N., 380, *387*
Daigneault, S., 162, *173*
Dalla Barba, G., 311—312, 314, 321, *323*
Dallas, M., 65, *71*, 138, 139, *175*
Damasio, A. R., 277, 278, 279, 280, 281, 283, 284, 288, 289, 290, *297, 302, 303*, 314, *323*, 386, *391*
Damasio, H., 277, 278, 279, 280, 281, 283, 284, 289, 290, *297, 303*, 314, *323*, 364, *390*
Daniel, D. G., 318, *324*
Dark, C. H., 350, *358*
Darley, J. M., 115, *127*, 184, *198*
Davidoff, J., 278, 279, 285, 287, *297*
Davis, B. J., 380, *387*
Davis, C. M., 94, *101*
Davis, G. C., 264, *273*
Davis, K. D., 335, *356*
Davis, K. E., 107, *129*
Davis, L., 155, *172*
Day, R. M., 85, *102*
De Ajuriaguerra, V., 321, *323*
Dean, J. T., 268, *274*
Dean, P., *391*
Debruille, B., 281, 284, *301*
Deese, J., 141, *173*
Deffenbacher, K., 192, *197*
De Haan, E. H. F., 278, 280, 282, 285, 286, 287, 288, 290, 291, 292, *296, 297, 298, 301, 303, 304, 305*
De Leonardis, D., 146, *176*
De Leonardis, D. M., 157, 158, *173, 178*
DeLuca, J., 166, *173*, 314, *323*
Dember, W. N., 81, *101*
Dembowsky, K. P., 348, *357*
Dement, W., 210, 211, 212, *216, 217*
Denes, G., 312, *323*
Dennett, D. C., 137, *173, 298*
Dennis, S. G., 350, *357*
Denny-Brown, D., 315, *323*, 367, 371, 377, *388*

Denoth, F., 219, 223
Denton, K., 228, 229, 230, 232, *242*
De Paulo, B. M., 183, 184, *198*, 293, *305*
de Paun, K. W., 286, *298*
de Pauw, K. W., 168, *174*
Deregowski, J., 96, *101*
De Renzi, E., 280, 281, 282, 283, 289, *298*, 363, 364, 369, 372, *388*
DeSchepper, B., 139, 161, *173*
De Schonen, S., 282, *298*
Desimone, R., 162, *173*, 317, *325*
DeSimone Leichtman, M., 10, *19*
D'Esposito, M., 165, 166, *174*, 314, *323*
De Tanti, A., 371, *388*
Deutsch, G., 164, *179*
Deutsch, H., 269, 270, 271, 272, *273*
Devor, M., 329, 331, 336, 337, 339, 340, 341, 343, 344, 345, 348, 349, 351, 352, *356, 357, 358, 359, 360*
Diamond, B. J., 286, *298*, 314, *323*
Diamond, I. T., 382, *388*
Diamond, R., 278, *297*
Diamond, S. P., 374, *388*
Dickman, S., 67, *71*
Diederich, J., 287, *298*
Dimsdale, J. E., 226, *241*
Dince, P. R., 267, *273*
Ditto, P. H., 111, 121, *128*
Dive, D., 221, *223*
Dixon, N. F., 66, *70*
Dobson, M., 145, *173*
Dodd, B., 376, *388*
Dodson, C. S., 146, 148, 149, *173*
Doherty, E., *198*
Dollard, L., 61, *70*
Domman, G. A., 368n, *388*
Donnelly, N., 287, 291, *300*
Doricchi, F., 219, *223*
Dorpat, T. L., 225, 227, 231, *241*
Doruo, E., 203, *217*
Dorus, W., *217*
Dostrovsky, J. O., 335, 348, *356, 359*
Dougherty, P. M., 348, 352, *357*
Dovidio, J. F., 108, *129*
Drever, J., 75, *101*
Driver, J., 375, 386, *388, 391*
Drooglever Fortuyn, J., 371, *392*
Dubner, R., 349, *357*
Ducarne, B., 280, *300*
Dudek, S. K., 272, *273*
Duggan, L. M. III, 188, *198*
Duncan, J., 162, *173*
Duncker, K., 138, *173*
Dunn, J. C., 139, *173*
Dunning, D. D., 185, *198, 390*
Dupont, R. M., 222, *223*

Dupré, E. M., 2, 5, 15, *19*
Durso, F. T., 145, 150, *173—174*
Duverger, P., 5, *19*
Dweck, C. A., 107, 124, *128*
Dywan, J., 190, *198*

E

Eagly, A. H., 142, 150, *172, 174*
Ebata, S., 280, *298*
Ebbesen, E. B., 183, *199*
Edwards, D., 151, *174*
Eggers, R., 158, *175*
Eich, E., 148, 161, *174*
Eichenbaum, H., 159, *173*
Ekman, P., 11, *19*
Ekstein, R., 270, *273*
Elaad, E., 284, *298*
Elbert, T., 353, *357*
Elizur, A., 283, *302*
Ellis, A. W., 282, 286, *296, 299, 304, 305*
Ellis, H. D., 167, 168, *174*, 277, 278, 279, 284, 286, 287, 289, 290, *298, 304*
Ellisman, M. H., 340, *358*
Endo, M., 279, *298*
Engkvist, O., 341, *357*
Enns, J. T., 73, 75, 77, 88, 92, 96, *101*
Epstein, S., 231, 238, *241*
Erdelyi, H. M., 110, *128*
Erdelyi, M. H., 66, 67, *70*, 230, 231, 232, *241*
Erickson, C., 335, 348, 352, *361*
Eriksen, C. W., 58, 67, *70*, 88, *101*
Escourelle, R., 280, *300*
Eskenazi, B., 364, *387*
Eslinger, P. J., 314, *323*
Etcoff, N. L., 279, *299*
Ettlin, T. M., 280, 283, *299*
Eugenio, P., 371, *390*
Evans, C. R., 98, *101*
Ewalt, J. R., 329, *357*
Eysenck, M. W., 233, 234, 235, 238, 240, *241, 242*

F

Faglioni, P., 280, 282, 289, *298*, 364, 372, *388*
Fairey, P. J., 113, *127*
Fallon, J., 380, *387*
Farah, M. J., 279, 280, 285, 286, 287, 293, *299, 304*
Farvolden, P., 193, 194, 195, *197*
Fast, I., 267, *273*
Favre, C., 280, *295*
Fay, D., 150, *174*
Fazio, F., 281, *298*
Feeney, D. M., 368, *388*
Feigenberg, I., 9, *19*, 375, *389*
Feinberg, I. M., 291, *299*

Feinberg, T. E., 280, *299*
Feinstein, B., 333, 345, *357*
Feldman, M. D., 6, *19*
Feldman, S., 380, *387*
Ferguson, S. A., 144, 145, 146, 157, 158, *174, 175, 176*
Fergusson, T. J., 192, *201*
Festinger, L., 11, 14, *19*, 106, 108, 109, *128*, 189, *198*
Feyerabend, P., 42, 45, *50*
Feyereisen, P., 280, 283, 285, *296*
Fiaschi, A., 278, *301*
Fiedler, K., 150, *174*
Fieschi, C., 380, *390*
Fingarette, H., 52, 53, 54, *70*
Finke, R. A., 146, 150, *174*
Fischer, D., 158, *175*
Fischer, R. S., 165, 166, *174*, 314, *323*
Fischhoff, B., *128*
Fisher, C., 212, *217*
Fisher, C. M., 309, 310, *324*
Fisher, R. L., 227, 229, 232, *241*
Fisher, S., 227, 229, 232, *241*
Fiske, S. T., 105, *128*
Fivush, R., 188, 190, *198*
Flandrin, J. M., 381, *392*
Fleisher, S., 205, *217*
Fleming, J. H., 184, *198*
Fleminger, S., 319, *324*
Fletcher, B., 230, *242*
Fletcher, G. J. O., 105, 106, 107, 111, *130*
Flor, H., 353, *357*
Florence, M., 278, 290, *298*
Flude, B. M., 282, *299, 304*
Flynn, R. E., 364, *391*
Fode, K. L., *130*
Fodor, J. A., 137, *174*, 293, *299*
Foley, M. A., 138, 141, 151, *174, 176*, 185, *199*
Folkman, S., 228, *242*
Fong, G. T., 110, 122, *130*, 183, *200*
Fonseca, J. S. da, 380, *389*
Ford, C. V., 245, 271, *274*
Forgus, R. H., 88, 94, *101*
Fortier, J., 219, 222, *223*
Foster, A. F., 187, *200*
Foulkes, D., 205–206, 210, 211, 211n, *217*, 219, 222, *223*
Franck, G., 221, *223*
Franco, G., 221, *223*
Frank, I., *357*
Frankfurter, A., 384, *387*
Franklin, N., 147, *175*
Franks, J. J., *197*
Freedman, M., 164, *178*
Freeman, R., 279, 283, *299*
Freud, S., 45, *50*, 54, *70*, 225, *241*

Frey, D., 108, 111, 121, *128, 131*
Friberg, L., 222, *223*
Fried, K., 340, *358*
Fried, Y., 47, *50*
Friedland, R. P., 363, 365, *392*
Friedman, S. W., 270, *273*
Friedrich, J., 118, 120, *128*
Frith, C. D., 278, *299*
Frost, D., 290, *301*
Furedy, J. J., 284, *296*
Fuster, J. M., 162, *174*, 314, *324*

G

Gainotti, G., 309, 311, *324*, 365, *389*
Gains, A. D., 11, *19*
Galambos, R., 380, *389*
Gall, N. G., 331, 342, *360*
Gallen, C. C., 352, *361*
Gallinek, A., 336, *358*
Gardner, H., 293, *299*, 310, 311, 312, 314, *325, 326*
Gardner, R, 212–213, *217*
Garey, L. J., 367, 382, *389, 392*
Garmezy, N., 320, *325*
Garrett, M. F., 137, *174*
Gati, I., 284, *296, 299*
Gazzaniga, M. S., 16, *20*, 55, *70*, 281, 283, 294n, *299*, 386, *392*
Gediman, H. K., 245, 269, *273*
Gelade, G., *71*
Gellner, E., 27, 37, *50*
Gentilini, M., 364, *388*
Gentner, D., 138, *174*
Georgopolous, A., 379, *390*
Gerard, G., 158, *174*
Gerard, H. B., *128*
Gerhard, D., 185, *200*
Gerrig, R. J., 150, *174*
Gervey, B., 124, *128*
Geschwind, N., 294n, *299*, 310, *324*, 365, *388*
Gibson, E. J., 78, 81, *101*
Gibson, J. J., 135, *174*, 375, *388*
Gick, M., 138, *174*
Gilbert, D. T., 113, *128*, 150, 151, *174*, 184, *198*
Giles, M., 237, *241*
Gillin, J. C., 222, *223*
Gilson, W. E., 335, 348, 352, *361*
Giltrow, M., 191, *199*
Ginzburg, R., 349, 350, *360*
Giolli, R. A., 385, *389*
Girgus, J. S., 98, 99, *100, 102*
Glickshon, J., 95, *103*
Glynn, C. J., 333, *356*
Godden, D. R., 148, *175*
Goetzl, E.J., 341, *357*
Goffman, E., 11, *20*

Gold, J. M., 317, *324*
Goldberg, B., 66, *70*, 230, 231, 232, *241*
Goldberg, E., 281, 288, 289, *299*
Goldberg, L., *241*
Goldberg, M. E., 379, 381, *388, 391*
Goldberg, T. E., 317, 318, 320, *324, 325*
Goldman-Rakic, P. S., 162, *175*, 384, *389*
Goldstein, A., 219, *223*
Gonzales-Darder, J. M., 350, *358*
Goodale, M. A., 14, *20*
Goodell, H., 348, *358*
Goodenough, D. R., *217*
Goodman, C. C., 94, *100*, 182, *198*
Goodman, G. S., 154, *175*
Goodwin, J., 268, *273*
Gopher, D., 370, *389*
Gordon, B., 380, *389*
Gordon, H. W., 318, *326*
Gorecki, J., 348, *359*
Govrin-Lippmann, R., 340, 351, *357, 358*
Gracely, R.H., 349, *358*
Graff-Radford, N. R., 314, *323*
Graybiel, A., 97, *100*, *389*
Greenacre, P., 246, 252, 271–272, *273, 274*
Greenberg, J., 113, 121, *129*
Greenson, R. R., 269, *274*
Greenwald, A. G., 16, *20*, 53n, 55, 59, 59n, 61, 64n, 66, 67n, 68, 69, *70*, 105, *128*, 295, *299*
Gregory, R. L., 78, 93, 99, *100, 101*
Gregory, W. L., 114, *128*
Grek, A., 314, *325*
Greve, K. W., 285, 286, 287, 288, 292, *297, 299*
Grice, H. P., 184, *198*
Griddin, D. W., *128*
Griffin, D. W., 126
Griffin, M., 149, *175*
Grinker, R. R., Jr., 272, *274*
Gross, J, 212, *217*
Gross, P. H., 115, *127*
Grossi, D., 280, 289, *298*
Grossman, W. I., 213, *217*
Grundvig, J. L., 308, 318, 321, *324*
Grüsser, O.-J., 12, 17, *20*
Guariglia, C., 380, *390*
Gudjosson, G. H., 312, *323*
Guilbaud, G., 348, *357, 358*
Guinan, E. M., 167, 168, *177*
Guiton, D., *389*
Gunderson, J. G., 266, *274*
Gur, R. C., 9, 11, *20*, 52, 53, 54, 58, 67, 68, *70*, 71, 105, *130*, 228–229, *241*, 291, 294, *302*, 317, *326*
Gur, R. E., 317, *326*
Gurtman, M. B., 108, *129*
Gutnick, M., 337, 339, *360*

H

Haan, N., *241*
Haber, W. B., 341, 350, 352, *358*
Habib, M., 281, *299*
Hackett, T. P., 226, *241, 243*
Hagbarth, K.-E., 337, 344–345, *359*
Haggard, H. W., 3, *20*
Halévy, E., 38, *50*
Hall, C. S., 212, *217, 227, 238, 241*
Hall, W. C., 382, *388*
Haller, L., 269, *273*
Halligan, P. W., 386, *390*
Hamby, S., 314, *326*
Hammond, K. R., 98, *101*
Hanley, J. R., 288, *300*
Harding, F. A., 287, 291, *300*
Hardy, J. D., 348, *358*
Harris, W. A., 380, *389*
Harsch, N., 183, 188, 192, *199*
Harting, J. K., 382, *388*
Hartman, W. M., 89, *102*
Hasher, L., 143, 149, 169, *175, 238, 241*
Hashmonay, R., 236, 237, *240, 241*
Hashtroudi, S., 133, 134, 140, 142, 144, 145, 146, 157, 158, 159, *174, 175, 176, 178,* 182, 185, 187, 188, 191, *199*
Haskins, R. G., 320, *324*
Hastie, R., 183, *199*
Hastorf, A., 182, *199*
Hatopf, W. H. N., 98, *101*
Hatta, T., 282, *300*
Haug, H., 158, *175*
Hay, D. C., 282, 289, *300, 304*
Hazlett, E., 222, *223*
Hecaén, H., 280, 281, 288, 289, *300, 303*
Hegley, D. C., 317, *325*
Heider, F., 106, *128*
Heilbrun, A. B., Jr., 226, 235, *241*
Heilman, K. M., 281–282, *296, 364, 389, 392*
Heimer, L., 385, *387*
Held, R., 290, *301*
Hellawell, D., 278, 285, 287, 288, *305*
Helmholtz, H., 374–375, *389*
Helson, H., 91, *101*
Henderson, W. R., 337, 342, 350, *358*
Henkel, L., 147, *175*
Henson, C. O., 380, *389*
Hepps, D., 154, *175*
Hervitz, E. F., 113, *130*
Hess, W. R., 382, *389*
Hicks, L. H., 318, 320, *324, 325*
Higgins, E. T., 115, 123, 124, *128*
Higgins, N. C., 228, 229, 230, 232, *242*
Hilgard, E. R., 55, *70*
Hillger, L. A., 282, *300*
Hilliard, R. D., 282, *300*

Hilton, J. L., 184, *198*
Hirayama, T., 348, *359*
Hirschman, J. E., 154, *175*
Hirst, W., 134, 139, 159, 161, 164, *175, 176*
Hochberg, J. E., 77, *101, 137, 175*
Hoffman, J. E., 149, *175*
Hogan, R. M., 146, 161, *175*
Hokfelt, T., 349, *358*
Holm, S., 222, *223*
Holmberg, D., 183, 191, *200*
Holmes, D. S., 67, *71*
Holt, K., 121, *129*
Holyoak, K., 138, *174*
Hong, Y., 107, *128*
Horenstein, G., 367, 379, *388*
Horevitz, R. P., 267, *274*
Horton, P. C., 269, *273*
Houle, S., 166, *180*
Howe, J. F., 353, *358*
Hubel, D. H., 380, *389*
Hume, D., 30, 31, *50*
Humphrey, N. K., 374, *389*
Humphreys, G. W., 135, *179, 278, 280, 287,* 288, 291, *300, 302, 305*
Huntley, C. W., 54, *71*
Hurtig, M., 284, 289, *302*
Hutchinson, W. D., 335, *356*
Huxley, A., 187, *199*
Hynes, L., 145, *178*
Hyvärinen, J., 379, 380, 382, *389, 390*

I

Iacono, R., 347, *360*
Imbert, M., 380, *388*
Imhof, H.-G., 281, *300*
Intraub, H., 149, *175*
Inzaghi, M. G., 371, *388*
Isen, A. M., 110, *128*
Isquith, P., *198*
Ivy, G. O., 158, *175*

J

Jacklin, C. N., 191, *199*
Jacobson, L., 114, *130, 341, 356*
Jacoby, L. L., 65, 68, *71, 138, 139, 144, 148, 175*
Jahangiri, M., 350, *358*
Jahoda, M., 105, *128*
Jaki, S., *50*
James, M., 289, *304*
Jänig, W., 339, 344, 345, 348, *357, 359*
Janis, I. L., 230, *241, 242*
Janowsky, J. S., 161, *179, 314, 324*
Jarvie, I. C., 25, 48, *50*
Jayatunga, A. P., 350, *358*
Jeannerod, M., 381, *392*
Jeeves, M. A., 282, *301*

Jeffers, J., 376, *389*
Jenkins, C. D., 236, *242*
Jensen, T. S., 329, 349, 350, *358*
Johnson, C. E., 278, *299*
Johnson, D. N., 135, *180*
Johnson, F. M., 318, 320, *324, 325*
Johnson, M. K., 133, 134, 135, 137, 138, 139, 140, 141, 142, 143, 144, 145, 146, 147, 148, 149, 150, 151, 152, 154, 156, 157, 158, 159, 160, 161, 162, 163, 164, 165, 166, 167, 170, *172, 173, 174, 175, 176, 177, 178, 179, 180,* 182, 185, 187, 188, 191, 194, *199,* 220, 221, 223, 308, 316, 317, *324*
Johnson-Laird, P. N., 134, *177, 389*
Johnston, R. A., 286, *296*
Jones, B., 282, *300*
Jones, E. E., 61, *71,* 107, *129*
Joscelyne, B., 266, *273*
Joseph, R., 166, 167, *177,* 314, *324*
Joslyn, D., 308, 318, 321, *324*
Jourard, S. M., 105, *129*
Juduca, A., 380, *390*
Jung, R., 380, *389*
Jus, A., 219, 222, *223*
Jus, K., 219, 222, *223*

K

Kaas, J. H., 352, *358*
Kahan, T. L., 147, *176*
Kahn, E, 211, *216*
Kahn, M. M. R., 269, *274*
Kahn, R. L., 310, 311, *326,* 364, 366, 381, 382, *387*
Kahneman, D., 123, *130*
Kajander, K. C., 344, *358*
Kalbert, L., 78, 79, 89, *102*
Kaplan, E., 158, *172*
Kaplan, L. J., 250, *274*
Kapur, N., 165, 166, *177, 180,* 308, 314, *324*
Karacan, I., 203, *217*
Karr, J. W., 184, 187, 188, *200*
Karush, A., 270, *274*
Kassell, N., 314, *323*
Kaszniak, A. W., 156, *179*
Katz, J., 329, 331, 350, 353, *356, 358, 360*
Kaufmann, W., 31, 46, *50*
Kay, J., 282, *299*
Kay, M. C., 282, 289, *301*
Kellerman, H., 226, *242*
Kelley, C. M., 144, 148, *175*
Kelley, G. A., 105, *129*
Kemper, T., 158, *177*
Kempler, B., 58, *71*
Kern, R. S., 314, 321, *324*
Kershaw, R. H., 368n, *391*

Kets de Vries, M. F., 245, *274*
Kierkegaard, S., 37, *50*
Kihlstrom J. F., 156, *179,* 190, 193, 194, *199*
Killackey, H. P., 352, *358*
Killbride, P. L., 96, *101*
Kilpatrick, F. P., 80, *101*
Kim, K. J., 339, *356*
King, B. H., 245, 271, *274*
King, G. A., 115, *128*
Kinsbourne, M., 312, *324*
Kintsch, W., 146, 161, *175*
Kirk, E. J., 344, *358*
Kirsner, K., 139, *173*
Kiss, Z. H. T., 335, *356*
Kleihues, P., 281, *300*
Klein, D., 282, *300*
Kleinman, J. E., 318, *324*
Kleitman, N., 210, *216, 217*
Klinger, M. R., 68, *70*
Klotz, I. M., 250, *274*
Knecht, S., 353, *357*
Knight, R. T., 160, *177*
Knyazeva, G. R., 287, *296*
Koch-Weser, M. P., 282, *297*
Koehler, D. J., 113, *129*
Koenig, O., 282, *300*
Koenken, G., 284, *298*
Kojetin, B. A., 184, *198*
Kolb, B., 163, 164, *177*
Kolers, P. A., 135, *177*
Koltzenburg, M., 339, 349, *357, 358*
Kopelman, M. D., 165, 167, 168, *177,* 310, 313, 314, *324*
Korenman, E. M. D., *359*
Korin, Y., 317, *323*
Kornhuber, H. H., 380, *389*
Koschorke, G. M., 339, *359*
Koshland, D. E., 317, *324*
Kosko, B., 2, *20*
Kosslyn, S. M., 138, *177*
Koulack, D., 212, *217*
Kouvumaki, J. H., 108, *130*
Kowler, E., 135, *177*
Kraepelin, E., 308, *325*
Kramer, T. H., 371, *390*
Krauss, R. M., 184, *199*
Krebs, B., 350, *358*
Krebs, D., 228, 229, 230, 232, *242*
Krech, D., 386, *390*
Kreinick, C. J., 364, *391*
Krieger, H. P., 352, *360*
Kritchevsky, M., 314, *324*
Krohne, H. W., 227, 228, *242*
Kroll, N. E. A., 160, *177*
Kruglanski, A. W., 127, *129*
Krumhansl, C. L., 137, *177*

Kugelberg, E., 337, *359*
Kugelmass, S., 317, *323*
Kuhl, S., 158, *175*
Kunda, Z., 105, 110, 111, 113, 121, 122, *129*, *130*, 183, *199*, *200*
Kuntz, H., 150, *174*
Kwan, H. C., 348, *359*
Kwan, P. C., 280, *299*
Kwapil, T. R., 317, *325*
Kwon, P., 145, *177*

L

Lachance, R., 219, 222, 223
Lachman, J. L., 238, *242*
Lachman, R., 238, *242*
Lackner, J. R., 97, *101*
Laird, J. D., 108, 109, *127*
Lakatos, I., 15, *20*
Lambert, W. W., 94, *101*
Lammers, W., 147, *179*
LaMotte, R. H., 348, *359*, *360*
Landauer, T. K., 146, 161, *177*
Landesman, T., 105, *129*
Landis, T., 12, 17, *20*, 279, 281, *297*, *300*, 318, *323*
Lane, S. M., 148, 149, 153, *180*
Langer, E. J., 107, *129*
Langfitt, J. T., *299*
Langton, J. N. K., 333, 345, *357*
Laor, N., *50*
Lapidot, M., 377, *387*
Larbig, W., 353, *357*
Lassen, N. A., 222, *223*
Lassiter, G. D., 184, *198*
Laterre, C., 280, 283, 285, *296*
Lazarus, R. S., 55, *71*, 105, *129*, 225, 227, 228, 230, *242*
Leavitt, C., 59, *70*
Le Bras, H., 280, *303*
Ledoux, J. E., 386, *392*
Leibowitz, H. W., 96, *101*
Leichtman, M., 154, *172*
Leinonen, L., 380, *390*
Lennon, A. M., 375, *392*
Lenz, F. A., 348, 352, *357*, *359*
Lenzi, G. L., 380, *390*
Lerer, B., 317, *323*
Leventhal, C. M., 81, *102*
Levi, M. D., 85, 98, *100*
Levin, H. S., 282, 289, *301*
Levine, D. N., 278, *300*, 314, *325*
Levine, H., 133, *179*, 221, *223*, 308, 314, *326*
Levine, J. D., 341, 348, *357*
Levine, M., *198*
Levinson, S., 183, *198*
Levitt, E. E., 307, *322*

Levy, J., 281, *300*
Levy, V. L., 9, *19*
Lewin, B. D., 252, *274*
Lewin, W., 221, 223, 314, *326*
Lewinsohn, P. M., 106, *129*
Lewis, P. D. R., 167, 168, *177*
Lhermitte, F., 13, *20*, 280, *300*, *325*
Li, L., 315, 317, *325*
Liberman, A., 111, 112, 113, 114, 116, 121, *129*, *130*, *172*, *179*
Libow, J. A., 257, *274*
Lieberman, A., 133, 142, *172*, *179*, 221, 223, 308, 314, *326*
Light, L. L., 156, *177*, 191, *198*
Lindsay, D. S., 68, *71*, 133, 134, 140, 142, 145, 146, 149, 153, 155, 159, *176*, *177*, *178*, 182, 185, 187, 188, *199*
Lindsay, P. M., 88, *101*
Lindsay, R. C., 192, *201*
Lindzey, G., 227, 238, *241*
Linn, L., 307, *325*
Lipps, T., 99, *101*
Lissauer, H., 288, *300*
Litman, R. E., 253, *274*
Livingston, K. E., 337, *359*
Livingston, W. K., 329, 333—334, *359*
Liwag, M., 182, *200—201*
Lockard, J. S., 11, *20*, 53, *71*, 294n, *300*
Lockhart, R. S., 238, *241*
Loesner, J. D., 347, *359*
Loewen, E. R., 158, *173*
Loftus, E. F., 67, *71*, 133, 154, 155, *172*, *177*, 183, 185, 187, 189, 193, 194, 195, *199*, *200*
Loftus, E. T., 314, *325*, 371, *390*
Loftus, G. R., 67, *71*, 195, *199*, 371, *390*
Lomazov, P., 336, 339, 343, *357*
Lombard, M. C., 348, *356*, *359*
London, N., 380, *392*
Lopez, D. F., 111, 121, *128*
Lovallo, W. R., 317, *326*
Luborsky, L., 233, *242*
Luce, J. C., 333, 345, *357*
Ludwig, A. M., 268, *274*
Lundberg, L. E. R., 348, *360*
Luria, A., 371, *390*
Luzzatti, C., 364, *388*
Lyerly, O. G., 312, *326*
Lykken, D. T., 283—284, *300*
Lynch, J. C., 379, *390*
Lynch, S. A., 349, *358*

M

Maccoby, E. E., 191, *199*
MacDonald, B., 281, *303*
MacDonald, J., 318, *325*, 377, *390*
MacFarlane, K., 190, *199*

Mach, E., *101*
MacKay, D. M., 315—316, *325*, 366, *390*
Mackey, A., 385, *390*
MacKinnon, S. E., 348, *356*
Macko, K. A., 135, *178*
MacLeod, C. M., 158, *175*, 233, 234, 240, *241*, *242*
MacRae, D., 280, *300*
Madigan, S. A., *199*
Madsen, P. L., 222, 223
Maher, B., 167, 168, *177*
Maher, B. A., 167, 168, *177*, 317, *325*
Maier, C., 348, *356*
Mailis, A., 342, *359*
Malitz, S., *326*
Malone, D. R., 282, 289, *301*
Malone, P. S., 150, *174*, 184, *198*
Maltzman, I., 16, *20*
Mandeville, B., 2, *20*
Mann, L., 230, *242*
Manschreck, T. C., 317, *325*
Maquet, P., 221, *223*
Marbach, J. J., 329, 331, *360*
Marcel, T., 282, *301*
Marchok, P. L., 364, *391*
Marikawa, K., 99, *101*
Markham, R., 145, *173*, *178*
Marks, L. E., 374, *390*
Markus, E. J., 158, *175*
Markus, H., 106, *129*, 183, *199*
Marr, D., 73, *101*, 135, *178*
Marsden, R. P., 98, *101*
Marshall, J. C., 290, 291, *304*, 365, 386, *390*, *391*
Martins, A. J., 135, *177*
Massaro, D. W., 376, *390*
Mateer, C. A., 294n, *300*
Mathews, A., 233, 234, 236, 240, *241*, *242*
Mathews, M., 235, 238, 240, *242*
Mathivet, E., 282, *298*
Matlin, M. W., 110, *129*
Matzner, O., 336, 339, 341, 343, *357*, *359*
Maunsell, J. H. R., 93, *100*
May, J., 235, *242*
Mayes, A. R., 159, *178*, 286, *298*
McAndrews, M. P., 292, *302*
McCallough, C., 87, *101*
McCarthy, R. A., 280, *301*, 309, *325*
McClellan, P. G., 97, 98, *101*
McClelland, J. L., 56, 64, *71*
McCormick, E. J., 97, *102*
McCready, D., 97, *102*
McDermott, K. B., 183, 187, *200*
McEntree, W. J., 158, *178*
McFarland, C., 191, *199*
McGeoch, J. A., 134, *178*
McGlynn, S. M., 290, 292, 294n, *301*

McGurk, H., 318, *325*, 377, *390*
McHaffie, J. G., 383, *390*
McNeil, J. E., 279, *301*
McWeeny, K. H., 282, *305*
Mead, G. H., 182, 187, 196, *199*
Meadows, J. C., 281, 289, *301*
Mehta, Z., 278, *301*
Meikle, T. H., Jr., 382, *391*
Melamed, L. E., 88, 94, *101*
Mele, A. R., 11, *20*, 48–49, *50*
Melzack, R., 327, 329, 333, 335, 336, 343, 347, 350, 353, *356*, *357*, *358*, *359*, 360
Memon, A., 155, *178*
Mencl, W. E., 159, *178*
Mercer, B., 310, 311, 312, *325*, *326*
Meredith, M. A., 370, 380, 381, 382, *390*, *391*
Merzenich, M. M., 352, *358*
Meso, J., 371, *390*
Mesulam, M.-M., 363, *390*
Metcalfe, J., 148, 159, 160, *174*, *177*, *178*
Meunch, J., *180*
Meyer, J. S., 367, 379, *388*
Meyer, R. A., 339, 348, *356*, *359*
Michael, S. F., 93, *102*
Michaelis, M., 339, 344, 345, *357*, *359*
Michon, J. A., 95, *102*
Michotte, A., 95, *102*
Middleton, D., 151, *174*
Milavetz, J. J., 317, *325*
Miller, D. T., 107, 113, *129*
Miller, E. D., 317, *325*
Miller, J. L., 376, *390*
Miller, N. E., 61, *70*
Miller, S. M., 227, *242*
Milner, A. D., 14, *20*
Milner, B., 159, *178*
Mintz, M., 17, *20*
Mischel, W., 106, *129*, 183, *198*, *199*
Mishkin, M., 135, *178*
Mitchell, R. W., 11, *20*
Mizuno, Y., 280, *298*
Mogg, K., 233, 234, 235, *242*
Molinari, S., 205—206, *217*
Molish, H. B., 307, *322*
Money, J, 212—213, *217*
Monk, A. F., *323*
Moray, N., *71*
Morrell, F., 380, *390*
Morris, H. H., 282, 289, *301*, 329, *357*
Morris, L. W., 158, *173*
Morris, R. G., 158, *173*
Moscovitch, M., 133, 161, 164, 166, 169, *178*, *180*, 182, *199*, 280, 282, 292, *296*, *300*, *302*, 311, 314, 316, 317, *325*
Moss, A., 289, *301*
Mountcastle, V. B., 379, *390*

Mowrer, O. H., 55, *71*
Mozley, L. H., 317, *326*
Mozley, P. D., 317
Multhaup, K. S., 134, 149, 157, *176, 178*
Munitz, H., 280, 283, *296*
Murphy, D., 318, *323*
Murphy, G., 52, *71*
Murphy, J. T., 348, *359*
Murri, L., 219, *223*
Myslobodsky, M., 10, 16, 17, *20*, 292, *301*, 318, 320, *324*, 366, 368, 373, 377, *387, 388, 391, 392*

N

Nachson, I., 279, 287, 292, 293, 295, *301, 325*
Nadel, L., 160, *178*
Nadvorna, H., 351, *356*
Nagera, H., 270, *274*
Nardelli, E., 278, 280, *301*
Narius, P., 106, *129*
Nashold, B. S., Jr., 347, 348, *359, 360*
Nathan, G., 372, *388*
Naumann, U., 150, *174*
Navona, C., 219, *223*
Neisser, U., 183, 185, 188, 192, 196, *199*, 232, 238, *242*
Nelson, K., 134, 150, 161, *178*
Nettleton, N. C., 364, 372, *388, 390*
Neumann, M. A., 283, *297*
Newby, I. R., 193, *200*
Newcombe, F., 278, 280, 282, 285, 287, 290, 291, *298, 301, 304*, 364, *390*
Newman, L. S., 189, 190, 194, 195, *199*
Neyraut, M., 5, *20*
Nicely, P. E., 376, *390*
Nichelli, P., 280, 289, *298*, 371, *388*
Nielsen, J., 350, *358*
Nisbett, R. E., 61, *71*, 95, *102*, 105, 107, *129*
Nissen, M. J., 139, *178*
Nitzan, D., 95, *103*
Noirot, E., 387, *387*
Nordin, M., 337, *359*
Nordlie, J. W., 291, *302*
Noreng, M. F., 350, *356*
Norita, M., *390*
Norman, D. A., 88, *101*, 162, *178*
Novelly, R. A., 364, *387*
Nurius, P., *129*
Nystrom, B., 337, 341, 344–345, *357, 359*

O

Obler, J. B., 5, *19*
Ochoa, E., 280, *299*
O'Connor, M., 165, 166, 170, *176, 178*
Ofshe, R. J., 189, *200*
Ogasawara, K., 383, *390*

Ogawa, M., 280, *298*
Ohta, S., 281, *303*
O'Keefe, J., 160, *178*
Oksenberg, A., 368, *392*
Onofrio, B. M., *359*
Openhimer, A., *102*
O'Reilly, R. C., 286, 287, *299*
Orne, M. T., 284, *303*
Osato, S. S., 314, 321, *324*
Osgood, C. E., 55, *71*
Osimani, A., 164, *178*
Ostdahl, R. H., 347, *359*
Otten, U. H., 348, *357*
Otto, R., 165, 166, *174*, 314, *323*
Ovesey, L., 251, 270, *274*
Owens, D. G. C., 278, *299*

P

Pallis, C. A., 278, 280, *301*
Pandya, D. N., 380, *391*
Pantano, P., 380, *390*
Pantev, C., 353, *357*
Paran, Y., 349, 350, *360*
Paré, A., *20*, 328, *359*
Parent, A., 385, *390*
Parker, L., 330, *360*
Parkes, C. M., 350, *359*
Parkin, A. J., 164, *178*, 282, *295*
Parry, F. M., 289, *301*
Passerini, D., 368, 381, *392*
Paulhus, D., 11, *20*
Pearson, N. A., 288, *300*
Pelissier, T., 348, *359*
Penfield, W., 335, 352, *359*
Perani, D., 281, *298*, 364, *388*
Perdue, C. W., 108, *129*
Perky, C. W., 170, *178*
Person, E., 251, *274*
Person, J. M., *390*
Peterhaus, E., 85, *102*
Petit, T. L., 158, *175*
Petry, S., 85, *102*
Phillips, R. J., 279, *301*
Piaget, J., 374, *390*
Pichert, J. W., 183, *197*
Pierrard, E., 280, 283, 285, *296*
Pierson, J. M., 372, *388*
Pierson-Savage, J. M., 364, 372, *390*
Pillon, B., 13, *20*, 280, *300*, 315, *325*
Pineda, G. S., *299*
Pinna, L., 277, *295*
Pires, A., 219, 222, *223*
Pizzamiglio, L., 380, *390*
Platt, S., 189, *200*
Pliskin, N. H., 317, *324*
Plutchik, R., 226, *242*

Podd, M. H., 317, *324*
Poirrer, R., 221, *223*
Pollack, J., 376, *391*
Pollack, M., 364, 366, 381, 382, *387*
Polster, M. R., 281, *301*
Pompeiano, O., 213, *217*
Poncet, M., 285, 286, *303*
Poole, D. A., 155, *178*, 189, *200*
Poppel, E., 290, *301*
Popper, K. R., 37, 47, *50*
Porac, C., 96, 98, 99, *101*
Porac, P., *102*
Portenoy, R. K., 348, *357*
Posner, M. I., 238, *242*
Postman, L., 105, 109, 111, *127*
Potemken, L., 370, *391*
Potter, J., 151, *174*
Prentice, D. A., 150, *174*
Pribor, E. F., 268, *274*
Price, D. D., 380, *392*
Puschel, J., 282, *301*
Putnick, M., 11, *19*
Pyszczynski, T. A., 113, 121, *129*

Q

Quattrone, G. A., 110, 122, *129*
Quillian, M. R., 139, *173*

R

Raber, P., 342, 351, *357*
Rabinowitz, J. C., 146, *179*
Radvansky, G. A., 89, *102*
Ragland, J., 318, *324*
Raines, J. M., 268, *274*
Raines, L. C., 268, *274*
Raja, S. N., 348, *356*
Rajan, P., 282, *301*
Rakerd, B., 89, *102*
Ramachandran, V. S., 352, 353, *360, 361*
Randall, G. C., **329, 357**
Randolph, C., 317, *324*
Rapcsak, S. Z., 281, *301*
Rasmussen, P., 329, 349, 350, *358*
Rasmussen, T., 335, 352, *359*
Ratclif, G., 364, *390*
Rawls, R. E., 279, *301*
Raye, C. L., 133, 134, 139, 140, 141, 142, 145, 147, 149, 151, *174, 176, 179*, 185, *199*
Raz, N., 141, 156, *179*
Read, J. D., 155, *177*
Rechtschaffen, A., 203, 210, 211, 212, 214, 214n, *217*, 220, *223*, 309, *325*
Rectem, D., 280, 283, 285, *296*
Redgrave, P., *391*
Reed, S. K., 238, *242*
Reeder, J. A., 137, 139, 140, 162, 163, 164, *176*

Regard, M., 281, *297, 300*, 318, *323*
Reid, T., 366, *391*
Reinitz, M., 147, *179*
Reisberg, D., 370, *391*
Reiser, B. J., 138, *179*
Reiss, L., 159, 160, *172*
Renault, B., 281, 284, 287, *297, 301*
Resnick, S. M., *326*
Révész, G., 75, *102*
Reynolds, D., 282, *301*
Rezak, M., 380, *387*
Reznick, S. M., 317
Rhodes, G., 278, 283, *301, 302*
Richards, A., 234, *242*
Riddoch, M. J., 135, *179*, 278, 280, 287, 288, 291, *300, 302, 305*
Rieberg, R. W., 318, *325*
Riecken, H. W., 189, *198*
Riva, L., 347, *360*
Rizzo, M., 284, 289, *302*
Rizzolatti, G., 282, *302*
Rizzuto, N., 278, *301*
Roberts, W., 94, *101*
Robertson, G., 317, *325*
Robertson, I. H., 365, *391*
Robinson, D. L., 381, *391*
Rock, I., 74, 75, 98, *102*
Rodin, G., 245, 249, *275*
Rodnick, E. H., 320, *325*
Roediger, H. L., 135, *177*
Roediger, H. L., III, 183, 187, *200*
Roffwarg, H. P., 211, 213, *216, 217*
Rogers-Ramachandran, D. C., 353, *360*
Rosati, G., 277, *295*
Rosen, V. H., 270, *274*
Rosenman, R. H., 236, *242*
Rosenquist, A. C., 384, 385, *388, 392*
Rosenthal, F., 340, *358*
Rosenthal, R., 114, *129, 130*, 293, *305*
Ross, B. M., 313, 320, *326*
Ross, E. D., *302*
Ross, H. E., 94, *102*
Ross, J., 282, 287, *301*
Ross, J. S., 168, *177*
Ross, L., 95, *102*, 105, 107, 126, *128, 129, 130*
Ross, M., 105, 106, 107, 111, 113, *129, 130*, 133, *179*, 183, 184, 187, 188, 191, 192, 193, 194, *199, 200*
Ross, P., 282, *302*
Ross-Kossak, P., 282, *302*
Rotenberg, V. S., 283, *302*
Roth, M., 309, *326*
Rothbaum, F., *200*
Roucoux, A., *389*
Rovee-Collier, C., 160, *179*
Rubens, B., 281, *301*

Ruda, M., 349, *357*
Rudy, L., 154, *175*
Rumelhart, D. E., 56, 64, *71*
Rumiati, R. I., 280, *302*
Rupert, A., 380, *389*
Rusconi, M. L., 368, 381, *392*
Russell, B., 23, 40, *50*
Russell, L. C., 341, *356*

S

Saadah, E. S. M., 333, *360*
Sabo, A. N., 266, *274*
Sackheim, H. A., 9, 11, *20*, 52, 53, 54, 58, 67, 68, 70, *71*, 105, *130*, 228–229, *241*, *302*
Sacks, O., 277, 279, 289, 291, 293, 294, 295, *302*
Sadzot, B., 221, *223*
Sakata, H., 379, *390*
Salmon, E., 221, *223*
Salomon, R. L., 94, *101*
Sandel, M. E., 286
Sanders, M. D., 290, 291, *304*
Sandroni, P., 368, *392*
Sandson, T., 170, *178*
Sanitioso, R., 110, 122, *130*
Santioso, R., 183, *200*
Saris, S. C., 347, *360*
Sass, N. L., 158, *175*
Saul, J. S. M., 289, *301*
Saykin, A. J., 317, *326*
Scandel, M. E., *298*
Schachter, S., 55, *71*, 188, *199*
Schacter, D. L., 66, *71*, 135, 139, 156, 161, *179*, 180, 287, 290, 292, 293, 294, 294n, *301*, *302*
Schafer, R., 52, *71*
Schank, R. C., 134, *179*, 183, *200*
Schankweiler, D. P., 369, *391*
Schapiro, J. S., 38, *50*
Scheflin, A. W., 193, 196, *200*
Scheiber, R., 370, *391*
Scheier, M. F., 227, 228, 230, *241*
Scheiner, J., *198*
Schiffman, H. R., 80, 81, 86, *102*
Schilder, P., 321, 323, 364, *391*
Schimek, J., 233, *242*
Schindler, R. J., 280, *299*
Schmidt, H., 87, *102*
Schneider, G. E., 382, *391*
Schneyer, M. L., 317, *325*
Schooler, J. W., 185, 187, *200*
Schreier, H. A., 257, *274*
Schuh, E. S., 68, *70*
Schwartz, A. S., 364, *391*
Schwartz, B. J., 352, *361*
Schwarz, N., 127, *130*
Schweich, M., 288, *302*

Scott, E., 205, *217*
Scott, J., 203, *217*
Scotti, G., 280, *298*, 364, 372, *388*
Seeman, M. V., 264, *274*
Segal, M. M., 252, *274*
Seltzer, B., 380, *391*
Seltzer, Z., 349, 350, *360*
Sengel, R. A., 317, *326*
Serdaru, M., 13, *20*, 315, *325*
Sergent, J., 278, 279, 280, 281, 282, 285, 286, 287, *302*, *303*
Seron, X., 280, 283, 285, *296*
Servin, S. L., 368n, *391*
Shain, D., 348, *359*
Shakow, D., 319, *326*
Shallice, T., 162, *178*
Shapin, S., 3, *20*
Shapiro, A., *217*
Shapiro, B. E., 310, *326*
Shargrough, F. W., 368n, *388*
Sherman, C. J., 330, 331, 342, 351, *360*
Sherman, R. A., 329, 330, 331, 338, 341, 342, 351, *360*
Sherman, S. J., 113, *130*, 133, 151, 170, *176*
Sherrick, M. F., 93, *102*
Shevrin, H., 67, *71*
Shilo, E., 90, *103*
Shimamura, A. P., 159, 161, *179*, 314, *324*
Shimko, T., 349, 350, *360*
Shyi, G. C. W., 146, 150, *174*
Sicottee, M., 222, *223*
Siegel, S., 85, *102*
Siegfried, J., 329, 347, *360*
Signoret, J.-L., 280, 281, 284, 287, *301*, *303*
Silverberg-Shalev, R., 318, *326*
Silveri, M. C., 281, *298*
Simmel, E., 271, *274*
Simmel, M. L., 333, 343, *360*
Simon, H. A., 192, *198*
Simone, D. A., 348, *359*
Singer, J. E., 55, *71*
Singer, M., 268, *274*
Skinner, B. F., 319, *326*
Skov, R. B., 113, *130*
Slater, E., 309, *326*
Smith, E. E., 55, 56, *71*, 154, *172*
Smith, F., 320, *326*
Smith, Y., 385, *390*
Smylie, C. S., 281, *299*
Smyth, G. E., 337, 342, 350, *358*
Snyder, C. R. R., 238, *242*
Snyder, F., 203, *217*
Snyder, M., 115, *130*, 183, *200*
Socarides, C. W., 252, *274–275*
Sokolov, E. N., 59, *71*
Solomon, R. C., 295, *303*

Solomon, S. K., 141, *176*
Soroker, N., 16, 17, *20*, 368, 373, 377, *388*, *391*, *392*
Sotgiu, M. L., 347, *360*
Souques-Poisot, A., 337, *360*
Sovijarvi, A. R. A., 380, *390*
Spelke, E. S., 375, *391*
Spence, C. J., 375, 386, *388*, *391*
Spence, D. P., 134, *179*, 183, *200*, 227, 231, 233, 242
Spence, K. W., 55, *71*
Spencer, W. D., 141, 156, *179*
Sperling, G., 137, *179*
Sperry, R., 294n, *303*
Sperry, R. W., 16, *20*, 294n, *303*
Spiegel, D., 193, 196, *200*
Spielman, L. A., 123, *127*
Spinelli, D. N., 380, *391*
Spinnler, H., 280, 282, *298*
Spiro, H. R., 248, 270, *275*
Spiro, R. J., 182, *200*
Spivak, H., 245, 249, *275*
Spivey-Knowlton, M. J., 92, *102*
Sprague, J. M., 382, 383, 384, 385, *391*, *392*
Springer, S., 164, *179*
Squire, L. R., 139, 159, 161, *173*, *179*, 314, *324*
Sroka, H., 280, 283, *296*
St. John, R. C., 282, *303*
Stafanini, A., 219, *223*
Stanton, G. B., 381, *391*
Starker, S., *217*
Starr, A., 380, *391*
Stein, B. E., 370, 380, 381, 382, 383, *390*, *391*, *392*
Stein, N. L., 182, *200–201*
Steinbach, T., 351, *356*
Steller, M., 185, 187, 188, *201*
Stengel, E., *275*, 364, *391*
Stern, L. B., 185, *198*
Stern, W., 191, *201*
Sternberg, S., 55, *71*, 317, *326*
Sterzi, R., 368, 381, *392*
Stevens, M., 278, *299*, 318, *326*
Stewart, M., 353, *360*
Stewart, O., 386, *391*
Stiles, W., 183, *198*
Stock, C. B., 113, *130*
Stoerig, P., 291, *297*, *303*
Stoker, B., 268, 272, *275*
Stone, J. I., 184, *198*
Story, I., 255, *275*
Strang, D. J., 110, *129*
Stroot, C., 282, *296*
Stuart, G. W., 85, *102*
Stuss, D. T., 133, 162, 164, 165, 166, 167, *172*, *179*, 221, *223*, 308, 314, *326*

Stypstein, E., 280, 283, 285, *296*
Subbotsky, E. V., 270, *275*
Suengas, A. G., 138, 144, 146, 151, 154, *176*, *180*, 185, *199*
Sully, J., 76, *102*
Suls, J., 230, *242*
Sumby, W. H., 376, *391*
Summerfield, A. Q., 376, *391*
Summers, D. A., 98, *101*
Sunderland, S., 337, 342, *360*
Suttleworth, E. C., Jr., 283, *303*
Suzuki, H., 380, *391*
Svenson, O., 106, *130*
Swann, W. B., Jr., *130*
Swearingen, C., 253, *274*
Sweet, W. H., 342, 346, 347, *361*
Switzer, R. C., 385, *387*
Syring, V., 283, *303*
Szasz, T. S., 329, *360*

T

Tafarodi, R. W., 150, *174*
Tajfel, H., 106, 108, *130*
Talland, G. A., 308, 310, 314, *326*
Tanaka, Y., 280, *298*
Tasker, R. R., 335, 348, *356*, *359*
Tata, P., 233, 234, *242*
Taub, E., 353, *358*
Taylor, P. S., 312, 317, *325*
Taylor, S., 11, *20*, *326*
Taylor, S. E., 105, 108, 110, 126, *128*, *130*, 183, *201*, 229, *242*
Taylor, T. H., 140, 142, 145, 149, *176*, *179*
Tehovnik, E. J., 382, *392*
Terr, L., 194, *201*
Terzian, H., 278, *301*
Teuber, H.-L., 352, *360*
Tharp, V. K., 203, *217*
Theodore, M. D., 335, 348, 352, *361*
Thompson, N. S., 11, *20*
Thomson, D. M., 134, 148, *180*
Tillman, D. B., 339, *359*
Tissot, R., 321, *323*
Tjellden, N. U., 350, *356*
Tolman, E. E., 316, *326*
Torebjork, E., 341, 348, *357*
Torebjork, H. E., 349, *358*, *360*
Torigoe, Y., 385, *389*
Torrey, E. F., 18, *21*, *324*
Toth, J. P., 68, *71*
Tour, R. L., 368n, *391*
Trabasso, T., 182, *200–201*
Tranel, D., 277, 278, 279, 280, 281, 283, 284, 289, *297*, *303*, 386, *391*
Treisman, A. M., *71*, 87, *102*, 161, *173*
Trivers, R., 53, *71*, 228, 229, *242*

Trolle, E., 280, *300*
Trope, Y., 112, 113, 114, 115, 116, 123, 124, *128, 130*
Troscianko, T., 287, 291, *300*
Trosman, H., 210, *218*
Tsai, E.-F., 348, *359*
Tsal, Y., 78, 79, 87, 89, *102*
Tulving, E., 134, 139, 148, 160, 161, *177, 180*
Turkewitz, G., 282, *302*
Turnbull, W., 183, *201*
Turner, J. C., 106, 108, *130*
Tversky, A., 110, 122, 123, *129, 130*
Tyler, R. B., 108, *129*
Tzavaras, A., 280, *303*

U

Ullman, S., 79, 92, *102*
Umilta, C., 169, *178*, 282, *302*, 316, *325*, 364, *392*
Undeutsch, U., 185, 188, 191, 192, *201*
Ungerleider, L. G., 135, *178*
Uranowitz, S. M., 183, *200*
Uranowitz, S. W., 115, *130*

V

Vaccarino, A. L., 350, *356, 358*
Vaillant, G. E., 226, *243*
Valdiserri, M., 156, *179*
Valenstein, E., 364, *389*
Valentine, T., 286, *298*
Vallar, G., 363, 368, 372, 381, *388, 392*
Van Allen, M. W., 284, 289, *296*
Van de Castle, R. L., 212, *217*
Van den Heydt, R., 85, *102*
Van Gorp, W. G., 314, 321, *324*
Van Gulick, R., 286, *303*
Van Hezewijk, R., 287, *303*
Van Hoesen, G. W., 277, 279, 280, 281, *297*
Vecera, S. P., 286, 287, *299*
Velge, V., 280, *296*
Velnstein, E., 364, *392*
Venables, P. H., *323*
Ventre, J., 381, *392*
Verdone, P., 210, *217*
Verfaellie, M., 159, 160, *172*, 284, *295*, 386, *387*
Vetter, H., 318, *325*
Vetter, R. J., 333, *360*
Vigna, C., 282, *300*
Villanueve, R., 219, 222, *223*
Villemure, J.-G., 279, 281, 287, *303*
Villenueve, A., 219, 222, *223*
Violani, C., 219, *223*
Vnek, N., 144, 157, *175*
Vogel, C., 339, *359*
Vogel, G, 205, *217*
Volkan, V., 255, 258, *275*
Volpe, B. T., 386, *392*

von Dongen, H. R., 371, *392*
von Frenckell, R., 221, *223*
Vorstrup, S., 222, *223*

W

Wade, J., 342, *359*
Wahren, L. K., 341, 349, *357, 358*
Waid, W. M., 284, *303*
Wakisaka, S., 344, *358*
Walbridge, M., 170, *178*
Walker-Andrews, A.S., 375, *392*
Wall, P. D., 327, 337, 339, 343, 344, 345, 349, 351, 352, *356, 357, 359, 360*
Wallace, M. A., 285, 286, *304*
Wallace, S. F., 384, 385, *388, 392*
Wallin, E., 337, 341, *357*
Wallin, U., *359*
Walther, E., 150, *174*
Wang, A. Y., 142, 145, *176*
Wapner, W., 310, 311, 312, 314, *325, 326*
Ward, A. A., 347, *359*
Ward, L. M., 73, 75, 77, 88, 92, 96, 99, *101, 102*
Warrington, E. K., 278, 279, 280, 281, 288, 289, 290, 291, *301, 304*, 309, *325, 326*
Wartel, M. O., 5, *19*
Wasserstein, J., 364, *387*
Watson, P. D., 94, *101*
Watson, R. T., 364, *392*
Webster, W. R., 367, *392*
Wechsler, D., 309, *326*
Weidner, G., 236, *242*
Weinberger, D. R., 162, 163, *180*, 317, 318, 320, *323, 324, 325*
Weinbruch, C., 353, *357*
Weiner, H., 213, *217*
Weinman, J., 233, 234, *242*
Weinstein, E. A., 310, 311, 312, *326*, 363, 365, *392*
Weinstein, N. D., 106, *130, 131*, 236, *243*
Weinstein, S., 331, 332, 333, 347, 352, *360*
Weintraub, J. K., 227, 228, 230, *241*
Weisberg, L. A., 158, *174*
Weiskrantz, L., 135, *180*, 290, 291, *304*
Weisman, A., 225—226, *243*
Weisstein, C. C., 317, *325*
Weisz, J., 368, 384, *392*
Wells, G. L., 192, *201*
Wells, L. A., 245, 246n, 252, 255, 270, 271, *275*
Wertheimer, M., 81, *102*, 371, 386, *392*
Westby, G. W. M., *391*
Wetzel, R. D., 268, *274*
Wheaton, J., 210, *217*
Whishaw, I., 163, 164, *177*
Whisnat, J. P., 368n, *388*
Whitaker, H. A., 162, *173*
White, D. M., 341, *357*

White, G. L., *128*
White, J. C., 342, 346, 347, *361*
White, L. E., 347, *359*
Whiteley, A. M., 278, 281, *304*
Whitty, C. W. M., 221, *223*, 314, *326*
Wickelgren, B. G., 380, *392*
Wiener, M., 58, *71*
Wier, C. S., 368, *388*
Wiersma, D., 269, *275*
Wiesenfeld-Hallin, Z., 349, *358*
Wilbrand, H., 277, 289, *304*
Wilcox, G. L., 349, *361*
Wildschoidtz, G., 222, *223*
Wilkinson, L. K., 380, *392*
Williams, D. D., 385, *389*
Wilson, B., 188, *197*
Wilson, L., 372, *388*
Wilson, S. C., 156, 168, *180*
Wilson, S. K., 284, *303*
Wilson, T. D., 133, *180*
Winocour, G., 280, *296*
Witherspoon, D., 65, *71*
Witkin, H. A., 96, *102*
Wittgenstein, L., 41, *50*
Wlbrand, H., *304*
Wolf, E. S., *177*
Wolf, H. G., 348, *358*
Wolff, W., 54, *71*
Woloshyn, V., 144, 148, *175*
Wolpert, E. A., 210, 211, 212, 213, *217, 218*
Wood, D. H., 283, *297*
Woodruff, D. S., 158, *180*
Woolf, C. J., 348, *361*
Woolsey, C. N., 335, 348, 352, *361*
Wortzman, G., 164, *178*

Wu, J., 222, *223*
Wyer, R. S., 111, 121, *131*
Wyke, M., 308, *326*
Wylie, R. C., 385, *392*
Wynn-Parry, C. B., 331, 347, *361*

Y

Yang, T. T., 352, *361*
Yantis, S., 135, *180*
Yapko, M. D., 195, *201*
Yarnitzky, D., 348, *361*
Yeomans, J., 164, *178*
Yeomans, J. S., 382, *392*
Yin, R. K., 279, *304*
Yoshida, M., 280, *298*
Young, A. W., 167, 168, *174*, 277, 278, 279, 280, 282, 284, 285, 286, 287, 288, 289, 290, 291, *296, 298, 300, 301, 304, 305*
Yutzy, S. H., 268, *274*

Z

Zacks, R. T., 143, 169, *175*, 238, *241*
Zahavi, A., 8, *21*
Zaidel, E., 282, 294n, *301, 305*
Zakay, D., 90, 95, *102–103*, 236, *243*
Zaragoza, M. S., 148, 149, 153, *180*
Zeiss, A. M., 183, *199*
Zhang, X., 349, *358*
Zimmerman, M., 329, *360*
Zimmerman, W. B., 204, *218*
Zuch, J., 212, *217*
Zuckerman, M., 293, *305*
Zyzanski, S. J., 236, *242*

Subject Index

A

Age, memory and, 156–158, 190–191
Alloacusis, 374
Aniseikonia, 79
Anorexia nervosa, 253–255
Anosognosia, 289–290
Anxiety
  denial and, 233–234
  memory and, 319–320
  The Apology of Socrates (Plato), 30–31
Apperception, 288–290
Aristotle, 34, 46
Aristotle illusion, 87
Asomatognosia, 365
Association, 288–290
Attention avoidance, 63
Audiovisual neglect. *See* Unilateral spatial
    neglect (USN)
Auditory neglect
  in unilateral spatial neglect (USN), 14,
    365–367
  ventriloquist illusion and, 379–382
Autokinetic movement, 93
Avoidance strategies, 56–64, 227–228

B

Baconian radicalism, 37–39
Bacon's doctrine of prejudice, 33–36
Behavioral confirmation, 114–115
Behaviorism, 29
Bias
  correspondence, 184
  wishful thinking and, 110–111, 113–116,
    123, 125
Binocular rivalry, 92
Blend illusion, 376–379

B

Blindsight, 290–291
Blocking, 240
Borderline disorders, 263–265, 267–268
Brain regions
  confabulations and, 12–14, 165–167, 221,
    314–315
  dreams and, 221–222
  MEM and, 162–165
  prosopagnosia and, 280–283
  source memory and, 159–170
  unilateral spatial neglect (USN) and, 379,
    382–385
Briquet's syndrome, 268

C

Capgras syndrome, 167
Caricature, imposture and, 270
Central nervous system (CNS) and phantom
    limb sensation
  centralization and, 350–351
  central sensitization and, 348–349
  central somatosensory maps, distortion
    of, 351–354
  ectopia originating in, 347–348
  long-term CNS changes and, 349–350
Charpantier illusion, 375
Cognitive defenses. *See* Denial; Knowledge
    avoidance; Self-deception
Cognitive dissonance, 108–109
Cognitive neuropsychiatry, 168
Cognitive style, defined, 96
Colliculi neurons, 382–383
Comprehension avoidance, 62–63
Compulsions, imposture and, 270
Confabulations

affective background and, 310–311
brain regions and, 12–14, 165–167, 221, 314–315
defined, 307–309, 322
as legitimized distortions, 311–312
material of, 312–313
provoked, 312–313
recall and, 315–317
schizophrenia and, 317–320
self-monitoring and, 309–310
spontaneous, 313
Connectionism. *See* Neural network modeling
Conscious awareness system (CAS), 292–293
Consensus criterion, 188–189
Context effects, 90–92
Context of recall criterion, 189–190
Coordinate unconscious, 56
Coping strategies, 56–64, 227–228
Criticism
in Bacon's doctrine of prejudice, 34–36
in new theory of rationality, 46–49

D

Deafferentation pain, 347
Deception
honesty and, 1–2
in mind-body relation. *See* Phantom limb sensation
prosopagnosia and, 293–295
prospective, 5–7
retrospective, 5–7
in unilateral spatial neglect (USN) rehabilitation, 385–387
Delusion, 168, 307, 319
Demonstrability, 40–42
Denial
anxiety and, 233–234
assessment of, 232–237
described, 9–10
information processing and, 230–235, 238–240
information rejection variants and, 225–230
paradox of, 231
Descartes, René, 37, 38
Discovering, as MEM process, 138
Dissociable Interactions and Conscious Experience (DICE), 292–293
Dissociation, 258–263, 265–268
Dorsal root ganglion, ectopia originating in, 344–345
Dreams, 17–18
brain regions and, 221
Freudian theory of, 213
imagination in, 108–109

isolation of consciousness in, 211–216
lucid, 206
poor recall of, 209–211
reflective awareness during, 204–208, 219–223
single-mindedness of, 203–211
thematic coherence in, 209
Duhem, Pierre, 34–35
Duhem-Quine thesis, 34

E

Ectopia in phantom limb sensation
defined, 339
originating in dorsal root ganglion (DRG), 344–345
originating in nerve end neuromas, 337–344
originating in the central nervous system (CNS), 347–348
Elaborations, 321–322
Emotions, source monitoring and, 144–145
Encoding
biased, wishful thinking and, 115
denial and, 239–240
as stage in recollection process, 182
Enlightenment movement of rationality, 28–30
Environmental dependency syndrome, 315
Eudaimony, Socratic doctrine of, 30–31
Examining, as MEM process, 135–137
Exposure avoidance, 63–64
Extended reasoning, 142
Extracting, as MEM process, 135

F

Fabrications, 314
Feature binding, 143–145
hippocampus and, 159–160
Feature integration theory, 87
Festinger, Leon, 36
Figural ambiguity, 78
Fraser illusion, 85
Freudian theory
of defense mechanisms, 230
of dreams, 213
of personality, 238
self-deception and, 44–46, 54
Frontal regions
confabulations and, 165–167, 221, 314–315
degrees of deficits in, 169–170
schizophrenia and, 317–318
source memory and, 162–170

G

Gender, memory and, 191–192
Geometrical illusions, 98–100

Guilty knowledge technique (GKT), 283–284

H

Hegel, Georg, 43, 44
Hemispatial neglect. *See* Unilateral spatial neglect (USN)
Hering grid, 86
Hippocampus, 159–160
Hoaxes, 249
Honesty, deception and, 1–2
Hypnosis, recovered memories and, 190, 195
Hypothesis testing, wishful thinking and asymmetric error costs and, 116–125
  confirmatory biases and, 113–116, 123–124
  pragmatic model of, 112

I

Identifying, as MEM process, 135
Illusions, cognitive, 107–109
Illusions, perceptual
  adaptive, 80, 89
  aftereffects, 81, 83, 87
  anatomical structure based, 86
  Aristotle, 87
  blend, 376–379
  Charpantier, 375
  cognitive processes and, 92–94, 94–96
  conflicting perceptual cues and, 92
  context effects and, 90–92
  contrasts, 81
  critical-cue *versus* multiple-cue approach, 97–98
  cultural influences and, 96–97
  defined, 75–76, 80
  "echoic," 319
  expectations and, 94
  Fraser, 85
  geometrical, 98–100
  high-level brain processes and, 94–98
  individual differences and, 96
  information interference and, 87–88
  information processing based, 82–98
  information shortage and, 89–90
  Jastrow, 75
  low-level brain process based, 84–85
  maladaptive, 80, 97
  McGurk (blend), 376–379
  motivation and, 94
  perception of causality and, 95–96
  perceptual organization and, 88–89
  physically based, 83–84
  physiologically based, 86–87
  scale, 89
  self-deception and, 8–9
  structural and strategy based, 82
  temporal, 94–95

ventriloquist, 14, 370, 379–382, 384
Illusory conjunctions, 87
Illusory contour stimuli, 85
Imagination, dreams and, 208–209
Implicit cognition, 65–66
Imposture
  anorexia nervosa and, 253–255
  borderline disorders and, 263–265, 267–268
  circumscribed or limited, 255–256
  dissociation and, 258–263, 265–268
  for gain, 246–247
  garden-variety, 257–258
  hoaxes, 249
  literary, 249–250
  multiple-personality disorder and, 258–263
  Münchausen's syndrome, 7, 247–248, 268
  by proxy, 256–257, 262, 263
  theory of, 268–272
  transvestism, 250–253
Inference avoidance, 60–62
Information processing. *See also* Memory
  denial and, 238–240
  perceptual illusions and, 82–98
Initiating, as MEM process, 138
Internal consistency criterion, 187
Intrusions, 321–322

J

Jastrow illusion, 75
Just-Noticeable-Difference (JND), 76–77

K

Kinetic depth effect, 78–79
Knowledge avoidance
  nonparadox of, 56–61
  ordinariness of, 62–64
Knowledge criterion, 188, 195

L

Lateral inhibition, 86
Leading questions, memory and. *See* Suggestibility
Levels-of-representation model, 56–61
Locating, as MEM process, 135
Lorenz, Konrad, 47

M

Magical repair, 270
Marx, Karl, 42–44
McGurk illusion, 376–379
Mechanosensitivity, 337–339
Medial-temporal region, 159–161

MEM. *See* Multiple-entry, modular (MEM) system
Memorability criterion, 186–187
Memory. *See also* Prosopagnosia
  age and, 156–158, 190–191
  behavioral neurology and, 11–14
  biased, and wishful thinking, 110, 115
  of dreams, 209–211
  episodic, 6, 142, 289
  false, 153–156, 193–196, 308
  gender and, 191–192
  levels-of-representation model, 56–61
  multiple-entry, modular (MEM) system,
    6–7, 135–140, 162–165, 171
  recall and confabulations, 315–317
  recollection process, 182–184
  repression of, 193–196
  schizophrenia and, 317–318
  source monitoring, 134, 140–159
  truth criteria and, 185–196
  validating, 184
Memory quality criterion, 185–186
"Method of monsters," 15
Misoplegia, 365
Mnemopoesis, 314, 321–322
Multimodal input processing, 379–382
Multiple-entry, modular (MEM) system
  described, 6–7, 135–140, 171
  frontal brain regions and, 162–165
Multiple-personality disorder, 258–263
Münchausen's syndrome, 7, 247–248, 268
Mysticism, 33–34
Mythomanias
  meaning of, 2–3
  obscurity of, 3–5
  as prospective duplicity, 6

N

Neural matrix of conscious sensation,
  335–336
Neural network modeling, 64–66
Neurology, behavioral, 11–15
Neuromas, ectopia in, 337–340
Noting, as MEM process, 138

O

Obsessions, imposture and, 270
Orienting reflex (OR), 16–17

P

Parallel distributed processing. *See* Neural
  network modeling
Pathology, normalcy and, 15
Perception
  adaptive, 83
  corrected veridical, 83

direct, 78
maladaptive, 83
as MEM subsystem, 135–137
self-deception and, 35–36
synthetic, 374–375
transactional theory of, 79–80
veridical, 83
vision and, 14
Perceptual aftereffects, 81, 83, 87
Perceptual defense, 109–112
Perceptual illusions. *See* Illusions, perceptual
Perceptual organization, 88–89
Perceptual phenomena, 73–75
Perceptual systems, purpose and task of,
  77–79
Peripheral nervous system (PNS) and phantom limb sensation, 336–345
Personal unity, self-deception paradox and,
  55–56
Phantom limb pain. *See also* Phantom limb
  sensation
  centralization of, 350–351
  described, 330–331
  dorsal root entry zone (DREZ) surgery for,
    347
  ectopia originating in central nervous sys-
    tem (CNS) and, 347–348
  exacerbating factors, 333, 340–341
Phantom limb sensation
  case history of, 333–334
  central sensitization and, 348–349
  changes with time of, 332–333
  defined, 327–328
  distortion of somatosensory maps and,
    351–354
  ectopia in
    defined, 339
    originating in dorsal root ganglion,
      344–345
    originating in nerve end neuromas,
      336–344
    originating in the central nervous sys-
      tem (CNS), 347–348
  ganglionectomy for, 346–347
  individual differences in, 341–342
  interaction with surroundings and, 332
  long-term CNS changes and, 349–350
  movement of limb in, 332
  nerve blocks and, 342–345
  neural origins of, 12, 331, 334–336
  "normal phantoms," 343–344
  quality of sensation in, 330
  rhizotomy for, 346–347
  telescoping limbs in, 351–354
  treatment failures in, 342
  without amputation, 331–332

Phantom organs. *See* Phantom limb pain;
  Phantom limb sensation
Phi movement, 94
Placing, as MEM process, 135
Plato, 30–31, 34, 46
Positivity bias. *See* Wishful thinking
Prefrontal cortex, source memory and,
  162–170
Proof theory, 40–42
Prosopagnosia
  anosognosia and, 289–290
  apperceptive, 288–289
  associative, 288–289
  bilateral lesions and, 280–281
  blindsight and, 290–292
  componential recognition of faces in,
    278–279
  covert recognition of faces in
    behavioral indices of, 284–285
    guilty knowledge technique (GKT)
      and, 283–284
    models of, 285–287
  defined, 17, 277
  dynamic theories and, 292
  heterogenous nature of, 287–288
  implicit-explicit knowledge and, 292–293
  left and right hemispheres and, 282–283
  manifestations of, 277–278
  motivational aspects of, 291–292
  self-deception and, 293–295
  specificity of face recognition in, 279–280
  unilateral lesions and, 281–282
Proteus syndrome, 7
Pseudologia phantastica, 269, 271, 307, 308, 313
Psychoanalytic theory, denial and, 227
Psychophysical function, 76–77
Purkinje shift, 86
Pygmalion effect, 114

R

Rationalism
  classical
    extreme, as self-deception, 39–42
    self-reliance and, 28–30
    social order and, 26–28
    thought and action in, 27–28
  Enlightenment movement of, 28–30
  fallibilist theory of, 47, 48
  new theory of, 46–49
  romanticism, 25
Reactionary thought, 39
Reactivating, as MEM process, 137–138,
  160–161
Reality monitoring, 141, 149–151
Recall
  confabulations and, 315–317

  of dreams, 209–211
  process of, 182–184
Reflection, as MEM subsystem, 135–139
Reflective awareness, in dreams, 204–208,
  219–223
Refreshing, as MEM process, 137, 161
Rehearsing, as MEM processs, 138, 161
Relativism, 43
Reliability criterion, 187–188
Reporting, as stage in recollection process,
  183–184
Resolving, as MEM process, 135
Retinal image, 73–74
Retrieval
  biased, and wishful thinking, 110, 115
  denial and, 238, 240
  as MEM process, 138, 161
  as stage in recollection process, 182–183
Romanticism, 25

S

Sadomasochism, 252–253
Schizophrenia, 317–320, 375
Self-assessment, wishful thinking and,
  106–109
Self-deception. *See also* Knowledge avoidance
  classic rationalism and, 25, 26–28
  criticism and, 34–36
  denial and, 9–10, 228–229
  disciplines interested in, 52–53
  Enlightenment movement and, 28–30
  error and sin and, 30–33
  extreme rationalism as, 39–42
  as fixation, 42
  Freudian theory and, 44–46
  general discussion of, 23–25
  illusion and, 8–9
  as inference avoidance, 60–61
  paradox of, 51–56, 67
  prosopagnosia and, 293–295
  self-reliance and, 37–39
Self-Deception (Fingarette), 53–54
Self-interest, doctrine of enlightened, 30–31
Self-reliance
  rationality and, 28–30
  self-deception and, 37–39
Self-testing, biased, 110–111
Shifting, as MEM process, 138
Socrates, 30–31
Somatosensory hemineglect syndrome, 328
Somatosensory psyche, 335–336
Source characteristics criterion, 190–193
Source memory
  frontal brain regions and, 162–170
  frontal deficits and, 169–170

medial-temporal brain regions and, 159–161
Source monitoring
    aging and, 156–158
    described, 134, 140–142
    errors and deficits in, 143–151
    heuristic and strategic processes in, 142–143
    suggestibility and, 153–156
    summary of, 151–153
Sprague effect, 384
Striato-nigro-tectal pathway, 383–384
Structuring, as MEM process, 137
Subordinate unconscious, 56–64
Suggestibility
    confabulations and, 312–313
    context of recall and, 189–190
    source monitoring and, 153–156
Synesthesia, 374

T

Thematic coherence, in dreams, 209
Tracking, as MEM process, 135
Transactionalism, 79–80
Transvestism, 250–253
Trust, 3
Truth. *See* Honesty
Truth criteria
    consensus, 188–189
    context of recall, 189–190
    internal consistency, 187
    knowledge criterion, 188, 195
    memorability of events, 186–187
    memory qualities, 185–186
    recovered memories controversy and, 193–196
    reliability, 187–188
    source characteristics, 190–193

using, 192–196

U

Unconscious cognition
    coordinate, 56
    relationship between conscious and, 66–69
    subordinate, 56–64
Unilateral spatial neglect (USN)
    auditory neglect in, 365–367
    brain-evoked potentials and, 368–369
    deception as rehabilitation for, 385–387
    deceptions in stimuli source and, 372–373
    described, 363–365
    McGurk (blend) illusion and, 376–379
    neuroanatomy of, 379, 382–385
    vision, role of in, 370–372

V

Ventriloquist illusion, 14, 370, 379–382, 384
Vision
    perception and, 14
    in unilateral spatial neglect (USN), 370–372

W

Weber, Max, 28
When Prophecy Fails (Festinger, Riecken, Schachter), 189
Wishful thinking
    asymmetric error costs in, 116–123, 124–125
    confirmatory biases in, 113–116, 123
    hypothesis testing and, 112, 126–127
    mental health and, 105–106, 126
    outcomes of, 7, 106–109
    processes of, 109–112